Putin's Russia

Eighth Edition

Edited by

Darrell Slider

with Stephen K. Wegren

ROWMAN & LITTLEFIELD
Lanham • Boulder • New York • London

Acquisitions Editor: Ashley Dodge
Editorial Assistant: Haley White
Sales and Marketing Inquiries: textbooks@rowman.com

Credits and acknowledgments for material borrowed from other sources, and reproduced with permission, appear on the appropriate page within the text.

Published by Rowman & Littlefield
An imprint of The Rowman & Littlefield Publishing Group, Inc.
4501 Forbes Boulevard, Suite 200, Lanham, Maryland 20706
rowman.com

86-90 Paul Street, London EC2A 4NE

British Library Cataloguing in Publication Information Available

Library of Congress Cataloging-in-Publication Data

Names: Slider, Darrell, editor. | Wegren, Stephen K., 1956– editor.
Title: Putin's Russia / edited by Darrell Slider with Stephen K. Wegren.
Description: Eighth edition. | Lanham: Rowman & Littlefield, [2022] | Includes bibliographical references and index.
Identifiers: LCCN 2022016750 (print) | LCCN 2022016751 (ebook) | ISBN 9781538148679 (cloth) | ISBN 9781538148686 (paperback) | ISBN 9781538148693 (epub)
Subjects: LCSH: Russia (Federation)—Politics and government—1991– | Russia (Federation)—Foreign relations. | Putin, Vladimir Vladimirovich, 1952—Political and social views.
Classification: LCC DK510.763 .P88 2022 (print) | LCC DK510.763 (ebook) | DDC 947.086—dc23/eng/20220429
LC record available at https://lccn.loc.gov/2022016750
LC ebook record available at https://lccn.loc.gov/2022016751

Contents

Preface

In February 2022, as this volume was being prepared for press, Vladimir Putin made an hourlong address to the Russian people about Ukraine that was, in fact, a declaration of war. (An official translation can be found at http://en.kremlin.ru/events/president/news/67828.)

In addition to a rambling and distorted retelling of the history of Ukraine, including the claim that America had taken control over all Ukrainian government institutions, Putin included criticism of the flaws and shortcomings of Ukraine's political-economic system. For Putin, the Ukrainian government was guilty of (1) massive corruption, including predation by oligarchs, that impoverished the population and destroyed the country's economic potential; (2) failing to establish an independent judiciary; (3) persecuting political opponents (many of whom, because of their moderate views, were unwilling to engage in illegal actions to resist); (4) subverting elections to obstruct representation of the genuine interests of the people; (5) muzzling independent media and censoring views that the authorities attributed to the influence of an outside power—in this case, Russia; and (6) suppressing the autonomy of regions where ethnic minorities sought the free use of their language and respect for their culture.

To anyone even vaguely familiar with the recent history of Russia, this set of accusations is an obvious projection of Putin-era policies onto a neighboring state, presented without any sense of irony or self-reflection, and understanding that most Russians would accept it as truthful, given the messaging presented in Russian state media. Meanwhile, Putin's main opponent, Alexei Navalny, was sitting in a prison cell in Corrective Colony No. 2, in Pokrov, Vladimir oblast, after surviving an attempt by the Kremlin to poison him. Why? Because Navalny was determined to expose realities about the Putin elite and present a political alternative. In Putin's Russia, this constitutes extremism and terrorism, and it is viewed as an existential threat to the regime that should be punished by death, exile, or life imprisonment.

This, the 8th edition of *Putin's Russia*, presents analyses by experts in the field of Russian studies on where Putin has taken Russia, encompassing a broad spectrum of policy areas both domestic and international. My profuse thanks to my fellow contributors; their chapters are dedicated to the goal that readers benefit from an informed analysis about the strengths and flaws of a Russia that is now indisputably Putin's. Most chapters were written in late 2021, before he launched his destructive war on Ukraine in February 2022, and then updated in April–May 2022. They collectively provide an analysis of how Putin transformed Russia into a country where a decision of such consequence can be made and implemented based on the will of a single person. The impact of this war on Russia's standing in the world could last for decades to come.

As editor of the current volume, I would like to acknowledge the role of the two previous editors. I am sure that when Dale Herspring came up with the idea for this text over twenty years ago, he never would have believed there would be an 8th edition and that it would still be titled *Putin's Russia*! The editorial role was taken on by my friend and colleague, Stephen Wegren, in 2009. Since Dmitry Medvedev had recently been elected as Russian president, that edition, the 4th, was optimistically called *After Putin's Russia*, while the 5th (published in 2013) became *Return to Putin's Russia*. Over the years, Steve expanded the number of authors and worked tirelessly to maintain the level of quality, for which all of us who contributed are grateful. Recognition is also due to the editors and staff at Rowman & Littlefield who have supported this work and shepherded the current volume to completion.

I would like to thank Victor Peppard and Golfo Alexopoulos, fellow professors in Russian studies during the many years that I taught at the University of South Florida (Tampa). Both are deeply knowledgeable about the country and its history and culture, and I have learned much from them.

Finally, I am indebted to my partner, Valentina Pushkar, who every day shows me that, despite everything, there are millions of reasons to be hopeful about Russia and its future when it is no longer "Putin's."

Darrell Slider

PART I

Domestic Politics

Chapter 1

Vladimir Putin in Historical Context

Darrell Slider

The political-economic system that has emerged in Russia after more than twenty years of Putin's rule is one based on authoritarian rule from the Kremlin, the center of power.[1] The regime has elevated the values of preserving unity and stability above all else. Any activity or institution that might be described with the adjective "independent"—free of state dominance or control—is suspected of threatening those values. Perceived threats to the regime have included independent political parties, prosecutors, courts and judges, parliaments and legislatures, governors, mayors, nongovernmental organizations, mass media, cultural and educational institutions, "oligarchs," business leaders, investment groups, and large corporations. As the chapters that follow demonstrate, by 2022 most autonomous actors in what could be described broadly as the "political" sphere had been either subdued, co-opted, marginalized, or eliminated.

Vladimir Putin's values and ways of seeing the world were shaped by his experiences during the Soviet period and after. This is not to argue that it was *inevitable* that Putin would end up with a particular worldview. Others from his generation with similar backgrounds drew different lessons and are on the opposite end of the political spectrum.[2] But one can see in Putin's expressed attitudes and policies direct parallels with what he knew and experienced as he grew into maturity. There was no single, uniform "Soviet system"; the Soviet Union was constantly changing. The history of the Soviet political life saw lengthy periods of reaction, repression, and stagnation interrupted by intense and chaotic spurts of relaxation and reform. The purpose of this chapter is to briefly outline the nature of the shifting political-economic systems that influenced Putin's worldview: How did these systems handle political opponents, diversity of thought and culture, and the representation of diverse interests?

The dominant characteristics of the Soviet Union were those of a highly authoritarian political system with a centralized and bureaucratized economy. Elite corruption and abuse of power have been constant elements of this historical pattern. A large repressive state apparatus was a necessary element of this system. Many Russians have come to accept this as normal, or even as a "special path" that ideally fits Russian geography, history, and national characteristics, but in comparative terms, it is rare that a bureaucratic, authoritarian system that frequently resorts to violent repression can survive and prosper in the long term. The alternative to this authoritarian model is a pluralist system with strong elements of competition. Markets, along with checks and balances in the form of what some political scientists call "veto players," and self-governing and autonomous institutions are characteristic of most Western liberal democracies.[3] Democratization, representation of diverse interests, market-based economies, anticorruption efforts, and norms that force the authorities to observe human rights and the rule of law are features common to almost all the world's richest and most technologically advanced countries.[4] Periodic reform efforts in Soviet and post-Soviet history have tried to incorporate elements of the liberal democratic model, a market economy, and civil society with mixed results.

The core element of the Soviet model starting in the late 1920s was state monopoly—in politics, in the economy, and in social organization. The leadership used a combination of methods, ranging from persuasion to violent repression, to eliminate autonomous actors and institutions. The advantages of an authoritarian system accrue to decision makers themselves: They enjoy greater power to concentrate resources for the purposes they value. It also can permit personal enrichment of the elite, hidden from public view. Disadvantages of a monopolistic political structure are many. Centralized decision-making requires a great amount of information for the deciders to make correct or approximately correct decisions. But monopoly in all spheres attenuates or destroys feedback mechanisms such as market-generated prices, election outcomes, reports from independent media, and advocacy from nongovernment movements and organizations. In theory, authoritarianism means that orders are issued from above and implemented below. Horizontal ties between citizens—civil society—were seen for most of the Soviet period as potentially dangerous attempts to evade party control. Horizontal ties between economic entities such as factories were also viewed with suspicion—as attempts to evade directives issued by the party and state. There is a lack of self-correcting or self-regulating mechanisms, evolutionary processes of change and development are precluded, and innovation in all spheres becomes less likely. A well-worn saying over the years of Soviet power was that "initiative is punishable." Inevitably, stability morphs into stagnation, and subsequent political-economic and social crises set the stage for new reform efforts—almost always from within the elite. Critics of the system created by Putin see Russia today as suffering from a stagnation that will continue to spiral downward.

STALINISM, 1928–1953

It was Stalin who, in the late 1920s, formed many of the core characteristics of the Soviet politico-economic system. Stalin's Soviet Union pioneered the creation of a modern, industrialized economy through a centralized, hierarchical, and highly bureaucratized state. Prior to this, from 1921–1928 during the so-called New Economic Policy period, the USSR was a mixed economy. Private ownership of small- and medium-sized businesses was allowed, along with private traders and the main elements of a market economy. Stalin and others among the Bolshevik leadership were alarmed that a continuation of this policy was undermining the ability of the Kremlin to exercise control. Beginning in 1928, the Soviet state began an historically unprecedented push to bring the economy and society under control, using massive nationalization—state ownership—as the main instrument. All economic entities, from factories to retail shops to restaurants, were soon brought under state control. The Bolsheviks recognized that support for the new order was weakest in the countryside. Private traders and the most effective peasant farmers, called kulaks, had prospered in the 1920s. In 1928, Stalin unleashed the forced collectivization of agriculture, confiscating property that was then turned over to the new collective farms. Many kulaks were killed, imprisoned, or sent into exile. Later, during the 1937 purges, hundreds of thousands more would be executed—even those who had been allowed to return home. Famine in 1932–1933 was another outcome of collectivization, as the state confiscated grain, which was exported to pay for industrial machinery. Stalin viewed

Table 1.1. Putin's Age During the Rule of Soviet and Russian Leaders

	Years in power	*Putin's age at the time*
Joseph Stalin (1879–1953)	1927–1953	<1
Nikita Khrushchev (1894–1971)	1955–1964	3–12
Leonid Brezhnev (1906–1982)	1964–1982	13–29
Mikhail Gorbachev (1931–)	1985–1991	33–39
Boris Yeltsin (1931–2007)	1991–1999	40–47
Vladimir Putin (1952–)	2000–	47–

Note: Does not include periods of significant power-sharing and transitional leaders in office for only a short time. From 2008–2012, Putin served as prime minister and continued to wield substantial power while Dmitry Medvedev was president.

rapid industrialization and building a strong military as necessary for the survival of the Soviet state in a setting characterized by "hostile capitalist encirclement," the main source for both internal and external threats to the regime.

State control was accompanied by the rapid buildup of government and communist party bureaucracies to make decisions for economic units that would normally be made by factory owners, individual farmers, and private retailers. The resulting "command economy" refused to be guided by laws of markets, such as prices sensitive to supply and demand. Centralized ministries controlled sectors of the economy to enforce the priorities of the regime. Government organs that managed the economy included variations of *Gosplan* (the State Planning Commission), *Goskomtsen* (State Committee on Prices), or *Gossnab* (the State Supply Commission), plus a wide array of state ministries for sectors of the economy such as railroads, agriculture, heavy industry (machine tools), light industry (consumer goods), and military industry. Each represented a self-contained hierarchy that zealously guarded its realm from encroachment by others.

Pluralism in the form of multiple political parties and political opposition was seen as a dangerous, existential threat. Already by 1918, the Bolsheviks had banned all political opposition, including the Left Socialist Revolutionaries and Mensheviks. The ideological justification for this came from the Leninist version of Marxism, which required a dictatorship of the proletariat to build a socialist, and eventually communist, society.[5] In 1936 the role of the vanguard party was formally enshrined in article 126 of the new "Stalin constitution" as "the progressive detachment of the working people in their struggle for strengthening and developing a socialist order, representing the guiding core of all organizations of the working people—both public and state." A secret police and spy agency, the *Cheka*—Extraordinary Commission for the Struggle Against Counter-Revolution and Sabotage—under the leadership of Feliks Dzerzhinsky, was created in December 1917 to serve as the "sword and shield" of the revolution. They openly described their initial operations as "red terror." Direct descendants of the Cheka included the OGPU, NKVD, KGB, and ultimately today's FSB—all of which proudly claimed the legacy of the original *"Chekisty."*[6]

Civil society was supplanted by state structures that appeared to perform the same functions. Strike committees of workers had been an important source of support for the Bolsheviks at the time of the revolution. Under Soviet rule, official trade unions supported state policy, mostly at the expense of worker interests. Religion also came under attack, and not simply because the ideology of Marxism-Leninism considered it a retrograde phenomenon. Prior to mass arrests of priests and the destruction of thousands of churches, the Russian Orthodox Church was an entity that violated the principle of monolithic control over education, socialization, and the propagation of values. Rather than destroy the Orthodox Church entirely, an outcome the state was easily capable of, the Soviet state brought the Church under control, and its activities and reach were severely curtailed. Over the years, the KGB extensively penetrated the Church hierarchy, so that it could no longer impede the goal of a monopoly by the Communist party over society.

Only one party was allowed, the Communist Party of the Soviet Union (CPSU).[7] Decision-making at all levels of the system was concentrated in the hierarchy of communist party organs, from the committee of the primary party organization in factories and other places of employment, to the highest decision-making bodies: the Politburo (Political Bureau) and Secretariat of the Central Committee. While one can imagine a one-party system with elements of competition and choice built in, the Soviet system centralized control over personnel matters (the *nomenklatura*). The party determined who should be members of "representative" bodies such as city councils (the Russian word "soviet" means council) or parliamentary bodies such as the Supreme Soviet.[8] Elections were held for these bodies, but the ballot consisted of the name of one candidate for each seat. Voter turnout was very high despite the lack of choice, a result of mobilization campaigns that included both carrots (food and alcohol, as well as some hard-to-find consumer goods were often on sale as one left the polling place) and sticks (party members would be held personally responsible for cajoling their fellow workers and neighbors to vote).

Newspapers and publishers were immediately banned or brought under state ownership. The party newspaper *Pravda*, which means "the truth," became the definitive source of Kremlin pronouncements. The monopoly on information meant banning foreign sources as well. With the beginning of the Cold War in the late 1940s, the Soviet state made it difficult for Soviet citizens to listen to shortwave radio broadcasts from the United States and Western Europe by jamming their signals. Cultural output of all kinds was also monitored closely for evidence of opposition or foreign influence—writers, artists, filmmakers, and even composers of classical music. Unions of filmmakers, writers, artists, composers, and theatrical workers were formed to control who was able to publish, perform, or show their work in public. *Glavlit*, created in 1922, was the main censor for printed material. Films were often previewed by Stalin personally, and he decided what should be shelved and what should be distributed widely.[9]

Paranoia about threats to his rule led Stalin to eliminate his main rivals for power, mostly in the mid-1930s, through sham judicial proceedings ("show trials") followed by swift executions. Purges in the late 1930s widened to target the higher ranks of the Communist Party itself, with "old Bolsheviks" being at highest risk. The last major rival to Stalin, Leon Trotsky, had earlier been exiled but continued to publish attacks on Stalin and the Soviet system from abroad. In 1940 Trotsky was killed by an assassin who was able to infil-trate Trotsky's household in Mexico and who was acting on orders from the Soviet secret police.

Stalin's repressive policies extended to large groups in the population. One interpretation, based on the notion of a "rational" agenda for someone suffering extreme paranoia, is that mass terror eliminated anyone who might become a threat to the regime, with excess killings justified as adding a safe margin of error.[10] Overall, *potential* enemies rather than actual ones were the targets. The characteristics that were seen as indicators of potential disloyalty included having worked or served abroad (including diplomats and military personnel), having had interactions with foreigners in the USSR, and receiv-ing a higher education before the revolution. The Soviet military leadership was left decimated by the late 1930s, and this had major repercussions in the early stages of combat operations starting in 1941. Certain ethnic minori-ties were automatically considered disloyal, and entire populations of Poles, Germans, and Koreans were exiled or killed before the war. Other factors included having the "wrong" social background or being a close relative of someone who had been an earlier target. A new article was even added to the 1937 criminal code, to punish a "Member of the Family of Traitors to the Homeland." Victims included citizens from all walks of life: scientists, engineers, writers, poets, theater directors, composers, actors. Millions were consigned by Stalin to the gulag (an acronym for "chief administration of the camps"). These camps predated Stalin but increased dramatically in size dur-ing his reign. Conditions in some of the camps were so harsh that they were effectively death camps.[11]

In the most severe period of repression, the state attempted to penetrate society even at the most granular level. This attempted "atomization" of society was not successful,[12] but levels of interpersonal trust in Soviet society were very low compared with other countries. Only at the level of family, close friends, and workmates could one openly complain or express opinions that could be considered antiregime.

The postwar period of "late Stalinism" established some characteristics that would persist for decades. The Cold War exacerbated earlier tendencies toward xenophobia, while the instability of the earlier "revolutionary" phase of Stalinism was replaced by a more predictable, bureaucratic model. In the words of the historian Evgeny Dobrenko, "the institutions of the new state were consolidated, as was the Soviet nation, with its fantasies of its own greatness and 'primacy'; its aspirations to a messianic role and conviction of its absolute moral superiority; its aggressive nationalism and imperialism; its resentment of and implacable resistance to the haughty West; and its deeply rooted authoritarianism, statism, paternalism, and anti-liberalism."[13]

Vladimir Putin was born in Leningrad (now St. Petersburg) during this period, in the last months of Stalin's rule. If one accepts the Soviet-era postulate that the country was divided into two groups—those who were prisoners and those who were their guards—Putin's family's roots were with the guards. His father's father, Spiridon Putin, had been a cook in the households of both Lenin and Stalin, a position that was highly sensitive given the Soviet leaders' fears that their enemies would try to poison them. Putin's father, Vladimir Spiridonovich Putin, served in an NKVD battalion during World War II and was wounded in combat. The family lived in conditions typical of postwar Leningrad: a small room in a shared, multifamily "communal" apartment.[14]

KHRUSHCHEV AND "THE THAW," 1953–1964

With Stalin's death, there began almost immediately a "de-Stalinization" of nearly every sphere of public life, which came to be known as "the thaw." (A recent book on the thaw published in Russia provides a day-by-day account of key changes in culture and politics from 1953 to 1968; it runs almost 1,200 pages.[15]) This process was sped up by the consolidation of power by Nikita Khrushchev, who used de-Stalinization to undermine the position of his rivals. Most prisoners who survived were released from the gulag and had their rights restored, while the legal system was reformed under the banner of "restoring socialist legality."

The 1953 revision of the Soviet constitution again placed the Communist Party at the center of the country's political life: It is "the progressive detachment of the working people for the building of a communist society and represents the guiding core of all organizations, both public and state." In 1956 Khrushchev's famous "secret speech" at the end of the twentieth party congress criticized the purges and Stalin's treatment of the Communist Party elite. Khrushchev and others in the top leadership stopped executing rivals for power who were ousted. Lavrenty Beria, head of the KGB and feared by all the other members of the ruling elite, was the last Politburo member to die as a result of losing out to his fellow Politburo members, in 1953. Later, members of the inner circle who fell from favor with Khrushchev, such as the "Anti-party group" that attempted to remove him in 1957—Politburo members Malenkov, Molotov, and Kaganovich—were not executed or imprisoned but demoted to unimportant positions far from the center of power.

The easing of rigid controls on culture was the element of the thaw best remembered in today's Russia. While Glavlit continued to function, censorship was relaxed, and points of view that had been suppressed or worse under Stalin now could get published or presented on stage and screen. Editors of major literary journals staked out enough autonomy to publish works that were highly controversial, such as Alexander Solzhenitsyn's *One Day in the Life of Ivan Denisovich*. The novella, published in a leading Soviet literary journal in 1962, was based on Solzhenitsyn's own experiences and depicted conditions in the gulag in stark terms. The Soviet film industry began a period of unprecedented creativity, including the 1958 Cannes festival winner, Mikhail Kalatozov's *The Cranes Are Flying*. The renowned filmmaker Andrei Tarkovsky was able to make his first film, fresh out of film school, in 1962. All his films included spiritual undertones that went against the official ideology that was supposed to govern all cultural output.[16]

Khrushchev exposed Soviet citizens to the outside world. A landmark event was the 1957 international youth festival held in Moscow, in which thousands of foreigners from around the world visited and interacted with Soviet youth. There were still limits, though—in the context of the Cold War, foreign radio broadcasts were still jammed, and international travel was still highly restricted through a system of "exit visas" under which citizens had to apply for the right to leave the country. (Restrictions on leaving the USSR had been in place since the late 1920s.)

Development of Soviet science, engineering, and technology reached its peak in the Khrushchev years. Achievements in rocketry, the first satellite—*sputnik*—and the first man in space were heralded around the world. Resources devoted to science increased. Khrushchev created a Siberian Branch of the Academy of Sciences in the new campus-like city of Akademgorodok, just outside Novosibirsk. Being far from Moscow meant that the traditional hold of the Moscow research institutes and bureaucracies was broken or at least attenuated. Even the social sciences benefited from this distance and relatively free atmosphere. Over two decades later, Siberian sociologists and economists were among the experts who helped guide Gorbachev's reform efforts.

There was no organized dissident movement in this period. There were, however, infrequent popular outbursts against regime policies, including mass protests in Tbilisi, Georgia—1956, against de-Stalinization; and in Novocherkassk, Russia—1962, against food price increases. Both were brutally put down by the KGB and the Soviet army using tanks and machine guns.[17]

Khrushchev set about to resolve what he considered the biggest drag on the economy—the rigid, centralized system of bureaucracy in the ministries and in the communist party itself. He deconcentrated decision-making by breaking up Moscow-based ministries and sending officials to regional centers. Khrushchev also split the party structure into agriculture and industrial branches. Administrative shakeups did little to improve economic performance, though they did cause disruption and resentment among the bureaucratic elite. Much of the Stalinist economic system remained intact: the collective farm system, state planning, centrally set prices, and the state monopoly on ownership. Agriculture, Khrushchev's self-proclaimed specialty, was hit by disastrous harvests. The Soviet Union began in 1962 to import grain and was thus able to maintain its level of meat output. There were also attempts to shift priorities to increase the production of consumer goods and the first major effort to build housing for an increasingly urban population.

Khrushchev's reforms alienated many in positions of power—other Politburo members, the military, police, and regional party leaders who made up the majority in the Central Committee of the CPSU. Fellow Politburo members conspired with Leonid Brezhnev to oust Khrushchev from the party leadership in October 1964. The conspirators went over Khrushchev's head to organize a meeting of the Party's Central Committee, who voted to force Khrushchev into early retirement. He died of natural causes in 1971, but not before dictating his memoirs in secret and publishing them in the West.[18]

BREZHNEVISM, 1965–1985

Vladimir Putin was little affected by the radical breakthroughs of Khrushchev era's thaw, since he was only twelve years old by the time Khrushchev was ousted. Putin's formative years as a teenager and as an adult coincided completely with the long-running Brezhnev era. Almost immediately, the Politburo under Brezhnev reversed Khrushchev's administrative reforms, which they labeled "harebrained schemes." Stability and "trust in cadres" became the guiding principles. Bureaucratization of economic decision-making increased while performance lagged; production bottlenecks and shortages were met with the creation of new ministries. Party hardliners considered economic reform to be a threat to their political control over the economy, even if the result of reforms would be improved economic performance. It was Brezhnev's good fortune that in the 1970s, the world market price of oil and gas rose sharply, just as the USSR was expanding its export potential. Thus, imports of technology and food were able to cover up at least some of the flaws in the system.

The Supreme Soviet and legislative bodies at lower levels played only a symbolic role in policymaking. The Communist Party's monopoly on political power was retained in the Brezhnev period and even enshrined in the new, 1977 Soviet Constitution. Article 6 stated that "the Communist Party of the Soviet Union is the leading and guiding force of Soviet society and the core of its political system, state and public organizations. The CPSU exists for the people and serves the people. Armed with Marxism–Leninism, the

Communist Party guides the overall development of society and the course of the domestic and foreign policy of the USSR, directs the great constructive activity of the Soviet people, and gives their struggle for the victory of communism a systematic and scientifically grounded character."

It was during the Brezhnev era that Vladimir Putin began his career in the KGB. He had been attracted in part by the Andropov-era[19] refurbishing of the KGB's image, particularly through film and television. The Soviet entertainment industry presented Soviet spies in heroic terms, but their actual work in the Brezhnev era was anything but heroic. Much of it was devoted to monitoring "dangerous" dissidents and Soviet citizens' contacts with foreigners. It is not known if, as a young KGB operative during the Brezhnev years, Putin was engaged in repressing dissent. One of his close associates at the time, Viktor Cherkesov, definitely was. Putin has never spoken in detail about his KGB activities prior to 1985.

The KGB took the lead in cracking down on independent thought in all areas. Universities and research institutes, where most of the Soviet intelligentsia was employed, were under strict party and KGB control. Every academic institution had a KGB-staffed office that monitored political views of students and faculty, as well as foreign contacts, and oversaw the protection of state secrets. The social sciences were singled out for enhanced repression, while the teaching of "scientific communism" took a central position in universities. Sociology and the nascent field of public opinion research was decimated by hardliners in the late 1960s. Repression of dissent became systematic in the Brezhnev era. Censorship was enhanced, and writers unable to publish their work began circulating copies that were "self-published" (*samizdat*, typed using carbon paper). Works that could be smuggled out through foreign correspondents or diplomats were often published abroad (called *tamizdat*, meaning published "over there").

The "thaw" had created a constituency among the intelligentsia for openness and free expression that bristled in the face of repression. Early in the Brezhnev era, in 1966, prosecutors brought the first case against dissident writers whose work appeared abroad, Andrei Sinyavskii and Yuli Dan'iel. The authorities, in effect, criminalized criticism of the Soviet system under the charge of "anti-Soviet agitation." In response to the writers' trial and increased repression, dissidents began to organize. *The Chronicle of Current Events*, an underground periodical, began to circulate as *samizdat* in 1968, reporting on protests, searches and arrests, and trials across the full spectrum of dissident activity. Soon after, the first dissident movement appeared, the "initiative group for the defense of human rights in the USSR." Other prominent groups were formed in 1975 after the Soviet Union signed the Helsinki Accords, which included provisions guaranteeing human rights. Helsinki

Watch Groups were founded in several Soviet cities to present evidence of Soviet violations of the Accords.

Dissidents never represented a serious political threat to the regime; they were few in number and had little influence beyond a narrow stratum of the population, and their voices were heard abroad through the reporting of Western correspondents. "Those who think differently" were perceived, nonetheless, as an ideological threat, a threat to the system's legitimacy. In the latter Brezhnev years, forced exile, combined with the loss of Soviet citizenship, became a common form of punishment for dissidents of all types. There were multiple and mutually incompatible strands of dissident thought, including most prominently Western-oriented liberals such as Andrei Sakharov (nuclear physicist, "father of the Soviet hydrogen bomb") and conservative, religious nationalists such as Solzhenitsyn. Sakharov, drawing on his experience in scientific research, called for the free exchange of ideas and an end to state censorship as essential to social progress.[20] After criticizing the Soviet intervention in Afghanistan, Sakharov was forced into internal exile in the Russian city of Gorky (now Nizhnii Novgorod) in 1980.[21] In 1976 Solzhenitsyn was sent into forced exile, most of which he spent writing in an isolated part of Vermont. He had earlier been deprived of his Soviet citizenship.

Other nonconformist writers and artists whose work was less overtly political were unable to publish in their homeland and were pressured to emigrate. Among them were the poet Joseph Brodsky (convicted of "parasitism"—not having a visible means of support—and later winner of the Nobel prize for literature) and Sergei Dovlatov, whose ironic storytelling would become popular in Russia in the 1990s. The filmmaker Andrei Tarkovsky, while working in Italy, decided not to return to the Soviet Union in 1979. Prior to this, his films were almost never shown to the public, and he died in exile in 1986. Even the work of classical music composers was subject to censorship and repression. The works of modern composers such as Alfred Schnittke, Sofia Gubaidulina, Gia Kancheli, and Arvo Pärt, all now widely performed by orchestras in both Russia and worldwide, were effectively banned from being performed in Brezhnev's time. Most of them made a living composing music for Soviet films as a side profession. Rock music was suspect as a vessel of Western values; it nevertheless developed "underground" with concerts in private apartments and basements. Vladimir Putin's Leningrad was one of the hotbeds of Russian rock, with its own unofficial "rock club" dating back to 1981. Even it was under close KGB supervision.[22] (Putin apparently had no interest in the rock music scene. At a 2010 meeting with cultural figures in his hometown, he acted as if he did not know Yuri Shevchuk, a Soviet-Russian rock icon who founded the popular group DDT. When Putin asked him to introduce himself, Shevchuk replied, "Yura, a musician.")

Over time, the KGB worked out an extremely effective system of measures to quell dissent. A wide range of tactics was applied, usually calibrated to dissuade dissidents from continuing their activities. *The Chronicle of Current Events* was eventually infiltrated, its organizers and contributors imprisoned or exiled, and it ceased publication at the end of 1982. Defense lawyers who were effective at using Soviet laws to defend dissidents in court were also targeted for repression. Treatment at the hands of the KGB could be extremely harsh; forced confinement to mental institutions was one of the most brutal types.[23] State psychiatrists came up with a specific diagnosis of "sluggish schizophrenia"—political opposition was designated as an inability to accept reality. That said, there were no known cases of Soviet dissidents being murdered by the KGB during the Brezhnev years.

GORBACHEV, YELTSIN, AND THE END OF THE SOVIET SYSTEM, 1985–1999

Though Brezhnev for years suffered serious health issues that affected his ability to perform his duties, he remained in power until his death in 1982. Yuri Andropov, a personal hero of Putin's, became party leader for a brief period until he died in office in 1984.[24] Konstantin Chernenko, formerly Brezhnev's top aide, took over for another brief term before he, too, succumbed to illness in 1985. In the aftermath, the overall vector of policies that characterized the Brezhnev era would soon be labeled as the "stagnation period."

The heavy legacy of Brezhnevism and incomplete de-Stalinization made the reform of the Soviet system a nearly impossible task. The new general secretary of the Communist Party, Mikhail Gorbachev, began to craft an agenda for change in the face of growing economic crises, made even more dire by a sharp drop in the price of oil. Most of the Soviet officials who conceived and carried out reforms in this period were born in the 1930s and had come of age politically during Khrushchev's thaw. Mikhail Gorbachev himself was a student in the law program at Moscow University during the 1950s and even shared a dormitory room with a foreigner. (His roommate, from Czechoslovakia, was Zdenek Milosz, who in 1968 was one of the architects of the "Prague Spring." He remained in touch with Gorbachev, and many elements of Gorbachev's reform program mirrored the course of liberalization in Czechoslovakia before the Soviet invasion.[25])

Gorbachev had several rivals for power, but none were arrested or imprisoned. Early competitors for the top party post in the Politburo were forced to retire. By 1988 onetime allies had turned against Gorbachev—Yegor Ligachev on the communist left, and Boris Yeltsin on the democratic right. Ligachev, who initially oversaw the media, was increasingly marginalized.

Gorbachev had brought Yeltsin to Moscow from Sverdlovsk to serve in the important post of Moscow city party chief. After publicly dissenting on the pace and scope of reforms, Yeltsin was removed from his post and the Politburo. While Gorbachev later regretted, only partly in jest, that he did not name Yeltsin ambassador to some African country, Yeltsin was allowed to remain in Moscow as a deputy minister of the construction sector. Yeltsin's popularity increasingly eclipsed that of Gorbachev between 1989–1991, and in 1991 Yeltsin was elected president of the Russian Federation.

Gorbachev began cautious economic reforms, including allowing for the first time since the 1920s the rise of a private sector. New businesses, called "cooperatives," were subject to many limitations, and Gorbachev refused to reject socialism as the fundamental principle of the Soviet system. It was not until the Soviet Union ceased to exist that large-scale privatization of state enterprises began in earnest. Privatization of housing began in the Gorbachev era and continued in the 1990s; in a lucrative game of musical chairs, most Soviet citizens could obtain without cost the rights to the apartments they were living in at the time.

Gorbachev released all political prisoners, understanding that his agenda included some of the policies they had been arrested for advocating. Officials hurriedly installed a telephone in Andrei Sakharov's Gorky apartment, in December 1986, so that he could receive a call from Gorbachev informing him that he was now free to return to his apartment in Moscow. "Informal" groups and organizations not under state tutelage, the building blocks of civil society, began to emerge during perestroika. Sakharov was one of the founders of "Memorial," the most important human rights organization to emerge in this period. The purpose of Memorial, founded in 1989, was to recover the names and stories of victims of Soviet political repression—taking up, retrospectively, the work begun earlier by the *Chronicle of Current Events.* It also had as its mission the defense of human rights in today's Russia.

Perhaps the most important reforms Gorbachev introduced came under the heading of democratization and "glasnost"—meaning openness, or "giving voice." Domestic media, especially newspapers and television, were in the forefront of glasnost, with many editors being willing to take risks in order to publish highly sensitive and controversial material. Jamming of foreign radio stations ceased, and under Yeltsin's rule they were even invited to open offices in Moscow. The cultural sphere also became freer, and there was an effective end to censorship. Alexander Solzhenitsyn's *Gulag Archipelago*, his monumental history of the Soviet prison camp system, was finally published in the Soviet Union, years after it had appeared in the West. His citizenship was restored in 1990, and he triumphantly returned to post-Soviet Russia in 1994. Sergei Dovlatov's short stories and novellas began to be published in the Soviet Union, and he became one of the most popular of contemporary

Russian authors.[26] Perestroika in the film industry began in 1986 with a shakeup in the Soviet filmmakers' union. Films that had been blocked from distribution or "shelved" after a limited showing were now shown across the country to broad audiences. New films such as *Repentance*, by the Georgian director Tengiz Abuladze, challenged viewers to question the Stalinist legacy, and by extension, the legitimacy of Stalin's successors.[27] New films explored topics that had been banned in the past: disillusioned youth, criminality, corruption, stifling bureaucracy, harsh conditions in Soviet prisons. This new freedom in cinema continued under Yeltsin, though the economic disruption made financing of films difficult. Most Russian films that were made in the 1990s had very low budgets, but they were made in an atmosphere of near total freedom. (Popular films from this period included Sergei Bodrov's *Prisoner of the Mountains*, Pavel Chukhrai's *The Thief,* Aleksei Balabanov's *Brother,* and Yuri Mamin's *Window to Paris.*) Critical, independent media continued to develop under Boris Yeltsin, even when Yeltsin was himself the target of biting satire and criticism. (See chapter 6.)

Democratization had several components. Political pluralism rapidly reemerged, with the first contested elections since the revolution. The landmark 1989 elections to the Congress of People's Deputies included many candidates who were opponents of the CPSU and who sought further democratic reforms. Yeltsin, who was allowed to run in the district representing the entire city of Moscow, made a dramatic political comeback as an outsider and an advocate of more radical reform. Conservative forces still comprised most representatives in the new body, and part of the body was chosen by organizations rather than through popular vote. Gorbachev did not subject himself to popular election, but instead led the slate put forward by the CPSU. Televised sessions of the first sessions led to the rise of several political stars among the "democrats." Andrei Sakharov, who had been elected on the slate representing the Academy of Sciences, was the most famous of the democrats, along with Boris Yeltsin. Another was a then-unknown law professor from Leningrad, Anatoly Sobchak, who in 1990 become chairman of the city council and later the elected mayor and a mentor to Vladimir Putin. The opposition for the first time organized a minority faction in a Soviet parliament—the "interregional deputies' group." Though initially opposed by Gorbachev, in March 1990 the Soviet parliament changed article 6 of the Soviet constitution, ending the CPSU's political monopoly. In 1990 the Russian Federation elected its own Congress of People's Deputies, and Yeltsin won by just a few votes the post of speaker. This proved to be the springboard to the newly created post of president of the Russian Federation, and Yeltsin was popularly elected president in June 1991. Among the deputies elected in 1990 was a young politician, Boris Nemtsov, a physicist and environmental activist from the Gorky region (soon to be called Nizhnii Novgorod) whom Yeltsin would later appoint as the region's governor.

The last year of Gorbachev's rule was marked by contradictory moves. He filled the top posts with advocates of more conservative views and was slow to see that centrifugal forces that were developing in many of the Soviet republics made preservation of the USSR increasingly untenable. His hard-line subordinates staged a brief coup, in August 1991, and held Gorbachev incommunicado at his state dacha in the Crimea. The coup failed when Yeltsin rallied the opposition in Moscow, and Soviet military and KGB units refused to follow orders to intervene. The coup plotters were arrested and tried, though all were freed only a few months later. The failed coup under-mined Gorbachev's power and sped up the collapse of the Soviet Union. (See chapter 12.) In late December, Yeltsin took over in the Kremlin as the leader of Russia, the largest of what now would be fifteen independent states.

Under Yeltsin, Russia's democratic development continued, though not without periodic crises and turmoil. Clashes between the president and an increasingly assertive parliament—the Russian Duma, which had been elected in 1990—led to an armed confrontation in October 1993. Tanks were ordered to shell the parliament building when the Russian vice president and the parliamentary speaker attempted to use force to seize power. They were arrested, but like the coup leaders from 1991, only served a few months in prison when the parliament amnestied them. Yeltsin's rivals for power were all treated quite humanely in defeat. Yeltsin's past nemesis, Gorbachev, was able to remain in Moscow after leaving office and headed his own foundation. Former vice president Aleksander Rutskoi, a leader of the 1993 coup attempt, won election as governor of Kursk region in 1996. In the aftermath of the October 1993 events, Yeltsin oversaw the drafting of a new Constitution, which went into effect at the end of 1993. It provided for a strong presidency but also guaranteed many democratic rights, including freedom of speech, a total ban on censorship, the right to assemble peacefully, and a near-universal right to vote and run for political office. A bicameral parliament was created, consisting of a lower house, the Duma, and an upper house to represent the regions, the Federation Council. Elections were largely free and fair—though there was evidence of significant fraud in the 1996 presidential elections—both for Yeltsin and for the communist party candidate Gennady Zyuganov.

Elections in the Yeltsin era gave voters a genuine choice between multiple political parties—in the 1995 Duma election, there were forty-three parties on the ballot, and if that were not enough, discerning voters could choose to vote "against all." Duma elections in late 1993 and 1995 produced majorities in opposition to Yeltsin. The Duma came close to impeaching Yeltsin. An important issue was the Chechen war, which was opposed by human rights advocates and liberal Yeltsin supporters such as Boris Nemtsov.

Post-Soviet Russia did not attempt to introduce "lustration," as in some Eastern European countries—banning former secret police and party officials from political life and major government posts. As a result, former cogs in the repressive apparatus from the late Soviet period continued to have influence for decades after Russia became "free." One example was Vladimir Putin. Putin not only missed "the thaw"; he also did not personally experience perestroika because of his job assignment in the KGB. In August 1985, just as Gorbachev was consolidating power, Putin received his highest posting as a KGB officer in Dresden, East Germany. So, while his home country was enthralled with the new hope generated by perestroika and glasnost, Putin was working in a country whose leadership resisted change to the end. East German communists, more than most in Eastern Europe, were alarmed by Gorbachev's attempts to reform the system. For a period, the GDR (German Democratic Republic) even banned Soviet journals and papers that were in the forefront of perestroika.

East Germany was an outlier among communist countries. On the one hand, it managed to achieve one of the highest living standards in the communist world. Putin was enamored of the economic successes he saw, and East Germans had a much higher standard of living than he was used to, even in the relatively affluent city of Leningrad. Consumer goods were of high quality by Soviet standards.[28] At the same time, the GDR distinguished itself with the size of the secret police apparatus and its deep penetration of East German society. The Stasi, while modeled on the Soviet KGB, played a much greater role in the political system. Massive surveillance was carried out through a large core of secret collaborators. By 1989, as the Soviet empire in Eastern Europe began to disintegrate, Putin was still in Dresden. East Germany was undergoing a revolution as popular disenchantment against the communist state grew. It is unlikely that Putin, whose circle of contacts comprised fellow Soviet KGB operatives and Stasi officers,[29] had any awareness or understanding of the popular mood and its origins. Stasi internal documents insisted that domestic political unrest was the product of Western subversion.[30] In 1989, Putin witnessed for the first time in his life popular protests that would cause the regime to fall. Putin was appalled, and from then on, he equated protests with rioting and mass disturbances.

Gorbachev quickly drew down the Soviet presence as Germany reunited. Putin and his family returned to Leningrad in January 1990, jobless and without significant savings—though he did have an automobile. Putin has since claimed that he made money on the side, as did many at the time, using his car as an unofficial taxi. He found employment in the international department of his alma mater,[31] Leningrad State University, and soon became an aide to his former law professor, Anatoly Sobchak, in city government. This proved to be the springboard to Putin's rise in politics, first in St. Petersburg and later in the Kremlin. During the 1990s, Putin directly experienced the deconstruction of the Soviet system and the chaotic rise of a new political and economic system based on pluralism, elections, private ownership, and markets but hampered by bureaucracy, poverty, cronyism, and criminality. Putin also had first-hand experience with some of the defects in representative democracy when extended conflicts developed between Sobchak and the Leningrad city council. Putin himself was accused of fraudulent dealings and was one of the first city officials in post-Soviet Russia to be the subject of a parliamentary investigation on corruption charges.[32]

Putin also had direct experience with competitive elections at this time, coming out on the losing side when he managed Sobchak's 1996 reelection campaign. The lessons learned did not endear Putin to electoral politics and the functioning of Russian democracy. He saw how voters could be easily manipulated by the media and how easily the loyalty of top officials could be bought. Loss of this election and his resignation from the St. Petersburg city administration is what led to Putin's hiring at the Kremlin and set in motion his meteoric and unexpected career rise—from head of the Control Administration (overseeing regional governance) to head of FSB for a brief period, then prime minister, and finally Yeltsin's designated successor as president.

PUTIN IN POWER, 2000–

Vladimir Putin, once he was elected president, almost immediately began to use his newly gained powers to reduce the role of autonomous political actors and institutions of all types. His first targets were governors, oligarchs (including Yeltsin's inner circle, or "family," which had supported his candidacy), and the media. All were brought under his control through a series of special operations in which much of the activity took place behind the scenes, covering up the direct role of the Kremlin. Putin gradually reversed the democratizing political reforms introduced by Gorbachev and Yeltsin. Political power in Russia became more concentrated, parliament was cleansed of opposition fractions, and elections became increasingly meaningless. In 2004, Putin completely halted elections of regional leaders; these resumed only after 2012 for most regions, but with limitations that enabled the Kremlin to usually determine the outcome. (See chapter 3.)

Having experienced unruly, opposition-dominated representative bodies in St. Petersburg, Putin was determined never to face that problem as president. The upper house of the parliament, the Federation Council, had frequently used its veto in the 1990s to thwart policies that hurt regional interests. It was soon reorganized, and the Presidential Administration dictated who would be appointed to the body by the regions. In the lower house, the Duma, Putin never had less than a majority. The 1999 Duma election gave Putin a working majority, and in subsequent elections, liberal, opposition parties were outmaneuvered and excluded. Elections during the Putin era became increasingly unfair, with frequent changes in the procedures and rampant fraud committed by election commissions at all levels. The runup to elections often predetermined the outcome: strong opposition candidates were usually prevented from registering.

The party of Putin loyalists, eventually to be called United Russia, has been the dominant party ever since he came to power. In 2007 it won a constitutional majority, a two-thirds majority allowing it to adopt any law and even change the constitution without the support of any other party. It preserved this status, with the help of the Central Election Commission and fraud perpetrated at lower levels, in subsequent Duma elections in 2011, 2016, and 2021. It has also achieved a dominant role in almost all regional parliaments and city councils. Putin's fear of any power centers not directly under his control meant that United Russia was given little autonomy and was closely controlled by the Presidential Administration and at times by his governors in the regions. Other parties represented in the Duma—the Communist Party of the Russian Federation (the Russian acronym is KPRF), the Liberal Democratic Party of Russia (LDPR), and, after 2006, A Just Russia (SR)—were all either creatures of, or coopted by, the Kremlin. They, too, were closely monitored by the Presidential Administration, and they ceased to act even as a minority opposition to United Russia. In the 2021 Duma elections, a new fifth party called "New People" also won seats in the Duma. The party promoted itself as a proponent of liberal values, but it, too, had been formed at the initiative of the Presidential Administration.[33]

Most laws were drafted either by the Presidential Administration or the ministries. They were passed with unanimous or nearly unanimous votes, echoing the pattern set by the Supreme Soviet in the USSR. The parties represented in the Duma came to be known as "within system" parties. No party could openly oppose Putin or his priorities if they wished to remain a part of the Russian political landscape. A party that rejected this condition was designated as being "outside the system" and was met with varying degrees of discrimination or repression. Over time, Putin effectively outlawed any organized political opposition. Vyacheslav Volodin, speaker of the Duma, on opening the new Duma in October 2021, used sophistic logic to justify loyalty to the regime: "independently of which party we represent, we all represent the legislative power of the Russian Federation, the highest legislative organ. It is impossible, while being in power, to be in opposition to it at the same time."[34]

The first significant police repression of the opposition in post-Soviet Russia began in 2006. Protesters, usually few in number, demanded the freedom of assembly guaranteed by article 31 of the constitution. In late 2011 and 2012, political protests increased in scale, with turnouts of well over one hundred thousand in Moscow and a few other cities. Putin refused to allow these protesters and their leaders to enter the formal political life of the country. Instead, they were surveilled, harassed, arrested, tried, and imprisoned. The first wave of convictions came after the 2012 presidential inauguration protests, and they increased in the years that followed. By 2021, the number of political prisoners approached that of Brezhnev's Soviet Union.[35] The number of Russian political exiles from all walks of life increased dramatically as well, exceeding the number of Soviet exiles thanks to open borders.[36] Regime opponents were tailed and harassed by the FSB, ironically by the section responsible for "preserving the constitutional order." In their understanding, the written constitution was subordinate to the de facto reality of an antiliberal, authoritarian regime. Supporters of democratic change and anticorruption reforms were the enemies of the state. There was a return to the late Soviet practice of forcibly committing dissidents to mental institutions. Another "innovation" adopted from the Soviet period was to harass and arrest family members of opposition leaders, activists, and their lawyers, also on trumped-up charges.[37]

Putin, adopting the mindset of the Cheka, NKVD, KGB, FSB, and the Stasi before him, viewed political opponents as agents of Western influence, a "fifth column." In 2012, the Russian parliament adopted a law on "foreign agents." The degree of foreign support for an organization was not weighed in making this determination; when it was lacking, fake contributions from abroad were initiated to justify the label. Once on the list of foreign agents, organizations were subjected to onerous reports on their activities and finances and were banned from engaging in loosely defined "political" activities. In essence, the Kremlin was returning to Soviet policies to prohibit dissent. Among those designated as a foreign agent, in 2016, was Memorial, the organization that Andrei Sakharov had helped create during perestroika to defend human rights and commemorate the victims of Stalinism. In late December 2021, Russian prosecutors won their case in the Russian Supreme Court to liquidate the organization. Initially, they claimed Memorial had neglected to add the "foreign agent" label to some of its publications. In court, prosecutors revealed the real motive: Memorial had created a "false" image of the USSR as a "terrorist state." Putin himself had criticized Memorial a few weeks earlier for its current activities, in support of "terrorist and extremist organizations."[38] At the same time, the FSB blocked access to the names of NKVD agents who fabricated cases that led to innocent victims being executed in the 1930s, claiming that these constituted "personal data" of intelligence officers who needed to be protected from public exposure. In a step that mirrored the KGB harassment of *The Chronicle of Current Events*, in December 2021 internet regulators blocked access to the site of *OVD-Info*, the leading source of real-time information on political arrests as well as a coordinator of legal assistance.[39]

Opponents of Putin were not simply arrested and imprisoned. In 2015, days after a state-sponsored march against "traitors" among the opposition, Boris Nemtsov was murdered on a bridge within sight of the Kremlin. Nemtsov had been a vocal opponent of Russia's military operations on Ukrainian territory, just as he had opposed Yeltsin's war in Chechnya. He was the only opposition leader who had previously served as a regional governor, government minister, party leader, and member of the Duma. Most likely, Putin did not have a direct role in Nemtsov's death, though it was discovered later that an FSB team tasked with the elimination of political opponents had shadowed his movements in the months before the assassination. Evidence instead points directly to the leader of Chechnya, Ramzan Kadyrov.[40] But the Kremlin created the political atmosphere around the murder and directly intervened to curtail the investigation when it began to get too close to Kadyrov, who is seen by Putin as critical to stability in the North Caucasus.

The rule of law promised by the 1993 constitution was shredded. Courts, at least on matters of concern to the state, became part of the "vertical of power." Despite a constitutional prohibition of censorship, authorities increasingly relied on courts to stop the spread of opposition views. Activist artists from the group Pussy Riot were convicted in 2012 of "hooliganism" when they attempted to stage a feminist, anti-Putin performance in Moscow's main cathedral. Afterward a law was passed making it a crime to offend someone's religious feelings.[41] Over time, the Soviet practice of preemptive censorship was applied to musicians, actors, and other performing artists—even rappers and stand-up comics—who supported opposition views. The authorities disrupted planned concerts and other events; typically, this would happen behind the scenes—a phone call from a local official to a concert venue would threaten difficulties if a planned event was not cancelled. Blacklists forbade the appearance of a long list of actors, directors, writers, musicians, and scholars on national television. Films, most of which could not be made without state support, could not feature actors who had supported the opposition in social media or by attending protests.[42] The Kremlin mobilized prosecutors, investigators, and financial auditors to put pressure on a range of liberal-leaning institutions in culture and higher education. A prime example was the "theater case" directed at the most famous contemporary director, Kiril Serebrennikov. Universities with a reputation for being bastions of liberal thought, such as the Higher School of Economics—were subjected to new restrictions and leadership changes. The role of FSB overseers ("curators") at universities and research institutes was restored and expanded.[43] Public opinion research institutes, working in a field that was reborn in the late 1980s and 1990s, were mostly brought under Kremlin control.[44]

Fear of mass protests, enhanced after the election-related protests of late 2011–2012, led to substantial increases in the size and budgets of internal security forces. A new police unit, the Russian National Guard (*Rosgvardia*), was formed in 2016 with former Putin bodyguard Viktor Zolotov in charge.[45] Control of mass protests was one of their major functions. The *siloviki*—the men in uniforms from the police and military—have played a central role in Putin's inner circle since the beginning. Efforts to maintain their loyalty was a core component of Putin's system of rule. The total number of personnel in uniform (police, army, prosecutors, judges, security guards, etc.) as a percent of the Russian workforce is among the highest in the world. The military and private security agencies alone employ around four million men.

The Navalny Threat and Putin's Response

The most serious challenge to Putin's rule had its origins in protests that emerged after widespread election fraud in the December 2011 Duma elections, particularly in Moscow. A previously little-known figure in Russian opposition politics, Alexei Navalny, emerged as the unofficial leader of the protests that followed the elections. Navalny's political views fall squarely in the liberal democratic camp. His program, which he often describes as building a "Beautiful Russia of the Future," was influenced by liberal advisers such as the economist Sergei Guriev. Navalny's opponents, including former fellow members of the Yabloko party, have tried to stigmatize Navalny as having nationalist proclivities, including a prejudiced view of non-Russians. In fact, this has not been an element of Navalny's political views since he rose to prominence.[46] His model of a future Russia is one with checks and balances, an independent judiciary, free press, and political pluralism. The focus of Navalny's political activities was exposing corruption among Russia's ruling elite. In September 2011 he established the Foundation for the Struggle Against Corruption (FBK is the Russian abbreviation), which investigated abuse of power and corruption among Putin's elite. The material was presented in an engaging way, typically combining the dry content of property and business records with drone footage of mansions, internet memes, and a heavy dose of mocking irony. FBK videos attracted millions of views on YouTube. Particularly popular was the 2017 exposé of former president Dmitry Medvedev, with the title "Stop Calling Him Dimon!"[47] The allegations made in the video sparked large protests in major Russian cities, and increasingly Navalny's efforts attracted younger protesters.

Navalny attempted repeatedly to engage in politics within the established constitutional order, organizing a nationwide political movement that he sought to register as a political party. Every time the documents were submitted to the Ministry of Justice, however, the applications were rejected. Navalny also organized a political campaign in hopes of running for president in 2018, and established offices led by his supporters in most Russian regions. The Kremlin sought over the years to rein in Navalny by tasking prosecutors with "finding" violations in his previous commercial activities. In one case, involving the French cosmetic retailer Yves Roche, Navalny was initially sentenced to prison, but after a large, impromptu protest in the center of Moscow, the court changed his sentence to probation. The European Court of Human Rights, the ultimate appeals court for all members of the European Council (including Russia), determined that Navalny had not received a fair trial. Nevertheless, Alexei Navalny's brother, Oleg, who was his business partner in a shipping contract for Yves Roche, was imprisoned for three and a half years, and Alexei Navalny's suspended sentence remained in force.

The one indulgence the Kremlin granted to Navalny was to allow him to run for the important post of Moscow mayor in 2013. Popular elections for regional leaders had just been reinstated. The Presidential Administration badly miscalculated, having assumed that the Kremlin's choice, Sergei Sobyanin, would win easily amid a large field of opposition candidates. (In elections for regional heads, if the top candidate receives less than 50 percent, a second round is held between the top two candidates.) Denied access to mass media or even billboard space, Navalny ran a sophisticated campaign with an army of young volunteers and made personal appearances throughout the city nearly every day. He came in a strong second to Sobyanin, with 27 percent of the official tally, while Sobyanin barely avoided a runoff—most likely helped over the top with vote fraud.

Street protests, all peaceful until the police tried to break them up, have been a major part of Navalny's activities since 2011, and perhaps this was the greatest irritant to the Kremlin and to Putin personally. In December 2016, Navalny announced that he was seeking to become a candidate for the Russian presidency in the 2018 election. He began traveling around the country to open local campaign headquarters. Navalny's attempts to get on the ballot were thwarted. But over the course of 2017–2018, he and his supporters in the regions organized protests that were national in scope. Few were authorized in advance by the local authorities, and they were treated by law enforcement as "mass disturbances."

In August 2020, while returning from a trip to film reports on regional politics from Tomsk, Siberia, Navalny collapsed on board his flight; immediately, poison was suspected as the cause.[48] Fortunately for him, the pilot chose to make a quick emergency landing in Omsk, where he received vital first aid.

Navalny spent three days there in a coma in a poorly equipped clinic; Putin finally agreed to demands that he be medevacked to Germany. There, traces of the nerve agent *novichok* were found in his system and on items that had been secured from his hotel room in Tomsk. This chemical was developed in Russia and has been banned by the international convention on chemical and biological weapons signed by Russia; stockpiles are under strict Russian government control by the FSB and GRU. (Previously the same substance had been used by Russian agents trying to kill a former GRU double agent, Sergei Skripal, in Salisbury, England.) Though the source of the poison and Putin's role in this attempted murder were obvious, it was thought that direct evidence and the names and affiliations of the attempted murderers would never be discovered. Russian authorities never even pretended to investigate this crime and claimed that Navalny was not poisoned, at least not in Russia.

Researchers from Bellingcat,[49] an organization of forensic journalists specializing in open-source research, soon discovered details about the identities of Putin's "death squad." Details about airplane passenger manifests, phone geolocation data, and contact lists were purchased on the darknet from Russian databases, information that was leaked by corrupt officials. They discovered multiple attempts to kill Navalny, apparently authorized just after he announced his run for the presidency. The multi-agency involvement in the plot meant that only Putin could have authorized the operation. Bellingcat painstakingly gathered data on Navalny's trips in recent years and checked the identities of other passengers who followed the same itineraries at about the same time. Phone data for many of these suspects, along with how they were described in telephone contact lists, revealed that they were from the FSB. When confronted, Putin confirmed FSB surveillance of Navalny, claiming the FSB had reason to believe that Navalny was an agent of American intelligence. What Putin did not know was that Bellingcat and Navalny's team had already discovered the backgrounds of these agents. Several were experts in medicine or chemical weapons and had repeated contacts with a known chemical weapons laboratory; in other words, these were highly specialized agents, not the type used for surveillance. Also, by the time of Putin's partial admission, Navalny had already recorded an extended call with one of his poisoners about the failed operation—which he then released on YouTube.[50]

Later findings by Bellingcat determined that foreign operations with death squads (under Russian counterintelligence, the GRU) date back to 2009,[51] while the FSB team apparently began operating in 2014. There were other well-known and lesser-known victims of poison attacks before Navalny, including the activist Vladimir Kara-Murza and the poet/writer Dmitry Bykov.[52] In this respect, Putin has exceeded even Stalin in the application of state violence. Domestically, Stalin made use of a quasi-legal process—show trials or tribunals and then executions to carry out death sentences of real and imagined opponents. Putin ordered his security forces to kill his opponents in Russia through secret, special operations for which he could deny responsibility. The advantage of poisoning is that the symptoms mimic illness, and death could be mistakenly attributed to natural causes. The drawback is that poisoning with a strong nerve agent such as *novichok* is hit or miss. When applied to a doorknob or smeared on clothing that a potential victim is expected to wear (as in Navalny's case), the poison's effective dosage is highly variable.

When Navalny returned to Russia after being treated in Germany, he was arrested at the airport and charged with violating the terms of his parole. He was sentenced to two and a half years in a corrective labor camp, in effect becoming Putin's personal captive. In 2022, Navalny was sentenced to an additional nine years for alleged fraud in his fund-raising efforts and for insulting a judge. Obviously without merit, the charges were filed to keep Navalny in prison longer . . . perhaps as long as Putin is president. Two days after Navalny's arrest, his associates released a documentary on YouTube: *Putin's Palace: History of the World's Largest Bribe.*[53] Previous FBK reporting had largely avoided direct attacks on the president, focusing on his inner circle and government ministers. Designed as a response to Putin's efforts to kill Navalny, the new documentary explored, graphically, a more-than-trillion-dollar palace for Putin and his closest friends near Gelindzhik on the Black Sea. The video was a major embarrassment for Putin, showing how money from state corporations was diverted for his personal aggrandizement. It also showed Putin trying to replicate a Czarist-type lifestyle, with some of the same gaudy design choices. Among the special features: an aqua disco, a "mud room" for storing spa treatments, a gambling room (Putin banned casinos in almost all of Russia in 2009), and a hookah lounge with a stripper pole. YouTube recognized Navalny's video as the most popular program of 2021 on the Russia segment of that service, obtaining over 120 million views worldwide. Over a period of just a few months, Navalny and his team had provided convincing proof that Putin was a murderer, a liar, and a thief.

By mid-2021, in advance of parliamentary (Duma) elections, the Kremlin began to use the criminal justice system to prevent opponents from running for seats. In previous elections, the regime used the electoral rules themselves to deny opposition candidates a place on the ballot—for example, by invalidating signatures needed to qualify. This time all potential candidates who had been part of Navalny's structures were eliminated in one broad stroke: Navalny's organization was declared to be "extremist," and the designation was applied retroactively—in violation of the Constitution—to anyone who had worked with or had contributed to Navalny's efforts. The result was the systematic destruction of Navalny's national political organization, and by the end of 2021, over one-third of his regional coordinators had left the country rather than face possible prosecution. It should be noted that the "extremist" activities targeted by prosecutors all took place before Navalny's organization was designated extremist; the organization had been legally registered with the Ministry of Justice, and Navalny's associates formally liquidated it in advance of the court decision.

When the campaign for the State Duma got under way, prosecutors and the Investigative Committee brought fabricated charges against almost all opposition figures who announced that they planned to run for the Duma and who had a public following. Many more who were politically suspect were deprived of even the formal political right to run for office possessed by citizens. It was estimated that over nine million Russians, including hundreds of thousands of Navalny supporters, were effectively banned from running for political office. Not since the Stalin era had so many citizens been deprived of their rights.[54] Navalny, despite being in prison, played an outsized role in the 2021 Duma election. His variant of strategic voting, which he called "smart voting," was seen by the Kremlin as dangerous, even though there were no Navalny-linked candidates on any ballot. The strategy was designed to increase the impact of protest votes in elections where there is no real choice of an opposition candidate.[55] In most single-member districts, the source of United Russia's dominance in the 2016 election, the percentage of the vote needed to win was relatively small, and the opposition could defeat a United Russia candidate if their voters were not dispersed among multiple candidates. Voters who signed up would be notified just before election day of the names of the candidate in their district who would do best against the UR candidate. The goal was to reduce or even eliminate the Duma majority of United Russia. In 2021, the smart voting strategy helped some candidates win Duma seats. Most often, smart voting recommendations called on supporters to vote for the KPRF candidate. In fact, the communists at that time were moving toward becoming a more genuine opposition both in regional legislatures and the Duma.

The Kremlin's fear of Navalny's smart voting strategy led it to take extreme steps to prevent the concept from reaching disenchanted potential voters. The following list represents just some of the steps devised by the Presidential Administration: The "smart voting" internet site was the target of multiple DDoS attacks before government IT regulators blocked it. The popular email domain mail.ru identified all "smart voting" messages as spam or blocked them entirely. After authorities threatened to prosecute Apple and Google employees based in Russia, both services dropped the "smart voting" app from their app stores.[56] Google Docs removed the "smart voting" recommended candidate lists from their files after leading Russian telecom companies began to block their service. Telegram and YouTube deleted related material shortly thereafter. (YouTube in the United States defended its participation in Russian government censorship by saying they were simply "obeying local laws" against "extremism.") A fast-track procedure was used to register the words "smart voting" as a trademark by a wool trader in the Stavropol region; it filed complaints when Google and Yandex search engines showed this word combination on the grounds that they were violating the company's trademark rights.[57] Police called or went to the residences of Russians on a leaked list of Navalny supporters to ask if they were registered on the "smart voting" site and suggested that doing so could be considered criminal behavior in support of extremism.

CONCLUSION (AND PUTIN-ERA CORRUPTION)

Historical parallels are always imperfect, but Putin's regime follows patterns set by Stalin and Brezhnev. Putin's treatment of his rivals, of political opposition, and of those who "think differently" lines up more with the behavior of Stalin and Brezhnev and East German leaders than with reformers like Khrushchev, Gorbachev, or Yeltsin. His continual attempts to "improve the efficiency" of the political system by eliminating autonomous elements have consequences: the end of democratization, federalism, the rule of law, free markets, and the development of an active, pluralist civil society. The new feature of Putin's form of authoritarian rule is that it has engendered massive corruption—corruption developed on a scale unseen under any previous Soviet or Russian leader and that has been intricately woven into the system of governance.

The Brezhnev-era elite certainly enjoyed privileges. Special stores open only to them were well-stocked with goods at subsidized prices, from Kamchatka crab to French champagne. Better and exclusive apartments, dachas, and the use of cars with chauffeurs meant that the party and economic elite of the country benefited from special status both officially and unofficially. Lower-ranking officials and bureaucrats often extorted bribes from citizens to issue documents or make favorable decisions. Nevertheless, there were de facto limits on corruption, not because the police worked to end the phenomenon, but because it was so difficult to hold on to and take full advantage of ill-gotten gains. Private property was virtually nonexistent, travel to the West was limited, rubles could not be easily and legally converted to foreign currency. Even top party leaders had to give up their state-owned apartments and dachas when they left power. There were limits on what one could buy with the fruits of corruption. The market in consumer goods was poorly supplied, though the black market helped provide some items. Well-known cases of corruption exposed among the elite in the 1970s and early 1980s were often illustrated with evidence that consisted of jewels and cash buried in jars on the grounds of an official's state-owned residence.

New opportunities for personal enrichment were apparent to Putin in his role in governing Russia's second largest city in the 1990s. St. Petersburg had a reputation for criminality second to none, and there were close links between crime bosses, businessmen, and local government.[58] Putin's first posting in the Kremlin when he moved to Moscow from St. Petersburg was to head the Kremlin's property department—an office that co-opted political opponents using incentives such as free apartments in Moscow—in essence, state bribery in exchange for loyalty. The biggest difference between the Putin era and the Soviet Union before 1990 was the emergence of private ownership and entrepreneurs. The new private sector provided some residual autonomy to ordinary Russians. If you were fired by a state corporation, you could find a job in a private company or start your own business. The private sector included islands of relative freedom even in spheres such as publishing and the mass media. This was limited, however, by state regulation of economic activity and by courts that tended to support the state over private owners. Keeping small business small and under pressure had a political advantage for the Kremlin. There was less chance of financial flows to opposition groups that might push for different rules of the game. And whenever a business grew and became more successful, there was increased danger of a hostile takeover orchestrated by the FSB or other state actors.

The state's role in the economy, especially state corporations with near-monopoly control in sectors that produced significant cash flow, increased dramatically over the Putin period. Private investors who were not part of the loyal Putin inner circle were pushed out as major stockholders of these corporations. The purpose of increasing the role of state ownership was not to produce a particular result, such as Stalin's rapid industrialization, but to pursue a more Brezhnev-like goal of retaining control. Now the control needed to be, not in the hands just of the state or party, but in the hands of loyal Putin associates. The apex of the Putin-era elite was made up of men with close personal ties to Putin dating back as far as childhood and extending into his early KGB years, his East Germany assignment, and the St. Petersburg government. Loyalty trumps competence in Putin's world.

Another source of corrupt elite predation is the sphere of state purchases—the spending of state budgetary funds by government agencies. Putin's close associates were often winners of tenders for projects with highly inflated price tags. Government officials were also allowed to siphon off a big part of state spending through the contracting process. In 2021, public administration experts at the Higher School of Economics surveyed anonymously over 1,200 companies that had been awarded state contracts. Over 70 percent said they were required to make corrupt payments. The average kickback required to win the bid—usually through a rigged "auction"—was 22.5 percent of the total value of the contract. If this was the average for all state contracts, the result would equal 6.6 trillion rubles, or 35 percent of Russian budget revenue and over 6 percent of the GDP. This is more than Russia spends in a typical year on health care and education combined.[59]

Unlike Soviet-era bureaucrats, the new Russian administrative hierarchy had both targets to fleece—the new private sector—and opportunities to convert, possess, and transfer ill-gotten gains to their families. The institution of private ownership made corruption easier and more lucrative. A whole new world of possibilities opened to the recipients of illicit wealth: ownership of foreign property and bank accounts, offshore corporations, and Russian real estate itself. The construction of "elite" housing became a priority of the Kremlin and the Moscow city government, and each apartment had market prices in the millions of dollars. Later, elite housing began to be built in leading Russian resorts in the south, including Sochi and, after 2014, Crimea. These were usually distributed by the Kremlin or regional governments without transparency. An implicit contract was offered to high-level officials: Do as you are told, remain loyal, and we will transfer to you a small portion of Russia's wealth.

When journalists exposed what was happening and who benefited, the authorities tried to cleanse from property registries the names of the true owners, designated investigative journalists "foreign agents" or "extremists," and blocked public access to their reporting. Genuine political opposition, investigative journalism, and anticorruption researchers, such as those with Navalny's Fund for the Struggle Against Corruption, presented an existential threat to the regime and what became the de facto "constitutional order." Putin and the new elite he created have a strong vested interest in staying in power and preventing a transition to a successor who does not have a stake in the system. Even designating a successor is fraught with danger. Just as in the Soviet system, a leader who has consolidated his personal power is virtually trapped in that position; any potential successor will become a threat—just as Gorbachev's and Yeltsin's vice presidents turned out to be (both led coups against their leaders).

Reforming the system itself represents a threat, though without reform the system becomes progressively less capable of responding to crises that present dangers of another magnitude. A recent example: Russia's response to COVID-19. Russia was well-positioned to show the world how a competent authoritarian government could cope with a national emergency. Russia was able to produce one of the first effective vaccines against the virus, called Sputnik-V, thanks largely to past Soviet investment in medical research. Yet, the Russian state failed to come up with a coherent policy on the pandemic and was unable to overcome problems caused by decades of underfunding the healthcare system. The regime's response was to lie about the magnitude of the problem, lie about the effectiveness and safety of other, foreign vaccines (and prevent them from being imported), and declare prematurely that the virus had been defeated—Putin did this three times. He also repeatedly claimed that, compared to other countries, Russia had responded effectively to the crisis. The Kremlin shied away from lockdowns after May 2020, fearing popular outrage. Putin was unwilling to spend "rainy day" funds to provide serious support to impacted businesses. The Kremlin was also hesitant to impose vaccine mandates. Russians were reluctant to get vaccinated, partly because they had learned that information and recommendations coming from the authorities were not to be trusted. By the end of 2021, only 46 percent of the population was fully vaccinated. Many refused to believe Putin's claim that he was vaccinated, seeing that he isolated himself in a "bunker" and was reluctant to meet with anyone who had not spent two weeks in quarantine. Consequently, Russia experienced the worst COVID outcome of any major country—approaching one million excess deaths over the course of the pandemic, while the average life expectancy dropped by two full years.[60] A study published in the journal *The Lancet* in 2022 found that likely COVID deaths in Russia in 2020–2021 were the highest in the world. For every 100,000 people, Russia lost 375 to COVID. (The global average was 120; the other worst performers were Mexico [325], Brazil [187], the United States [179].)[61]

Putin's disastrous decision to invade Ukraine (see chapter 12), in late February 2022, also is rooted in the failings of the system he built. Like the ill-conceived Soviet decision to send troops to Afghanistan in December 1979, a small group of advisors trusted by the leader made a fateful decision without consultation with other officials and without even giving them any advanced warning. The 1979 intervention was apparently approved by Brezhnev after a consensus decision by three officials: Defense Minister Dmitry Ustinov, Foreign Minister Andrei Gromyko, and KGB chief Yuri Andropov.[62] Bloomberg News reported, based on interviews with several Kremlin insiders, that the core decision on Ukraine was made by Putin in consultation with Minister of Defense Sergei Shoigu, Security Council head Nikolai Patrushev, and chief of the military's general staff Valery Gerasimov, all policy "hawks."[63] As with Ukraine, a major factor in the Afghanistan decision was fear of "losing" the country to US influence. In an effort to reduce popular opposition, Soviet officials refused to call the Afghanistan intervention a war—instead, a "limited military contingent" was fulfilling its "fraternal international obligations" to Afghanistan. Russian officials forbade calling the Ukraine invasion a war; it was merely a "special military operation." Anyone posting information on how the war was actually being fought or protesting the war was subject to criminal prosecution for "discrediting the Russian armed forces."

The impact of the war on the Russian political system was to impose even tighter controls on information and political discourse, to a degree not seen since the pre-Gorbachev Soviet Union. We do not know if a nascent Putin plan for an attack on Ukraine was behind the crackdown on political opposition in recent years, but it certainly removed the potential for any organized resistance.[64] Putin returned to his past "fifth column" and "national traitor" rhetoric to describe opponents. In one speech in March, he mocked his opponents as mentally living in the West with their taste for "foie gras, oysters, and so-called gender freedoms." Putin invoked a Stalinist mindset to view opponents as "enemies of the people" who must be exposed: Traitors are part of a Western plot to divide and destroy the country, but the Russian people can easily recognize them and "spit them out, like a gnat that happened to land in their mouth." Putin said he was "convinced that such a natural and necessary self-cleaning of society will only strengthen our country, our solidarity, cohesion, and readiness to respond to any challenges."[65]

Ordinary Russians responded as in Soviet times, with neighbors, colleagues from work, students, teachers, and even close family members informing on one another. There was one technical innovation—it was now possible to denounce someone anonymously online. The ruling party United Russia's St. Petersburg branch devised an app for reporting anti-war activity.[66]

A Russian demographer who specializes in emigration data estimates that around 150,000 Russians left the country in the weeks after the war began,[67] a mass exodus not seen in such a short period since the 1917 revolution. The Russian border was not closed for emigrants as it was from the late 1920s to the late 1980s; in effect, this was an unspoken invitation for those opposed to Putin's system to leave. The number is less significant than the composition of who left and how their loss will affect Russia's immediate future. Almost all had higher education. Among those leaving were most of the remaining independent journalists, Navalny supporters, human rights activists, and leading social scientists (especially political scientists who focused on Russian domestic politics). From the sphere of culture, departures included some of the best theater directors and playwrights, writers, artists, musicians, and several well-known popular culture personalities. The largest group to leave was comprised of IT professionals—explained less by politics than by the shrinking of career prospects as Russia increasingly cuts itself off from the digital world.

Russian officials, by contrast, remained loyal. Of those known to the public, only Anatoly Chubais left the country, a "system liberal" who had carried out privatization under Yeltsin and previously worked with Putin in the St. Petersburg city government. Even he did not publicly criticize the Ukraine invasion when he left.

SUGGESTED READINGS

Brown, Archie. *The Gorbachev Factor.* Oxford: Oxford University Press, 1997.

Colton, Timothy J. *Yeltsin: A Life.* New York: Basic Books, 2008.

Frye, Timothy. *Weak Strongman: The Limits of Power in Putin's Russia.* Princeton, NJ: Princeton University Press, 2021.

Gevorkyan, Nataliya, Natalya Timakova, and Andrei Kolesnikov. *First Person: An Astonishingly Frank Self-Portrait by Russia's President Vladimir Putin.* New York: Public Affairs, 2000.

Hill, Fiona, and Clifford G. Gaddy. *Mr. Putin: Operative in the Kremlin.* Washington, DC: Brookings, 2013.

Taylor, Brian D. *The Code of Putinism.* Oxford: Oxford University Press, 2018.

DISCUSSION QUESTIONS

1. What events from Vladimir Putin's past could, under the right circumstances, have led him to adopt a different worldview and a different set of policies?

2. What factors might explain why, over the past one hundred years of Soviet/Russian history, periods that are relatively free of repression always seem to be short and are followed quickly by periods of repression and stagnation?

3. Why is a cultural atmosphere of innovation and experimentation incompatible with authoritarianism in the Soviet/Russian context?

4. Why does Putin fear Aleksei Navalny and other advocates of liberal policies?

NOTES

1. As in the Soviet era, the shorthand term for the center of power is a physical location—"the Kremlin" (*kreml'* in Russian means "fortress") in the center of Moscow adjoining Red Square. The headquarters of the Kremlin bureaucracy, easily the most powerful institution, are located not far from the Kremlin on *Staraya ploshchad'* (the Old Square). This is the Presidential Administration; in Soviet times, it was the Secretariat of the Central Committee of the Communist Party—the top stratum of the party bureaucracy that provided reports and guidance to the top decision-making body, the Politburo, headed by the General Secretary of the Communist Party.

2. Alexander Lebedev, for example, was born seven years after Putin, in 1959, and like Putin, was a KGB officer until he resigned in 1992. Yet he went on to become a successful businessman who helped finance the independent, liberal newspaper in Russia, *Novaya gazeta,* whose editor won the Nobel Peace Prize in 2021. Lebedev

now lives mostly in London and owns two British newspapers, *The Evening Standard* and *The Independent*.

3. The "veto player" concept comes from the political scientist George Tsebelis; he argues that any political system can be described in terms of the number of actors or institutions whose agreement is needed to change the status quo. It defines the complexity and sequence of compromises needed to get a policy adopted and implemented. Authoritarian systems typically have only one veto player, as do single-party dominant democracies. George Tsebelis, *Veto Players: How Political Institutions Work* (Princeton: Princeton University Press, 2002).

4. A rare exception among developed countries is the city-state of Singapore, which has prospered under authoritarian rule and yet successfully fought corruption. Illiberal economic development can be successful to a point: China and Vietnam are examples that combine relatively free markets with authoritarian political systems and show high rates of growth. Yet both remain relatively poor countries, and archaic political systems are likely to encounter future turbulence.

5. In the historical scheme of Marxism-Leninism, socialism was the first phase, with state ownership and a continued need for incentives to work; communism was the final phase of historical development, with voluntary labor and free distribution of goods. Soviet leaders never claimed to have gone further than "developed socialism."

6. Soviet films created an image of the Cheka as heroic and romantic, and Putin was an admitted fan. For a more realistic depiction of the role of the Cheka in the period after the revolution, see the film by Alexander Rogozhkin, *Chekist* (1992). Much of the film consists of repetitive images of executions by firing squads of innocent civilians in a cellar and the subsequent carting away of their bodies for mass burial, as the Cheka officer who signs off on the killings loses his mind.

7. Founded by Vladimir Lenin in 1903 after splitting off from a more moderate socialist party, the party underwent several name changes over its history: Russian Social Democratic Labor Party (Bolsheviks) until 1918; Russian Communist Party (Bolsheviks) to 1925; All-Union Communist Party (Bolsheviks) to 1952; and finally, CPSU until the end in 1991.

8. This took the form of the *nomenklatura* system, a system of lists of key positions and candidates for positions that were either allocated directly by communist party organs at the next higher level—for a factory, this might be at the province or city level—or that had to be approved by those party organs. For factories of "all-union significance," decisions on key personnel were made by departments of the CPSU Central Committee Secretariat.

9. See Richard Taylor and Derek Spring, eds., *Stalinism and Soviet Cinema* (Routledge, 1993). Documents showing Stalin's personal role were published in *Kremlevskii kinoteatr 1928–1953: dokumenty* (ROSSPEN, 2005).

10. Paul R. Gregory, Phillip J.H. Schroder, and Konstantin Sonin, "Dictators, Repression, and the 'Median Citizen': An 'Eliminations Model' of Stalin's Terror," CEFIR/NES Working Paper no. 91 (November 2006).

11. A vivid, illustrated rendering of the Soviet state's violence against its own people is depicted in the graphic book by Igort, *The Ukrainian and Russian Notebooks: Life and Death under Soviet Rule* (New York: Simon and Schuster, 2016).

12. For an innovative exploration of the limits of atomization, see Jonathan Waterlow, *It's Only a Joke, Comrade!: Humour, Trust and Everyday Life Under Stalin* (Oxford: Oxford University Press, 2018).

13. Evgeny Dobrenko, *Late Stalinism: The Aesthetics of Politics* (New Haven: Yale University Press, 2020). Quote on pp. 33–34.

14. For an online exploration of what it was like to live in a communal apartment, see the site "Communal Living in Russia: A Virtual Museum of Soviet Everyday Life," https://russlang.as.cornell.edu/komm/index.cfm.

15. Sergei Chuprinin, *Ottepel': Sobytiia. Mart 1953—avgust 1968 goda* (Novoe literaturnoe obozrenie, 2020).

16. Tarkovsky's first full-length film was *Ivan's Childhood*, a war drama. Other well-known Tarkovsky films include *Andrei Rublev*, based on the life of an icon painter, and *Solaris*, a science fiction film.

17. A 2020 Russian film by the director Andrei Konchalovsky, *Dear Comrades*, is set during the events in Novocherkassk and depicts the massacre of protesters. The most complete account of "mass disorders" in the Khrushchev and Brezhnev period is Vladimir A. Kozlov, *Massovye besporiadki v SSSR pri Khrushcheve i Brezhneve (1953-nachalo 1980-x gg.)*, (Sibirskii khronograf, 1999).

18. The multiple volumes of the memoirs published as *Khrushchev Remembers* could not be published in the Soviet Union until the Gorbachev era. They were smuggled out and appeared in the West starting in 1970—causing a scandal that forced Khrushchev to disavow their authenticity.

19. Yuri Andropov was head of the KGB from 1967 to 1982, and when Brezhnev died, Andropov briefly served as party general secretary.

20. Sakharov's political manifesto was published in the West as *Progress, Coexistence and Intellectual Freedom* (New York: W.W. Norton, 1968). He was awarded the Nobel Peace Prize in 1975.

21. This decision was taken at the level of the Politburo. Gorky was a "closed" city, meaning that foreigners could not travel there for security reasons. This blocked Western correspondents from interviewing him. Exile was ruled out because of his past access to state secrets as a nuclear physicist.

22. https://www.npr.org/2021/08/14/1027689237/russias-iconic-leningrad-rock -club-celebrates-its-40th-anniversary.

23. See Sidney Bloch and Peter Reddaway, *Psychiatric Terror: How Soviet Psychiatry Is Used to Suppress Dissent* (New York: Basic Books, 1977).

24. Acting President Putin in December 1999 restored a memorial plaque honoring Andropov on the façade of KGB headquarters, where he had worked. The plaque had been removed in 1991 after the failed August coup.

25. See his book *Nightfrost in Prague: The End of Humane Socialism* (New York: Karz, 1980).

26. Dovlatov did not live to see how his work was received. He died in New York in 1990 at the age of forty-eight.

27. The film was made in 1984, before perestroika, when Georgia was under the relatively liberal leadership of Eduard Shevardnadze, whom Gorbachev later chose to be his foreign minister. *Repentance* was released across the Soviet Union in 1987.

28. East Germans did not see themselves as well off. For them, the standard of comparison was not the USSR, but West Germany. Much better conditions in the West were visible to most East Germans through viewing West German television, accessible despite intermittent jamming efforts.

29. Putin worked closely with the Stasi, and the Dresden police archives have a copy of a Stasi ID card in his name. Several of his Stasi contacts continue to be members of Putin's circle of trusted friends.

30. See Richard Popplewell, "The Stasi and the East German Revolution of 1989," *Contemporary European History* 1, no. 1 (March 1992), 37–63.

31. A position almost always held by former FSB agents.

32. The main charge concerned a deal for food supplies to the city that were paid for but never delivered. See Karen Dawisha, *Putin's Kleptocracy: Who Owns Russia?* (New York: Simon and Schuster, 2014), 106–25.

33. Tatiana Stanovaya, "Playing at Politics: Manufacturing Russia's Parliamentary Parties," Carnegie Moscow Center, September 30, 2021. In 2021, the party "A Just Russia" merged with two smaller parties and became "A Just Russia-Patriots-For Truth."

34. http://duma.gov.ru/news/52408/.

35. In October 2021, the Russian human rights organization Memorial published a list of 420 known political prisoners. Members of banned religious organizations made up the largest single group. https://memohrc.org/ru/news_old/v-preddverii -2021-goda-memorial-publikuet-obnovlyonnye-spiski-politzaklyuchyonnyh.

36. Most political exiles went to the Baltic states, Ukraine, or Georgia.

37. This practice was especially widespread in Chechnya, where Ramzan Kadyrov took family members hostage to pressure his critics who had emigrated.

38. "Meeting of Council for Civil Society and Human Rights," http://en.kremlin.ru /events/councils/by-council/18/67331 (December 9, 2021).

39. The project began in 2011 to document human rights violations. A court in Moscow oblast issued the ban, charging that the site promoted "terrorism and extremism" by publishing information on the arrest of members of organizations so labeled by the authorities. https://tass.ru/obschestvo/13299153.

40. Video surveillance around the scene of the crime provided evidence that led to the killer and his associates. They were arrested, convicted, and are in prison. All are from Chechnya, and all were active members of Kadyrov's security forces.

41. In October 2021, a man and woman became the first to be convicted under this law. They each received ten-month prison sentences for taking a photo where they, fully clothed, simulated a sexual act on Red Square with St. Basil's cathedral in the background.

42. "'U nas zapret na real'nost.' Pochemu v rossiiskom kino i serialakh vse bol'she tabu," *BBC Russia*, November 12, 2021.

43. "'Kuratory' ot FSB v rossiiskikh vuzakh. Kak ustroena sistema, unasledovannaya ot SSSR," *The Insider* (December 20, 2021).

44. VTsIOM, the All-Russian Center for the Study of Public Opinion, that had been founded in 1987 was taken over by Kremlin loyalists in 2003. "Refugees" from the center formed the independent Levada Center in 2004. In 2016, the Ministry of

Justice designated Levada Center a "foreign agent," and it was banned from publishing data on the popularity of parties and candidates in advance of Russian elections.

45. Mark Galeotti, "The Silovik-Industrial Complex: Russia's National Guard as Coercive, Political, Economic, and Cultural Force," *Democratizatsiya* 29, no. 1 (Winter 2021), 3–30.

46. Amnesty International briefly dropped Navalny from its list of "prisoners of conscience" based on these false claims in early 2021. See the analysis by Masha Gessen, "The Evolution of Alexey Navalny's Nationalism," *New Yorker* (February 15, 2021).

47. By 2021 it had been viewed over forty-four million times. A version with subtitles in English can be accessed at https://www.youtube.com/watch?v=Wgd -E1XnNBI.

48. Navalny's colleagues put together an extensive website with links on all that is known about the poisoning and subsequent investigation, both in Russian and in English. https://novichok.navalny.wiki/en.

49. Christo Grozev was the lead investigator. For an account on Bellingcat and open-source methods by the founder (written before the Navalny investigation), see Eliot Higgins, *We Are Bellingcat: Global Crime, Online Sleuths, and the Bold Future of News* (Bloomsbury, 2021). The poisoning and subsequent detective work were the subject on an excellent documentary produced by CNN/HBO, *Navalny* (2022).

50. A December 14, 2020 video describes the results of the investigation: https://www.youtube.com/watch?v=smhi6jts97I; Navalny's conversation with the agent appeared a week later: www.youtube.com/watch?v=ibqiet6Bg38.

51. Putin had resurrected Stalin's practice of seeking to assassinate "traitors" or enemies both abroad and in the context of the conflict in Chechnya. Earlier, Boris Yeltsin had approved the targeted killing of the elected Chechen president, Dzhokar Dudaev, in 1996, with a rocket that homed in on his satellite phone during a call. The next elected Chechen president who turned rebel leader during the Second Chechen War, Aslan Maskhadov, was killed in 2005 by a grenade tossed in his bunker. The first known use of poison by the FSB was the killing of Chechen rebel commander Ibn al-Khatab—by poisoned letter, delivered in 2002. Alexander Litvinenko, an ex-FSB agent who had self-exiled to London, where he authored books attacking Putin, was killed in 2006 by exposure to radioactive polonium. It had been mixed into his tea by two "former" Russian intelligence agents.

52. Like Navalny, both survived, thanks to quick medical treatment. Others, such as the political analyst Nikita Isaev, who was poisoned in November 2019, were not as lucky. "Navalny Poison Squad Implicated in Murders of Three Russian Activists," Bellingcat.com, January 27, 2021.

53. A version with English subtitles is at https://www.youtube.com/watch?v =mMxqTae75Fs.

54. The largest group banned from running were those with citizenship or residence rights in a foreign country. Also, anyone convicted of participating in "illegal" demonstrations or sentenced for crimes such as narcotics possession (often planted by police). Based on the report by Golos: "Novye 'Lishentsy': Za chto grazhdan Rossii massovo porazhaiut v prave byt' izbrannymi na vyborakh v 2021 godu," dated June

22, 2021. https://www.golosinfo.org/articles/145272. On the use of this practice in early Stalinism, see Golfo Alexopoulos, *Stalin's Outcasts: Aliens, Citizens, and the Soviet State, 1926–1936* (Ithaca, NY: Cornell, 2003).

55. On the strategy's effectiveness in St. Petersburg's 2019 municipal elections, see Mikhail Turchenko and Grigory Golosov, "Smart enough to make a difference? An empirical test of the efficacy of strategic voting in Russia's authoritarian elections," *Post-Soviet Affairs* 37, no. 1 (2021): 65–79.

56. See Justin Sherman, "In Russia, Apple and Google Staff Get Muscled by the State," *Wired* (September 26, 2021).

57. "Kompaniia po prodazhe shersti, zaregestrirovavshaya brend 'Umnoe golosovanie,' svyazana s silovikami," *The Insider*, September 6, 2021.

58. See Catherine Belton, *Putin's People: How the KGB Took Back Russia and Then Took on the West* (Farrar, Straus and Giroux, 2020), 84–114.

59. "*Eksperty otsenili srednii razmer otkatov pri goszakupkakh*" (December 20, 2021). https://www.rbc.ru/economics/20/12/2021/61bc5d059a794770833e7b51.

60. "Excess deaths" are calculated based on the difference in the number of deaths between the last normal year (in this case, 2019) and the pandemic years. The United States, another country that failed to respond adequately to the pandemic, also had around one million excess deaths, but the United States has over twice the population of Russia.

61. "Estimating Excess Mortality Due to the COVID-19 Pandemic: A Systematic Analysis of COVID-19-Related Mortality, 2020–21," *The Lancet* 399 (March 2022): 1513–36.

62. Artemy Kalinovsky, "Decision-Making and the Soviet War in Afghanistan," *Journal of Cold War Studies* 11, no. 4 (Fall 2009): 46–73.

63. "Kremlin Insiders Alarmed Over Growing Toll of Putin's War in Ukraine," *Bloomberg News* (April 20, 2022).

64. Daniel Treisman, "Putin Unbound: How Repression at Home Presaged Belligerence Abroad," *Foreign Affairs,* 101, no. 3 (May/June 2022): 40–53.

65. Speech at videoconference on social-economic support for Russian regions. http://kremlin.ru/events/president/news/67996.

66. "Edinaya Rossiia v Peterburge sozdala bot dlia 'priema signalov' o feikakh pro voijnu," *Mediazona* (April 21, 2022).

67. Yuliya Florenskaya interviewed in "Skol'ko liudei uekhalo iz Rossii iz-za voiny?," *Meduza* (May 7, 2022).

Chapter 2

Political Leadership

Richard Sakwa

It is clearly too early to assert that, this time, Russia will complete her real convergence with the West. But it is not too early to assert that, in the normal course, she hardly has anywhere else to go. . . . As has ever been the case since Peter, if Russia wants to be strong, she will have to Westernize. With her Communist identity gone, and with no other ideological identity possible, she has little choice but to become, as before 1917, just another "normal" European power, with an equally normal internal order.

—Martin Malia[1]

The Putin phenomenon remains an enigma. Putin studied law but then spent a large part of his formative adult years in the security apparatus, and then, following the fall of the communist system in 1991, he threw in his lot with the democratic leader of St. Petersburg, Anatoly Sobchak. Elected president for the first time in March 2000, Vladimir Putin presided over the development of a market economy and frequently reiterated his commitment to democracy, yet following reelection for his second term in 2004, the system veered toward a type of state capitalism. Dirigisme in the economy was accompanied by suffocating restrictions on the free play of political pluralism and democratic competition in society. Putin came to power committed to the "normalization" of Russia, in the sense of aligning its internal order with the norms practiced elsewhere and establishing Russia's foreign policy presence as just another "normal great power," yet there remained something "extraordinary" about the country. In May 2008 Putin left the presidency, as prescribed by the constitution adopted in December 1993. Power was transferred to his nominee, Dmitry Medvedev, while Putin himself became prime minister and was thus able to ensure that "Putinism after Putin" would continue.

The "tandem" form of rule during 2008–2012 ensured that neither the liberalizing aspirations of Medvedev nor Putin's more conservative inclinations could be given free rein. This was a prescription for stalemate and stagnation, as well as frustration for those who hoped that Medvedev's liberalizing rhetoric would be translated into more concrete action. His presidency was unable to reconcile the contradiction between the regime's avowed commitment to the development of a modern capitalist democracy, accompanied by declarations in favor of "modernization," with the consolidation of a rapacious power system that absorbed all independent political life and stifled the autonomy of civil society. The contradictions continued into Putin's renewed presidency.

In May 2012 Putin returned to the Kremlin, while Medvedev swapped positions with him to become prime minister. The move was formally legitimized by elections, yet it was clear that Putin's decision was decisive. The regime had become increasingly personalistic, focused on Putin himself, and his character towered over every substantive decision. Medvedev's continued membership on the reconfigured Putin team indicated that modernization and reform remained on the agenda, yet the moderate political reforms enacted in early 2012 in response to the wave of popular protest that accompanied Putin's return to power were gutted of their substantive content. Instead, elections became more formulaic and less competitive, and state corporations increasingly dominated the economy.

On September 12, 2017, Putin passed Leonid Brezhnev to become the longest-serving leader since Stalin's death in 1953, a total of eighteen years. In March 2018 he was reelected for a fourth term in a landslide victory, winning 77 percent of the vote with 67 percent turnout. While there was some vote stuffing, it was clear that Putin enjoyed the support of the overwhelming majority of the Russian people, although the depth of that support may be questioned. Few expected major changes in Putin's renewed presidency, and his fourth term was characterized by drift until the 2022 war. The question of the succession became increasingly urgent, since Putin would come to the end of his second constitutionally mandated two terms in 2024. To solve the problem and to prevent intra-elite conflicts in the runup to the expected change of leader, Putin in 2020 launched an accelerated process of constitutional reform that "zeroed" the term limits for himself, allowing Putin to run again in 2024, and theoretically even in 2030. Institutional change only accentuated the personalistic character of the regime. The task of this chapter is to indicate some of the dimensions of Russia's continuing engagement with the problem of "becoming modern" and to present an analysis of the leadership dynamics accompanying this challenge.

THE DUAL STATE AND POLITICS

Under the leadership of Boris Yeltsin in the 1990s, Russia emerged as a dual state. The divergence between, on the one hand, the formal constitutional order, the rule of law, and the autonomous expression of political and media freedoms and, on the other hand, the instrumental use of law and attempts to manage political processes by an administrative regime was already evident in the 1996 presidential election, which was effectively stolen by Yeltsin with the help of Western advisers. Under Putin, the gulf widened and defined his system of rule. Putin's administration was careful not to overstep the bounds of the letter of the constitution, but the system of "managed democracy" allowed the regime to conduct itself with relative impunity and lack of effective accountability. The regime worked in the gray area of para-constitutionalism, a style of governance that remains true to the formal institutional rules but devises various strategies based on technocratic (rather than democratic) rationality to achieve desired political goals. Putin's para-constitutionalism did not repudiate the legitimacy of the constitution, but in practice undermined the spirit of constitutionalism. For example, from 2012 regional governors were once again elected, but a "municipal filter" was introduced (requiring a candidate to be endorsed by a set proportion of local councilors) that allowed undesirables to be filtered out. This prevented a return to the situation of the 1990s, when all sorts of criminals and gangsters had become governors, but it also filtered out those who were politically undesirable, as seen from the perspective of the Kremlin. Equally, in most normal cases the legal system operates with a high degree of impartiality, but in political cases the judicial system is suborned. The lack of judicial independence is particularly evident in "raiding" attacks on business, which continues to damage the Russian business environment.

The interaction of real constitutionalism and nominal para-constitutionalism in Russia can be compared to the development of the dual state in Germany in the 1930s. Ernst Fraenkel described how the prerogative state acted as a separate law system of its own, although the formal constitutional state was not dismantled. Two parallel systems of law operated, where the "normative state" operated according to sanctioned principles of rationality and impartial legal norms while the "prerogative state" exercised power arbitrarily and without constraints, unrestrained by law.[2] The contrast between the *constitutional state* and the *administrative regime* defines contemporary Russia. To reflect the distinctive features of Russian development, I use these terms in place of Fraenkel's "normative" and "prerogative" states. The fundamental legitimacy of the regime is derived from its location in a constitutional order that it is sworn to defend, yet it places itself above the constitution to apply the law in ways that subvert the independence of the judiciary. The most egregious case of such abuse was the attack on Mikhail Khodorkovsky, the head of the Yukos oil company. In October 2003 he was arrested, and in the following year Yukos was dismembered, with most of the spoils going to the state-owned oil company, Rosneft. The rule of law in Russia remains fragile and susceptible to manipulation by the political authorities, but until 2020 no full-fledged prerogative state emerged. Instead, the administrative regime granted itself considerable latitude but formally remained within the letter of the constitution. Russia remained trapped in the gray area between a prerogative and a genuine constitutional state. The regime ruled *by* law when it suited its purposes, but the struggle for the rule *of* law continues. This was evident in the 2020 amendments, which changed the constitution to solve a political problem—the question of the succession—and thereby weakened the foundations of constitutionalism.

Nevertheless, the political systems continue to operate in parallel. On the one hand, there is the system of open public politics, with the relevant institutions described in the constitution and conducted with detailed regulation. At this level parties are formed, elections are fought, and parliamentary politics are conducted. However, at another level, a second para-political world exists based on informal groups and factions operating within the framework of the inner court of the presidency. This Byzantine level never openly challenges the leader but seeks to influence the decisions of the supreme ruler. This second level is more than simply "virtual" politics, the attempt to manipulate public opinion and shape electoral outcomes through the exercise of manipulative techniques.[3] However, by reducing the inevitable contradictions that accompany public politics into a matter of technocratic management, tensions between groups become part of factional conflict within the regime rather than being conducted openly through the constitutional institutions of a competitive democracy. Putin places a high value on civil peace and thus opposes a return to the antagonistic politics typical of the 1990s, but this reinforces the pseudo-politics typical of court systems. The restraints on public politics intensify factional conflicts within the regime. Putin's political genius lies in ensuring that no single faction predominates over the others, while also ensuring that he remains the arbiter over them all.

The divisions of the dual state are exacerbated by the modernization program pursued by Putin. His rule was committed to the development of Russia as a modern state and society comfortable with itself and the world, although after 2014, as the Second Cold War intensified, the security aspect of development took priority over competitiveness. The Putin system seeks to overcome the failings of what it considers to be the excesses of the 1990s under Yeltsin, notably the pell-mell privatization, the liberalism that gave rise to inequality epitomized by the enormous wealth of a handful of "oligarchs," and the "anarcho-democracy" characterized by the hijacking of the electoral process by business-dominated media concerns and regional elites.[4] However, instead of strengthening the state, it was the administrative system that flourished. This encouraged officialdom to rule with arrogant high-handedness and the security apparatus to insinuate itself back into the control of daily life, accompanied by a high level of corruption. Personal freedoms for the mass of the population are at an unprecedented level, including the right to travel abroad, acquire property, and choose their own careers and lifestyles (the latter within the framework of a revived conservative ethos). However, for intellectual, political, and business elites, the suffocating hand of the administrative regime weakens initiative and the freedoms proclaimed in the constitution. Elements of the atmosphere of the late Soviet years has returned, known as the period of stagnation. Although Putin achieved his goal of improving the business climate, recognized by Russia's significant rise in the World Bank's ease of doing business index, the economic environment remains hazardous because of the weakness of the rule of law and the general indefensibility of property rights against raiders. This encourages capital flight and inhibits inward investment, notably in the relatively underdeveloped small and medium enterprise (SME) sector. It also degrades the quality of governance, with the so-called vertical of power requiring a high degree of personal intervention to get anything done.[5] Even the president's word was far from law.

Some 1,800 policy-relevant decrees issued by Putin during his first eight years as president were not implemented, and this remains the case to this day.[6] This was the price to pay for the attempt to manage everything from a single center.

The Medvedev interregnum between 2008 and 2012 marked a notable moment when reform was on the agenda, although in the end very little was achieved. Medvedev's programmatic article "Forward, Russia!" was published in September 2009 and articulated Medvedev's conviction that continued political drift was no longer an option, but it also suggested uncertainty over what was to be done.[7] The fundamental question was whether Russia, with its "primitive economy" and "chronic corruption," had a future. Medvedev attacked not Putin, but the system that Putin represented, a balancing act that blunted his message. The goal was to consolidate the constitutional state by strengthening the rule of law and tackling corruption, but without challenging the prerogatives of the administrative regime, little could be changed. Outside factors also helped to derail the program of gradual political decompression, with renewed confrontation with the United States and the West in general. The Five-Day War of August 2008 with Georgia demonstrated to hardliners in the Kremlin that the country once again, as in Soviet times, faced a choice between modernization and militarization.

As prime minister from 2012 to 2018, Medvedev was forced to compromise, especially in conditions of political reaction. Putin returned to the Kremlin in 2012, chastened by the unprecedented challenge to his rule. The whole system had been rocked by the mass protest against electoral fraud in the December 2011 parliamentary election, demonstrating that Medvedev's reformism had a significant popular base. The list of reforms advanced by Medvedev is impressive, but none were able to transform the political situation. As far as Putin is concerned, there is no need for "reform," a word that he never uses. In Putin's view, the experience of the disintegration of the perestroika years between 1985 and 1991 and then the chaos of the 1990s acted as a salutary warning of what happens if liberalization is too radical and speedy. Hence, under his leadership there would be no "perestroika 2.0," no repeat of Mikhail Gorbachev's runaway reform process from 1985, which ended up with the dissolution of the communist system and the disintegration of the country in 1991.

Putin's third term was marked by sluggish economic growth and then a recession as oil prices plunged from late 2014, and growth was only restored in 2016. The imposition of sanctions by the Western powers in response to Russia's actions in Ukraine following the overthrow of President Viktor Yanukovych in February 2014 worsened the economic climate, although encouraging the further diversification of the economy and the development of such sectors as the agri-food complex. (See chapter 10.) Nevertheless, as Putin entered his fourth term in 2018, it was clear that the economy needed to be rejuvenated, and although he remained popular, the institutions of governance stagnated.

Four main themes emerge from this. The first is the remedial element. Putin's policy agenda emerged not only out of the legacy of seventy-four years of communism and the way it was overcome, notably the disintegration of the Soviet Union in 1991, but also out of the need to overcome the perceived excesses of the 1990s, above all the development of inequality, mass poverty, oligarch domination of the media, and the political ambitions of the new business elite. The second feature is the type of developmental program that Putin ultimately favored, with a strong role for the state to ensure that the business of business remained business, not politics, and to remain firmly in control of economic policymaking, accompanied by support for national champions in the energy, military defense, and manufacturing sectors. Already from his second term, the overall economic strategy became increasingly securitized, focused on self-reliance, the development of native industries, localization, import substitution, and the reduction of external dependencies. The third feature is the political managerialism designed to counter what was perceived to be the irresponsibility engendered by an untutored democratic process, a theme that provoked an obsession with security by the *siloviki* (representatives of the security and military) in Putin's team. These three elements combined to create a profoundly tutelary regime that was in some ways reminiscent of the "trustee" democracy practiced in Singapore.[8] However, the fourth theme should not be forgotten: the ability of the regime to generate plans for development. Numerous strategies were devised, including for the modernization of the military, the energy sector, welfare, and just about everything else. However, the pension reform of 2018, in which the retirement age was raised from fifty-five to sixty-three for women and from sixty to sixty-five for men, provoked a popular backlash from which the regime's popularity never recovered. This only reinforced the Kremlin's aversion to structural reform, and instead the administration played for time.

There is a profound historical reality behind the emergence of the guardianship system. This was apparent in the constitutional reform of 2020. Announced in Putin's annual state-of-the-nation speech on January 15, within just a few months, 206 amendments were made to Russia's 1993 constitution. Putin initially suggested seven changes that were at first seen as rebalancing the separation of powers by granting greater authority to the State Duma and the Federation Council (the lower and upper houses, respectively, of the bicameral Federal Assembly). In the event, the presidency emerged even more powerful than the already established "super-presidential" system. Above all, a last-minute amendment in March introduced the "zero" option (*obnulirovanie*), meaning that although the new version of the constitution limited future presidents to a maximum of two terms, the periods already served by sitting or earlier presidents were discounted. This means that Putin (and theoretically Medvedev) had the option of running again in 2024, when his current incumbency would come to an end. A number of social rights now became part of the constitution: The Russian language is now defined as "state-forming," marriage is defined as between a man and a woman, and the independence of Constitutional Court judges and of local government was weakened. Overall, a minimal redistribution of power took place, and instead a conservative centralizing ethos predominated. A "popular vote" on July 1 (postponed from April because of the COVID-19 pandemic) overwhelmingly ratified the changes. However, by using constitutional change to solve the political problem of the succession, Putin weakened the constitutional foundations of the polity.

As in so many other "third wave" countries that have embarked on the path toward greater political openness since 1974,[9] democracy in Russia was forced to create the conditions for its own existence. This is a type of giant bootstrapping operation described by Ernest Gellner in his work on the development of civil society in Russia and other postcommunist countries.[10] The social subjects of capitalist democracy were being created in the process of establishing capitalist democracy, a circular process that engendered numerous contradictions. The relationship between the various subsystems of a dynamic democracy, notably a functioning multiparty system, had to be devised. Instead, the tutelary role of the administrative regime tended to become an end itself. Its developmental functions came to substitute for, and became an impediment to, the development of autonomous structures in society. The mechanical management of political affairs hindered the development of more spontaneous and organic forms of political engagement and integration. Thus, there is a profound paradox about Putin's leadership and the nature of his developmental agenda, an ambivalence that is characteristic of Russia's long-term modernization in which adaptation to the technological and economic standards of the West has been accompanied by resistance to the fundamental elements that would make modernization work.[11]

All these contradictions were evident in Putin's leadership.[12] His presidency was shaped by a combination of domestic and external factors. The political reforms launched in the wake of the protests in 2012 soon lost their transformative edge. It now became much easier to form parties and to participate in elections. By 2021 there were over seventy registered parties, with about a dozen represented in regional legislatures, but "non-systemic" parties (that is, those who refused to compromise with the regime) were usually not allowed to register. The regime maintained its firm grip on political life. This was reflected in the process known as the nationalization of elites, forcing top officials and legislators to withdraw their assets from abroad (a process known as "deoffshorization") and to commit themselves to Russia. Trumpeted as a measure to reduce corruption, this reduced their political independence. The tightening of domestic screws was exacerbated by the sharply deteriorating international environment. The Ukraine crisis from November 2013 that led to the overthrow of President Victor Yanukovych in February 2014 provoked Russia to intervene. In highly controversial circumstances, Putin supported a referendum in Crimea that on March 18, 2014, saw the territory returned to Russian jurisdiction (it had been part of Russia until 1954, when it had been transferred to Ukraine). Shortly thereafter, an uprising in two of Ukraine's regions, Donetsk and Lugansk (together known as the Donbas), against the nationalistic Kiev government provoked a further deterioration in relations with the West. Various waves of sanctions were imposed on Russia, affecting individuals close to Putin and the banking and oil sectors. Putin's domestic popularity soared for a time, but the poisonous relations with the West reinforced the process that had long been in train of building links with the East, above all China. Putin's plan to achieve deeper Eurasian integration continued in rather less ambitious forms than originally envisaged, and on January 1, 2015, the Eurasian Economic Union (EEU) was born. Finally, the personalization of Russian politics was intensified, with Putin reelected in 2018 and set to serve his final presidency to 2024. There was no one who came close to challenging his preeminence. A whole epoch in Russian history is stamped by this man.

PROBLEMS OF POWER CONCENTRATION

Democracy in Russia was faced with the task of creating the conditions for its own existence. To this postulate, Putin implicitly added that this could not be done by following the rules of democracy itself.[13] Therein lay a further level of duality—between the stated goals of the regime and its practices, which permanently subverted the principles that it proclaims. Putin's team dismantled the network of business and regional relationships that had developed under Yeltsin, and although in policy terms, there was significant continuity between the two periods, where power relations are concerned, a sharp gulf separates the two leaderships. Putin recruited former associates from St. Petersburg and the security forces, and on this he built a team focused on the Presidential Administration in the Kremlin that drove through the new agenda.[14] The power of the most egregiously political oligarchs was reduced, and in exile they plotted their revenge, further stoking the paranoia of the *siloviki*. With the fear of the oligarchic Jacobites abroad, continuing insurgency across the North Caucasus, and the specter of color revolutions, it is not surprising that the regime exhibited all the symptoms of a siege mentality. After 2012 the "fortress Russia" syndrome included a turn to conservative social policy, restrictions on independent NGOs (the "foreign agents" law of 2012), and greater controls on elections and competitive politics in general. All these trends intensified after 2014, as did the confrontation with the Atlantic powers.

The Yukos affair not only ensured that business leaders stayed out of politics, but also brought the state back into the heart of business life.[15] This was achieved not so much by renationalization as by "de-privatization." Economic policy was no longer a matter for autonomous economic agents but had to be coordinated with the state, while the state itself became a major player in the economic arena (in particular in the energy sector) through its "national champions," above all Gazprom and Rosneft. A number of state corporations were created, including the giant "Russian Technologies" (Rosstec) holding company owning hundreds of factories and plants, including the giant "Avtovaz" automobile company in Togliatti.

The equivalent of de-privatization in the political sphere is "de-autonomization." The ability of political actors to act as independent agents was reduced through a not-so-subtle and at times brutal system of rewards and punishments, while the economic bases of independent political activity were systematically dismantled. The "imposed consensus" of

Russia's elite, as Gel'man notes, was achieved through the Kremlin's use of "selective punishment of some elite sections and selective co-optation of others."[16] As long as the Kremlin had adequate resources, in material, political capital, and authority terms, to rein in potentially fractious elites, the system could continue, but there was an ever-present threat of defection. In Putin's first two terms, an unprecedented decade-long economic boom, accompanied by windfall energy rents, reinforced the position of the power elite. This allowed a new type of "neo-Stalinist compromise" to be imposed: a type of "social contract" whereby the government promised rising standards of living in exchange for restrictions on independent popular political participation, a pact that could only be sustained, as Gorbachev discovered to his cost in the late 1980s, so long as the economy could deliver the goods. The country weathered the economic crisis of 2008–2009 because of the healthy financial reserves it had built up in the good times, and these reserves once again allowed the regime to survive the fall in oil prices and sanctions from 2014.

Putin also reengineered the domestic political system. Yeltsin tried several times to create a "party of power" that would serve to push through the regime's legislative agenda in parliament, but it was Putin who succeeded in this task. In 2001 he forced the merger of some political parties to create United Russia (UR), which increasingly dominated the party system and elections while firmly subordinated to the executive. The establishment of UR created a structure in whose name a government could be formed and through which legislation could be rammed through parliament.[17] Fear of the autonomous development of an independent political force in the past ensured that no party of power managed to make a credible showing in a second election, but UR's triumph in the December 2003 elections demonstrated that a new type of politics had been created. This was confirmed by its even more convincing victory in the December 2007 Duma elections, and although it lost its constitutional majority in 2011, it remained by far the single largest party. In both the 2016 and 2021 Duma elections, UR retained a constitutional majority, with over two-thirds of the 450 seats. Amendments to the law on parties in 2012 eased restrictions on the registration of new parties, but the emergence of numerous small parties did not threaten UR's dominance. Four "systemic" parties that regularly entered parliament were joined for the first time by a fifth, New People, in 2021.

Putin effectively headed the party, but he demonstratively did not join it. In May 2012 Medvedev became UR's leader, and he also became a party member. The creation of the All-Russia People's Front (ONF) in May 2011 was a typical Putin move, creating a nonparty body whose work paralleled that of UR but in core respects does not duplicate its electoral and parliamentary functions. The ONF rallied public activists and social organizations to Putin's banner, while not sharing in the opprobrium that became attached to

UR's name. In 2011 the anticorruption campaigner Aleksei Navalny famously dubbed UR as "the party of thieves and swindlers."

The Putinite social contract—stability, security, and regular wages in exchange for political exclusion and passivity—was vulnerable to internal and external shocks. The fundamental problem of a concentrated power system is to ensure adequate renewal to avoid rendering itself so inward looking as to become dysfunctional. The reliance on a small coterie of trusted followers and the resulting weakness of competent personnel leads to reduced governmental capacity and poor policy performance. The early Putin years were marked by a remarkable "stability of cadres," but from his third term onward Putin sought to renew the governing elite as a way of avoiding more serious structural reforms. At the regional level, a new generation of younger and more technocratic governors was appointed.

THE CHARACTER OF LEADERSHIP

A whole arsenal of terms has been devised in an attempt to capture the hybrid nature of Russian reality, including "managed democracy," "managed pluralism," "electoral authoritarianism," and "competitive authoritarianism."[18] Following the Orange Revolution in Ukraine in late 2004, Russia's presidential administration launched the term "sovereign democracy" based on the idea that Russia would find its own path to democracy and that democracy in the country would have Russian characteristics. This was a theme Putin stressed in his state-of-the-federation speech on April 25, 2005. He took issue with those who suggested that Russia was somehow not suited to democratic government, the rule of law, and the basic values of civil society: "I would like to bring those who think like that back to political reality. . . . Without liberty and democracy there can be no order, no stability and no sustainable economic policies." Responding to Western criticism, however, Putin stressed that the "special feature" of Russia's democracy was that it would be pursued in its own way and not at the price of law and order or social stability: "Russia . . . will decide for itself the pace, terms and conditions of moving towards democracy."[19] In other words, while the content of policy would be democracy, its forms and the tempo of development would be a directed and managed process, a distinction that sustained the dual state. In this speech Putin argued that the collapse (*krushenie*) of the Soviet Union was a "major geopolitical catastrophe of the twentieth century," but he certainly did not mean that the USSR could be re-created. The phrase has been misinterpreted and taken out of context to suggest an attempt to re-create some sort of empire by taking over neighboring countries.

The theme of Russia's autonomy in domestic and foreign policy has been reinforced in a policy that could be called neorevisionism—the attempt to reshape the practices of the major powers in the international system while strengthening the institutions of international society, notably the United Nations and other instruments of global governance. Putin's challenge to the advance of the Atlantic system (NATO and the European Union) to Russia's borders provoked a sharp deterioration in relations with the West. Putin was demonized, and Russia was characterized as an authoritarian country.[20] Why did Russia take a turn toward authoritarianism? Did the cause lie in the political culture of the people, who perhaps need to be guided by an external authority in the absence of developed traditions of self-reliance, active citizenship, and civil society? Is it the "natural resource curse" that is to blame, whereby energy rents allow the political system to insulate itself from popular control? Or does the problem lie in a flawed institutional design, namely, the excessive powers granted the presidency by the 1993 constitution?[21]

No doubt a combination of these factors contributed to the crisis of Russian democracy. The potential for democratic development remains in society, with a new generation emerging tired of the suffocating tutelary system. The dual-state model suggests that the Russian polity is multilayered and dynamic, with a constant interplay between the constitutional and administrative levels that prevents Russia from becoming a full-fledged democracy, but by the same token there are systemic obstacles to Russia becoming an outright dictatorship. In recent years "soft" authoritarianism has given way to harder forms of repression, but the two systems still operate in parallel. The regime needs the legitimacy derived from the constitutional order to survive, while the regime defends the state from capture by powerful social and regional forces.

A further factor is Putin's own personality. Russia's development as a democracy was already stunted under Yeltsin in the 1990s, but Putin's charismatic personality and extraordinary rapport with the Russian people undermined the autonomy of the institutions of democracy (notably parliament, competitive parties, and elections) while allowing a complex and dynamic system to emerge. Putin constantly emphasizes the need for evolutionary development, renouncing the "revolutionary" jumps that in his view inflicted so much damage on Russia in 1917 and 1991. This was one of the key points of his "Millennium Manifesto" issued just before he took over the presidency in December 1999.[22] Evolutionary and centrist politics are by definition contradictory, since instead of trying to resolve contradictions, the refusal to reform means that contradictions become constitutive elements of the political system. Centrism is dragged to become more extreme as a result of social pressures. Hence the fundamental contradiction identified in this chapter between the constitutional and the administrative state remains unresolved and imbues the system with a chameleonlike character. Some people see authoritarianism while defenders of the system insist that democracy remains, whereas in fact the system is an unresolved combination of the two.

Is the country still in "transition" to an arguably more democratic system, despite numerous detours and recent substantial reverses, a perspective that can be dubbed the "democratic evolutionist" view? Or is what emerged under Putin more or less "it," stuck in some post-communist syndrome where democratic accoutrements adorn a society and polity that in fact has restored much of the authoritarianism of the Soviet system that was dismantled in 1991, the "failed democratization" approach?[23] In the latter camp, Steven Fish is unequivocal: "By the time of Vladimir Putin's reelection as president of Russia in 2004, Russia's experiment with open politics was over."[24] The failure to free the economy from the grip of the bureaucracy inhibited the development of a vibrant economy, notably in the small and medium business sector. Contrary to what critics of the privatization of the 1990s argue,[25] Fish insists that more liberalization was required. The stunted development of an independent business sector deprived political life and the media of sources of independent support, accompanied by widespread corruption and a corrosive venality in public life. The Yukos affair was a clear manifestation of the attempt to achieve economic goals by administrative means, using the law to achieve political purposes. While Putin's administration was clearly in favor of the creation of a capitalist market integrated into the world economy, it feared the free operation of market *forces*. In his 1997 doctoral dissertation, Putin argued for the creation of national champions, and this long-standing policy goal was reinforced by the concerns of the *siloviki* in Putin's team.[26] The security apparatus gradually won back much of the power that it lost in 1991, and then went on to restore its privileges and wealth.[27] This allowed strong economic growth in the early years, but from 2013 it was clear that the economy was beginning to stagnate, while sanctions from the following year threatened living standards as a whole.

The institutional choices embedded in the 1993 constitution, above all the establishment of a "super-presidential" system, are considered by many to have driven Russia toward monocracy. However, defenders of the constitution, such as one of its authors, Viktor Sheinis, argue that the black letter of the constitution is not the central issue, but the key problem is that the spirit of constitutionalism is lacking. Democratic evolutionists see plenty of potential for the development of a more robust adherence to the spirit of legality, despite present setbacks. Although the word "democracy" is not all that popular in Russia after the traumas of perestroika and the 1990s, its fundamental characteristics are: free and fair elections, civic dignity, the rule of law, defensible property rights, and accountable government.[28]

The tutelary role of the regime helped stabilize the state, but the quality of democracy suffered. The system in formal institutional terms is a liberal democracy, and this is what endows the present system with its legitimacy, but practice clearly falls short of declared principles. The amendments of 2020 were not allowed to change the fundamental rights and principles outlined in the first two chapters of the 1993 constitution, however much their spirit was eroded through amendments to later chapters. The constitution remains a liberal document enshrining fundamental human rights, the rule of law, separation of powers, federalism, and accountable governance, but the powers of the executive are enormous and allow the emergence of a relatively autonomous power center unconstrained either vertically or horizontally. The dual state model calls this power center the administrative regime, to a degree unlimited by the constitutional constraints of the formal state order from above and relatively unaccountable to the representative system from below.[29] Nevertheless, the administrative regime can only survive in its present form by drawing on the normative and practical resources of the constitutional order. Without at least formal obedience to liberal constitutional norms, the regime would be exposed as little more than a dictatorship. The Constitutional Court remains an authoritative body, and there have been sustained attempts to give muscle to the independence of the judicial system, including the widespread introduction of jury trials. However, in practice the various Putin administrations, while certainly remaining within the letter of the constitution (with the letter itself changed in 2020), undermined the motivating spirit of democracy, political pluralism, and judicial impartiality.

The two pillars of the dual state are in a condition of permanent tension. This degrades the coherent operation of both and undermines effective long-term strategic governance, but it does provide space for ambiguity and resistance. The inner logic of the operation of the constitutional state cannot be given free rein, but at the same time, the authoritarian and corrupt inclinations of the administrative system are challenged by civic associations and ultimately even the systemic political opposition. The Communist Party of the Russian Federation (CPRF) has the potential to emerge once again (as in the 1990s) as a serious opposition.

The logic of duality is reinforced by the international context. The geopolitical dilemmas facing Putin have a strong historical resonance. Frustrated by the failure to achieve a viable framework for political relations between the post-Soviet states in Eurasia, the resolute geopolitical struggle with external great powers (America and the European Union) in the region, and his exasperation with domestic liberal and democratic forces, Putin became ever more a conservative legitimist of the type that Alexander I turned into in his final years before his death in 1825.[30] Putin's innate antirevolutionism fears the emergence of social movement "network" revolutions, which adopted a number of colors (rose, orange, and tulip), but which in all cases threatened incumbent regimes. He failed to recognize the underlying credibility of the demands of the "white" movement in the winter of 2011–2012 (the white ribbon became the symbol of the protest movement) and suggested that the demonstrators were in the pay of foreign governments. With a career in the security apparatus and witness to the chaotic fall of communism in the German Democratic Republic in 1989, Putin had a deeply conservative view of how political change should take place. In foreign affairs Putin could not understand why Russia was not treated as just another of the great powers since in his view there was no longer anything to fear from Russia. He assumed that the West would have "the serenity of spirit to understand her more."[31] Putin believed that Russia was developing according to the same universal laws as the West, but at its own pace, but the 2020 constitutional changes undermined the credibility of this position. A Cold War spirit was revived by all sides. The breakdown of relations with the West and what in effect became a proxy war over Ukraine in 2022 was only the culmination of the long-term failure to create an inclusive and mutually equitable security system since 1991.[32]

Fears of external intervention and the continuing competitive dynamic to relations with the West is one of the reasons for the enduring "extraordinary" elements in Russian politics. Another is the cultural problem of adaptation to contemporary modernity. We can briefly characterize this as a process of partial and dual adaptation.[33] Political adaptation is necessarily a partial process, since only in postcolonial and postwar contexts can one country try to copy wholesale the institutions of another. It is the nature and parameters of this difference that are important. Traditionalists of all stripes, including neo-Eurasianists, neo-Soviet imperialists, and Russian nationalists (as well as many of the *siloviki*), insist that the gulf separating Russia from the West is enormous and therefore favor yet another *Sonderweg* (own path) that would affirm Russia's distinctive native traditions (*samobytnost'*). The security-focused part of the elite points to the danger to national security and national interests from full adaptation to external models. For economic liberals, the elements of difference are precisely dysfunctional, and hence in their view Russia should adapt fully and unreservedly to the global economic order. These two worldviews up to 2022 had been in rough balance, allowing a centrist authority to consolidate. The essence of Putin's leadership is the attempt to negotiate a new balance between adaptation and affirmation. Over time, a system of "partial adaptation" emerged, appealing to Russian political culture and shaped by security concerns while at the same time integrating into the international economy (notably, by joining the World Trade Organization in 2012). The partial nature of Putin's adaptation strategy was derived in part from the belief that excessive adaptation could be as dangerous as too little.

While committed to a certain type of top-down democratization, the Putin leadership insisted that democracy needs to be rooted in, and congruent with, national conditions.

The strategy of partial adaptation is therefore a balancing act torn by its inherent dualism. On the one hand, it looks to the norms and standards prevalent in the countries of advanced modernity; on the other, it seeks to root the adaptive process in a native discourse (managed and interpreted, of course, by the regime) while refusing to succumb to traditionalist insularity. This dualism characterizes most democratic institutions and processes in Russia and provides the framework for the dual state. The Putin strategy for political and economic modernization could not depend on the strata or institutions traditionally relied on by modernizing regimes, such as the army or Western-educated elites, and while forced in part to adapt to the social milieu in which it finds itself, it feared above all being absorbed by that milieu, in particular the social forces created by the transition process itself (notably, the oligarchs), as well as the unleashing of populist and nationalist sentiments. Nevertheless, new forces are emerging, notably a more active class of citizens who demand inclusion in the political system on an equal and universal basis. Even before the political protests of 2011–2012, there had been clear manifestations that the Putinite system of tutelary politics was challenged by groups who demanded genuine constitutionalism, civic dignity, and accountable government. However, traditionalists argue that the process of adaptation has gone too far. Putin steered a middle course, but with the wave of patriotic enthusiasm released by the return of Crimea to Russia and a renewed Cold War, the regime tightened the screws domestically and became more assertive abroad.

Putin's centrist, modernizing, technocratic regime was in danger of becoming isolated, bereft of substantive support from abroad (although alignment with China deepened) and unable to rely on the emerging sociopolitical structures domestically (above all, the rising class of entrepreneurs, professionals, intelligentsia, and service workers). Instead, it became reliant on traditional sources of power, above all the security apparatus and the bureaucracy, both of which were oriented to the power system itself. The existence of this state-dependent mass provides some scope for innovation since it furnishes critical support to the leadership, but at the same time it subverts the development of the autonomous agents of a genuinely modern society. The striving for regulation and control by the security state threatens liberty itself. The room for maneuver of the centrist regime declined. Putin had to choose between strengthening the constitutional state and with it enhanced political pluralism, free and fair competitive elections, and the consolidation of independent courts, or intensifying administrative regulation, the micromanagement of politics, manipulation of the state-owned media, and a combative foreign policy. In the classic Putinite manner, he balanced between the two, but he increasingly tilted toward the latter. The question of a stable succession in 2024 became the overriding concern. Putin looked to secure his status as a great Russian leader, but as so often happens in history, the attempt to cling on to power too long precisely undermines the legacy.

CONCLUSION: THE POWER OF CONTRADICTION

Putin appealed to the principles of stability, consolidation, evolutionary development, and the reassertion of the prerogatives of the state. However, the concepts of consensus, centrism, and the idea of "normal" politics were beset by some fundamental contradictions. The central problem facing any analysis of Putin's leadership is to assess the nature of his statism. Putin came to power promising to restore the state after the depredations of earlier years, yet his focus was on building the resources of the administrative regime. He did not entirely neglect the state, undertaking a liberal reform of the judicial system in his early years and ensuring that government workers were paid on time and that the army and security apparatus received increased funds. But instead of letting the state, together with its broader representative institutions such as parliament, get on with its business, his leadership constantly intervened in manual mode to perpetuate its power but thereby hollowed out the state. The regime sought to insulate itself as far as possible from ideological and popular pressure, but by the same token, it lost touch with popular aspirations.

Putin's centrism carried both a positive and a negative charge. The normative resources of the constitutional state were balanced against the arbitrariness of the administrative regime managed by a security-minded centrist authority. Putin emphasized the "dictatorship of law" and thus encouraged the development of a genuine rule-of-law state, but it did not subordinate itself to the pluralistic political process enshrined in the constitution. Once again traditions of the "revolution from above" were perpetuated, and patterns of lawlessness and arbitrariness were replicated. Up to 2020 Putin was a constitutional conservative, refusing to make substantive changes to the 1993 document, but in trying to manage the succession in the name of stability, he undermined the very stability that he sought. Putin's leadership is characterized by the absence of the spirit of constitutionalism, and this in turn undermined faith in the evolutionary potential of the constitution. There were few restraints on presidential power, and parliament and society were unable to call the authorities to account. Medvedev sought to overcome the gulf between the constitutional (normative) state and the administrative regime, but his halfhearted reforms achieved little.

There are many contradictions in the "project" espoused by Putin, but, paradoxically, these tensions themselves are the source of much of his power. Putin was able to appeal to a variety of constituencies, many of whom would be exclusive if his ideas were enunciated more clearly. The essence of Putin's statecraft is the ability to reconcile antagonistic and contradictory social programs. He transcended narrow party politics and affiliation with either left or right not by evasion but by a distinct type of political praxis that was itself transcendent of the classic political cleavages of the modern age. It would be hard to label Putin's policies as president, prime minister, and once again president as either "left" or "right." Putin has been described as a "liberal conservative," an oxymoron that typifies the contradictory nature of his leadership. In an age when politics is based less on interests or ideologies than on identities and values, Putin reconciled policies and groups that in an earlier period would have been in conflict. Putin's style is antipolitical, although as a leader confronted by the need to reconcile conflicting interests and views, he proved a highly adept politician. The self-constitutive character of democracy in Russia imbued its politics with a contradictory dynamic. These contradictions became increasingly exposed, forcing Putin in his fourth presidential term to apply a greater measure of authoritarianism.

The contradiction between liberal democratic aspirations and the state's inability to act as a coherent vessel to fulfil these ambitions became ever sharper. A strong state is often seen as an essential precondition for the development of liberalism,[34] but others see it as the greatest threat to those liberties. However, it is more dangerous when the state is challenged by an administrative system that it can barely constrain and when power is exercised by a technocratic, but often corrupt, elite that sees its own perpetuation as synonymous with stability, security, and development. At that point, only the evolutionary but rapid consolidation of the constitutional state may avert the onset of a renewed era of revolutionary upheavals. There is a natural cycle to leadership—of rise, consolidation, decline, and fall. Putin defied the laws of political gravity for a remarkably long time, but he could not do so forever. The supreme test of his leadership would be the way that his rule came to an end. The fate of Russia was in his hands.

AUTHOR'S POSTSCRIPT

Putin's decision to launch a full-scale invasion of Ukraine in February 2022 would be decisive for his leadership and how he would be viewed by history. For some, Putin recklessly gambled Russia's future and his achievements on a military campaign that by its very nature would have an uncertain outcome. Thirty years of post-communist economic and social development was jeopardized, and the stability that Putin had so assiduously nurtured was undermined. Why did Putin do it? Russia faced a genuine security dilemma, one that Putin felt he had to resolve one way or another, and in his view the sooner the better, given that Ukraine was being armed and trained by the Atlantic powers. This was a war that was predictable and had been predicted, but it was also avoidable. This takes us to the character of Russian political development in the Putin years. Russia had been excluded from the proclaimed indivisible European security order after the end of the Cold War in 1989, but there were different ways of managing this. Instead of trying to mitigate the effects of exclusion, Putin after 2012 exacerbated them. This was accompanied by tightening repression at home and a more assertive foreign policy abroad. The management of political affairs became even more concentrated in the Kremlin, a phenomenon exacerbated by the COVID-19 pandemic from early 2020. The survival of the regime appeared to gain greater prominence at the expense of the development of the formal attributes of the constitutional state—competitive elections, the rule of law, and political accountability. When it came to the Ukraine crisis, it was clear the decision was taken by Putin in consultation with a close group of like-minded security colleagues. The response from the Atlantic powers was swift and severe, with the imposition of an unprecedented raft of sanctions. In response, Russia dug in for a long war of attrition, while the rest of the world looked on in dismay. The Global North once again plunged into an extended period of conflict. There would be no winners in this war, yet some pathway to peace ultimately would have to be found. By then the world would have irrecoverably changed, and a different Russia would have been forged.

—2022

DISCUSSION QUESTIONS

1. What is the dual state, and how does it affect the dynamics of Russian politics?
2. To what degree do external factors shape the evolution of the Russian polity?
3. If drawing up a balance sheet of Putin's leadership, list the features that would go into the pro and contra columns.

SUGGESTED READINGS

Gill, Graeme. *Building an Authoritarian Polity. Russia in Post-Soviet Times.* Cambridge: Cambridge University Press, 2015.

Greene, Samuel A. and Graeme B. Robertson. *Putin v. the People: The Perilous Politics of a Divided Russia.* New Haven, CT: Yale University Press, 2019.

Hale, Henry E. *Patronal Politics: Eurasian Regime Dynamics in Comparative Perspective.* New York: Cambridge University Press, 2015.

Hale, Henry E., Maria Lipman, and Nikolay Petrov. "Russia's Regime-on-the-Move." *Russian Politics*, No. 4 (2019): 168–95.

Ledeneva, Alena V. *Can Russia Modernise?* Sistema, *Power Networks and Informal Governance.* Cambridge: Cambridge University Press, 2013.

Monaghan, Andrew. *The New Politics of Russia: Interpreting Change.* Manchester: Manchester University Press, 2016.

———. *Power in Modern Russia.* Manchester: Manchester University Press, 2017.

Robinson, Neil, and Gareth Schott. *Russian Politics: An Introduction.* Cambridge: Polity, 2018.

Sakwa, Richard. *Russian Politics and Society.* 5th ed. London: Routledge, 2020.

———. *The Putin Paradox.* London and New York: I. B. Tauris, 2020.

Sakwa, Richard, Henry Hale, and Stephen White, eds. *Developments in Russian Politics 9.* Basingstoke: Palgrave Macmillan; Durham, NC: Duke University Press, 2019.

NOTES

1. Martin Malia, *Russia under Western Eyes: From the Bronze Horseman to the Lenin Mausoleum* (Cambridge, MA: Belknap, 2000), 411–12.

2. Ernst Fraenkel, *The Dual State: A Contribution to the Theory of Dictatorship,* trans. from the German by E. A. Shils, in collaboration with Edith Lowenstein and Klaus Knorr (New York: Oxford University Press, 1941; repr., Clark, NJ: Lawbook Exchange, 2006).

3. Andrew Wilson, *Virtual Politics: Faking Democracy in the Post-Soviet World* (New Haven, CT: Yale University Press, 2005).

4. Gulnaz Sharafutdinova, *The Red Mirror: Putin's Leadership and Russia's Insecure Identity* (Oxford: Oxford University Press, 2020).

5. Andrew Monaghan, "Defibrillating the Vertikal? Putin and Russian Grand Strategy" (research paper, Russia and Eurasia Programme, Chatham House, London, October 2014).

6. Timothy Frye, *Weak Strongman: The Limits of Power in Putin's Russia* (Princeton, NJ: Princeton University Press, 2021).

7. Dmitry Medvedev, "Rossiia, vpered!," http://www.gazeta.ru/comments/2009/09/10_a_3258568.shtml.

8. See, for example, Mark R. Thompson, "Whatever Happened to 'Asian Values,'" *Journal of Democracy* 12, no. 4 (2001): 154–63.

9. Samuel P. Huntington, "Democracy's Third Wave," *Journal of Democracy* 1, no. 2 (1991): 12–34. The argument was developed at length in Samuel P. Huntington, *The Third Wave: Democratization in the Late Twentieth Century* (Norman: University of Oklahoma Press, 1991).

10. Ernest Gellner, *Conditions of Liberty: Civil Society and Its Rivals* (New York: Viking, 1994).

11. Richard Sakwa, *The Putin Paradox* (London and New York, I. B. Tauris, 2020).

12. For a detailed analysis, see Richard Sakwa, *Putin Redux: Power and Contradiction in Contemporary Russia* (London: Routledge, 2014).

13. For analysis, see David Lewis, *Russia's New Authoritarianism: Putin and the Politics of Order* (Edinburgh, Edinburgh University Press, 2020).

14. On the size and role of the siloviki in Putin's administration, see Ol'ga Kryshtanovkaya and Stephen White, "Putin's Militocracy," *Post-Soviet Affairs* 19, no. 4 (2003): 289–306; and for later figures, Ol'ga Kryshtanovkaya and Stephen White, "Inside the Putin Court: A Research Note," *Europe-Asia Studies* 57, no. 7 (2005): 1065–75.

15. See William Tompson, "Putin and the 'Oligarchs': A Two-Sided Commitment Problem," in *Leading Russia: Putin in Perspective*, ed. Alex Pravda (Oxford: Oxford University Press, 2005), 179–202; and William Tompson, "Putting Yukos in Perspective," *Post-Soviet Affairs* 21, no. 2 (2005): 159–81.

16. Vladimir Gel'man, "Political Opposition in Russia: A Dying Species?," *Post-Soviet Affairs* 21, no. 3 (2005): 242.

17. Pavel Isaev, "Ob'edinennaia partiia vlasti vystraivaet svoiu regional'nuiu vertikal' so skandalom," *Rossiiskii regional'nyi biulleten'* 4, no. 6 (2002).

18. For an overview, see Harley Balzer, "Managed Pluralism: Vladimir Putin's Emerging Regime," *Post-Soviet Affairs* 19, no. 3 (2003): 189–227.

19. See http://kremlin.ru/text/appears/2005/04/87049.shtml; *Rossiiskaia gazeta*, April 25, 2005.

20. For example, Masha Gessen, "The Dictator," *New York Times*, May 21, 2012.

21. For a comparative analysis, see Henry E. Hale, *Patronal Politics: Eurasian Regime Dynamics in Comparative Perspective* (New York: Cambridge University Press, 2015).

22. Vladimir Putin, "Russia at the Turn of the Millennium," in *First Person: An Astonishingly Frank Self-Portrait by Russia's President Vladimir Putin*, by Vladimir Putin, with Nataliya Gevorkyan, Natalya Timakova, and Andrei Kolesnikov, trans. Catherine A. Fitzpatrick (London: Hutchinson, 2000), 212. The text was originally published as Vladimir Putin, "Rossiya na rubezhe tysyacheletiya," *Rossiiskaya gazeta*, December 31, 1999.

23. See Richard Sakwa, "Two Camps? The Struggle to Understand Contemporary Russia," *Comparative Politics* 40, no. 4 (2008): 481–99.

24. M. Steven Fish, *Democracy Derailed in Russia: The Failure of Open Politics* (New York: Cambridge University Press, 2005), 1.

25. For example, Peter Reddaway and Dmitri Glinski, *The Tragedy of Russia's Reforms: Market Bolshevism against Democracy* (Washington, DC: United States Institute of Peace Press, 2001).

26. See Harley Balzer, "Vladimir Putin's Academic Writings and Russian Natural Resource Policy," *Problems of Post-Communism* 53, no. 1 (2006): 48–54; and Vladimir Putin, "Mineral Natural Resources in the Strategy for Development of the Russian Economy," *Problems of Post-Communism* 53, no. 1 (2006): 49–54.

27. Two books forcefully, although controversially, make the point: Karen Dawisha, *Putin's Kleptocracy: Who Owns Russia?* (New York, Simon and Schuster, 2014); and Catherine Belton, *Putin's People: How the KGB Took Back Russia and Then Took on the West* (London, William Collins, 2020).

28. For an early study making this point, see Ellen Carnaghan, *Out of Order: Russian Political Values in an Imperfect World* (University Park: Pennsylvania State University Press, 2007); and see Henry E. Hale, "The Myth of Mass Russian Support for Autocracy: The Public Opinion Foundations of a Hybrid Regime," *Europe-Asia Studies* 63, no. 8 (2011): 1357–75.

29. For earlier discussions, see Richard Sakwa, "The Regime System in Russia," *Contemporary Politics* 3, no. 1 (1997): 7–25; Richard Sakwa, *Russian Politics and Society*, 3rd ed. (London: Routledge, 2002), 454–58; Richard Sakwa, *Putin: Russia's Choice* (London: Routledge, 2004), 86–88.

30. Malia explains Alexander I's position as follows: "Hemmed in by his position as one of the chief architects and guarantors of the Vienna system, and increasingly frustrated by his failures to effect reform at home, [Alexander] became ever more preoccupied with preserving 'legitimacy' and the established order throughout Europe." Malia, *Russia under Western Eyes*, 91.

31. Malia, *Russia under Western Eyes*, 167.

32. Richard Sakwa, *Russia against the Rest: The Post–Cold War Crisis of World Order* (Cambridge: Cambridge University Press, 2017).

33. The theme of partial adaptation is explored in my "Partial Adaptation and Political Culture," in *Political Culture and Post-Communism*, ed. Stephen Whitefield (Basingstoke: Palgrave Macmillan, 2005), 42–53, from which this paragraph draws.

34. For example, Marcia A. Weigle, *Russia's Liberal Project: State-Society Relations in the Transition from Communism* (University Park: Pennsylvania State University Press, 2000), 458, where she talks of the need for a "state-dominated liberalism."

Chapter 3

Regional Politics

Nikolai Petrov and Darrell Slider

When Vladimir Putin was first elected president in 2000, one of the first areas he identified for attention was the relationship between Russia's regions and the central government. Former president Boris Yeltsin, in the face of political and financial weakness, was forced to make considerable concessions to the regions. Regional leaders increasingly took on responsibilities that would normally be carried out by federal agencies, and they used these opportunities to entrench themselves in power while often willfully flouting federal laws and presidential decrees.

Putin came to the Kremlin after having spent the early part of the 1990s as a regional government official. He witnessed the extent of regional-center problems from a different perspective when he supervised Russia's regions for Yeltsin from March 1997 to July 1998. At that time, Putin was head of the department within the presidential administration (called the Main Oversight Department, or *glavnoe kontrol'noe upravlenie*) that gathered evidence on violations of federal laws and policies in the regions. Putin's predecessor as head of the department was Aleksei Kudrin, who was later Putin's minister of finance and deputy prime minister, and his successor was Nikolai Patrushev, who became head of the Federal Security Service (FSB), which had replaced the KGB, and was later promoted to head the Kremlin's Security Council in 2008. Both men were key figures in implementing elements of Putin's policy toward the regions. All three, not coincidentally, were from Russia's second city, St. Petersburg.

This chapter examines the policies toward regional leaders. Center-region relations continued to be a key area of concern in Putin's second term and during the Medvedev presidency. Instead of attempting to develop or refine federalism in the Russian context, Putin aggressively pursued an antifederal policy designed to take away or circumscribe many powers exercised by regional leaders. His goal was to establish a unitary, centralized state under the guise of "restoring effective vertical power in the country," to use Putin's own description of his intentions. In keeping with Putin's background in the KGB (the secret police in Soviet times and early post-Soviet Russia), the main emphasis was on discipline and order. These institutional and personnel choices, however, produced a number of negative consequences. As early as 2005, some Russian officials began to propose what might be described as "re-decentralization" in order to correct some of the deficiencies in a centralized model. To date, however, centralized rule remains the defining principle in Russian regional politics.

BEFORE PUTIN: FEDERALISM BY DEFAULT

Even after the other fourteen former Soviet republics became independent, Russia remained the world's largest country; thus, it is perhaps inevitable that there would be serious problems in administering its far-flung territories. This was true both before and after the establishment of the Soviet state. The traditional approach of Russian rulers was to tighten control from the center. Despite some outward trappings of federalism (the Russian republic, for example, was called the RSFSR—Russian Soviet Federative Socialist Republic), the Soviet Union was a unitary state supplemented by parallel hierarchies: the Communist Party of the Soviet Union (CPSU) and an extensive state bureaucracy. Even under Stalin, however, "family circles" or cliques based on personal relations and patronage ties arose in the regions, insulating local politics from Moscow and allowing regional elites a free hand in many matters.[1]

In several of the former communist states of Eastern Europe—particularly in countries whose leaders embarked on a reformist agenda—a comprehensive redrawing of subnational administrative boundaries took place. In Poland, the Czech Republic, the former German Democratic Republic, Hungary, and Croatia, communist-era regional entities were eliminated or replaced by new ones. In part this was done to meet European Union (EU) entry requirements, but often another important motivation was to break up political and economic power at the regional level that had emerged under communist rule.[2] No radical redrawing of the political boundaries took place in Russia, and communist-era elites retained their power at the regional level. Russia's administrative structure closely mirrored that of the Russian republic under communism. Republics within Russia, designated "autonomous republics" in the Soviet period, received elevated status because they were home to a non-Russian ethnic group. Most often, though, Russians were the largest ethnic group even in republics; the exceptions were Dagestan, Chuvashia,

Chechen-Ingushetia (divided into two separate republics in 1992), Tuva, Kabardino-Balkaria, North Ossetia, Tatarstan, and Kalmykia. The most numerous administrative entities were *oblasts* (provinces) and *krais* (territories). The cities of Moscow and St. Petersburg also had the status of "subjects of the federation." Smaller autonomous *okrugs* (districts) located within the territory of other entities were merged with larger entities to simplify control from the center. As a result, Russia went from having eighty-nine administrative entities in 2000 to eighty-three by 2008. Adding Crimea and Sevastopol brought the total to eighty-five in 2014, a number that has remained constant since then.

Russian and Soviet history had never seen an attempt to apply a federal model as the basis for organizing the relationship between national and regional authorities. The policies of President Boris Yeltsin represented a revolutionary break from past methods of rule. The constitution adopted in 1993 made federalism a core component of the Russian political system. Article 71 of the constitution defines the areas of federal jurisdiction, Article 72 defines joint jurisdiction, and Article 73 grants all other functions to the regions. Many of these relationships remained to be defined by legislation, however, and Yeltsin did not take the goal of developing federal principles seriously. What prevented Yeltsin from building a more balanced system of federalism was the center's political and economic weakness. This weakness was exploited by republic presidents and governors to carve out substantial autonomy. By the time Yeltsin resigned from office at the end of 1999, Russia's federal system remained a work in progress, the result of an improvised series of compromises.

In the late Soviet period, the regions became an arena for political struggle. In 1990–1991 both Gorbachev and Yeltsin sought the support of regional elites, particularly those in the ethnically based autonomous republics within the fifteen union republics that became independent in late 1991. It was in this context that Yeltsin in 1990 famously encouraged republic leaders to "take as much sovereignty as you can swallow." In most of the republics, local leaders followed Yeltsin's lead and created the popularly elected post of president.

After the collapse of the Soviet Union in late 1991, Yeltsin faced a new and lengthy conflict—this time with the Russian legislature. Their disputes centered on the relative powers of the parliament versus the president and economic reform strategy. In this struggle, Yeltsin sought the support of regional executives—the governors whom he then had the right to appoint and dismiss—and the elected republic presidents. Ruslan Khasbulatov, the speaker of the Russian parliament who became Yeltsin's nemesis, appealed to the regional legislatures to build an alternative national power base. Since republic leaders had more independence than governors, Yeltsin rewarded the republics with larger budget subsidies and greater relative autonomy.[3] These concessions were often codified in the form of bilateral agreements signed by Yeltsin and individual leaders. The most generous terms were granted to Tatarstan, Bashkortostan, and Yakutia, the republics with the most potential leverage because of their natural resource wealth (oil and diamonds).

This battle culminated in the events of September–October 1993, when Yeltsin issued a decree dissolving the parliament. When Khasbulatov and Alexander Rutskoi, Yeltsin's vice president, resisted and attempted to seize power by force, Yeltsin responded by having tanks shell the building. The new political context led to fundamental changes in regional politics.

First was the drafting of the 1993 constitution that enshrined the concepts of federalism, including the creation of a new legislature with an upper house to represent the regions—the Federation Council—with the right to veto laws passed by the lower house, the State Duma. A second consequence of the 1993 events was the dissolution of regional legislatures (though not in the republics) that had been elected in 1990. Political power in the regions shifted dramatically toward the executive branch of government, and this would be further strengthened when Yeltsin gave in to the demand by regional executives for popular elections of governors. Yeltsin's last set of appointments to the post of governor took place in late 1995–early 1996, when he appointed thirteen.[4] After that, all governors were elected to office. This gave governors added legitimacy and made their removal by Yeltsin almost impossible.

In 1994–1995, new regional legislatures were elected. The new assemblies were smaller in size than the soviets of 1990, and their powers were substantially reduced. With just a few exceptions, the new deputies tended to be local officials, employees from sectors funded by the government (education and health care), or the regional economic elite—all groups that were dependent on the executive. Only a small proportion of deputies were full-time legislators, and in their legislative role they were both unwilling and unable to challenge the region's governor or president. Very few legislatures had more than token representation by national political parties.[5]

A year after the October 1993 attack on parliament, Yeltsin once again attempted to use force to solve a political problem—this time in Chechnya. Unlike other republics, Chechnya refused to enter into a dialogue with the Kremlin and pressed for full independence. Under the leadership of General (and president) Dzhokhar Dudaev, Chechnya created its own military forces and expelled representatives of virtually all central Russian ministries, including the FSB and the Ministry of Finance. The Russian leadership did not make a serious attempt to achieve a negotiated solution to Chechnya's complaints, which strengthened the Chechens' resolve to secede. In December 1994, Yeltsin ordered Russian Army and Interior Ministry troops into Chechnya in hopes of a quick military victory. The result was a disaster: The army was ill prepared for a guerrilla war and suffered many casualties while directing much of its military might against the civilian population.

The war in Chechnya and ineffective policies in other areas threatened defeat for Yeltsin in the 1996 presidential election, and he again turned to regional leaders (as well as the business elite) for help. With the help of regional "administrative resources," such as control over the local press, government workers, and simple vote fraud in some cases, Yeltsin came from behind to win reelection in 1996. Following his victory, Yeltsin further strengthened the status of regional leaders by changing how the Federation Council was formed. From 1996 to 2000, governors and speakers of regional legislatures would automatically have seats in the Federation Council.

These serial political crises took place against a background of persistent economic emergencies that were stabilized in the mid-1990s only by resorting to "virtual" economics and financial trickery. These schemes eventually collapsed in the August 1998 devaluation and default. One common mechanism to formally balance tax receipts and expenses, which was used both by central agencies and regional governments, was sequestering funds—in other words, reducing expenditures by not paying salaries and not meeting obligations to suppliers of goods and services. In this way, the federal government effectively lost control of many of its agencies in the regions. Shortfalls in tax collection and nonpayment meant that regional leaders were almost forced to step in to provide funds or in-kind payments (office space, transportation, heat, hot water, electricity, and even food) in order to support the continued operation of federal institutions such as the criminal police, tax police, prosecutors, courts, and even Yeltsin's presidential representatives (created in 1991 to serve as his "eyes and ears" in the regions). Inevitably, federal entities in the regions shifted their loyalty from the center to the regions. Even the Russian military became increasingly dependent on regional leaders. The result was "a sustained trend towards increasing compartmentalization and regionalization of military structures, driven primarily by the shortage of resources and underfinancing."[6] This was not a power play by regional leaders. In the face of the failure by the Kremlin to carry out its responsibilities, the regions were simply trying to cope. The result was federalism by default.

Another feature of Yeltsin's policies toward the regions was the personalized and bilateral nature of center-region relationships. This was a continuation of the informal operation of regional lobbying of the central institutions during the Soviet era; both Yeltsin and most regional leaders had practical experience in this dating back to the Brezhnev era. Bilateralism was formally institutionalized in treaties negotiated between the Yeltsin administration and regional leaders. The first of these agreements was with republics; it provided a set of exceptions and exemptions that went far beyond what other regions were allowed. In the mid-1990s, over twenty new bilateral treaties with *oblasts* and *krais* were signed. These agreements made Russian federalism extremely asymmetrical, but in ways that were unsystematic and nontransparent.[7] Much of the enabling documentation at the ministerial level was kept secret. Later, most *oblasts* and *krais* also negotiated bilateral treaties with the center, though under less-favorable terms. The personalization of politics meant that Yeltsin often turned a blind eye to violations of federal laws and the constitution if regional leaders demonstrated loyalty to him in federal elections.

Overall, the institutional framework and dynamics of "federalism, Russian style," had many dysfunctional elements and allowed regions control over areas of federal responsibility that were atypical of a normal federal system.[8] The nature of federal relations also undermined efforts to democratize the political system and create a market economy. Governors and republic presidents obstructed the development of a national party system and used their powers to harass political opponents and independent media. To protect local industries and markets, regional leaders created barriers to free trade between regions. They also preserved an economic climate that was hostile to outside investment and the rise of small business.[9]

PUTIN'S RECENTRALIZATION

Unlike Yeltsin, Vladimir Putin began his first term with the advantages of both firm control over central political institutions and an economy that was beginning to prosper. The improvement of the Russian economy after the August 1998 crisis cannot be overestimated in this regard. Growing oil revenues, the result of skyrocketing prices on the world market, provided Putin with resources to remold Russian government structures. This led to enhanced tax collection and greater budgetary resources that could be used to pay off past debts and to finance federal institutions. Putin's election to the presidency was closely linked to the Second Chechen War (1999–2004), which eventually restored federal control over that region by brute force. At the same time, he began a more sophisticated, multipronged strategy to restore central control over all Russian regions. One early change was in budgetary policy. Since the center had easy access to a larger revenue stream, it revised the tax code to increase the center's share, from roughly a 40/60 split in favor of the regions to 60/40 in favor of the center. As a result, regions became much more dependent on the central authorities for budgetary allocations—a factor that greatly increased their vulnerability to pressure from the Kremlin.

Federal Districts and Presidential Representatives

The first major institutional change adopted by Putin was the creation of a new level of administration between the center and the regions in the form of seven federal administrative districts (*federal'nye okruga*) headed by specially appointed presidential representatives. Each of these "super-regions" was headed by a presidential envoy, called the plenipotentiary presidential representative—*pol'nomochnyi predstavitel' prezidenta*, or *polpred* for short. The ultimate purpose of this new structure was not to replace existing regions, but rather to increase the ability of the center to coordinate the operation of federal agencies in the regions through a framework that was totally controlled by the Kremlin. The federal districts and their administrative headquarters corresponded completely to the regional command structure of the Soviet/Russian Interior Ministry troops.[10]

The term *polpred* had been used by Yeltsin in 1991 to designate his personal representative in each region. Putin abolished this post in the regions, replacing them with "chief federal inspectors" who would be directly subordinate to (and appointed by) the presidential representative for the corresponding administrative district. The decree creating presidential envoys provided for their direct accountability to the president. Yeltsin had initially given the same degree of access to his representatives, but later they were subordinated to a department within his administration.[11] While Putin appointed each of his representatives, they did not report solely to the president. The *polpreds* were still part of the presidential administration, which meant they were supervised by the head of Putin's staff. This was a source of consternation among the presidential representatives, since they wanted to be closer to the ultimate source of authority at the top of the administrative ladder. The *polpreds* were also allowed to participate in regular meetings of the president's Security Council and the Russian government cabinet chaired by the prime minister.

Putin's "magnificent seven," as they were initially referred to with some irony in the media,[12] were drawn for the most part from the *siloviki*, or "power ministries": FSB, military, police, and prosecutors. The contrast with the early Yeltsin period could not be more vivid. Many of Yeltsin's *polpreds* were drawn from the ranks of radical democrats who had worked with Yeltsin in the Soviet and Russian parliaments. In effect, the early Yeltsin appointees to this post were the type of people that several of the Putin appointees had worked to put in prison camps or psychiatric wards! (Later, though, Yeltsin replaced his initial appointees with career bureaucrats, including several FSB officials.)

Presidential envoys were denied many of the instruments of real power to control developments in the regions—the right to direct financial flows from the center, for example, or the power to appoint federal officials in the regions. Depending on their skills and resourcefulness, many presidential representatives increased their leverage by expanding their links with important regional actors, such as the business community. *Polpreds* influenced personnel decisions by federal agencies and the president in their district through their recommendations for promotions. Over time, they helped create a web of cadres in the district that facilitated the center's "penetration" of the regions.

Much of the work performed by presidential representatives was secret; as a result, their actual role remained hidden.[13] The functions of the office changed over time. They devoted considerable effort initially to overseeing the process of bringing regional legislation (including republic constitutions and regional charters) into conformity with federal law and the constitution. Given that Russia has yet to address seriously the problem of establishing the rule of law, a massive effort to improve the content of laws appeared to be premature. Russia, and this is even truer of the regions, is a country where the letter of the law often counts for little in the face of arbitrariness, incompetence, politicization, and corruption in the judicial system and the bureaucracy.

Another task the Kremlin assigned the *polpreds* was to facilitate centralized control over policymaking. The bilateral treaties that had been signed between regions and Yeltsin were eventually phased out. Cities and rural districts, the third level of government, were subjected to increasing restrictions on their autonomy in the interest of restoring top-down control. Under Yeltsin, the constitution had proclaimed "local self-management," which meant that popularly elected mayors enjoyed considerable powers, often leading them into conflicts with governors. Putin's 2003 Law on Principles of Organizing Local Self-Management increased the control of regional authorities over local officials, gradually pushing mayors into the "vertical of authority." Many mayors of big cities resigned their posts, frustrated both by these changes and inadequate budgetary resources. For those who didn't get the message, prosecutors began targeting mayors with corruption charges in an apparent campaign of intimidation. Another innovation introduced under Putin replaced elected mayors in favor of "city managers" chosen by city councils—bodies that were more easily manipulated by governors and the Kremlin. By 2011 the capital cities of over half of all regions had shifted from popularly elected mayors to appointed city managers. In 2014 a new "reform" of local government permitted regional parliaments (all of which by then had United Russia majorities) to eliminate the popular election of mayors of large cities, replacing them with city managers appointed by regional assemblies. Governors and the ruling party now determine who will become the mayors of cities in their regions. The 2020 changes to the Russian constitution were the final step in bringing local government into the administrative hierarchy;

it created a "unified system of public authority," which was codified in laws adopted in December 2021.

Over time, the Kremlin introduced additional institutional changes in an attempt to grapple with persistent regional problems. Continued instability in the North Caucasus led former president Medvedev to create a new, eighth federal *okrug* in January 2010 that encompassed the non-Russian republics of the North Caucasus along with the predominantly Russian Stavropol region. The *polpred* was made a member of the Russian cabinet at the vice premier level, thus giving him additional powers to coordinate federal policy toward the region. Later, this morphed into a new Ministry for Economic Development of the North Caucasus. Another problematic region, the Russian Far East, was stagnating economically and losing population. In May 2012 the Kremlin sought to deal with the problem by creating a new federal ministry, the Ministry for Development of the Far East. In September 2014, the federal Ministry of Regional Development that had been created ten years earlier was abolished, in part because its functions in key problem regions had been taken over by the new, specialized ministries.

Parallel Vertical Structures

Centralization was accomplished by strengthening federal agencies' activities in regions and making sure that their chain of command was "from above" and not from regional governors. Regaining control over appointing and monitoring personnel in federal agencies in the regions was a key element. This process of centralization was accompanied by a massive expansion in the number of federal officials in the regions. Between 2001 and 2006, the number of federal executive branch employees in the regions (not including law enforcement agencies) grew from 348,000 to 616,000, according to the Russian Statistical Agency.

New territorial structures were established in the federal districts by the most important federal agencies and ministries—in all, about twenty federal agencies. To illustrate, within a year of Putin's reform, there were nineteen federal agencies represented in the Volga federal district. These included the prosecutor's office, the Ministry of Justice, the Tax Police, the Federal Tax Service, the Federal Agency on Governmental Communication, the Ministry of the Interior for Internal Troops, the Federal Criminal Police, the Federal Service on Financial Restructuring and Bankruptcy, the State Courier Service, the Committee on State Reserves, the Federal Securities Commission, the Property Ministry, the Federal Property Fund, the Ministry for Publishing and TV and Radio Broadcasting, the Ministry of Natural Resources, the Pension Fund, the Ministry of Transportation, the Health Ministry, the State Committee on Statistics, and the Ministry of Anti-Monopoly Policy (the latter two had other regional branches within which they established federal district departments).[14]

Priority was given to returning central control over military, police, and security organs. This had been largely accomplished by 2002. Central control rapidly increased over other federal organs in the regions, including courts, prosecutors, election commissions, and even the mass media. Some of the most important changes in administrative subordination took place in the Ministry of Internal Affairs (MVD). When Putin came to power, there was a symbiosis between police generals and regional leaders that seemed to be unbreakable. Putin employed chess-like maneuvers to reassert dominance over this key lever of control. In June 2001 governors lost their effective veto on appointments of regional MVD chiefs. Instead of immediately appointing his own men as the top police official in each region, he began by establishing a new intermediate level of seven MVD district directorates, each headed by high-ranking police officials who were directly subordinate to the minister of internal affairs and appointed by decrees issued by Putin. It took only a year of personnel transfers at the regional level to disentangle existing networks of relationships, restoring control by the central ministry over regional police chiefs. In subsequent years, Putin maintained these gains by forcing high rates of turnover among regional police heads, regularly moving officials from region to region.

None of the heads of the new district agencies were subordinate to the *polpred*. While such a change would make sense from the standpoint of a clear and single vertical chain of command, it would represent a major assault on the prerogatives of the Moscow-based ministries. Ever since Khrushchev's attempt to undermine the ministries and transfer their powers to regional economic councils (the *sovnarkhozy*), the ministries have effectively fought reorganizations that would decentralize power to the district or regional level. The *polpred* typically could not order the federal agencies in his district to do anything, though he could complain to Putin if they ignored his advice.

The FSB was one of the few federal ministries that did not create a new territorial structure based on the federal districts. However, in February 2006, Putin announced the creation of a new federal structure, the National Anti-Terrorism Committee, headed by the FSB chair. Each region's antiterrorism committee (none were created at the federal district level) would be headed by the governor or president of the region. The result was a new "antiterror vertical." On matters concerning terrorism and its prevention, which can be broadly construed, governors were subordinate not just to Putin, but also to the chairman of the FSB. In each region, the local FSB head (also subordinate to the FSB chief, not the regional leadership) served as the head of the operational staff for antiterror operations and preparations.

Another vertical hierarchy established to increase central control over the regions was the new political party that Putin helped found, United Russia. While it got off to a slow start in many regions, United Russia rapidly expanded its regional party structures after 2004. Following the pattern of its predecessor "parties of power," United Russia was spread into the regions by recruiting key officials at all levels. It was not accidental that the party was called United Russia. The party was highly centralized, always under the control of Putin loyalists, and designed as a kind of straitjacket to bring under control what had been autonomous or governor-controlled regional political institutions. There was virtually no intraparty democracy; major party person-nel decisions were made by the party's curators in the Kremlin. Putin himself served as chairman of the party from 2008 to 2012 while serving as prime minister. Medvedev took over as party leader in May 2012 when he again became prime minister, and he continued to head the party after he lost the prime minister post.

Political parties that had significant support among regional elites were undermined or forced from the playing field. The 2001 law on political par-ties effectively banned regionally based parties, thus reducing the role of governor-dominated political organizations. In 2003, the Kremlin changed the rules on electing regional legislatures to require that at least half the deputies be chosen by a proportional representation system—by party list. The same advantages given to United Russia at the national level allowed it to establish a dominant role in most regional legislatures by 2006 and in all regions by 2010.

In July 2021, each federal district was assigned to a deputy prime minister who would work to better coordinate the actions of federal ministries in the regions. Their main focus would be on social-economic development and the investment climate. This gives the central government even greater control over regional affairs.[15]

Controlling Regional Governors

The popular election of governors gave them a status that was difficult for the Kremlin to overcome. Before 2005, the Kremlin succeeded in prevent-ing some incumbent governors from winning reelection. Methods included exerting influence on elections by instructing or pressuring the election com-mission or the local courts to remove a candidate from the ballot. In some cases, *kompromat* (compromising material) gathered on regional leaders was employed to persuade them not to seek another term in office. In 2003–2004, for the first time, serious criminal investigations were launched against sev-eral sitting governors, most typically those the Kremlin labeled as weak and ineffective. While none of these cases were brought to trial, they helped Putin establish his primacy in the period before he began appointing regional leaders. Over one-third of Russia's regional leaders were replaced during Putin's first term.

A critical component of Putin's policy restoring central control over regions was the decision to end direct popular elections of regional leaders. This occurred in the aftermath of the terrorist attack in Beslan, North Ossetia, in September 2004. Rebels, mostly from the neighboring republic of Ingushetia, took over a school on the opening day of classes, and the poorly coordinated effort to save the hostages resulted in over three hundred deaths. Elected governors must justify their reelection to voters; appointed governors have an electorate of one: Vladimir Putin.

To deflect criticism that Russia was abandoning democratic principles, the appointment process was fitted with a veneer of democratic choice. Three candidates had to be nominated, initially by the presidential envoy in the federal district in which the region was located, and they were expected to consult with major political forces in the region. From the beginning, the authenticity of the process was brought into question when outsiders who were unknown in the region ended up as nominees and then governors. Another element of formal democracy was that the president's choice, once nominated, had to be approved by the regional legislature. In every case, however, regional legislatures ratified the president's choice. If they did not, the law provided for the dissolution of the legislature and new elections. After Putin began appointing governors, most of those who had not yet become members of United Russia rushed to join. By the time of the 2007 Duma elections, almost all governors had become members of the party, and they had a direct interest in ensuring the best possible performance for United Russia in subsequent regional and national elections. Governors who organized massive vote fraud were rewarded for their actions and never faced punishment.

Perhaps because of his dependence on regional leaders who could produce the electoral results he needed, Putin was extremely cautious in his dealings with strong, popular regional leaders. During his second term, governors and republic presidents who had been elected to their posts prior to 2005 and were perceived to be "loyal" were allowed to remain in power. A procedure was adopted that allowed governors to seek Putin's "vote of confidence," most often through a personal meeting with him, prior to the end of their term in office. In most cases, Putin responded favorably without even considering other candidates and submitted the current governor's name to the regional assembly for reappointment. An important consequence of the end of elections was the de facto suspension of term limits for Russia's regional leaders. There was some speculation that this was the main purpose of the change: It would permit the reappointment of leaders viewed by the Kremlin as hard to replace.

As president, Dmitry Medvedev introduced a change in the system for nominating candidates for governor that provided further gloss to the democratic veneer. Starting in 2009, the nomination of the three candidates was transferred from the *polpred* to the largest party in the regional assembly. This meant turning the nomination process over to United Russia, since it had become the largest party in every regional parliament. Given the Kremlin's leverage over all these political actors, the charade that unfolded was obvious to all. Each of the actors in the spectacle would dutifully follow the Kremlin's script, and nominees became candidates who became governors. As a rule, the decisions about who would be nominated and who would be approved were made by the internal politics department of the presidential administration in the Kremlin.

It was Medvedev who presided over the most significant change in the corps of Russia's regional leaders. The so-called regional heavyweights who had won election many years earlier and had consolidated control over regional political and economic institutions were systematically targeted for removal starting in 2009. The victims included some of the most prominent figures on the Russian political scene, such as Mintimir Shaimiev, who had led Tatarstan since 1989, and Murtaza Rakhimov, head of Bashkortostan since 1989. Most governors saw the writing on the wall and agreed to resign quietly. The exception was the powerful mayor of Moscow, Yury Luzhkov, who resisted efforts to force him out in October 2010. Luzhkov, who had been mayor since 1992, was relieved by Medvedev with the formulation that he had "lost confidence" in Luzhkov. Later, Medvedev would claim that several of the governors had been removed because of evidence against them of corruption, though none of them were subjected to criminal prosecution. Many had held leadership positions in United Russia until the end and had repeatedly demonstrated their loyalty to the Kremlin.

Massive popular protests in Moscow in the aftermath of elections to the Duma in December 2011 led Putin and Medvedev to reverse themselves on the issue of popular elections of governors. Only a couple of years earlier, Medvedev had said that gubernatorial elections would not be reinstated even in "a hundred years." A law was quickly passed in early 2012 that again made the post an elected one. Steps were taken to minimize the scope of elections under the new law. One provision, the "municipal filter," required that candidates get signatures of support from as many as 10 percent of the deputies in local legislatures. Given the high percentage of local deputies affiliated with United Russia, the chances for opposition candidates to qualify were severely limited. In most regions, only a candidate supported by the KPRF (communists) could pass through this "filter." Several regions were allowed to opt out entirely from gubernatorial elections starting in 2013 in order to preserve ethnic harmony or "stability." These regions retained the post-2004 system of regional legislature approval of governors. Initially, republics in the North Caucasus were the only ones to opt out, and the de facto presidential appointment process remained in place in Dagestan, Ingushetia, and Kabardino-Balkaria. The elimination of popular elections for governor was later extended to three autonomous *okrugs* "nested" within the Tiumen' and Arkhangel'sk *oblasts*, all of which are rich in oil and natural gas— Khanty-Mansi, Yamalo-Nenetsk, and Nenetsk.

Between 2012 and 2021, there were 171 elections of governors. Candidates favored by Putin won all but four. The exceptions, all of which resulted from a runoff election after the favored candidate failed to get over half the votes, were in 2015 in Irkutsk (Levchenko—KPRF), and three in 2018: Vladimir (Vladimir Sipyagin—LDPR), Khabarovsk (Sergei Furgal—LDPR), and Khakasia (Valentin Konovalov—KPRF). (Note: Of these four, only Konovalov was still governor in 2021. Levchenko resigned under pressure in 2019 and was not allowed to run again in 2020; Furgal was arrested in 2020 and charged with murder; Sipyagin resigned in 2021 to take a seat in the Duma.) The Kremlin learned that if a gubernatorial election went to the second round, the chances of the incumbent winning were poor; after 2018 no strong opposition candidate would be allowed to register as a candidate. Also, when secret polls conducted for the Presidential Administration showed that an incumbent governor was in trouble, he or she was removed in the months before the election. The "acting" governor generally had little time to generate popular hostility and would be able to win easily. The margins of victory in governors' races were typically very high, from 50 to 70 percent.[16] The absolute record in this regard was the 2021 reelection of Ramzan Kadyrov in Chechnya; the official tally gave him 99.7 percent of the vote. At the end of 2021, a new law on regional government removed term limits for governors and preserved the president's power to dismiss any governor who "lost his confidence."

Beginning in 2015, the Kremlin decided that governors, who now owed their positions to Putin personally, needed additional stimuli to guarantee their loyalty. A new campaign of arrests of sitting or recently replaced governors unfolded, with charges of abuse of authority and corruption. Governors were arrested and put on trial from Sakhalin, Komi, Kirov, Mari El, Udmurtia, Khabarovsk, and Penza. Deputy governors were also targeted for prosecution in some regions, a clear signal to the governors who appointed them that they could be next. While these arrests were presented in the state media as evidence that in Russia "no one is above the law," in fact this was a highly selective campaign against governors who were targeted apparently because they had encroached on the interests of officials with stronger Kremlin connections. Decisions about whom to investigate (and plant evidence on, if needed) were made in the Kremlin's Domestic Politics Department, then carried out by the FSB's "Department K."[17] Overall, since 2015, criminal cases are brought each year against roughly 2 percent of high regional officials, including governors, deputy governors, and mayors of regional capitals.

The Kremlin established yet another mechanism to enhance control over governors—this time in the digital realm. Regional Management Centers (RMCs) were set up in every region to gather citizens' complaints from social media. This provides an additional channel of input about a governor's performance, one that is less vulnerable to manipulation by the governor. RMCs focus above all on the quality of government services in a region. The system went into operation in December 2020.[18]

"Corona Federalism"

When the COVID-19 pandemic hit Russia in the spring of 2020, Putin declared that the main responsibility for public health decisions would be placed on regions and their governors. That led to some optimism that once again Russian federalism would begin to have substance, that "corona federalism" would allow regional officials to make decisions based on local conditions. As was true in every large country, the virus spread first in major metropolitan areas and only much later to more distant and rural regions. It would make sense, then, to allow regional leaders to set the timing of anti-COVID measures. Instead, there was a broad lockdown nationally when the first wave of the pandemic hit, though it was implemented with varying degrees of strictness. Moscow, which had by far the most deaths early on, led the way with a radical lockdown, and Mayor Sergei Sobyanin was given a major role in early pandemic policy development at the federal level. But as soon as regional pandemic policies came in conflict with Putin's political calendar, governors were forced to open up in ways that helped the virus to spread at critical junctures. Putin insisted on holding a referendum on constitutional amendments in the summer of 2020, as well as elections in the fall of 2020 and 2021.

Regions were given additional financing to make up for past underfunding of health care, and many substantially increased the number of hospital beds available for the most seriously afflicted patients. But regional funding from federal sources was inadequate to support business and individuals through a long lockdown. The Kremlin refused to release "rainy day" funds for this purpose. Instead, businesses and factories were allowed to reopen quickly, thus avoiding economic disaster, mass unemployment, and protests. Later partial lockdowns were imposed in some regions, but they often were lifted at the first signs of public dissatisfaction.

The results of central and regional policy failures in meeting the challenges of the pandemic were devastating. Comparisons of "excess deaths" (comparing monthly deaths to those in pre-pandemic years) per capita show that Russia performed worse than any other major country. By the end of 2021, excess deaths were over one million. Russian official statistics on attributing deaths to COVID-19 were among the most distorted of any country, and most excess deaths were not officially linked to COVID. Regional variations in data reliability were the key determinant of this distortion. Sevastopol and St. Petersburg produced more accurate numbers, but ethnically non-Russian republics such as Tatarstan and Bashkortostan severely understated the pandemic's impact.

While Russia was the first country to approve a vaccine for emergency use (Sputnik-V), it quickly lagged in vaccinating the population. The substantial regional variations in vaccination rates bore little relationship to where the pandemic was spreading fastest. By autumn 2021, when Russia was experiencing a sustained third wave of the pandemic, the percent fully vaccinated hovered around 30 percent. Both regional and national leaders were guilty of doing too little to guarantee supplies of the vaccine and too little to encourage—or require—vaccination. Only in October 2021 did regions begin to require vaccination for workers and employees who come in contact with the public. More serious vaccine mandates for anyone over the age of sixty began to be introduced in some regions in November 2021. This was an unpopular measure, and the slow pace at which it was implemented—only a few regions per week—indicated that this was a slow-motion, centrally adopted plan designed to minimize protests.

KRYM—NASH (CRIMEA IS OURS)

When Maidan protesters and demonstrations forced Ukrainian president Viktor Yanukovych to seek asylum in Russia in February 2014, Putin took advantage of the disorder. Russian state television stoked fears of a new, anti-Russian regime in Kiev, and the predominantly ethnic Russian region of Crimea was encouraged to separate from Ukraine. A pro-Russian government was installed, and a hurried referendum was held, both aided by the presence—denied at the time—of Russian special forces. In a surprise move, Putin decided that Crimea should be immediately incorporated into Russia without any negotiations and without regard to Ukrainian law. Ukraine had had jurisdiction over Crimea since 1954, and the Russian argument was that annexing the region constituted the righting of a historical injustice.

The incorporation of Crimea added 2.2 million people to the Russian population and resulted in two new subjects of the federation, Crimea and the "federal city" of Sevastopol. (Previously, only two cities had this status: Moscow and St. Petersburg.) The process of integrating Crimea into Russia resembled the postwar redrawing of Soviet borders to encompass the Baltic states and western Ukraine, as well as parts of Romania (Moldova) and Tuva. Stalin telescoped the implementation of Soviet policies that had taken decades into a few years in these newly acquired territories, stirring local resentment that is still tangible seventy years later.

Incorporation of Crimea into Russia presented a whole series of unanticipated difficulties for the Kremlin. Kiev ruled Crimea under a set of laws and institutions that were substantially different from those operating in Russia, and virtually every institution needed to be restructured to conform to Russian standards.

The international community—most vocally the United States and the European Union—rejected the annexation of Crimea as a violation of international norms governing the sovereignty of established states and their territorial integrity. Sanctions and future legal action vastly complicate the process of integrating the new entities. Crimea's airports, critical to the region's tourist economy, cannot accept international flights since they are formally under the jurisdiction of Ukraine in the eyes of international aviation authorities. The flow of tourists from outside of Russia dropped dramatically; paradoxically, the largest number came by car from the now-hostile neighbor, Ukraine. Russian banks and companies, including state-dominated corporations, avoid the region out of fear of possible Western sanctions. The same is true of foreign companies. For example, in late 2021, the Chinese telephone giant Xiaomi stopped providing services to owners of its smartphones in Crimea out of fear of sanctions. Even Crimea's football (soccer) teams are in limbo, not allowed to compete in Russian leagues: The major world soccer organizations have agreed with complaints by Ukraine that these teams remain Ukrainian.

Crimea has required significant new economic investment, inevitably at the expense of other Russian regions and other priorities. Water, fuel, and electricity must all be supplied from Russia, and past infrastructure—including the railroad—came through Ukrainian territory. This factor, in the context of a planned economy, was a major factor in the 1954 decision by the Soviet leadership to attach Crimea to Ukraine. When Putin decided to invade Ukraine in February 2022, one of the first Russian military incursions came from Crimea. Russian forces immediately opened the canal on the Dniepr river that Ukraine had closed, restoring water supplies to the region. When Putin's initial plan to seize all of Ukraine failed, the fallback strategy was to seize enough Ukrainian territory in the east to create a land bridge between Crimea and the self-proclaimed republics centered on the cities of Lugansk and Donetsk. Of course, this also would restore a land link between Russia and Crimea. In June 2022, Russia claimed it had restored rail connections to Crimea through occupied Ukrainian territories.

An early alternative to the land bridge idea was to build a bridge for automobile and rail traffic across the Kerch Strait. When opened in 2018, it solved some problems, but it turned into the most expensive bridge ever constructed. The main contractor, coincidentally, was Putin's friend from childhood, Arkady Rotenberg. Meanwhile, the economy of Crimea requires substantial Russian financial support, including pensions promised at the rate paid to Moscow residents, which is significantly higher than the Russian average. Currently, Crimea and Chechnya are by far the most heavily subsidized regions in Russia.

Following the same pattern previously outlined, the annexation of Crimea was accompanied by administrative changes as Putin placed overall supervision of Crimean developments in the hands of Dmitry Kozak, the presidential troubleshooter who had previously been tasked with overseeing the North Caucasus and the Sochi Olympics. Following the example of the North Caucasus and the Far East, a new Ministry for the Economic Development of Crimea was created—but then after a year, the ministry was disbanded. A new, ninth federal district for Crimea and Sevastopol was also created and disbanded, and the two new regions were added to the Southern Federal District.

Russia gained not just Crimea, but two new, potentially restive minorities that preferred to be ruled from Kiev: Ukrainians living in Crimea and Crimean Tatars, who together made up at least 25 percent of the population based on post-annexation Russian statistics. Repression and intimidation were the initial responses by Russia's newly appointed regional leaders. Prominent leaders of the Tatar Mejlis, or people's assembly, were expelled from the region and are living in exile in Ukraine, and protests were prohibited as in Russia proper. Crimean Tatar members of a peaceful Islamic political group, banned in Russia but legal in Ukraine, have been arrested on charges of extremism and terrorism.

CONCLUSION: IS REFORM POSSIBLE UNDER PUTIN?

The state of center-region affairs under Yeltsin was not sustainable—the regions had become too strong at the expense of the center. But Putin swung the pendulum too far in the opposite direction. His policies curtailed both federalism and democratic development in Russia.

The methods used by Putin and his team were in large part derived from the standard operating procedures of the KGB and its successor organization, the FSB. These included gathering compromising materials against "targets," using this information to blackmail the targets to gain their cooperation, planning and carrying out extralegal operations with a maximum degree of secrecy, and using diversions and feints to direct attention away from the real purpose of an operation. In the case of the shift of powers to the federal districts, a part of Putin's strategy seemed to be to create new institutions that at first seem merely to duplicate functions of existing institutions but that could later take their place. The emphasis on discipline, carrying out orders without question, and strict hierarchical relations also reflects the internal ethos of the KGB. The Putin approach to the regions seemed to suffer from a set of limitations that reflected his life experiences and background. There is a Soviet-era joke about a machinist from a defense plant who made Kalashnikovs (machine guns). When he retired from the factory, he decided to make toys for the children in his neighborhood. But whatever he tried to make, whether it was a rocking horse, a doll, or a model ship, it always came out looking like a Kalashnikov! Putin's choice of instruments and personnel made it almost inevitable that his policies for dealing with the regions would end up "looking like a Kalashnikov," a recentralized, unitary system.

Russia's leaders from the outset had only a hazy notion of what constitutes federalism or liberal democracy. To an extent, this paralleled Soviet-era misunderstandings about the nature of a market economy. The absence of a planned or command system for allocating resources was equated with chaos and anarchy. Democracy and an effectively operating federal system rely on political institutions for resolving disputes with an emphasis on transparent, lawful action and the use of methods such as negotiation, persuasion, and compromise. If one sets aside the obvious exception of Chechnya, the Yeltsin presidency relied heavily on compromise and negotiation to achieve settlements with the regions. Putin, with much higher levels of public support, an effective working majority in the Duma, and a much more favorable economic and budgetary situation, could dispense with democratic procedures and still get results. Putin preferred to use his strength to force the changes he wanted largely without bargaining and without employing constitutional mechanisms.

How did Putin's policies work in practice? The new policies did restore central control over the military, police, and federal agencies that rightfully belonged under federal jurisdiction. But there was little recognition among Putin's inner circle that this strategy could go too far, or that excessive centralization was one of the weaknesses of the Soviet system. It is clear from Putin's statements on "restoring" vertical power that his main reference point was the USSR. To someone who was a product of the Soviet system, the elimination of checks and balances appears to increase the manageability and effectiveness of the political system. This may have been true in the short run, but there was a serious downside. A highly centralized system runs the risk of collapsing in the face of a crisis or rapidly changing conditions.

A high degree of centralization is problematic in any political system, but this was especially true of a country as diverse as Russia. Natal'ya

Zubarevich has argued that there are four different Russias.[19] First there is the Russia of big cities (from 21 to 36 percent of the total population), where the middle class is concentrated and where skilled, white-collar professions dominate. Second is what remains of industrial Russia (around 25 percent of the population), where regions are dominated both by blue-collar workers and *budzhetniki*—pensioners, teachers, and others dependent on the federal and regional budgets. This Russia includes an important subset of "mono-cities," dominated by one large factory or industry, that are especially vulnerable to changes in state contracts or subsidies. The third Russia (about 38 percent of the population) is poor, peripheral, and mostly rural. It is less dependent on government policy and survives on the natural economy. Finally, a fourth Russia is made up of the poorest republics of the North Caucasus and southern Siberia (Tuva, Altai). Dominated by clans, these regions are highly dependent on direct transfers from the federal budget.

The fate of Putin's 2012 "May Directives" (*ukazy*) show how excessive centralization can impact regions. After his inauguration to a third term, Putin set specific policy targets that every region would be expected to meet in a variety of areas. Targets were set for demographic and health indicators, such as life expectancy, birth rate, infant mortality, and cardiovascular deaths. Economic and business targets included growth in real wages, lower mortgage interest rates, and ease of doing business ratings. Special importance was assigned to underpaid *budzhetniki* in education and health care, who were to have their salaries increased to exceed the average income in their region. Funding from the center only partially covered the new demands on regional budgets, and the results were predictable: Regions' debt levels increased, and they were forced to divert discretionary funds from high-priority problems to show progress on fulfilling the presidential directives. Whenever Putin met with governors one-on-one, he expected an update on how his policy goals were being met. The budget squeeze led to various tricks by regional bureaucrats to report achievements that existed only on paper. For example, to increase pay for medical personnel, some nurses and orderlies were put on part-time contracts not subject to the decree, or their jobs were reclassified as "cleaning staff." To show progress in reducing deaths from cardiovascular disease, doctors were ordered to report other maladies or "unknown" as the cause of death.

The difficulties produced by the May Directives did not help Putin grasp the limits of centralization. After his 2018 inauguration, Putin issued another (this time in a single document) "May Directive" containing a long list of ambitious policy goals with no visible means to carry them out at the regional level. About a dozen federal programs designed to implement portions of the directive were planned, with uncertain implications for regional budgets.

The default option for a Kremlin that insisted on centralized decision-making was to design policies that corresponded to the worst-case scenario in the regions; in practice, this meant the North Caucasus republics. This region suffered from serious economic and political difficulties, such as low levels of development, high unemployment, inequality, and poor governance. One could make the case that Putinism in regional policy was an attempt to bring to the entire country the "successful" lessons learned from dealing with Chechnya after the war there.[20] Putin put in place a handpicked regional leader, Ramzan Kadyrov, who restored order by dealing ruthlessly with his opponents, demonstrated total loyalty to the Kremlin, shamelessly manipulated election results to the advantage of United Russia and himself, and implemented a state-dominated reconstruction program financed both from central and local resources. Yet, as was shown by the disastrous results of Russia's response to the COVID-19 pandemic, centralized policymaking was not capable of formulating policies that would be effective in the varied settings that comprise the Russian Federation. Chechnya-type policies applied in Moscow in 2010 and 2011 alienated a significant stratum of the population, producing massive anti-Putin demonstrations starting in December 2011. The protest mood changed dramatically in the aftermath of the Crimean annexation, and even the populations of large Russian cities came to view protests through the lens of Ukrainian events—as a factor that could precipitate instability or even civil war.

What are the prospects that Putin could adopt policies that would begin the process of returning the pendulum in center-region relations back toward the regions? There were several signs that such a reassessment was under way in 2011. Working groups headed by two of the most important officials tasked with regional policy, deputy prime ministers Dmitry Kozak and Alexander Khloponin, headed commissions to develop proposals that would reallocate government functions and budgetary resources from the center to the regions. Nothing of substance resulted from this effort. Similarly, efforts to reform the Federation Council and the State Council—a body made up of governors and government ministers that advises the president—in ways that would increase regional interest representation also produced nothing. In the end, Putin's desire to maintain centralized control exceeds his willingness to pursue reforms that would allow regions to govern themselves more effectively. The lack of regional representation in central government decision-making makes the political system vulnerable to unexpected shocks, crises, and future street protests, a consequence of policies that fail to meet regional needs.

DISCUSSION QUESTIONS

1. How did the basic institutional framework of region-center relations change from Yeltsin to Putin?
2. What elements of Russian federalism were incompatible with Putin's approach to governing?
3. Why is it that administrative complications arose after Russia annexed Crimea in 2014?
4. How likely is it that Russia will attain true federalism under Putin? Give evidence to justify your answer.

SUGGESTED READINGS

Evans, Alfred B., and Vladimir Gel'man, eds. *The Politics of Local Government in Russia*. Lanham, MD: Rowman & Littlefield, 2004.

Gill, Graeme, and James Young, eds. *Routledge Handbook of Russian Politics and Society*. London: Routledge, 2011.

Reddaway, Peter, and Robert W. Orttung. *The Dynamics of Russian Politics: Putin's Reform of Federal-Regional Relations*, vols. 1 and 2. Lanham, MD: Rowman & Littlefield, 2004 and 2005.

Reisinger, William M., and Bryon J. Moraski. *The Regional Roots of Russia's Political Regime*. Ann Arbor: University of Michigan Press, 2017.

Reuter, Ora John. *The Origins of Dominant Parties: Building Authoritarian Institutions in Post-Soviet Russia*. Cambridge: Cambridge University Press, 2017.

Ross, Cameron. *Local Politics and Democratization in Russia*. London: Routledge, 2009.

———, ed. *Russian Regional Politics under Putin and Medvedev*. London: Routledge, 2011.

Ross, Cameron, and Adrian Campbell, eds. *Federalism and Local Politics in Russia*. London: Routledge, 2009.

Zubarevich, Natal'ya. "Four Russias: Human Potential and Social Differentiation of Russian Regions and Cities." In *Russia 2025: Scenarios for the Russian Future*, ed. Maria Lipman and Nikolai Petrov. London: Palgrave, 2013.

NOTES

1. See Graeme Gill, *The Origins of the Stalinist Political System* (Cambridge: Cambridge University Press, 1996); and Gerald Easter, *Reconstructing the State: Personal Networks and Elite Identity in Soviet Russia* (Cambridge: Cambridge University Press, 1996).

2. Peter Jordan, "Regional Identities and Regionalization in East-Central Europe," *Post-Soviet Geography and Economics* 42, no. 4 (2001): 235–65.

3. Daniel Triesman, "The Politics of Intergovernmental Transfers in Post-Soviet Russia," *British Journal of Political Science* 26, no. 3 (1996): 299–335; and Daniel Triesman, "Fiscal Redistribution in a Fragile Federation: Moscow and the Regions in 1994," *British Journal of Political Science* 28, no. 1 (1998).

4. Michael McFaul and Nikolai Petrov, *Politicheskii Al'manakh Rossii 1997*, vol. 1 (Moscow: Carnegie Center, 1998), 149.

5. Darrell Slider, "Elections to Russia's Regional Assemblies," *Post-Soviet Affairs* 12, no. 3 (1996): 243–64.

6. Pavel K. Baev, "The Russian Armed Forces: Failed Reform Attempts and Creeping Regionalization," *Journal of Communist Studies and Transition Politics* 17, no. 1 (2001): 34.

7. Steven Solnick, "Is the Center Too Weak or Too Strong in the Russian Federation?," in *Building the Russian State*, ed. Valerie Sperling (Boulder, CO: Westview, 2000).

8. Alfred Stepan, "Russian Federalism in Comparative Perspective," *Post-Soviet Affairs* 6, no. 2 (2000): 133–76.

9. Darrell Slider, "Russia's Market-Distorting Federalism," *Post-Soviet Geography and Economics* 38, no. 8 (1997): 445–60.

10. Nikolai Petrov, "Seven Faces of Putin's Russia: Failed Districts as the New Level of State Territorial Composition," *Security Dialogue* 33, no. 1 (2002): 219–37.

11. Mathew Hyde, "Putin's Federal Reforms and Their Implications for Presidential Power in Russia," *Europe-Asia Studies* 53, no. 5 (2001): 719–43.

12. The reference is to the movie *The Magnificent Seven*, which was one of the first American films to be widely shown in the Soviet Union during the Cold War. The film, a western about seven gunslingers hired by a poor Mexican village to protect it from bandits, was extremely popular in the 1960s, when Vladimir Putin was growing up.

13. The most detailed examination of the early role of the federal districts and *polpreds* is Peter Reddaway and Robert W. Orttung, *Putin's Reform of Federal-Regional Relations*, vol. 1, *The Dynamics of Russian Politics* (Lanham, MD: Rowman & Littlefield, 2004). The second volume of this study (2005) shows the impact of Putin's federal reforms on law enforcement, the courts, the Federation Council, local government, political parties, and business.

14. An additional eighteen federal agencies had regional offices in another location, while forty-three had no intermediate structures between their central headquarters and regional branches. "Federal Agencies on the Territory of Nizhniy Novgorod *Oblast*," chart prepared by the Volga federal district administration (2001).

15. https://www.rbc.ru/politics/19/07/2021/60dca8979a7947079ed59ffb.

16. Yevgeny Ivanov and Nikolay Petrov, "Transition to a New Model of Russian Governors' Appointments as a Reflection of Regime Transformation," *Russian Politics* vol. 6, no. 2 (June 2021): 153–84.

17. Confirmation of this came in the form of a YouTube video posted in April 2018 by Alexander Shestun, the mayor of Serpukhov in Moscow *oblast*. He secretly

recorded threats made to him by the FSB general in charge of prosecuting regional officials and the head of the Kremlin's Domestic Politics Department. See http://www .youtube.com/watch?v=whPAGmeE6O4. Shestun was arrested shortly thereafter, and in 2020 was convicted on charges of corruption and abuse of power. He is serving a fifteen-year sentence.

18. Nikolay Petrov, "Ukho gosudarevo. Kak Kreml' sozdaet novuyu strukturu vneshnego kontrolya za regionami," *The Insider* (March 11, 2021).

19. Natal'ya Zubarevich, "Four Russias: Human Potential and Social Differentiation of Russian Regions and Cities," in *Russia 2025*, eds. Maria Lipman and Nikolay Petrov (London: Palgrave Macmillan, 2013), 67–85.

20. See Robert Ware, "Has the Russian Federation Been Chechenised?," *Europe-Asia Studies* 63, no. 3 (2011): 493–508.

Chapter 4

The Rule of Law

Kathryn Hendley

Law has had a checkered history in Russia. The rule of law, as evidenced by an independent judiciary that applies the law in an evenhanded manner to all who come before it, has been mostly absent. During the Soviet era, the leaders of the Communist Party used law in a blatantly instrumental fashion, a situation that began to change in the late 1980s when Gorbachev put forward the goal of a *pravovoe gosudarstvo*, or a "state based on the rule of law."[1] The leaders of post-Soviet Russia have reiterated this goal, yet their actions reflect ambivalence. The heavy-handed prosecutions of political opponents of the Kremlin suggest that the willingness to use law as a weapon to achieve short-term goals is a vestige of Soviet life that lives on in post-Soviet Russia. Though these prosecutions have become the most well-known feature of the Russian legal system, both domestically and internationally, they do not tell the whole story. They have occurred within a legal system that has undergone remarkable institutional reforms over the past three decades.

The contemporary Russian legal system is best conceptualized as a dual system, under which mundane cases are handled in accordance with the prevailing law, but when cases attract the attention of those in power, outcomes can be manipulated to serve their interests.[2] To put it more simply, justice is possible and maybe even probable, but it cannot be guaranteed. This lack of predictability is unfortunate, but it does not make Russia unique. Law is inherently messy. Many countries aspire to the rule of law, but none has yet achieved it in full measure. Articulating the rules is always easier than applying them to concrete circumstances. Some gap between the law on the books and the law in practice is inevitable. The efforts to bridge this gap in Russia are the subject of this chapter.

HISTORICAL OVERVIEW

The role of law in any society is not dependent solely on written law and formal legal institutions but is also influenced by how these laws and institutions are understood and by how they are used (or not used) by both the powerful and the powerless within that society.[3] These attitudes, often referred to as legal culture, are neither uniform nor consistent. They are influenced by many factors. Primary among them are the common perceptions of the responsiveness of law and legal institutions to the interests of society. For some, these perceptions are shaped by their own experiences. But in Russia, much as in the rest of the world, the vast majority of citizens have had no firsthand encounters with the formal legal system. For them, their attitudes toward the legal system are influenced by beliefs about how law has worked in the past as well as by mass media accounts about how the legal system is presently functioning and/or anecdotal accounts of the experiences of friends or family. As a result, making sense of the role of law in contemporary Russia requires some knowledge of what came before.

The Soviet Union is often referred to as a lawless society. Taken literally, this was not true. The Soviet Union possessed all the elements of a typical legal system.[4] It had a complex body of statutory law as well as a series of constitutions. It had a hierarchy of formal courts that mirrored what would be found in any Western democracy, as well as a well-developed system of alternative dispute resolution that allowed for neighborhood mediation in so-called comrades' courts. But all of these institutions were firmly under the thumb of the Communist Party. Though the constitution prominently proclaimed their commitment to the principle of judicial independence, the absence of judicial review made the constitution largely symbolic. The legislature, though composed of representatives who were ostensibly popularly elected, operated as a rubber stamp for decisions made by party leaders. Likewise, judges tended to follow the party line.[5] All understood that anyone who diverged would not be invited to stand for reelection, and the short five-year terms ensured that judges were kept on a short leash. At the same time, this should not be taken to mean that party officials dictated the outcomes of all cases. Judges were left alone to resolve many (perhaps most) of the cases they heard in accord with the law and their consciences.[6] But judges knew that at any moment the telephone might ring and they might be told how to decide a specific case. The specter of "telephone law" hung over all cases and gave rise to a culture of dependency within the judiciary. Over time, fewer and fewer calls were needed as judges developed an instinct for what the party wanted. Not surprisingly, ordinary citizens grew skeptical of the power of the law to protect their interests. This legal culture of distrust persists to some extent to the present day and has stymied efforts to reform the legal system. A 2017 public opinion poll shows that Russians are evenly divided on the question of whether courts should be independent or should be controlled by the executive branch.[7]

Gorbachev was the first Soviet leader to make a systematic effort to change the role of law.[8] He regularly invoked the goal of creating a rule of law–based state or *pravovoe gosudarstvo* in his public statements. Moreover, he took concrete actions to that end. His reforms to the electoral system brought an end to the era of rubber-stamp legislatures. Under his tenure, the judicial selection system was overhauled, eliminating the Communist Party's stranglehold and granting judges life tenure. Though these reforms were certainly necessary to achieving judicial independence, they were far from sufficient. Judges could not shake off the mantle of dependency so easily. Citizens were likewise slow to abandon their skepticism regarding the capacity of judges to rule in an evenhanded manner without clear proof of a shift in judicial behavior. Along similar lines, Gorbachev introduced the principle of judicial review to Russia for the first time. He created the Committee on Constitutional Supervision, which, while not a full-fledged constitutional court, was empowered to review acts of the executive and legislative branches, making it an early (albeit feeble) attempt at checks and balances. Its impact was largely symbolic. How far Gorbachev would have pushed the legal reform had he not lost power is unknowable.

Reform to the legal system was less of a marquee issue under Boris Yeltsin but continued throughout the 1990s. In some ways, the challenges were mitigated by the disintegration of the Soviet Union. No longer did reformers have to concern themselves with how reforms would play out in all the republics, which became independent countries in 1992, but the immense size of Russia, as well as the wholesale nature of the transformation, left reformers with their hands full. Yeltsin's decision to abandon the halfway reforms that characterized perestroika and to embrace the goals of creating a democracy and a market economy meant that comprehensive reforms were needed. The institutional infrastructure for both democracies and markets is grounded in law. Much of the Soviet-era legislation and legal institutions were inadequate to the task. Russian reformers turned to Western advisers for assistance in writing the new laws and creating the necessary institutions. Many of these advisers approached Russia as if it was a tabula rasa, disregarding what existed on paper as well as the prevailing legal culture. Almost no area of law was left untouched by the legislative whirlwind of the 1990s. The top-down nature of these reforms and the unwillingness to pay attention to the needs of those who would be impacted felt familiar to Russians, who recognized the modus operandi from their Soviet past, albeit under a new banner.[9] The result was a continued skepticism toward the usefulness of law, a sentiment that was only deepened as the new institutions were rocked by a series of corruption scandals.

Snapshots of the judicial system taken at the beginning and end of the 1990s would reveal dramatically different pictures. Though the basic court system remained intact and continued to handle the bulk of cases, other more specialized courts were introduced. The most well known is the stand-alone Constitutional Court, which represented a dramatic break with Russia's auto-cratic tradition. Through its power of judicial review, the court could declare legislative and executive acts unconstitutional, thereby making the judicial branch an equal partner for the first time in Russian history. In its early days, the court took some highly controversial positions, most notably siding with the legislature against Yeltsin in the leadup to the October Events of 1993.[10] Yeltsin disbanded the court during this crisis, and when it was reconstituted in early 1994, the justices, having learned their lesson, shied away from disputes with political overtones. Less well known, but essential to the development of a market economy, was the emergence of the *arbitrazh* courts in 1992. These courts were not created out of whole cloth but were built on the foun-dation of the Soviet-era system for resolving disputes between state-owned enterprises. Critical changes were made in terms of the status of the decision makers (raised from arbiters to judges) and jurisdiction (expanded to include disputes involving private firms as well as bankruptcy), but the *arbitrazh* courts represent a creative adaptation of Soviet-era institutions to serve the needs of the new Russia.[11]

In addition to the structural innovations, the depoliticization of the judicial selection process was consolidated under Yeltsin (though, as discussed below, there has been some backtracking in recent years under Putin).[12] The con-stitution, approved by popular referendum in December 1993, provides that judges be appointed by the president, with the proviso that nominations to any of the top courts be confirmed by the Federation Council. The seemingly unchecked power of the president to select lower-level judges might seem to be an example of the expansive powers granted to the president by this consti-tution. In reality, however, it constituted the final step in a system designed to preference competence over political reliability, a noteworthy reversal from the previous system in which judges served at the pleasure of the Communist Party. Under the reformed system, which persists to the present day, open positions are publicized, and anyone with the requisite qualifications can apply.[13] Under this competitive process, their applications are assessed by judicial qualification commissions (JQCs), who forward their recommenda-tions up the bureaucratic chain, culminating in a presidential appointment. All Russian judges enjoy life tenure, subject to a mandatory retirement age of seventy.[14] Allegations of judicial corruption and other malfeasance are handled by the JQCs, which have the power to sanction and remove judges.

Both of Yeltsin's successors, Putin and Dmitry Medvedev, came to the presidency with legal training. Their attitude toward law was undeniably shaped by their work experiences. Putin's years in the KGB seem to have taught him the importance of discipline and predictability. Not surprisingly, he has consistently espoused a philosophy of "supremacy of law" (*gospodstvo zakona*) that complements the "power vertical" and emphasizes the importance of law and order over the protection of human rights.[15] Medvedev, by contrast, spent several years on the law faculty at St. Petersburg State University and has a subtler view of law. While president (from 2008–2012), he proved more willing to meet with rights activists, and his rhetoric was notably less bombastic than Putin's. In terms of action, however, Medvedev rarely challenged Putin, either when he served as president or prime minister.

LEGISLATIVE REFORMS

Putin's consolidation of power within the Duma and his emasculation of the Federation Council allowed for legislative reforms that eluded Yeltsin. During the 1990s, a number of key pieces of legislation stalled due to opposition within the Duma. As a result, those affected had to hobble along using either stopgap presidential decrees or Soviet codes, which had been amended so many times that they had come to resemble a patchwork quilt. Not only did this undermine the predictability of law by making it difficult to discern what the rules were, but it left the guiding principles of the Soviet era in place, at least on paper. During Putin's first two terms, this legislative logjam was broken. The way laws were passed seemed to signal a return to the Soviet style of rubber-stamp legislatures. Under both Putin and Medvedev, United Russia (the Kremlin-affiliated party) was able to take advantage of both its majority and the ability of its leaders to enforce party discipline and build coalitions to enact the Kremlin's legislative agenda.

The criminal procedure code in effect when Putin took office was originally passed under Khrushchev. A new code, which enhanced the rights of judges at the expense of the police, got bogged down in the Duma in the latter years of Yeltsin's tenure. This new code was finally passed and came into effect in 2002.[16] Under its terms, the police are required to obtain warrants for investigative activities that previously could be carried out without judicial supervision. The code also limits the circumstances under which the accused may be kept in pretrial detention. Whether all of these procedural niceties are being observed in practice is a different question. The question of whether judges do a better job of safeguarding individual rights has also come into question. The Khodorkovsky case, in which the Yukos chief was jailed while awaiting trial on fraud charges despite not meeting the prerequisites of the code, shows that the rules regarding pretrial detention can and will be disregarded when convenient for the Kremlin.[17] Judging a system solely on high-profile cases can be dicey. The extent to which the state lives up to its obligations in more mundane cases is unclear, but the strong culture of backdoor dealings between judges and procurators (or prosecutors) creates grounds for suspicion.[18] The procuracy is a uniquely Russian component of the legal system that is not only charged with prosecuting crime but also with supervising justice more generally. It has stubbornly held out against numerous reform efforts aimed at making its activities more transparent.[19]

Since 2000, a Soviet-era tactic of drafting laws with intentionally vague language has reemerged. Such legislation offers maximum flexibility to officials and minimal predictability to citizens. Examples of this practice include amendments introduced in 2012 to the law governing Russian nongovernmental organizations (NGOs), which required them to register as "foreign agents" if they received financial support from outside Russia. NGOs resisted identifying themselves as "foreign agents," finding the Cold War connotations of the label to be distasteful. Authorities used the law as a pretext to conduct unscheduled audits of the records of NGOs that were not supportive of Kremlin policies. Although activists challenged the law, the Constitutional Court upheld its constitutionality.[20] In 2019, amendments expanded the reach of the law to include many journalists and public interest lawyers. Likewise, the law on extremism, which was passed in 2002 to fight terrorism, has been used to outlaw political movements not in sync with the Kremlin and to ban Jehovah's Witnesses. The seemingly innocuous requirement that candidates submit the petitions supporting their candidacy as well as for permits authorizing demonstrations have been used to stymie opponents of the Kremlin. These actions demonstrate the Kremlin's willingness to use law instrumentally.

JUDICIAL POLITICS

The dualistic nature of the present-day Russian legal system can undermine the independence of the courts. "Telephone law" did not disappear with the Communist Party, and it continues to hold sway in cases with political resonance as well as in cases where the economic stakes are high.[21] When such cases arise, court chairmen take care to assign them to pliant and politically reliable judges. On the other hand, judges follow the law on the books in mundane claims, which are handled expeditiously.[22] Many who bring civil or administrative cases are able to proceed without lawyers, thanks to the straightforward nature of the procedural rules and the willingness of judges to help neophyte litigants. Indigent criminal defendants are provided with lawyers at no charge.

Judicial Selection and Supervision

The method of selecting judges and supervising them once they are on the bench has profound implications for the independence of the judicial system. Ideally, judges should look only to the law in resolving disputes; politics should not factor into their decisions. But when judges feel beholden to a political benefactor for their appointments or fear being thrown off the bench if their decisions displease those in power, their impartiality can be compromised. Lifetime tenure is a potential solution, but it runs the risk of creating a judicial corps detached from society, answerable to no one. Judges, even those with lifetime appointments, must be held accountable for misbehavior. Some oversight is necessary. Yet it requires a delicate touch; otherwise, it risks undermining independence. As this suggests, the mechanics of maintaining an independent judicial system are excruciatingly difficult and highly political. Striking an acceptable balance between independence and accountability can be elusive.

Locating this equilibrium point in post-Soviet Russia has proven to be particularly vexing. Under Putin's leadership, concerns about the lack of judicial accountability gave rise to subtle but important changes in the selection system.[23] The composition of the JQCs was altered. Judges no longer enjoyed a monopoly but still made up two-thirds of the membership of the JQCs at all levels. In theory, opening JQC membership to nonjudges might seem to be democratic, in that it creates an avenue for societal concerns to be expressed. Judges saw it differently, fearing an effort by the Kremlin to politicize the process. The JQCs, however, do not have the last word. Their proposals are sent to a commission in the presidential office that makes the final recommendations to the president. Although chaired by the chief justice of the Supreme Court, its membership is dominated by court outsiders, raising the specter of politics. In recent years, it has rejected around a quarter of the candidates forwarded by the JQCs.

In addition to selecting judges, the JQCs have responsibility for disciplining trial-level judges. This brings some level of accountability into the mix. Possible sanctions range from private reprimands to dismissals. The number of complaints brought to JQCs by litigants has hovered around fifty thousand in recent years, which represented less than 0.3 percent of cases brought before Russian courts.[24] The 2020 amendments to the constitution establish a different procedure for the removal of higher-level judges. The JQC is authorized to make recommendations to the president on this score. The Federation Council, on the advice of the president, now has the right to dismiss these judges when they have undermined the honor and dignity of the court.[25] Some commentators argue that the effect will be to undermine the independence of the higher courts.[26] Whether this happens depends on the conditions under which this newfound power is exercised.

In contrast to the judicial system in the United States, where legal professionals go on to the bench after a lengthy career in some other legal arena, becoming a judge in Russia is a career choice made at a much earlier stage of life. There are two basic career paths for those interested in becoming a judge.[27] Judges who handle criminal cases are drawn from the ranks of criminal investigators and prosecutors, whereas judges who handle noncriminal cases typically go to work for the courts as an assistant to a judge immediately after completing their legal education to gain the necessary experience to apply for a judicial post. Once they get onto the bench, most stay for their entire work life. As of 2018, women constituted 61 percent of the judicial corps.[28] Though the prestige of the judiciary has risen considerably since the demise of the Soviet Union, it remains lower than in the United States. As in other countries with a civil law legal tradition, Russian judges view themselves as civil servants, not as policymakers.[29] Recognizing that status is linked to salary and staff support, the funding for the courts increased more than twenty-fold under Putin and Medvedev.[30] Even so, recruiting a sufficient number of judges to staff the courts remains difficult. Institutional efforts aimed at enhancing the status of the judiciary represent a starting point but are effective only if accompanied by societal trust. This has been slow to develop, as evidenced by public opinion polls indicating that most Russians approach the courts with skepticism.[31]

As part of an effort to build legitimacy for the courts, a law was passed mandating that, as of July 2010, all courts create websites on which schedules for upcoming hearings are posted as well as most judicial decisions. Taking account of the massive workload of justices of the peace, low-level courts are required only to notify parties of the outcome of simple cases. They need write out full opinions only when one of the parties requests it. Such websites have been created, though their quality varies widely.[32] A market has grown up for more easily useable websites that aggregate these cases. Notwithstanding the fact that lower-court decisions do not constitute binding precedent, some litigants have made active use of the information posted to investigate how the judges assigned to their cases have ruled in previous analogous cases. They believe that compiling this information helps them to persuade judges to be consistent in their rulings.

Constitutional Court

The Constitutional Court is a post-Soviet innovation. Its purpose is to ensure that the constitution remains the preeminent legal authority in Russia. To that end, it is empowered to invalidate legislative and/or executive acts as unconstitutional. From a technical legal point of view, the Constitutional Court stands on equal footing with the Supreme Court (see figure 4.1), but it is unlike the Supreme Court in several important respects. First, it does not stand at the apex of an elaborate hierarchy of courts that stretch across Russia. It is a stand-alone court.[33] Second, it is a much smaller court, with only eleven judges.[34] The background of these judges is quite different from that of their counterparts on the Supreme Court, most of whom have worked as judges for their entire careers. By contrast, many members of the Constitutional Court are drawn from the top ranks of legal scholars and come to the bench only after several decades of working in universities or research institutes. This means they are free of the legacy of dependence that hangs over the rest of the

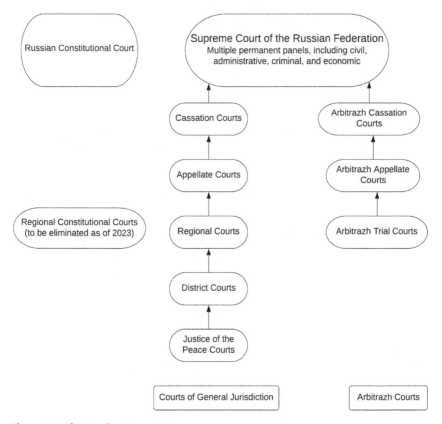

Figure 4.1. The Russian Court System

Russian judiciary. Because they mostly come from a scholarly background, their opinions are longer and more literate, providing a clearer window into their thinking than is possible with opinions from the other courts. For most of its life, judges' right to write dissenting opinions enhanced the transparency of this Court. In fall 2020, the law was changed to forbid the publication of dissenting opinions or any discussion of the inner workings of the Court.[35] Decisions of the Constitutional Court continue to be a source of law and, as such, are binding on the other branches of government as well as on other courts.

Between 2008 and 2016, the number of petitions sent to the Constitutional Court ranged between twelve thousand and nineteen thousand per year, though the number has been decreasing. In 2020, the Court received 12,838 petitions.[36] Almost all come in the form of individual complaints centering on alleged violations of constitutional rights. The remaining cases stem from claims initiated by the president, a group of legislators (at least 20 percent of the members of either chamber), or regional governments. Its decisions take several forms. Not all involve an up-or-down vote on the constitutionality of a particular law or regulation. Many of its rulings lay out the justification for the constitutionality of legal norms. These so-called "authoritative interpretations" can have the effect of rewriting the law under the guise of ensuring its constitutionality. They have given the court tremendous influence in many areas of law (including taxes, contracts, and social benefits) that would not appear to fall under its jurisdiction. The court has further expanded its jurisdiction by issuing rulings that declared contested legal norms "noncontradictory to the constitution," but their interpretations of these laws are considered binding on all Russian courts.[37]

Since its reconstitution following the October Events of 1993, the Constitutional Court has been reluctant to immerse itself in political controversy. Its ability to do so has been institutionally constrained by the decision to limit its jurisdiction to cases brought to it; the court can no longer take up cases on its own initiative. The court has also adopted a more deliberative pace for resolving cases. In contrast to the chaotic practices of the early 1990s, when decisions were sometimes issued on an overnight basis, cases now take eight or nine months to wind their way through the system, allowing time for the sorts of back-and-forth discussions among the judges that are familiar to students of the US Supreme Court.[38] Students of the Constitutional Court have been struck by the pragmatic approach taken during the Putin era. They argue that it "decides cases that matter to the regime in a politically expedient way, while giving priority to legal and constitutional considerations in other cases, thereby recognizing the reality of a dual state."[39] The 2020 amendments to the constitution give the Court the right to review draft laws at the request of the president.[40] Some have argued that, while this appears to expand the powers of the Court, the true beneficiary is the president. Rather than having to wait to exhibit his displeasure with a law until presented with it as a fait accompli, the president can force reconsideration of laws by sending (or even threatening to send) a law to the Court.[41] The ability of outside observers to understand the thinking of justices was curtailed in 2020, when the legislature changed the law to forbid them from publishing dissenting opinions.

Getting its decisions enforced is a problem that the Constitutional Court shares with the courts of general jurisdiction and the *arbitrazh* courts. Enforcing judgments is not just a problem in Russia; it is a problem that plagues courts everywhere. For the most part, litigants are expected to live up to the obligations imposed by the courts out of a combination of respect for the institution and a fear of being identified as noncompliant and shamed. The lack of societal trust in courts turns these assumptions upside down in Russia. Flouting judicial orders brings no disgrace. The Constitutional Court has attempted to remedy the problem by creating a department charged with monitoring its decisions. But the small size of the department (four people) and intransigence of the underlying political issues have hampered efforts at improving the record on implementation. Perhaps the most notable example of resistance involves a series of decisions by the Constitutional Court declaring municipal residence permits to be unconstitutional, viewing them as contradicting the right to freedom of movement. Facing a never-ending stream of Russians and migrants keen to take advantage of the economic opportunities available in large cities (especially Moscow), the mayors of these cities have consistently turned a blind eye to the Court's rulings.[42]

The Courts of General Jurisdiction

The courts of general jurisdiction are the workhorses of the Russian judicial system. Any case that is not specifically allocated to the Constitutional Court or the *arbitrazh* courts lands in their lap. In 2020, the workload of these courts, constituting over twenty-one million cases, was over thirteen times greater than that of the *arbitrazh* courts. They handle all criminal cases, as well as any civil or administrative case that affects an individual (rather than a firm). The number of cases heard by these courts more than tripled between 1995 and 2020.[43] The increase has been driven by civil cases; the number of criminal cases has actually decreased in recent years. The rise in civil claims is particularly intriguing, given that most of these cases are brought by private actors. Whether this reflects a fundamental shift in attitudes toward the legal system, namely a greater willingness on the part of Russians to use the courts to protect their interests, is unclear.[44]

The courts of general jurisdiction can be found in every administrative district, making them the most accessible of the Russian courts. This has only increased under Putin with the introduction of a new layer of courts, the justice of the peace (JP) courts (see figure 4.1). The JP courts were first authorized in late 1998 and were intended to provide a way to siphon off simple cases, thereby alleviating the burden on the already existing courts.[45] Creating thousands of new courts proved to be easier said than done. When Putin took over in 2000, none existed, but by 2009, JP courts could be found in every part of Russia. From an institutional perspective, they have lived up to their promise. By 2019, these courts were handling two-thirds of all civil cases, one-third of all criminal cases, and almost 90 percent of all administrative cases.[46] Thanks in large measure to this, delays throughout the entire system have been lessened. The JP courts have also benefited litigants by making courts more accessible, both geographically as well as in terms of simplified procedures. As figure 4.1 indicates, those dissatisfied with the JP courts are entitled to appeal the judgment to a higher court.

Most cases that have not been diverted to the JP courts originate in the district courts, which are located in each rural or urban district. More serious matters are heard for the first time by the regional courts (which also serve as courts of appeal for the district courts).[47] In 2018, two new levels of appellate courts were introduced. Each of the five new appeals courts hear cases from fifteen to twenty regional courts and each of the nine cassation courts has jurisdiction over ten to fifteen regions (see figure 4.1).[48] The court of last resort is the Supreme Court of the Russian Federation. Like the Constitutional Court, the decisions of this court serve as binding precedent. In addition to its pure judicial function of reviewing individual cases, the court is also charged with overseeing the general development of judicial practice. To this end, it periodically issues guiding explanations of legislation that has been interpreted in contradictory fashion by lower courts. These explanations are binding on the lower courts. Ironically this gives the Russian Supreme Court greater institutional latitude than that enjoyed by the US Supreme Court, though few would argue that the political clout of the Russian court approaches that of its American counterpart.

Putin's control of the legislature allowed for thorough reforms of the three procedural codes (administrative, civil, and criminal) that govern the day-to-day operations of the courts of general jurisdiction. Some of the innovations of the new criminal procedure code have been discussed above. The code also changed the operation of the courts by institutionalizing jury trials throughout Russia. The first jury trial was held in 1993. In 2001, the right to a jury trial was made available to defendants charged with certain serious felonies. Juries have become increasingly popular. In 2019, jury trials accounted for 20.2 percent of the caseload of regional courts, compared with 8.3 percent in 2003.[49] Defendants tend to fare better with juries than with judges. Overall acquittal rates have long been less than 1 percent. By contrast, almost a quarter of defendants in jury trials were acquitted in 2019.[50] Jury verdicts, including acquittals, have been subject to appeal from the outset. After the Kremlin was embarrassed when juries acquitted defendants in several politically sensitive cases, the law was changed in 2008 to eliminate the right to a jury trial in cases of espionage, treason, terrorism, and other crimes against the state. As of 2018, however, the right to a jury trial was expanded to district courts.[51]

The broader impact of the availability of jury trials on Russians' attitudes toward the legal system is unclear. Elsewhere, juries have been justified on the grounds that they allow defendants to be judged by their peers and that they provide jurors with hands-on experience in how a democratic system operates. The relatively small number of Russians who have served on juries undermines any argument that they are building support for democracy. Public opinion polls confirm Russians' ambivalence about their merits. More than 30 percent of those surveyed between 2006 and 2020 said they trusted juries more than judges. About 20 percent (17 percent in 2020) said juries were less trustworthy. The biggest shift between the surveys was in those who saw no significant difference between verdicts issued by judge and juries. This percentage increased from 19 in 2006 to 30 in 2020.[52]

The *Arbitrazh* Courts

The jurisdiction of the *arbitrazh* courts is threefold: (1) disputes between firms (irrespective of ownership structure), (2) disputes between firms and the state, and (3) bankruptcies. At the outset, almost all cases fell into the first category, but over time the docket has shifted. Comparing the case distributions in 1997, 2005, and 2020 illustrates the point well. In 1997, disputes between firms dominated the docket, constituting over 80 percent of the cases decided by these courts. By 2005, these disputes accounted for about a quarter of the cases decided, and the number of cases involving the state made up 74 percent of the docket. The picture had shifted again by 2020. Once again, interfirm disputes dominated, constituting 72 percent of all cases. Disputes involving the state had receded, making up around 20 percent of the docket. Bankruptcy cases, fueled by the introduction of personal bankruptcy in 2015, made up almost 7 percent of all cases.[53] These shifts are the result of the changing economic fortunes of Russia as well as changes in the underlying law.

The number of cases brought to the *arbitrazh* courts grew sixfold from 1995 to 2020. The willingness of economic actors to submit their disputes to the court is driven by the comparatively low costs and the speed of the process. This is not to say that litigation is the only or even the preferred mechanism of resolving disputes. For Russian managers, much as for their counterparts elsewhere, turning to the courts is a last resort, used only when efforts at negotiation have failed. Rather, the point is that litigation is a viable option for commercial disputes in Russia.

The continued viability of the *arbitrazh* courts came into question with the decision to merge what had been the top court of this system, the Higher *Arbitrazh* Court, with the Supreme Court. Putin announced this plan in mid-2013, prompting immediate protests from the business community, who had come to respect the competency of the *arbitrazh* courts. Disregarding these protests, the legislature moved with lightning speed to achieve Putin's goal, pushing through changes to the procedural codes and initiating the necessary amendments to the constitution. By August 2014, the Higher *Arbitrazh* Court was only an institutional memory. The Supreme Court now serves as the court of last resort for the *arbitrazh* courts. To accommodate this institutional reform, separate chambers have been created to handle final appeals from the courts of general jurisdiction and the *arbitrazh* courts. At present, the *arbitrazh* courts continue to operate according to their own procedures.

The European Court of Human Rights

When Russia joined the Council of Europe in 1996 and it ratified the European Convention on Human Rights in 1998, it became subject to the jurisdiction of the European Court of Human Rights (ECHR) in Strasbourg. Were Russians as nihilistic about law as is typically assumed, this would have made no difference. But Russians have flocked to the ECHR when their domestic courts have failed them. A 2010 survey confirmed that two-thirds of Russians were aware of the ECHR. In 2020, Russians submitted 22 percent of all petitions, putting them in first place.[54] This suggests that Russians still believe justice is possible and that they are searching out ways of holding their courts and government to account. At the same time, the fact that almost all of these Russian petitions were declared inadmissible (as was the case for many other countries), reveals that many petitioners were unclear about the precise function of the ECHR. In the wake of the invasion of Ukraine, Russia withdrew from the Council of Europe in March 2022. Its announcement came hours before the Assembly of the Council of Europe voted to expel Russia. As a result, Russians are no longer able to appeal to the ECHR.

Prior to this, the Russian government had a mixed record at the ECHR. When damages were assessed against it, they have generally paid without question. But when the court called for changes in policy, Russia's record was less impressive. A 2015 law granted discretion to the Constitutional Court to override ECHR decisions.[55] To that end, when the ECHR ruled in 2017 that Russia's so-called gay propaganda law was discriminatory and encouraged homophobia, imposing damages of over €43,000, one legislator said that the decision would not be honored "because it contradicts the Russian Constitution."[56] This hostility to the ECHR was reinforced by the 2020 amendments to the constitution, which mirrored the earlier legislation by stating that decisions of international tribunals that contradict the constitution will not be enforced.[57] Yet the availability of recourse to the ECHR undoubtedly affected judicial behavior. Russian judges, worried that their opinions would become the subject of appeals to the ECHR, took care to live up to their procedural obligations. Though it might have been more gratifying if such behavior had stemmed from a commitment to the rule of law, fear of public humiliation turned out to be a powerful stimulant. Whether this conscientiousness on the part of judges will persist without the "stick" provided by the ECHR remains to be seen.

Russians' Experiences with the Courts

The bulk of cases brought to the courts have no political resonance. They involve garden-variety crimes, complaints about mistakes in tax assessments, noisy neighbors, and/or nonpayment of child support. Results in such cases are predictable; judges hew closely to the written law. The same cannot be said for cases with political resonance. These range from high-profile cases involving prominent Kremlin opponents, such as Alexei Navalny and Pussy Riot, to cases in which multitudes are arrested and charged with protesting illegally. In such cases, the law on the books takes a back seat to "telephone law." Yet the same judges hear both categories of cases. They are able to read the signals, both formal and informal, and typically fulfill the expectations of the regime. Judges who fail to heed the signals tend to get hauled before the JQC on vague charges of having dishonored the courts and are typically removed from the bench.

Politicized cases are an old story in Russia. Millions were sent to the gulag under Stalin, convicted of anti-Soviet activities on the basis of vaguely worded statutes. Due process, including having legal representation, was notable by its absence. In the post-Stalin era, the numbers affected were fewer. When put on trial, the so-called dissidents were allowed to have lawyers (though only those vetted by the security services) and to put on an affirmative defense (both in the courtroom and in the international press), but the outcome was never in doubt.

Sadly, politicized cases did not disappear when the Soviet Union collapsed in 1991. As in the post-Stalin era, their numbers are small, representing a tiny percentage of all cases heard by the Russian courts. Some have argued that politically charged prosecutions initiated under Putin harken back to the dark days of the Stalinist purges.[58] To be sure, there are troubling similarities. As was common practice in the past, these recent cases have been grounded in deliberately vague statutes that afford maximum discretion to the authorities. And they have been assigned to pliant judges who toe the line, rendering their outcomes foregone conclusions. Tactics of suspended punishment, which allowed Soviet authorities to gain leverage over large swaths of the population, have returned. The propensity to keep irksome individuals incarcerated by conveniently finding and convicting them on new charges while already in prison, which was commonplace under Stalin, has likewise returned. The experience of Alexei Navalny illustrates these practices.[59] In 2014, he was convicted on charges of fraud that he claimed were politically motivated. His sentence was suspended. When he failed to live up to the conditions for this suspended sentence, the court sent him to prison. His explanation for his failure to comply, namely that he was in Germany for treatment after an attempt to poison him, fell on deaf ears. As was so often true in the Soviet era, the judge's decision lived up to the letter of the law but not its spirit. In August 2021, new charges were filed against Navalny. If successful, he will languish in prison until after the next scheduled presidential election in 2024.[60] Although not applied to Navalny, Russian courts have also reverted to Soviet-era tactics of sentencing political dissidents to psychiatric hospitals on the grounds that their noncompliance with political norms reflects mental illness.[61]

But there are several critical differences. First is the role of publicity. Defendants are able to rally the public to the ramparts. Though traditional media outlets tout the party line, those victimized by the system are able to get their message out through social media. Sometimes it helps, as in the case of Ivan Golunov, a crusading journalist who was arrested for drug possession in the spring of 2019. Thousands protested his arrest, arguing that the drugs had been planted as way to silence Golunov, and he was released.[62] In other instances, as with Navalny, protests proved ineffective. Despite having Russians across the country take to the streets to express their displeasure with his detention, Navalny was still imprisoned for three years, many of those protesting his treatment were arrested, and his organization was hounded into non-existence. A second difference between politicized cases in the past and present is the role of lawyers. Defendants are no longer limited to a list of lawyers pre-approved by the security services. They are free to hire anyone and, if they lack the resources to do so, an *advokat* will be appointed for them. Not all Russian lawyers are interested in, or willing to, participate in political cases but there are a cadre of committed public interest lawyers who do not shy away from these cases.[63] Some, including the lawyers for Khodorkovsky and Navalny, have been targeted themselves by the regime.[64] Thus far, efforts to have them disbarred have been unsuccessful.

For the defendants in politicized cases, the fact that their rights are not trampled as thoroughly as were their predecessors is likely cold comfort. For students of the Russian court system, the reaction is more mixed. On one hand, the propensity of the regime to dictate the outcome of court cases involving its detractors explains why Russia typically scrapes the bottom of indexes aimed at measuring the rule of law. The cornerstone of the rule of law concept is that everyone is equal before the law. Despite Putin's rhetoric endorsing the rule of law, his regime's behavior tells a different story. On the other hand, the transparency of the regime's actions, as evidenced by the multiple documentaries and voluminous studies (both scholarly and journalistic) based on these politicized cases, represents a step in the right direction. It surely would have been unthinkable in the Soviet era.

THE POLITICS OF THE LEGAL PROFESSION

In many countries, lawyers are potent catalysts for legal reform. Their comprehensive knowledge of the law makes them well qualified to identify where changes are needed. Such changes may be either iterative or fundamental. Their willingness to embrace these changes and to operationalize them through their clients can have a profound impact. Merely passing a law is only a first step. More difficult is integrating new norms into daily life. Lawyers can be integral in this process.

The legal profession in Russia has not traditionally performed this sort of role. The reasons are complicated. As in other countries with civil law traditions, lawyers tend to act more as technicians than as social activists. The divided nature of the profession in such countries also contributes to its political passivity. In Russia, for example, there is no single organization that speaks for lawyers, nor is there any uniform system for licensing lawyers. This inevitably gives rise to a fragmented profession. The Soviet heritage, under which lawyers were heavily regulated and their independence was constrained, only deepened this natural instinct.

In the post-Soviet era, young people have been increasingly drawn to legal education. The number of law schools has increased from fewer than 100 in the 1980s to more than 600 today.[65] During this time, the transition to the market gave rise to new opportunities for lawyers, including specializations in corporate law, bankruptcy, and intellectual property. Between 2003 and 2015, the market for legal services doubled in size.[66] Yet even millennial lawyers are not terribly interested in rocking the boat. A 2016 survey of law students on the cusp of graduation revealed that a minority (44.7 percent) were interested in taking advantage of opportunities in the private sector. A majority (55.3 percent) planned a career in state service.[67]

Most of the Soviet-era regulations governing lawyers have been eliminated and/or ignored in practice. The traditional distinction between litigators (*advokaty*) and business lawyers (*iuriskonsul'ty*) broke down during the 1990s. Private law firms, which had been outlawed during the Soviet era, sprang up and included both varieties of lawyers. Courts treated them similarly. This permissiveness was viewed with dismay by many *advokaty*, who had long viewed themselves as the elite of the legal profession. Becoming an *advokat* had always required persevering through a rigorous and selective process, in contrast to becoming a *iuriskonsul't*, which simply required advanced legal education. *Iuriskonsul'ty* have taken advantage of the laxness of the regulatory regime to establish themselves as experts in business law, a specialization that had been more-or-less nonexistent during the Soviet era and an area of law not much exploited by *advokaty* (who tended to focus on criminal defense work). Prosecutors and judges are separate categories of lawyers. The disaggregated nature of the legal profession complicates determining the total number of Russian lawyers, though in 2013 Medvedev estimated that there were at least 1.3 million.[68]

Drafts of a law that would restore the *advokaty* to their preeminent role were floated but never passed during the 1990s. Under Putin, this state of affairs changed. His legislative dominance allowed for the passage of a law dealing with the legal profession in 2002. The law took an important step toward institutionalizing the independence of *advokaty* by establishing a privilege for their communications with clients.[69] The law created a monopoly on courtroom practice for *advokaty* in criminal cases. In civil or administrative cases, however, litigants were free to pick anyone to assist them in court or to go it alone. It was only in 2018 that representatives in such cases were even required to have a law degree.

CONCLUSION

This review of the role of law in contemporary Russia illustrates that easy conclusions are not possible. The reasons for criticism of his regime on this score are obvious. Under both Putin and Medvedev, the Kremlin's legislative agenda was pushed through with a heavy hand and often had the result of curtailing human rights. Putin's willingness to use the courts as a weapon for punishing his political opponents quite rightly calls their independence into question. Such policies would be troubling in any context but are particularly disquieting in post-Soviet Russia. They are disturbingly reminiscent of problem-solving tactics employed by Soviet leaders that would seem to have been renounced as part of the transition to a rule-of-law-based state (*pravovoe gosudarstvo*). On the other hand, the post-Yeltsin era brought critical institutional innovations. The introduction of the JP courts increased the responsiveness of courts to citizens and eased the strain on the district and regional courts. The use of courts has continued to grow, suggesting a societal willingness to turn over disputes to the courts.

These seemingly contradictory indicators make sense only when the Russian legal system is analyzed as a dualistic system. The institutional progress cannot be dismissed as mere window dressing. After all, the vast majority of the millions of cases heard each year within the Russian judicial system are resolved on the basis of the law on the books, as interpreted by the judge, and without any interference from political authorities. Justice is not out of reach in Russia; it is the likely outcome in most cases. But the continued willingness of those with political power to use law in an instrumental fashion to achieve their short-term goals means that justice can sometimes be out of reach. It also means that the commitment to the basic principle of the rule of law, namely that law applies equally to all, irrespective of their power or connections, is not yet complete. A gap between the law on the books and the law in practice exists in Russia, as in all countries. Surely it has receded from the chasm it was during the Soviet era. But whether it will increase or decrease as time goes on remains to be seen.

DISCUSSION QUESTIONS

1. What are the advantages to the Putin regime of vaguely worded legislation?
2. How has the institutional structure of the courts changed since the collapse of the Soviet Union? What impact have these changes had on citizens' access to justice?
3. What efforts have been made to enhance judicial independence in post-Soviet Russia? Is judicial independence possible in present-day Russia?

SUGGESTED READINGS

Gessen, Masha. *Words Will Break Cement: The Passion of Pussy Riot.* New York: Riverhead Books, 2014.

Henderson, Jane. *The Constitution of the Russian Federation: A Contextual Analysis.* Portland, OR: Hart Publishing, 2011.

Hendley, Kathryn. *Everyday Law in Russia.* Ithaca, NY: Cornell University Press, 2017.

Maggs, Peter B., Olga Schwartz, and William Burnham. *Law and Legal System of the Russian Federation*. 7th ed. New York: Juris Publishing, 2020.

Paneyakh, Ella. "Faking Performance Together: Systems of Performance Evaluation in Russian Enforcement Agencies and Production of Bias and Privilege." *Post-Soviet Affairs* 30, nos. 2–3 (2014): 115–36.

Solomon, Peter H. Jr., and Todd S. Foglesong. *Courts and Transition in Russia: The Challenge of Judicial Reform*. Boulder, CO: Westview, 2000.

Teague, Elizabeth. "Russia's Constitutional Reforms of 2020." *Russian Politics* 5, no. 3 (2020): 301–28.

Trochev, Alexei, and Peter H. Solomon Jr. "Authoritarian Constitutionalism in Putin's Russia: A Pragmatic Constitutional Court in a Dual State." *Communist and Post-Communist Studies* 51, no. 3 (September 2018): 201–14.

NOTES

1. For background on the meaning of *pravovoe gosudarstvo*, see Harold J. Berman, "The Rule of Law and the Law-Based State (*Rechsstaat*)," *Harriman Institute Forum* 4, no. 5 (May 1991): 1–12.

2. The conceptualization of the Russian legal system as dualistic was first suggested by Robert Sharlet with regard to the Stalinist system. "Stalinism and Soviet Legal Culture," in *Stalinism: Essays in Historical Interpretation*, ed. Robert C. Tucker (New York: Norton, 1977), 155–56. He, in turn, was drawing on the ideas of Ernst Fraenkel, *The Dual State: A Contribution to the Theory of Dictatorship* (London: Oxford University Press, 1941). For more on the dualistic nature of the contemporary Russian legal system, see Kathryn Hendley, *Everyday Law in Russia* (Ithaca, NY: Cornell University Press, 2017).

3. For an overview of the rule of law, see Lon L. Fuller, *The Morality of Law* (New Haven, CT: Yale University Press, 1965); and Phillipe Nonet and Philip Selznick, *Law and Society in Transition* (New York: Harper and Row, 1978).

4. Harold J. Berman, *Justice in the U.S.S.R: An Interpretation of Soviet Law* (Cambridge, MA: Harvard University Press, 1963).

5. George Ginsburgs, "The Soviet Judicial Elite: Is It?," *Review of Socialist Law* 11, no. 4 (1985): 293–311.

6. George Feifer, *Justice in Moscow* (New York: Simon & Schuster, 1964).

7. "Reputatsiia sudov i sudei," Fom.ru, September 23, 2020, http://fom.ru/bezopasnost-i-pravo/ 14459 (accessed March 25, 2021).

8. Kathryn Hendley, *Trying to Make Law Matter* (Ann Arbor: University of Michigan Press, 1996), 34–45.

9. Kathryn Hendley, "Legal Development in Post-Soviet Russia," *Post-Soviet Affairs* 13, no. 3 (July–September 1997): 228–51.

10. In addition, the court famously took on the question of the legality of the Communist Party, giving rise to a lengthy and rather bizarre trial. David Remnick, *Lenin's Tomb: The Last Days of the Soviet Empire* (New York: Vintage, 1994), 494–530. The

text of the court's decision is available in *Vestnik Konstitutsionnogo Suda*, nos. 4–5 (1993): 37–64.

11. Kathryn Hendley, "Remaking an Institution: The Transition in Russia from State Arbitrazh to Arbitrazh Courts," *American Journal of Comparative Law* 46, no. 1 (1998): 93–127.

12. Peter H. Solomon Jr. and Todd S. Foglesong, *Courts and Transition in Russia: The Challenge of Judicial Reform* (Boulder, CO: Westview, 2000).

13. All candidates for the bench must be Russian citizens with university-level law degrees who have clean criminal records. The minimum age and years of work experience in the legal field vary depending on the post sought. For example, those applying to be a justice of the peace, the lowest level of the court system, must be at least twenty-five years old with five years of experience, whereas those seeking a position on the constitutional court must be at least forty years old with fifteen years of experience.

14. Justices of the peace receive life tenure only after a three-year probationary period.

15. There are two words for "law" in Russian: *pravo* and *zakon*. The former conveys a notion of law that incorporates human rights, while the latter invokes a more positivistic notion of statutory law. Although the phrases used to capture the goals of legal reform in Russia used by Gorbachev (*pravovoe gosudarstvo*) and Putin (*gospodstvo zakonnosti*) seem similar on the surface, they actually capture very different notions of the role of state and society.

16. William Burnham and Jeffrey Kahn, "Russia's Criminal Procedure Code Five Years Out," *Review of Central & East European Law* 33, no. 1 (2008): 1–93.

17. Mikhail Khodorkovsky was arrested in the fall of 2003 on charges of fraud, tax evasion, and theft of state property in the course of privatization. At every stage of the process, the authorities skirted on the edge of legal proprieties, typically obeying the literal letter of the law (though not always) but trampling on its spirit. His case became a cause célèbre among the international human rights community, acting to confirm the common wisdom about the dysfunction of the Russian legal system. In December 2013, Putin pardoned Khodorkovsky and released him from prison. For background on this case, see Richard Sakwa, *Putin and the Oligarch: The Khodorkovsky-Yukos Affair* (New York: Palgrave Macmillan, 2014).

18. Ella Paneyakh, "Faking Performance Together: Systems of Performance Evaluation in Russian Enforcement Agencies and Production of Bias and Privilege," *Post-Soviet Affairs* 30, nos. 2–3 (2014): 115–36.

19. Gordon B. Smith, "Putin, the Procuracy, and the New Criminal Procedure Code," in *Public Policy and Law in Russia: In Search of a Unified Legal and Political Space*, ed. Robert Sharlet and Ferdinand Feldbrugge (Leiden: Martinus Nijhoff, 2005), 169–85.

20. Vladimir Ryzhkov, "Putin's War on NGOs Threatens Russia's Future," *Moscow Times*, July 29, 2014, https://themoscowtimes.com/articles/putins-war-on-ngos-threatens-russiasfuture-37786 (accessed March 3, 2018). Rebuffed by Russian courts, affected NGOs have taken their claims to the European Court of Human Rights. Charles Diggins, "Russia to Answer for Its 'Foreign Agent' Law in European Court

of Human Rights," *Bellona*, October 5, 2017, http://bellona.org/news/russian-human
-rights-issues/russian-ngo-law/2017-10-russia-to-answer-for-its-foreign-agent-law-in
-european-court-of-human-rights (accessed March 3, 2018).

21. Alena Ledeneva, *Can Russia Modernise? Sistema, Power Networks and Informal Governance* (New York: Cambridge University Press, 2013).

22. Filing fees are calculated as a percentage of the damages sought but are waived for many categories of cases, including consumer complaints. Court websites include a link that calculates these fees for litigants. As to delays, Solomon and Foglesong report that in the mid-1990s, the statutorily imposed deadlines for resolving cases were not met in more than 25 percent and 15 percent of criminal and civil cases, respectively. *Courts and Transition in Russia*, 118–19. The 2020 data collected by the courts indicate that over 99 percent of civil and 83 percent of criminal cases were resolved within the deadlines established by law, http://www.cdep.ru/index.php?id=79 (accessed August 3, 2021). Even so, delays remain a serious concern. Litigants are entitled to seek compensation from the court when cases are unreasonably delayed. In extreme instances, parties can take their complaints to the European Court of Human Rights.

23. Alexei Trochev, "Judicial Selection in Russia: Towards Accountability and Centralization," in *Appointing Judges in an Age of Judicial Power: Critical Perspectives from Around the World*, ed. Peter H. Russell and Kate Malleson (Toronto: University of Toronto Press, 2006).

24. For a summary of the activities of the JQCs, see http://www.vkks.ru/category/8/ (accessed August 2, 2021).

25. Arts. 83, 102, Constitution. http://pravo.gov.ru/proxy/ips/?docbody=&nd=102027595 (accessed August 2, 2021).

26. Elizabeth Teague, "Russia's Constitutional Reforms of 2020," *Russian Politics* 5, no. 3 (2020): 301–28.

27. Vadim Volkov and Aryna Dzmitryieva, "Recruitment Patterns, Gender, and Professional Subcultures of the Judiciary in Russia," *International Journal of the Legal Profession* 22, no. 2 (2015): 166–92.

28. European Commission for the Efficiency of Justice, "Dynamic Database of European Judicial Systems," https://public.tableau.com/app/profile/cepej/viz/CEPEJ-Genderequalityv2020_1_0EN/GenderEquality (accessed August 24, 2021).

29. On the differences between common law and civil law legal traditions, see John Henry Merryman, *The Civil Law Tradition: An Introduction to the Legal Systems of Western Europe and Latin America*, 2nd ed. (Stanford, CA: Stanford University Press, 1985).

30. In 2000, 8.3 billion rubles were allocated to the courts. By 2019, this figure had increased to 190.5 billion rubles. Compare the budget law for 2000 (http://kremlin.ru/acts/bank/18024) with the budget law for 2019 (http://publication.pravo.gov.ru/Document/View/0001202010150075) (accessed on August 3, 2021).

31. In a series of polls conducted between 1994 and 2020, Russians were asked whether they trusted state institutions, including courts. Over that time, the percentage of those surveyed who completely trust the courts fluctuated between 8 and 31 percent. A plurality of respondents has taken a middle-of-the-road position, while those

who distrust the courts has held steady at about 20 percent. See http://www.levada .ru/2016/10/13/ institutsionalnoe-doverie-2; https://www.levada.ru/2019/10/24/ institutsionalnoe-doverie-5/; https://www.levada.ru/2020/09/21/doverie-institutam/ (accessed March 24, 2021).

32. Infometr, "Voprosy opublikovaniia sudebnykh aktov na saitakh sudov obshchei iurisdiktsii," http://infometer.org/analitika/voprosyi-opublikovaniya-sudebnyix-aktov -na-sajtax-sudov-obshhej-yurisdikczii (accessed March 3, 2018).

33. The fifteen regional constitutional courts are not institutionally linked to the Russian Constitutional Court. Alexei Trochev, "Less Democracy, More Courts: The Puzzle of Judicial Review in Russia," *Law & Society Review* 38, no. 3 (September 2004): 513–38.

34. The 2020 amendments to the constitution reduced the number from nineteen to eleven. Art. 125, http://pravo.gov.ru/proxy/ips/?docbody=&nd=102027595 (accessed August 2, 2021).

35. Federal'nyi konstitutsionnyi zakon ot 9 noiabria 2020 g. No. 5-FKZ "O vnesenii izmenenii v Federal'nyi konstitutsionnyi zakon 'O Konstitutsionnom Sude Rossiiskoi Federatsii," *Rossiiskaia gazeta*, November 11, 2020, https://rg.ru/2020/11/11/ ks-dok.html (accessed August 22, 2021).

36. http://ksrf.ru/ru/Petition/Pages/StatisticDef.aspx (accessed May 23, 2021).

37. Trochev, *Judging Russia: Constitutional Court in Russian Politics, 1990–2006* (Cambridge: Cambridge University Press, 2008), 122–23.

38. Trochev, *Judging Russia*, 120–21.

39. Alexei Trochev and Peter H. Solomon Jr., "Authoritarian Constitutionalism in Putin's Russia: A Pragmatic Constitutional Court in a Dual State," *Communist and Post-Communist Studies* 51, no. 3 (September 2018): 201–14, 201.

40. Art. 125, Constitution.

41. Teague, "Russia's Constitutional Reforms," 324.

42. Trochev, *Judging Russia*, 97–98, 245–6.

43. See http://www.cdep.ru/index.php?id=79 (accessed March 24, 2021).

44. Kathryn Hendley, "The Puzzling Non-Consequences of Societal Distrust of Courts: Explaining the Use of Courts in Russia," *Cornell International Law Journal* 45, no. 3 (Fall 2012): 527–58.

45. Kathryn Hendley, "Assessing the Role of Justice-of-the-Peace Courts in the Russian Judicial System," *Review of Central and East European Law* 37, no. 4 (2012): 373–93.

46. http://www.cdep.ru/index.php?id=79 (accessed March 23, 2021).

47. In 2019, less than 1 percent of cases originated in the regional courts. "Obzor sudebnoi statistiki o deiatel'nosti federal'nykh sudov obshchei iurisdiktsii i mirovykh sudei v 2019 godu." http://www.cdep.ru/index.php?id=80 (accessed March 24, 2021).

48. These courts were introduced at the urging of the European Court of Human Rights, which had long argued that the structure of Russia's courts failed to comply with article 2 of protocol 7 to the European Convention on Human Rights, which guarantees criminal defendants the right to have their conviction reviewed by a higher court. Peter B. Maggs, Olga Schwartz, and William Burnham, *Law and Legal System of the Russian Federation*, 7th ed. (New York: Juris Publishing, 2020): 105–7.

49. "Obzor sudebnoi statistiki o deiatel'nosti federal'nykh sudov obshchei iuris-diktsii i mirovykh sudei v 2019 godu. http://www.cdep.ru/index.php?id=80 (accessed March 24, 2021); "Obzor deiatel'nosti federal'nykh sudov obshchei iurisdiktsii i mirovykh sudei v 2004 godu," *Rossiiskaia iustitsiia*, no. 6 (2005): 29. When taken as a percentage of the total criminal cases, the share of cases heard by juries is infinitesimal.

50. The low acquittal rate in nonjury trials is a bit misleading. In 2020, two-thirds of criminal cases were resolved through the Russian version of plea bargaining without a full-fledged trial. http://www.cdep.ru/index.php?id=79 (accessed August 2, 2021). On plea bargaining, see Olga B. Semukhina and K. Michael Reynolds, "Plea Bargaining Implementation and Acceptance in Modern Russia," *International Criminal Justice Review* 19, no. 4 (2009): 400–32.

51. Maggs, Schwartz, and Burnham, *Law and Legal System of the Russian Federation*, 958–60.

52. There was a corresponding decrease in those who refused to express an opinion. "Reputatsiia sudov i sudei."

53. "Osnovanye pokazateli raboty arbitrazhnykh sudov v 1996–1997 godakh," *Vestnik Vysshego Arbitrazhnogo Suda*, no. 4 (1998): 21–23; "Spravka o rassmotren-nykh delakh arbitrazhnymi sudami sub'ektov Rossiiskoi Federatsii v 2012–2013 gg.," "Sudebno-arbitrazhnaia statistika o rassmotrennykh delakh arbitrazhnymi sudami Rossiiskoi Federatsii v 2002–2005 godakh," *Vestnik Vosshego Arbitrazhnogo Suda*, no. 5 (2006): 22–23; "Otchet o rabote arbitrazhnykh sudov sub'ektov Rossiiskoi Fed-eratsii v 2020," http://www.cdep.ru/index.php?id= 79&item=5670 (accessed August 3, 2021).

54. "European Court of Human Rights: Analysis of Statistics 2020," http://www .echr.coe. int/Documents/Stats_analysis_2020_ENG.pdf (accessed March 23, 2021). See generally Freek ven der Vet, "Protecting Rights in Strasbourg: Developing a Research Agenda for Analyzing International Litigation from Russia," *Laboratorium* 6, no. 3 (2014): 105–18.

55. "O vnesenii izmenenii v Federal'nyi konstitutsionnyi zakon 'O Konstitutsion-nom Sude Rossiiskoi Federatsii,'" Federal'nyi zakon ot 14 dekabria 2015 g. No. 7-FKZ, *Rossiiskaia gazeta*, December 16, 2015, https://rg.ru/2015/12/15/ks-site-dok .html (accessed March 3, 2018).

56. Sewell Chan, "Russia's 'Gay Propaganda' Laws Are Illegal, European Court Rules," *New York Times*, June 20, 2017, https://www.nytimes.com/2017/06/20/world/ europe/russia-gay-propaganda.html (accessed March 3, 2018). On Russia's record for implementation, see Rene Provost, "Teetering on the Edge of Legal Nihilism: Russia and the Evolving European Human Rights Regime," *Human Rights Quarterly* 37, no. 2 (2015): 289–340.

57. Art. 79, Constitution.

58. E.g., Vladimir Kara-Murza, "Russia Just Took a Big Step Back Toward the Soviet Union," *Washington Post*. May 4, 2021; Andrei Kolesnikov, "The Return of Stalinist Show Trials," *Moscow Times*, February 11, 2020; Masha Gessen, "Is It 1937 Yet?" *New York Times*, May 5, 2015.

59. Anton Troianovski, "A Life in Opposition: Navalny's Path From Gadfly to Heroic Symbol," *New York Times*, February 13, 2021.

60. Anton Troianovski, "Russia Brings a New Criminal Charge Against Navalny," *New York Times*, August 11, 2021.

61. Robert Coalson and Olga Beshlei, "Increasingly, Russian Activists Find Themselves Sentenced to Compulsory Medical Treatment," *Radio Free Europe Radio Liberty*, July 20, 2021. https://www.rferl.org/a/russian-activists-compulsory-medical -treatment/31386001.html (accessed August 17, 2021).

62. Neil MacFarquhar, "In Stunning Reversal, Russia Drops Charges Against Reporter," *New York Times*, June 11, 2019.

63. Kathryn Hendley, "Assessing the Potential for Renegades Among Russian Millennial Lawyers," *Demokratizatsiya* 28, no. 1 (2020): 143–75; Freek van der Vet, "Spies. Lies, and Trolls: Political Lawyering against Disinformation and State Surveillance in Russia," *Law & Social Inquiry* 46, no. 2 (May 2021): 407–34.

64. E.g., Anton Troianovski, "My Conscience Is Clean. And Yet They Came for Me," *New York Times*, June 4, 2021.

65. Ekaterina Moiseeva, "Iuridicheskoye obrazovanie v Rossii" Seriia "Analiticheskie obzory po problemam pravoprimeneniia" (St. Petersburg: IPP EUCPB, 2018), https://enforce.spb.ru/images/analit_zapiski/IRL_analit_obzor_legal_education_ moiseeva.pdf (accessed March 26, 2021); http://www.edu.ru/abitur/act.106/fgosp.39/ index.php (accessed March 26, 2021).

66. Ekaterina Moiseeva and Dmitrii Skugarevskii, "Rynok iuridicheskikh uslug v Rossii: chto govorit statistika," Seriia "Analiticheskie obzory po problemam pravoprimeneniia" (St. Petersburg: IPP EUCPB, 2016), http://enforce.spb.ru/images/ lawfirms_report_e_version.pdf (accessed March 3, 2018).

67. Kathryn Hendley, "Nature versus Nurture: A Comparison of Russian Law Graduates Destined for State Service and for Private Practice," *Law & Policy* 41, no. 2 (April 2019): 147–73, 155.

68. Vladimir Bagaev, "Chislennost' rossiiskikh iuristov obradovala prem'era," *zakon.ru*, May 15, 2013. https://zakon.ru/discussion/2013/5/15/chislennost_ rossijskix_yuristov_obradovala_premera_pravovedy_debyutirovali_na_novoj_scene _mariinsko (accessed August 3, 2021).

69. For an analysis of the challenges associated with inculcating professional ethics among Russian lawyers, see Katrina P. Lewinbuk, "Perestroika or Just Perfunctory? The Scope and Significance of Russia's New Legal Ethics Laws," *Journal of the Legal Profession* 35, no. 1 (2010): 25–80.

Chapter 5

Civil Society and Social Movements

Alfred B. Evans Jr. and Elizabeth Plantan

Scholars in the social sciences think of civil society as the sphere of activity that is initiated, organized, and carried out primarily by citizens and not directed by the state. Larry Diamond, for example, characterizes civil society as "the realm of organized social life that is voluntary, self-generating, at least partially self-supporting, autonomous from the state, and bound by a legal order or set of shared rules."[1] Scholarly writings on civil society in Russia bear the imprint of two different perspectives. Those scholars whose perspective is shaped by the "democratization framework" argue that a robust civil society would contribute to the growth and consolidation of democratic political institutions in Russia.[2] That point of view, which is rooted in British and American historical experiences, raises the hope that civil society will serve as a counterweight to the power of the state and thus expects that there will be continuing conflict between social organizations and the state.[3] Another group of writings on civil society has a more pragmatic orientation,[4] primarily addressing the question of whether nongovernmental organizations (NGOs) in Russia "help people solve their problems."[5] Scholars of that school of thought emphasize the usefulness of partnership between NGOs and agencies of the state in providing services to groups of people,[6] though those scholars note that NGOs that collaborate with the state may still try to preserve a degree of independence.

In this chapter, we argue that these two different perspectives on civil society in Russia are two sides of the same coin. On the one hand, civil society and social movements make demands of the state that could undermine the regime or even lead to democratization. On the other hand, some civil society organizations or social movements could prove beneficial to the authorities

111

by providing public services or drawing attention to local governance issues. These two different possible roles for civil society have led the Russian government to enact various policies that have essentially created "two civil societies": one that is perceived as regime-supporting and beneficial, and one that is deemed politically risky and regime-threatening.[7] Throughout this chapter, we trace the development of civil society and social movements in Russia, explain this dual approach to societal management, and examine important current and future trends in state-society relations in post-Soviet Russia.

HISTORICAL BACKGROUND

The political regime of the Soviet Union was hostile toward the idea of civil society because its leaders saw any independence of organized groups as threatening their monopoly of power. Russian historians have confirmed that even during the earliest years of the Soviet system, the Communist Party wanted to eliminate independent groups, and that the party intensified its control of social organizations from the 1920s to the 1930s.[8] During the 1950s and 1960s, a variety of informal and unofficial social groups did come into existence quietly, and there are reports that the number of groups that were not sponsored by the Communist Party increased during the 1970s and early 1980s.[9] A dissident movement voiced open criticism of the Soviet regime by the 1960s, often at great personal cost for its members, but the active participants in that movement were a tiny minority. It is likely that most people in the Soviet Union who had heard of the dissenters were indifferent or even hostile toward them, so that dissidents "failed to strike a responsive chord among the masses at large."[10]

After he came to power in 1985, Mikhail Gorbachev opened the way for a major shift in the relationship between the state and society. Part of his program of radical reform allowed citizens to create "informal" groups (*neformalye*), which were not controlled by the Communist Party. The number of those groups grew very rapidly; in 1989, the party newspaper, *Pravda*, said that around sixty thousand informal groups had come into existence.[11] Those groups were devoted to a wide range of activities, but many of them asserted demands for change in the policies of the state, and some called for change that was more basic than Gorbachev had wanted. Soon some Western scholars spoke very optimistically about the emergence of civil society in the Soviet Union, even suggesting that the shift in power between society and the state could not be reversed.[12]

CIVIL SOCIETY IN POST-SOVIET RUSSIA

The Chaotic 1990s

Assessments of civil society in Russia several years after the collapse of rule by the Communist Party and the breakup of the USSR painted a largely negative picture. Among scholars there was a consensus that the boom in civil society organizations under Gorbachev had been followed by a slump in post-Soviet Russia in the 1990s.[13] The legacy of the Soviet system in political culture was a source of problems for organizations that sought to unite groups of Russians for the pursuit of common interests. Ken Jowitt contends that the experience of living under communist rule led citizens to see a dichotomy between the official realm and the private realm.[14] In the unofficial culture of such citizens, the sphere of political life was regarded as "suspect, distasteful, and possibly dangerous,"[15] and as sharply distinct from the sphere of private life, the only area where intimacy could be found and ethical conduct was possible.[16] Nongovernmental organizations were seen as part of the public sphere. On the basis of data from surveys, Marc Morjé Howard concluded that "most people in post-communist societies still strongly mistrust and avoid joining any kind of formal organizations,"[17] and he showed that the rate of membership in voluntary associations is lower in post-communist countries than in the older democracies, or in post-authoritarian countries that had not been under communist control.[18]

Another serious problem for Russian civil society and social movements in the post-Soviet period was the deep dislocation in that country's economy during the 1990s. Because of interruptions in the payment of wages and pensions and a high rate of inflation, most people in Russia were preoccupied with the struggle for economic survival and did not have the means to offer financial support to nongovernmental organizations, even if they had wanted to do so. Thus it is not surprising that most of those organizations did not even attempt to raise funds by expanding the ranks of their members or soliciting donations from potential supporters.[19] In surveys, the leaders of nongovernmental organizations in Russia often said that their biggest problem was a lack of financial support for their activities.[20] During the 1990s, a few of those organizations received grants from foreign sources,[21] but that kind of support had mixed effects, on the one hand raising the level of professional competence of the leaders of the organizations, but on the other hand discouraging the leaders of such groups from seeking to build a base of support in their society.[22] Furthermore, protests during the Yeltsin era reflected the challenges of the period. During the 1990s, protests more often took the form of direct action (such as strikes), were geographically scattered among Russia's regions, and focused on economic woes like unpaid wages.[23] In summary, civil society in Russia was weak, on the whole, by the end of the 1990s, and the two main reasons for the marginal condition of most of the organizations in civil society were the distrust of the public sphere and the unfavorable economic circumstances for social organizations or social movements.

Putin's First and Second Terms (2000–2008)

After Vladimir Putin became president of Russia in 2000, he consolidated control over the political system, subordinating the parliament, regional governments, political parties, and television networks to domination by the national executive leadership. Within a few years, Putin turned his attention to bringing civil society into an integrated system of support for the centralized state.[24] While his speeches frequently mentioned the importance of civil society, they made it clear that he envisioned social groups as assisting the state in addressing tasks that serve the needs of the whole nation.[25] Putin is suspicious toward nongovernmental organizations in Russia that receive funding from abroad, especially if those organizations are at all involved in politics. In 2006 the parliament passed changes in the regulations for NGOs. Some groups complained that the requirements for registration and reporting under the new laws were onerous, but it is not clear whether the new procedures forced any genuinely active organizations to close down.[26] Putin's suspicion about possible foreign influence on civil society in Russia seemed to grow after protests played a major role in toppling leaders in other states that formerly had been part of the Soviet Union, in events in Georgia, Ukraine, and Kyrgyzstan. It is safe to say that Putin's insistence on suppressing any potential for a similar "color revolution" in Russia has conditioned some of his policies toward civil society in his country.

On the other hand, Putin also enhanced positive incentives for organizations in civil society to provide the kinds of services that the state considered most valuable. In 2006 the federal government began to award grants to Russian NGOs through a competitive process, offering an alternative to Western funding.[27] The political regime also took the initiative in forming groups that some scholars have called "government-organized nongovernmental organizations," or GONGOs. Perhaps the most prominent of these were a series of state-sponsored youth groups, but the fact that each of these groups has been replaced or has become inactive[28] implies that none has been very successful. Another innovation of the Putin leadership that was intended to ensure a closer relationship between the state and civil society was the Public Chamber of the Russian Federation.[29] In 2004 Putin proposed the establishment of a public chamber, "as a platform for extensive dialogue, where citizens' initiatives could be presented and discussed in detail,"[30] and a law adopted by the parliament made it possible for that body to begin functioning in early 2006. The president plays a major role in appointing the members of the Public Chamber, who are said to be representatives of organizations in civil society. Though some of the members of that body have spoken out as individuals on controversial issues, over time there has not been enough of a consensus among the members to make it possible for them to attempt to exert influence on the resolution of any major controversial question. Similarly, public chambers at the regional and local levels do not seem to have played a significant role in resolving issues raised by citizens.[31]

From Medvedev's Presidency to Bolotnaia (2008–2012)

When Dmitry Medvedev was elected president, some signs were pointing to a more cooperative relationship between state and civil society. As president-elect in March 2008, Medvedev proclaimed that an increased role for civil society was central to his vision for Russia's modernization.[32] In April 2009, Medvedev met with the Presidential Council for Civil Society and Human Rights (PCCSHR) and admitted that changes to the laws governing NGOs were necessary.[33] True to his word, in July 2009, Medvedev signed amendments to the NGO law that removed some of the most onerous restrictions from the 2006 revision. The US-Russia Bilateral Presidential Commission, set up that summer under the Obama and Medvedev administrations, even included a working group on civil society.[34]

Still, there were other developments that suggested a less cooperative and welcoming view of civil society and their foreign funders within the Russian political establishment. In July 2008, Putin, in his role as prime minister, signed a decree that dramatically reduced the number of foreign-based NGOs with tax exempt status from 101 down to 12, which subjected the 89 removed organizations, including the Ford Foundation, World Wildlife Fund, and the MacArthur Foundation, to a 24 percent tax rate on all grants within Russia.[35] As for domestic funding, the presidential grant program, which was first launched at the end of Putin's second term as president, had come under scrutiny for its lack of transparency, Moscow-centrism, and high administrative costs, which led to a significant drop in applications from 2008 to 2010.[36]

The Medvedev presidency also coincided with several major Russian social movements that relied on protest tactics, culminating in the 2011–2012 protests against electoral fraud. Compared to the Yeltsin era in the 1990s, protests from 2007–2011 were more often symbolic demonstrations, more frequently located in Moscow and St. Petersburg, and advanced more abstract claims.[37] One of the first major protest movements during the Medvedev interregnum was against a tax on foreign-made cars in late 2008 and early 2009 in the Far Eastern city of Vladivostok. Others that followed included a movement against routing a St. Petersburg-Moscow highway through Khimki forest, which at its height attracted over five thousand people to a protest rally and concert in Moscow's Pushkin square in August 2010. That same year, motorists in Moscow protested elite abuse of blue emergency flashers (*migalki*) on top of their cars to speed through traffic. Also that year, in Eastern Siberia, local environmentalists protested the re-opening of a paper and pulp mill on Baikal's shores. Although Moscow and St. Petersburg saw an increase in mass protest compared to the 1990s, the majority of protest during the Medvedev era was spread across Russia's regions.[38]

Then, in December 2011, massive protests broke out in response to allegations of electoral fraud in the Duma elections. Earlier that fall, Putin and Medvedev had announced their plans to "switch" roles, which fueled anger and disappointment from those who were expecting Russia to move down a more democratic path. The protests "For Fair Elections" (*za chestniye vybory*) raged from December 2011 through Putin's third inauguration as president in May 2012, drawing tens of thousands of citizens to the streets not only in Moscow and St. Petersburg, but also in other parts of Russia.[39] Although scholars note that these protests were in many ways a continuation of longer trends,[40] they were still considered significant for their scale and resonance[41] as well as their ability to forge new ties between existing protest groups.[42]

Putin's Third Term (2012–2018)

After the 2011–2012 protests subsided, Vladimir Putin returned to the presidency in May 2012 ready to punish the perceived perpetrators of the 2011–2012 movement. That summer, several new laws and regulations were promulgated that restricted some aspects of civil society, social movements, and protest. Russian lawmakers increased fines on unsanctioned protests, kicked out the United States Agency for International Development (USAID), and passed the so-called law on "foreign agents." The "foreign agent" law requires NGOs receiving foreign funding and engaging in ambiguously defined "political activity" to register with the Ministry of Justice as such or face steep fines. Scholars have shown that the law selectively targets human rights and environmental organizations.[43] In May 2015, Putin signed a follow-up law on "undesirable" organizations that allows Russian authorities to shut down blacklisted foreign NGOs and ban their operation in Russia. These laws and measures reflected the Kremlin's worries about certain NGOs, their foreign funders, and unsanctioned protests at the beginning of Putin's third term.

At the same time, several other new policies supported the growth and development of civil society organizations. This included the revamped presidential grants system in 2017, which responded to the earlier criticism by making the process more transparent, increasing the funding available, and making significant grants to NGOs in Russia's regions, following the model of the more successful but short-lived Ministry of Economic Development program from 2011–2015.[44] In addition, while regulations to support "socially oriented" NGOs (SONGOs) had begun in the 2010s, legislation that came into effect in January 2015 allowed government entities to "outsource" public service provision to SONGOs. Scholars have argued that these supportive policies are part of the "welfare track" within the Russian government's response to civil society organizations, while measures like the law on "foreign agents" and "undesirable" foreign organizations constitute the "security track."[45] Thus, Putin's third term as president saw a bifurcation, stronger than ever, between two civil societies: those deemed beneficial and "socially oriented" and those deemed "undesirable" or "foreign agents."

There were also other major events during Putin's third term that impacted state-society relations. On the negative side, this included the 2014 annexation of Crimea, the sentencing of those charged with leading the 2011–2012 protests, and the 2015 assassination of Boris Nemtsov. Many prominent Russian activists interpreted these events as signs that the regime was becoming more authoritarian and chose to flee Russia in fear of repression, which intensified during Putin's third term.[46] Despite these developments, activism in Russia continued, and Putin's third term was also marked by an increase in local activism to protect urban spaces. This included a movement around Moscow against housing demolition, movements to protect local parks all across Russia, and a long-haul truck driver protest in multiple Russian regions in 2015 and 2016. In March 2017, a viral video about Medvedev's personal wealth titled "Stop Calling Him Dimon!" sparked the largest and most widespread protests since the 2011–2012 movement. Certainly, increased fines on unsanctioned protests and laws about "foreign agents" and "undesirable" organizations did not stop Russians from taking their demands to the street.

Putin's Fourth Term: A Post-Pandemic Civil Society? (2018–present)

Putin's fourth term as president, which has coincided with a global pandemic, has in some ways solidified the bifurcated nature of the regime's response to civil society. In terms of NGOs, the picture is still mixed. Even in the wake of the "foreign agent" law, a small percentage of Russian NGOs continue to receive funding from abroad. According to the Russian Ministry of Justice, approximately 3,500 Russian NGOs received about 72 billion rubles in funding from foreign sources in 2020.[47] (Although this figure is from the Russian Ministry of Justice, which may have its own interests in reporting this information, it is the best source of data available on the volume of foreign grants to Russian NGOs.) However, there were approximately 213,000 registered NGOs in Russia in 2019,[48] meaning only about 2 percent of Russian NGOs receive foreign funding. Instead, more and more Russian NGOs are receiving their funding from domestic sources, including crowdfunding, charitable donations, and government grants. As an example, the number of federally financed SONGOs has grown from 3,826 in 2018 to 4,248 in 2019, with most of the funding coming through the Presidential Grants Fund.[49] Since its relaunch in 2017, the Presidential Grant program has supported more than twenty thousand projects at a level of 41.2 billion rubles.[50] Scholars have examined these grants, however, and find that the majority go to those working on the provision of public services,[51] whereas foreign funding can still be an important lifeline for groups working on human rights, environmental protection, or election monitoring.

There have also been several significant protest movements in the years leading up to the pandemic. When Putin first returned to the presidency, the Russian government initiated a widely unpopular pension reform that provoked mass protests in September 2018 across several Russian cities. In June 2019, citizens gathered in Moscow to protest the arrest of investigative journalist Ivan Golunov. Later that summer, there were additional protests in the capital city over the refusal to register some opposition candidates for the Moscow City Duma, and over 1,300 people were arrested.[52] In September 2019, thousands again gathered in Moscow to protest the harsh sentencing of those involved at the July protests. Besides these major political grievances, there were also social movements and related protests about more "everyday" problems at the beginning of Putin's fourth term, such as a movement against plans to ship Moscow's trash 1,200 kilometers northeast to a landfill in Shiyes, multiple movements against landfills and trash incinerators in the Moscow region, and a movement to protect a city park from the construction of a church in Yekaterinburg. These protests, both in the streets and online, continued throughout 2020 and 2021 despite the COVID-19 pandemic. In March 2020, for example, the "Stop-Shiyes" coalition helped to coordinate a united day of environmental protest that brought together more than 40 cities across the region.[53] In June 2020, the protestors prevailed when the Arkhangelsk government terminated its contract to build the landfill.[54] In addition, in August 2020, a local grassroots protest movement in Bashkortostan successfully halted plans for mining at a sacred hill, Mt. Kushtau, as described later in this chapter. Many others took their protests online. In April 2020, Russian netizens in multiple cities organized a virtual rally by marking their location in the same place on Yandex.Maps and Yandex.Navigator, protesting harsh lockdown and self-isolation measures.[55] Russia's Fridays for Future activists, who normally participate through in-person single-person pickets, also started to participate online and other environmental activists set up Ecowiki, in order to better coordinate online actions for the environment during the pandemic.[56]

By May 2020, Putin's approval rating had hit a historic low.[57] Still, the regime pushed forward with a delayed vote on several constitutional amendments, including a provision that would allow Putin to hold the presidency until 2036. In July 2020, the constitutional amendments passed by a huge margin and protests of the result were relatively muted. Unexpectedly, however, the arrest of Khabarovsk Krai governor Sergei Furgal about a week after the constitutional referendum unleashed massive and sustained protests in the Russian Far East that continued for weeks. These also coincided with the protests against the August 2020 election results in Belarus, leading to solidarity demonstrations between the two.

Other protest movements in 2020 and 2021 were less successful than Shiyes and Kushtau. One of the most prominent examples are the protests in support of leading opposition figure Alexei Navalny in early 2021. Navalny was poisoned on a flight between two Siberian towns in September 2020 and airlifted to Germany to make a full recovery. When he returned to Moscow in January 2021, he was arrested upon arrival for violating the parole terms of an earlier suspended sentence. This provoked major protests from Kaliningrad to Vladivostok, which were met with higher-than-average detention rates. According to the watchdog OVD-Info, over five thousand protesters were detained at the protests on January 31, surpassing the detentions the week prior by one thousand.[58] Although protests continued in February and April 2021, the authorities' reactions were much more muted, with fewer arrests. Then, in summer 2021, Navalny's political network and anti-corruption foundation were listed as "extremist" organizations, bringing potential criminal penalties to anyone involved.[59] Several top opposition politicians either backed out of the 2021 Duma race, or fled Russia in exile, like Dmitry Gudkov and Lyubov Sobol.[60]

The pandemic has thus had mixed effects on the trajectory of civil society and social movements in Russia. On the one hand, the lockdowns in early 2020 no doubt deterred some protestors and made it more difficult for social organizations to provide their in-person services. However, as detailed above, many protestors defied lockdown orders and took to the streets and many civil society groups used digital tools to continue their activism or to organize to mutual aid. In response, some have alleged that the Russian authorities have used the pandemic as an excuse to deny protest permits and to charge opposition-minded activists with violating pandemic-related restrictions.[61] In some regions of Russia, the authorities cited the pandemic as the reason for prohibiting even single-person protests. As the number of COVID-19 cases decreased, many other restrictions were lifted, but the ban on solo pickets remained.[62] In many regions of Russia there have been protests opposing mandatory vaccination against COVID-19, though the number of participants in each protest is small.[63] Many objections to regulations requiring checking vaccination with the use of QR-codes circulated in social media and blogs. Polls showed that over two-thirds of Russians opposed requiring vaccination for entry into stores, theaters, schools, buses, and subways.[64] In social media, opponents of compulsory vaccination sent hundreds of videos appealing to Vladimir Putin for assistance.[65] It did not appear that one organization coordinated such expressions of opposition to measures that were being taken on various levels in the state. The spontaneous movement opposing mandatory vaccination evidently reflected deep-seated distrust of statements from their government among the majority of Russians, including many who would be reluctant to go into the streets to join in protests. The political leadership chose a cautious course in reaction to that movement, which was reflected in the lack of arrests of those who took part in anti-vaccination demonstrations. However, the Russian government has also supported volunteer initiatives like "We Are Together" ("My Vmeste") and voluntarism in Russia grew in response to pandemic-driven needs in 2020.[66] If anything, the pandemic has exacerbated the divide between Russia's "two civil societies."

RECENT TRENDS IN CIVIL SOCIETY AND SOCIAL MOVEMENTS IN RUSSIA

As described in the introduction to this chapter, the management of civil society and social movements in post-Soviet Russia involves both facilitation and repression. On the one hand, civil society organizations or movements that are deemed to be "threatening" to the political authorities are increasingly targeted by repression and coercion. On the other hand, there are many other types of civil society organizations or movements that could be beneficial to the political authorities. In contrast to the former group, this latter group is often co-opted, channeled, or encouraged to continue their activities, which indirectly or even directly support state priorities.[67] We have argued that this creates a bifurcation between "two civil societies" in post-Soviet Russia, providing evidence for the historical development of this trend in the previous section. In this section, we examine some of the differences in the constraints and opportunities facing these two different civil societies. First, we examine and assess the puzzling opportunities for formal collaboration between the state and formal civil society organizations. Next, we examine the other not-so-lucky group of civil society organizations who have experienced increasing repression in recent years. As we show, these groups have responded to increased constraints with innovation as they navigate their changing operating environment. Finally, we turn to the question of how social movements fit into these two broader trends for facilitation and repression, and how they are in turn navigating both opportunities for and constraints on their behavior.

Opportunities for Formal Collaboration with State Actors

As mentioned in the background section, new regulations on NGOs during Putin's third and fourth terms have created some opportunities for civil society organizations to receive governmental support for their activities, such as through state-contracting to "socially oriented" NGOs for the provision of social services as well as increased opportunities for federal-level funding through the Presidential Grant program.[68] In addition to these official federal-level designations and support programs, this group of beneficial NGOs also enjoys another important privilege: access to political authorities.

Even in electoral authoritarian Russia, there are numerous policy or governance networks that bring together state and civil society to discuss specific policy problems and their potential solutions. These include the formal civil society consultative bodies like the public chambers and the advisory councils at various administrative levels within the formal state bureaucracy.[69] Scholars have shown that these governance networks are particularly open to "loyal" organizations and, in turn, these organizations benefit from increased access to resources, networks, and influence in the policymaking process.[70] For example, Bindman, Kulmala, and Bogdanova (2018) explore how Russian child welfare NGOs in Moscow were able to act as policy entrepreneurs to influence federal-level policymaking from agenda setting to policy formation and adoption.[71] Part of their success came from their involvement in formal institutions for civil society consultation in governance, such as public councils and hearings, and connections to officials in the presidential administration, federal government, Ministry of Education, and other lawmakers. Similarly, in their study of Russian veterans' organizations, Kulmala and Tarasenko (2016) find that political connections, particularly with local and regional authorities, allow these organizations to access policymakers and lobby on behalf of their constituents.[72] Even informal connections to policymakers are critically important for civil society groups to gain more credibility and funding and this is often the driving force behind joining consultative bodies.[73] As these examples show, some Russian civil society organizations are able to work through formal institutions for public participation in governance to impact policymaking through "limited pluralism."[74] However, as the concept of "limited pluralism" implies, there are limits to policy networks in Russia, since these institutions are only advisory bodies with limited power to make or implement policy.[75]

Although NGOs that are seen as more beneficial, such as those who engage in social service provision, are more likely to receive a positive response from government officials through these channels for limited civil society partici-pation in governance, even NGOs that have faced the designation of "foreign agent" or other forms of repression can still enjoy working relationships with particular sub-national officials or officials in certain national-level minis-tries. For example, activists within the Russian branch of the transnational environmental organization Greenpeace often clash with political authori-ties, leading a Duma official to call for Greenpeace Russia to be listed as an "undesirable" organization in December 2020.[76] However, the group has so far dodged the label, and there are also programs where they work closely with like-minded local and regional officials. For example, in August 2021, Greenpeace volunteers joined forces with firefighters from the Ministry of Natural Resources and Natural Reserve Rangers to extinguish forest fires near Lake Ladoga.[77] Furthermore, the head of Greenpeace Russia sits on the Presidential Council for Civil Society and Human Rights, a high-level consultative body that has access to the presidential administration.[78] Even for a more contentious area like environmental politics, local, regional, and even federal officials within the Russian government are sometimes willing to work directly with civil society actors.

NGO Innovation in Response to State-Created Constraints

While some Russian NGOs have been encouraged to take part in formal insti-tutions for civil society participation in governance, not all civil society orga-nizations have this luxury. As detailed in the background section, at the same time that the state expanded federal grantmaking and government contracting to socially oriented or other beneficial NGOs, state organs also introduced new constraints on certain types of NGO behavior, such as through the laws on "foreign agents" and "undesirable" organizations. The law on "foreign agents," in particular, has had an intentionally uneven impact on civil society groups, targeting human rights and environmental NGOs more than organiza-tions operating in any other issue area.[79] Furthermore, Russian officials have sometimes used anti-extremism laws to shut down civil society organizations ranging from religious groups such as the Jehovah's Witnesses to political and anticorruption organizations associated with Alexei Navalny.[80]

Still, even in the face of increasing repression, many Russian NGOs have figured out how to navigate constraints on their behavior and how to innovate in response. In their study of the impacts of the "foreign agent" law, Tysiachniouk, Tulaeva, and Henry (2018) create a typology of NGO responses. In their case study of environmental NGOs, they find that most organizations are able to secure their survival by operating in new ways given these constraints.[81] Similarly, Plantan (2020) finds that one unintended consequence of the law on "foreign agents" is to incentivize organizations to deregister and operate informally, which creates additional challenges for state organs charged with managing these groups.[82] Other NGOs have reregistered as commercial entities in order to get around the law.[83] This shift from formal to informal work, or from nonprofit to commercial work, illustrates how civil society organizations in Russia can innovate to get around state-created political constraints. However, the state can also catch on to these innovations and shift its response to match. For example, the "foreign agent" law was recently amended to allow the Ministry of Justice to list even unregistered, informal organizations, a designation that has recently been applied to the election monitoring group Golos.[84]

Recent Trends in Social Movements and Protests

In recent years, while some nongovernmental organizations in Russia have faced tighter constraints, many new social movements have sprung up, often presenting problems for the functioning of the state. An important precedent for recent movements was created in an earlier period; in 2005 massive protests erupted after the state cut its subsidies for services for certain groups of Russians, including pensioners.[85] In response to those protests the leadership backed off from some of the changes that it had introduced. Since Russians may remember that sometimes protests with strong support can get results, it is not surprising that more recently at the local level, protests against actions by local governments and businesses have continued. Recent protests that have attracted a great deal of attention in Russia and have put intense pressure on local officials have been provoked by problems created by landfills for garbage. The number of legally permitted landfills has decreased during the last several years, while the amount of garbage coming from cities has increased. When the accumulation of garbage in a landfill has gone beyond its intended limits, environmental problems for nearby towns have intensified, often provoking protests by local residents. The most dramatic results came from a movement focused on a proposed landfill in a remote place in the far North. Shiyes is the location of a railway station in Arkhangel'sk region that had been chosen for a landfill, which eventually would have stored a huge amount of garbage from Moscow. Protesters erected a camp of tents at that site, and their bitter opposition to the creation of that landfill was eventually successful in bringing the abandonment of that plan.[86] The turmoil that such protests had caused even led to the replacement of the governor of the Arkhangel'sk region and the head of the neighboring Komi Republic. Private security guards and police officers had repeatedly attacked the protesters at Shiyes, and charges of violating criminal laws and administrative regulations were introduced against some of the activists.[87] Even after the authorities canceled the plan to store waste at Shiyes, the government of Arkhangelsk made no effort to appear conciliatory in relation to the movement that had opposed that plan. In September 2020, when Aleksander Tsybul'skii, the new governor of the region, visited Shiyes, he blamed the protesters for the delays in removing the remaining construction from that site, and said that he had no authority to prevent criminal prosecution of activists.[88] Arrests and fines for people who had taken part in the protests regarding Shiyes continued. (None of those who had violently attacked protesters were charged with crimes.) Leaders of the protests were still being arrested and charged with violations of laws in 2021, showing a vindictive attitude toward their activities.[89] Also, a bulldozer destroyed the camp that the protesters tried to maintain at Shiyes in order to watch for signs of new construction. Nevertheless, Shiyes had become the symbol of a successful movement that opposed a plan that had powerful political backing.

That movement helped to inspire the people who struggled to protect a mountain in another region of Russia.[90] Kushtau is a small mountain in Bashkortostan, a republic in south-central Russia. In the tradition of the Bashkir ethnic group Kushtau is one the mountains (the *shikhany*) that are regarded as sacred. After the Bashkir Soda Company received approval for mining in that mountain, a movement in that republic sought to protect Kushtau from the exploitation that eventually would have destroyed it. In August 2020, that controversy came into the open in a dramatic fashion, when it was discovered that workers had come to Kushtau to start cutting down trees in preparation for the beginning of mining operations. Local residents confronted those workers, and some of those defending the mountain set up tents at the foot of Kushtau. During the following days, the number of tents grew, and people from nearby towns gathered to join the ecological activists. During the night of August 9, a force of three hundred or more private security guides arrived, brought in by buses to threaten or attack the people in the tents.[91] In response, a flashmob of three thousand to five thousand people assembled to join in the defense of the mountain, chanting slogans, including "Kushtau, Zhivi!" ("Kushtau, Live!") and "Kushtau Nash!" ("Kushtau Is Ours!"). Soon the private security was joined by OMON police (riot police), members of the Russian Guard, and men who were not in uniform.[92] The clashes at the foot of the mountain became more violent.

As the conflict on Kushtau grew in scale, it attracted the attention of the national media, reportedly evoking sympathy across the country. As a result, the federal authorities intervened in the conflict over the fate of Kushtau. It seems very likely that Radii Khabirov, the head of Bashkortostan, was directed by the federal center to put an end to that conflict as soon as possible. On August 21, Khabirov announced that Kushtau would be given the status of a nature preserve and would not be mined. On August 24, he requested that the federal ministry of nature and the environment (Minprirody) make

Kushtau an especially protected natural territory (OOPT) of regional designation, which would give it further protection from commercial exploitation.

The story of the movement that had focused on Shiyes was a source of inspiration for the people who took part in the effort to save Kushtau. In February 2020, protesters at Kushtau proclaimed that "the residents of Shiyes have been celebrated throughout the whole country."[93] At that time some of the activists who had protested at Shiyes went to Bashkortostan to show their support for those who strove to defend Kushtau.[94] The protesters from Shiyes shared lessons from their experiences with those participating in the movement to protect Kushtau.[95] Some of those in the movement to protect Kushtau referred to the events at that mountain as constituting a "new Shiyes," a "Bashkir Shiyes," or a "second Shiyes, only in Bashkortostan."[96] As an example of specific influence, the activists who sought to protect Kushtau created a camp of tents, "according to the Shiyes model" (*po obraztsu Shiesa*).[97] That language suggests that the leaders of the movement to defend Kushtau regarded the experience of those who had opposed the creation of a landfill at Shiyes as an example that could guide them.

In turn, after the movement against mining on Kushtau achieved a successful result, its example inspired groups that used protests to protect the environment in other parts of Bashkortostan. One commentator has said that the victory of activists at Kushtau "awakened the protest agenda in the republic,"[98] and another has asserted, "the effect of Kushtau is being disseminated."[99] Also there are some signs that the influence of the movement to save Kushtau has been felt outside the Bashkir republic. Activists who have opposed construction projects in Moscow that are planned by the company Tashir have made a film that is titled "Moskovskii Kushtau" (Moscow's Kushtau), which explains why some Muscovites are dissatisfied with those plans.[100] And in December 2020, a representative of an "initiative group" that strives to defend the Troitskii Forest in Moscow from proposed road construction observed, "there are successful examples of the defense of natural territories, for example, Shiyes or the shikhans."[101] So the experience of the movement to defend Kushtau has even become a positive example for some residents in Russia's capital.

The example of the movement to protect Kushtau also shows that a movement that might seem to have little importance because of its narrowly focused objectives can have broader implications, because it raises essential questions about the relationship between citizens and the authorities, its thinking resonates with groups in society, and finally because of the potential for the diffusion of the influence of a movement that emerges in one region or in one part of society. The success of the activists who opposed the creation of a large landfill at Shiyes served as an inspiration for activists in Bashkortostan. Further, the movement that focused on Shiyes has become a model that appeals to the leaders of environmentalist movements in other parts of Russia, and the example of the movement to protect Kushtau also encourages other protesters. Horizontal communication makes it possible to transfer strategies for change across physical distances. Of course, the model developed at Shiyes is attractive to activists in other locations because it achieved a high degree of success. And the fact that its victory is highly respected in other parts of Russia implies that it is unusual for any social movement in that country to reach its goals when it is battling against powerful, entrenched interests.

Local Activism and Electoral Politics

Some Russian civil society and social movement activists are also increasingly running for political office and engaging in electoral campaigns. Over the last decade, local civil society activists in Moscow have increasingly won office through municipal elections, thanks to initiatives like United Democrats (*Ob'edinnennye demokraty)* that helped to train local activists to run as opposition party candidates or independents.[102] Besides running for municipal council seats, many activists have become candidates—or tried to become candidates—for higher office. Yevgeniia Chirikova, the leader of the Khimki Forest movement ran for mayor of Khimki in 2009 and 2012. Krasimir Vranski, a St. Petersburg-based urban and environmental activist, announced his intent to run for governor of St. Petersburg in 2019, but was ultimately unable to get on the ballot. Oleg Mandrykin, a representative of the Stop-Shiyes coalition, was Yabloko's nominee for Governor of Arkhangelsk in 2020, but also unable to register as a candidate. Chirikova and Galyamina have paid a high price for their involvement in high-profile opposition politics—Chirikova fled Russia for Estonia in 2015 and Galyamina received a two-year suspended sentence following participation in unauthorized opposition protests in 2020. However, despite this, many other Russian activists continue to enter electoral politics to further their causes and some of them have even won their local level elections.

Even though most activists are unable to even get on the ballot, let alone be elected for these high-profile elected positions, they cite other reasons for wanting to engage in electoral politics. Running as a candidate can make it easier to gather people for rallies and the campaign itself could attract media attention to an activist's cause. Others, however, fully shifted from civil society activists to opposition politicians after getting involved in elections. There are several examples of high-profile opposition members who got their start within social movements, such as Yevgeniia Chirikova and Yulya Galyamina, who later became leaders within the opposition movement or vocally supported Alexei Navalny and his Smart Voting (*Umnoye golosovaniye)* initiative. Although the Russian authorities clamped down on opposition candidates ahead of the 2021 Duma elections, including by labeling Navalny's organizations as "extremist," some local civil society activists are likely to continue to use electoral politics in the future, whether as a tool to advance their movement's goals or as full participants in Russia's political opposition.

A SUMMARY OF RECENT TRENDS

The preceding sections have described distinct trends in three areas of civil society in Russia in recent years: first, the tightening of restrictions on NGOs that are seen as potentially undermining political stability; second, the growth of opportunities for collaboration with the state for organizations that are not seen as a challenge to its authority and instead help to improve services for citizens; and third, the proliferation of social movements that protest against problems that affect the everyday lives of groups of citizens. The leaders of the political regime in Russia might see different levels of success in those three areas. First, they may have reason to be satisfied with the results of the intensified repression of organizations that are suspected of having the potential to cause instability. Few Russians now feel safe to participate in the activities of those organizations or believe that they have a real chance of bringing major improvements, and in any case groups that call for change in the political system have a narrow base of support in society. Second, the state has found that devoting more resources to socially oriented NGOs has enhanced the effectiveness of its performance in some areas, while the opportunities for NGO leaders to seek the reorientation of practices are limited to certain "safe" areas of policy. The state has been successful in channeling the efforts of those activists in society who accept the limits that are associated with collaboration with the authorities.

In relation to the third trend, however, the state has been inconsistent in reacting to social movements that protest against the actions of local officials and businesses, and the results of such protests have been mixed, to say the least. Some of those movements have achieved success in gaining concessions from the state and reversing decisions that they opposed. Even in those cases, however, the state has harassed the leaders of those movements and has even put some of them in prison, sending the message that there are negative consequences for any open challenge to authority. It seems likely that most protests in response to local problems fail to gain any change; the regime hopes that such examples convey the futility of resorting to protests, which reflects the regime's reliance on a sense of powerlessness among citizens as a condition for political stability. Yet a result of such apparent short-term successes by officials is that many citizens are convinced that the process of governing is biased against them, and the state is insensitive to their complaints. In addition, even though victories by protesters may be exceptions to the usual pattern, each successful movement serves as an example that is remembered and inspires the hope of a similar achievement in another setting. In other words, there is horizontal diffusion of information about protest movements, which is facilitated by widespread access to social media and other resources on the internet. And it is also possible that examples of protest movements can spread across national boundaries. It has been said for many years that Vladimir Putin has worried about the possibility that the model created by "color revolutions" might be applied in Russia. In 2020 exceptionally large protests erupted in neighboring Belarus, emphatically challenging the legitimacy of that country's political regime. A perceptive Russian scholar, Lev Gudkov, argues that the protests in Belarus "greatly frightened the authorities" in Russia and "compelled them to raise the harshness and scale of repression [in Russia] to a qualitatively higher level."[103]

CONCLUSION

Some of the change in interaction between protesters and the state is revealed by a striking contrast. In response to allegations of fraud in the 2011 Duma elections, there were large protests. More than one hundred thousand people took part in the largest protest rally in February 2012 in Moscow. One of the main speakers at that meeting was Alexei Navalny, and the non-systemic opposition[104] determined the mood of the protest. But though there have been accusations of fraud in the Duma elections in September 2021, there have been no large protests by the non-systemic opposition. The Communist Party of the Russian Federation, a party that is part of the permitted opposition and thus is relatively tame, announced its intention to hold protests against irregularities in the elections. The crowd that gathered at the largest of those rallies was relatively small, with about one thousand participants.[105] The organizations that reject the basic features of the political regime were reduced to following the lead of the in-house critics (consistent with Navalny's electoral strategy of "smart voting"). Navalny could only issue a statement from the labor camp in which he is imprisoned. At this point, the non-systemic opposition to Putin's regime appears to have been stymied.

In the light of such conditions, some journalists have argued that civil society in Russia has been virtually wiped out.[106] The basis for such alarming assertions is the assumption that the scope of civil society does not extend beyond the boundaries of political opposition to the ruling elite. But that viewpoint does not correspond to the interpretation of the meaning of civil society that is accepted by most scholars and was presented in this chapter.

This chapter has suggested a much broader and more complex reality. As we have seen, the experiences of nongovernmental organizations in Russia can be comprehended by a tale of two civil societies. On the one hand, some organizations have faced ever more severe burdens, and while some have found ways to persist, others have been driven underground or have simply closed up shop. On the other hand, some NGOs have enjoyed more favorable conditions, receiving increased support from the state, business, or private donors. All the while, many Russians have shown they are capable of striving openly for the defense of their interests through a variety of social movements that have emerged at the grassroots level.

AUTHORS' POSTSCRIPT

Russia's war in Ukraine will have widespread consequences not only for lives and livelihoods in Ukraine, but also for Russian society. Soon after the invasion, the media atmosphere considerably tightened. The last remaining independent news sources were shuttered, a law was passed to criminalize "false information" about Russian state entities abroad with up to fifteen years in prison, and political activists, journalists, and commentators alike have been labeled as individual "foreign agents" for their criticism of the war. Recently a proposed change in law has been introduced in the lower house of Russia's national legislature, under which the category of "foreign agents" would be broadened to include not only organizations and individuals who receive funding from abroad but also those who are "under foreign influence" or who gather information that "can be used against the security of the Russian Federation."[107] We may be sure that if that change is adopted, those categories will be interpreted very broadly. Many Russians have fled the country in what some are calling a major "brain drain," but among those leaving are some of the most outspoken civic activists.[108]

Russia's anti-war movement, however, has continued despite repression and emigration. More than fifteen thousand people were arrested for participating in anti-war protests between February 24 and March 20, 2022, alone.[109] While the larger protests of late February and March were fleeting, they have been followed by a steady stream of single-person pickets protesting the war. This has led to several viral videos on social media showing the absurdity of Russian repression of anti-war activities, including single-person picketers arrested for holding placards with euphemisms for "no war," including "two words" (*dva slova*),[110] "*** *****," or even a blank piece of paper.[111] Russians have also found other ways to protest, including bumper stickers, graffiti, and art installations or performances.[112] Furthermore, many activists who have fled Russia—whether during this most recent wave of emigration or earlier—are engaging in anti-war activism and helping Ukrainian refugees outside of Russia.[113]

Even those civil society activists who are not criticizing the war will feel its repercussions. Already, the Russian economy is projected to decrease by 11.2 percent in 2022.[114] This will no doubt impact how the Putin regime allocates its budget, perhaps making it more difficult for Russian NGOs to apply for domestic sources of funding. Even if Russian NGOs win domestically funded grants, soaring inflation in Russia will decrease the mileage of those funds. Furthermore, Russian NGOs are likely to be affected by Western sanctions, as well. Although there are many foreign NGOs and foundations that have been listed as "undesirable" over the years and forced to disband their operations in Russia, there were still many groups that were making grants to Russian NGOs. With Western sanctions, it will be even more difficult—if not impossible—for many international charities and grant-making organizations to continue making grants to Russian organizations.[115] In short, the already constrained supply of foreign funding is likely to get smaller.

On the other hand, as we have seen, some nongovernmental organizations have achieved success in collaborating with the state. We do not expect much change for those organizations. But even more than before, it will be crucial for them to convince key officials that their organizations are striving to fulfill the goals of the political regime. And they will face the reality that in most areas of policy, financial resources will be more limited because of difficult conditions in the economy.

It is uncertain what the future will hold for movements that call for solutions for specific problems while they signal that they are loyal to Putin and his government. The leadership's heightened demand for conformity could furnish a pretext for clamping down on such movements. (The situation already looks even worse for environmental organizations.[116]) But in conditions of declining living standards, such an approach by the regime could prove dangerous. The example of the recent movement against the enforcement of vaccine mandates might cause sobering reflections by Russia's leaders. The leadership backed down hastily from its demands in the face of large-scale dissatisfaction among groups of indignant citizens.[117] (It is likely that most of those who voiced opposition to such mandates were not usually among Putin's critics.) And local movements by "initiative groups" and activists against particular actions by local authorities that arise from resentment, such as the incursion of development into urban parks and the closing of a sports stadium, certainly continue, apparently not discouraged by wider developments.[118]

—2022

DISCUSSION QUESTIONS

1. How were the problems faced by organizations in civil society in the Soviet Union different from those that civil society organizations have faced in Russia since the collapse of the Soviet Union in 1991?
2. There are two general perspectives on civil society in Russia, one of which is within a "democratization framework" and the other of which has a more pragmatic orientation. What questions does each of these perspectives lead us to ask as we study civil society in contemporary Russia? How much have organizations in civil society in post-Soviet Russia satisfied the expectations of each of these perspectives?
3. How has the political environment for civil society and social movements in post-Soviet Russia changed over time? What are some of the possible explanations for these shifts? What are some of the new trends in civil society and social movements in recent years?

SUGGESTED READINGS

Cook, Linda J., Elena Iarskaia-Smirnova, and Anna Tarasenko. "Outsourcing Social Services to NGOs in Russia: Federal Policy and Regional Responses." *Post-Soviet Affairs* 37, no. 2 (2021): 119–36.

Henry, Laura A., "People Power in Putin's Russia: Social vs. Political Protests." In Nathan Stoltzfus and Christopher Osmar, eds. *The Power of Populism and People: Resistance and Protest in the Modern World.* London: Bloomsbury, 2022, 137–61.

Javeline, Debra, and Sarah Lindemann-Komarova. "Financing Russian Civil Society." *Europe-Asia Studies* 72, no. 4 (2020): 1–42.

McCarthy, Lauren A., Katherine Stolerman, and Anton V. Tikhomirov. "Managed Civil Society and Police Oversight in Russia: Regional Police-Public Councils." *Europe-Asia Studies* 72, no. 9 (2020): 1498–533.

Owen, Catherine, and Eleanor Bindman. "Civic Participation in a Hybrid Regime: Limited Pluralism in Policymaking and Delivery in Contemporary Russia." *Government and Opposition* 54, no. 1 (2019): 98–120.

Plantan, Elizabeth. "Not All NGOs Are Treated Equally: Selectivity in Civil Society Management in China and Russia." *Comparative Politics*, forthcoming, 2022.

Toepler, Stefan, Ulla Pape, and Vladimir Benevolenski. "Subnational Variations in Government-Nonprofit Relations: A Comparative Analysis of Regional Differences within Russia." *Journal of Comparative Policy Analysis: Research and Practice* 22, no. 1 (2020): 47–65.

NOTES

1. Larry Diamond, *Developing Democracy* (Baltimore, MD: Johns Hopkins University Press, 1999), 221.

2. Meri Kulmala, "Post-Soviet 'Political'? 'Social' and 'Political' in the Work of Russian Socially Oriented CSOs," *Demokratizatsiya* 24, no. 2 (2016): 208. An example of a scholarly analysis that is shaped by the democratization framework is Mark R. Beissinger, "'Conventional' and 'Virtual' Civil Societies in Autocratic Regimes," *Comparative Politics* 49, no. 3 (2017): 351.

3. Sarah L. Henderson, "Shaping Civic Advocacy: International and Domestic Politics toward Russia's NGO Sector," in *Advocacy Organizations and Collective Action*, ed. Aseem Prakash and May Kay Gregory (Cambridge: Cambridge University Press, 2010), 255; Janet Elise Johnson, Meri Kulmala, and Maija Jäppinen, "Street-Level Practice of Russia's Social Policymaking in Saint Petersburg: Federalism, Informal Politics, and Domestic Violence," *Journal of Social Policy* 45, no. 2 (2016): 290.

4. Henderson, "Shaping Civic Advocacy," 255.

5. Johnson, Kulmala, and Jäppinen, "Street-Level Practice," 296–97.

6. Henderson, "Shaping Civic Advocacy," 255.

7. Other authors have also noted the dual nature of civil society management in Russia but use slightly different approaches. See, for example: Elena Bogdanova, Linda J. Cook, and Meri Kulmala, "The Carrot or the Stick? Constraints and Opportunities of Russia's CSO Policy," *Europe-Asia Studies* 70, no. 4 (2018): 501–13.

8. Alfred B. Evans Jr., "Civil Society in the Soviet Union?," in *Russian Civil Society: A Critical Assessment*, ed. Alfred B. Evans Jr., Laura A. Henry, and Lisa McIntosh Sundstrom (Armonk, NY: M. E. Sharpe, 2006), 30.

9. Evans, "Civil Society in the Soviet Union?," 42.

10. Walter D. Connor, *Socialism's Dilemmas: State and Society in the Soviet Bloc* (New York: Columbia University Press, 1988).

11. Evans, "Civil Society in the Soviet Union?," 45.

12. Evans, "Civil Society in the Soviet Union?," 45.

13. Alfred B. Evans Jr., "Recent Assessments of Social Organizations in Russia," *Demokratizatsiya* 10, no. 3 (2002): 322–42.

14. Ken Jowitt, *New World Disorder: The Leninist Extinction* (Berkeley: University of California Press, 1992), 287. Jowitt believes that his generalization applies to all countries that have been under "Leninist," or communist, rule.

15. Jowitt, *New World Disorder*, 293.

16. The annual report of Russia's Public Chamber for 2011 confirmed that Russians typically see the "circle of trust" as extending only to family members and close friends. Obshchestvennaia Palata Rossiiskoi Federatsii, *Doklad o sostoianii grazhdanskogo obshchestva v Rossiiskoi Federatsii za 2011 god* (Moscow: Obshchestvennaia Palata Rossiiskoi Federatsii, 2012), 9.

17. Marc Morjé Howard, *The Weakness of Civil Society in Post-Communist Europe* (Cambridge: Cambridge University Press, 2003), 26.

18. Howard, *The Weakness of Civil Society*, 63.

19. Valerie Sperling, *Organizing Women in Contemporary Russia: Engendering Transition* (Cambridge: Cambridge University Press, 1999), 46, 171–72.

20. In 2012 the annual report of Russia's Public Chamber said that NGOs in Russia "for the most part are extremely weak economically and often are barely surviving." Obshchestvennaia Palata, *Doklad o sostoianii grazhdanskogo obshchestva*, 18.

21. Debra Javeline and Sarah Lindemann-Komarova, "Indigenously Funded Russian Civil Society" (PONARS Eurasia Policy Memo No. 496, November 2017), 1, report that the proportion of all NGOs in Russia receiving funding from Western donors reached a high of 7 percent in 2009.

22. Sarah L. Henderson, *Building Democracy in Contemporary Russia: Western Support for Grassroots Organizations* (Ithaca, NY: Cornell University Press, 2003), 154–55, 165; Lisa McIntosh Sundstrom, *Funding Civil Society: Foreign Assistance and NGO Development in Russia* (Stanford, CA: Stanford University Press, 2006), 99–101.

23. Graeme Robertson, "Protesting Putinism: The Election Protests of 2011–2012 in Broader Perspective," *Problems of Post-Communism* 60, no. 2 (2013): 11–23.

24. Alfred B. Evans Jr., "Putin's Design for Civil Society," in *Russian Civil Society: A Critical Assessment*, ed. Alfred B. Evans Jr., Laura A. Henry, and Lisa McIntosh Sundstrom (Armonk, NY: M. E. Sharpe, 2006), 149.

25. Evans, "Putin's Design," 149; Sarah L. Henderson, "Civil Society in Russia: State-Society Relations in the Post-Yeltsin Era," *Problems of Communism* 58, no. 3 (2011): 18.

26. Debra Javeline and Sarah Lindemann-Komarova, "A Balanced Assessment of Russian Civil Society," *Journal of International Affairs* 63, no. 2 (2010): 173–75.

27. Henderson, "Civil Society in Russia," 20; Javeline and Lindemann-Komarova, "A Balanced Assessment," 176–80; Johnson, Kulmala, and Jäppinen, "Street-Level Practice," 15.

28. Ol'ga Churakova and Elena Mukhametshina, "'Edinaia Rossiia' sozdast gruppy bystrogo reagirovaniia dlia uchastiia v ulichnykh aktsiiakh," *Vedomosti*, March 19, 2018.

29. James Richter, "Putin and the Public Chamber," *Post-Soviet Affairs* 25, no. 1 (2009): 39–65. Public chambers also have been established in most regions of Russia and in some cities.

30. Evans, "Putin's Design," 151.

31. Abbas Galliamov, "Obshchestvennye palaty okazalis' vredny v krizisnykh situatsiiakh," *Novye izvestiia*, April 16, 2018.

32. Oleg Shchedrov, "Russia's Medvedev Urges Stronger Role for Civil Society," *Reuters*, March 19, 2008.

33. Vladimir Shishlin, "Medvedev zastupilsia za NPO," *Interfax*, April 15, 2009.

34. "U.S.-Russia Relations: 'Reset' Fact Sheet," White House Office of the Press Secretary, June 24, 2010.

35. Yuliya Taratuta and Aleksandr Voronov, "Zagrantotryad," *Kommersant*, July 3, 2008.

36. Javeline and Lindemann-Komarova, "A Balanced Assessment," 661.

37. Robertson, "Protesting Putinism."

38. Tomila Lankina and Alisa Voznaya, "New Data on Protest Trends in Russia's Regions," *Europe-Asia Studies* 67, no. 2 (2015): 327–42.

39. Tomila Lankina, "The Dynamics of Regional and National Contentious Politics in Russia: Evidence from a New Dataset," *Problems of Post-Communism* 62, no. 1 (2015): 26–44.

40. Robertson, "Protesting Putinism."

41. Virginie Lasnier, "Demobilisation and Its Consequences: After the Russian Movement *Za Chestnye Vybory*." *Europe-Asia Studies* 69, no. 5 (May 28, 2017): 771–93.

42. Samuel A. Greene, "Beyond Bolotnaia." *Problems of Post-Communism* 60, no. 2 (March 1, 2013): 40–52.

43. Maria Tysiachniouk, Svetlana Tulaeva, and Laura A. Henry, "Civil Society under the Law 'On Foreign Agents': NGO Strategies and Network Transformation," *Europe-Asia Studies* 70, no. 4 (2018): 615–37; Elizabeth Plantan, "Not All NGOs Are Treated Equally: Selectivity in Civil Society Management in China and Russia," *Comparative Politics*, forthcoming, 2022.

44. Debra Javeline and Sarah Lindemann-Komarova, "Financing Russian Civil Society," *Europe-Asia Studies* 72, no. 4 (2020): 662.

45. Bogdanova, Cook, and Kulmala, "The Carrot or the Stick?"

46. Laura Henry and Elizabeth Plantan, "Activism in Exile: How Russian Environmentalists Maintain Voice after Exit," Manuscript submitted for publication.

47. Marina Tretiakova, "Financirovanie NKO voz'mut pod polnyj kontrol'," *Parlamentskaia Gazeta*, June 9, 2021.

48. "V Miniuste otmenili umen'shenie chisla nekommercheskikh organizatsij," *TASS*, March 31, 2020.

49. "Doklad o deiatel'nosti i razvitii sotsial'no orientirovannykh nekommercheskikh organizatsij," Ministry of Economic Development of the Russian Federation, September 1, 2020.

50. "Obyavleny poluchateli grantov Prezidenta na razvitie grazhdanskogo obshchestva," Office of the President of Russia, Press Release, June 11, 2021.

51. Marlene Laruelle and Laura Howells, "Ideological or Pragmatic? A Data-Driven Analysis of the Russian Presidential Grant Fund," *Russian Politics* 5, no. 1 (2020): 29–51.

52. Ivan Nechepurenko, "Moscow Police Arrest More Than 1,300 at Election Protest," *The New York Times*, July 27, 2019.

53. Tatiana Britskaia, "V otstavku—i v tiurmu!" *Novaia Gazeta*, March 16, 2020.

54. Vlasti Pomor'ia ob"iavili o 'planovom zakrytii proekta' po stroitel'stvu musornogo poligona 'Shiyes,'" *Mediazona*, July 9, 2020.

55. https://meduza.io/en/feature/2020/04/20/cities-across-russia-see-virtual-protests-against-self-isolation-restrictions.

56. For more information on the project, see https://ecowiki.ru/category/temy/.

57. Levada Center, "Odobrenie institutov vlasti i doverie politikam," May 6, 2020.

58. Jim Heintz and Vladimir Isachenkov, "Over 5,100 Arrested at pro-Navalny Protests across Russia," AP, January 31, 2021.

59. "Alexei Navalny: Moscow Court Outlaws 'Extremist' Organizations," BBC News, June 10, 2021.

60. Anton Troianovski, "Exile or Jail: The Grim Choice Facing Russian Opposition Leaders," *New York Times*, August 30, 2021.

61. See, for example, Andrew E. Kramer, "In Russia, a Virus Lockdown Targets the Opposition," *New York Times*, March 19, 2021.

62. Alexey Shumkin, "Going Solo: The 'Solitary Picket' Was Once a Key Method of Public Protest in Russia. Here's How the Authorities Did Away with It," *Meduza*, July 26, 2021. The state had increasingly tightened the restrictions on single-person pickets for years since 2012.

63. Ivan Medvedev, "Rossiane vykhodit na QR-protesty," *BFM.RU*, November 15, 2021; Kirill Gromov, "V rossiiskikh gorodakh prodolzhaiutsia mitingi protiv prinuditel'noi vaksinatsii i QR-kodov," *Readovka*, November 15, 2021.

64. Vladimir Solodovnikov, "Novye protest protiv QR-kodov idut po vsei Rossii," *FederalCity,ru*, November 15, 2021.

65. Irina Korbat, "Protesty antivakserov dobavliaiut massovost' za schet chuzhogo mitinga. Feik raspoznali ne vse." *Fontanka.ru*, November 16, 2021.

66. "V Rossii zametili rost chisla volontyorov na fone pandemii," Lenta.ru, December 25, 2020.

67. Elizabeth Plantan, "Not All NGOs Are Treated Equally."

68. On contracting for social services, see: Vladimir B. Benevolenski and Stefan Toepler, "Modernising Social Service Delivery in Russia: Evolving Government Support for Non-Profit Organizations," *Development in Practice* 27, no. 1 (2017): 64–76; Linda J. Cook, Elena Iarskaia-Smirnova, and Anna Tarasenko, "Outsourcing Social Services to NGOs in Russia: Federal Policy and Regional Responses," *Post-Soviet Affairs* 37, no. 2 (2021): 199–236. On the presidential grant program and other funding opportunities, see: Marlene Laruelle and Laura Howells, "Ideological or Pragmatic? A Data-Driven Analysis of the Russian Presidential Grant Fund," *Russian Politics* 5, no. 1 (April 2, 2020): 29–51; Debra Javeline and Sarah Lindemann-Komarova, "Financing Russian Civil Society, *Europe-Asia Studies* 72, no. 4 (2020): 644–85.

69. On the Public Chamber, see James Richter, "Putin and the Public Chamber," *Post-Soviet Affairs* 25, no. 1 (2009): 39–65.

70. Aadne Aasland, Mikkel Berg-Nordlie, and Elena Bogdanova, "Encouraged but Controlled: Governance Networks in Russian Regions," *East European Politics* 32, no. 2 (2016): 148–69.

71. Eleanor Bindman, Meri Kulmala, and Elena Bogdanova, "NGOs and the Policy-Making Process in Russia: The Case of Child Welfare Reform," *Governance* 32, no. 2 (2019): 207–22.

72. Meri Kulmala and Anna Tarasenko, "Interest Representation and Social Policy Making: Russian Veterans' Organisations as Brokers between the State and Society," *Europe-Asia Studies* 68, no. 1 (2016): 138–63.

73. Aadne Aasland, Sabine Kropp, and Anastasia Y. Meylakhs, "Between Collaboration and Subordination: State and Non-state Actors in Russian Anti-drug Policy," *Voluntas* 31 (2020): 431, 432.

74. Catherine Owen and Eleanor Bindman, "Civic Participation in a Hybrid Regime: Limited Pluralism in Policymaking and Delivery in Contemporary Russia," *Government and Opposition* 54, no. 1 (2019): 98–120.

75. Aasland, Berg-Nordlie, and Bogdanova, "Encouraged but Controlled."

76. "V Gosdume predlozhili priznat' Greenpeace nezhelatel'noi v Rossii organizatsiei," *Vedomosti,* December 10, 2020.

77. Yulia Davydova, "Record Breaking Fires in Siberia," *Greenpeace.org*, August 18, 2021.

78. For a full list of members, see: http://www.president-sovet.ru/members/constitution/.

79. Plantan, "Not All NGOs Are Treated Equally."

80. Igor Slabykh, "How the Russian Government Uses Anti-Extremism Laws to Fight Opponents," *Institute of Modern Russia*, June 4, 2021.

81. Tysiachniouk, Tulaeva, and Henry, "Civil Society under the Law 'On Foreign Agents.'"

82. Elizabeth Plantan, "A Tale of Two Laws: Managing Foreign Agents and Overseas NGOs in Russia and China," in *Citizens and the State in Authoritarian Regimes: Comparing China and Russia*, eds. Karrie J. Koesel, Valerie J. Bunce, and Jessica C. Weiss (New York, NY: Oxford University Press, 2020).

83. Tysiachniouk, Tulaeva, and Henry, "Civil Society under the Law 'On Foreign Agents.'"

84. "Miniust RF sozdast eshche odin reestr inoagentov," *Interfax.ru*, February 19, 2021.

85. Linda J. Cook, *Postcommunist Welfare States: Reform Politics in Russia and Eastern Europe* (Ithaca, NY: Cornell University Press, 2007), 179.

86. Irina Andrionova, "The Shies Camp: How Moscow's Trash Became Treasure for a Group of Environmental Protestors," *Bellona*, January 21, 2020.

87. Laura A. Henry, "The Politics of Waste in Russia: Everyday Environmentalism and Shifting State-Society Relations," paper presented at the Annual Meeting of the Association for Slavic, East European, and Eurasian Studies, November 2020, 10; Tat'iana Britskaia, "Shies v gorle," *Novaia gazeta*, September 2, 2019.

88. Tat'iana Britskaia, "Kak ego posadish'? Na derevo!" *Novaia gazeta*, September 18, 2020.

89. Tat'iana Britskaia, "Siloviki zaderzhali na Shiese shesterykh aktivistov," *Novaia gazeta*, February 18, 2021.

90. Alfred B. Evans Jr., "The Struggle for Kushtau: The Movement to Protect a Mountain in Russia," paper presented at the annual meeting of the Western Political Science Association, April 2021.

91. Karina Gorbacheva, "Vstali goroi za bashkirskii Shies: kak spasaiut Kushtau," *Real'noe vremia*, August 12, 2020; Karina Gorbacheva, "Kakie uroki Bashkortostan izvlekla iz Kushtau?" *Real'noe vremia*, September 11, 2020.

92. Ivan Zhilin, "Sodovody Bashkortostana," *Novaia gazeta*, August 20, 2020; Ivan Zhilin, "'Beskontrol'noe vykachivanie deneg—eto pechal'naia istoriia': Putin raskritoval sodovuiu kompaniiu, sobiravshuiusia snesti sviashchennuiu bashkirskuiu goru Kushtau," *Novaia gazeta,* August 20, 2020.

93. Nadezhda Valitova, "V Bashkirii v aktsii 'Zhivaia tsep' Kushtau' priniali uchastie aktivisty Shiesa," *Mkset.ru*, February 24, 2020.

94. Ibid.

95. Andras Toth-Czifra, "The Voice of the Regions," *No Yardstick*, September 23, 2020.

96. Oleg Zurman, "Bez 'Sodovoi,' pozhaluista. Kak ekoaktivisty otstoiali shikhan Kushtau." *Mediazona*, August 17, 2020,

97. Andrei Pertsev, "Pokhishchenie gory," *Meduza*, August 16, 2020.

98. Kirill Zotov, "Shikhan Kushtau razbudil protestnuiu povestku v Bashkirii," *Regnum IA*, September 17, 2020.

99. Nataliia Pavlova, "S chuvstvom glubokogo bureniia," *Kommersant (Ufa)*, September 22, 2020.

100. Lora Suslova, "'Moskovskii Kushtau': Pochemu moskvichi protestuiut protiv stroek 'Tashira,'" *MBKh Media*, October 6, 2020.

101. Dar'ia Alifanova, "V Novoi Moskve mogut unichtozhit' desiatki gektarov Troitskogo lesa," *Moskovskaia gazeta*, December 24, 2020. The person who was quoted is Ol'ga Slastunina.

102. Yana Gorokhovskaia, "From Local Activism to Local Politics: The Case of Moscow," *Russian Politics* 3, no. 4 (2018): 577–604.

103. Nadezhda Guzheva, "Lev Gudkov: U nas net ni massovykh besporiadkov, ni massovykh repressii," *Sobesednik*, June 21, 2021.

104. The "systemic" (or "inside-the-system") opposition is represented by political parties that appear to be in opposition to the ruling party, but do not challenge the basic features of the political regime and are tolerated by the top leadership. Those parties have some of the seats in the Duma and lower-level legislative bodies. The "non-systemic" (or "outside-the system") opposition calls for transformation of the political regime and faces many obstacles in competing for offices; it has no seats in the Duma.

105. Aleksei Chernikov, "Na Pushkinskoi ploshchadi storonniki KPRF potrebovali otmenit' itogi elektronnogo golosovaniia," *Moskovskaia gazeta*, September 25, 2021.

106. "Putin Is Destroying What Is Left of Russian Civil Society. Biden Must Keep the Pressure On," *Washington Post*, August 10, 2021.

107. "I drugie litsa: v reestr inoagentov mogut byt' vkliucheny ikh rodstvenniki," *Izvestiia*, April 25, 2022, https://iz.ru/1324846/natalia-bashlykova-maksim-khodykin/i-drugie-litca-v-reestr-inoagentov-mogut-byt-vkliucheny-ikh-rodstvenniki; 'Закон безграничного применения: скоро иноагентами будут признаны все инакомыслящие," *Novye Izvestiia*, April 26, 2022, https://newizv.ru/article/general/26-04-2022/zakon-bezgranichnogo-primeneniya-skoro-inoagentami-budut-priznany-vse-inakomyslyaschie.

108. Laura Henry and Elizabeth Plantan, "Putin Called Fleeing Russians 'Traitors.' Who's Actually Leaving?" *Washington Post*, March 31, 2022, https://www.washingtonpost.com/politics/2022/03/31/russian-activists-exile-putin-protests/.

109. According to data reported by OVDInfo. For the most recent numbers, see https://ovdinfo.org/.

110. "Video Shows Back-to-Back Arrests of Anti- and Pro-War Activists in Moscow," *Moscow Times*, March 14, 2022, https://www.themoscowtimes.com/2022/03/14/video-shows-back-to-back-arrests-of-anti-and-pro-war-activists-in-moscow-a76917.

111. Isabel Van Brugen, "Russia Arrests Multiple People for Holding Up Blank Signs," *Newsweek*, March 14, 2022, https://www.newsweek.com/russia-ukraine-war-invasion-protests-police-arrest-activists-holding-blank-signs-paper-1687603.

112. "Antivoyennye aktsii v Rossii i mire," *Activatica*, 2022, https://activatica.org/content/2f87e7e2-4d58-4509-8c78-c0f62d5741b5/2404-antivoennye-akcii-v-rossii-i-mire.

113. Pjotr Sauer, "Red Is Dead: Russian Anti-War Protesters Fly a New Flag for Peace," April 3, 2022, *Guardian*. https://www.theguardian.com/world/2022/apr/03/red-is-dead-russian-anti-war-protesters-fly-a-new-flag-for-peace.

114. Michael Winfrey, "Ukraine Economy to Fall 45% in 2022, Russia 11%, World Bank Says," *Bloomberg*, April 10, 2022, https://www.bloomberg.com/news/articles/2022-04-10/ukraine-economy-to-fall-45-in-2022-russia-11-world-bank-says.

115. Corrine Bonnerwith and Rebekah Siddique, "New Sanctions on Russia: What Donors Need to Know," CAF America Insider Blog, February 28, 2022, https://www.cafamerica.org/ukraine-what-donors-need-to-know/.

116. "Siloviki ishchut 'sviaz' ekologicheskikh protestov v Bashkortostane s 'sobytiiami v Ukraine,'" *Idel.realii*, April 9, 2022, www.idelreal.org/a/31794693.html.

117. Elisha Hart, "Canceling QR-Codes: Russian Lawmakers Withdraw Controversial Vaccine Pass Bill from Consideration," *Meduza*, January 17, 2022, https://meduza.io/en/feature/2022/01/17/canceling-qr-codes.

118. Andrei Kozlov, "Opaseniia zashchitnikov Titsevskogo lesa podverzhdaetsia?" FederalCity.ru, April 14, 2022, https://federalcity.ru/index.php?newsid=13194; Pavel Vinogradov, "V Peterburge mestnye zhiteli b'iutsia za sokhranenie stadiona 'Olimpiiskie nadezhny,'" FederalCity.ru, April 26, 2022, https://federalcity.ru/index.php?newsid=13300.

Chapter 6

The Media

Maria Lipman

Russia's invasion of Ukraine followed by a brutal and devastating war on Ukrainian territory is inseparable from the dramatic transformation of the Russian political regime. The radical rupture of relations with the West and the ensuing turn toward economic autarky is accompanied by a rapid and somewhat chaotic crushing of any form of dissent. The first two months of the war were marked by utter destruction of the nongovernmental media realm. As the Kremlin has used its TV propaganda weapon full force to ensure public support for its "special military operation,"[1] it has blocked, shut down, or forced to close those nongovernmental media that would not follow the official line. Blatant censorship, whether defined by hastily adopted legislation or enforced by zealous administrators, has become daily reality. According to Roskomsvoboda, the Russian nongovernmental organization that champions freedom of information, by early May 2022 about three thousand websites have been subject to various forms of "wartime censorship,"[2] among them major social networks, such as Facebook, Twitter, and Instagram. Cases of prosecution and incarceration of journalists have not been very numerous; intimidation, harassment, and labeling journalists "foreign agents" are much more common methods used to "cleanse" the Russian information space. As of this writing, the Russian government's policy appears to be generally aimed at forcing defiant journalists into exile, rather than locking them up in prison. Many of the exiled journalists have resumed operation from abroad, but in Russia their texts, podcasts, or videos are now inaccessible without special means, such as VPNs. Besides, the financing of Russian outlets operating away from home is problematic. There was still high interest in the Russian voices of dissent in May, over two months into the war, and the émigré publications and journalists can draw on grants and donations from various sources, but with time, this interest is bound to decline.

Control over media has been of primary concern for Vladimir Putin's government ever since his ascent to the Russian presidency in 2000. The main target was national TV channels with news broadcasting. By the end of Putin's first term, all three major national TV channels were securely under the Kremlin control. Smaller-audience outlets, however, could exercise relative freedom of expression and pursue nongovernment editorial lines—as long as the Kremlin stayed assured that those "niche" media had virtually no effect on a mass audience, the political process, or policymaking. During the "tandem rule" of 2008–2011, when Putin anointed for the presidency his loyal associate Dmitry Medvedev and took for himself the position of the prime minister, the government grew a bit more permissive, and the nongovernment media took advantage of a more auspicious environment.

The permissiveness associated with the tandem rule gave way to hardened policies after Putin's return to the Kremlin in 2012 accompanied by mass anti-Putin protests. After the 2013 political crisis in Ukraine and the annexation of Crimea the next year, the Kremlin shifted toward ever deepening confrontation with the West. Characteristically, that was also when Russia Today (RT), originally designed to improve Russia's image abroad, irrevocably reinvented itself as a Kremlin weapon in the information war with the West. Domestically, Putin's government has opted for a conservative,[3] increasingly antiliberal and anti-Western course; the regime has become more repressive, more authoritarian, and more personalistic.

State-controlled media, first and foremost national television, have been used ever more intensely as the Kremlin's mouthpieces, while constraints on the public realm, including nongovernment media, have been further tightened.

It should be noted, however, that throughout the 2010s, while the Kremlin resorted to violence against political activists, in its effort to harness the defiant press it still relied on softer, manipulative means. The "niche" liberal media outlets found themselves under pressure, some were forced to moderate their editorial lines or to switch to nonpolitical coverage. Some media outlets that were disfavored by the government suffered economically as their non-grata status scared away advertisers.

Despite the Kremlin's hardened policy, the second half of the 2010s was marked by an improbable rise of investigative reporting facilitated by a rapid advance of social media. Young Russian journalists mastered the skills of data journalism and made full use of state-of-the-art communications technologies and information platforms.

Beginning in 2020, however, the Kremlin launched a frontal assault on its opponents. In the summer of 2020, Aleksey Navalny was poisoned by a nerve agent. Upon his return to Russia from Germany, where he had recovered from the poisoning, he was arrested and sentenced to a jail term. His arrest caused street protests across Russia that were suppressed with unprecedented brutality; the Kremlin's crackdown included large-scale persecutions of political activists and the destruction of civic and political organizations. Dozens of media outlets and individual journalists have been labeled "foreign agents," a discriminatory measure that at best strongly interferes with their professional operation or at worst makes it impossible. Several outlets have been forced to close down; dozens of journalists remained jobless. Never before had Putin's regime attacked journalists so directly or on such a large scale. What the journalists, their audience, and most likely their government persecutors did not know at the time was that this unprecedented attack would turn out to be a prelude to the radical cleansing of the Russian media realm that followed the invasion of Ukraine.

This chapter focuses mostly on the national media or the outlets operating in, or broadcasting from, Moscow. Moscow is the center of Russia in more ways than most national capitals: It is a powerful magnet for anyone with ambition, whether it be making money, a career in government or in management, in literature, in fashion, in academia or the arts. Media is no exception.

PUBLIC/PRIVATE SPHERES IN POST-COMMUNIST RUSSIA

After the collapse of Soviet communism and the establishment of Russia as a post-communist state, President Boris Yeltsin's reforms created new opportunities for political, social, and economic activities not controlled by the state. The 1990s witnessed a largely unconstrained press, though the causes of this freedom were many. In the fierce political battles of the last years of the Soviet Union, Yeltsin evolved as an ardent anticommunist, and this turned him into a proponent of an independent press and a natural ally of new Russian journalists who also saw the Communist Party as a grave threat to Russia's democratic development.[4] Yeltsin's government almost never intervened to mute criticism of the president himself or his policies. Very early in Yeltsin's tenure, his government succeeded in passing a very progressive law on mass media.[5] But the government of the 1990s was also weak. Fighting many political and economic battles simultaneously, the Russian state simply did not have the capacity to control the media even if policymakers had wanted to.

THE RISE OF PRIVATELY OWNED MEDIA

Market reforms initially helped to stimulate the growth of media outlets not controlled by the state, including, most importantly, national television that reached viewers in the tens of millions.[6] NTV, the first private television network, was launched in 1993 by one of Russia's major first-generation business tycoons, Vladimir Gusinsky.[7] NTV quickly earned its credentials as a serious news organization when it provided critical coverage of the First Chechen War (1994–1996). Every day, the horrible scenes from Chechnya appeared on television screens in Russian homes and generated broad anti-war sentiments, not unlike the way the coverage of the Vietnam War had shaped opinions of the US audience. Partly as a result of media coverage, Yeltsin was forced to initiate a peace process with Chechnya; otherwise, he had no chance for reelection in 1996. NTV also produced the puppet show *Kukly* (Puppets), a political satire that spared no one. NTV quickly achieved a level of post-Soviet professionalism, quality, and style that its rival channels, Ostankino and RTR, struggling to overcome their Soviet background, lacked.

Before starting NTV, Gusinsky had already launched his own daily newspaper, *Segodnia* (Today). He also bought a stake in a popular radio station, Ekho Moskvy (Echo of Moscow), that began broadcasting in 1990 and gained prominence during the days of the attempted coup by hardliners in August 1991. In 1995 he founded a weekly magazine, *Itogi*, published in partnership with *Newsweek*, making his company, Media-Most, a media powerhouse. Other financial tycoons followed Gusinsky, believing that the media, especially television, were an important political tool. Through an inside deal arranged by the Kremlin, Boris Berezovsky acquired part ownership and de facto control of Ostankino, Russia's largest television network, which was renamed ORT (*Obshchestvennoe Rossiiskoe Televidenie*, Russian Public Television).[8] This "public" status, however, hardly meant anything, except the emergence of another powerful media tycoon and another national television asset under private control.

In the Russian media environment of the 1990s, adherence to the high principles of editorial independence professed by many editors and journalists soon grew problematic. Russia's media tycoons who emerged during Yeltsin's presidency were hardly consistent advocates of a free and independent press. Rather, they were profit seekers with questionable business ethics and controversial political agendas. As a result, media outlets were frequently biased, as the new tycoons would use them to pursue their own political and business goals. Yet the very fact that they were owned or controlled by non–state actors endowed those post-Soviet media with immense importance: After decades of tight ideological control by the Soviet state, they could offer alternative coverage, not guided by the interests of the government. Besides, those early tycoons permanently engaged in fierce rivalries, so if the media environment of the 1990s did not meet high democratic and ethical principles, at least it ensured pluralism of coverage and opinion.

The power of television as a political tool was in plain view in 1996 when Yeltsin was to stand reelection. By that time his support rating dwindled down to single-digits, and his communist rival looked to be a sure winner. Terrified of the prospect of a communist comeback, the media oligarchs joined efforts with the Kremlin administration. The national TV channels were virtually turned into Yeltsin's campaign tools and helped him defeat his communist challenger.[9]

The emerging media tycoons proved as susceptible as others to what one Moscow-based Western diplomat called the "incestuous" relationship between business and government.[10] This made them potentially vulnerable to government oversight. The state—or more aptly in Russian, *vlast'* (the power)—may have been dramatically weakened after the political turmoil following the collapse of the USSR and the ensuing economic meltdown, but it retained some leverage in different strategic sectors, including the national broadcast media. For example, while Berezovsky effectively controlled ORT, the Russian federal government remained its majority shareholder. The government also owned 100 percent of the state radio and TV company, even as its regional subsidiaries were de facto captured by local governors. As the Kremlin was preparing for the highly contested election cycle of 1999–2000, the government began to reclaim its media territory. A major step was the creation of a government agency in charge of the media and a consolidation of state broadcasters under federal auspices. In 1998, regional TV subsidiaries were brought together and subordinated to VGTRK (All-Russian State Radio and Television Company). Its main asset was the national channel RTR, renamed Rossiia in 2001.

RECONSOLIDATION OF THE STATE

When Vladimir Putin became Russia's new president in 2000, his primary goal was to reassert the power of the state. In *First Person*, Putin's book of interviews published in time for the outset of his presidency, he said, " . . . at some point many people decided that the president was no longer the center of power. . . . I'll make sure . . . that no one ever has such illusions anymore."[11] Putin effectively fulfilled his pledge before the end of his first term. Since the beginning of his rule, all political power has been steadily concentrated at the top of the executive branch, and government decision-making was concealed

Maria Lipman

from the public eye; gradually Putin emerged as Russia's uncontested and unchallenged leader.

As for the media, state-owned television was strengthened organizationally and financially for the upcoming election cycle of 1999–2000. The oligarchic media played a very significant role in that political campaign. But unlike the 1996 presidential election, when the media tycoons Gusinsky and Berezovsky combined their TV resources in the effort to get Yeltsin reelected, this time they ended up on different sides. Berezovsky committed his channel, ORT, to support the Kremlin.[12] Gusinsky and his channel, NTV, however, would not support the Kremlin's hastily masterminded party Edinstvo (Unity) in the parliamentary race, nor would they back Putin, Yeltsin's anointed successor, in the March 2000 presidential election.

In December 1999 the pro-Kremlin Edinstvo outperformed its main challenger—the party of the Moscow mayor, Yury Luzhkov, and former prime minister Yevgeny Primakov, and in March 2000, Putin was elected president. The Kremlin thus defeated its rivals. This made Berezovsky the winner (and, in his view, Putin's kingmaker) and Gusinsky the loser. But the consequences for their media properties, as well as for themselves, were similar. Soon thereafter, both were stripped of most of their media assets and forced into exile.

THE CAMPAIGN AGAINST OLIGARCHIC MEDIA

Expanding state control over national TV media was a major element of Putin's strategic goal of reasserting state power. On a tactical level, his primary task was to get rid of Gusinsky, a powerful actor who chose to play against him. Within days of Putin's inauguration in May 2000, Gusinsky and his media holdings came under massive attack.[13] The Kremlin, however, carefully avoided harassing or persecuting journalists or editors. Instead, the attack was mostly disguised as business litigation against Gusinsky's media properties. In late 2000, Gusinsky was forced to flee abroad and never returned to Russia. In the spring of 2001, Gusinsky's media company was taken over by Gazprom-Media, the media subsidiary of the state-controlled giant Gazprom. Media-Most, once the biggest privately owned media group in Russia, was dismantled. Eventually, though not immediately, the new management of NTV transformed the channel's editorial policy to keep it firmly in line with the Kremlin's political goals.

Since the takeover of Media-Most was disguised as business litigation against a "fat cat," such as Gusinsky, and none of the NTV journalists was persecuted, the majority of the Russian public would not see the attack at NTV/Media-Most as a threat to freedom of the press. After the decade of political turmoil and radical weakening of the state under Putin's predecessor,

Boris Yeltsin, the people at large appreciated the reconsolidation of state control undertaken by Putin.[14]

ORT, the channel controlled by Berezovsky, was reclaimed by the state at about the same time as NTV. Regaining control over ORT took much less time than the takeover of NTV and was mostly hidden from the public eye. It was not until the 2011 litigation in the High Court of London between two major Russian tycoons, Berezovsky and Roman Abramovich, that the story was finally revealed to the public. According to testimony at the hearings, Berezovsky had been pressured to sell his 49 percent stake in ORT to a Kremlin-chosen buyer, Roman Abramovich, who had earlier done special, secret, and costly favors for Putin. Secretly buying ORT on Putin's, or the Kremlin's, behalf was one such favor. Abramovich never claimed control over the channel, and the Kremlin has since used it as its political resource.[15]

In 2001–2002, there were two failed attempts to launch new, privately owned, national television channels. Through various techniques, the Kremlin made sure that both projects would be short-lived.[16] In 2002 NTV's highly popular *Kukly* show was canceled. By the middle of 2003, all three federal TV channels, whose outreach far surpassed all other Russian media, were turned into political tools of the Kremlin. Putin thus achieved major success, strategic (reconsolidating state control), as well as tactical (getting rid of two very powerful actors).

MANAGED TELEVISION COVERAGE

The coverage of three tragedies—the 2000 sinking of the submarine *Kursk*, the 2002 terrorist siege of a Moscow theater, and the 2004 terrorist attack on a school in Beslan—illustrates the Kremlin's expanded control over television broadcasting. Back in 2000, the media, including national television, tried their best to cover the *Kursk* catastrophe, which took the lives of all 118 sailors on board. While officials, both uniformed and civilian, sought to cover up the inefficiency of the rescue operation and the poor condition of the Russian navy, Russian journalists undertook thorough investigations to report what the government sought to hide, which, of course, made Putin, then very early in his presidency, look incompetent and weak. Putin was furious: He lashed out at "people in television" who "over the past ten years have destroyed that same army and navy where people are dying today."[17] Soon thereafter, the state assumed control over ORT.[18]

In October 2002, a group of terrorists seized a Moscow theater with over eight hundred people inside. In a badly bungled rescue operation, at least 129 hostages were killed, almost all of them by the poisonous gas used by the rescuers. This time, federal television was mostly tame, but the journalists of NTV, though it had been taken over by Gazprom the previous year, still retained their professional instincts, supported by the channel's new top manager, Boris Jordan. (Jordan, an American entrepreneur, had vowed to maintain NTV's integrity, and he did not interfere with the way the channels' journalists reported those tragic developments.) NTV's recalcitrance deeply displeased Putin.[19] Within three months of the event, Jordan was replaced by a more amenable figure.

In September 2004, over 1,100 people, most of them children, were taken hostage in a school in Beslan in the North Caucasus region of North Ossetia. During the siege and subsequent storming of the school building, at least 334 hostages were killed. The rescue operation left serious doubts about the competence of those in charge. By 2004, however, the government had secured full control over all three major federal television channels. For their top managers, cooperation with the government had become a higher priority than professional skills or ethics.[20] This time, Putin had no complaints about the coverage or TV reporters' performance.

TIGHTENED CONTROL OVER POLITICAL AND PUBLIC SPHERES

The government used the tragedy at Beslan as a pretext to tighten controls, launching what eventually amounted to full-blown political reform that endowed the Kremlin with a virtually unlimited capacity to bar unwelcome forces or figures from Russian political life.[21]

The end of 2004 was also marked by the Orange Revolution in Ukraine, which the Kremlin saw as a Western plot to install a pro-Western regime on Russia's border with the help of foreign-funded nongovernmental organizations (NGOs). The "orange scare" pushed the Kremlin to further tighten its grip on power. NGOs sponsored from abroad became the primary target of this campaign. State-controlled media, first and foremost national TV channels, engaged in smearing foreign-funded NGOs as agents of the West seeking to do damage to Russia.[22]

By the middle of his second term, Putin presided over a deeply personalized political system; he did not have to worry about political competition or public accountability. National TV channels steadily and effectively generated a sense that there was no alternative to Putin's leadership. The high and rising price of oil enabled the government to generously deliver to the people; Putin's approval rating hovered above 80 percent,[23] and the dominant public mood was one of quiescence.

Any political action or organization opposing the government was strongly discouraged, and the remaining independent political groups and activists were scarce, fragmented, and generally reduced to irrelevance. In this environment, the government could afford a degree of permissiveness toward niche liberal media that afforded some freedom of expression to the more modernized and critically minded minority, yet it remained politically irrelevant and generally unnoticed by the broad public.

CONTROLLED TELEVISION AS THE KREMLIN'S POLITICAL RESOURCE

Control over national television networks constituted a major element of the political system and the pattern of state-society relations that Putin built. State control over TV was (and remains) by no means a coercive operation: Top TV managers are staunch loyalists who have committed their professional skills, creative talents, and their organizations' capacities to advancing the government's goals in close cooperation with the Kremlin Administration. Alexey Gromov, the Administration's first deputy chief of staff, has been for many years a key manager of public policy for mass media.[24]

The mass-audience channels, especially Channel One (ORT was renamed Channel One in 2002) and Rossiia, as well as NTV, have been effectively used as tools to shape public perceptions by boosting certain developments, playing down others, or ignoring them altogether, and by praising or smearing certain figures or groups.[25]

The 2003 State Duma election, which further consolidated the Kremlin's control, was criticized by the Organization for Security and Cooperation in Europe (OSCE) monitoring mission, which pointed to biased media coverage favoring the incumbent.[26] Putin's reelection in 2004 was a heavily manipulated affair with a preordained result: Putin won handily, with 71 percent of the vote.[27]

Before Putin left the presidency in 2008, he had handpicked a successor, his protégé Dmitry Medvedev. As a presidential candidate, Medvedev was featured on television almost as prominently as Putin and gained 70 percent of the vote. Putin became the prime minister in Medvedev's government. Although technically his position was inferior to Medvedev's, in fact Putin remained the most powerful man in Russia. The coverage of the three major TV channels was deftly adjusted to what came to be referred to as "tandem rule" and helped maintain high approval ratings for both leaders.[28]

The role of television as the Kremlin's indispensable political resource is inseparable from its business aspect. While the three federal broadcasters did not compete in news coverage—hardly different from channel to channel—they fiercely competed for advertisers' rubles by offering the audience a broad choice of entertainment shows and high-quality TV series. Advertisers attracted by the channels' broad outreach eagerly committed their budgets to government-controlled TV. On top of that, the federal TV channels, as a key element in the structure of state power, were also assured of government subsidies.[29] Further, entertainment programming performed an important sociopolitical function by keeping people pacified and demobilized; glued to the TV screens by their favorite shows, viewers stay on the same channels for the pro-Kremlin news coverage.

ECONOMIC RISE

In the 1990s there was still hope—or a dream—that the Russian media would evolve as a public institution holding the government to account. During the first decade of the 2000s, the Kremlin thoroughly eliminated any chance that the media would fulfill this public mission. But as an industry and as a lucrative business, media flourished. The rising price of oil boosted economic growth and contributed to a steady rise of the advertising market (it reached R131 billion in 2011),[30] making media a promising and prestigious business venture. Russian media groups perfected their business models and expanded to include movie production, printing and distribution businesses, as well as telecommunications.

In the course of the 2000s, the Kremlin continued to redistribute and con-solidate media holdings. After getting rid of the two major media tycoons, Gusinsky and Berezovsky, the Kremlin approved or orchestrated deals in which media assets ended up in the hands of loyal owners. While Putin's government took pride in ridding Russia of oligarchic media, media assets amassed during Putin's own tenure are enormous and substantially exceed those held by Gusinsky or Berezovsky in the 1990s. In contrast to the 1990s, now loyalty to the president became the order of the day, and big business in general as well as holders of media assets in particular pledged full allegiance to the man in the Kremlin.

The largest-audience media outlets, the Kremlin's essential political resource, have been entrusted to magnates who made their fortunes in the energy sector or banking after Putin's rise to the presidency. By the late 2000s, National Media Group (NMG), controlled by business structures associated with Yury Kovalchuk, broadly reported to be a member of Putin's innermost circle of old friends,[31] emerged as one of three major media hold-ings alongside state-owned VGTRK and Gazprom-Media. NMG includes two national media channels with news coverage (REN TV and Channel Five) and an entire range of other TV, print, and internet resources. In early 2011, NMG vastly increased its holdings by purchasing a 20 percent share in Channel One.[32] In 2016, the value of NMG was estimated at R150 billion

($2.2 billion).[33] In addition to media assets, Kovalchuk's Bank *Rossiya* bought shares in Russia's largest advertising sales house, VI (formerly Video International).[34] The concentration of media properties eventually produced a "media oligopoly"[35] with huge media holdings (including nearly all of the two dozen federal TV channels, some with news coverage, some purely entertainment) concentrated in the hands of just the three entities mentioned above. In 2016, however, it was reported that neither Kovalchuk personally, nor Bank Rossiya any longer had control of NMG.[36] Ownership ties among the "Big Three" are complex, data on the media ownership structure are generally hard to obtain, and published reports are impossible to verify.

Another step toward further concentration of media properties in the business structures controlled by Putin's allies was taken in December 2021, when metal tycoon and billionaire Alisher Usmanov announced the sale of his stake in internet-holding company VK, which controls two major Russian social networks: Vkontakte and Odnoklassniki. The stake is to become the property of state-owned bank Gazprombank and insurance company Sogaz, which is controlled by Yuri Kovalchuk and his family.[37]

BEYOND DIRECT CONTROL, BUT AT
THE KREMLIN'S DISCRETION

By 2008 it became common among the critically minded, modernized, and liberal minority in Russia to dismiss news coverage of national TV broadcasters as heavy-handed and boring propaganda. This constituency drew instead on a range of alternative, nongovernmental sources of information—print, radio, internet, and smaller-audience television channels—that pursued editorial independence of varying degrees, among them dailies such as *Kommersant, Vedomosti* (a business daily, until 2015 published jointly by the *Wall Street Journal* and the *Financial Times*), or *Novaia Gazeta*; weeklies, such as *The New Times, Kommersant-Vlast'*, or *Russian Newsweek* (closed on the initiative of its German publisher in 2010); or the radio station Ekho Moskvy (this list is far from being exhaustive). A variety of websites offered a combination of news, analysis, and opinion unconstrained by censorship or other modes of state control (the internet in Russia still remained generally free). REN TV, a formerly independent channel with a sizable audience had at least one show left with an independent voice—*Nedelia* (The Week), a weekend news wrap-up show hosted by Marianna Maksimovskaya). REN TV was an example of a redistribution of media assets to loyal owners; in 2008 it was included in the NMG holding; it has since repeatedly changed its editorial policy and generally stayed away from news coverage.

Some journalists continued to engage in investigative reporting and exposed abuses of offices by high-ranking government officials. The picture of Russia that emerged from the above-mentioned relatively independent outlets was entirely different from the image offered by federal TV channels. In a more open political environment, some of the stories reported by those "alternative" media would become the subject of a parliamentary discussion or probe; others would generate political scandals. But in Putin's Russia competitive politics had been virtually eliminated, the legislature had been turned into an arm of the Kremlin executive, judicial rulings were bent to the Kremlin's will whenever needed, and autonomous political activism was thoroughly marginalized. In these conditions, the surviving elements of free media remained politically irrelevant.[38]

The Kremlin made sure that the nongovernmental media stay marginal and be restricted to their "niche" of preaching to the converted. And if marginalization was not enough, the government had an array of administrative, legal, and other tools to use against excessively audacious outlets. At that point, however, those instruments were infrequently applied and served to intimidate defiant media outlets and remind them that they existed at the Kremlin's discretion: If they went too far and incurred the wrath of the powerful upon themselves, nothing would protect them.[39] For instance, Raf Shakirov, the editor-in-chief of *Izvestia* daily, was forced to resign after publishing full-page-size, poster-like photos from the scene of the above-mentioned terrorist attack in Beslan; it was broadly assumed that his resignation followed the Kremlin's orders.[40]

Unlike the Soviet Union where a system of prior censorship ensured that every word on paper or on air conformed with the Communist Party line, Putin's Kremlin did not seek to stifle every voice. In fact, media that pursued editorial independence could even be useful for the Kremlin as a safety valve that helped the critically minded let off steam. The problem with media freedom in Putin's Russia was, therefore, not the absence of alternative sources of information. Rather, it was the tightly controlled political system and the social environment in which a vast majority showed no interest in alternative sources of news. Both factors made "alternative" media irrelevant and defenseless in the face of state power. Though they continued to operate, the atmosphere grew increasingly inauspicious. Some journalists felt discouraged and opted for nonpolitical beats or even other occupations; some adjusted to the controlled political environment and engaged in self-censorship.[41]

TANDEM RULE: VERBAL LIBERTIES
AND THE "DIGITAL DIVIDE"

The environment of general public quiescence began to change with the transition to "tandem rule." The more cynical may have regarded Dmitry Medvedev's presidency as merely a public relations trick—putting a "soft face" to Putin's authoritarian regime. But Medvedev's liberal rhetoric (he famously said that "freedom is better than nonfreedom"; the word "modernization" became the mantra of the tandem period), his younger age, and his enthusiasm for gadgets and the digital world appealed to certain constituencies, especially younger urban Russians. Besides, the very fact that there were two men at the top instead of just one loosened the system a bit and emboldened some members of the elites, as well as political opponents of the regime who remained marginal after Putin had consolidated state power. The phrase "political thaw" entered the political lingo of the tandem's early period.[42]

The somewhat softer environment unleashed more criticism by the media. Though federal television channels remained fully under state control, beyond the everyday operation on federal TV a mild degree of new audacity could be found in the television community. For instance, annual TV awards were repeatedly granted to "non grata" TV journalists who had been barred from national television, or to those from smaller-audience TV channels who had retained a relatively independent voice. At the awards ceremony in 2010, Leonid Parfyonov, a top TV star in the 1990s forced out of NTV in 2004, gave a speech in which he harshly denounced federal broadcasters:

> For a correspondent of federal television the top government executives are not newsmakers, but the bosses of their bosses . . . a correspondent is not a journalist, he is a bureaucrat guided by the logic of allegiance and subordination. . . . Nothing critical, skeptical or ironic about the president or the prime minister can be aired on federal channels.[43]

The tandem rule was also marked by the emergence of new media outlets or the politicization of those that previously had remained largely nonpolitical. Kommersant, which since its inception back in 1990 had been a well-established print media holding, in 2010 launched Kommersant FM, a well-informed news and analysis radio. *TV Dozhd* (TV Rain) was launched the same year as an almost unique example of (medium-scale) entrepreneurs, Alexander Vinokurov and his wife Natalia Sindeeva, openly funding a media outlet that pursued nongovernmental editorial policy. TV Rain was able to substantially broaden its outreach and its profits after it was included in cable packages. Several thick glossies, such as *GQ*, *Citizen K*, or *Esquire*, also turned to political themes (*Esquire* made this choice even earlier), apparently responding to an emerging interest in social and political matters among their reasonably prosperous, well-traveled, Westernized audiences. *Bolshoi Gorod* (*Big City*), a biweekly magazine about Moscow city life, was reformatted and offered strongly politicized, sometimes angry coverage. *Afisha* (*Billboard*) magazine, originally focused on culture and leisure, now developed a defiant political voice.

The newly energized "alternative" media realm was filled with reportage, critical policy analysis by experts, as well as angry opinions and poisonous jokes. The tandem period was also marked by rapidly growing internet penetration; most major print and radio outlets developed internet platforms; and web, print, audio, and video were also merging. Though television remained the main source of news for a majority of Russians (and the only one to those living in remote places), a growing number of people in large urban centers were drawing on the internet. Two Russian social networks, VKontakte and Odnoklassniki, both launched in 2006, were rapidly gaining popularity. Advanced web users in greater numbers switched to Facebook, where they found references to media publications made by their like-minded liberal "friends." The number of social network users was growing faster in Russia than anyplace else in Europe. In 2012, 24 percent of Russians in a national poll said they relied on the internet for news,[44] up from 11 percent less than one year earlier.

The penetration of the web was not yet universal, yet broad enough to generate a "digital divide," with more sophisticated users being generally more critically minded and drawing on alternative, nongovernment sources of information. The internet was awash with reports, submitted by professional journalists and ordinary citizens writing about lawlessness, injustice, or abuse by government or police authority. The number of bloggers increased, some of them gaining huge popularity and becoming voices of authority for tens of thousands of loyal followers. The popularity of social networks facilitated the exchange of information, strengthened social linkages, and promoted interest in civic causes. Civic activism was on the rise.[45] The fragmented "islets" of nongovernment media seemed to be merging into something of an archipelago. Then Putin announced that he was returning to the presidency.

PUTIN'S RETURN TO THE KREMLIN: HARDENED AUTHORITARIANISM

By the end of the tandem period, Russia's economy began to slow down, so even before he returned to the Kremlin, Putin arguably knew he would no longer be able to maintain his regime's legitimacy by generously delivering to the people. This in itself called for a change of policy away from permissiveness toward tighter controls.

The shift toward harder and more authoritarian policy was triggered by mass street protests that broke out in December 2011 and continued in 2012—that the protests erupted less than one year after the Arab Spring arguably looked even more ominous to the Kremlin. The outrage over the "castling" trick—with Putin and Medvedev announcing that Putin, not Medvedev, would run for president in 2012 and Medvedev would take the office of prime minister—was further deepened by egregious rigging during the parliamentary election of December 2011. Mass protest rallies brought out tens of thousands in the Russian capital (reaching one hundred thousand at its peak) and other large urban centers; the protesters chanted "Putin, Go!" or "Russia without Putin!" Many among the new generation of journalists were at the very center of the protest.[46] The new media provided enthusiastic coverage of the protests, and social networks served as an excellent tool to organize rallies and disseminate information among the protest community.

The Kremlin showed tolerance toward the protests up until Putin's successful election for a third term. After his inauguration in May 2012, the Kremlin launched a counteroffensive against the newly politicized and defiant Russian citizenry. Beatings, detentions, and years-long sentences were accompanied by an aggressive campaign on state-controlled television that viciously pitted the conservative majority against their excessively modernized compatriots. TV smear campaigns and "documentaries" attacked the anti-Putin protesters, civic and political activists, as well as liberal journalists. Terms such as "national traitors" and "fifth column" entered the language of the TV news and talk shows.

FIRST CRACKDOWN ON NONGOVERNMENTAL MEDIA

Nongovernmental media which to that point had enjoyed relative freedom of expression came under pressure as part of a general crackdown that followed the protest wave. The fact that most major media had been redistributed to loyal owners greatly facilitated the Kremlin's task. Business tycoons concerned about their vast holdings in nonmedia spheres could be fully relied on to adjust their outlets' editorial lines to the Kremlin's interests and get rid of unwanted writers or editors, sometimes even anticipating and preempting the Kremlin's requests. This spared the Kremlin the trouble of direct interference, harassment, or persecution of individual journalists.

Beginning in late 2011, quite a few leading editors were fired or forced to resign by the owner. The editor in chief of *Vlast'*, the *Kommersant* weekly magazine (owned by billionaire Usmanov), was forced to quit after publishing a photograph of a voting ballot with an expletive applied to Putin.[47] Then the general director of the Kommersant publishing house was replaced, as well as the editor in chief of Kommersant FM radio. In short order, *Kommersant*, until then a high-quality mainstream daily, lost several other prominent journalists, grew much tamer, and fell way below its earlier editorial standards. The editor in chief of *Bolshoi Gorod* had to go, and since then the magazine has generally avoided sensitive political subjects. In 2014, Marianna Maksimovskaia's above-mentioned weekly show, *Nedelia*, was closed by the REN TV network.

One of the major blows in the media realm was the radical reformatting in late 2013 of the Russian state news agency RIA-Novosti (this decision was taken by Putin personally).[48] RIA-Novosti had been a successful operation headed by a highly professional and respected manager, Svetlana Mironyuk, who was now replaced by Dmitry Kiselev, a TV host known for his raving attacks on air at anyone whom the Kremlin regarded as an enemy of Russia: Ukrainian politicians, gays, Americans, and so on. Around the same time, TV Rain came under pressure. Under the pretext of an unethical question to the viewers posted on TV Rain's website, all cable operators, one after another, terminated their contracts with the channel (there is every reason to believe that the operators' decisions were prompted by the Kremlin).[49] TV Rain's audience, which by then had reached about seventeen million, dramatically shrank to under one hundred thousand when the channel was forced to reduce its distribution to paid internet subscriptions.

The next to fall under attack was Galina Timchenko, the editor in chief of Lenta.ru, a political website owned by billionaire Alexander Mamut, a major owner of internet media. Timchenko and her team had turned their outlet into a must-read for those interested in high-quality news coverage. The fact that Timchenko's audacious and independent website was rapidly gaining popularity was probably enough reason for the owner to fire her to avoid (or preempt) the Kremlin's discontent.[50] Almost all members of her team quit as a sign of protest. With a group of her former *Lenta* staffers, Timchenko launched a new website called Meduza.io. [51] *Meduza*, however, was operating from Latvia.

The forced redistribution of media assets that had been practiced since the early 2000s was applied again in 2014: Pavel Durov, the founder of Russia's most popular social network, VKontakte, was forced to sell his network to a partner of billionaire Usmanov[52] and subsequently left Russia. In 2016, three top editors at media-holding RBC (owned by billionaire Mikhail Prokhorov) were dismissed or quit after publishing reports and investigations on politically sensitive subjects. The next year Prokhorov sold his media holding to a staunch loyalist Grigory Berezkin, who was not a major media holder, but who owned the pro-Kremlin tabloid *Komsomolskaya Pravda*, Russia's largest circulation daily. One of the RBC former top editors, Yelizaveta Osetinskaya, who had turned RBC into a highly professional and successful holding, left Russia and, with a group of RBC journalists who had quit in solidarity, launched The Bell, a Russian-language website operating out of the United States and focused on business news and commentary.[53]

Following the political crisis in Ukraine and the annexation of Crimea in 2014, a highly intense campaign of jingoistic propaganda was launched on Russian national television. Mass-audience TV channels began attacking Ukrainian "fascists" and their Western "masters." The TV news shows became much longer than usual and almost entirely focused on Ukraine, with only a small fraction of airtime devoted to Russia proper. This propaganda onslaught further boosted the rally-around-the-leader effect generated by the annexation of Crimea. The return of Crimea to the Russian fold, as broadly seen by the Russian people, served to demonstrate their country's strengthened global stature: following the collapse of the Soviet Union Russia had been long taken for granted, yet it was now the West that looked weak, forced to accept the annexation of Crimea as a *fait accompli*. Putin's approval rating, which had dropped to 60 percent before his return to the Kremlin in 2012, jumped up to over 80 percent and remained at this level through the end of his third term and his reelection in 2018.

THE KREMLIN STEPS UP REPRESSIONS

The Kremlin's crackdown on protesters and political activists that began in the spring of 2012 never quite subsided. Protest waves came and went, and, although on some occasions, the government showed tolerance, the overall trend was one of growing pressure and persecutions. Besides, the Duma was adopting an increasing number of legal constraints on civil liberties, especially on the freedom of assembly. Over time, more and more activists, human rights defenders, lawyers, and others were persecuted and prosecuted. Encroachment on freedom of speech included persecution of bloggers and those reposting "extremist" materials (anti-extremism legislation originally framed to tackle radical Islam or hate crimes has been increasingly applied to punish online expressions of political disloyalty). For instance, on numerous occasions individuals were prosecuted for reposting information about upcoming protest rallies.[54] During the same period, the national TV channels launched aggressive political talk shows, filled with loud-mouthed attacks directed at America, Ukraine, liberals, and whomever else the Kremlin deemed Russia's enemies.

The treatment of Alexey Navalny is a graphic illustration of how the Kremlin's policy hardened since the protest wave of 2011–2012. Although national television ignored him, Navalny was gaining broad public awareness (just 18 percent said they never heard of him in 2020, down from almost 60 percent who were unaware of him in 2013[55]). He continued his relentless fight against elite corruption and organized repeated mass protests that by the end of the 2010s spread to many cities across Russia. During that decade, Navalny was harassed, kept under house arrest, physically attacked, and fined. While he spent about forty days in detention during the period of 2011–2015, from 2017 until his return to Russia in early 2021 his time in detention amounted to two hundred days.[56]

Meanwhile, the "Crimean consensus" began to fade, precipitated by the unpopular 2018 pension reform that raised the retirement age, as well as by the economic slowdown and the ensuing decline in living standards. Putin's approval rating dropped from its sky-high post-Crimea levels and fluctuated between 60 and 70 percent. The decline of Putin's rating, Navalny's expanded activism and growing popularity, as well as the expanded geography of street protests were among the most important factors behind the Kremlin's new, radical clampdown of 2020–2021.

THE IMPROBABLE RISE OF INVESTIGATIVE JOURNALISM AND AN UNPRECEDENTED ATTACK ON JOURNALISTS

Compared to activists and protesters, by the end of the 2010s journalists were still not badly mistreated. Throughout that decade, the Kremlin mostly maintained its habitual practice of targeting media outlets, rather than individual journalists. Paradoxically, the end of the 2010s, when the government further hardened its clampdown on oppositionist activism, was marked by what the *New York Times* referred to as a "flourish of investigative journalism."[57] Young reporters, well-versed in modern communications technologies, engaged in data journalism drawing on digitized public records, as well as the "dark web" marketplace where one can buy personal cellphone geolocation or air travel records. The web filled with investigations of egregiously unsavory practices and ill-gotten gains of very important people, such as the formidable head of the state company Rosneft, the head of Russian Foreign Intelligence, Putin's former son-in-law, high-ranking members of the Moscow government, etc. "One week can bring you five large pieces full of previously unknown facts about public officials and their illegal moneymaking schemes," Maxim Trudolyubov, a longtime Russian columnist and editor wrote in summer of 2019.[58]

A new, independent media award, called Redkollegia, was established by a private foundation *Sreda*. Redkollegia grants one or more awards every month to journalists of Moscow, as well as regional outlets who "keep up high professional standards at a time when free, high-quality journalism is under state pressure."[59] All the awarded materials are republished on the *Redkollegia* website; this way the award-winning reporters are introduced to an audience beyond their publications.

In Russia, as elsewhere in the world, citizen journalism, bloggers, as well as websites of informal public initiatives or nonprofit organizations, have attracted large audiences, sometimes larger than those of "conventional" media. Aleksey Navalny's YouTube videos are a striking example. In those videos Navalny made allegations of corruption among highest-ranking government officials based on the data collected by his Anti-Corruption Foundation. The video exposing the exorbitant wealth of the then prime minister Dmitry Medvedev, promptly gained twenty-five million views.[60] After Navalny's arrest in January 2021, his team published a video titled *Putin's Palace* that collected over one hundred million views.[61]

An explosive growth of YouTube gave rise to highly popular shows not infrequently dwelling upon politically sensitive subjects. Yuri Dud's YouTube interviews with prominent Russian figures and his YouTube documentaries gained him nationwide fame. In late 2020, younger audiences of YouTube and Instagram named Dud the most popular Russian blogger.[62]

The rapid rise of YouTube and Instagram further deepened the "digital divide" that in recent years has generated a widening rift between younger Russians and their older compatriots. The "competition" among various means of communication has radically shifted from the TV image versus online text to TV footage versus online video, with the internet "defeating" TV among younger audiences. Young Russians increasingly rely on their phones as the source of knowledge and style, as well as values and authority figures. By early 2021, twenty- to thirty-year-old Russians constituted "one of the most critically minded social groups."[63] In early 2021, at the time of mass protests against Navalny's arrest, even TikTok grew politicized and rapidly evolved as a "protest venue."[64]

The "disloyal youth" factor arguably exacerbated the Kremlin's anxiety over the gradual erosion of the government legitimacy. The government's clampdown on freedoms now went beyond political activists, civic organizations, and media outlets and—for the first time—targeted individual journalists. The "foreign agents" legislation that originally had been adopted in 2012 to constrain the operation of unwelcome nonprofit organizations, was expanded in 2017 to target foreign media organizations, such as Radio Liberty and its associated outlets, as well as domestic outlets deemed disloyal. Two years later, it was amended to introduce a notion of individual journalists as "foreign agents." As of the fall of 2021, about sixty journalists, many of them engaged in investigative reporting, and about thirty media organizations, among them Meduza and TV Rain, had been labeled "foreign agents."[65] At least one online outlet—Proekt, registered in the United States—that had exposed highly influential officials' wrongdoings was labeled an "undesirable organization," which implies a de-facto ban on Proekt's very existence (most of Proekt's journalists left Russia; Proekt briefly continued its operation under a different name; starting in March 2022 it resumed publication under its old name, Proekt[66]). Some of the outlets were forced to close; those that continued to operate found themselves in a highly precarious situation. Many journalists were left jobless and chose to leave Russia.[67]

Another major line of attack included stepped up constraints on internet freedom. The Kremlin had long worked toward controlling the internet by a range of technological, legislative, and administrative means. For a while, however, it seemed that the government could not catch up with tech-savvy Russians who found ways to overcome the new restrictions. In a striking example, the Kremlin "surrendered" after its attempts to block the Telegram messaging app resulted in serious "collateral damage."[68] The year 2021, however, not only marked a major assault on the internet freedom, but it also demonstrated that the government agencies in charge of surveillance, barring unwelcome content, etc., had made substantial progress. "The state's crackdown on individual online freedoms, opposition forces and internet infrastructure has escalated to a fever pitch," Tanya Lokot, an internet expert wrote in the fall of 2021.[69] She cited blocking websites without notification, putting pressure on Google and Apple forcing them to remove undesired content, levying huge fines on Facebook, Twitter, and WhatsApp, as well as introducing bans on circumvention providers, such as VPNs. The Kremlin's "sovereign internet" policy, disguised as a means to counter external threats, is geared toward the gradual isolation of the Russian internet from the rest of the world.

CONCLUSION

The political regime of Vladimir Putin's first decade in power can be seen as an "informational autocracy,"[70] a soft authoritarianism that draws on propaganda, censorship, and co-optation, rather than ideology, coercion, or violence. Control over national television, Russia's largest-audience media, was a key element of that system. By the end of Putin's first term, all three national TV channels with news coverage had been taken under state control and turned into the Kremlin's political resource—an effective instrument of shaping public opinion in the Kremlin's interests. The Kremlin generally refrained from direct persecution of individual journalists and relied, first and foremost, on redistribution of media assets to loyal owners as its strategy of choice. Loyal owners were expected to rein in excessively audacious journalists and editors—and they did so at the slightest hint from the Kremlin. Still, during the first decade of Putin's leadership, the government showed tolerance toward a range of niche media that pursued editorial independence. Tight control over politics and policymaking kept these niche nongovernment outlets politically irrelevant. The Kremlin could afford a degree of lenience toward independent media outlets, as long as it could deliver prosperity and stability and ensure public quiescence; in other words, as long as it felt reasonably unthreatened.

When mass anti-Putin protests broke out in 2011–2012, the Kremlin responded with a crackdown on the disloyal elements of society. Many of the independent outlets came under pressure, yet the Kremlin still targeted outlets, not individual journalists. Compared to the increasingly repressive treatment of political activists and civic organizations, independent journalists could still exercise a degree of freedom and provide alternative information, analysis, and opinion about Russia and the world. (It should be noted, however, that public interest in such alternative sources remained limited.) The explosive growth of YouTube, Instagram, and the general advance of digital technologies created new opportunities for young reporters, which resulted in "an increasingly vibrant journalistic scene," as one observer wrote in 2019.[71] Around the same time, pollsters registered a widening "digital divide" between younger and older Russians, the younger ones broadly sharing critical views of government policies. Combined with a stagnant economy and declining living standards, as well as Aleksey Navalny's political organizing, this apparently caused serious concerns in the Kremlin. The poisoning of Navalny in 2020 and his jailing the next year marked a watershed: Russian informational autocracy inexorably evolved into dictatorship. The government grew more violent toward political oppositionists, protesters, and civic activists. Its repressive policies were expanded to include media organizations, and for the first time, also individual journalists. The broader and more sophisticated constraints on the internet freedom present a new, dramatic obstacle to independent journalism.

Many of those journalists targeted by the Kremlin's onslaught were left jobless, some were virtually banned from practicing journalism and chose to leave Russia. By the end of 2021, the Russian media scene substantially shrunk, but it was still not scorched earth. The amount of space left for independent journalism, however, remained at the Kremlin's discretion. In early March 2022, within days of Russia's invasion of Ukraine, the government's assault on nongovernmental media radically hardened.[72] Very soon the territory of Russia was thoroughly cleansed of nongovernmental media.[73]

DISCUSSION QUESTIONS

1. What constitutes media freedom, and what are its safeguards? Why did media freedom of the early post-communist period prove to be easy to suppress?
2. What were the oligarchic media of the 1990s, and how were they different from the concentration of media assets in the late 2000s–early 2010s?
3. What are the causes, targets, methods, and results of the Kremlin's media policy during Putin's first term?
4. How and why did the media scene change during Dmitry Medvedev's presidency, also referred to as the "tandem rule"? Do you see a problem with journalists being at the forefront of the mass protests of 2011–2012?
5. How and why has the media scene changed since Putin's return to the Kremlin in 2012 and again in 2020–2021?

SUGGESTED READINGS

Baker, Peter, and Susan Glasser. *Kremlin Rising: Vladimir Putin's Russia and the End of Revolution*. New York: Lisa Drew/Scribner, 2005.

Federman, Adam. "Moscow's New Rules." *Columbia Journalism Review*, January–February 2010. http://www.cjr.org/feature/moscows_new_rules.php?page=all.

Gatov, Vasily. "How the Kremlin and the Media Ended Up in Bed Together." *Moscow Times*, March 11, 2015, https://www.themoscowtimes.com/2015/03/11/how-the-kremlin-and-the-media-ended-up-in-bed-together-a44663.

Hoffman, David. *The Oligarchs: Wealth and Power in the New Russia*. New York: Public Affairs, 2002.

Idov, Michael. "The New Decembrists." *New York Magazine*, January 22, 2012. http://nymag.com/news/features/russian-revolutionaries-2012-1.

Koltsova, Olessia. *News Media and Power in Russia*. New York: Routledge, 2006.

Lipman, Maria. "Freedom of Expression without Freedom of the Press." *Journal of International Affairs* 63, no. 2 (2010): 153–69.

———. "Russia's Nongovernmental Media under Assault." *Demokratizatsiya: The Journal of Post-Soviet Democratization* 22, no. 2 (2014): 179–90.

Lipman, Maria, Anna Kachkaeva, and Mikhail Poyker. "Media in Russia: Between Modernization and Monopoly." In *The New Autocracy: Information, Politics, and Policy in Putin's Russia*, ed. Daniel Treisman. Washington, DC: Brookings Institution, 2018.

Ostrovsky, Arkady. *The Invention of Russia: The Journey from Gorbachev's Freedom to Putin's War*. London: Atlantic Books, 2015.

Reiter, Svetlana. *"Toxic Assets": How Russia's Invasion of Ukraine Tore Yandex Apart*. Meduza, May 6, 2022. https://meduza.io/en/feature/2022/05/06/toxic-assets.

Soldatov, Andrey, and Irina Borogan. *The Red Web: The Struggle between Russia's Digital Dictators and the New Online Revolutionaries.* New York: Public Affairs, 2015.

Yaffa, Joshua. "The Kremlin's Creative Director." *New Yorker,* December 16, 2019, https://www.newyorker.com/magazine/2019/12/16/the-kremlins-creative-director.

NOTES

1. As soon as the Russian invasion in Ukraine began, the government has dramatically increased the funding of the major government media. https://www.moscowtimes.ru/2022/04/12/milliardi-na-propagandu-rashodi-byudzheta-na-gossmi-podskochili-vtroe-na-fone-voini-a19511.

2. https://roskomsvoboda.org/post/voennaya-cenzura-3000-saytov/.

3. For an analysis of the conservative shift following Putin's return to the Kremlin and annexation of Crimea, see Marlene Laruelle, "Putin's Regime and Ideological Market: Difficult Balancing Game," March 16, 2017, http://carnegieendowment.org/2017/03/16/putin-s-regime-and-ideological-market-difficult-balancing-game-pub-68250.

4. On the anti-communist "united front" of Yeltsin's administration and the post-communist media, see Michael McFaul, *Russia's 1996 Presidential Election: The End of Polarized Politics* (Stanford, CA: Hoover Institution Press, 1997).

5. The Russian law on mass media, adopted in December 1991, was preceded by a Soviet media law framed the previous year by the same group of liberal experts inspired by a desire to provide legal safeguards of media independence from the state. See http://www.medialaw.ru/e_ pages/laws/russian/massmedia_eng/massmedia_eng.html.

6. Ellen Mickiewicz, *Changing Channels: Television and the Struggle for Power in Russia* (Oxford: Oxford University Press, 1997).

7. See the chapter about Vladimir Gusinsky in David E. Hoffman, *The Oligarchs: Wealth and Power in the New Russia* (New York: Public Affairs, 2002), 150–74.

8. Russian Public Television (ORT) gained control of the first national television channel in Russia through presidential decree no. 2133 on November 29, 1994, and began broadcasting on April 1, 1995. Several private companies purchased 49 percent; Berezovsky's Logovaz owned 8 percent of the shares, while the share of the state owners totaled more than 50 percent. Nonetheless, Berezovsky used side payments and bribes to gain control of the company's operations and editorial policy. See Paul Klebnikov, *Godfather of the Kremlin: Boris Berezovsky and the Looting of Russia* (New York: Harcourt, 2000), 159–61.

9. Hoffman, *The Oligarchs,* 325–64.

10. Glenn Waller, an Australian diplomat quoted in Hoffman, *The Oligarchs,* 322.

11. Nataliya Gevorkyan, Natalya Timakova, and Andrei Kolesnikov, *First Person: An Astonishingly Frank Self-Portrait by Russia's President Putin, Vladimir Putin,* trans. Catherine A. Fitzpatrick (New York: Public Affairs, 2000).

12. The 1999 parliamentary election turned out to be Russia's last truly competitive national election, and the competition was fierce and at times ugly. The operation of

Berezovsky's television was shocking even by Russian standards. The use of television as a tool for smearing the Kremlin's political rivals was driven to grotesque proportions by TV journalist Sergei Dorenko, hired to fulfill this mission by Boris Berezovsky. See Hoffman, *The Oligarchs*, 464–70.

13. For more detail about the campaign against Gusinsky and his media, see Maria Lipman and Michael McFaul, "Putin and the Media," in *Putin's Russia: Past Imperfect, Future Uncertain*, 2nd ed., ed. Dale R. Herspring (Lanham, MD: Rowman & Littlefield, 2005), 59–64; and Hoffman, *The Oligarchs*, 442–85.

14. Though the campaign against NTV caused public protest and two large protest rallies were held in Moscow, national polls suggested that "only 4 percent of the public regarded the NTV takeover as a government attempt to limit media freedom." Floriana Fossato, "The Russian Media: From Popularity to Distrust," *Current History* 100, no. 648 (2001): 343.

15. "Tainaia zapis': Abramovich i Berezovsky o Putine," BBC Russian, November 9, 2011, http://www.bbc.co.uk/russian/russia/2011/11/111108_abramovich_berezovsky_tape.shtml; "Berezovsky vs Abramovich: Abramovich kupil ORT za $10 mln," http://www.gazeta.ru/ business/2011/11/07/3825378.shtml1/2.

16. The fates of two channels, TV-6 and TVS, are discussed in more detail in Lipman and McFaul, "Putin and the Media," 64–67.

17. Peter Baker and Susan Glasser, *Kremlin Rising: Vladimir Putin's Russia and the End of Revolution* (New York: Lisa Drew/Scribner, 2005), 89. Putin's even more emotional statements were quoted in *Kommersant-Vlast'*, "Vstrecha s rodnymi," August 29, 2000, https://www. kommersant.ru/doc/17499.

18. According to the testimony in the above-cited litigation between Abramovich and Berezovsky, the coverage of the *Kursk* disaster by ORT was the final reason why Putin demanded that Berezovsky relinquish control of the largest national TV channel. Putin was cited as saying that he would be personally in charge of ORT.

19. Baker and Glasser, *Kremlin Rising*, 174–75. https://www.svoboda.org/a/24192493.html.

20. Baker and Glasser, *Kremlin Rising*, 34–35.

21. For a detailed description of the electoral reform, see Nikolai Petrov, "Kakaia vlast'—takie i vybory, kakie vybory—takaia i vlast' (ob itogakh izbiratel'nogo tsykla 2007–2008 gg.)," *Carnegie Moscow Center Briefing Paper* 10, no. 2 (2008).

22. Putin personally set the tone for this campaign by emphasizing that "he who pays the piper calls the tune." See "Vstrechi s predstaviteliami razlichnykh soobshchestv," July 5, 2005, http://archive.kremlin.ru/appears/2005/07/20/1801_type63376type63378type63381_91644. shtm.

23. According to the Levada Center's polls, Putin's approval rating in 2007–2008 ranged between 79 and 88 percent. See http://www.levada.ru/indeksy.

24. Vasily Gatov, "How the Kremlin and the Media Ended Up in Bed Together," March 11, 2015. https://www.themoscowtimes.com/2015/03/11/how-the-kremlin-and-the-media-ended-up-in-bed-together-a44663.

25. Over the years, targets of TV smearing campaigns included Mikhail Khodorkovsky, once Russia's richest man, deemed a dangerous rival by Putin and some in his close circle. Khodorkovsky was prosecuted, served ten years in jail, and

eventually was forced out of Russia; another target was foreign-funded nongovernment organizations. Russian television fomented anti-Georgian sentiments in the time of the Georgian war in 2008. In 2010, national TV vilified Moscow mayor, Yury Luzhkov, who wouldn't resign at the Kremlin's request. Following the annexation of Crimea, federal TV channels became a tool of raw anti-American and anti-Ukrainian propaganda.

26. In its final report on the Russian 2004 presidential election, the OSCE/ODIHR Election Observation Mission stated, "the State-controlled media comprehensively failed to meet its legal obligation to provide equal treatment to all candidates, displaying clear favoritism towards Mr. Putin," March 14, 2004, https://www.osce.org/odihr/elections/russia/33101? download=true.

27. Maria Lipman, "In Russia It's No Contest," *Washington Post*, December 1, 2004, http:// www.carnegieendowment.org.

28. "Rankings of Russian Leaders and the Situation in the Country," Levada Center, March 4, 2010, http://www.levada.ru/press/2010030404.html. See also Mikhail Fishman and Konstantin Gaaze, "Efir dlia dvoikh," *Russian Newsweek*, August 4, 2008, accessible at http://www.compromat.ru/page_23142.htm; Maria Lipman, "Freedom of Expression without Freedom of the Press," *Journal of International Affairs* 63, no. 2 (2010): 153–69.

29. On various forms of government subsidies to media, see Gatov, "How the Kremlin and the Media Ended Up in Bed Together." For instance, the state subsidizes signal transmissions to smaller cities (under two hundred thousand residents).

30. Channel One and Rossiia were by far the largest in terms of capitalization and were the largest recipients of advertising revenues. In 2010 these two major federal television channels received about 40 percent of all the TV advertising revenues in Russia.

31. An investigation conducted in 2014 by the internet resource rbc.ru produced a fairly complex chart illustrating the ownership structure of the National Media Group. Since the companies and individuals mentioned in the publication refused to comment, the authors opted for evasive phrases, such as "companies controlled by Yury Kovalchuk." The investigation maintains that three other major tycoons belonging to Putin's inner circle—the Rotenberg brothers and Gennady Timchenko, as well as Putin's friend of many years, musician Sergei Roldugin—also have stakes in NMG. Igor Terentiev, "Iashchik Rotenbergov: kak milliardery sviazany s Natsional'noi media gruppoi," November 17, 2014, https://www.rbc.ru/business/17/11/2014/5468ae40cbb20f2878362373. See also Maria Lipman, Anna Kachkaeva, and Michael Poyker, "Media in Russia: Between Modernization and Monopoly," in *The New Autocracy: Information, Politics and Policy in Putin's Russia*, ed. Daniel Treisman (Washington, DC: Brookings Institution, 2018), 159–90.

32. Konstantin Gaaze, "Otdel'no vziatyi telekanal," February 9, 2011, http://www.forbes.ru/ ekonomika-opinion/vlast/63087-otdelno-vzyatyi-telekanal. According to one estimate, by the end of 2013, the NMG media empire de facto controlled eleven of the largest Russian TV channels, 60 percent of the television audience, and 80 percent of the television advertisement revenues. Dmitry Kamyshev, Olga Beshlei, and

Zhanna Ul'ianova, "Kooperativ 'Ozero': efir vziat," *New Times*, December 2, 2013, http://www.newtimes.ru/articles/detail/74981?sphrase_ id=237051.

33. Polina Rusiaeva and Yelizaveta Surganova, "Mediakompanii Kovalchuka i Mordashova otsenili v 150 mlrd rublei," March 31, 2016, http://www.rbc.ru/technology_and_media/31/03/2016/56fcf20c9a7947dd35dbd00f?from=main.

34. Bank Rossiia acquired VI in 2010. Kseniya Boletskaya, "'Video International' smenil khozyaev," June 28, 2010, http://www.vedomosti.ru/business/articles/2010/06/28/video-interneshnl-smenil-hozyaev.

35. About "media oligopoly," see Maria Lipman et al., "Media in Russia."

36. Ksenia Boletskaya, "National Media Group Will Be Headed by Olga Paskina" ("Natsionalnuyu media gruppu vozglavit Olga Paskina"), Vedomosti, www.vedomosti.ru/technology/articles/2016/03/17/634079-nmg.

37. "Russia Takes Direct Control of Top Social Media Networks." The Bell. December 6, 2021, https://thebell.io/en/russia-takes-direct-control-of-top-social-media-networks/?fbclid=IwAR3ttLXgYjySXRanvHRCb67yaAefbTpAOnfqviZmn ubbENOovwUHMjXap2U.

38. Maria Lipman, "Constrained or Irrelevant: The Media in Putin's Russia," *Current History* 104, no. 684 (2005): 319–24.

39. For example, radio *Ekho Moskvy* was repeatedly threatened when its coverage angered Putin. See David Remnick, "Echo in the Dark," *New Yorker*, September 22, 2008, https://www. newyorker.com/magazine/2008/09/22/echo-in-the-dark. In 2012, *Ekho Moskvy* was threatened once again. See Maksim Ivanov, "My vsegda na kriuchke," *Kommersant*, March 30, 2012, https://www.kommersant.ru/doc/1903903.

40. https://www.rferl.org/a/1054709.html.

41. Aleksandr Gorbachev and Ilya Krasil'shchik, eds., *Istoriia russkikh media 1989–2011* (Moscow: Afisha, 2011), 295–97.

42. One of Medvedev's moves that inspired hopes of liberalization was his meeting with the top editor of *Novaia gazeta* (his first visit to a print outlet), a paper known for its exposure of the government's wrongdoings and its criticism of the Kremlin policies.

43. See Parfyonov's address at "Vlast' predstaet dorogim pokoinikom: o nej tol'ko khorosho ili nichego," November 25, 2010, http://www.kommersant.ru/doc/1546420. The coverage of the TV awards ceremonies censored out the unwanted lines.

44. Levada Center, March 20, 2012, http://www.levada.ru/20-03-2012/chislo-polzovatelei-interneta-rastet.

45. On examples of civic activism, see Masha Lipman, "Sleeping Giant, " Foreign Policy, August 19, 2010, https://foreignpolicy.com/2010/08/19/sleeping-giant/. For a more detailed account, see "Obshchestvo i grazhdane v 2008–2010 gg," Maria Lipman and Nikolay Petrov (eds.), Working Papers, Moscow Carnegie Center 2010, # 3, 2010, https://carnegieendowment.org/files/WP_3_2010_society.pdf.

46. Michael Idov, "The New Decembrists," *New York Magazine*, January 22, 2012, http:// nymag.com/news/features/russian-revolutionaries-2012–1.

47. "Koval'sky uvolitsia iz Kommersanta po soglasheniyu storon," December 16, 2011, https://lenta.ru/news/2011/12/16/kovalsky.

48. "Putin Orders Overhaul of Top State News Agency," RT, December 9, 2013, https:// www.rt.com/news/ria-novosti-overhaul-putin-960.

49. Masha Lipman, "Asking the Wrong Question on Russian TV," *New Yorker*, February 5, 2014, http://www.newyorker.com/news/daily-comment/asking-the -wrong-question-on-russian-tv.

50. David Remnick, "Putin Moves against the Press," *New Yorker*, March 12, 2014, http:// www.newyorker.com/news/daily-comment/putin-moves-against-the-press.

51. Anna Nemtsova, "Russia's Freest Website Now Lives in Latvia," November 29, 2014, http://www.thedailybeast.com/articles/2014/11/29/russia-s-freest-website-now -lives-in-latvia. html?via=desktop&source=facebook.

52. Nickolay Kononov, "The Kremlin's Social Media Takeover," *New York Times*, March 10, 2014, http://www.nytimes.com/2014/03/11/opinion/the-kremlins-social -media-takeover. html. In 2018, Pavel Durov found himself at the center of attention when the government moved to block his messenger Telegram.

53. Masha Lipman, "The Demise of RBC and Investigative Reporting in Russia," *New Yorker*, May 18, 2016, https://www.newyorker.com/news/news-desk/the-demise -of-rbc-and-investigative-reporting-in-russia. The editors hired to replace those who were dismissed or quit made it clear to the RBC team that their editorial policy would be more cautious. See https:// meduza.io/feature/2016/07/08/esli-kto-to-schitaet-chto- mozhno-pryamo-voobsche-vse-eto-netak. In another episode of media redistribution in favor of staunch loyalists, in June 2017 Prokhorov sold control of his troublesome media asset to energy tycoon Grigory Berezkin. Berezkin is not a major media holder, but he owns the pro-Kremlin tabloid *Komsomolskaya Pravda*, Russia's largest circu- lation daily; his loyalty to the Kremlin is not in doubt. See Max Seddon, "Mikhail Prokhorov Sells Control of Russian Media Outlet RBC," June 16, 2017, https://www .ft.com/content/37fd60b8-66b4-3b38-9286-4e7062c45229.

54. For a detailed report on the most recent repressive trends see https://liberal.ru/ lm-ekspertiza/god-navalnogo.

55. https://www.levada.ru/2021/07/09/otnoshenie-k-alekseyu-navalnomu/.

56. https://www.dw.com/ru/navalnyj-aresty-2011-2019-infografika/g-45620488.

57. https://www.nytimes.com/2021/02/21/business/media/probiv-investigative -reporting-russia.html.

58. Maxim Trudolyubov, "Russia's Half-Full Glasnost," The Russia File, Wil- son Center, July 15, 2019. https://www.wilsoncenter.org/blog-post/russias-half-full -glasnost. This article cites many publications contributing to what the author describes as a "vibrant media scene."

59. *Redkollegia* is Russian for "newsroom," http://redkollegia.org.

60. Aleksey Navalny's video on Dmitry Medvedev's amazing wealth was posted on March 2, 2017. "Don't Call Him 'Dimon,'" https://www.youtube. com/ watch?v=qrwlk7_GF9g.

61. *Putin's Palace. History of World's Largest Bribe.* https://www.youtube.com/ watch?v=ipAnwilMncI.

62. By late 2020, Dud's YouTube channel had over eight million subscrib- ers, and his regular audience is close to two million. http://m-m-g.ru/news/2020

/analiticheskaya-platforma-mmg-blogger-track-predstavlyaet-reyting-top-10
-blogerov-dlya-molodezhnoy-a/.

63. https://www.levada.ru/2021/02/03/smena-pokolenij-ne-budet-bystroj-i
-beskonfliktnoj/.

64. https://www.bbc.com/russian/features-55757215.

65. For updated lists of "foreign agents," see OVD.INFO, a civic human-rights organization that keeps track of political persecutions in Russia, https://ovdinfo.org /inoteka. In late December 2021, the government blocked the OVD.INFO website; on the Website of the Ministry of Justice, the list of individual journalists labeled "foreign agents" reached seventy-five, and that of media organizations amounted to thirty-six, https://minjust.gov.ru/ru/documents/7755/. For an account of the government's 2021 onslaught on media and journalists, see https://www.newyorker.com/ news/dispatch/the-victims-of-putins-crackdown-on-the-press.

66. In early May 2022 Proekt published a detailed investigation of why the Russian invasion of Ukraine did not go as planned. https://www.proekt.media/narrative/ kak-planirovali-voinu/.

67. Vasily Gatov, "Media in 2021: It's About to Get Worse," *Riddle*, December 22, 2021. https://ridl.io.en/media-in2021-it-s-about-to-get-worse/.

68. https://www.washingtonpost.com/world/europe/russia-telegram-kremlin-pavel -durov/2020/06/27/4928ddd4-b161-11ea-98b5-279a6479a1e4_story.html.

69. Tanya Lokot, "Ahead of September Elections, Russia Tightens Grip on Remaining Online Freedoms." *Global Voices*, September 16, 2021. https://globalvoices.org /2021/09/16/ahead-of-september-elections-russia-tightens-grip-on-remaining-online -freedoms/.

70. Sergei Guriev and Daniel Treisman, "Informational Autocrats," *Journal of Economic Perspectives* 33, no. 4 (Fall 2019): 100–27, https://pubs.aeaweb.org/doi/ pdfplus/10.1257/jep.33.4.100.

71. Trudolyubov, "Russia's Half-Full Glasnost."

72. See Steve Lee Myers, "With New Limits on Media, Putin Closes a Door on Russia's 'Openness'. "*New York Times*, March 7, 2022. htps://www.nytimes. com/2022/03/07/world/europe/russia-ukraine-putin-media.html.

73. Xenia Loutchenko, "Novoe russkoe slovo. S kem i o chem budet govorit' rossiiskaya zhurnalistika v izgnanii," *Republic*, May 26, 2022.

PART II

The Economy and Society

Chapter 7

Economic Policy

Laura Solanko and Pekka Sutela

The decade of the 1990s was not kind to the Russian economy. According to official statistics, during the decade the economy contracted up to 50 percent in industrial output, and another 40 percent of agricultural production was lost. In all, from 1990 to 1995, Russia's GDP declined by an estimated 50 percent, although some analysts argue that the true decline may have been somewhat less. Unemployment and labor unrest spiked. Russia experienced mass poverty. Inflation peaked at 2,509 percent in 1992, when most consumer prices were freed, and declined thereafter but failed to reach single digits during the remainder of the decade. The Russian government ran up enormous debt. The federal budget deficit fluctuated between 5 and 10 percent of GDP. As the decade wore on, budget deficits were financed by issuing short-term ruble-denominated government debt (government short-term obligations, or GKOs). Due to the size of the financial need, together with political and economic uncertainty, the GKOs could only be sold with very high yields, which ultimately reached 100 percent annually. The debt spiral was clearly unsustainable. Worse, about one-third of GKOs were held by foreigners, which added to exchange rate risk. The litany of economic troubles culminated in the ruble crisis of August 1998, when the state had to announce a partial default on its debt, and the ruble collapsed against foreign currencies. The ruble crisis had two main effects. First, Russia's credibility as a borrower was lost. Second, the crisis changed the framework for Russia's macroeconomic policy. A political consensus for macroeconomic stabilization had been reached in principle by 1995, but turning the consensus in principle into consistent practical policies had proven impossible.

The 1998 crisis marked an end to one phase in Russia's economic transformation. Thereafter, a new and stronger consensus emerged on economic policy. The new approach was introduced by the leftist Primakov-Masliukov government in 1998–1999 (against their early announcements) and continued to the end of the Yeltsin period. The new economic consensus had several ingredients, which defined the political economy of Putin's Russia.[1] The purpose of this chapter is to examine the elements of the post-1998 economic stabilization consensus and the new challenges in the post-2008 world.

THREE TASKS FOR THE EARLY 2000S

Draconian Fiscal Adjustment

The first task facing the new Putin regime in 2000 was balancing the budget. Continued accumulation of debt was not only potentially destabilizing but also in conflict with the goal of attaining economic sovereignty. Russia needed to do away with the need to finance its debt from external lenders. The only way to do this in the short term was to reduce expenditures, in particular the complex and nontransparent web of subsidies that had emerged behind the veil of economic liberalization in the 1990s at the federal, regional, and local levels. From 1997 to 2001 a fiscal adjustment of some 10 percent of general government balance was enacted, primarily by cutting expenditures, especially subsidies to companies.[2] In the short term, there was little alternative to this fiscal shock, as a return to monetizing deficits was excluded by the bitter experiences of the early 1990s. There was still a fiscal deficit of 4 percent of GDP in 1999, but thereafter the country experienced surpluses until the financial crisis of 2008–2009. Public foreign debt shrank from 66.8 percent of GDP in 1999 to 2.7 percent in 2007; total public debt remained less than 15 percent of GDP after 2005.[3] Russia, one of the grandest fiscal failures of the 1990s, emerged as a model for fiscal conservatism in just a few years. Necessity caused by failure was turned into virtue.

Russia's quest to balance the budget was helped by traditional export commodities—oil, gas, minerals, and, later, agricultural production. Exporters reaped great benefits from the cheap ruble and later from high prices, although their export volumes were often constrained by production and transport capacity. Russia was able to increase exports of oil and some minerals while exports of pipeline-tied gas stagnated. The world had an unprecedented golden period of economic growth during 1992–2008. Russia, with its newly privatized companies, was at last able to join booming global markets. From the trough of early 1998 to the peak in summer 2008, the export price of oil increased tenfold. Prices of Russia's other export commodities also increased, though generally not as much. Evsey Gurvich and Aleksei Kudrin estimate that the oil windfall alone reached up to 15 percent of GDP annually, while economists Clifford Gaddy and Barry Ickes give even higher estimates.[4] The price of oil was important for Russian incomes and budgets, but Russia was not able to live on oil revenue alone.

Reforming Oil Taxation

The second task was to fix the tax system. The state had fought a losing battle for more effective company taxation in the 1990s, especially under Minister of Finance Boris Fyodorov. The true state of company finances was hidden in nonmonetary exchanges and webs of implicit subsidies, especially at the regional level. It is estimated that only one-fifth of all transactions in and around the domestic energy sector were conducted in rubles. The state routinely accepted nonmonetary clearing of tax obligations. A construction company could have its tax arrears offset by contributing to a public construction project. What prices were used in calculating a proper offset remained unclear. With a ballooning export revenue windfall, this situation could no longer be accepted. Oligarchs, regional governors, and others had to be subordinated to an emerging "power vertical," to use Putin's words.

The share of the federal government in tax revenue increased, and most regions became dependent on tax transfers from the Moscow center. A stiff oil revenue taxation regime was introduced: the average tax rate rose to 60 percent, and the marginal tax rate even surpassed 90 percent.[5] The former figure is not exorbitant in international comparison, but the latter was, leaving hardly any incentives to increase upstream oil production. The confiscatory tax rate was corrected only years later. In 2014, the burden of oil-sector taxation shifted from taxing export revenue to taxing oil production.

Distributing the revenue windfall became a key policy issue that had not existed in the 1990s because of low oil prices. Logically there were three alternatives. The first alternative was that monies could be distributed among the population, to be used for consumption or private investment as households wished. In view of the income decline and hugely increased income differentials in the 1990s, this would have been a politically popular solution, but it was rejected by the regime as populism. Many resource-rich countries had shown evidence of the "Dutch disease" due to using high export revenue to increase money and wealth of the population, presumably for the general good, but actually leading to high inflation, an overvalued exchange rate, and lost competitiveness in non-resource production. The Putin regime was politically strong enough to avoid this option.

A second alternative had stronger political support and suggested using oil-sector tax revenue for investment in the economy at large. Though investment ratios were very high under Soviet socialism, evidence showed that much of the money used by the state had actually disappeared in hidden inflation, with little if any impact on actual production capacity. Russia thus inherited a capital stock that was smaller, older, and more worn out than official statistics claimed. What had been inherited from the Soviet Union was not what the emerging market economy needed. In addition, while official GDP had dropped by almost one-half in the 1990s, the collapse of investment was even steeper, some four-fifths. The country badly needed high real investment to grow in a sustainable way. Moreover, there was a need to close plants in and around the military sector, which produced very little of what was needed in a market economy. This side of capitalist creative destruction was, however, hardly raised in Russian debates. Protecting existing jobs has always been a priority that constrained economic choices in the Putin regime. One key question for the future is whether this basically conservative attitude will continue.

Because there was little optimism that foreign investment was sufficient to fund modernization, the argument was made that export revenue windfall should be invested into the economy, not only in roads, railways, and airports, but also in health, education, housing, innovation, and other such purposes that were seen as the responsibility of the state. This argument for development was made, not surprisingly, by the Ministry of Economic Development. Investment in the economy was to receive a major boost by the introduction of four "national programs" that took effect in 2006 with great fanfare, in health, housing, education, and agriculture. Dmitry Medvedev, as first deputy prime minister, was responsible for their implementation. Looking not at the budget plans but at their actual implementation, however, shows that the national programs' share as a proportion of all state expenditures never increased.

A final alternative proved the winner of policy debate. Russia opted for a fiscally conservative strategy of maintaining a budget surplus, paying back most public debt, and accumulating reserve funds. This course was pursued by Aleksei Kudrin, who served as the minister of finance from May 2000 to September 2011. The decisive voice for fiscal conservatism was that of Vladimir Putin. Steep taxation of oil export revenue was in place by 2004. Accumulation of a stabilization fund was started the same year. By the end of 2007 it amounted to $156.8 billion and a year later to $225.1 billion.[6] The growth was stupendous. As part of the official reserves of the country—peaking at just over $600 billion in mid-2008—these monies had a key role in combating the 2008 crisis. Just before the crisis, the stabilization fund had been divided into a reserve fund (for stabilizing fiscal revenue) and a national welfare fund (mostly for supporting the pension system).

Remonetizing Economic Transactions

The third task was transforming Russia from an economy based on barter to one based on rubles; in other words, the economy had to be monetized. A monetized economy increases the productivity of labor compared to an economy based on barter. In Russia, barter chains could have a number of participants, and the transaction costs involved in establishing and maintaining such chains were great. Barter has little transparency, exchange pricing could be arbitrary, avoiding taxation was easy, and the whole barter economy was prone to corruption. When barter was used in lieu of taxation, the efficiency of public finance obviously suffered. Goods obtained in barter can only be used for limited purposes. On the other hand, money facilitates risk control, saving for investment, and economic growth. There is considerable evidence that monetary and financial systems contribute to economic growth. Berkowitz and DeJong show that financial development has been the key domestic driving force for Russia's economic growth.[7]

States usually wish to have complete or at least shared (in currency unions) control over the money circulating within their borders. It is a matter of prestige—sovereign currency being one of the defining features of a state—but more important is the economic benefit. Beyond that, sovereign currency opens up the possibility of monetary policy; its scope depends on foreign trade and trade payments. Russia liberalized its foreign trade in the early 1990s, but capital mobility was officially announced as a major achievement of economic policy only in 2006, and this attitude remains to this day. Russia has not introduced capital controls even in the face of the macroeconomic adversity of 2014–2015.

There was some speculation in the 1990s that Russia's nonmonetary market economy was nationally specific, an outcome of the Soviet economy. However, as predicted by standard economic theory, the Russian economy monetized and de-dollarized quickly as inflation was brought under control and the exchange rate stabilized. At its peak in late 1998, barter accounted for 61 percent of manufacturing turnover. The ratio normalized to about 10 percent within a few years.[8]

The ruble had lost much of its credibility in the early 1990s, and continued high inflation made it difficult to reestablish. Savings held in rubles were lost in 1992, to some degree in 1994, and again more widely in 1998. Dollars remained for a few years rare in Russia, but the share of foreign currency deposits as a percentage of all deposits peaked at more than 40 percent after 1998.[9] From 1999 to 2007 deposit dollarization declined gradually, especially after 2003 when the ruble began to appreciate due to high export revenue. In early 2008 deposit dollarization hit a minimum of 12 to 13 percent, but the possibility of dollarization remains real. This was seen at the peak of the financial crisis and again in 2014, when lower oil prices and economic stagnation led both to a weaker ruble and avoidance of using it as a currency reserve.

ECONOMIC POLICIES TAKING SHAPE

Monetary Policy

Russia's transformation into a money-based economy was one of the major positive changes of the early 2000s. However, Russian financial markets still remained small and underdeveloped relative to the size of the economy, which had implications for the conduct of monetary policy.

Toward Inflation Targeting

Turning first to inflation, table 7.1 indicates that inflation was on a downward trend, from 13.7 percent in 2003 to 9.7 percent in 2006. In 2008 it again increased. Some of the increase may be explained by external factors: the global economy was in overdrive, global food prices increased, and though Russia is among the three biggest exporters of grain, it imports many other foodstuffs. There was also domestic overheating with excess demand for skilled city-based labor and construction materials in particular. Fiscal policy was procyclical as it targeted the budget surplus. As revenue was increased by higher export tariff incomes, expenditures increased as well. The ruble devaluation of fall 2008 raised import prices.

Table 7.1. Russian Economic Indicators (year-on-year change in percent)

	2003	2004	2005	2006	2007	2008	2009	2010	2011
Inflation	13.7	10.9	12.7	9.7	9.0	14.1	11.7	6.9	8.4
Broad Money (M2)	50.4	35.8	38.5	48.7	43.5	0.8	17.7	31.1	21.0
GDP	7.3	7.2	6.4	8.2	8.5	5.2	−7.8	4.5	4.3
Fixed investments	12.7	16.8	10.2	17.8	23.8	9.5	−13.5	6.3	10.8
Household real incomes	14.6	11.2	11.7	14.1	13.1	3.9	1.8	5.9	1.2

	2012	2013	2014	2015	2016	2017	2018	2019	2020
Inflation	5.1	6.8	7.8	15.5	7.1	3.7	2.9	4.5	3.4
Broad Money (M2)	12.2	14.7	1.5	11.3	9.2	10.5	11.0	9.7	13.5
GDP	4.0	1.8	0.7	−2.0	0.2	1.8	2.8	2.0	−3.0
Fixed investments	6.8	0.8	−1.5	−10.1	−0.2	4.8	5.4	2.1	−1.4
Household real incomes	5.8	4.8	−0.8	−3.6	−4.5	−0.2	1.4	1.7	−2.6

Source: BOFIT Russia Statistics, Rosstat.

After 2008, inflation continued to decline to 6 percent in 2011. Many Russians blame inflation on the monopolized structure of the economy, but that is a valid explanation only if monopoly profits increase continuously or the efficiency of monopoly producers keeps declining. Some of the stubborn level of inflation is due to needed hikes of tariffs for gas, electricity, and transportation. More importantly, before the switch to a free float in the end of 2014, fighting inflation was not the Central Bank's sole priority.

Most central banks concentrate on inflation control, perhaps together with maintaining an acceptable level of employment, as the Federal Reserve does. The Russian Central Bank has targeted both keeping inflation on a downward trend and stabilizing the ruble exchange rate. The latter has been desirable due to the continuing risk of dollarization. In practice, as long as export revenue kept increasing, the Central Bank increased the ruble supply, as shown in table 7.1.

A booming ruble supply should preferably have been sterilized, that is, withdrawn from the market by selling government or Central Bank bonds. As bond markets remained very small—and the state did not need them for financing budget deficits—this option did not work. The Central Bank did issue its bonds, but not so much to sterilize as to offer an asset in which to park excess liquidity. There has been no distinct effect on the financial markets stemming from Central Bank issuance of bonds.[10]

The Central Bank of Russia first shifted its strategy to inflation targeting and full exchange rate flexibility as longer-term goals around mid-decade. Russia finally announced that inflation targeting would take place in the beginning of 2015. As the ruble came under pressure in the currency market, the shift was brought forward to November 2014. A shift to inflation targeting implies a shift from rough policy instruments like reserve ratios to more market-based policy instruments like interest rates. A critical precondition for the shift is that the financial markets are sophisticated enough to be responsive to changes in Central Bank key rates. A country that has segmented markets, lack of trust, negative real interest rates, and excess liquidity in the banking system was not an obvious candidate.

The Central Bank had the clear backing of the political leadership in pushing through the shift. The nominal interest rate was raised to 17 percent in December 2014, making real interest rates positive. While extremely tight monetary policy discouraged bank lending, it had the desired effect on inflation. Toward the end of 2017, market participants have begun to adjust to the new monetary policy regime. Both headline inflation and inflation expectations have declined to levels never before experienced in Russia. The inflation rate fell back to single digits after 2015 and remained below 5 percent in 2017–2020. Recent studies note a clear break in the Central Bank's policy rules in early 2015.[11]

Exchange Rate Policy

The Central Bank chose to maintain a stable nominal exchange rate up to 2009, first pegging to the dollar and then to a bi-currency basket that reflected the structure of Russia's foreign trade (55 percent USD/45 percent euro). The value of the ruble was maintained by interventions in foreign exchange markets. There was pressure on the ruble to appreciate, as much of the ballooning export revenue was exchanged into rubles, thus strengthening demand for domestic currency. The Central Bank sold rubles and bought foreign currency. There is no hard evidence that the ruble was overvalued in 1998, but it was clearly undervalued after the devaluation. As no country with an open economy can choose a real exchange rate of its liking, real appreciation of the ruble was inevitable in the 2000s. As the nominal exchange rate was kept stable, real appreciation had to happen through domestic inflation that was higher than abroad.

Targeting the nominal exchange rate was understandable given Russia's history of dollarization and the goal of de-dollarization. Shifts in asset allocation between the ruble and foreign currencies have been sensitive to the real exchange rate between currencies, a matter of rational market behavior. Targeting the exchange rate may also have been inevitable as the Central Bank did not have a monetary policy channel through which to choose a suitable money supply. There was a lot of uncertainty about demand for money. Fine-tuning the money supply was also impossible as the behavioral patterns of the small but fast-growing banking sector were largely untried. In the early 2000s, the Russian Central Bank mostly concentrated on fighting money laundering and other violations of regulation, in the process learning little of actual bank behavior. There was a target for annual money growth, but that was traditionally missed by wide margins, with no negative consequences for the Central Bank. Nor could the Central Bank easily use interest rates to regulate demand for money. With little market for interest-bearing assets and negative real interest rates, the interest rate channel was of little importance.

Beginning in 2009, the Central Bank gradually withdrew from foreign exchange markets, and the exchange rate policy moved to a managed float. The width of the corridor changed over time. The exchange rate was allowed to move freely within the corridor. If it approached either of the set corridor boundaries, the Central Bank intervened. If the change in markets was deemed permanent, the corridor itself was shifted. This situation changed in December 2014 when the Central Bank allowed the ruble to float freely along with the fall in the price of oil. Most central banks, including Russia's, combine inflation targeting with a floating exchange rate.

The adjustment to floating exchange rate was not an easy one. All economic agents had to adjust to a volatile exchange rate—not a simple task in an economy where many contracts and, for example, rental agreements in prime locations were still specified in dollars. Nevertheless, the floating ruble has brought tangible benefits for the economy. Since 2014 fluctuations in oil prices have had a much smaller effect on public finances and the economy as a whole as the weakening ruble has taken most of the hit.

FISCAL POLICY

Taxation

Before 2010 the main responsibility for fighting inflation remained with fiscal policy. Most windfall oil export revenue was and still is taxed by the state. Energy-sector taxation—including export tariffs and natural resource exploitation payments—has accounted for roughly one-half of federal fiscal revenue. Russia is dependent on energy for exports and tax revenue, but not directly for jobs. Less than 2 percent of all Russian jobs are in extracting and transporting basic energy.[12]

Taming the oil sector for taxation has been a major challenge. Oil companies have been able to minimize their taxation by using such vehicles as transfer pricing[13] and both domestic and offshore tax havens. Consequently, many analysts have concluded that official statistics grossly underestimate the energy sector's true contribution to GDP (probably somewhere between 20 and 30 percent, rather than below 10 percent as shown in official statistics).[14] Tax authorities have been unable to trust the bookkeeping values and profits of oil companies. Company taxation has therefore not been based on profits but on trade turnover.

Taxation of oil and oil companies is also complicated by the changing structure of production. As long as almost all production took place in conditions similar to those of the traditional supergiant fields of Western Siberia, the taxation system did not matter too much. Production, however, must now increasingly move into high-cost and widely differing far eastern and northern conditions. Taxation by turnover discriminates severely against investment in such fields, which are needed for maintaining national production levels. Consequently, both oil and gas producers have received tax exemptions, first in the Far East and in the North as well. Turnover-based taxation that was supposed to be similar for all has thus given way to negotiated taxation, a certain recipe for influence peddling and outright corruption in the heart of Russia's export and tax revenue. This situation helps to explain why energy-sector taxation has been in turmoil for decades. The current shift from export revenue taxation toward a key role of natural resource exploitation payments hardly changes the situation.

Contrary to most advanced market economies, Russia receives very little revenue from the taxation of personal income, accounting for only a couple of percent of GDP; most government revenue comes from foreign trade, commodity taxes, and profit tax, as well as from social security contributions. Income tax avoidance has traditionally been rife. Russia therefore did not engage in a huge fiscal risk when it was one of the first Central and Eastern European countries to introduce a flat tax of 13 percent on all income in 2001. The goal was to decrease tax avoidance. Studies show that the impact on tax avoidance was much greater than on labor supply.[15] Russia's adoption of a flat income tax is seen as one of the major economic policy achievements of the early Putin regime. Introducing progressive income taxation regularly figures in further tax reform proposals, especially in those coming from experts with a European egalitarian value orientation. The prospects for abandoning the flat income tax, however, remain weak. It is likely to remain a feature of Russian capitalism.

Regional Revenue

Russia is, according to the 1993 constitution, a federation. Since 1992, relations between the center and regions have changed thoroughly. During the Yeltsin years, regions were much more independent and less beholden to the center. In the 1990s, regional revenues as a share of total state revenues increased from 40 percent in 1992 to about 55 percent in 1997–1998.[16] One might have expected the regions to do their utmost to widen the tax base by promoting new entrepreneurship. Instead, existing large enterprises, which had their roots in Soviet-era conglomerates, captured the state. Both regional and local authorities tended to protect existing jobs through taxation, regulation, and corruption.[17] This situation was partly due to the importance of several hundred one-company towns, usually based on military-industrial companies, that had little future. Simultaneously, regional expenditures as a share of total expenditures also rose from less than 30 percent to about 55 percent.

The relationship between the center and regions changed in many ways when Putin came to power. Putin took several steps to reestablish the primacy of centralized power beginning in 2000. Establishing "the vertical of power," the Putin regime aimed at controlling regional political and economic elites. The share of regional expenditures declined only slightly, to about one-half of total expenditures. In contrast, the share of regional revenues fell significantly, to about 35 percent in 2005.[18] On average, therefore, regions became dependent on transfers from the center. Even though direct elections of regional governors were reinstated in 2012, the president retained the de facto right to dismiss and nominate any candidate. Thus, regions and regional leadership remained dependent on financial support by the Kremlin. Loyalty to the party in power is awarded by promotions or financial assistance. Loyalty is measured by voter turnout and share of votes for the party in power, not by a region's economic prosperity.[19]

Budget Rules

Budget expenditures tend to increase when the economy is booming. This was clearly the case in Russia in the latter half of the 2000s, when budget expenditures contributed to overheating the economy. Current expenditure decisions often imply longer-term spending commitments. Basing expenditure decisions on temporarily high, but intrinsically volatile, oil revenue is fiscally irresponsible. For well over a decade, the International Monetary Fund has argued that fiscal policy should be based on maintaining a constant "non-oil" deficit, defined as expenditure minus revenue, assuming some "normal" oil price and ensuing revenues. While the argument for using a non-oil deficit constraint on expenditure commitments is compelling, the apparent simplicity of the non-oil deficit concept is deceptive.

In spring 2012, Russian authorities debated whether the "normal oil price" should be the average of the past ten years (as the fiscally conservative Ministry of Finance argued) or the past three years (as preferred by the high-spending Ministry of Economic Development). This seeming technicality does not have a self-evident answer but implies huge differences in expenditure levels, as the average oil price of 2010–2012 was much higher than for 2001–2012.

The revised budget rule, finally adopted in late 2012, restricted the federal budget deficit to 1 percent of annual forecasted GDP from 2013 to 2015. The collapse of oil prices in late 2014 and the subsequent recession made it impossible for the government to adhere to the rule. The newest budget rule was adopted in summer 2017. Under the current rule, the federal primary budget balance must be zero or positive with estimated budget revenues. The estimate uses a base average oil price of $40 per barrel that is increased by 2 percent each year. All budget revenue from production and export of oil and gas above the base oil price is to be transferred to the National Welfare Fund.[20] The base oil price, a very conservative estimate of future oil prices, reflects a hard-earned understanding that a world of permanently high oil prices may be illusory. The promise of a huge transfer of income to Russia's next generation no longer seems guaranteed.

RESPONSES TO EXTERNAL SHOCKS

The 2008–2009 Financial Crisis

The global financial crisis that started in late 2008 and extended through 2009 revealed how dependent the Russian economy is on swings in global markets. The first impact was on export prices, led by oil and followed by minerals and then gas. When the crisis hit, there was a lot of uncertainty about the coming pattern of the crisis. Although some expected a fast dip followed by an equally fast global recovery (a v-shaped crisis), the majority opinion in Russia, as elsewhere, foresaw a long recession (a u-shaped crisis). Amid the uncertainty, the collapse of global commodity prices occurred faster and deeper than was justified in retrospect. When fears of a u-shaped recession gave way to optimism for a v-shaped upswing, global oil prices also recovered quickly.

The second impact was on Russia's export volumes. For example, steel exports were cut in half practically overnight, as European construction activity was curtailed. More important for the long run, in the beginning of 2009, Russia and Ukraine got involved in another dispute over gas prices, transit tariffs, and the settlement of accumulated Ukrainian debt for gas. At the time four-fifths of Russian gas exports to Europe crossed Ukrainian territory, and supplies to Central Europe were disrupted exactly at the time when relatively cheap liquefied natural gas (LNG) was entering markets in large amounts. Russia's reliability as gas supplier was compromised, and its gas export prices seemed inflated. The Russian-Ukrainian crisis has further undermined Europe's willingness to depend on Russia for a quarter of its gas consumption.

The third and arguably most important impact was that global investors started pulling their monies out of all peripheral markets. Russian public and private entities were not deep in debt, but existing debt was short term, it had increased quickly, and investors grew pessimistic about Russia's overall economic prospects since they tended to see them through the prism of oil prices. Foreign short-term finance had maintained what existed as interbank markets, and now that it was withdrawn, the wheels of Russian finance were quickly slowing down. Another full-scale financial crisis was threatening Russia, and were financial markets to stall, the impact on production, incomes, and employment would be drastic as well.

In responding to the 2008–2009 financial crisis, Russia chose an expensive policy alternative. Some $200 billion in official reserves were used to satisfy demand for foreign currencies. But this money did not just disappear. Some of it was used to service private foreign debt, which declined by about $100 billion during the crisis.[21] The remainder of the reserves that were expended were shifted from public reserves into private assets. Most important, devaluation did not lead to a continuous spiral fed by further expectations of further devaluation as experts had expected. What had failed elsewhere somehow succeeded in Russia.

Like other countries, the Russian government supported both its financial sector and the real economy. A large portion of the support was channeled to huge manufacturing enterprises whose profitability was questionable at best. The crisis measures helped in keeping employment high but also cemented old and inefficient production structures for years to come. Not only did the non-oil deficit widen to almost 15 percent of GDP, but large commitments were also left as a fiscal burden for future years.

The Recession of 2015–2016

Recovery from the effects of the global financial crisis was rapid, as oil prices returned to precrisis levels by early 2011. After the rapid recovery, growth rates began to slow. Investment growth turned negative in 2013. For reasons that are unclear, domestic investors assessed that the rate of return to risk was better elsewhere. When oil prices collapsed again in the latter half of 2014, the Russian economy was hardly growing at all. Moreover, the global environment was less benign than at any time since the collapse of the Soviet Union.

The illegal annexation of Crimea and the war in eastern Ukraine led Western countries to impose economic sanctions on Russia. The sanctions severely restricted the access of several of Russia's largest corporations and commercial banks to global financial markets. Russia retaliated by banning imports of certain foodstuffs from the European Union, the United States, and other countries. These countersanctions naturally increased consumer prices and contributed to a decrease in household real incomes.

The fiscal policy reaction to the crisis was expected. The budget rule was temporarily lifted, and federal expenditures were allowed to remain intact. The monetary policy framework changed dramatically as the Central Bank shifted to inflation targeting. Suddenly the ruble was allowed to fluctuate freely, leading to a sizable devaluation. A weaker ruble made domestic production more attractive and smoothed the effect of falling oil prices on government revenue. At the same time, however, monetary policy became extremely tight. To fight ballooning inflation and support the currency, the Central Bank's key rate was raised from 5.5 to 17 percent in December 2014.

The resulting recession was milder than in 2009, wiping out less than 3 percent of Russian GDP in 2015–2016. In contrast to the previous crisis, real incomes took a serious hit. Household real incomes were almost 10 percent lower in 2016 than in 2013. Economic recession and the increasing role of the state in the economy may have seriously hampered social upward mobility, lowering the potential growth rate in the future.

The Double Shock of 2020

As oil prices rose and the immediate effects of the sanctions turned out to be less devastating than some pessimists feared, the Russian economy again recovered relatively quickly. Russian GDP surpassed its 2014 level in 2018 and, fueled by increasing exports, grew by a further 2 percent in 2019. To support oil prices Russia participated in OPEC production cuts in 2017–2019, but domestic opposition to further cuts constantly increased. As the OPEC+ agreement ended in March 2020, Russia surprised everyone by walking away from further negotiations. Oil prices duly collapsed. At the end of February 2020, Urals crude traded at 50 usd per barrel, by the end of March one barrel was worth less than 20 usd.

These Russian negotiation tactics managed to collapse oil prices precisely when the COVID-19 pandemic hit the global economy and the first wave of infections threatened to overwhelm the domestic healthcare system. It took only a few days for the authorities to realize the self-inflicted damage, and a new agreement on oil production cuts was signed by mid-April. To ease the pressure on health care, most businesses were ordered to close for the month of April, and the national referendum on constitutional amendments was postponed from April to July.

Overall, the pandemic-related restrictions were relatively mild in Russia, a fact that was reflected in very high excess mortality in 2020–2021. The Russian economy, however, fared relatively well, and the drop in GDP (–3 percent) was clearly smaller than in most European economies or in the United States. While the relatively mild pandemic-related restrictions did play a role in averting deeper recession, the main reason was a combination of fiscal policy response and the inherited structure of the economy. The share of services in Russian GDP is still slightly lower than in high-income economies. The difference is especially pronounced in the hospitality sector, which tended to suffer most from COVID-19 related restrictions.

Conservative fiscal policies ensured sizable fiscal surpluses and low debt levels. Once the economic effects of the COVID-19 pandemic became visible, fiscal policy could react fast. The measures included temporarily broadening social support for the most vulnerable groups and various forms of support to the businesses. When debt guarantees and capital injections are included, the total cost of additional fiscal measures was 4.5 percent of GDP in 2020—mostly financed by domestic borrowing. Moreover, the Central Bank had ample room to maneuver. The CBR supported the economy by cutting the key rate from 6.5 percent to a historical low of 4.25 percent and by temporarily relaxing various banking regulations.[22] Once more, buffers created via conservative fiscal and monetary policies helped to maintain economic stability.

NEW TASKS FOR THE 2020S

New Policy Programs to Tackle Old Problems

Toward the end of the 2000s, the critical tasks of post-1998 economic stabilization had been achieved. Thanks to rising oil prices and a greatly streamlined tax system, the federal budget was running sizable surpluses, and the economy had been successfully remonetized. As the urgency of fixing the system waned, a wide consensus emerged that Russia's economic development could not be based on oil and gas. Experts projected that oil production would increase little, if at all. Maintaining current export volumes demanded major improvement in the notoriously low energy efficiency of the economy. Gas prices in particular had to be increased to reach international levels. Households and jobs could no longer be subsidized by artificially low energy prices. Modernization and diversification were badly needed. That was the message of the first "Russia 2020" economic program that was passed in late 2008. The 2008 global crisis, however, postponed most attempts to implement the program. Its goal of making Russia an innovation-based society by 2020 was utopian at best.

The problems were real enough, and another attempt was needed. In January 2011, then prime minister Vladimir Putin gave the Russian economic expert community the task of "writing the economic program of the post–May 2012 government." The document produced by more than one thousand experts was published in March 2012.[23] At 864 pages, it is not a policy program but rather a wide-ranging survey of policy tasks, many of them complex and demanding. Within two months, this vast document had been condensed into "May Decrees" (*Maiskie ukazi*) that President Putin signed in conjunction with his inauguration address on May 7, 2012.[24] The May Decrees required the Medvedev government to fulfill a range of tasks varying from increasing the country's overall labor productivity by 150 percent to increasing the share of domestically produced critical medicine to 90 percent. Little remained of the original program document's notions of enhancing the public-private partnership or reforming the country's social policy framework.

The approach taken in the May 2012 Decrees underlines three broad issues. First, the Putin regime increasingly believes in state-led development. Private enterprise and free competition, with all the uncertainty inherent in a free market economy, is not favored. The worldview of the decrees is one of "manual control," whereby economic development occurs by establishing and fulfilling detailed targets singled out by the president. Second, the leadership acknowledges that the growth model of the 2000s is no longer relevant. Many of the drivers of past growth were transient, and the world economy can no longer be expected to provide as benign an environment for Russia as before.

Third, the regime clearly lacks a strategic view on how Russia is supposed to prosper. This lack of vision has resulted in a multitude of narrow, sector-specific development programs that in many cases support vested interests with the aim of maintaining employment.[25] In this respect, the approach of the May 2012 Decrees was closer to reality than that of the Russia 2020 strategy.

Following the practice of previous election cycles, preparation of new economic policy strategies for the post–May 2018 presidency began in late 2016. This time the task was assigned to two competing groups. The first group was led by the conservative Stolypin Club, while the second aligned around the liberal-minded Center for Strategic Studies. Both groups acknowledged that Russia badly needed more investment, the pension system required reform, and the competitiveness of domestic industries had to be improved. Neither program was officially published, but the "May Decree" that President Putin signed in conjunction with his fourth inauguration in May 2018 mentions many of the ideas favored by the more liberal group. The underlying approach to economic development, however, is no different from the previous decrees. The focus remained in fine-tuning the existing structures, not in reforming them.

The May 2018 Decree ordered the Medvedev government to create twelve national programs for years 2018–2024 in areas ranging from digital economy to demography to guarantee that the country achieves "breakthroughs in science and technology and socioeconomic development."[26] The new national programs were duly launched in early 2019, but, as before, implementation has not been impressive. The new Mishustin government was clearly expected to prioritize national programs, but fighting the COVID-19 pandemic naturally has taken precedence since early 2020. The national programs include several important and ambitious targets in health care and education, for example, but there are no mentions of reforms to improve the business climate, streamline public administration, or foster competition. All of these would be necessary to support economic well-being in the future.

New Challenges Emerging

The current regime clearly believes in state-led economic development driven by sectoral programs and executive orders. This approach is hardly suited to address the structural weaknesses of the Russian economy. And it may make addressing new challenges especially difficult.

Due to increases in social benefits (especially pensions) the share of people living below the official poverty line declined from about 30 percent in the early 2000s to 13 percent in 2010, and the share has remained at about 12 percent for the last decade. Income inequality as measured by the Gini index has actually decreased since the global financial crisis. As a result, Russia's income inequality is still higher than in almost any other European country, but lower than in the United States or in most Latin American economies. One reason for relatively high income inequality is Russia's flat tax system. Personal income taxes are not progressive and have a flat rate of 13 percent. Moreover, mainly due to the Soviet legacy, most social benefits are not means-tested or targeted to the poor. Additionally, the costs of moving to big cities for better-paying jobs are often prohibitively high, keeping inter-regional mobility in Russia at very low levels.[27]

The June 2020 decision to increase income tax to 15 percent for the top earners can be seen as a baby step toward recognizing the problem. The real effects of the amendment are likely to be minor. As introducing a meaningful tax or benefits reform is out of the question, social policies are left with very few means. In recent years the focus has been in increasing social support for families with small children. The aim of those policy decisions has not been in supporting the poor or decreasing income inequality but rather in increasing the birth rate to reverse the unfavorable demographic development. The Russian population is aging fast, shaking the sustainability of the pension system. Increasing old age pension benefits, improving life expectancy, low birth rates, and low pension age is a toxic combination for public finances. The decision to gradually increase retirement age to 55 for women and 60 to men is only a partial answer to calls for a real reform in the pension system.

The huge inequalities in Russian society are mainly created by wealth inequality. The difference in wealth between the super-rich and the rest is staggering, and Russia is often listed among the most unequal economies globally. Partly unequal wealth distribution is linked to how privatization proceeded in the early 1990s. Housing wealth was distributed practically free of charge. As a result, households living in centers of large cities in the end of the 1980s got a huge advantage compared to households in remote regions or small villages. Enterprise privatization by vouchers and via loans-for-shares eventually resulted in ownership ending in the hands of a very few businessmen, who were called oligarchs because of their political influence under Yeltsin.

Extreme wealth inequality easily creates a sense of unfairness and decreases support for the regime. Tackling the problem would, however, seriously harm the economic prospects of the elites, making any such policy highly unlikely.

Wealth inequality may cause long-lasting harm for economic development, especially if it is coupled with close connections between business and politics.[28] Unfortunately, Russia is a prime example of such an economy.

Despite economic growth and no marked increase in poverty, real disposable income of an average Russian has not increased since 2013. In 2020 real incomes dropped below the levels of 2010. At the same time financial wealth of the super-rich has continued to increase, making the gap (both perceived and real) between the rich and the majority even bigger. Addressing concerns about inequalities in the society is difficult for policy makers everywhere. But a combination of slow economic growth, stagnant real incomes, staggering wealth inequality, weak institutions, and very limited room for legal political opposition may make the task an impossible one.

Hopes for serious reforms that would address the structural weaknesses of the Russian economy are not high. The regime feels no urgency to embark on necessary reforms that are by their nature complex and difficult to implement. And the incumbent industrial firms have no interest in making the economy more transparent or competitive. The Russian economy is still capable of generating a tolerable standard of living for most of the population. But the lack of structural reforms signifies weak growth prospects for the majority of the population. This may partly explain the regime's desire to nurture patriotic feelings and to suppress political opposition.

This looming stagnation raises fundamental issues. How can the business environment be improved to facilitate long-term investment? Assuming that Western sanctions are not lifted, where can financial resources be raised? And where should investment be made? How can upward social mobility be enhanced to increase productivity growth? Currently, Russia has a competitive advantage in natural resources, agriculture, and—potentially at least—information technology services. The growing importance of import-substitution policies makes it increasingly difficult to assess if any of these would be competitive in an open economy.

CONCLUSION

The economic policies of Putin's third and fourth terms have been based on conservative fiscal policies, a relatively independent inflation-targeting Central Bank, and increasingly protectionist trade policies. All of this has allowed the economy to weather the recessions of 2015–2016 and 2020 relatively unscathed but has resulted in declining real incomes and a growing role of the state in the economy.

For the most part, the future does not look very promising. Success in some sectors, for example in agriculture, which has been growing faster than national GDP since 2013, has not translated into economy-wide improvements.[29] Russian GDP grew on average by 7 percent annually in 2000–2008. The average growth in 2010–2020 was 1.6 percent. Most forecasters expect similar growth to prevail in the coming years, once the recovery from the 2020 recession is over.

To find new sources of growth, Russia needs a strategic view on how to prosper in the low-carbon future. Such a strategic view has been completely lacking since 2012. The focus in economic policies has increasingly shifted towards the Soviet tradition of fulfilling federally mandated numerical targets embedded in various national programs. After the extremely unpopular pension reform was finally approved in September 2018, mentions of any structural reforms have all but disappeared from policy discussions. The remaining economic policy discussion is limited to how to use the money that has accumulated in the National Welfare Fund. The Ukrainian crisis and subsequent geopolitical tensions have made deep structural reforms much less probable than optimists wished for a decade ago.

Current and future challenges are complex and difficult, and Russia is highly unlikely to match its growth performance of the 2000s. Russia's investment rate is alarmingly low for an emerging economy, its labor force is shrinking for demographic reasons, and the international environment is much less favorable than earlier. Russia has only itself to blame for most of these predicaments. Most importantly, the Putin regime has failed to make needed reforms and adjustments. The reason is not a shortage of sensible reform programs or detailed road maps. Summoning the political will to address systemic deficiencies is the key economic challenge of the current regime.[30]

EDITOR'S POSTSCRIPT

In February 2022, Russia gradually entered a new and potentially deep economic crisis—this one resulting from the impact of another political decision, the decision to launch a brutal and unprovoked war against Ukraine. Western sanctions and boycotts threaten to cause serious economic consequences that will be felt for decades to come. Most estimates of the decline in Russian GDP for 2022 ranged from 10 to 15 percent. Inflation was the first consequence of the war to be experienced directly by the population. While some of this came because of shortages induced by panic buying, the decline in the true exchange value of the ruble meant that imports and imported components became more expensive. Estimates of the likely annual inflation rate for 2022 ranged from 15 to 25 percent.

Putin appears to have made his decision to invade Ukraine without informing members of his economic team. Over half of Russia's "rainy day" financial cushion, the National Welfare Fund, was on deposit in Western banks.
Western leaders, in a move unprecedented against a country of the size of
Russia, froze those funds and later sought legal ways to confiscate them as
reparations for Ukraine. Nevertheless, income from oil and natural gas sales,
at least during the early months of the war, continued to provide a comfortable surplus for the state budget.

Putin appears to have significantly underestimated the degree to which
the Russian economy had become dependent on the global economy in the
post-Soviet period. One estimate put the percent of Russian-made goods with
foreign components at around 70 percent. The immediate response from the
Russian political elite, as usual, was to respond to sanctions with a call for
economic mobilization and import substitution. There are several problems
with this: First, Russia does not represent a large portion of the world's GDP,
less than 2 percent. It is not a large enough market to sustain self-sufficient
production in most sectors of a modern economy. It is also too small to compensate the risk of secondary sanctions on potential sanction-busters such
as China or Kazakhstan (sanctions on sanction violators). Second, banned
technology exports to Russia will cripple whole industries. The USSR was
able to produce on its own relatively primitive planes, trains, and automobiles, for example, without depending on technology supplied from abroad
(though the assembly lines of some of its automobile factories were equipped
by companies such as Ford and Fiat). As technology has advanced over the
past fifty years, however, it relies to a greater extent on a global supply chain.
Russia has no significant potential to make microchips, for example. Russian
automobile plants do not make automatic transmissions or airbags but import
them along with most other high-tech components. Automobiles produced in
plants in cities such as Kaluga and Tolyatti had to shut down, and prospects
for reopening are slim. The Soviet Union used to produce its own passenger
aircraft; all current and projected planes rely on parts—sometimes the entire
engine—made by Western manufacturers who are now banned from working with Russian companies. Almost all Russian airlines used planes that
were leased from Western companies that are now being recalled and cannot
legally be flown or serviced.

Commercial and logistical isolation of Russia from the West will produce
cascading shortages. For example, one of the first items to disappear from
shelves was standard office paper. Russia is a major producer of paper, but
it turns out that the chemicals used to bleach paper white are all imported;
instead, Russian paper mills began to offer lower quality off-white paper. In
a move only partly related to sanctions, many leading Western and Japanese
brands that had entered the Russian market in the 1990s and 2000s announced

they would cease operations in the Russian market—including McDonald's, Starbucks, and IKEA.

A decline in the standard of living for most of the population and growing unemployment would appear to be the inevitable long-term consequences of the political decision to invade Ukraine.

—2022

DISCUSSION QUESTIONS

1. What were the three economic tasks the Putin regime had in 2000 to put the Russian economy on the right track?
2. How have Russia's fiscal policies changed over time?
3. How have Russia's monetary policies changed over time?
4. What is the main economic policy challenge facing Russian leadership over the next five years?
5. Are you optimistic or pessimistic about Russia's economic future? Why?

SUGGESTED READINGS

Alexeev, Michael, and Shlomo Weber, eds. *Handbook of the Russian Economy*. Oxford: Oxford University Press, 2013.

Åslund, Anders. *Russia's Capitalist Revolution*. Washington, DC: Peterson Institute for International Economics, 2007.

Sutela, Pekka. *The Political Economy of Putin's Russia*. London: Routledge, 2012.

Treisman, Daniel. *The Return: Russia's Journey from Gorbachev to Medvedev*. New York: Free Press, 2011.

NOTES

1. Pekka Sutela, *The Political Economy of Putin's Russia* (London: Routledge, 2012).

2. David Owen and David O. Robinson, eds., *Russia Rebounds* (Washington, DC: International Monetary Fund, 2003).

3. BOFIT Russia Statistics, https://www.bofit.fi/en/monitoring/statistics/russia -statistics (accessed May 10, 2018).

4. Alexey Kudrin and Evsey Gurvich, "A New Growth Model for the Russian Economy," *Russian Journal of Economics* 1, no. 1 (2015): 30–54; Clifford G. Gaddy

and Barry W. Ickes, "Russia after the Global Economic Crisis," *Eurasian Geography and Economics* 50, no. 3 (2010): 281–311.

5. Michael Alexeev and Robert Conrad, "The Russian Oil Tax Regime: A Comparative Perspective," *Eurasian Geography and Economics* 49, no. 2 (2009): 93–114.

6. BOFIT Russia Statistics, https://www.bofit.fi/en/monitoring/statistics/russia -statistics (accessed May 10, 2018).

7. Daniel Berkowitz and Daniel N. DeJong, "Growth in Post-Soviet Russia: A Tale of Two Transitions," *Journal of Economic Behavior & Organization* 79, nos. 1–2 (2011): 133–43.

8. Russian Economic Barometer, http://ecsoc.ru/en/reb (accessed June 11, 2012).

9. Seija Lainela and Alexey Ponomarenko, "Russian Financial Markets and Monetary Policy Instruments," *BOFIT Online*, no. 3 (2012).

10. Lainela and Ponomarenko, "Russian Financial Markets," 26.

11. Iikka Korhonen and Riikka Nuutilainen, "Breaking Monetary Policy Rules in Russia," *Russian Journal of Economics* 3, no. 4 (2017): 366–78.

12. Employment share obviously grows when a wider definition of the energy sector is used, including refining, trading, and manufacturing branches that are dependent on providing energy producers with pipes, machinery, and so forth. The figure grows further if jobs dependent on low energy costs are added, but doing that makes distinguishing the energy and the nonenergy parts of the economy impossible.

13. Abusive transfer pricing refers to the practice of selling goods or services between various units of one single business conglomerate at below-market prices. The incentive for transfer pricing is great if tax treatment in different jurisdictions or in different stages of production differs markedly.

14. Sutela, *The Political Economy of Putin's Russia*, 94–95.

15. Denvil Duncan and Klara Sabirianova Peter, "Does Labour Supply Respond to a Flat Tax? Evidence from Russian Tax Reform," *Economics of Transition* 18, no. 2 (2010): 333–63.

16. Migara A. De Silva, Galina Kurlyanskaya, Elena Andreeva, and Natalia Golovanova, *Intergovernmental Reforms in the Russian Federation: One Step Forward, Two Steps Back?* (Washington, DC: World Bank, 2009).

17. Ekaterina Zhuravskaya, "Federalism in Russia," in *Russia after the Global Economic Crisis*, ed. Anders Åslund, Sergey Guriev, and Andrew W. Kuchins (Washington, DC: Peterson Institute for International Economics, 2010), 59–78.

18. De Silva et al., *Intergovernmental Reforms*.

19. Thomas Remington, Irina Soboleva, Anton Sobolev, and Mark Urnov, "Governors' Dilemmas: Economic and Social Policy Trade-Offs in the Russian Regions (Evidence from Four Case Studies)," *Europe-Asia Studies* 65, no. 10 (2013): 1855–76.

20. BOFIT Weekly 17/2017, https://www.bofit.fi/en/monitoring/weekly/2017/ vw201729_1 (accessed April 26, 2018).

21. BOFIT Weekly 16/2009, https://www.bofit.fi/en/monitoring/weekly/2009/ venajan_ ulkomainen_velka_supistui (accessed April 26, 2018).

22. "IMF Policy Responses to COVID-19: Russia," https://www.imf.org/en/Topics /imf-and-covid19/Policy-Responses-to-COVID-19#R (accessed June 30, 2021).

23. "Strategiia-2020: novaia model rosta—novaia sotsialnaia politika," http://www. 2020strategy.ru (accessed March 21, 2012).

24. Ukazov Presidenta Rossii ot 7 Maya 2012 No. 596–606, http://government.ru/orders/ selection/406 (accessed April 26, 2018).

25. Yuri Simachev, Natalia Akindinova et al., *Strukturnaya politika v Rossii: novie uslovia i vosmozhnaya povestka* (Moscow: Higher School of Economics, 2018).

26. "Executive Order on National Goals and Strategic Objectives of the Russian Federation through to 2024," http://en.kremlin.ru/events/president/news/57425 (accessed May 10, 2018).

27. Sergei Guriev and Elena Vakulenko, "Breaking Out of Poverty Traps: Internal Migration and Interregional Convergence in Russia," *Journal of Comparative Economics* 43(3) (August 2015): 633–49.

28. Sutritha Bagchi and Jan Sveinar, "Does Wealth Inequality Matter for Growth? The Effect of Billionaire Wealth, Income Distribution, and Poverty," *Journal of Comparative Economics* 43(3) (August 2015): 505–30.

29. See Stephen K. Wegren, Alexander Nikulin, and Irina Trotsuk, *Food Policy and Food Security: Putting Food on the Russian Table* (Lanham, MD: Lexington Books, 2018); and Stephen K. Wegren and Christel Elvestad, "Russia's Self-Sufficiency and Food Security: An Assessment," *Post-Communist Economies* 30, no. 5 (2018).

30. This chapter was revised by Laura Solanko based on a jointly authored earlier version. Due to a long illness, Pekka Sutela was unable to participate in the revisions, and he passed away in December 2021.

Chapter 8

Crime and Corruption

Louise Shelley

More than two decades after the collapse of the Soviet Union, organized crime and kleptocratic corruption remain intractable problems for the Russian state. The Kremlin leadership is closely tied by corruption to the powerful oligarchs who dominate the Russian economy. Violent crime rates have declined since the collapse of the USSR, although ethnically related violence exacerbates these rates.[1] Organized crime is no longer as visibly violent and battling over turf and control over key sectors of the economy as was the case in the 1990s. However, the extent of the crime problem has not diminished; its form has merely changed over time. Organized crime groups are now significant leaders of lucrative computer crime, an activity now often supported or tolerated by the state.[2] Powerful organized crime groups are no longer as influential because the functions and activities of organized crime have been subsumed by the increasingly authoritarian Russian state and the president's political cronies.[3]

With the enormous growth of Russia's drug markets, its crime groups are now more deeply involved in the narcotics trade than in the past. This is a problem that may get worse as the Taliban needs to enhance its income in Afghanistan and use the Northern Drug Route to generate income. Moreover, the pervasive problem of corporate raiding,[4] by which valuable businesses are taken over by force and legal manipulation, reflects the fact that organized crime often serves as enforcers for powerful officials who seek to obtain the property of political rivals and competitors.[5]

The Russian state, because of an absence of political will and pervasive corruption within its ranks, has been ineffective in dealing with these problems. Moreover, the long-term rule of President Putin and his close associates has proven the adage that "absolute power corrupts absolutely."[6] Compounding the problem is the political-criminal nexus and the fact that politicians who assume political office have legal immunity from investigation and prosecution.[7] The specialized police units that combated organized crime were abolished in September 2008 without any alternative enforcement strategy.[8] Moreover, the problem of corruption has become a highly political issue that drove tens if not hundreds of thousands of Russian protesters to the streets. The anticorruption efforts of blogger Aleksei Navalny made him a highly popular political figure within Russian society.[9] The FSB, the security police, has been linked to the effort to murder Navalny by placing the poisonous chemical novichok in his underwear.[10] At present, Navalny is in prison on trumped-up charges, and the Kremlin has coerced US tech companies to remove his voting strategy app.[11]

Russia's crime problems are not just national; they are international. Russian criminals were among the first to take full advantage of globalization.[12] Some had links to officials in the Kremlin, and others came out of the security apparatus. Many criminals who initially set up operations overseas were the so-called *vory-v-zakone* (thieves-in-law), or the traditional elite of the Soviet-era criminal world who lived according to rigidly established rules.[13] In addition, many smaller groups of criminals from the former USSR are operating in many regions of the world, often in support of Russian state interests. They are involved in serious organized crime, corruption, tax evasion, and money laundering.[14] Russian-speaking organized crime has assumed an important role in the darknet, on which they sell products harmful to computer systems such as malware and botnets.[15] Products such as malware can also facilitate entry into foreign bank accounts and deprive citizens of their savings. Russian cybercriminals were indicted in the United States for running an exchange that facilitated the use of cryptocurrency, which has made large-scale criminal activity more feasible.[16] Subsequently, six members of Russian intelligence were indicted in an American court in 2020 for destructive use of malware.[17] This is only one example of criminal activity serving the interests of the Russian state.

Crime groups often unite Russian criminals with their compatriots from other post-Soviet states. Whereas their activities were once focused primarily on the acquisition of key sectors of the Russian economy, more recently they have become greater participants in the international drug trade and in computer crime, complementing their international role in the trade of women, arms, endangered species, and illegal timber.[18] Moreover, the technical capacity of the criminals has pushed them to the forefront of computer crime, with major involvement in the production of child pornography marketed through the internet, "phishing," and even wholesale coordinated attacks on the internet and on websites of foreign countries such as Estonia and Georgia, viewed as unfriendly to Russia.[19] The largest generator of spam on the internet for a period, before it shut down under pressure, was an online pharmaceutical business run by Russian criminals.[20] Russian criminals have also attacked US infrastructure by means of ransomware, as occurred with the Colonial Pipeline in 2021.[21]

In Russia, there is a unique integration of the licit and illicit economies. Key sectors of the economy are controlled by oligarchs with criminal pasts or close ties to organized crime. But the parallels that many commentators once tried to draw between the oligarchs and the robber barons have been proven invalid. Robber barons used corruption and coercion to eliminate competition and intimidate laborers and take over large elements of American infrastructure. In Russia, the order was reversed. Criminality was crucial to the acquisition of key sectors in energy, aluminum, and natural resources. Then violence was used to eliminate competitors. Russia has not diversified its economy in needed ways and remains heavily dependent on natural resource extraction of oil and natural gas to fuel its economy.

Russia's licit and illicit economies operate on a natural resources model, which is not surprising, as illicit business is shaped by the same cultural and historical factors that shape the legitimate economy. The illicit economy mirrors the patterns of the legitimate one. Historically, Russia was never a society of traders. Before the 1917 revolution, Russian trade was dominated by non-Russians: Armenians, Greeks, Germans, and others, who lived in distinct districts of Moscow. Russians did not trade. Instead, they sold natural resources such as fur, timber, and the natural mineral wealth of their vast empire. With the reintroduction of capitalism in 1992, old patterns of business quickly reemerged. The sale of oil, gas, and petroleum products represented about half of the federal budget in 2015.[22] Russia is also reliant on other natural resources such as ores and metals as well as fish and timber, many of which are illicitly extracted. Russia suffers from the natural resource curse, failing to invest in human capital, as do other oil-rich countries that lack the rule of law.[23]

The trafficking of women operates on the natural resources model. Russian criminals sell off the women like a raw commodity, selling them to other crime groups who will exploit the women in the destination countries, maximizing their profits.[24] The Russian state shows little will to protect its citizens, even though it is facing a severe demographic crisis, and the export and sale of its women of childbearing age threatens the very survival of the Russian nation. The natural resources model of both licit and illicit trade is extremely harmful to the long-term health of the Russian economy and the Russian state. Russian legislation to combat trafficking has failed to result in a significant number of prosecutions.[25]

This chapter is based on a wide variety of sources, including analyses that have been carried out in Russia by researchers affiliated with TraCCC (Terrorism, Transnational Crime and Corruption Center) centers in Russia for over fifteen years, until political developments in Russia made this collaboration difficult. This multidisciplinary research focused on particular aspects of crime, such as human trafficking, money laundering, the role of crime groups in the process of privatization, corporate raiding, overall crime trends, and many other topics.[26]

Interviews have been conducted with large numbers of law enforcement agents in Russia and in other parts of the world concerned with post-Soviet organized crime. Legal documents of criminal cases in Russia and abroad have been studied to understand the mechanisms of organized crime activity and the rise of cybercrime activity and the phenomenon of corporate raiding. Document caches that have been leaked such as Troika Laundromat and Panama and Pandora Papers have contributed to an understanding of illicit financial flows. Civil litigation in the West among key industrial figures with criminal pasts has also been examined to shed light on the acquisition of businesses through criminal tactics.[27]

In addition, the chapter draws on the Russian press and national and regional data to understand the evolution and geography of crime in Russia. The chapter also uses Western scholarship on crime and policing in Russia, which has increased in recent years.[28] Analysis of crime data reveals striking regional differences from west to east, in part a legacy of the Soviet era where labor camps were concentrated in Siberia and new industrialized cities gave rise to particularly high rates of criminality.[29]

OVERALL TRENDS IN CRIME

The growth of crime and the absence of an effective law enforcement response[30] have affected the quality of daily life, the longevity of the population, and the economy. Beccaria, the Enlightenment thinker, wrote that the certainty of punishment is more important than its severity. In Russia, at the present time, there is no certainty of punishment, which has contributed to significant crime rates. The prosecutor general reported that there were 2.1 million crimes reported in Russia in 2014, 2.2 million in 2013, and 2.3 million in 2012. In 2015, there was a noted increase in crime rates of almost 7 percent.[31] These statistics should be treated with certain skepticism as Russian law enforcement has long understated the extent of crime to prove their efficiency. Moreover, citizens are often reluctant to report crimes to the police.[32] There may not be certainty, but there is severity for those who are caught and either cannot pay bribes to get out of the criminal justice system or who are subjects of particular political concern to the government, such as the former oil magnate Mikhail Khodorkovsky.[33] Khodorkovsky was released from his second prison term in December 2013, but not pardoned.[34]

The framing of political opponents on trumped-up charges continues to remain a problem. The following trends characterize Russian crime and organized crime:

- High rates of violence
- High rates of drug abuse and a key locale on an international drug route
- High level and extensive cybercrime that can have political dimensions
- Large-scale human smuggling and trafficking from, into, and through Russia
- Corporate raiding resulting in insecure property rights and undermining entrepreneurship
- Organized crime involvement in all sectors of the economy
- Significant complicity of organized crime and law enforcement[35]
- High level corruption undermines citizen faith in the political system
- Organized crime involvement in the foreign policy of Russia[36]

Homicide and Violent Crime

In the immediate post-Soviet period, Russia had very high rates of homicide, the result both of high rates of interpersonal violence and contract killings associated with organized crime. Increased violence was also explained by the availability of weapons, which had been tightly controlled during the Soviet period.[37] The availability of arms, facilitated by the small-weapons trade of Russian organized crime and former military personnel, made many ordinary acts of crime more violent than in the past.[38] The decline in Russian medical care meant that many individuals who were merely assault victims in the past now became homicide victims. Even though contract killings have declined, intrapersonal violence remains very high, partly explained by enduring problems of alcohol abuse. According to a scholar of Russian violence, "post-communist Russia's homicide mortality rate has been one of the highest in the world, exceeding that of European countries by a factor of 20–25, and for most of the post-communist period has also been significantly higher than that of other ex-Soviet states."[39] In 2015, the homicide rate was 11.3 per one hundred thousand, a rate that far exceeded the rates of most European countries, which are consistently in the low single digits.[40] In 2019, it was 7.7, representing a marked decline but exceeding that in Western Europe.[41]

Youth Crime and Child Exploitation

Youth crime and child exploitation, very serious problems after the collapse of the Soviet Union. were problems in Russia; this can be explained by high rates of abandoned children, street children, and the number of institutionalized children whose parents have left them or whose parents have been declared incompetent to raise their children.[42] Parents have been determined to be unfit because of alcoholism, drug use, domestic violence, and child sexual exploitation. The number of homeless or abandoned children in the early post-Soviet period was estimated to be at the same level as after World War II. There were seven hundred thousand orphans and two million illiterate youth.[43] According to the prosecutor general's office in 2010, over 2 percent of Russian children were homeless, totaling over six hundred thousand.[44] Children exposed to high levels of violence in their youth often replicate those patterns in adolescence and adulthood. Moreover, the absence of programs to help deinstitutionalized youth after eighteen return to their communities has made many of the females susceptible to sex traffickers. Presently, the Russian state fails to identify many child victims of trafficking.[45] Therefore, the rate of victimization is not clearly reported. The annual State Department Report on Trafficking states that the children of many migrants within Russia are subject to forced labor.[46]

Drug Abuse

Drug addiction has skyrocketed in Russia in recent decades, and the problem has increased during the COVID-19 pandemic.[47] This increase has occurred in the number of users, the geographical reach of the problem, and the variety of drugs used. Heroin remains the drug of choice but there are both other natural and synthetic drugs in the market. As the market has grown, there also appears to be a presence of large and more powerful organized crime groups involved, although no monopolization of markets has yet emerged. According to official figures, almost 6 percent of the total population,[48] or some 8.5 million people,[49] are drug addicts or regular users, and treatment programs for addiction are almost nonexistent.[50]

Drug-related deaths increased in 2020 over 2019. In 2020, 7,316 people died from drug overdoses, up from 4,569 deaths in the previous year.[51] This number is far below the figures recorded in the US opioid crisis, where the figure in 2020 was 93,000 deaths.[52] In Russia, deaths from alcohol are approximately seven times those resulting from drug abuse.[53]

After the collapse of the Soviet Union, the number and distribution of Russian drug abusers increased. For example, in 1985, the Ministry of Internal Affairs had identified only four regions in Russia with over ten thousand serious abusers of drugs. By the beginning of the twenty-first century, that figure had climbed to over thirty regions, and there was hardly a city in Russia in which there are not drug addicts.[54] Drug abuse is not evenly distributed.[55] Whereas 310 addicts were registered per 100,000 people in Russia as a whole in January 2004, the figure in the Russian Far East was 542 per

100,000.[56] In a very short period, Russia has developed one of the world's most serious problems of drug abuse.

The drug problem in Russia does not consist of only one commodity. Cocaine sales are limited to major urban centers. Cocaine enters from Latin America brought by Latin Americans to Europe for transshipment, and Russians are operating in Colombia and elsewhere.[57]

Synthetic drugs are increasingly in use and are smuggled from China or produced in clandestine labs in Russia. Many drugs are being sold through the dark web, which accounts for 80 percent of drug sales. Thirteen thousand packages of these drugs are traded daily in Russia.[58] A designer drug called *krokodil*, or crocodile, related to morphine, spread rapidly in Russia in recent years.[59] Another drug called salts, referred to in the United States as PABS, or psychoactive bath salts, is consumed intravenously in Russia, with devastating consequences for Russian women, who are the prime consumers.[60]

Russia is a major transshipment route for drugs out of Afghanistan, especially heroin.[61] These drugs are then consumed intravenously giving Russia a very serious problem of HIV.[62]

Russia has become a transit country for drugs from Afghanistan, Pakistan, and Iran into European markets.[63] The so-called Northern Route linked Afghanistan via Central Asia (Tajikistan and Kyrgyzstan, or Uzbekistan and Turkmenistan) for the purpose of heroin smuggling. Its use will probably increase as the Taliban in Afghanistan need more revenue.[64] The northern route[65] and the entry of drugs from the Golden Crescent and Central Asia, according to Russian authorities, undermines Russian national security.[66]

The Russian situation also recalls the Colombian situation, where drug trafficking has been used to finance nonstate violent actors, including separatist and terrorist movements.[67] Dagestan, a region adjoining Chechnya, was a major entry point for drugs into Russia until a brutal crackdown.[68] Although the links between insurgencies and the drug trade are not as strong in Russia as in Colombia, there has been an important link in both drug markets between drugs and violent conflict. Organized crime, including drug trafficking, has been a factor in the proliferation of violence in the North Caucasus. There is less violence in the Russian areas close to Central Asia because the drug trade is consolidated and controlled by the leaders of some Central Asian countries.[69]

Human Smuggling and Trafficking

Human trafficking persists on a large scale both for labor and sexual exploitation. Initially, in the first decades of the post-Soviet period, the focus was on the trafficking of Russian women for sexual exploitation abroad. For over a decade, labor exploitation has become the dominant problem even though it receives little attention.[70]

Those who suffer from labor exploitation are Russians, North Korean workers who are contracted by the North Korean state to work in the Russian Far East and other regions, as well as millions of workers from Central Asia, many of whom are in Russia illegally.[71] As Mary Buckley has written, "Russians themselves may unwittingly get drawn into unfree labour situations in their own country, be it on farms, in brickworks, in prostitution, in metal work, in begging rings or in forced theft."[72] Moreover, there is a significant illegal migrant population and there is little success in integrating them into Russian society.[73] Many of the workers are exploited. There is also an increasing problem of the exploitation of the children of illegal migrants who have no legal status and cannot attend school.[74]

Sexual trafficking remains a serious problem within Russia, and Russian women are still exported overseas for exploitation. Despite the passage of laws to combat human trafficking by the Russian legislature, there has been little implementation of these laws by the police.[75] Illustrative of this are the limited programs to prevent, prosecute, or protect victims of human trafficking.[76] Many of the sexually exploited youth come from alcoholic families and others have been in foster homes after having been taken away from their families. Those victimized are often motivated by the desire for financial improvement in their lives.[77]

Three of the approximately six to twelve million labor migrants in Russia lack the necessary documents, and many of these are in forced labor situations.[78] "Instances of labor trafficking have been reported in the construction, manufacturing, logging, textile, and maritime industries, as well as in sawmills, agriculture, sheep farms, grocery and retail stores, restaurants, waste sorting, street sweeping, domestic service, and forced begging. There are reports of widespread forced labor in brick factories in the Dagestan region."[79] Work conditions and vulnerability have gotten worse in Russia during the pandemic, and many sought to but could not leave Russia.[80] Many of the migrants left Russia during the pandemic. Russian authorities in 2021 sought to force remaining workers to leave and return to Central Asian states.[81] Their uncertain and often illegal status compounded their vulnerability and risk of labor exploitation.

Despite this massive exploitation, aiding Russian and foreign trafficking victims is not a priority for either Russian citizens or the state. Some Russian businesses are trying to establish and abide by labor standards,[82] but the difficult financial conditions accompanying the pandemic have increased the hardship of the most vulnerable. Moreover, there is very little concern for individual rights, a legacy of the Soviet period and even prerevolutionary traditions that results in the failure of the state to allocate human and financial capital to aid the most vulnerable.[83] Civil society, under siege in contemporary Russia, is unable to fill the void.

Corporate Raiding

Corporate raiding combines the use of illegal acts and the misuse of criminal law to deprive business owners of valuable property. It takes place on a broad scale in Russia. The problem has increased dramatically between 2014 and 2019, growing by over 50 percent.[84] The problem of corporate raiding is not merely a problem of insecure property rights but also involves significant threats to the life and welfare of individuals whose property is sought by highly protected and connected individuals. *Reiderstvo* (raiding) is often initiated at the behest of powerful government people and is often executed by law enforcement officials. Therefore, its victims are not just threatened by private citizens but are persecuted with the full force of the state. Tom Firestone, a long-serving US Department of Justice prosecutor assigned to the American embassy in Moscow, explains,

> "Reiderstvo" differs greatly from the U.S. hostile takeover practice in that it relies on criminal methods such as fraud, blackmail, obstruction of justice, and actual and threatened physical violence. At the same time, though, "reiderstvo" is not just simple thuggery. In contrast to more primitive criminals, Russian "reideri" rely on court orders, resolutions of shareholders and boards of directors, lawsuits. In short, it is a new more sophisticated form of organized crime.[85]

In 2019, over 317,000 economic crimes were prosecuted, many associated with corporate raiding.[86] This represented a 136 percent rise over the previous year. Therefore, 80 percent of entrepreneurs in Russia think it is unsafe to do business in the country.[87] Wealthy businesspeople are targets of corporate raiding. While the raid is under way, many of them are confined on trumped-up charges, and some agree to the charges to escape the brutal treatment they can expect while in confinement. If they manage to depart from Russia, some are subject to Red Notices through Interpol, which demand that the country where they reside deport them to Russia.[88]

Organized Crime

Post-Soviet organized crime is distinct from organized crime in many regions of the world because it initially focused on the legitimate economy and only more recently assumed a larger role in the drug trade and other aspects of the illicit economy.[89] Organized crime was able to grow so rapidly in the 1990s because of pervasive corruption among government officials, the incapacity of demoralized law enforcement, and the perception by criminals that they could act with near total impunity.[90] During the Soviet period, party sanctions placed some curbs on government misconduct, but with the collapse of the Communist Party, and in the absence of the rule of law, there were no limits on the conduct of government officials. The crime groups could function effectively because they corrupted or co-opted government officials and were rarely arrested and incarcerated.[91] Corruption, bribery, and abuse of power escalated rapidly, but there was a sharp drop in prosecutions for these offenses.[92] The failure to prosecute well-placed individuals as well as officials for corruption is an ongoing problem in Russia.[93]

The law enforcement system was decimated by poor morale and dangerous work conditions, as well as by the dismissal and departure of many senior personnel at the end of the Soviet period. For these reasons it was ill equipped to deal with the increasing number of serious crimes. Moreover, law enforcement's inexperience with investigating and prosecuting crimes in a market economy gave organized crime groups the opportunity to expand their financial reach enormously. A whole business of private protection evolved, often staffed and run by organized crime, and crime groups extracted payments from those in need of protection rather than actually providing a service. They have been named "violent entrepreneurs" by the Russian researcher Vadim Volkov.[94]

The diversity of post-Soviet organized crime is one of its hallmarks. The traditional criminal world of thieves-in-law continued and evolved to the new market conditions.[95] Crime groups are multiethnic and often involve cooperation among groups that are antagonistic outside the criminal world.[96] Foreign groups not only operate on Russian territory but also provide partnerships with Russian crime groups to carry out their activities. For example, Japanese Yakuza work with Russian organized crime in the Far East to illegally secure needed timber in exchange for used Japanese cars for the Russian market.

Organized crime groups are not involved exclusively in one area of criminal activity. Crime groups may specialize in drug trafficking, arms trafficking, or auto theft, but most crime groups are multifaceted, spanning many aspects of the legitimate and illegitimate sectors of the economy simultaneously. In any one region of the country, most forms of illicit activity will be present. There are regional differences as well; for example, organized crime involvement with environmental crime is greater in Siberia and the Far East than in the more densely populated regions of western Russia.[97] But it is a serious problem throughout Russia.[98] There has also been a significant involvement of organized crime in regional politics.[99]

The involvement of Russian organized crime in the banking sector undermined the integrity of the financial system and facilitated massive money laundering out of Russia during the 1990s. Russian money laundering, as distinct from capital flight, was so significant in the 1990s that it drained Russia of much of its investment capital.[100] Only after the Russian financial collapse in 1998, and after Russia was cited by the Financial Action Task Force for noncompliance with international money laundering standards early in the following decade, were substantial improvements made in the banking sector.[101] But there are still problems with organized crime having influence over some banks and capital flight associated with it.[102] Russians continue to launder money on a grand scale into the UK[103] through countries such as Moldova. Money is also sent through Latvia,[104] Lithuania, and Cyprus.[105] In 2017, Russians estimate that $31 billion left the country.[106] The revelations of the Pandora Papers in late 2021 reveal the hidden riches of Putin's intimates.[107]

THE GEOGRAPHY OF CRIME

The vastness of Russia's enormous territory results in significant variations in crime by region. Compounding these geographical differences is the fact that many regions of Russia, such as the North Caucasus, Tatarstan, and parts of the Volga region, have strong ethnic influences that also shape the characteristics of crime. Furthermore, there are certain regions characterized by particularly high rates of crime, such as the major cities of Moscow, St. Petersburg, and Yekaterinburg, as well as the regions of Siberia and the Russian Far East. The Crimea since annexation by Russia in March 2014 is also the locus of crime and smuggling. Many Russian crime groups have moved to Ukraine.[108] The crime rates rise as one moves from the western part of the country to the east. This phenomenon is a legacy of Soviet-era policies of strict population controls, a massive institutionalized penal population that often settled close to their former labor colonies in Siberia after release, and the development of new cities east of the Urals without necessary infrastructure and social support systems.

Siberia and the Urals

During the Soviet era, new cities were established, particularly in Siberia, which were populated primarily by young men, and there was no planning to attract women to the same communities. The internal passport and registration system in place at that time restricted mobility; women could not move to these communities without employment. Therefore, these new cities quickly became areas with high rates of alcohol consumption, violent crime, and other forms of criminality.

At the end of the Soviet period, these communities that were the basis of Soviet industrial production went into sharp decline. The rich natural resources of the Urals and Siberia, however, provided large revenues for corrupt bureaucrats and crime groups that appropriated this state property as their own. A vast illicit trade in natural resources such as timber ensued.[109] Furthermore, the Urals region was a major center of the Soviet Union's military-industrial complex. With the decline of Soviet military production, many of these factories ceased to function, leaving many citizens without jobs or incomes. The economic crisis that hit this region helps explain the large number of children at risk. Although economic prosperity has come to many cities in the area since 2000, serious problems endure, and addiction is particularly pronounced in Siberia and the Far East.

There is an enormous diversity of organized crime groups operating in Siberia. The Trans-Siberian Railroad that traverses Russia is a key transportation hub along which crime groups can operate.[110] Moreover, the railroad's proximity to China contributes to the active presence of crime groups, facilitated by serious problems of corruption along the border. In addition to such powerful local crime groups as the Bratsk criminal society, there are groups from Central Asia and the Caucasus, including Ingush and Chechen organizations.[111]

The Russian Far East

The Russian Far East has seen a significant decline in population since the collapse of the Soviet Union. The absence of economic development in the region and its isolation from the more populous western regions of Russia have provided a strong motivation for citizens to leave. The region had extremely high crime rates in the 1970s, and the region continues to be characterized by very high rates of crime and violent crime. Making the situation worse, criminal elements have also moved into local government. Epitomizing this problem was Vladimir Nikolayev, an organized criminal with the *klichka*, or criminal nickname, of Winnie the Pooh, who was elected mayor of Vladivostok in 2004.[112] His ouster in 2007 was made all the more difficult because he was second in command in the region's ruling United Russia Party. Sergei Darkin, the criminal governor of Primorskii *krai* in the Russian Far East, was forced out in 2012.[113] The pattern of corruption in Vladivostok and the region continues. In 2016, the mayor of Vladivostok, Igor Pushkarev, similar to his predecessors, faced corruption charges.[114] In 2019, he was sentenced in Moscow to fifteen years in prison for bribery and abuse of his position and in 2021 further investigations of his malfeasance were announced by Russian investigative bodies.[115] Following the 2020 elections in Khabarovsk, a scene of antigovernment protests, the region's governor was arrested for ordering murders when he was a businessman in the early 2000s.[116]

Organized crime groups from the Russian Far East work with South Korean, Japanese, Chinese, and Vietnamese crime groups. Much of the criminality is connected with the ports and the massive shipping that flows through this region. Many of the shipping and fishing companies are dominated by organized crime.[117] The impoverished military in the region contributed to massive unauthorized arms sales to foreign governments and organized crime groups. A sale of Russian helicopters to North Koreans was averted in the late 1990s only when members of the police, who were not part of the scheme, stumbled on the helicopters just prior to delivery.[118]

Much of the crime is connected with the exploitation of natural resources. Fish and timber a decade ago represented 93 percent of the exports from the Russian Far East. Seafood from overfished waters, according to crime data from the organized crime authorities in the Russian Far East, winds up in Japanese and Korean markets.[119] Since the fall of the Soviet Union, there has been a fourfold decline in forested land.[120] Russia in 2019 exported $12 billion worth of hardwood and half of that is believed to be illegally exported,[121] a massive trade facilitated by corrupt officials often in conjunction with criminal networks. Illegally logged timber from Siberia[122] and the Russia Far East is transported to Europe[123] and much goes to China.[124]

Crime in Major Urban Centers

Moscow, as Russia's largest city and economic powerhouse, is home to the largest and most important crime groups, such as the Solntsevo and Izmailovo gangs. These groups had penetrated the most lucrative sectors of the economy, such as banks, real estate, and raw materials. But the power of these groups has diminished as they have been pushed out of lucrative sectors as insiders close to Putin have acquired key sectors of the economy.

The crime groups are part of a very diverse picture of criminality in the city. Ethnic crime groups have been deeply involved in markets selling food and consumer goods. Restaurants, clubs, and casinos have been centers of criminal activity and investment. But in this rich investment environment, it is often hard to differentiate where the criminality ends and the corruption of government officials begins.

Moscow in the early 2000s was one of the most expensive cities in the world, but it had lost this distinction by 2019 due to a sharp drop in its economy and the value of the ruble. Corruption led to distorted real estate prices in Moscow as well as St. Petersburg, with many of Putin's associates from his St. Petersburg days benefiting.[125]

Moscow is still a major center of money laundering, despite enhanced controls. The close relationship between the banks and people in power, a cash-reliant economy, and the lack of effective regulation of financial markets still make it relatively easy to launder the proceeds of corrupt and criminal money. The presence of such substantial Russian money in the Panama and Pandora Papers, in the UK, and in key financial centers overseas attests to this problem. Much of this money has been laundered into real estate in the United States and the UK.[126]

CONCLUSION

Crime rates were suppressed in the Soviet years, a consequence of its high levels of social control, high rates of incarceration, and controls over places of residence. With liberalization during the Gorbachev era, fundamental changes occurred in Soviet crime patterns. Crime rates rose rapidly, and organized crime became a formidable actor in the new economy. The 1990s were traumatic. Many Russians lost their life savings in bank failures. Unemployment rose dramatically, particularly among women. The social safety net collapsed. In the absence of effective state enforcement, organized crime filled the vacuum and became a visible force in society, not only through its displays of violence and its role in private protection but also through the key role it played in privatization and politics in the transitional period.

Organized crime linked to kleptocratic corruption and to the drug trade continues. High levels of money laundering and export of capital have continued to deprive Russia of the capital it needs for investment. Export of capital continues with Russia under sanctions from the West and many businessmen fearing the loss of their assets through corporate raiding.

Under Putin's leadership, even more sinister aspects of the crime problem have emerged. There are strong indications that Russia used criminals in its invasion of Ukraine, especially in the Crimea.[127] Criminals are increasingly used as tools of state policy, especially in the areas of cybercrime. Ransomware has been used by Russian criminals allied with the state to extract large sums from businesses and other institutions abroad. Moreover, they have been used to shut down critical infrastructure, such as the Colonial Pipeline along the east coast of the United States in 2021.[128]

Crime problems have evolved over the years, yet crime remains an important element of the structure of the Russian economy, society, and political system. Drug problems are serious and functioning increasingly online. Violence remains a problem although less than in the early post-Soviet period. Conflicts over property are no longer decided by shootings but often instead by expensive litigation in the West, particularly London, where many of Russia's richest citizens have placed their assets.[129]

Despite the centrality of the crime and corruption problem, there has been no concerted state action commensurate with the size of the problem. Rather, the administration of President Putin has attempted to exploit rather than eliminate the criminal groups. Law enforcement and the courts are so corrupt and subservient to the state that they are unable to effectively address the problem nor address the widespread labor abuses, especially of migrants.[130] Without an effective law enforcement apparatus, an empowered civil society, or a free media, it is very difficult to curb the rise of organized crime or pervasive corruption. The awarding of the 2021 Nobel Peace Prize to the editor of *Novaya Gazeta*, a courageous newspaper reporting on crime and corruption, many of whose writers have been killed, is emblematic of the problem.[131] In his Nobel address, he said, "My colleagues have exposed money laundering schemes and ensured that billions of stolen rubles have been returned to the Treasury, they have revealed offshore accounts and stopped barbaric logging of Siberian forests."[132]

The criminal and corruption trajectories set in motion in the early post-Soviet period have continued. Organized criminals have so much power because they assumed critical investment positions in key sectors of the economy in the transitional period. Massive collusion with and corruption of politicians have ensured this continued ownership. In fact, many criminals have sought governmental positions to acquire immunity from prosecution and hold positions on the national and regional level.

Crime in Russia is a major political and economic influence on society. The heavy involvement of criminals and corrupt politicians in the legitimate economy is a key explanation for the absence of transparency in Russian financial markets. This contributed to the especially precipitous decline of the Russian markets relative to other international exchanges in the fall of 2008, and the massive capital flight and money laundering in recent years is further evidence that needed change has not occurred. Furthermore, the existence of widespread monopolies because of organized crime and oligarchic dominance of the economy has led to high prices and a failure to diversify the economy. Pervasive criminal activity is an enormous impediment to entrepreneurship and the emergence of small and medium-sized businesses that are crucial to long-term economic development and a middle class that could be the backbone of a more democratic society.

Corruption also remains endemic. The long-term destabilizing influence of this corruption should not be underestimated. It has contributed to human brain drain, capital flight, and a disillusionment of many citizens with government, not just in Moscow but in many more remote regions as well.[133] The massive rallies all over Russia in support of the opposition politician, Alexei

Navalny, in the spring of 2021, testify to his galvanizing message of anti-corruption.[134] But Navalny, like so many before him, who have challenged the Kremlin's leadership faced death and now incarceration under brutal conditions.[135] The state's need to suppress such an opponent of corruption testifies to the centrality of this issue to Russian political life.

DISCUSSION QUESTIONS

1. What are some of the macro-characteristics of Russian crime?
2. In what forms is corruption manifest in Russia?
3. Summarize the geography of crime. In which regions is the problem of crime and corruption the worst?
4. Why is cybercrime such a serious problem in Russia? How is it linked to the political process?
5. How has the government's approach to crime and corruption changed since Putin returned to office in 2012?

SUGGESTED READINGS

Buckley, Mary. *The Politics of Unfree Labour in Russia: Human Trafficking and Labour Migration.* Cambridge and New York: Cambridge University Press, 2018.

Bullough, Oliver. *Moneyland: Why Thieves & Crooks Now Rule the World & How to Take It Back.* London: Profile Books, 2018.

Dawisha, Karen. *Putin's Kleptocracy: Who Owns Russia?* New York: Simon & Schuster, 2014.

Galeotti, Mark. *The Vory Russia's Super Mafia.* New Haven, CT: Yale University Press, 2018.

Karklins, Rasma. *The System Made Me Do It: Corruption in Post-Communist Societies.* Armonk, NY: M. E. Sharpe, 2005.

McCarthy, A. Lauren. *Trafficking Justice: How Russian Police Use New Law, from Crime to Courtroom.* Ithaca, NY: Cornell University Press, 2015.

Orttung, Robert, and Anthony Latta, eds. *Russia's Battle with Crime, Corruption and Terrorism.* New York and London: Routledge, 2008.

Stephenson, Svetlana. *Gangs of Russia: From the Streets to the Corridors of Power.* Ithaca, NY: Cornell University Press, 2015.

Varese, Federico. *Mafias on the Move: How Organized Crime Conquers New Territories.* Princeton, NJ: Princeton University Press, 2011.

———. *The Russian Mafia: Private Protection in a New Market Economy.* Oxford: Oxford University Press, 2005.

Volkov, Vadim. *Violent Entrepreneurs: The Use of Force in the Making of Russian Capitalism.* Ithaca, NY: Cornell University Press, 2002.

NOTES

1. Natalia Yudina, "Xenophobia in Figures: Hate Crime in Russia and Efforts to Counteract It in 2017," SOVA Center for Information Analysis, February 12, 2018, http://www.sovacenter.ru/en/xenophobia/reports-analyses/2018/02/d38830 (accessed May 5, 2018).

2. Ellen Nakashima and Craig Timberg, "Russian Government Hackers Are Behind a Broad Espionage Campaign That Has Compromised U.S. Agencies, Including Treasury and Commerce," *Washington Post*, December 14, 2020, https://www.washingtonpost.com/national-security/russian-government-spies-are-behind-a-broad-hacking-campaign-that-has-breached-us-agencies-and-a-top-cyber-firm/2020/12/13/d5a53b88-3d7d-11eb-9453-fc36ba051781_story.html; Kanishka Singh, "Russian Extradited to U.S. to Face Cyber Crime Charges," *Reuters*, October 29, 2021, https://www.reuters.com/world/russian-national-extradited-us-face-charges-alleged-role-cyber-crime-2021-10-28/; Dmitri Alperovitch, "America Is Being Held for Ransom. It Needs to Fight Back," *New York Times*, September 20, 2021, https://www.nytimes.com/2021/09/20/opinion/ransomware-biden-russia.html.

3. Hannes Adomeit, "The 'Putin System': Crime and Corruption as Constituent Building Parts," *Europe-Asia Studies* 68, no. 6 (2016): 1067–73.

4. Thomas Firestone, "Criminal Corporate Raiding in Russia," *International Lawyer* 42, no. 4 (2008): 1207–29; Yulia Krylova, Judy Deane, and Louise Shelley, "Reiderstvo 2.0: The Illegal Raiding Pandemic in Russia," Reiderstvo.org, June 2021, https://reiderstvo.org/wp-content/uploads/2021/06/Reiderstvo-2.0-The-illegal-raiding-pandemic-in-Russia-1.pdf; Louise Shelley and Judy Deane, "The Rise of Reiderstvo: Implications for Russia and the West," Reiderstvo.org, May 2016, http://reiderstvo.org/sites/default/files/The_Rise_of_Reiderstvo.pdf; Michael Rochlitz, "Corporate Raiding and the Role of the State in Russia," *Post-Soviet Affairs* 30, nos. 2–3 (2014); Ararat Osipian, "Predatory Raiding in Russia: Institutions and Property Rights after the Crisis," *Journal of Economic Issues* 46, no. 2 (2012): 470.

5. An illustration of this is the arrest of an oligarch in September 2014. See "Russian Oligarch Yevtushenkov Arrested," *Radio Free Europe/Radio Liberty*, September 17, 2014, http://www.rferl.org/content/evtushenko-arrested-russia-sistema-money-laundering-charge/ 26588656.html (accessed April 29, 2018).

6. Karen Dawisha, *Putin's Kleptocracy: Who Owns Russia?* (New York: Simon & Schuster, 2014).

7. Roy Godson, ed., *Menace to Society: Political-Criminal Collaboration around the World* (New Brunswick, NJ: Transaction, 2003); Leslie Holmes, "The Corruption-Organised Crime Nexus in Central and Eastern Europe," in *Terrorism, Organised Crime and Corruption: Networks and Linkage*, ed. Leslie Holmes (Cheltenham, UK: Edward Elgar, 2007), 84–108.

8. Mark Galeotti, "Medvedev's First Police Reform: MVD Loses Specialised Organised Crime Department," http://inmoscowsshadows.wordpress.com/2008/09/11/medvedevs-first-police-reform-mvd-loses-specialised-organised-crime-department (accessed April 29, 2018).

9. See Russia's Anticorruption Foundation, https://fbk.info/english/about (accessed April 29, 2018).

10. Luke Harding, "Navalny Says Russian Officer Admits Putting Poison in Underwear," *Guardian*, December 21, 2020, https://www.theguardian.com/world/2020/dec/21/navalny-russian-agent-novichok-death-plot.

11. Anton Troianovski and Adam Satariano, "Google and Apple, Under Pressure from Russia, Remove Voting App," *New York Times*, September 17, 2021, https://www.nytimes.com/2021/09/17/world/europe/russia-navalny-app-election.html.

12. They have globalized and moved to different locales to increase their business opportunities in different markets. See Federico Varese, *Mafias on the Move: How Organized Crime Conquers New Territories* (Princeton, NJ: Princeton University Press, 2011).

13. These organized crime groups are not the product of post-Soviet society; they also flourished under the Soviet regime. Federico Varese, *The Russian Mafia: Private Protection in a New Market Economy* (Oxford: Oxford University Press, 2001); Yakov Gilinskiy and Yakov Kostjukovsky, "From Thievish Cartel to Criminal Corporation," in *Organised Crime in Europe*, ed. Cyril Fijnaut and Letizia Paoli (Dordrecht: Springer, 2004), 181–202; Mark Galeotti, *The Vory Russia's Super Mafia* (New Haven, CT: Yale University Press, 2018).

14. Europol, *Organised Crime Threat Assessment 2011*, May 4, 2011, http://www.europol.europa.eu/content/press/europol-organised-crime-threat-assessment-2011-429 (accessed April 29, 2018); Walter Kegö and Alexandru Molcean, *Russian Speaking Organized Crime Groups in the EU* (Stockholm: Institute for Security and Development Policy, 2011), 26.

15. Del Quentin Wilber, "Ransomware Hackers Remain Largely out of Reach Behind Russia's Cybercurtain," *Los Angeles Times*, June 10, 2021, https://www.latimes.com/politics/story/2021-06-10/ransomware-hackers-remain-largely-out-of-reach-behind-russias-cyber-curtain.

16. "Russian National and Bitcoin Exchange Charged in 21-Count Indictment for Operating Alleged International Money Laundering Scheme and Allegedly Laundering Funds from Hack of Mt. Gox," US Department of Justice, July 26, 2017, https://www.justice.gov/usao-ndca/pr/russian-national-and-bitcoin-exchange-charged-21-count-indictment-operating-alleged (accessed April 19, 2018).

17. U.S. Department of Justice, "Six Russian GRU Officers Charged in Connection with Worldwide Deployment of Destructive Malware and Other Disruptive Actions in Cyberspace," Press Release, October 19, 2020, https://www.justice.gov/opa/pr/six-russian-gru-officers-charged-connection-worldwide-deployment-destructive-malware-and.

18. For trade of women, see Louise Shelley, *Human Trafficking: A Global Perspective* (Cambridge: Cambridge University Press, 2010), 174–200; G. M. Zherebkin, *Otvetstvennost' za nezakonnuiu rubku lesnykh nasazhdenii. Analuz nelegal'nykh rubok na rossiiskom Dal'nem Vostoke i metodika ikh rassledovaniia* (Vladivostok: Apel'sin, 2011); Nicholas Schmidle, "Disarming Victor Bout: The Rise and Fall of the World's Most Notorious Weapons Trafficker," *New Yorker*, March 5, 2012, 54–65.

19. "Marching Off to Cyberwar: The Internet; Attacks Launched over the Internet on Estonia and Georgia Highlight the Difficulty of Defining and Dealing with 'Cyberwar,'" *The Economist*, December 4, 2008, http://www.economist.com/node/12673385 (accessed April 29, 2018).

20. Damon McCoy, Andreas Pitsillidis, Grant Jordan, Nicholas Weaver, Christian Kreibich, Brian Krebs, Geoffrey M. Voelker, Stefan Savage, and Kirill Levchenko, "PharmaLeaks: Understanding the Business of Online Pharmaceutical Affiliate Programs," http://www.cs.gmu. edu/~mccoy/papers/pharmaleaks.pdf (accessed April 29, 2018).

21. William Turton and Mehrotra Kartikay, "Hackers Breached Colonial Pipeline Using Compromised Password," *Bloomberg*, June 4, 2021, https://www.bloomberg.com/news/articles/2021-06-04/hackers-breached-colonial-pipeline-using-compromised-password.

22. Russian Exports 1994–2018, TradingEconomics.com, https://tradingeconomics.com/ russia/exports (accessed April 19, 2018).

23. Daniel Treisman, "Is Russia Cursed by Oil?," *Journal of International Affairs*, April 15, 2010, http://jia.sipa.columbia.edu/russia-cursed-oil (accessed April 29, 2018).

24. Shelley, *Human Trafficking*, 113–21.

25. Lauren A. McCarthy, *Trafficking Justice: How Russian Police Use New Law, from Crime to Courtroom* (Ithaca, NY: Cornell University Press, 2015); U.S. Department of State, "2020 Trafficking in Persons Report: Russia," U.S. Department of State, Office to Monitor and Combat Trafficking in Persons, 2020, https://www.state.gov/reports/2020-trafficking-in-persons-report/russia/.

26. For some of this research, see "Publications from the Vladivostok Center," Terrorism, Transnational Crime and Corruption Center (TraCCC), n.d., https://traccc.gmu.edu/international-centers/russia/vladivostok/publications-from-the-vladivostok-center/; "Russia," Terrorism, Transnational Crime and Corruption Center (TraCCC), n.d., https://traccc.gmu.edu/international-centers/russia/.

27. Simon Goodley, "Oleg Deripaska Accuses Rival Bringing £1.6bn Suit of Running Protection Racket," February 13, 2012, https://www.theguardian.com/world/2012/feb/13/oleg-deripaska-rival-crime-claims (accessed April 29, 2018).

28. Gilles Favarel-Garrigues, *Policing Economic Crime in Russia: From Soviet Planned Economy to Privatization*, trans. Roger Leverdier (New York: Columbia University Press, 2011); Brian Taylor, *State Building in Putin's Russia: Policing and Coercion after Communism* (Cambridge: Cambridge University Press, 2011); Vadim Volkov, *Violent Entrepreneurs: The Use of Force in the Making of Russian Capitalism* (Ithaca, NY: Cornell University Press, 2002); Svetlana Stephenson, *Gangs of Russia: From the Streets to the Corridors of Power* (Cornell University Press, 2015), https://doi.org/10.7591/9781501701689; Mark Galeotti, *The Vory: Russia's Super Mafia* (New Haven: Yale University Press, 2018).

29. Louise Shelley and Yuri Andrienko, "Crime, Violence and Political Conflict in Russia," in *Understanding Civil War: Evidence and Analysis*, ed. Nicholas Sambanis (Washington, DC: World Bank, 2005), 87–117; Elina Alexandra Treyger, *Soviet Roots of Post-Soviet Order* (PhD diss., Harvard University, June 2011); A. Lysova,

N. G. Shchitov, and W. A. Pridemore, "Homicide in Russia, Ukraine and Belarus," in *Sourcebook of European Homicide Research*, ed. M. Liem and W. A. Pridemore (New York: Springer, 2011), 451–69.

30. Lauren McCarthy and Mary Elizabeth Malinkin, "Every Day Law Enforcement in Russia," Wilson Center, September 8, 2015, https://www.wilsoncenter.org/article/everyday-law-enforcement-russia (accessed April 18, 2018).

31. "Russia Sees 2015 Crime Spike," *Moscow Times*, September 16, 2015, https://themoscowtimes.com/news/russia-sees-2015-crime-rate-spike-49597 (accessed April 18, 2018); "Crime Rate in Russia from 1995 to 2000," Statista, n.d., https://www.statista.com/statistics/1045439/russia-crime-rate/.

32. Lauren A. McCarthy et al., "Who Reports Crime? Citizen Engagement with the Police in Russia and Georgia," *Europe-Asia Studies* 73, no. 1 (January 27, 2021): 8–35, https://doi.org/10.1080/09668136.2020.1851354.

33. Serge Schmemann, "The Case against and for Khodorkovsky," *International Herald Tribune*, October 19, 2008, http://www.nytimes.com/2008/10/20/opinion/20mon4.html (accessed April 29, 2018); Alena Ledeneva, "Telephone Justice in Russia," *Post-Soviet Affairs* 24, no. 4 (2008): 324–50; Kathryn Hendley, "Telephone Law and the 'Rule of Law': The Russian Case," *Hague Journal on the Rule of Law* 1, no. 2 (2009): 241–64.

34. Holly Yan and Dick Wright, "Russian Dissident Mikhail Khodorkovsky Speaks Out," CNN, December 22, 2013, http://www.cnn.com/2013/12/22/world/amanpour-mikhail-khodorkovsky-interview (accessed April 29, 2018).

35. Illustrative of this is the Magnitsky case, in which an individual who attempted to whistle-blow on police corruption died in prison. See http://www.bbc.com/news/world-europe-20626960 (accessed April 29, 2018). A law in honor of him was passed at the end of 2012 in the United States and other countries. In the United States, it is called the Global Magnitsky Act, https://www.state.gov/e/eb/tfs/spi/globalmagnitsky (accessed April 29, 2018).

36. This has been seen in regard to the invasion of Ukraine by Russia as well as the previously mentioned cyberattacks. See Mark Galeotti, "Crime and Crimea: Criminals as Allies and Agents," November 3, 2014, http://www.rferl.org/content/crimea-crime-criminals-as-agents-allies/26671923.html (accessed April 29, 2018).

37. Louise I. Shelley, "Interpersonal Violence in the Soviet Union," *Violence, Aggression and Terrorism* 1, no. 2 (1987): 41–67.

38. N. F. Kuznetsova and G. M. Minkovskii, *Kriminologiia: Uchebnik* (Moscow: Vek, 1998), 553.

39. Treyger, *Soviet Roots of Post-Soviet Order*, 8; see also W. A. Pridemore, "Social Structure and Homicide in Post-Soviet Russia," *Social Science Research* 34, no. 4 (2005): 732–56.

40. Russian Federation—Homicide Rate, https://knoema.com/atlas/Russian-Federation/topics/Crime-Statistics/Homicides/Homicide-rate (accessed April 19, 2018); United Nations Office on Drugs and Crime, *Global Study on Homicide 2013*, 12, https://www.unodc.org/documents/gsh/pdfs/2014_GLOBAL_HOMICIDE_BOOK_web.pdf (accessed April 19, 2018).

41. "Russian Federation Homicide Rate, 1990–2020," Knoema, accessed November 1, 2021, https://knoema.com//atlas/Russian-Federation/Homicide-rate.

42. Clementine K. Fujimura, Sally W. Stoecker, and Tatyana Sudakova, *Russia's Abandoned Children: An Intimate Understanding* (Westport, CT: Praeger, 2005).

43. "V Rossii—'tretiia volna' bezprizornosti, beznadzornosti, negramotnosti, i prestupnost' podrostov (statistika)," NewsRu.com, June 1, 2005, http://www.newsru.com/russia/01jun2005/ generation.html (accessed April 29, 2018).

44. Olga Khvostunova, "Russia's Invisible Children: The Unrelieved Plight of Russia's Homeless Youth," May 31, 2012, http://imrussia.org/en/society/245-besprizorniki (accessed April 21, 2018).

45. U.S. Department of State, "2020 Trafficking in Persons Report: Russia."

46. Ibid.

47. "Drug Deaths in Russia Spike 60 Percent During Pandemic," *Radio Free Europe/Radio Liberty*, July 19, 2021, https://www.rferl.org/a/drug-deaths-russia-pandemic/31365534.html.

48. Mark Galeotti, "Narcotics and Nationalism: Russian Drug Policies and Futures," Center for 21st Century Security and Intelligence, Brookings Institution, 2016, https://www.brookings.edu/wp-content/uploads/2016/07/galeotti-russia-final.pdf.

49. My Lilja, "Russian Political Discourse on Illegal Drugs: A Thematic Analysis of Parliamentary Debates," *Substance Use & Misuse* 56, no. 7 (June 7, 2021): 1010–17, https://doi.org/10.1080/10826084.2021.1906275.

50. U.S. Department of State, "International Narcotics Control Strategy Report, Volume 1" (Bureau for International Narcotics and Law Enforcement Affairs, March 2020), 218, https://www.state.gov/wp-content/uploads/2020/06/Tab-1-INCSR-Vol.-I-Final-for-Printing-1-29-20-508-4.pdf; Galeotti, "Narcotics and Nationalism: Russian Drug Policies and Futures."

51. "Drug Deaths in Russia Spike 60 Percent During Pandemic," *Radio Free Europe/Radio Liberty*, July 19, 2021, https://www.rferl.org/a/drug-deaths-russia-pandemic/31365534.html.

52. Michael Devitt, "Drug Overdose Deaths Reached New High in 2020, Says CDC," American Academy of Family Physicians, August 6, 2021, https://www.aafp.org/news/health-of-the-public/20210806overdosedeaths.html.

53. "Drug Deaths in Russia Spike 60 Percent During Pandemic," *Radio Free Europe/Radio Liberty*, July 19, 2021, https://www.rferl.org/a/drug-deaths-russia-pandemic/31365534.html.

54. B. Tselinsky, "Sovremennaia Narkosituatsiia v Rossii: Tendentsii i Perspektivii," *Organizovannaia Prestupnost, Terrorizm, i Korruptsiia*, no. 4 (2003): 21.

55. A. G. Museibov, "Regional'nye praktiki po preduprezhdeniiu nezakonnogo oborota narkotikov," *Sotsiologicheskie issledovaniia*, no. 7 (2003): 125–30.

56. Based on the analysis of the Vladivostok branch of the Transnational Crime and Corruption Center, http://www.crime.vl.ru/index.php?p=1202&more=1&c=1&tb=1&pb=1 (accessed May 5, 2018).

57. Aaron Beitman, "Perspectives on Illicit Drugs in Russia," Schar School of Policy and Government, George Mason University, December 5, 2011, http://traccc

.gmu.edu/2011/12/05/ perspectives-on-illicit-drugs-in-russia (accessed April 29, 2018); Oleg Yegorov, "$61 Million in Cocaine: The Mysterious Haul That Has Russia and Argentina in Cahoots," Russia Beyond, February 18, 2018, https://www.rbth.com /lifestyle/327679-61-million-of-cocaine-russia-argentina (accessed May 5, 2018).

58. U.S. Department of State, "International Narcotics Control Strategy Report, Volume 1" (Bureau for International Narcotics and Law Enforcement Affairs, March 2020), 218, https://www.state.gov/wp-content/uploads/2020/06/Tab-1-INCSR-Vol.-I -Final-for-Printing-1-29-20-508-4.pdf.

59. Simon Schuster, "The Curse of the Crocodile: Russia's Deadly Designer Drug," June 21, 2011, http://www.time.com/time/world/article/0,8599,2078355,00 .html (accessed April 29, 2018).

60. Anna Nemtsova, "The Drug Decimating Russia's Women," *Daily Beast*, November 18, 2017, https://www.thedailybeast.com/the-drug-decimating-russias -women (accessed April 21, 2018).

61. Country Report: Russia, Bureau of International Narcotics and Law Enforce-ment Affairs, *2014 International Narcotics Control Strategy Report (INCSR)*, http:// www.state.gov/j/ inl/rls/nrcrpt/2014/vol1/223000.htm (accessed May 5, 2018); United Nations Office on Drugs and Crime, "Afghan Opiate Trafficking Along the Northern Route" (Vienna, June 2018), https://www.unodc.org/documents/publications/NR _Report_21.06.18_low.pdf.

62. Peter Meylakhs et al., "A New Generation of Drug Users in St. Petersburg, Rus-sia? HIV, HCV, and Overdose Risks in a Mixed-Methods Pilot Study of Young Hard Drug Users," *AIDS and Behavior* 23, no. 12 (December 2019): 3350–65, https://doi .org/10.1007/s10461-019-02489-6.

63. Tselinsky, "Sovremennaia Narkosituatsiia v Rossii," 23; Kairat Osmonaliev, "Developing Counter-Narcotics Policy in Central Asia, Washington and Uppsala: Silk Road Paper," Central Asia-Caucasus Institute and Silk Road Studies Program, 2005; "Drug Dealers, Drug Lords, and Drug Warriors-cum-Traffickers: Drug Crime and the Narcotic Market in Tajikistan," Schar School of Policy and Government, George Mason University, http://traccc.gmu. edu/?s=drug+dealers+and+drug+lords (accessed May 5, 2018); Letizia Paoli, Victoria A. Greenfield, and Peter Reuter, *The World Heroin Market: Can Supply Be Cut?* (Oxford: Oxford University Press, 2009).

64. United Nations Office on Drugs and Crime, "Afghan Opiate Trafficking Along the Northern Route" (Vienna, June 2018), https://www.unodc.org/documents/ publications/NR_Report_21.06.18_low.pdf.

65. Nabil Bhatia, "Opioids in the Golden Crescent: Production, Trafficking and Cooperative Counternarcotics Initiatives," March 13, 2017, http://natoassociation .ca/opioids-in-the-golden-crescent-production-trafficking-and-cooperative-counternarcotics-initiatives (accessed May 5, 2018); *World Drug Report 2017*, 18, https://www.unodc.org/wdr2017/field/Booklet_1_ EXSUM.pdf (accessed May 5, 2018).

66. Ombeline Lemarchal, "Tackling the Illicit Drug Trade: Perspectives From Russia," Russian International Affairs Council, September 14, 2020, https:// russiancouncil.ru/en/analytics-and-comments/columns/eurasian-policy/tackling-the -illicit-drug-trade-perspectives-from-russia/; My Lilja, "Russian Political Discourse

on Illegal Drugs: A Thematic Analysis of Parliamentary Debates," *Substance Use & Misuse* 56, no. 7 (June 7, 2021): 1010–17, https://doi.org/10.1080/10826084.2021 .1906275; United Nations Office on Drugs and Crime, "Afghan Opiate Trafficking Along the Northern Route" (Vienna, June 2018), https://www.unodc.org/documents/ publications/NR_Report_21.06.18_low.pdf.

67. Tamara Makarenko, "Terrorism and Transnational Organised Crime: The Emerging Nexus," *Transnational Violence and Seams of Lawlessness in the Asia-Pacific: Linkages to Global Terrorism* (Hawaii: Asia Pacific Center for Strategic Studies, 2004); Kimberley Thachuk, "Transnational Threats: Falling through the Cracks?," *Low Intensity Conflict & Law Enforcement* 10, no. 1 (2001); Sabrina Adamoli et al., *Organized Crime around the World* (Helsinki: HEUNI, 1998); Barbara Harris-White, *Globalization and Insecurity: Political, Economic and Physical Challenges* (Hampshire: Palgrave Macmillan, 2002); Ian Griffith, "From Cold War Geopolitics to Post-Cold War Geonarcotics," *International Journal* 49, no. 1 (1993–1994): 1–36; R. Matthew and G. Shambaugh, "Sex, Drugs, and Heavy Metal: Transnational Threats and National Vulnerabilities," *Security Dialogue* 29, no. 2 (1998): 163–75; Louise I. Shelley, *Dirty Entanglements: Corruption, Crime and Terrorism* (Cambridge: Cambridge University Press, 2014).

68. Louise I. Shelley and Svante E. Cornell, "The Drug Trade in Russia," in *Russian Business Power: The Role of Russian Business in Foreign and Security Relations*, ed. Andreas Wegner, Jeronim Perovic, and Robert W. Orttung (London: Routledge, 2006), 200; https://www.themoscowtimes.com/2018/01/16/chechnya-initiated-brutal -crackdown-on-drugs-last-year-investigation-says-a60194.

69. Alexander Kupatadze, "Kyrgyzstan—A Virtual Narco State?," *International Journal of Drug Policy* 25, no. 6 (2014): 1178–85; Alexander Kupatadze, "Bribe, Swindle, Steal," April 9, 2018, http://bribeswindleorsteal.libsyn.com/website /corruption-in-the-caucasus (accessed May 5, 2018).

70. Elena Tyuryukanova, "THB, Irregular Migration and Criminal Gains" (paper presented at OSCE-UNODC-CYPRUS Regional Meeting on Human Trafficking and Money Laundering, Larnaca, Cyprus, September 18–19, 2008).

71. US State Department, *Trafficking in Persons Report, 2017, Russia*, https://www .state.gov/j/tip/rls/tiprpt/countries/2017/271269.htm (accessed April 28, 2018).

72. Mary Buckley, *The Politics of Unfree Labour in Russia: Human Trafficking and Labour Migration* (Cambridge: Cambridge University Press, 2018), https://doi .org/10.1017/9781108325639, 23.

73. Dmitry V. Poletaev, "Adaptation and Integration of Labour Migrants from the EAEU in Russia on the Example of Migrants from Kyrgyzstan," *Politics and Economics*, no. 1 (April 9, 2020). Gale Academic OneFile; https://link.gale.com/apps /doc/A620041568/AONE?u=anon~67176f7d&sid=googleScholar&xid=2b705025; Maria Smekalova, "Dmitry Poletaev: Up to 50% of Migrants in Russia Are Illegal," Russian International Affairs Council, November 21, 2016, https://russiancouncil .ru/en/analytics-and-comments/interview/dmitriy-poletaev-do-50-migrantov-v-rossii -nelegalnye/.

74. See this synopsis of the work of Dmitry Poletaev in Aaron Beitman, "Addressing the Problem of Labor Exploitation of Foreign Migrant Children in Russia," Schar

School of Policy and Government, George Mason University, August 21, 2013, http://traccc.gmu.edu/2013/08/21/addressing-the-problem-of-labor-exploitation-of-foreign-migrant-children-in-russia (accessed April 28, 2018).

75. Lauren A. McCarthy, *Trafficking Justice: How Russian Police Enforce New Laws, from Crime to Courtroom* (Ithaca, NY: Cornell University Press, 2015), https://doi.org/10.7591/9781501701375.

76. U.S. Department of State, "2020 Trafficking in Persons Report: Russia."

77. Buckley, *The Politics of Unfree Labour in Russia: Human Trafficking and Labour Migration,* 65–66.

78. U.S. Department of State, "2020 Trafficking in Persons Report: Russia."

79. Ibid.

80. Ivan Nechepurenko and Sergey Ponomarev, "For Migrants in Russia, Virus Means No Money to Live and No Way to Leave," *The New York Times,* June 15, 2020, https://www.nytimes.com/2020/06/15/world/europe/russia-coronavirus-migrant-workers.html.

81. "Russia Tells Illegal Migrants from Post-Soviet Countries to Leave by June 15," *The Moscow Times,* April 16, 2021, https://www.themoscowtimes.com/2021/04/16/russia-tells-illegal-migrants-from-post-soviet-countries-to-leave-by-june-15-a73623.

82. Office of the Special Representative and Coordinator for Combating Trafficking in Human Beings OSCE, "Ensuring That Businesses Do Not Contribute to Trafficking in Human Beings: Duties of States and the Private Sector" (Occasional Paper Series, no. 7, Vienna, November 2014), 71–78.

83. U.S. Department of State, "2020 Trafficking in Persons Report: Russia."

84. Krylova, Deane, and Shelley, "Reiderstvo 2.0: The Illegal Raiding Pandemic in Russia," 8.

85. Firestone, "Criminal Corporate Raiding in Russia," 1207.

86. Krylova, Deane, and Shelley, "Reiderstvo 2.0: The Illegal Raiding Pandemic in Russia," 8.

87. Ibid., 9.

88. Red Notice Abuse Report, http://rednoticeabuse.com (accessed April 28, 2018).

89. Svetlana Glinkina, "Privatizatsiia and Kriminalizatsiia—How Organized Crime Is Hijacking Privatization," *Demokratizatsiya* 2, no. 3 (1994): 385–91.

90. Louise Shelley, "Organized Crime Groups: 'Uncivil Society,'" in *Russian Civil Society: A Critical Assessment,* eds. Alfred B. Evans Jr., Laura A. Henry, and Lisa McIntosh Sundstrom (Armonk, NY: M.E. Sharpe, 2006), 95–109.

91. G. F. Khokhriakov, "Organizovannia prestupnost' v Rossii: 60-e gody-pervaia polovina 90-x godov," *Obshchestvennye nauki i sovremmenost',* no. 6 (2000): 62–74.

92. See Louise Shelley, "Crime and Corruption," in *Developments in Russian Politics,* ed. Stephen White, Alex Pravda, and Zvi Gitelman (Houndmills: Palgrave, 2001), 239–53; Alena Ledeneva, *How Russia Really Works: The Informal Practices That Shaped Post-Soviet Politics and Business* (Ithaca, NY: Cornell University Press, 2006); Leslie Holmes, "Crime, Organised Crime and Corruption in Post-Communist Europe and the CIS," *Communist and Post-Communist Studies* 42, no. 2 (2009): 265–87.

93. Adomeit, "The 'Putin System.'"

94. Volkov, *Violent Entrepreneurs*; Vadim Volkov, "Silovoe predprinimatel'stvo v sovremennoi Rossii," *Sotsiologiecheskie issledovaniia*, no. 1 (1999): 55–65.

95. Mark Galeotti, *The Vory: Russia's Super Mafia* (New Haven, CT: Yale University Press, 2018).

96. Varese, *The Russian Mafia*; Alexander Kupatadze, *Organised Crime, Political Transitions and State Formation in Post-Soviet Eurasia* (Houndmills: Palgrave Macmillan, 2012).

97. EIA, "Liquidating the Forests," 2013, https://eia-global.org/reports/liquidating-theforests-report (accessed April 29, 2018).

98. "Russian Polluters Evading Huge Environmental Fines," May 11, 2015, https:// themoscowtimes.com/articles/russian-polluters-evading-huge-environmental-fines-46462 (accessed May 5, 2018).

99. Sophie Pinkham, "Normal Is Over for Russia's Hinterland," *Foreign Policy*, August 7, 2020, https://foreignpolicy.com/2020/08/07/khabarovsk-furgal-putin-siberia-normal-isnt-ever-coming-back-to-russias-hinterland/.

100. Center for Strategic and International Studies, *Russian Organized Crime and Corruption, Putin's Challenge* (Washington, DC: CSIS, 2000), 32–39.

101. For continuing problems with Russian money laundering, see Bureau of International Narcotics and Law Enforcement Affairs, *2012 International Narcotics Control Strategy Report (INCSR)*, vol. 2, March 7, 2012, http://www.state.gov/j/inl/rls/nrcrpt/2012/vol2/184117. htm#Russia (accessed May 5, 2018).

102. N. A. Lopashenko, *Begstvo kapitalov, peredel sobstvennosti i ekonomicheskaia amnistiia* (Moscow: Iuridicheskie programmy, 2005); Anna Repetskaya, *Ekonomicheskaya Organizovannaya Prestupnost' V Rossii* (Moscow: Palmarium Academic Publishing, 2012).

103. Oliver Bullough, *Moneyland: The Inside Story of the Crooks and Kleptocrats Who Rule the World* (New York: St. Martin's Press, 2019).

104. Charles Davidson et al., "Countering Russian Money Laundering: Lessons from Latvia" (Hudson Institute, Washington, DC, October 5, 2018), https://www.gmfus.org/news/countering-russian-money-laundering-lessons-latvia.

105. "Russian Money in Cyprus Hit by Savings Seizure," The Motley Fool, March 18, 2013, https://www.fool.com/investing/general/2013/03/18/russian-money-in-cyprus-hit-by-savings-seizure.aspx.

106. Votonovskaya, "Capital Flight from Russia."

107. Luke Harding, "Pandora Papers Reveal Hidden Riches of Putin's Inner Circle," *Guardian*, October 3, 2021, https://www.theguardian.com/news/2021/oct/03/pandora-papers-reveal-hidden-wealth-vladimir-putin-inner-circle.

108. Mark Galeotti, "How the Invasion of Ukraine Is Shaking Up the Global Crime Scene," November 6, 2014, http://www.vice.com/read/how-the-invasion-of-ukraine-is-shaking-up-the-global-crime-scene-1106 (accessed May 5, 2018).

109. Anna L. Repetskaya, "Regionalization and Expansion: The Growth of Organized Crime in East Siberia," in *Global Organized Crime and International Security*, 1st Edition (Routledge, 1999).

110. "Siberian and Far East Regions Hit by Drugs Menace, Shows a New League Table," *Siberian Times*, September 22, 2015, http://siberiantimes.com/other/others/news/n0416-siberian-and-far-east-regions-hit-by-drugs-menace-shows-a-new-league-table/; "Russia's HIV Rates Highest in Three Siberian Cities," *Moscow Times*, July 24, 2017, sec. news, https://www.themoscowtimes.com/2017/07/24/hiv-in-siberia-a58477.

111. Mark Galeotti suggests that Chechen organized crime may be seen as a franchise, as there is more Chechen organized crime than Chechens. See "'Brotherhoods' and 'Associates': Chechen Networks of Crime and Resistance," in *Networks, Terrorism and Global Insurgency*, ed. Robert J. Bunker (London: Routledge, 2005), 175; Aaron Beitman, "Organized Crime in Western Siberia," part 3, discusses Repetskaya's research on the crime groups present in Western Siberia, April 26, 2012, http://traccc.gmu.edu/2012/04/26/organized-crime-in-western-siberia-part-3 (accessed April 29, 2018).

112. "Vladivostok Mayor Stripped of Power among Corruption Investigation," Associated Press, March 1, 2007, http://www.nytimes.com/2007/03/01/world/europe/01iht-russia. 4763829.html (accessed April 29, 2018).

113. "Russian Far East Governor Steps Down," RIA-Novosti, February 28, 2012, http:// sputniknews.com/society/20120228/171590672.html (accessed May 5, 2018).

114. Dmitry Frolovskiy, "Vladivostok: The Many Loves of Russia's Far East Capital," *Diplomat*, September 3, 2016, https://thediplomat.com/2016/09/vladivostok-the-many-lives-ofrussias-far-eastern-capital (accessed April 29, 2018).

115. See: "Ex-Mayor of Vladivostok Receives Long Jail Term for Corruption," *Moscow Times*, April 10, 2019, https://www.themoscowtimes.com/2019/04/10/ex-mayor-of-vladivostok-receives-long-jail-term-for-corruption-a65167.

116. Sophie Pinkham, "Normal Is Over for Russia's Hinterland," *Foreign Policy*, August 7, 2020, https://foreignpolicy.com/2020/08/07/khabarovsk-furgal-putin-siberia-normal-isnt-ever-coming-back-to-russias-hinterland/.

117. See website of the Vladivostok Center, http://www.crime.vl.ru (accessed April 29, 2018), which has extensive material on corruption in the Far East Region.

118. V. A. Nomokonov, ed., *Organizovannia prestupnost': tendentsii, perspektivy bor'by* (Vladivostok: Dalnevostochnogo universiteta, 1998).

119. P. V. Korovnikov, "Problemy dekriminalizatsii sfery prirodopol'zovaniia Primorskogo kraiia i nekotorye puti ikh resheniia," in *Rossiia i ATR Problemy bezopasnosti, migratsii i prestupnosti* (Vladivostok: Dal'nevostochnogo universiteta, 2007), 88–89.

120. Dal'nii Vostok: Khronika organizovannoi prestupnosti (Obzor pressy 1997–August 2003), http://www.crime.vl.ru/index.php?p=2640&more=1&c=1&tb=1&pb=1 (accessed April 29, 2018).

121. "Report: Illegal Russian Lumber Flooded Europe despite Timber Laws," Mongabay, December 17, 2020, https://news.mongabay.com/2020/12/report-illegal-russian-lumber-flooded-europe-despite-timber-laws/.

122. Natalie Sauer, "The Fight for the World's Largest Forest," Climate Home News, August 10, 2019, https://www.climatechangenews.com/2019/10/08/siberia-illegal-logging-feeds-chinas-factories-one-woman-fights-back/.

123. Ibid.

124. Steven Lee Myers, "China's Voracious Appetite for Timber Stokes Fury in Russia and Beyond," *New York Times*, April 9, 2019, https://www.nytimes.com /2019/04/09/world/asia/chinas-voracious-appetite-for-timber-stokes-fury-in-russia -and-beyond.html.

125. Dawisha, *Putin's Kleptocracy.*

126. Craig Unger, "Trump's Businesses Are Full of Dirty Russian Money. The Scandal Is That It's Legal." *Washington Post*, March 29, 2019, https://www .washingtonpost.com/outlook/trumps-businesses-are-full-of-dirty-russian-money-the -scandal-is-thats-legal/2019/03/29/11b812da-5171-11e9-88a1-ed346f0ec94f_story .html.

127. Galeotti, "Crime and Crimea."

128. Dmitri Alperovitch, "America Is Being Held for Ransom. It Needs to Fight Back," *New York Times*, September 20, 2021, sec. Opinion, https://www.nytimes.com /2021/09/20/opinion/ransomware-biden-russia.html.

129. "Court Battle between Roman Abramovich and Boris Berezovsky Ends," *Guardian*, January 19, 2012, http://www.theguardian.com/world/2012/jan/19/court -battle-abramovich-berezovsky-ends (accessed May 5, 2018); Bullough, *Moneyland.*

130. Buckley, *The Politics of Unfree Labour in Russia.*

131. Ilya Yablokov, "Nobel Peace Prize: How Dmitry Muratov Built Rus-sia's 'Bravest' Newspaper, *Novaya Gazeta*," *The Conversation*, 2021, http:// theconversation.com/nobel-peace-prize-how-dmitry-muratov-built-russias-bravest -newspaper-novaya-gazeta-169560.

132. "The Nobel Peace Prize 2021," NobelPrize.org, October 8, 2021, https://www .nobelprize.org/prizes/peace/2021/press-release/.

133. See, for example, "Astrakhan Focus of Anti-Putin Protests," Euronews, April 14, 2012, http://www.euronews.com/2012/04/14/astrakhan-focus-of-anti-putin -protests (accessed May 5, 2018).

134. "Alexei Navalny: Thousands across Russia Defy Ban on Protests," *BBC News*, April 21, 2021, https://www.bbc.com/news/world-europe-56834655.

135. "'Psychological Violence': Alexei Navalny Says He Is Forced to Watch Eight Hours of State TV a Day," *Guardian*, August 26, 2021, https://www.theguardian .com/world/2021/aug/26/alexei-navalny-russia-prison-state-tv-china-labour-camp -psychological-violence.

Chapter 9

Gender and Politics

Janet Elise Johnson and Alexandra Novitskaya

Women have a huge presence in Russia. Women make up a higher proportion of senior management positions in small to midsize businesses in Russia—around 40 percent—than anywhere else in the world.[1] Tatiana Bakal'chuk, the founder of internet retailer Wildberries, with a 2021 net worth of $13 billion, is Russia's richest woman and one of the richest women in the world. The late dissidents-turned-civil-rights-activists Liudmila Alekseeva, Natalia Gorbanevskaia, and Valeria Novodvorskaia have been replaced with a new generation, such as Alena Popova and Mari Davtyan, who are fighting for victims of domestic violence; Lyubov Sobol, who was a lawyer at Alexei Navalny's Anti-Corruption Foundation until its forced closure in 2021; and Yulia Tsvetkova, who has been imprisoned since 2019 for her body-positive and LGBTQ activism. Gaining international fame after performing near the Kremlin, the feminist punk band Pussy Riot became the symbol of the 2011–2012 opposition in Russia, joining other women, such as Evgeniia Chirikova, an environmental activist, who had dared to criticize Putin's rule (and who fled Russia in 2015). TV journalist Ksenia Sobchak ran against Putin in the 2018 presidential elections. Not immune to violence, women politicians (Galina Starovoitova in 1998), journalists (Anna Politkovskaia in 2006 and Anastasia Baburova in 2009), and human rights activists (Natalia Estemirova in 2009) have been prominent among those murdered for their activism.

These achievements reflect not only the extraordinary efforts of these women but the Soviet legacy. In the Soviet Union, women had been heavily recruited into the labor force because of Marxist ideology's promise of equality and the imperative of catching up with industrialization in the West. In the 1920s, with pressure from Inessa Armand and the feminist Aleksandra Kollontai, who were the first two women to head the newly formed Women's Department of the Communist Party, the Bolshevik government created what could be considered highly progressive legislation in support of women, such as paid maternity leave, subsidized day care, legalized abortion, easily accessible divorce by either spouse, and restrictions on sexual harassment. The Soviet system also advanced women into local politics, surpassing their Western counterparts.

However, these advances were mostly for cis-gender heterosexual women—with female same-sex desire framed as a mental illness and trans issues only addressed periodically with crude operations[2]—and overall, women gained more duties than liberation or equal rights. After World War II—when there were twice as many women aged twenty to twenty-nine than men—women were summoned to rebuild the ruined country and to replenish its lost population, to produce and reproduce. Throughout, Soviet women faced a triple burden of work, home, and procurement of scarce basic goods. In contrast to the propaganda of women on tractors, women were restricted from around five hundred of the most lucrative jobs on the pretense of protecting their fertility. There was only one woman, Ekaterina Furtseva, who was a member of the ruling Politburo, but only for four years (1957–1961) before being shifted to the much less powerful position of minister of culture. In the Soviet Union, women's inclusion was not about gender equality but about equal mobilization of everyone in society.[3] It was faux emancipation.

In the post-Soviet period, gender equality for women has remained elusive and complicated. New problems—such as sex trafficking and widespread sexual harassment—emerged among the new freedoms. The shrinking of the welfare state put many women, especially single mothers and disabled women, into poverty, even as they may qualify for benefits. Even middle-class women have had trouble making ends meet, as families were put on a roller-coaster ride of economic insecurity. Most precarious have been women migrants, who often lack legal residence rights and are often not ethnically Russian, which makes them more vulnerable to crime and corruption as well as subject to virulent xenophobia. Most limited in their rights are women in the North Caucasus, where male leaders, backed by the Kremlin, have called for a revival of religious "traditions" such as bride kidnapping, female genital mutilation, arranged marriage, and polygamy; with the Russian government's tacit support, Chechnya's leader has authorized a reign of terror, including defending brutal "honor" killings of women, and attacks on lesbian and bisexual women as well as transgender persons.[4]

Since Putin came to power in 2000, there has been the appearance of more inclusion of women in politics. Valentina Matvienko governed Russia's second city, St. Petersburg, from 2003 until 2011, when she became chair of the upper house, the highest government position held by a woman since Catherine the Great. Since 2013, Elvira Nabiullina, a longtime member of Putin's government, has headed Russia's Central Bank, the first woman to head a central bank in one of the world's biggest economies. Though still lagging behind the world average, women in the bicameral legislature reached the highest proportions in post-Soviet Russian history in 2021, with 22.2 percent in the Federation Council and 16.4 percent in the State Duma.

But these increases in women in politics have been a bait and switch, a con in which the appearance of gender equality is given while the reality is backsliding.[5] Though still a legal and provided part of state-funded health care, abortion has been increasingly restricted since 2003, for the first time since Stalin, and motherhood promoted as the best choice for women. Though there were some small reforms on domestic violence in 2016, they were reversed six months later, when Orthodox Church–sponsored groups worried that the reforms meant that it was not okay to slap your children or your wife.[6] A comprehensive law on domestic violence, required by Russia's international obligations, was proposed in 2019, but was again waylaid by conservative groups and then the pandemic. The most prominent gender-related policy is the "maternity capital," introduced in 2007, in which the government promised a contribution to children's education, housing, or mothers' retirement to women (later single fathers also) who have more than one child.[7] (In 2020, the program's eligibility was extended to first-time mothers.) Such a payment—about $7,000 in 2016—may provide a small kind of assistance to mothers but ignores the underlying problems of health care, child care, and irresponsible fathers that contribute to Russia's declining population. Three of four eligible women do not use it, either because they still wouldn't be able to afford a mortgage or because they do not trust the government-run banks to protect their pension savings.[8]

The repressive legislation passed in the aftermath of the 2011–2012 protests has had particularly negative consequences for women. The 2012 law requiring organizations engaging in political activities and receiving foreign funds to register as "foreign agents," which was expanded over the next several years, has been used against more than a dozen feminist and lesbian organizations, incurring great costs for the organizations even when they then win in court.[9] The 2013 law banning "gay propaganda" toward minors threatens non-heterosexual women, particularly lesbian mothers, and legitimizes attacks on and social control over all women as well as people whose gender and sexuality do not fit the standard established by the government.

This chapter explains the limitations placed on women in politics and the importance of feminism in opposition. We also make a deeper critique, arguing that gender constitutes the essential, internal supports of the edifice of the regime that has been consolidated under Putin. It is not just that, as the feminist-identified protest punk band Pussy Riot explained, "Putin is a symbol of sexism and patriarchal attitudes . . . present in every unit of the society."[10] We argue that only by seeing gender can Russian politics be understood.

MALE DOMINANCE OF POLITICS

Over the last two decades, political science has moved beyond the transition paradigm with its focus on Russia's level of democratization.[11] With Putin's rise to power, observers labeled Russia first as a hybrid regime, then electoral authoritarian and, by 2021, authoritarian but increasingly recognize that such regimes have their own particular dynamics. The attention turned toward informal politics, the informal institutions and practices that undermine the formal institutions and procedures laid out in the Russian constitution.[12] Instead of a meaningful formal political system, Russia, like other Eurasian countries, has a hybrid of empty rules and regulations mixed with the institutionalization of informal rules and practices that sometimes use the formal rules but more often subvert them. The system is neo-patrimonial, characterized by personalistic relations such as nepotism (favoring relatives) and cronyism (favoring friends), even as the formal-legal sometimes matters.

This new regime dynamics paradigm is more ideologically neutral and promises much insight into how such regimes work; however, most political scientists who study Russia are blind to gender.[13] By gender, we mean rules about how men and women are to behave that operate as central organizing forces in intersection with other structures of power such as class, ethnicity, race, and sexuality. While the first generation of gender scholars thought more about women, more recent theorizing considers the role of masculinity and how gender gets embedded in social and political institutions in the form of male dominance.[14] Extending the scholarship showing that post-communism is gendered, we argue that gender is embedded in and essential to Russia's informal politics.[15] Our intent is not about blaming men but to see how gender can stabilize regimes, something that is especially important for regimes like Russia, where formal constitutions cannot provide predictability.

Most obviously, the high-glossed image of Putin illustrates the power of "hegemonic masculinity," the masculine ideal for political leaders.[16] More so than in most other countries, the Kremlin has been explicit in its attempt to establish Putin as the ideal man-leader. Pictures of tough-guy Putin, often with a bare sculpted chest or illustrating his manly prowess hunting, racing, or practicing judo are propagated (with a new set of bare-chested photos released in August 2017), but they are mere phantasms, as Putin is never in real danger.[17] His image has also been sexualized to show that he is the only man that women—and the whole country—should want. As a result, his masculinity is unlike other statesmen, who must appear with their wives (and children) at their sides. Putin's former wife was virtually invisible, and most Russians saw no problem when his divorce was made public in 2013. Even his alleged extramarital relationships, with ex-housekeeper Svetlana Krivonogikh and former rhythmic gymnast Alina Kabaeva, perhaps even fathering their children and sending millions of dollars and plum positions their way, have been unremarkable. This informally constructed masculinity, not the typical symbols of constitutionalism and the flag, has been central to legitimating Putin's leadership and the post-Soviet regime.[18]

Despite the assertions that this hegemonic masculinity with its embrace of heterosexuality is traditionally Russian, this masculinity is revisionism that offers alternatives to what many saw as the powerless, emasculated Soviet man. Hegemonic masculinity also uses the Soviet model of gender discourse in which sexuality was silenced and conflict within heterosexual relationships was hidden.[19] Finally, this masculinity evokes an old myth of the sexual innocence of Russians, a new conservatism, where homosexuality is viewed as foreign.[20] That the Kremlin has had to do this much cultural work shows that Putin's position is more precarious than most Westerner observers assume.[21]

Over the last several years, Putin's masculinity project has been bolstered by the consolidation of an alliance with the Russian Orthodox Church based on a shared critique of Western "gender ideology."[22] (The church's Patriarch Kirill openly supported Putin's return to the presidency as "God's miracle," and Putin had an official celebration for Kirill at the Kremlin.[23]) The new church-state "anti-gender" campaign opposes gender equality, reproductive rights, sex education, and LGBTQ rights marked by the antigay legislation.[24] These moves helped Putin claim global leadership of illiberal populism around the world and his party, United Russia, to continue to win enough seats to retain power. To enlist popular support for Putin protecting constitutional amendments in 2020, the regime included an amendment reifying that marriage was only between a man and a woman. This hegemonic masculinity also helps explain Putin's warmongering in Georgia, Ukraine, and Syria, which, because of the financial costs, does not seem rational. Russia had never gotten rid of its imperial ambitions, but Putin's land grab in Crimea reads as a reassertion of his masculinity through imperialist lenses: History would have never "forgiven" him for failing to act, so he had to act.

Russia's regime also illustrates the informal power of "homosociality," how being of the same sex can help individuals "understand and thus [can] predict each other's behavior."[25] In most places around the world, elite networks have historically been "predominantly accessible for other men as well as more valuable when built between men." Homosociality protects networks and provides predictability, rational goals for elite men in any regime, but especially ones that do not have predictable formal institutions. In Russia, homosociality is most evident in the key elite networks that dominate Russian politics and which have included very few women. This is particularly true among the *siloviki*. The dominance of men is essential to the network: they draw personnel from the Soviet coercive structures such as the KGB that were predominantly men. In addition, the *silovik* mentality is about hegemonic masculinity and homosociality. They call for more order engineered by a strong state staffed by men, with imported cultural traditions such as secrecy that help keep women out.[26] Putin's relationship with the *siloviki* may be uneasy at times, but his idealization of the KGB culture—a homosocial experience virtually impossible for women to share—began in his early childhood.[27] Putin has even been open about the importance of homosociality, asserting at the 2011 International Women's Forum that it is easier to work with men than women.[28]

While seeing that informal elite networks—made up of those with economic and/or political power—have proven more reliable than Russia's unclear institutions and weak parties,[29] most political scientists of Russia have missed the importance of hegemonic masculinity and homosociality to the building and maintenance of the personal relationships within the networks. For example, Alena Ledeneva has pointed to the Kremlin's revival of the tradition of enforced solidarity and mutual cover-up (*krugovaiia poruka*), but failed to note the gender of this practice, as evidenced in her illustrative political cartoon: men in suits stand in a circle with guns pointed at each other.[30] Similarly, the use of compromising materials (*kompromat*) by the Kremlin has been seen as a key strategy to keep elites from stepping out of line, but this observation has missed the way *kompromat* tends to mix allegations of abuse of office, disloyalty, or incompetence with titillating questions about sexual behavior, orientation, or sufficient masculinity. For example, in 1999 when Putin was head of the Federal Security Service, or FSB, which is the post-Soviet successor to the KGB, a video of Russia's prosecutor general—or someone who looked a lot like him—in bed with two women was shown on TV, causing the prosecutor to lose his job; he had been investigating corruption in the Kremlin. Putin's job at the KGB, as the Soviet Union collapsed, was not as a spy but as a case officer who gathered information about people in order to be able to manipulate them, a skill he appears to have translated into the post-Soviet era.[31]

The threat of *kompromat* works so well now that the actual use of it against the inner circle is rare. In one case where *kompromat* was deployed and not just threatened, the former defense minister Anatoly Serdiukov's affair was made public in order to undermine his protection from his father-in-law (Viktor Zubkov), a former deputy prime minister and friend of Putin. Critics and opposition leaders fare worse, several of whom have been caught in a "honeypot" by a woman who offers herself up and then brings out drugs or bondage to catch them on video in compromising positions. Before the 2016 election for the State Duma, a videotape of Mikhail Kasyanov, a former prime minister and opposition leader, was played on national television, which showed him having sex with a female member of the opposition, followed by pillow talk in which Kasyanov appears to admit to skimming money, dismiss his fellow opposition leaders, and agree to make sure his lover gets a position in the Duma "with a fat paycheck."[32]

WOMEN IN POLITICS UNDER PUTIN

In addition to holding the regime together, hegemonic masculinity and homosociality establish a bulwark of male dominance that restricts women in politics. Feminist theorists point out that hegemonic masculinity comes with "emphasized femininity," ideals of women who are compliant to male domi-nance.[33] Emphasized femininity in Russian politics is illustrated most color-fully in Putin's comments about Hillary Clinton. In a remark understood as a derisive penis joke, he questioned her ability to lead: "At a minimum, a head of state should have a head."[34] Later, responding to Clinton's comparison between Putin and Hitler (for annexing Crimea), Putin said that "it's better not to argue with women," adding that Clinton had never been "too graceful" in her statements, and that strong accusations usually illustrate weakness, but "maybe weakness is not the worst quality for a woman."[35]

Though made about an American politician, these comments serve as oblique, public threats to women participating in Russian politics. The threat also appears in the guise of pseudo-respect for Russian women as the most beautiful and in sexist assumptions about them. For example, in the early 2000s, a party campaigned against Matvienko with the slogan "Being Governor Is Not a Woman's Business."[36] In the 2016 Duma election, *Life-News*, a tabloid with links to the Kremlin, published nude pictures of a Moscow member of the opposition and her (female) chief of staff. In her 2018 presidential bid, Ksenia Sobchak faced a barrage of sexist commentary in the media and from male politicians, including being called a "disgusting bitch."[37] This was set in the context of a plethora of images of sexualized women encouraging (male) citizens to vote for Putin, as well as an ad warn-ing Russians that, if they did not vote, a candidate like Sobchak (who had expressed support for LGBTQ rights) would win and help gay people take over.[38] These informal rules of the gender game have been so institutional-ized in Russia that they only need to be rarely enforced in order to signal the severe consequences facing women who do not stay in line.

The result is that male dominance has simultaneously enabled a small num-ber of women to access positions of some power, while severely limiting their opportunities to represent women and push for gender equality. As in other countries, women tend to be excluded from the more "powerful" positions on issues related to law enforcement, military, and international diplomacy and are relegated to what are traditionally viewed as care-related issues of family, children, health, and welfare. This has been especially true for social and health policy issues in which heads of ministries and legislative committees are informally reserved for women. During the COVID-19 crisis, two women—Anna Popova, a doctor who heads Russia's agency for consumer rights and well-being, and Tatiana Golikova, the deputy prime minister with responsibility over health, the social sphere, and pension provision—have been the most prominent public health spokespersons, but they have been unable to instill confidence in Russia's vaccine.

Outside of these "feminized" ministries, women are brought in as "cleaners" to sweep messes under the rug so that the men leaders look good. For example, to insiders, Matvienko was brought to "clean up" St. Petersburg, but she failed to keep corruption under wraps (that is, to keep up Putin's cover story of bringing order to Russia). Her final landing place, chairing the Federation Council, is a position that provides few patronage perks. In other cases, women famous for achievements outside of politics are used as "showgirls"—to use the Russian nomenclature—to enlist support for the regime's political party. This is a feminized version of the Russian practice of "locomotives": nominating big names such as celebrities, singers, and athletes (including an opera singer, a rhythmic gymnast, and a former Playboy model) to attract voters.[39] Their roles are portrayed as being kissed on the hand by their male counterparts, putting on makeup, or acting beautiful and silly.[40] In the 2016 Duma election, nationalism was attached to the showgirl role, exemplified by the election of the "sex symbol" Natalia Poklonskaya. Poklonskaya, once a Ukrainian citizen, changed sides when Crimea was annexed in 2014 and was appointed the general prosecutor of Crimea for Russia (and then prosecuted pro-Ukrainian activists). In 2021, Poklonskaya was forced out for not following the party line but left with some important spoils (high-priced apartments in Crimea and Moscow); Maria Butina, convicted as an unregistered foreign agent in the United States in 2018 for ingratiating herself in conservative circles, took up the mantle of the Duma's nationalist showgirl.

Other members of parliament, most notably Irina Yarovaia, Elena Mizulina, and Ekaterina Lakhova, have been "loyalists," known for sponsoring hastily conceived, ideological bills to signal their allegiance with Putin; Mizulina and Lakhova are particularly striking because they once identified as feminists. Mizulina, who has changed her party affiliation several times and gained notoriety during her 2008–2015 tenure as the head of what is left of the Duma Committee on Family, Women, and Children's Affairs, authored laws restricting abortion and banning "gay propaganda" while proposing taxing divorce, taking children away from same-sex parents, and adding Orthodoxy to the preamble of the constitution. She also spearheaded the successful campaign to undo progress on domestic violence. Lakhova, once head of the woman-only faction Women of Russia, championed the law banning adoption of Russian children by Americans, helping her to secure a move to the Federation Council in 2014. Yarovaia coauthored the "foreign agent" law that threatens nongovernmental organizations, as well as a 2016 package of legislation (known as the Yarovaia law) under the guise of "antiterrorism," which greatly increases the regime's ability to surveil citizens' online activities. Instead of having to demonstrate loyalty to the regime, male deputies are more likely to leave the Duma to go into private or state-owned enterprises, indicating their greater access to the long-term spoils of patronage and political entrepreneurship.[41]

In all these roles, women must have powerful (male) patrons or demonstrate ultimate loyalty to the regime. Even the head of the Central Bank, Elvira Nabiullina, with strong economist credentials and mostly supported by an economically liberal coalition, is the protégé of Putin's close friend and is married to a chief theorist for Putin's economic policy. All these roles come with limited power. In the best case, they are akin to throwing women off a "glass cliff" by bringing them into failing businesses.[42] The worst-case scenario is illustrated by Maria Maksakova, a prominent opera singer, who was elected in 2011 as a showgirl but later spoke out against the "gay propaganda" law.[43] In October 2016, she and her husband (also a deputy) fled to Ukraine, claiming they had been hounded by the FSB for their views, even to the point of Maksakova's miscarrying (her husband was then shot and killed in 2017, apparently by the FSB, though she now rejects this assertion). In 2021, the most prominent advocate in the Russian parliament for women and LGBTQ people, Oksana Pushkhina, former TV talk show host and deputy chair of the Committee on Family, Women, and Children, was not allowed to run for reelection.

Looking at the inclusion of women in Russian political arenas also indicates the relative power of these arenas in the regime. With the introduction of competitive elections, the proportion of women in the legislatures dropped by more than half, and then continued to drop through the 1990s (see figure 9.1). Since Putin came to power, there have been increases of women in the Duma, the Constitutional Court, and the Public Chamber, arenas that are showplaces of constitutionalism or representation. Even so, women continue to be underrepresented. At the top of the regime, the president and the prime minister have never been women. As of 2021, there have only been six women governors since the end of the USSR and only one head of a federal district (the presidential envoy who oversees a set of regions; see chapter 3), Matvienko, for six months. In other bastions of power, the Presidium of the

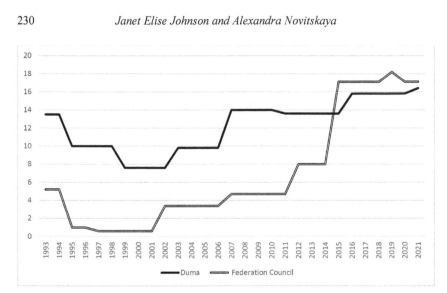

Figure 9.1. Percent of Women in Russia's Legislatures, 1993–2021 (*Sources:* Inter-Parliamentary Union Parline. "Monthly ranking of women in national parliaments," September 27, 2021, https://data.ipu.org/women-ranking. Russian State Duma. "Status i polnomochiya, poryadok formirovaniya i Reglament Gosudarstvennoy Dumy" [Status and powers, formation procedure and regulations of the State Duma]. October 12, 2021, http://duma.gov.ru/duma/about/.)

State Council and the Security Council, there have been very few women. This pattern of "the higher, the fewer" women in politics is common to most political systems, including the Soviet one, but the Russian case helps reveal how much this pattern is now about informal politics. The most informal gatherings—perhaps in the sauna at Putin's various homes—likely have no space for women at all.

FEMINIST ACTIVISM RESISTING MALE DOMINANCE

Perhaps unsurprisingly given these limitations on women and representation, the primary arena of resistance to male dominance in Russia's politics has been outside the political system. In the first decade after the Soviet collapse, feminism gained only a small toehold in Russia in some gender studies centers and women's crisis centers, where the former focused on academic apprehension of feminist theory and gender studies and the latter addressed violence against women.[44] During that period, feminism in Russia did not become mainstream nor was it even properly understood by the masses. Many Russians embraced "traditional" gender roles—in theory more than practice—because of the Soviet faux emancipation. While women tended to staff the nongovernmental organizations that proliferated after communism, many were focused on social issues, extending women's traditional caregiving roles from their own children to the broader society, and most did not see themselves as organizing as women, let alone as feminists.[45] Those who were interested in promoting gender equality tended to use the weaker language of "women's rights" common in the Western donor community rather than the confrontational feminisms that had emerged in the 1960s and 1970s in the West.[46]

After 2000, small pockets of more radical feminism began to emerge with the growth of social media and increased availability of internet access across the country. Russia's first prominent online feminist platform, Feministki (http://feministki.livejournal.com), founded in 2006, grew to several thousand subscribers and prompted lively debate, including over whether women should live separately from men. Other early groups included the radical intersectional Moscow Feminist Group, the separatist Womenation, and the sexist media–tackling Za Feminizm (Pro Feminism). Although most eschew direct involvement in politics, the opposition party Yabloko created an active "gender faction" headed by a self-identified feminist that has provided more public visibility to the small groups.

Pussy Riot arose as part of these developments.[47] In December 2011 at the beginning of protests against electoral fraud, they took the stage near Red Square in multicolored balaclavas that covered their faces, and then, in February 2012, they briefly occupied Moscow's showplace church calling on the "Mother of God [to] Drive Putin Away." As their lyrics explicitly took on Putin, homophobia, sexism, and the regime's alliance with the Russian Orthodox Church, Pussy Riot became the first feminist-identified group to openly and directly confront the regime.

For the first time, the regime felt threatened by feminism, arresting the three members of the group that they could find and then, after a show trial reminiscent of the Soviet period, sentencing them to two years in a labor camp. The trial of Pussy Riot also showed how the gender of the persecuted artists could be used against them (from accusations of being bad mothers to being somebody else's puppets, since such young women could not possibly have come up with all those profoundly critical ideas by themselves).[48] Putin stated that he pitied the imprisoned members, not for being incarcerated under harsh conditions, but for losing their "feminine dignity" by their protest.[49] For Putin, a woman who would participate in a demonstration or, even worse, facilitate protest action is a deviant and does not possess "real" or "proper" femininity.[50] Much of the Russian public was swayed by the show trial—leaving the group misunderstood as blasphemers more than political dissidents.[51] The prosecution gave Pussy Riot international prestige, making this feminist punk band a symbol of resistance to Russia's regime.

Since Pussy Riot's imprisonment, the repression of feminist projects has been stepped up as part of the overall restrictions on independent political expression, including on social media. After Russia's invasion of Ukraine in 2014, feminism became a specific target amid the omnipresent nationalist propaganda predicated on hegemonic masculinity and emphasized femininity. Feminist ideas challenging these norms were branded as anti-Russian. The most prominent women's crisis center, ANNA, was put on the "foreign agent" list in 2016, apparently because of its domestic violence activism during Duma debates.[52] A number of other women's NGOs and university gender studies centers were subsequently declared "foreign agents," including, in 2020, a prominent women's rights group, Moscow-based Nasiliyu. net (No to Violence), as well as a number of individual activists, such as feminist artist Daria Apakhonchich.[53] Finally, artist and former drama teacher Yulia Tsvetkova from Komsomolsk-on-Amur (Russia's Far East) faced state persecution in 2020–2021 when she was charged with violating the "gay propaganda" law and disseminating pornography for drawing feminist and LGBTQ-affirming art. The feminist and LGBTQ community responded to her trial with a series of protests which spread beyond the insularity of feminist and LGBTQ activism and involved support from various artists and the progressive media.[54]

However, feminists resist, using both conventional and innovative forms. Feminists marched in their own column in an October 2012 protest for the first time in post-Soviet Russian history and have continued to do so, as in the 2014 May Day parade.[55] In 2012–2013, a group of feminist activists organized such exhibitions of feminist art as the *Feminist Pencil* in Moscow and in St. Petersburg, uniting women artists from various regions and artistic traditions. V-Day, an international campaign against gender violence, reached Russia in 2013–2014. In 2014, Eve Ensler's *The Vagina Monologues* play ran for three days with great success (all three performances were sold out), with all proceeds going to support crisis centers for women. These events brought gender violence and widespread sexism, both safer issues than directly challenging the regime, to the public space. In 2016, activists protested against a reform that would decriminalize battery and briefly won a concession that made domestic violence a more serious crime (but this moderate success was reversed six months later). Feminists in St. Petersburg have taken sides on the sex work/prostitution divide, with Silver Rose formed by former sex workers and their allies to provide psychological and legal assistance to sex workers, versus Eve's Ribs (Rebra Evy), which advocates the abolition of prostitution. In 2018, a student in international relations at St. Petersburg State University protested on International Women's Day by making posters of sexist statements made by the faculty, such as "women do not have a place in politics," and the head of the department threatened an investigation into the student.[56] Essential resistance to hegemonic masculinity has come from LGBTQ groups, some of which include feminism. Side by Side, which runs an annual LGBTQ film festival and successfully fought a "foreign agent" allegation in the courts, has even had feminist and women's organizations come to them for advice.[57]

Since the mid-2010s, feminist bloggers and influencers on social media have been steadily gaining popularity and recognition. Many organize and participate in a broad range of grassroots politics combining artistic expression with activism and a feminist agenda with a wider array of social justice issues such as environmental causes, support for Russia's political opposition, migrants and refugees' rights, prisoners' rights, and so on. For example, St. Petersburg DJ and social media blogger Lölja Nordic, with an audience of around twenty thousand, has founded an anti-domestic violence project Ne Vinovata (Not Guilty), but also advocates for animal rights and ecology.[58] Moscow-based poet and artist Daria Serenko, who has a combined social media audience of over thirty-two thousand, created "Tikhii Piket" (Quiet Picketing), a performance art series consisting of her carrying posters with feminist statements on the Moscow subway. She also organized, in August 2020, "chains of solidarity and love," feminist public protests in solidarity with the women in Belarus facing oppression after the antigovernment protests, and again in February 2021 to support imprisoned Alexey Navalny's wife, Yulia Navalnaia.[59] Another feminist blogger from St. Petersburg, Maria Tunkara, who publishes reviews of sex toys and beauty products to the audience of 103,000 followers on Instagram under the name of Young Masha, has raised issues of beauty standards, women's sexuality, and the nationalism and racism faced by non-Slavic and mixed-raced women in Russia.[60] Another example of intersectional, feminist and anti-nationalist activism is the work of the collective behind the online beauty zine Agasshin, dedicated to highlighting the experiences of Russia's ethnic minorities.[61] Although it might be tempting to dismiss many feminist bloggers and influencers' focus on lifestyle, in the words of gender scholar Ella Rossman, in contemporary Russia the women's movement and "internet feminists" specifically are crucial influences in the politicization of the youth: by reading feminist blogs, young Russian women learn that "personal is political" and thus, via such intimate topics as "day-to-day life, personal freedom, the body, and relationships, they enter a larger political dimension" and develop their own agency.[62]

The rise of social media has also been instrumental in larger flashes of mobilization. In 2016, tens of thousands of women—and some men—organized a virtual flash mob sharing their stories of rape, sexual assault, incest, and sexual harassment on social media, started by a Ukrainian woman's Facebook post using the hashtag #Iamnotafraidtospeakout (*#yaneboius'skaza ti/#yaneboius'skazat'*). Sympathizing with those who had spoken out, Russian and Ukrainian celebrities shared their personal stories of sexual assault. More than just discourse, the online flash mob led to the resignation of a school principal for negligence and a criminal conviction of a popular teacher (for "engaging in any sexual activities with a child under sixteen years of age") at one of Moscow's most prominent public schools (No. 57, portrayed in the 2010 documentary film *My Perestroika*). Despite its similarity to the #Iamnotafraidtospeakout campaign, the Russian public's initial reaction to the US-initiated #Metoo movement was a mix of skepticism and ridicule, as prominent politicians and TV personalities—including the chair of the Duma's Committee on Family, Women, and Children, Tatiana Pletneva—asserted that sexual harassment was foreign to Russia.[63] However, another online flash mob broke out in 2018 when the Duma Ethics Committee found nothing wrong with the behavior of Deputy Leonid Slutski, whom several women journalists alleged had groped them. The flash mob collected 13.9 million signatures calling for his resignation.[64] Several national media outlets started boycotting the Duma as an "unsafe space for women." Since the 2017 decriminalization of domestic violence, feminists have been reenergized. The largest post-Soviet feminist street protest was in support of the three Khachaturyan sisters, who, seeing no other option in the face of no protective mechanisms from the state, killed their father after years of physical, emotional, and sexual abuse. In 2019 activists staged an online flash mob #Ididnotwanttodie (#*Yanekhotelumirat'*) in which they used makeup to portray battered women.

The cross-mobilization between gay rights and feminist activism has also helped foster a change in support of LGBTQ issues among the opposition. The once-nationalist-and-not-particularly-progressive opposition leader Aleksei Navalny included the possibility of solving inheritance and civil union issues and permitting pride marches on his agenda.[65] His promises, while incomplete, were strikingly different from the way Russian politicians had dealt with LGBTQ issues in the past. Similarly, during the 2021 Duma elections campaign, several opposition candidates included LGBTQ and feminist rights in their agenda, including two Moscow politicians—independent (and former Yabloko member) Anastasia Brykhanova, and Yabloko member Nikolay Kavkazskii. Although neither won, their open embrace of feminism and support for LGBTQ rights demonstrate a significant change in a society where both pro and anti-regime forces readily use homophobia as a successful tactic for demeaning the political enemy.[66]

CONCLUSION

Scholars and students of Russian politics often do not see gender, a blindness that the Russian regime cultivates even as it uses gender. Gender, along with other differences such as race, ethnicity, and sexuality, is cast as natural and thus outside of politics. Bringing gender into focus helps observers grasp the operation of informal politics—bolstered by support beams of hegemonic masculinity and homosociality—underneath the increasingly thinning veneer of constitutionalism and democracy. Understanding these gendered informal politics also helps explain the increase in the number of women in formal politics since Putin came to power. As feminist political scientists have been arguing, the mere presence of women in formal political arenas does not secure gender equality because the practices and norms of male dominance remain. In Russia, the regime restricts women's positions and limits their opportunities, reserving only a few options—regime-worshiping loyalists, workhorses in fields typically understood to be feminine, temporary political cleaners in messy situations, or mere showgirls—and requires a powerful (male) patron.

Seeing gender also helps explain the emergence of Pussy Riot, with its seemingly crass lyrics designed to counter the regime's crass masculinity and homosociality in politics, as well as the regime's overreaction to these "girls" whom most Russians do not support. Contesting the regime's consolidated male dominance challenges institutionalized corruption—the issue that drove the 2011–2012 protests—much more so than anticorruption legislation, which has often been used against the regime's opponents. The regime's crackdown on feminist and LGBTQ protests reveals just how limited are the opportunities for any political expression in Russia today.

All these gendered informal politics help explain the paradox between increasing numbers of women in office under Putin's rule and the lack of progress in gender equality. The maternalist policies of Putin's regime, such as restrictions on abortion and maternity capital, fit with emphasized femininity, while tackling structural gender inequality (including criminalizing domestic violence) does not. Policies limiting the rights of LGBTQ citizens also fit the gendered informal politics of this kind of regime. The gender of informal politics also explains why the regime only cursorily attends to society's problems, while leaving most women, men, and their families on a roller coaster of financial instability. Facing traditionalist propaganda unchallenged by a strong feminist or women's movement, most women in Russia remain under the burden of not only work but also housework, childbearing, and child rearing, in conventional (if not always married) heterosexual relationships.

The informal obstacles in Russia have implications for explaining weak gender equality across post-communist states, even as almost all have passed gender equality and domestic violence legislation. While the smaller post-communist states needed the appearance of gender equality represented by these legislative reforms as they sought membership in European institutions, Russia is a former superpower that has focused on a reenergizing military and foreign policy and increasingly distancing itself from the West. In all post-communist states, real equality remains elusive, a puzzle in a world with some visibly powerful strong women. Raising questions about how hegemonic masculinity and homosociality get institutionalized uncovers new layers in this equality paradox of formal laws but weak implementation.

AUTHORS' POSTSCRIPT

As this book was going to press, Russia's male-dominated authoritarianism, with its increasingly anti-Western stance, took a horrifying turn by launching a full invasion of Ukraine. Much can be gained from using a gendered perspective here, as well. First, gender and sexuality discourses have been deployed front and center in Russia's justification of the war. In the year leading up to the 2022 invasion, Putin turned toward the elites promoting war; these "hawks" also tended to espouse social conservatism, which included sexism and LGBTQ-phobia, and Putin signaled his support for these elites by mirroring these attitudes in his public speeches. Speaking at the Valdai Discussion Club in October 2021, he proclaimed teaching children about gender fluidity to be "truly monstrous" and "verging on a crime against humanity."[67] At his December national news conference, Putin went further, asserting his support for the "traditional approach that a woman is a woman, a man is a man, a mother is a mother, and a father is a father."

Then, as the war began in February 2022, Putin evoked gender several times in speeches that justified the war and attacked Russia's internal enemies. He rationalized the war by, among other things, Russia's need to protect its "traditional values" (centered on heteronormative families) and branded all anti-war Russian citizens as pro-Western traitors who care more about "foie gras, oysters, and so-called gender freedoms" than about national interests.[68] Patriarch Kirill of the Russian Orthodox Church, an important ally of Putin, has been even more explicit about the link between the war and anti-genderism. Two weeks after Russia started the war, he gave a sermon making the patently false claim that there was a need to protect people in the Russian-occupied Donbas who had been at risk of "extermination" from Ukraine and the West for their refusal to hold gay pride parades.[69]

Second, the war has been gendered and homophobic in its violence, with building evidence of systematic rape and sexual assault of Ukrainian women, girls, and some men by Russian soldiers.[70] While much has been made about the professionalization of Russia's military over the last decade, it appears to be continuing the Soviet army's practice of war rape, such as in the "emancipation" of Eastern Europe after World War II. The regime does not appear to have rid itself of the symbiosis between "nationalism, militarism, and patriarchal masculinity [that was established] in Stalinist Soviet society."[71]

Third, few elites, let alone the more precarious women elites, have spoken out against the war, as the retaliation has been severe and swift. Nina Beliaieva, member of a municipal council in the Voronezh region, is one of the few elected officials who publicly condemned the war. She was immediately expelled from the Communist Party and then put under criminal investigation, and she had to flee the country for her safety.[72]

At the same time, women's rights, feminist, and queer activists have been an important part of civil society's anti-war efforts.[73] Pussy Riot quickly created a mechanism to raise money for Ukraine, but the most innovative has been the Feminist Antiwar Resistance, a transnational network of Russian feminist activists.[74] Staying mostly anonymous to try to avoid state persecution, they have been staging targeted actions in Russia to show that it is a full-scale war that the state-controlled media have been hiding from Russian citizens. In the words of one anonymous activist from provincial Russia, "The propaganda is so loud it's deafening. . . . Although we do not have access to the television, we have access to the streets: unlike social media posts and links, an antiwar poster will reach a person at a bus stop regardless of their political interests."[75] To date, the Feminist Antiwar Resistance's initiatives have included placing makeshift crosses in residential neighborhoods to commemorate civilian deaths in besieged Mariupol, leaving anti-war statements in public places like grocery stores and apartment blocks, and carrying around anti-war messages attached to clothes and accessories.[76] Under Russia's recent anti-dissent laws, all such actions are considered a crime punishable by up to fifteen years in prison. The activists insist that they have no leaders and pursue a horizontal, or grassroots structure: Anyone is welcome to join and contribute. Thus, most of the activism is nameless and small-scale, but those who have gotten caught, like artist Sasha Skochilenko, who put price tags with anti-war proclamations on groceries in a St. Petersburg supermarket, have received harsh and cruel punishment.[77]

In addition, other women, both formally with the Union of Committees of Soldiers' Mothers, which has been advocating on behalf of conscripted soldiers and their families since the 1980s, as well as some previously non-politicized mothers of soldiers killed in the war, have been marking the war losses in public ways, trying, for example, to hold officials accountable for the deaths of their sons, or to break through the wall of silence and censorship surrounding Russia's military losses in the war.[78] Such initiatives are political acts in themselves in a new repressive environment where the regime denies the reality of the war.

Finally, many progressive Russians have assessed that fleeing Russia is their only alternative to imprisonment or forced silence. This leaves Russia more conservative and more authoritarian, but activists in exile are scrambling to stop Russia's mass murder and destruction in Ukraine.

—2022

DISCUSSION QUESTIONS

1. What are the main achievements of women in Russian politics?
2. What are the main obstacles to women's participation and representation in Russian politics?
3. What kinds of feminisms exist in Russia, and how successful are they at challenging male dominance?
4. How does "seeing gender" clarify the way in which Russia's politics work?

SUGGESTED READINGS

Alyokhina, Maria. *Riot Days*. New York: Metropolitan Books, 2017.

Borenstein, Eliot. *Pussy Riot: Speaking Punk to Power*. Bloomsbury Publishing, 2020.

Dogangün, Gökten Huriye. *Gender in Turkey and Russia: From State Feminism to Authoritarian Rule*. Bloomsbury Publishing, 2019.

Fábián, Katalin, Janet Elise Johnson, and Mara Lazda, eds. *The Routledge Handbook of Gender in Central-Eastern Europe and Eurasia*. Routledge, 2021.

Healey, Dan. *Russian Homophobia from Stalin to Sochi*. London: Bloomsbury, 2017.

Ilic, Melanie. *The Palgrave Handbook of Women and Gender in Twentieth-Century Russia and the Soviet Union*. London: Palgrave Macmillan, 2017.

Johnson, Janet Elise. *The Gender of Informal Politics: Russia, Iceland and Twenty-First Century Male Dominance*. Basingstoke: Palgrave Macmillan, 2018.

Lomasko, Victoria. *Other Russias*. Translated by Thomas Campbell. United Kingdom: Penguin, 2017.

McCarthy, Lauren A. *Trafficking Justice: How Russian Police Enforce New Laws, from Crime to Courtroom*. Ithaca, NY: Cornell University Press, 2015.

Sperling, Valerie. *Sex, Politics, & Putin: Political Legitimacy in Russia.* Oxford: Oxford University Press, 2015.

Suchland, Jennifer. *Economies of Violence: Transnational Feminism, Postsocialism, and the Politics of Sex Trafficking.* Durham, NC: Duke University Press, 2015.

NOTES

1. Grant Thornton's 2014 International Business Report as reported in "Russia Is World's No. 1 Employer of Women Managers, Report Says," *Moscow Times*, June 18, 2014, http://www.themoscowtimes.com/business/article/russia-is-worlds-no-1-employer-of-women-managers-report-says/502168.html. Other reports find lower proportions of women. See OECD, "Percentage of Employed Who Are Senior Managers, by Sex," 2012, http://www.oecd. org/gender/data/proportionofemployedwhoareseniormanagersbysex.htm.

2. Laurie Essig, *Queer in Russia: A Story of Sex, Self, and the Other* (Chapel Hill: Duke University Press, 1999).

3. Gail Warshofsky Lapidus, *Women in Soviet Society: Equality, Development, and Social Change* (Berkeley: University of California Press, 1978), 200–32.

4. "RJI Submits Shadow Report to UN Women's Committee on Women's Rights in the North Caucasus," Stitching Justice Initiative, October 13, 2015, https://www.srji.org/en/news/ 2015/10/rji-submits-shadow-report-to-un-women-s-committee-on-women-s-rights-in-thenorth-caucasus/?sphrase_id=674500; Queer Women of North Caucasus, "Survival Strategies of Homosexual and Bisexual Women and Transgender Persons in the North Caucasus" (Moscow, 2020), https://outrightinternational.org/content/survival-strategies-homosexual-and-bisexual-women-and-transgender-persons-north-caucasus.

5. Janet Elise Johnson, *The Gender of Informal Politics: Russia, Iceland and Twenty-First Century Male Dominance* (Basingstoke: Palgrave Macmillan, 2018).

6. Janet Elise Johnson, "Gender Equality Policy: Criminalizing and Decriminalizing Domestic Violence," *Russian Analytical Digest*, no. 200 (March 28, 2017): 2–5, http://www.css.ethz.ch/content/dam/ethz/special-interest/gess/cis/center-for-securities-studies/pdfs/RAD200. pdf.

7. Linda J. Cook, "The Political Economy of Russia's Demographic Crisis: States and Markets, Migrants and Mothers," in *The Political Economy of Russia*, ed. Neil Robinson (Lanham, MD: Rowman & Littlefield, 2013), 97–119. Also, http://www.pfrf.ru/family_capital.

8. Ekaterina Borozdina, Anna Rotkirch, Anna Temkina, and Elena Zdravomyslova, "Using Maternity Capital: Citizen Distrust of Russian Family Policy," *European Journal of Women's Studies* 23 (2016): 60–75.

9. Johnson, *The Gender of Informal Politics*, 118.

10. Vladislav Moiseev, "Bunt Feminizma: Zachem Obrazovannye Devushki Provodyat Pank-Moleben v Khrame Khrista Spasitelya," *Russky Reporter*, February 24, 2012, http:// rusrep.ru/article/2012/02/24/pussy_riot.

11. Thomas Carothers, "The End of the Transition Paradigm," *Journal of Democracy* 13, no. 1 (2002): 5–21.

12. Scott Radnitz, "Review Article: Informal Politics and the State," *Comparative Politics* 43, no. 3 (2011): 351–71.

13. Janet Elise Johnson, "Fast-Tracked or Boxed In? Informal Politics, Gender, and Women's Representation in Putin's Russia," *Perspectives on Politics* 14, no. 3 (2016): 643–59.

14. R. W. Connell and James W. Messerschmidt, "Hegemonic Masculinity: Rethinking the Concept," *Gender & Society* 19, no. 6 (2005): 829–59; Elin Bjårnegard, *Gender, Informal Institutions and Political Recruitment: Explaining Male Dominance in Parliamentary Representation* (Houndmills, Basingstoke: Palgrave Macmillan, 2013).

15. See Association of Women in Slavic Studies, "Bibliographies (Women East-West)," October 15, 2014, http://www.awsshome.org/bibliographies.html.

16. Connell and Messerschmidt, "Hegemonic Masculinity," 849.

17. Janet Elise Johnson and Aino Saarinen, "Twenty-First-Century Feminisms under Repression: Gender Regime Change and the Women's Crisis Center Movement in Russia," *Signs: Journal of Women in Culture & Society* 38, no. 3 (2013): 543–67; Helena Goscilo, *Putin as Celebrity and Cultural Icon* (New York: Routledge, 2013); Valerie Sperling, *Sex, Politics & Putin: Political Legitimacy in Russia* (New York: Oxford University Press, 2015).

18. Sperling, *Sex, Politics, & Putin*, 13–15, 20–21.

19. Anna Temkina, "Nastoyashchii muzhchina," Polit.ru, June 12, 2013, http://polit.ru/article/2013/06/12/temkina; Dan Healey, "Chto takoe 'tradizionnye sexualnie otnoshenia'?," in *Na Pereputie: Metodologia, teoria i praktika LGBT i kvir-issledovanii* (sbornik statei), ed. Alexander Kondakov (Sankt Peterburg: Tsenter Nezavisimykh Sotsiologicheskih Issledovanii, 2014), 60.

20. Dan Healey, *Homosexual Desire in Revolutionary Russia: The Regulation of Sexual and Gender Dissent* (Chicago: Chicago University Press, 2001).

21. Temkina, "Nastoyashchii muzhchina."

22. Kevin Moss, "Russia as the Savior of European Civilization: Gender and the Geopolitics of Traditional Values," in *Anti-Gender Campaigns in Europe: Mobilizing against Equality*, ed. Roman Kuhar and David Paternotte (Lanham, MD: Rowman & Littlefield, 2017), 195–214.

23. Sperling, *Sex, Politics, & Putin*, 13–15, 273.

24. Moss, "Russia as the Savior of European Civilization."

25. Bjårnegard, *Gender, Informal Institutions and Political Recruitment*, 24.

26. Richard Sakwa, *The Crisis of Russian Democracy: The Dual State, Factionalism, and the Medvedev Succession* (Cambridge: Cambridge University Press, 2011), 118.

27. Putin: "Even before I graduated from school, I wanted to work in intelligence. It was a dream of mine, although it seemed about as likely as a flight to Mars. . . . But then books and spy movies . . . took hold of my imagination. What amazed me most of all was how one man's effort could achieve what whole armies could not. One spy could decide the fate of thousands of people. At least, that's the way I understood it.

. . . I wanted to be a spy." Vladimir Putin, Nataliya Gevorkyan, and Natalya Tima-kova, *First Person: An Astonishingly Frank Self-Portrait by Russia's President Putin, Vladimir Vladimirovich*, trans. Catherine A. Fitzpatrick (New York: Public Affairs, 2000), 22.

28. Elena Semenova, "Continuities in the Formation of Russian Political Elites," *Historical Social Research* 37, no. 2 (2012): 74.

29. Gulnaz Sharafutdinova, *Political Consequences of Crony Capitalism Inside Russia* (Notre Dame, IN: University of Notre Dame Press, 2010), 28.

30. Alena Ledeneva, *How Russia Really Works: The Informal Practices That Shaped Post-Soviet Politics and Business* (Ithaca, NY: Cornell University Press, 2006), 105–6, 270.

31. Fiona Hill and Clifford Gaddy, "Putin and the Uses of History," *National Interest* 117 (January 2012): 30.

32. Mikhail Klikushin, "Former Russian Prime Minister Caught on Camera Having Sex with Opposition Leader: Secret Video of Mikhail Kasyanov Having Sex," *Observer*, April 5, 2016, http://observer.com/2016/04/former-russian-prime-minister -caught-on-camera-having-sex-with-opposition-leader.

33. Connell and Messerschmidt, "Hegemonic Masculinity," 848.

34. "Things You Didn't Know about Russian President Vladimir Putin," News. com.au, March 5, 2014, http:// www.news.com.au/world/europe/things-you-didnt -know-about-russian-president-vladimir-putin/story-fnh81p7g-1226845669588.

35. Jake Miller, "Hillary Clinton: Vladimir Putin May Not Like My New Memoir," CBS News, June 11, 2014, http://www.cbsnews.com/news/hillary-clinton-vladimir -putin-may-not-like-my-new-memoir.

36. Elisabeth Duban, *CEDAW Assessment Tool Report for the Russian Federation*, ABACEELI (Moscow, 2006), 56–58.

37. Andrei Gatinski and Yevgenia Kuznetsova, "Zhirinovski i Sobchak reshili pozhalovatsya drug na druga Chaike," March 2, 2018, https://www.rbc.ru/politics/02 /03/2018/5a996d219a7947a686e1956c.

38. Mikhail Shibankov, "Ksenia Sobchak Leaves Russia's Most Recent Presidential Debate in Tears," *Meduza*, March 15, 2018, https://meduza.io/en/news /2018/03/15/ksenia-sobchakleaves-russia-s-most-recent-presidential-debate-in-tears; "Zhirinovsky obrugal Sobchak matom vo vremya debatov na 'Rossiya 1,'" February 28, 2018, https://meduza.io/video/2018/02/28/zhirinovskiy-obrugal-sobchak-matom-na-debatah-sobchak-oblila-ego-vodoy; Amelia McBain, "Homophobic Russian Ad Warns That the Gays Will Take Over if People Don't Vote," Out.com, February 19, 2018, https://www.out.com/news-opinion/2018/2/19/homophobic-russian-ad-warns -gays-will-take-over-if-people-dont-vote.

39. Elena Semenova, "Ministerial and Parliamentary Elites in an Executive-Dominated System: Post-Soviet Russia 1991–2009," *Comparative Sociology* 10, no. 6 (2011): 914, 919.

40. This is illustrated in a tongue-in-cheek slide show at http://www.kommersant .ru/gallery/ 2140440#id=842137.

41. Semenova, "Ministerial and Parliamentary Elites," 923.

42. See Michelle Ryan and Alex Haslam, who coined this term. Michelle K. Ryan and S. Alexander Haslam, "The Glass Cliff: Evidence That Women Are Over-Represented in Precarious Leadership Positions," *British Journal of Management* 16, no. 2 (2005).

43. Anna Nemtsova, "Russian Whistleblowers Turn on Putin—But Can They Be Trusted?," *Daily Beast*, February 17, 2017, http://www.thedailybeast.com/articles /2017/02/17/russian-spy-whistleblowers-turn-on-putin-but-can-they-be-trusted; "Lutsenko Nazval Zakachika Ubiistva Voronenkova," *Novoe Vremya*, October 9, 2017, https://nv.ua/ukraine/events/lutsenkonazval-familiju-zakazchika-ubijstva -voronenkova-1995045.html.

44. Elena Kochina, "Sistematizirovannye Nabroski 'Gendernye Issledovaniia v Rossii: ot Fragmentov k Kriticheskomu Peresmyshleniiu Politicheskikh Strategii," *Genderenye Issledovaniia* 15 (2007) 109–11, http://www.kcgs.org.ua/gurnal/15/03/. pdf; Johnson and Saarinen, "Twenty-First-Century Feminisms under Repression," 552.

45. Kochkina, "Sistematizirovannye nabroski," 118. Three-fourths of NGO staff were women in 2004.

46. Kochkina, "Sistematizirovannye nabroski," 102.

47. Vera Akulova, "Pussy Riot: Gender and Class," in *Post-Post-Soviet? Art, Politics and Society in Russia at the Turn of the Decade*, ed. Marta Dziewanska, Ekaterina Degot, and Ilya Budraitskis (Warsaw: Museum of Modern Art, 2013), 279–87; Masha Gessen, *Words Will Break Cement: The Passion of Pussy Riot* (New York: Riverhead Books, 2014); Janet Elise Johnson, "Pussy Riot as a Feminist Project: Russia's Gendered Informal Politics," *Nationalities Papers: The Journal of Nationalism and Ethnicity* 42, no. 4 (2014): 583–90.

48. "Pussy Riot i seksizm-chastnyi sluchai obshchego otnosheniia," October 19, 2012, http://feministki.livejournal.com/2369110.html.

49. Press Conference by Vladimir Putin, December 19, 2013, http://kremlin.ru/ transcripts/19859.

50. Women protesting can even be at risk of violence from the special forces, whom Putin has labeled "healthy guys," contradicting the accounts of special forces physically assaulting women participants of protest rallies. See http://avmalgin.livejournal .com/4220864.html.

51. Marina Yusupova, "Pussy Riot: A Feminist Band Lost in History and Translation," *Nationalities Papers* 42, no. 4 (2014): 604–10.

52. "O deiatel'nosti ne kommercheskikh organizatsii: Informatsionnyi portal Ministersterstva iustitsii Rossiiskoi Federatsii," November 10, 2014, http://unro.minjust .ru/ NKOForeignAgent.aspx.

53. "Dar'iu Apakhonchich priznali inostrannim agentom iz-za zarplati ot 'Krasnogo Kresta' i postakh v podderzhku dela 'Seti' i Yulii Tsevtkovoi," *Sever.Realii*, April 5, 2021, https://www.severreal.org/a/31187755.html.

54. Sarah Cascone, "A 27-Year-Old Artist Is on Trial in Russia After Publishing Cartoonish Drawings That Promote an Accepting View of the Female Body," *Artnet News*, April 14, 2021, https://news.artnet.com/art-world/yulia-tsvetkova-trial -1958935; Samantha Berkhead, "Russian Women Rally Behind Feminist 'Political

Prisoner,'" *Moscow Times*, July 6, 2020, https://www.themoscowtimes.com/2020/07/06/russian-women-rally-behind-feminist-political-prisoner-a70768.

55. Akulova, "Pussy Riot: Gender and Class," 280.

56. "Mozg aspirantki zatochen na zamuzhstvo: Studentka SPbGU povesila u sebya na fakultete plakaty s tsytatami prepodavatelei o zhenschinakh," *Meduza*, March 7, 2018, https://meduza.io/feature/2018/03/07/mozg-aspirantki-zatochen-na-zamuzhestvo-studentka-spbgu-povesila-usebya-na-fakultete-plakaty-s-tsitatami-prepodavateley-o-zhenschinah.

57. Manny de Guerre, interview by the authors, March 15, 2014, New York.

58. Dmitrii Pervushin, "DJ, khudozhnitsa i aktivistka Liel'a Nordik—o domashnem nasilii, kritike kapitalizma i rossiiskoi molodezhi," Sobaka.ru, August 14, 2019, https://www.sobaka.ru/city/society/94302.

59. Oleg Zurman, "'My znaiem, gde zhiviet tvoi muzh, my ub'iem tvoikh zhivotnikh': Posle 'zhenskoi tsepi solidarnosti' femnistka Daria Serenko sotn'ami poluchaiet ugrozy," *Mediazona*, February 16, 2021, https://zona.media/article/2021/02/15/serenko.

60. "Young Masha o standartakh krasoti, rasizme i travle v Rossii," The Blueprint, June 18, 2020, https://theblueprint.ru/beauty/shoot/young-masha.

61. Anastasiia Fedorova,"Agasshin Is the Beauty Zine Giving Russians of Color the Front Page," *Calvert Journal*, October 7, 2020, https://www.calvertjournal.com/features/show/12210/agasshin-beauty-zine-russians-of-colour-russia-z.

62. Ella Rossman, "Udivitel'no videt,' kak posle napadok na 'Yandex' i 'Tanuki' mnogikh zainteresovalo 'Muzhskoie gosudarstvo,'" *Facebook,* September 6, 2021.

63. Marina Ivanova and Stanislav Zakharkin, "Kto i zachem v Rossii blokiruyet zakon o zaschite ot seks-domogatelstv," November 2, 2017, https://ura.news/articles/1036272817.

64. The number of signatures may be found at https://socialdatahub.com/ru/sluckiy_1521672047.

65. Ksenia Sobchak, interview with Aleksei Naval'ny, July 22, 2013, http://ksenia-sobchak.com/sobchak-zhivem-aleksej-navalnyj-22-07-2013.

66. Sperling, *Sex, Politics, & Putin.*

67. Valerie Sperling, Alexandra Novitskaya, Janet Elise Johnson, and Lisa McIntosh Sundstrom, "Vladimir Putin, the Czar of Macho Politics, Is Threatened by Gender and Sexuality Rights," *The Conversation*, April 11, 2022, https://theconversation.com/vladimir-putin-the-czar-of-macho-politics-is-threatened-by-gender-and-sexuality-rights-180473.

68. Ibid.

69. Janine di Giovanni, "The Real Reason the Russian Orthodox Church's Leader Supports Putin's War," *Foreign Policy*, April 26, 2022, https://foreignpolicy.com/2022/04/26/ukraine-war-russian-orthodox-church-support-patriarch-kirill-homophobia/.

70. Amie Ferris-Rotman, "Ukrainians Are Speaking Up About Rape as a War Crime to Ensure the World Holds Russia Accountable," *Time Magazine*, April 20, 2022, https://time.com/6168330/rape-war-crime-russia-ukraine/.

71. James W. Messerschmidt, "The Forgotten Victims of World War II: Masculinities and Rape in Berlin, 1945," *Violence Against Women* 12, no 7 (2006): 708.

72. *Meduza*, "V Voronezhe Zaveli Delo o 'Feikakh' pro Rossiiskuiu Armiiu na Deputata ot KPRF, Kotoraia Osudila Voinu v Ukraiine na Zasedanii Raisoveta," April 29, 2022, https://meduza.io/news/2022/04/29/v-voronezhe-zaveli-delo-o-feykah -pro-rossiyskuyu-armiyu-na-deputata-ot-kprf-kotoraya-osudila-voynu-v-ukraine-na -zasedanii-raysoveta.

73. Sperling, Novitskaya, Johnson, and Sundstrom, "Vladimir Putin, the Czar of Macho Politics, Is Threatened by Gender and Sexuality Rights."

74. Amnesty International, "Kak Zashchitnitsy Prav Zhenshchin Stali Litsom Anti-voiennogo Dvizheniia v Rossii," April 19, 2022, https://eurasia.amnesty.org/2022/04 /19/kak-zashhitniczy-prav-zhenshhin-stali-liczom-antivoennogo-dvizheniya-v-rossii -rasskazyvaet-amnesty-international/.

75. *7X7: Gorizontal'naia Rossi'ia*, "Moia Li'ubov' k Rodine Bezotvetna: Kak Femsoprotivleniie Stalo Glavnym Rossi'iskim Dvizheniiem Protiv Sobytii V Ukraine," April 19, 2022, https://semnasem.org/articles/2022/04/19/moya-lyubov-k -rodine-bezotvetna.

76. Ibid.

77. *Meduza*, "'The Rules Don't Require it': Jailed Protester Sasha Skochilenko Has an Autoimmune Disease. Prison Officials are Ignoring Her Needs," April 29, 2022, https://meduza.io/en/feature/2022/04/29/the-rules-don-t-require-it.

78. Robyn Dixon, Sudarsan Raghavan, Isabelle Khurshudyan, and David L. Stern, "Russia's War Dead Belie Its Slogan That No One is Left Behind," *The Washington Post*, April 8, 2022, https://www.washingtonpost.com/world/2022/04/08/russia-war -dead-soldiers-bodies/.

Chapter 10

Putin's Food Policy

Stephen K. Wegren

The classic approach to food policy emphasizes the role of the state and its direct impact on producers, distributors (wholesale and retailers), and consumers.[1] A somewhat different approach looks less at direct control by the state over markets and more at complementarity and "getting institutions right."[2] State-defined food policy institutions distribute resources and enforce rules, thereby creating winners and losers in the food system. Both approaches have strengths and weaknesses, but we can agree that state interventions vary by regime type and country. In Russia, state interests are inherent to food policy. In Russia, while the private sector is active in investment—food production and food export—at the core of food policy are myriad ways that the state manages food policy.

Framing the salience of state interventions in food policy are three premises. The first is that food policy extends beyond the economic imperative to put food on consumers' tables, but rather should be understood as a political strategy to facilitate stability. The second premise is that governments are self-serving when it comes to creating and implementing food policy for their nation. What that means is that governments, to the extent possible, construct food policies that are likely to achieve food security for their population, thereby garnering support for and loyalty to the regime. The ideal outcome in most cases is a win-win in which producers, consumers, and the state all benefit from food policy. That said, food policy outcomes are not always positive because decision makers make mistakes. Alternatively, perhaps nature and/or economic circumstances do not cooperate. Or maybe the government is "captured" by special interests that direct food policy to benefit one group or one commodity at the expense of others.[3] But generally, governments have more interest in a food-secure population than a food-insecure population. There are exceptions to this general rule that occur when political leaders use food as a weapon against domestic groups who are considered disloyal, sometimes resulting in famine. Stalin's man-made famine in Ukraine during 1932–1933 certainly stands as one example, and there are others in which food supply was deliberately withheld from regions and certain populations in Bengal, Ethiopia, and China.[4] Incompetence, periods of political turmoil, and conflict also contribute to the outbreak of famine, but the point remains that this is an outcome that normally leaders want to avoid.

The third premise is that Russian President Vladimir Putin puts a premium on political stability, both within Russia and on its borders, as reflected in different speeches over the years. Since 2008, food security has been a core feature of Russia's food policy and an important part of the equation for its national security and foreign policy.[5] The quest for political stability is important because the comparative literature argues that authoritarian regimes with high corruption,[6] unfair elections, and myriad social problems are especially vulnerable to instability when food insecurity is added to the mix.[7] Russia's federal government has primary responsibility for defining the policies and goals that comprise food policy, so I begin the discussion with those aspects.

One approach to food policy is to examine how it affects different actors in the system, for example, the impact of policy on food producers, food distributors, and consumers. This author has used food policy as an independent variable in previous research.[8] Here, food policy is treated as a dependent variable to address two policy issues. (1) How a trifecta of goals defines food policy (those goals are to increase food production; reduce food imports; and expand the value and volume of food exports). (2) How state interests shape food policy. While Russia's contemporary food policy is not as heavily regulated as during the Soviet period, state interests are pervasive. Much of the time state and private sector interests are concordant; at other times, state interests conflict with the private sector.

OVERVIEW OF FOOD POLICY
PRIORITIES AND GOALS

The backdrop to Russia's contemporary food policy is a significant change in state capacity. In the 1990s, Russia's government was weak and bankrupt, which meant that food policy, to the extent it existed at all, was ineffective. After 2000, as Vladimir Putin strengthened the central government's capability to shape food policy improved. State capacity was used to achieve three goals in food policy.

GOAL 1: INCREASE FOOD PRODUCTION

The first goal of Russia's food policy is to increase food production. The state's interest in higher food output is to achieve "food independence" for the country and to provide a sufficient diet to the population. Both of those aspects were absent during the 1990s, when Russia's domestic agricultural production plummeted, and food insecurity was high due to tens of millions of people living in poverty. To compensate for falling domestic production, food imports rose, and their dollar value exceeded the value of domestic production. When Putin came to office, the primary goals of Russia's food policy were to stabilize and then increase domestic production, help domestic producers become competitive with imported food, and increase consumers' food security. Toward these ends, concerted efforts were made to increase domestic food production on farm enterprises (former state and collective farms), but also extending to private farms. The 2010 and 2020 versions of Russia's Food Security Doctrine make explicit mention that food independence is a priority goal. The state's primary policy instruments used to increase food production have been: (1) an infusion of monetary resources to agriculture, consisting of budgetary transfers; (2) tax concessions; and (3) trade-related support. I discuss the first two here, and trade support is discussed later in the chapter.

Federal budgetary transfers have increased substantially, including direct production and transportation subsidies, and subsidized loans and credits that act as indirect subsidies. Data from Russia's Ministry of Agriculture show that federal financial support from national programs and projects grew from R16.2 billion in 2006 to a high of R311.5 billion in 2019 before declining to R283.6 billion in 2020.[9] To put it somewhat differently, the sum of federal support to agriculture during 2018–2020 totaled R844.6 billion, or about the total of federal support during 2006–2013.[10] A study by the OECD indicates that as much as 73 percent of Russian government support to agriculture is trade-distorting, behavior that the World Trade Organization discourages.[11] Trade-distorting support gives an unfair advantage by making exports cheaper than competitors' prices and therefore states are not supposed to engage in this behavior according to WTO rules. Russia's trade-distorting behavior includes subsidies based on output, market price support, and subsidies for transporting food via land and water.

In addition to budget transfers, the ruble value of tax concessions to agriculture is roughly equal to budgetary transfers.[12] One example of a tax concession was the suspension of the 20 percent value added tax on the acquisition of high-yield pedigree cattle, pigs, and poultry, which was originally introduced in October 2016 and ran through December 2020. On November

11, 2020, the Duma approved the third reading of a bill that extends the term to the end of 2022.[13] The bill was approved by the Federation Council on November 18, 2020, and it was signed by President Putin on November 23, 2020. The law is important because Russia imports tens of thousands of high-yield cattle per year.[14]

The influx of monetary resources from the federal government and to a lesser extent regional governments—plus private sector investment from agroholdings—allows farm enterprises to purchase modern machinery and equipment, obtain high yield livestock, increase their use of synthetic fertilizers, modernize and expand livestock facilities, improve storage capabilities, and construct processing facilities onsite. Some farms obtain advanced technology such as driverless tractors, drones, robotics, and digital technologies. All these actions directly or indirectly facilitate an increase in food production and farm efficiency.

The primary beneficiaries from government subsidies have been farm enterprises, a category that includes agroholdings, or mega-sized farms. A structural change among food producers occurred after 2004 which allowed farm enterprises to reclaim the top position in terms of ruble value of production and volume of output.[15] In 2020, for example, farm enterprises accounted for 58 percent of production in ruble value, up from 45 percent in 2000.[16] The ruble value of production from enterprises was followed by households at 27 percent, down from 52 percent in 2000, thereby continuing their long-term decline.[17] In 2020, private farmers accounted for 14 percent of the total ruble value of food production, up from 3 percent in 2000.[18]

In recent years the agricultural sector has performed well and may be considered one of the sectoral "winners" since countersanctions were introduced in August 2014. Thanks largely to the rebound in production on farm enterprises, the nominal ruble value of agri-food production increased from R742 billion in 2000 to over R6.1 trillion in 2020. The nominal ruble value of crop production rose from R394.7 billion in 2000 to R3.2 trillion in 2020, accounting for 52 percent of total agricultural production.[19] Crops such as wheat experienced a notable increase in production, thereby facilitating a rise in exports as discussed below. The growth in average annual grain production is shown in table 10.1.

The table shows that during 2014–2020 the average annual production of wheat, corn, and barley increased substantially over the 2009–2013 average, thereby meeting domestic needs and facilitating exports. (Those crops were chosen because they are the top grain commodity exports.) Average total production of grain was up 43 percent during 2014–2020 over 2009–2013; wheat production rose by 47 percent; corn for human consumption grew by 91 percent; and barley product increased by 47 percent during 2014–2020.

Table 10.1. Russia's Grain Production, 2009–2020, million tons

	Total Grain Production	Wheat	Corn (used for human consumption)	Barley
2009-2013 annual average	83.1	49.9	6.8	14.5
2014	105.2	59.7	11.3	20.4
2015	104.7	61.8	13.1	17.5
2016	120.7	73.3	15.3	18.0
2017	135.5	86.0	13.2	20.6
2018	113.3	72.1	11.4	17.0
2019	121.2	74.5	14.3	20.4
2020	133.5	85.9	13.4	20.9
2014–2020 annual average	119.0	73.3	13.0	21.3
Annual % increase of 2014–2020 over 2009–2013	43%	47%	91%	47%

Sources: Rosstat, *Sel'skoe khoziaistvo v Rossii 2019* (Moscow: Rosstat, 2019), 47; Rosstat, *Rossiiskoi statisticheskii ezhegodnik 2020,* 407; Ministry of Agriculture; author's calculations.

Note: Production totals are post-cleaning.

The nominal ruble value of animal husbandry production increased from R347.8 billion in 2000 to R2.8 trillion in 2020.[20] Within the total rise, the most successful sectors were poultry meat production, which grew from 768 thousand tons in 2000 to 5 million tons in 2020; and pork production, which rose from 1.5 million tons in 2000 to 4.2 million tons in 2020.[21] Less successful sectors are beef and milk, both of which experienced a decline in the number of cows and a drop in production. Those two sectors have stabilized in recent years as output per cow is up, thanks to the import of pedigree cattle. Milk production has slowly increased since its nadir in 2016 and reached 32.2 million tons in 2020.[22] Overall, in 2020 Russia met its food self-sufficiency targets for grain, vegetable oil, meat and meat products, fish and fish products, and sugar.[23]

GOAL 2: REDUCE FOOD IMPORTS

Another goal in food policy has been to reduce food imports. The state's interest in reducing food imports is to improve food self-sufficiency (independence) and to help make Russian farm enterprises more internationally competitive which in turn aids profitability and ultimately increases government tax revenue. The policy goal to reduce imports has been pursued using three strategies, which are discussed below.

The first strategy entails an increase in domestic food production that fills store shelves with Russian products, the hope being that Russian consumers would prefer Russian products. Survey data proved that to be true, especially after 2014.[24] The government also hoped to make domestic food products the preferred option for Russian consumers by improving consumer confidence in Russian products. In the past few years, the Russian government has emphasized food quality and food safety through its certification and digital labeling policies that reduce unsafe practices and falsification of contents.

A major step in food safety was taken with the introduction of digital bar codes for dairy products, which have been subject to high levels of falsified content. In December 2019, the government approved the labeling of products using a Data Matrix code (QR code). Bar coding for food products was enacted by a December 2020 resolution. The voluntary use of bar codes for dairy products started in January 2021, and mandatory bar coding came into effect for cheese products and ice cream from June 2021. Dairy products produced by households are not required to have a QR code. According to the law, from September 2021, bar coding became obligatory for dairy products with a shelf life of more than forty days. Starting December 2021, bar coding was obligatory for dairy products with a shelf life of less than forty days. From December 2022, dairy products sold by private farmers were required to be bar coded. Companies that do not comply face fines and other penalties, including being banned from doing business in Russia. In June 2021, Putin signed a law that levies financial penalties against companies that do not comply, starting December 2021. The fines started at R50,000–100,000 plus confiscation of the products. Repeat offenders could be fined from R100,000 to R500,000.[25] In July 2021 the law was revised to include criminal penalties. A company that knowingly mislabels its products could be fined R300,00 or the responsible person could face prison up to three years and a R80,000 fine. A group of persons who conspire to falsify the content of products face prison terms up to four years in prison and a R100,000 fine. A large consignment of falsified goods comes with a three-year prison term and a R400,000 fine.[26] Subsequently, penalties were revised so that effective December 2021, individuals who sell milk products without a digital code could be fined between R5,000–R300,000, and companies from R50,000 up to R1 million, including prison terms for the responsible person or persons.[27] Persons who operate a private plot—*lichnoe podsobnoe khoziaistvo*—are not required to code their milk products, so one can imagine that some companies may try to exploit this loophole.

Russia's system is arguably the strictest food product tracking and tracing system in the world. A server called "Chestnyi znak" (Honest sign) is operated by the Center for Research in Perspective Technologies (CRPT) as a public-private partnership. The system tracks and traces products, and upon final sale allows consumers to see which companies have been accredited and which company produced the product being purchased. According to the CRPT, in the first week of June nearly 100 percent of cheese producers and 89 percent of companies that produce ice cream were registered in the system. The system is an enormous undertaking, with 1.2 billion QR codes distributed in the first three weeks of the program. As might be expected, there was some pushback from companies who complained about costs of buying the needed machinery and complexity of training people how to use the system. They warned of shortages and stoppages. During the first few months of the program, there were reports of attempted evasion and confiscation of newly illegal products. Nevertheless, a report from August 2021 stated that 80 percent of companies had registered and were ready for phase two of coding that was to begin in December 2021. The remaining 20 percent were still installing the necessary equipment.[28] Digital coding began for bottled mineral water in November 2021, and in that same month Rossel'khoznadzor suggested expanding digital coding to canned meat products.[29]

A second strategy to reduce food imports has been soft protectionism in the form of tariff rate quotas (TRQs) for meat and meat products. The policy started in 2003 and continues to the present, although it has changed over time. TRQs limit the quantity of imports with a low import tariff. Imports outside the low quota faced much higher tariffs. The intent was to protect, to some degree, domestic meat producers from foreign competition. Soft protectionism was not especially effective in restraining meat imports, indicated by the fact that meat imports grew from 1.2 million tons in 2000 to 1.8 million tons in 2013, a 50 percent increase for the period.[30] The total dollar value of Russia's food imports increased from $12 billion USD in 2003 to over $43 billion USD in 2013. During this period the volume of meat imports—pork, beef, and poultry—accounted for most of the dollar value of total food imports. In 2020, the TRQ for pork was ended and Russia went to a flat import tariff of 27.5 percent. With domestic production of pork at a record level of 4.2 million tons, pork imports dropped from 1.25 million tons in 2009 to an estimated 10,000 tons for 2020 and 2021 according to the Foreign Agricultural Service within the United States Department of Agriculture.[31] The TRQ for fresh and frozen beef was to be replaced by a flat 25 percent tariff starting in 2022. Due to higher food inflation in 2021, however, in November 2021 the Ministry of Agriculture indicated that it was moving toward tariff-free imports for the first 200,000 tons of frozen beef and 100,000 tons of frozen pork during the first six months of 2022, with the hope that these supplies would stabilize retail prices.[32]

More broadly, by 2020 a confluence of factors reduced meat imports. Those factors included COVID-19, which changed shopping habits; devaluation of the ruble that made imports more expensive; import tariffs; an increase in domestic meat production; and a rise in consumer confidence in the safety of Russian meat products. This combination resulted in the decline in total meat imports to about 600 thousand tons in 2020, down from 1.8 million tons in 2013.[33]

A third strategy to reduce imports has been selective hard protectionism, used from August 2014 in the form of the food embargo (countersanctions) against several Western states. Russia's countersanctions target only certain Western states—the United States, Canada, the EU, Australia, and Norway—which are major food traders in the international food system. Countersanctions are selective in that Russia chooses what to ban and what to allow. While most processed and manufactured food is banned from Western nations, as are many raw agricultural commodities, Russia continues to import high-yield livestock. In 2019, Russia imported nearly 113,000 head of cattle, including over 73,000 breeding cattle.[34]

All of that said, the food embargo should be understood as political retaliation for the economic sanctions that Western nations placed on Russia in 2014. Russia's countersanctions were extended through 2022 and, given the deterioration of relations following the invasion of Ukraine, are likely to be continued indefinitely. Although political in intent, the economic effects of the food embargo have been highly favorable to Russia because they allowed it to disregard some World Trade Organization (WTO) rules by invoking protection of national security to discriminate against a set of nations. Since the introduction of countersanctions in 2014, Russia's agricultural producers and especially farm enterprises have benefited. Russia has emerged as a leading global exporter of wheat; the agricultural sector has seen annual growth rates exceed that of national GDP; the gap in dollar value between food imports and exports narrowed until 2020 when the value of exports exceeded imports; Russia reduced its meat imports by a factor of four; and the average annual level of food consumption by Russian consumers increased. Based on these positive trends, it is no wonder why farm enterprises and other food interest groups have been very vocal about wanting countersanctions to continue.

GOAL 3: INCREASE FOOD EXPORTS

A third goal of Russia's food policy has been to increase the dollar value and volume of its food exports. The state's interest in expanded food exports became explicit in May 2018 with Putin's decree on national development that stated overall exports should reach $250 billion by 2024, with food exports totaling $45 billion. That goal subsequently was modified to $34 billion by 2024, and the $45 billion target was pushed back to 2030.[35] As part of this goal, regions have developed export plans and are required to report on their progress. Financial support has been linked to fulfillment of regional export targets. In addition, there is a drive to increase the export of processed foods that have a higher mark-up value than raw food products, and therefore Putin and other leaders have called for priority development of high-value commodities.[36] Grain exports will remain the largest generator of foreign revenue among agri-food exports. Another initiative is the "deep processing" of grain. The basic idea is that turning grain into processed products adds more value and earns more in foreign trade than raw grain. At this point, hard data on progress about deep processing are scarce, but it is worth noting that resources are being invested into other processed products for export such as Russian wine, chocolate, and a variety of hard and soft cheeses.

The dollar value of Russia's food exports has increased significantly during the past decade. In 2010, for example, the value of Russia's agri-food exports was just $9.4 billion, rising to $30.7 billion in 2020 according to the Ministry of Agriculture's Analytical Center. Grain exports generated the highest revenue, $9.7 billion in 2020, followed by exports of fish and seafood ($5.2 billion), oilseeds ($4.6 billion), and processed food ($4.1 billion).[37] In 2020 China was Russia's single largest food export market with a value of $4 billion, with fish and seafood the single largest category at $1.5 billion; China was followed by the European Union at $3.2 billion, with fish and seafood the single largest category at $1 billion; and Turkey in third place at $3.0 billion, with grains the single largest commodity at $1.7 billion.[38] Together, those three purchasers accounted for about 36 percent of the total dollar value of Russia's agri-food exports in 2020. As of mid-November 2021, Russia exported $29.5 billion of food and was on track to surpass $30 billion for a second year in a row. Food exports to the European Union and Turkey were up a combined 77 percent compared to the same period in 2020.[39]

Russia's emergence as a significant food exporting country is relatively recent, so it has had to build up an export infrastructure. In terms of obstacles to overcome, Russia has had to increase storage capacity and build grain elevators that can protect grain from vermin and spoilage; increase rail transport capacity by replacing old train wagons with new ones; and modernize and expand seaport capacity. As a longer-term project, Russia needs to ensure sufficient cargo capacity by building larger container ships and bulk carriers.

To help facilitate exports, an analytical center within the Ministry of Agriculture produces guides and market surveys on commodities and specific countries that are freely available on the ministry's website. It also provides consulting advice and assistance for the negotiation and signing of contracts.[40] The government has also expanded the number of foreign attaché offices. Through August 2021 the Ministry of Agriculture opened fourteen new foreign attaché offices and expected to open a similar number by the end of the year.[41] The intellectual infrastructure for exports is also supported by federal and regional educational institutes where students can study international trade; branch unions that are engaged in agricultural trade; and non-state commercial organizations.

Still, it is necessary to note that the development of Russia's export infrastructure remains a work in progress. In many cases, there is a mismatch between needed skills and available personnel. Most export-oriented organizations are located in Moscow or St. Petersburg, where personnel are not agricultural specialists and not trained in agricultural trade. Instead, export organizations in large cities consist of centers for certification, agencies for developing foreign economic ties, agencies to develop business, or centers to support small businesses. Regional personnel lack training, information, and knowledge about international food markets.

Other shortcomings include: difficulty obtaining reliable information about the costs and risks of exporting different products; a long procedure to complete an export transaction; underdevelopment of customs and communication infrastructure in Russia's regions; difficulty for small businesses to enter foreign markets; logistical difficulties due to large distances from regions to large markets; high transportation costs; a shortage of specialists who are trained in the operation of exports; and insufficient mechanisms for transferring non-financial state support to exporters.[42]

FOOD POLICY AND STATE INTERESTS

So far, we have seen how state-defined food policy benefits private sector actors in the food system. State and private sector interests are concordant for food production, food imports, and food exports. An increase in food production benefits farms, consumers, and potentially exporters (depending on the actual level of production and the commodity). The reduction in food imports protects domestic farms and food processors from foreign competition and gives them an advantage in the Russian marketplace. An increase in food exports benefits exporters and potentially domestic farms as revenue and profits rise.

That said, the state does not merely serve the interests of private sector actors in Russia's food system. State interests are independent, which is to say that the state may act in its own interests in ways that are not beneficial to private sector producers or distributors. An example of the state shaping food policy for its own interests came in 2020 and 2021 when the Russian government restricted grain exports and ultimately reinserted itself into retail price formation. The purpose was to directly influence the supply of food within Russia and depress inflationary pressures; indirectly, the intent was to prevent a rise in food insecurity from potential shortages and price spikes.

The political concern was that potential instability could occur from a rise in food insecurity, combined with preexisting grievances over economic stagnation, widespread corruption, the unpopularity of the "party of power," United Russia, and the treatment of Alexei Navalny, which included his poisoning in 2020 and an unjust trial and prison sentence in 2021. As a result of those concerns, the government moved decisively to prioritize domestic food security over food exports.

The backdrop to the Russian state promoting its interests in food policy was a rise in global commodity prices that reached an eleven-year high in 2021, partly explained by breakdowns in supply chains due to COVID-19. This rise was fueled by a slight drop in world wheat production in 2020 while utilization experienced a sustained increase since the 2012–2013 agricultural season.[43] As international grain prices rose, grain exporting companies and speculators in Russia were motivated to capitalize by exporting as much as possible.

Although Russia had strong harvests in 2019 (121 million metric tons [mmt]) and in 2020 (133 mmt), the government intervened in the grain market by introducing restrictions that hurt the interests of producers and exporters. From April 1 to June 30, 2020, the Russian government placed a limit of 7 mmt on exports. Although Russia still exported more than 34 mmt of wheat during the 2019–2020 season,[44] it lost its leading role to the EU as Russian traders were hesitant to sign contracts that would exceed the quota. During the second half of the 2020–2021 agricultural year (January–June), the Russian government again introduced an export quota on grain, extending from February 15, 2021, through June 30, 2021. The export quota was set at 17.5 mmt of grain. The Russian government has indicated its intent to use an export quota on grain again in 2022, but at the time of writing the size of the quota and its duration had not been established.

The 2021 export quota was coupled with an export tariff. Starting February 15, the tariff was 25 euro per ton, which doubled to 50 euro per ton on March 1, 2021.[45] From June 2021 a flexible tariff was used for wheat, corn, and barley sold outside the Eurasian Economic Union. The tariff was equal to 70 percent of the difference between the contract price and the base price of $200 per ton for wheat and $185 for corn and barley.[46] Thus, as the price of grain rose, so too would the tariff. The export tariff was, in effect, a tax on exports and designed to discourage those exports. The direct purpose of state restrictions on grain exports was to ensure sufficient domestic supply, thereby helping to reduce inflationary pressures on bread, flour, pasta, buckwheat, and other grain-based consumer edibles.

In reaction to the government's restrictions, grain exporters increased the export of grain during the first half of the agricultural year in advance of the quota and tariff. But the impact of export tariffs was evidenced by the fact that while total food imports were up 20 percent during the first eleven months of 2021, wheat exports were down 3 percent. Moreover, grain interest groups representing producers and exporters complained about the loss of hundreds of billions of rubles in revenue from the quota and the uncertainty caused by a flexible tariff.[47] For example, as the global price of wheat rose in the second half of 2021, Russia's export tariff increased from about $51 per ton in September 2021 to nearly $80 per ton in November, a direct cost to the exporter. Grain sector interests appealed to President Putin not to support export tariffs, but without success.[48] Putin's response was that it had been a "mistake" to subsidize food exports (especially grain) when exporting was so profitable. He blamed a lack of government oversight for the continuation of state support when the financial condition of exporters did not warrant it.[49]

A second significant state intervention concerns rising retail food prices. The government had not intervened in retail food prices since food shortages followed the disastrous harvest of 1997 that led to rapid food price spikes. In 1998, the federal government asked regions to impose limits on wholesale and retail price mark ups. Unlike 1998, however, in 2020–2021 government action was not spurred by domestic food shortages, but rather by global influences, some degree of speculation by domestic traders, and a fear of excessive exports. In late 2020, retail prices for some food commodities started to increase by double digits, paralleling a global rise in commodity prices. During his December 2020 press conference, Putin questioned why Russia's domestic food prices were increasing faster than world market prices.[50] Food prices were already higher than average in Russia's Far North, Siberia, and Far East, but lower than average in several regions in central European Russia.[51]

In recent years, Russia's food inflation had been modest. As shown in table 10.2, food inflation has declined significantly since the recession years

Table 10.2. Russia's Food Inflation, 2011–2020

	Food inflation, not including alcoholic beverages
2011	10.7%
2012	3.4%
2013	6.2%
2014	15.7%
2015	14.5%
2016	4.3%
2017	2.8%
2018	1.7%
2019	5.5%
2020	5.2%

Sources: Rosstat, *Sotsial'no-ekonomicheskoe polozhenie Rossii*, various years and pages.

of 2014–2015. In 2020, however, food inflation rose, and this trend continued into 2021. In 2020, Russia's official inflation rate was less than 5 percent, but food inflation from December 2019 to December 2020 was 7.2 percent.[52] As food prices rose in 2020, Prime Minister Mikhail Mishustin accused producers and wholesale distributors of "greed" that was causing higher prices.[53] Russia's federal government, fearful of potential political fallout from rising food prices, responded. First, the Ministry of Agriculture "recommended" that regions try to curtail food price increases. Next, the Ministry of Trade and the Federal Anti-Monopoly Agency negotiated with supply chain actors and retailers to restrain prices. In December 2020, the Ministry of Agriculture, Ministry of Trade, and a series of players in wholesale and retail markets signed an agreement that established upper limits on wholesale prices and retail prices for sunflower oil and sugar until April 2021.[54] As commonly happens when prices are controlled, black markets appear and canners reported that they were unable to find sugar at the state-set prices.[55] Subsequently, the wholesale and retail price caps were extended to June 2021 for sugar and October 2021 for sunflower oil.[56] For flour, the government announced a subsidy of R4.5 billion to flour millers to compensate them for higher wheat prices in the hope to keep prices down for bread. Small bakeries, which produce up to fifteen tons of bread a day, were eligible for a subsidy of R1 million per month, while large bakeries producing 60 tons or more of bread a day could receive R3.6 million per month. Enterprises that received a subsidy had to agree to fixed retail prices.[57]

At the end of December 2020 Prime Minister Mishustin signed a resolution that gave the federal government the right to cap retail food prices for major food groups.[58] The resolution permitted the government to set upper limits on retail prices for food commodities that rose more than 10 percent over a sixty-day period, and price caps could remain in effect for up to ninety days.[59] Vice Premier Viktoria Abramchenko admitted that it was unlikely that the government would actually freeze prices for ninety days, stating that this was an "extreme measure" that no one wanted.[60]

Food inflation was again expected to surpass the general rate of inflation by as much as two percentage points in 2021.[61] What had to be worrisome to political leaders was the warning from bread producers to retailers in July 2021 that prices would increase an average of 7–12 percent in the second half of the year due to a 38 percent rise in the price of margarine, a 26 percent rise in the price of packaging, and a 9 percent increase in the price of sugar.[62] Bread, of course, is a staple of the Russian diet and thus rising prices would touch every Russian family.

The annual food inflation rate reached 11 percent by November 2021 (year on year), but some products rose much more than that. Staples to the Russian diet such as cabbage were up 94 percent since January 2021, and potatoes rose 74 percent, due in part to a poor harvest. In addition, by November 2021 (year on year), pork was up 16 percent and beef 14 percent. To restrain food prices, the federal government tried to get producers to voluntarily hold back their price increases.

The idea to limit retail prices was criticized by private sector producers. The president of one of Russia's largest agroholding companies, Viktor Linnik of Miratorg, said that government limits on prices served no useful purpose and undermined incentives to invest in modernization. He instead advised that a better policy would be to increase the incomes of people and provide government support to the neediest segments of the population.[63] Other private sector actors sounded a similar note. The general director of the agroholding MolSib (and member of the National Union of Milk Producers) warned that limits on retail prices would lead not only to monetary losses for producers but also to food shortages for consumers as producers cut back production to reduce their losses.[64] In contrast to opposition from different actors and interests in the food system, as prices rose the percentage of Russian families who spent one half of their budget on food increased. According to one survey, 60 percent of Russians spent one half or more of their budget on food and 20 percent of respondents expressed support for direct governmental price controls in retail stores.[65]

Food price spikes are important because they exacerbate conditions for people who live in poverty and may push other families below the poverty line. In 2020, Russia had just under eighteen million people living below the official poverty line.[66] In the fourth quarter of 2020, the poverty threshold was defined as an income subsistence minimum of R11,312 per month for the entire population, and R12,235 per month for able-bodied persons.[67] Several million more people live just above the poverty threshold and have lifestyles that do not differ significantly from people in poverty. As is true in other countries, Russian poverty is highly correlated with food insecurity. The poor consume fewer calories, fewer grams of protein, carbohydrates, and fats than the non-poor each day.

These extraordinary government interventions—restricting agri-food exports despite a national project to increase exports and capping retail prices without food shortages—are important for three reasons. First, the willingness to regulate food prices reflects the degree to which concerns about food security continue to resonate with political leaders, a concern that is reflected in policy statements since 2008. Second, price caps place inherent limits on producers' and distributors' income earning potential. In the case of producers, lower income could lead them to reduce output. Third, restrictions on exports call into question the ability to meet the goals of the 2018 national project on food exports and the viability of the project itself if it can be so easily overridden by other policy needs. There can be little doubt that these market-regulating interventions were intended to minimize the risk of food-based political instability, and in that way food policy was shaped to protect state interests.

CONCLUSION

This chapter analyzes three core goals in Putin's food policy. State and private sector interests are concordant regarding an increase in food production. Private sector producers earn more and the state benefits from a food-secure population. State and private sector interests are concordant regarding protectionism and the goal to reduce food imports from selected Western nations. Private sector actors are protected from competition and can increase their domestic market share. The state benefits by showing resolve and strength vis-à-vis foreign adversaries. State and private sector interests are concordant regarding increasing the volume and value of food exports. Private sector actors increase foreign earnings and either establish or expand their presence in foreign markets. The state benefits from tax revenue on foreign earnings, plus enjoys prestige and status from becoming a global food supplier.

An important takeaway from this chapter is that private sector and state interests sometimes do not align, as occurred during 2020 and 2021. During these two years, state interventions restricted grain exports and placed export tariffs on grain, contrary to the interests of traders and export companies. Further, the state intervened in the retail price formation process to restrain price increases. While that effort may have benefited retail consumers in the short-term, it contradicted the interests of distributors and retailers who argued that their profits would fall. The unpopularity of state-defined wholesale prices for sugar and sunflower oil was reflected in the fact that less than 1 percent of producers and distributors who signed the original agreement in December 2020 agreed to continue complying with the price caps after the initial agreement ended on April 1, 2021.[68]

Thus, our understanding of Russia's food policy is illuminated by recognizing that the state and the private sector often have concordant interests, but when their interests diverge the priorities of the state will triumph.

AUTHOR'S POSTSCRIPT

Russia's brutal, unprovoked attack on Ukraine exacerbated global energy inflation and tight food supplies. Ukraine's wheat and corn will mostly be removed from global supply chains during the 2022–2023 marketing season. For its part, Russia faced political and financial obstacles in its foreign food trade. Russia's agricultural exports totaled $37.7 billion in 2021, $11.4 billion of which came from grain. In 2021, Russia's largest export market for foodstuffs was the European Union at $4.7 billion. Although Russia's agricultural products were not specifically targeted by Western sanctions, Russia will lose most of its European food market as countries refuse to buy Russian grain, and banks consider it too risky to do business with Russian companies. In addition, Western ports refused to accept Russian fertilizer exports, depriving Russia of millions in lost revenue.

A reduction in foreign food trade revenue was less important to the Putin regime than domestic food security. A series of policies were introduced to shore up domestic food security in the short term. Prior to the war, Russia's previously announced 11 mmt export quota for exports to states outside the Eurasian Economic Union went into effect and ran from February 15, 2022, until June 30, 2022. In the immediate aftermath of Russia's invasion, the Russian government introduced temporary bans on the export of grains and sugar to countries in the Eurasian Economic Union. The export of grains—wheat, rye, barley, and corn—was banned from March 15, 2022, to June 30, 2022, and sugar exports were banned until August 31, 2022. The Eurasian Economic Union followed Russia's move by placing quotas on the export of grain, sunflower oil, and sugar until June 30, 2022. Starting April 1 and running to August 31, 2022, Russia banned the export of sunflower seeds and rapeseeds. Russia's soybean exports were allowed to continue, but only through Russian ports located in the Far East.

Other short-term steps were also introduced. Additional money in the form of subsidized credit was allocated to the agricultural sector to ensure a successful spring sowing season. Russia was expected to plant 81.3 million hectares in 2022, up from 80.4 million hectares in 2021. Regulatory and administrative rules for food companies were relaxed. Proposals for a moratorium on digital coding of dairy products to 2028 were made in the State Duma. All these steps made it likely that domestic food supplies would be sufficient for 2022, despite rising food prices from inflation. The official line from the government was that food shortages were not expected, although the selection of imported food had narrowed.

Beyond 2022, however, Russia's food security faces obstacles if the war and sanctions continue. Russia imports a high percentage of its farm machinery, seed, and pedigree animals. Foreign vaccines are used to vaccinate livestock. If Russia cannot access its foreign reserves, its ability to subsidize future harvests and planting seasons may suffer. In sum, the short-term prospects for domestic food security are positive, but much less certain in the medium term.

—2022

QUESTIONS FOR DISCUSSION

1. Why is food policy an important political variable?
2. What are the foundational beliefs that underlie food policy in Russia?
3. What are three main goals of Russia's food policy, and how well have the goals been met?
4. How has the state intervened in Russia's food policy to protect its interests?
5. What are examples of state and private sector interests diverging?

SUGGESTED READINGS

Barrett, Christopher B. "Food or Consequences: Food Security and Its Implications for Global Sociopolitical Stability." In *Food Security and Sociopolitical Stability*, ed. Christopher B. Barrett. Oxford: Oxford University Press, 2013, 1–34.

Paarlberg, Robert. *Food Politics: What Everyone Needs to Know*. Oxford: Oxford University Press, 2013.

Pinstrup-Andersen, Per and Derrill D. Watson II, *Food Policy for Developing Countries: The Role of Government in Global, National, and Local Food Systems*. Ithaca, NY: Cornell University Press, 2011.

Timmer, C. Peter, Walter P. Falcon, and Scott R. Pearson, *Food Policy Analysis*. Baltimore: MD: Johns Hopkins University Press, 1983.

Wegren, Stephen K., Alexander Nikulin, and Irina Trotsuk. *Russia's Food Revolution: The Transformation of the Food System*. London: Routledge Publishers, 2021.

Wegren, Stephen K., Alexander Nikulin, and Irina Trotsuk. *Food Policy and Food Security: Putting Food on the Russian Table*. Lanham, MD: Lexington Books, 2018.

Wegren, Stephen K., Alexander Nikulin, and Irina Trotsuk. "The Russian Variant of Food Security," *Problems of Post-Communism* 64, no. 1 (2017): 47–62.

NOTES

1. C. Peter Timmer, Walter P. Falcon, and Scott R. Pearson, *Food Policy Analysis* (Baltimore: MD: Johns Hopkins University Press, 1983), 9.

2. Per Pinstrup-Andersen and Derrill D. Watson II, *Food Policy for Developing Countries: The Role of Government in Global, National, and Local Food Systems* (Ithaca, NY: Cornell University Press, 2011), 31–33.

3. In the United States during 1945–1975, cotton and wheat interests favored protection from the global market and supply management, while corn interests were opposed to protection and supply management. This political axis united southern Democrats and Congressional Republicans from the Wheat Belt against Republicans

262 *Stephen K. Wegren*

in the Corn Belt. See Bill Winders, *The Politics of Food Supply: U.S. Agricultural Policy in the World Economy* (New Haven, CT: Yale University Press, 2009), 77–104.

4. There are many good books on the 1932–1933 famine in Ukraine, but two of my favorites are R. W. Davies and Stephen G. Wheatcroft, *The Years of Hunger: Soviet Agriculture 1931–1933*. New York: Palgrave Macmillan, 2009; and Anne Applebaum, *Red Famine: Stalin's War on Ukraine* (New York: Doubleday, 2017). On famines in Bengal, Ethiopia, and China, see Cormac O´Grada, *Famine: A Short History* (Princeton: Princeton University Press, 2009); and Cormac O´Grada, *Eating People Is Wrong and Other Essays on Famine, Its Past, and Its Future* (Princeton: Princeton University Press, 2015).

5. Stephen K. Wegren, Alexander Nikulin, and Irina Trotsuk, *Food Policy and Food Security: Putting Food on the Russian Table* (Lanham, MD: Lexington Books, 2018).

6. See https://www.transparency.org/en/, countries. In 2020, Russia's corruption score was 33 out of 100 according to Transparency International.

7. See Christopher B. Barrett, "Food or Consequences: Food Security and Its Implications for Global Sociopolitical Stability," in *Food Security and Sociopolitical Stability*, ed. Christopher B. Barrett (Oxford: Oxford University Press, 2013), 1–34.

8. Stephen K. Wegren, Alexander Nikulin, and Irina Trotsuk, *Russia's Food Revolution: The Transformation of the Food System* (London and New York: Routledge Publishers, 2021).

9. Tat'iana Kulistikova, "Trilliony na perezagruzku," *Agroinvestor*, no. 1 (January 2021): 17.

10. Ibid.

11. OECD, "Russian Federation," in *Agricultural Policy Monitoring and Evaluation 2020* (Paris, France: OECD, 2020). https://doi.org/10.1787/928181a8-en, accessed April 2, 2021.

12. Natalia Karlova, Olga Shik, Eugenia Serova, and Renata Yanbykh, "State of the Art in Russian Agriculture: Production, Farm Structure, Trade, Policy and New Challenges," *Russian Analytical Digest*, no. 264 (February 22, 2021): 2.

13. "Zabyla pro importozameshchenie," *Sel'skaia zhizn'*, November 13–19, 2020, 2.

14. The Dairy News, "Dzhambulat Khatuov: Ezhegodno my zavozim 60 tysiach plemennykh korov iz-za rubezha," January. 28, 2021. https://www.dairynews.ru/news /dzhambulat-khatuov-ezhegodno-my-zavozim-60-tysyach.html, accessed January 28, 2021.

15. V. A. Saraikin, "Ekonomicheskie i struktrunye izmeneniia v sel'-skokhoziaistvennom proizvodstve Rossii za period s 2006 po 2016 god," *Ekonomika sel'skokhoziaistvennykh i pererabatyvaiushchikh predpriiatii*, no. 1 (January 2021): 16–23.

16. Rosstat, *Rossiia v tsifrakh 2021* (Moscow: Rosstat, 2021), 137.

17. Stephen K. Wegren, "Understanding the Decline of Smallholders in Contemporary Russia," *Outlook on Agriculture* 50, no. 1 (2021): 72–79. DOI: 10.1177/0030727020969201.

18. Rosstat, *Rossiia v tsifrakh 2021*, 137.

19. Ibid.

20. Ibid.

21. Ibid.

22. Ibid., 147.

23. Production fell short of targets for potatoes, milk and dairy products, fruits and berries, and vegetables. See Ministerstvo sel'skogo khoziaistva Rossiiskoi Federatsii, *Natsional'nyi doklad o khode rezul'tatakh realiatsii v 2020 godu gosudarstvennoi programmy razvititiia sel'skogo khoziaistva i regulirovaniia rynkov sel'skokhoziaistvenoi produktsii, syr'ia i prodovol'stviia* (Moscow: Ministry of Agriculture, 2021), 20–21.

24. Stephen K. Wegren, Alexander Nikulin, and Irina Trotsuk, "The Russian Variant of Food Security," *Problems of Post-Communism* 64, no. 1 (2017): 47–62.

25. TASS, "Putin podpisal zakon o shtrafakh za oborot nemarkirovannoi produktsii," June 15, 2021. https://www.dairynews.ru/news/putin-podpisal-zakon-o-shtrafakh -za-oborot-nemarki.html, accessed June 15, 2021.

26. TASS, "Putin podpisal zakon ob ugolovnom nakazanii za poddel'nye sredstva markirovki," July 1, 2021. https://www.dairynews.ru/news/putin-podpisal-zakon-ob -ugolovnom-nakazanii-za-pod.html, accessed July 1, 2021.

27. The Dairy News, "Shtrafy za narushenie pravil markirovki dlia iuridicheskikh lits dostigaiut 1 mln rublei," November 19, 2021. https://www.dairynews.ru/news /shtrafy-za-narushenie-pravil-markirovki-dlya-yurid.html, accessed November 19, 2021.

28. The Dairy News, "80% molochnykh predpriiatii RF gotovy k startu vtorogo etapa obiazatel'noi markirovki," August 25, 2021. https://www.dairynews.ru/news/80 -molochnykh-predpriyatiy-rf-gotovy-k-startu-vtor.html, accessed August 25, 2021.

29. RIA Novosti, "Rossel'khoznadzor predlozhil vvesti markirovku konservov," November 18, 2021. https://kvedomosti.ru/?p=1086299, accessed November 18, 2021.

30. Rosstat, *Rossiiskoi statisticheskii ezhegodnik 2015* (Moscow: Rosstat), 643.

31. Foreign Agricultural Service, United States Department of Agriculture, "Livestock and Products Annual," GAIN Report RS2020–0045, September 2020. https: //apps.fas.usda.gov/newgainapi/api/Report/DownloadReportByFileName?fileName =Livestock%20and%20Products%20Annual_Moscow_Russian%20Federation_09 -01-2020, accessed September 8, 2021.

32. Kristina Stashchenko, "Podkomissiia odobrila vvedenie kvoty na vvoz v Rossiiu zamorozhennoi goviadiny i svininy," November 10, 2021. https://kvedomosti.ru/ ?p=1085840, accessed November 10, 2021.

33. TASS, "Import miasa v Rossiiu v 2020 godu sostavit okolo 600 tys. tonn," December 11, 2020. https://kvedomosti.ru/news/https-tass-ru-ekonomika-10227843 .html, accessed December 11, 2020.

34. Foreign Agricultural Service, "Livestock and Products Annual."

35. Ekaterina Shokurova, "Minsel'khoz skorrektiroval plany eksporta produktsii APK," November 16, 2020. https://www.agroinvestor.ru/analytics/news/34801 -minselkhoz-skorrektiroval-plany-eksporta-produktsii-apk/, accessed November 16, 2020.

36. RIA.ru, "Putin: v APK nado podderzhivat' eksport s vysokoi dobavlennoi stoimost'iu," April 5, 2021. https://www.dairynews.ru/news/putin-v-apk-nado -podderzhivat-eksport-s-vysokoy-do.html, accessed April 5, 2021.

37. Ministerstvo sel'skogo khoziaistva Rossiiskoi Federatsii, "Operativnyi obzor eksporta produktsii APK," December 27, 2020. https://mcx.gov.ru/ministry/ departments/departament-informatsionnoy-politiki-i-spetsialnykh-proektov/industry -information/info-analiticheskie-obzory/, accessed March 31, 2021.

38. Ibid.

39. Ministry of Agriculture, "Operativnyi obzor eksporta produktsii APK," November 14, 2021, https://mcx.gov.ru, accessed November 14, 2021.

40. For more information about the functions of the Center, see its website at: https://mcx.gov.ru/ministry/departments/departament-informatsionnoy-politiki-i -spetsialnykh-proektov/industry-information/info-podderzhka-malogo-i-srednego -biznesa/.

41. TASS, "Minsel'khoz v 2021 godu napravil za rubezh 14 sel'khozattashe," September 3, 2021. https://agrovesti.net/news/indst/minselkhoz-v-2021-godu-napravil-za -rubezh-14-selkhozattashe.html, accessed September 3, 2021.

42. E. Semenova, "Organizatsionnyi mekhanizm razvitiia eksportnoi infrastruktury," *APK: ekonomika, upravlenie*, no. 12, December 2020: 36–46.

43. Food and Agricultural Organization, *Food Outlook. Biannual Report on Global Food Markets* (Rome: FAO, 2020).

44. An agricultural year extends from July 1 of one year to June 30 of the next year. An agricultural year is also sometimes called an agricultural season. I use the two terms synonymously.

45. RIA Novosti, "Rossiia vdvoe povyshaet poshlinu na eksport pshenitsy—do 50 evro za tonnu," March 1, 2021. https://agrovesti.net/news/indst/rossiya-vdvoe -povyshaet-poshlinu-na-eksport-pshenitsy-do-50-evro-za-tonnu.html, accessed March 1, 2021.

46. Parlamentskaia gazeta, "V Rossii s 2 Iiunia budet deistvovat' gibkaia eksportnaia poshlina na pshenitsu," February 9, 2021. https://kvedomosti.ru/news/https -www-pnp-ru-economics-v-rossii-s-2-iyunya-budet-deystvovat-gibkaya-eksportnaya -poshlina-na-pshenicu-html.html, accessed February 9, 2021.

47. RIA Novosti, "Agrarii RF boiatsia ubytkov i spada proizvodstva posle vvedeniia poshlin na zerno," February 5, 2021. https://agrovesti.net/news/indst/agrarii -rf-boyatsya-ubytkov-i-spada-proizvodstva-posle-vvedeniya-poshlin-na-zerno.html, accessed February 5, 2021.

48. Ekaterina Shokurova, "RZS poprosil Vladimira Putina ne podderzhivat' uzhestochenie ogranichenii na eksport zerna," February 8, 2021. https://www .agroinvestor.ru/markets/news/35252-rzs-poprosil-vladimira-putina-ne-podderzhivat -uzhestochenie-ogranicheniy-na-eksport-zerna/, accessed February 8, 2021.

49. "Priamoe obshchenie s liud'mi," *Sel'skaia zhizn*,' December 18–24, 2020, 3.

50. Ibid., 3.

51. Natal'ia Churkina, "Tseny rastut iz-za dorogoi logistiki," January 14, 2021. https://www.agroinvestor.ru/column/natalya-churkina/35094-tseny-rastut-iz-za -dorogoy-logistiki/, accessed January 14, 2021.

52. Rosstat, *Sotsial'no-ekonomicheskoe polozhenie Rossii*, no. 12 (2020), 149.

53. RIA Novosti, "Proizvoditeli produktov ne soglasny s mneniem o svoei zhad-nosti: u otrasli net sverkhpribyli," May 13, 2021. https://agrovesti.net/news/indst/proizvoditeli-produktov-ne-soglasny-s-mneniem-o-svoej-zhadnosti-u-otrasli-net-sverkhpribyli.html, accessed May 13, 2021.

54. TASS, "Torgovuye seti sobliudaiut soglasheniia o sderzhivanii tsen—glava FAS," January 26, 2021. https://www.dairynews.ru/news/torgovye-seti-soblyudayut-soglasheniya-o-sderzhiva.html, accessed January 26, 2021.

55. Tat'iana Kulistikova and Elena Maksimova, "Konditery ne mogut pokupat' sakhar po fiksirovannoi tsene," January 25, 2021. https://www.agroinvestor.ru/markets/news/35157-konditery-ne-mogut-pokupat-sakhar-po-fiksirovannoy-tsene/, accessed January 25, 2021.

56. RIA Novosti, "Prodlevaiutsia soglasheniia o stabilizatsii tsen na podsolnechnoe maslo i sakhar," April 2, 2021. https://kvedomosti.ru/news/https-ria-ru-20210401-tseny-1603721036-html.html, accessed April 2, 2021.

57. Ekaterina Shokurova, "Pravitel'stvo vydelit bolee 4.5 mlrd rublei dlia sderzhivaniia tsen na khleb i muku," January 21, 2021. https://www.agroinvestor.ru/markets/news/35145-pravitelstvo-vydelit-bolee-4-5-mlrd-rubley-dlya-sderzhivaniya-tsen-na-khleb-i-muku/, accessed January 21, 2021.

58. The groups included meat, chicken, frozen fish, milk, butter, eggs, sugar, salt, tea, flour bread, rice, vermicelli, and other pastas.

59. RBC.ru, "Mishustin dal pravitel'stvu pravo vvodit' predel'nye tseny na produkty," December 31, 2020. https://www.dairynews.ru/news/mishustin-dal-pravitelstvu-pravo-vvodit-predelnye-.html, accessed December 31, 2020.

60. The Dairy News, "Rossiia mozhet otkazat'sia ot gosregulirovaniia tsen na edu," July 28, 2021. https://www.dairynews.ru/news/rossiya-mozhet-otkazatsya-ot-gosregulirovaniya-tse.html, accessed July 28, 2021.

61. Regnum.ru, "Prodovol'stvennaia infliatsiia v RF prevysit obshchuiu—ekonomist VShE," July 15, 2021. https://www.dairynews.ru/news/prodovolstvennaya-inflyatsiya-v-rf-prevysit-obshch.html, accessed July 15, 2021.

62. RIA Novosti, "Khlebozavody predupredili o povyshenii tsen na svoiu produktsiiu," July 19, 2021. https://kvedomosti.ru/news/https-ria-ru-20210719-tseny-1741785438-html.html, accessed July 19, 2021.

63. RBK, "Glava Miratorga ne uvidel strategicheskoi pol'zy v gosregulirovanii tsen," July 4, 2021. https://kvedomosti.ru/news/https-www-rbc-ru-economics-04-07-2021-60e1008e9a7947b5805a3158.html, accessed July 4, 2021.

64. The Dairy News, "Gosudarstvennaia politika sderzhivaniia tsen privedet k ubytkam v sel'skom khoziaistve—Igor Eliseenko," May 17, 2021. https://www.dairynews.ru/news/gosudarstvennaya-politika-sderzhivaniya-tsen-prive.html, accessed May 17, 2021.

65. The Insider, "60% Rossiian tratiat na produkty polovinu svoego dokhoda," July 15, 2021. https://theins.ru/news/243478, accessed July 26, 2021. I thank Darrell Slider for this source.

66. Rosstat, *Sotsial'no-ekonomicheskie indikatory bednosti 2013–2020 gg.* (Moscow: Rosstat, 2020), 15.

67. Ibid., 10. In urban Russia, poverty rates are lowest in cities with one million or more people, and higher as the size of the population decreases, with the highest poverty rate in towns with fifty thousand or fewer residents.

68. TASS, "V Minpromtorge zaiavili, chto iz soglashenii o tsenakh na maslo i sakhar vyshlo menee 1% kompanii," April 16, 2021. https://agrovesti.net/news/indst/v-minpromtorge-zayavili-chto-iz-soglashenij-o-tsenakh-na-maslo-i-sakhar-vyshlo-menee-1-kompanij.html, accessed April 16, 2021.

PART III

Russia and the World

Chapter 11

Russia's Relations with the United States

Maria Snegovaya

The United States and Russia have not had an easy relationship in the twentieth century. During the Cold War, the conflict between two ideological systems—the Soviet Union seeking to expand Communism to other regions and the United States seeking to counter it—led to a number of direct and indirect clashes between them, including wars in Vietnam and Korea, the Cuban Missile Crisis and Berlin Blockade, and the buildup of the Berlin Wall. The collapse of the Communist system, together with a perception of the "End of History,"[1] spread a feeling of optimism about United States–Russia relations. At first, the optimism strengthened due to initially amicable relations between the Russian and US presidents.

However, subsequent relations took a wrong turn, going through several rounds of a downward spiral, worsening after each crisis (including the NATO bombings of Yugoslavia, the "color revolutions" in post-Soviet space, Russia's 2008 war with Georgia, Russia's 2014 war with Ukraine and 2015 war in Syria, Russia's interference in the US elections in 2016). As of today, United States–Russia relations are at the lowest point since the end of the Cold War. Many observers wonder to what extent such an outcome was inevitable, and who is to blame for it?

Various explanations for the deterioration in the United States–Russia relations may be divided into two broad categories. The first one puts more blame on the United States, accusing it of unilateral exercise of unrestrained power after the Cold War and ignoring Russia's national interests. The second explanation argues that Russia, historically aggressive and imperialistic, under the rule of Vladimir Putin, a political leader with a background in the

Soviet security services, has returned to its traditional pattern of confrontation with the West.

This chapter explores the key developments in the United States–Russia relations under Putin, the current dynamic status quo, as well as Russia's attacks against the West and the United States, more specifically, in the form of the so-called hybrid warfare or influence operations.

THE UNITED STATES–RUSSIA RELATIONS
AFTER THE SOVIET COLLAPSE

By some estimates, the relationship between Russia and the United States today is the worst that it has been since 1985.[2] According to Gallup's data, in 2021 Americans' opinion of Russia reached a record low with about 77 percent of them having an unfavorable view of the country (as opposed to only 29 percent back in 1989).[3] Similarly, in Russia, 54 percent of respondents had a bad attitude toward the United States in 2021 (almost eight times the number of those in 1990–7 percent).[4]

But the United States–Russia relations have not always been so bad. In fact, they have gone through a number of ups and downs.

The 1990s

Throughout most of the twentieth century, two great powers opposed each other in an ideological and geopolitical contestation for global influence, known as the Cold War. Soviet rulers viewed the alleged bellicose rhetoric, arms buildup, and interventionist approach to international relations by the United States as all being aimed at undermining the Communist system.[5] Americans were wary of Soviet expansionism in Eastern Europe during and after the Second World War and were concerned about the possibility of Communist ideology spreading into Western societies. At least in part, Soviet expansionism and desire to oppose the United States was driven by a fundamental insecurity of the Soviet leadership. George Kennan, a US ambassador to the USSR, in his Long Telegram, argued that the insecurity was driven by Soviet leaders' realization that their system was deeply flawed in comparison to Western models.[6] Throughout the Cold War, both powers deployed nuclear arsenals and conventional military in multiple world regions and ran a series of proxy wars, propaganda campaigns, and espionage operations against each other.

However, after the collapse of the USSR, the relationship between the two countries substantially improved under the rule of a new president of now-democratic Russia, Boris Yeltsin. Yeltsin's liberal policymakers proclaimed that, at the core, Russia was socially and culturally "Western" and that it should shed its imperial past and enter the community of liberal, democratic states.[7]

As Russia transitioned toward a market-oriented, democratic system and dropped its imperialistic ambitions in Europe, Moscow no longer presented a security threat to the United States. Russia also appeared to be open to collaborating with and learning from the experiences of Western democracies. American political and economic advisers traveled to Moscow to work with state and society representatives to promote democracy and markets. Both countries also successfully cooperated on a number of domestic and foreign policy issues. A friendly relationship between Boris Yeltsin and US President Bill Clinton also helped. In 1993, Clinton publicly backed Russia's President Yeltsin in his standoff with the Communist-controlled parliament.[8] The United States and Russia negotiated agreements to halt the sale of Russian rocket parts to India, remove Soviet-era nuclear missiles from Ukraine, Belarus, and Kazakhstan in exchange for Russian assurances of Ukraine's sovereignty and security,[9] withdraw Russian troops from the Baltic states, institutionalize cooperation between Russia and an expanding NATO, lay the groundwork for the Baltic states to join the alliance, ensure the participation of the Russian military in Balkan peacekeeping and of Russian diplomacy in the settlement of NATO's air war against Serbia, and reduce strategic nuclear weapons (START II agreement).[10] In 1997, Russia also joined the G7 (an inter-governmental political forum of Canada, France, Germany, Italy, Japan, the UK, and the United States), which then became known as the G8.

However, by the end of the 1990s, this relationship between the two countries took a negative turn following the Yugoslavia bombings. In late 1990s, tensions between Albanian and Serbian communities erupted into major violence in Kosovo, a province within the Yugoslav constituent republic of Serbia located in Southeast Europe. The Kosovo Liberation Army (KLA), an ethnic Albanian separatist militia, sought the separation of Kosovo from the Federal Republic of Yugoslavia. In response Yugoslav President Slobodan Milošević had launched an ethnic cleansing campaign against Kosovo's Albanians; subsequently, roughly a million ethnic Albanians fled or were forcefully driven from Kosovo. The fast escalation of the situation threatened to repeat the Srebrenica massacre that consumed Bosnia in the early 1990s. The recent memory of 1994 Rwanda genocide, in which hundreds of thousands were massacred, provided an additional impetus for the international community to act in an effort to avoid the possible deaths of hundreds or thousands of Kosovar Albanians and a major humanitarian crisis. The situation escalated fast, threatening to become a genocide of a scale witnessed previously in Rwanda in 1994.[11] The international community was horrified and committed to stop Milošević. But military action proposed by the United

Nations was blocked by Russian and Chinese UN delegates. Even a fairly pro-Western Russian president Boris Yeltsin had difficulty agreeing to the idea of a military action against Serbia, Russia's historical ally in the Balkans. The Kremlin was concerned that Kosovo could set a precedent for further interventions by Western countries, particularly those in Russia's "near abroad"—the former Soviet republics. Despite the lack of UN authorization, allies launched the United States–led NATO military operation on behalf of the KLA. The operation began in March 1999 through a series of airstrikes against Yugoslavia. This development was very negatively viewed in Russia. As a symbolic gesture, Russia's Prime Minister Primakov, who was flying to the United States, ordered his crew to turn the plane around in mid-flight over the Atlantic and went back to Moscow to protest NATO's impending bombardment of Serbia.[12]

The NATO bombings triggered a serious rethinking of Russia's role in the post–Cold War world within the Russian policymaking community and opened a door for a return to more hawkish foreign policy. For hardline Russian elites, the Yugoslavia bombings had demonstratively proved that Russia's cooperative stance throughout the 1990s was a strategic mistake. According to this line of thought, the United States–led NATO military operation against Serbia showed that the United States did not treat Moscow as an equal partner, and its interests, particularly in countries like Serbia, Russia's long-term strategic partner, were not respected. Many in the Kremlin, therefore, concluded that Russia had lost its relevance to the West by being too cooperative. Looking at the foreign policy opinions of the Russian elites, one can see that it is precisely in 1999 that there is a sharp surge in anti-American sentiment.[13]

Political scientist Keith Darden, who analyzed Russia's official security documents, has discovered that NATO's offensive military operations in Kosovo constituted the critical turning point in Russian perceptions of threat coming from the United States. Prior to that point, Russia's security assessments did not view the United States as a threat. And while the NATO expansion, which began in the mid-1990s, was not well received in Russia, it alone was insufficient to raise the specter of a threat to Russia's territorial integrity. In contrast, the NATO bombing of Yugoslavia radically shifted perceptions; it showcased NATO's willingness to intervene in the internal affairs of a sovereign state without UN approval using offensive out-of-area operations. Russia's security documents soon came to view the link between the external (US/NATO) military power with internal opposition (the Kosovo Liberation Army) as a new model of warfare and the foundation of a unipolar world. Published right after the Kosovo war, October 1999 National Security Concept identifies external influence in Russia's *internal* politics as a threat and offers expansion of the state *domestic* control as a strategic necessity to prevent external actors from undermining Russia's internal security.[14]

Thus, while the 1990s were generally a period of very good and cooperative relations between the United States and Russia, they ended on a sour note.

The 2000s

New Russian President Vladimir Putin, who came to power in 2000, projected an image of youth, strength, and energy, in a stark contrast to Yeltsin, who, at the end of his rule, often looked ill and intoxicated. At first, the US-Russia relationship under Putin was off to a good start. Russia stressed the need to cooperate with its "Western partners." Putin was the first foreign leader to contact US President George W. Bush after the 9/11 attacks, supported the US campaign against terrorism in 2001, and assisted the United States in the first phase of the war in Afghanistan, providing the United States with supplies and the information Russia had collected from the Soviet decade-long war there.[15] Russia assisted with the establishment of the NATO-Russian Council in May 2002 and accepted new rounds of NATO expansion in the early- to mid-2000s and the US withdrawal from the Anti-Ballistic Missile Treaty.[16]

However, this original optimism waned after the United States, under President George W. Bush's administration, entered Iraq in 2003. Yet again the invasion reconfirmed the Kremlin suspicions about US interventionist tendencies, which first surfaced after Yugoslavia. Moscow objected to the Iraq war. Putin personally called the war "unjustifiable and unnecessary" and an assault against "the system of international security."[17] The Russian parliament passed a resolution declaring the invasion an act of "aggression." The US willingness to go to war alone reinforced the perception that Washington did not consider Moscow to be an equal, but rather a junior partner, whose interests and positions could be disregarded. Putin and his security team also received confirmation that the United States was seeking pretexts to overthrow regimes potentially obstructive to its interests.[18] The war in Iraq marked the adoption in Kremlin's foreign policy thinking of the language of American hegemony, multipolarity,[19] and renewed discussions of Russia's status in the international system.[20]

Things between Russia and the United States got even worse after a stream of color revolutions shook the post-Soviet countries. This included Georgia in 2003, Ukraine in 2004, and Kyrgyzstan in 2005.[21] Putin, whose rule by the mid-2000s had taken an increasingly autocratic turn, grew more and more concerned that those developments could also trigger pro-democratic movements inside Russia and eventually threaten his own hold on power. President George W. Bush's remarks welcoming color revolutions suggested that

Maria Snegovaya

similar events might take place in countries like Belarus, and his backing of US initiatives in support of popular movements against authoritarian regimes elsewhere did not help alleviate Moscow's concerns.[22] The Kremlin viewed post-Soviet protests, not as a result of popular movements for freedom and democracy, but like the KLA in the case of Kosovo, as organizational pro-Western proxies America used to oust unfriendly leaders.[23] Kremlin elites grew increasingly convinced that the CIA and other Western intelligence services had encouraged if not launched these color revolutions. Hence the Kremlin now equated regime change with US subjugation, which put more and more strain on United States–Russia relations.

These overtones are noticeable in Putin's Beslan speech delivered after a terrorist attack on Russia's elementary school.[24] Moscow interpreted Beslan as a moment of truth, which exposed Russia's fragmented power system and weak international position.[25] In his September 4, 2004, speech, Putin declared that the terrorist attacks were part of a coordinated assault by international terrorism and tied the international terrorism to an outside force that sought to weaken and "remove the threat of Russia as a major nuclear power."[26] Similar official statements then followed, together with an intensified effort to tighten controls and cut off avenues of possible foreign influence.[27]

Since the mid-2000s, Russian security doctrines described countering the US unipolarity, not simply as a matter of reinforcing Russian military capability to counterbalance US military strength, but also as a necessity to limit the US "freedom agenda," viewed as a vehicle for the extension of the US power and subtle intervention. Russian leaders argued that the United States extended its influence through infiltration and subversion of unfriendly governments, exploited domestic and international law in a way that suited its relentless pursuit of power, and that much of the existing international order is a mechanism for imposing US influence and designs.[28] By 2005, Russian state-linked media were openly declaring that Russia was the target of a new Cold War, waged "by political provocation, played out with the help of special operations, media war, political destabilization, and the seizure of power by an aggressively activated minority . . . with the help of velvet, blue, orange, etc. revolutions." To minimize the risks of similar developments taking place in Russia, the Kremlin orchestrated a wave of repression against perceived domestic threats, including the independent media, opposition, and oligarchs. The more repression took place, the more critical the United States became of these developments, which put further strain on the relationship between the two countries.[29] Russia also strongly opposed US missile defense plans, which led to the announcement in July 2007 that Russia would suspend its compliance with the Conventional Forces in Europe (CFE) Treaty.[30]

Putin's confrontational stance against the United States was reinforced by the perceived growth of Russia's economic strength. Scholarship has demonstrated that petrostates (countries with an annual net oil export of at least 10 percent of GDP), like Russia, tend to become more assertive in their foreign policy as oil prices grow. The Kremlin's behavior fits this pattern perfectly. In the early 2000s, when Putin was pursuing cooperation with the United States, the price of oil was $25 a barrel. By 2007, around the time of the Munich speech, oil prices hit their first peak, at $75 a barrel.[31] Economically, Russia was growing fast, at 5 to 8 percent per year. A rise in relative material power contributed to a corresponding expansion in the ambition and scope of Russia's foreign policy activity.

This new thinking expressed itself in blatantly confrontational rhetoric toward the West and the United States–led international order expressed in Putin's 2007 Munich Security Conference speech.[32] In this speech, Putin lambasted American unilateralism and the hyper-use of force. He also warned the United States against pursuing further NATO expansion, which in his view would destabilize Europe and threaten Russia's security.[33] It did not take long for the confrontation to come to life. In April 2008, at the Bucharest Summit, NATO allies offered a vaguely worded promise to two post-Soviet countries, Georgia and Ukraine, that they would someday become members of the Alliance. In August 2008, four months after the Bucharest Summit, Russia invaded Georgia in a five-day war, defeating it and occupying 20 percent of its internationally recognized territory. Russia subsequently recognized as sovereign states two Georgian regions it occupied, Abkhazia and South Ossetia. These steps were taken in violation of international law and the principles of the Organization for Security and Co-operation in Europe. But the result was a de facto veto Russia now held over Georgia's NATO membership; the presence of a frozen conflict on Georgia's territory jeopardized its aspiration to join NATO in the foreseeable future. If Georgia was granted NATO membership, then under NATO's Article 5 Security Guarantee (the principle of collective defense), it could mean an immediate conflict with Russia over these occupied regions. Hence NATO is likely to avoid that scenario by not accepting Georgia.[34]

The Russo-Georgian war had a profound effect on United States–Russia relations. The war signaled Kremlin's resolve to "actively contest the US vision for European security, veto NATO expansion in its neighborhood, and challenge Washington's design for a normative international order where small states can determine their own affairs independent of the interests of great powers."[35] The "first European war of the twenty-first century," made abundantly clear the Kremlin's commitment to challenge the existing security framework in Europe and NATO's role in it as the principal security agent. But for Russia, the war also exposed profound deficiencies in its armed forces inherited from the Soviet times, including the poor performance of its air power, the inability of different services to work together, problems with command and control, gaps in capability, and poor intelligence.[36] Russia has subsequently launched a comprehensive army reform to modernize its military.

The 2010s

Despite United States–Russia relations becoming strained as result of these developments, the 2009–2012 period marked an attempted "reset" of the relationship with Russia, initiated by the Obama administration, with Russia's new president, Dmitry Medvedev, who held the throne in-between Putin's two consecutive terms. The US thinking underlying the reset policy was that after the rupture over the Russo-Georgian war, new opportunities for cooperation in areas of shared interest would emerge.[37] To be fair, the reset period, which lasted about four years, did achieve some progress in cooperation on arms control, Afghanistan, Iran, and a range of other issues; however, it came under severe strain following the multistate NATO-led coalition intervention in Libya[38] and the alleged US support for the mass protests in Russia that took place in 2011–2012.

In September 2011, Vladimir Putin announced he would run for the presidency again in 2012, switching places with Medvedev, who would become prime minister. In combination with blatant falsifications of parliamentary elections in December 2011, these events triggered mass protests across Russia, which continued into 2012. Organized by the leaders of the opposition parties and non-systemic opposition, the protests massively aggravated the Kremlin's concerns that the long-feared color revolution in Russia was around the corner. Then–Secretary of State Hillary Clinton's statement that "the Russian people, like people everywhere, deserve the right to have their voices heard and their votes counted" added fuel to the fire.[39] Kremlin interpreted this declaration as more evidence that the United States was backing the alleged destabilization of Russia.

In 2012, Putin returned to the Kremlin convinced that Hillary Clinton and the US State Department had been behind the demonstrators who had protested his return to power.[40] This marked yet another round of deterioration of United States–Russia relations. The counterattack soon followed. In 2013, the Kremlin responded to what it viewed as US interference in Russia's domestic affairs by granting political asylum to Edward Snowden, the NSA contractor who stole millions of classified documents, and subsequently refused President Obama's request to return him.[41] Domestically, Russian officials and state media embraced the narratives of external actors interfering in Russia's internal affairs and protestors being paid by Western institutions. The Kremlin responded to these alleged threats by expelling the USAID, passing a law demanding that entities receiving foreign funding register as "foreign agents," and adding new restrictions on protest participation.[42]

These tensions worsened dramatically after Ukraine's Euromaidan uprising. A wave of demonstrations and civil unrest in Ukraine began in November 2013, sparked by Ukraine's pro-Russia President Viktor Yanukovych's decision to suspend the signing of an association agreement with the European Union and instead choosing to push for closer ties to Russia and the Eurasian Economic Union. After months of popular protests, in February 2014 Yanukovych fled to Russia and was replaced by a pro-Western government. Almost immediately, the Kremlin deployed Russian troops to occupy and annex the Crimean Peninsula, which had been part of Ukraine since 1954. This annexation, the most blatant land grab in Europe since World War II,[43] also violated the terms of the 1994 Budapest Memorandum in which Russia, Ukraine, the United States, and the UK promised to uphold Ukraine's territorial integrity. In subsequent months, Russian-backed separatists and Russian no-insignia troops (the so-called little green men) moved in to occupy large parts of Eastern Ukraine, the Donbas and Luhansk regions, ousting the legitimate local authorities. The protracted conflict, which continues until now, has led to at least fourteen thousand dead.

In an August 2014 speech in Yalta, Crimea, Putin voiced Russia's now open rejection of the US and Western vision of the post–Cold War order. In the Yalta speech, Putin proposed that the world order be returned to the previous post-WWII framework established at the Potsdam and Yalta conferences, when the three allied powers—the United States, the UK, and the USSR—decided the fate of Europe and agreed to rearrange borders, ignoring the opinions of the defeated powers and smaller countries. Putin suggested that the United States and Russia get together again in a "new Yalta."[44] The strong version of this proposal implies an implicit recognition of Russia's special status in regions of Europe and Eurasia that once constituted part of the Soviet empire. The weaker version demands non-alignment or neutrality in several post-Soviet states, primarily Ukraine.[45] Neither option is acceptable to the United States in light of its liberal vision of the world and existing commitments to European allies. Nor is it compatible with America's values.

The impact of Russia's war with Ukraine on United States–Russia relations is hard to overestimate. It sparked "Europe's worst security crisis since the 1990s Yugoslav wars"[46] and fundamentally repositioned Putin's Russia as a long-term threat to NATO, the EU, and the United States. Russia's actions in 2014 also raised wider concerns about its intentions elsewhere in Eastern Europe and Central Asia. It has complicated possibilities for cooperation between United States and Russia on other issues, including terrorism and arms control. Until now, the conflict in Ukraine remains unfinished, threatens constant escalation, and has the potential to further worsen United States–Russia relations if Russia were to expand its presence in Ukraine.[47]

Since February 2015, France, Germany, Russia, and Ukraine, the so-called Normandy Four, have attempted to negotiate a cessation in war actions through the Minsk Accords. However, these agreements suffer from a number of problems, such as mentioning Russia as a mediator in a conflict in which it was the aggressor and instigator or placing unfeasible demands on Ukraine to implement constitutional reforms.[48] Despite continued meetings of the Normandy Four, with the last meeting in this format being held in December 2019 in Paris with little to no progress, many observers argue that, as of today, the Minsk agreements are de facto dead.[49]

In response to major violation of Ukraine's sovereignty, the United States and Europe imposed visa and financial sanctions on Russia and individuals close to Putin. The effect of these sanctions on Russia's economic situation is hard to evaluate. Various estimates suggest that combined economic impact of sanctions could have reduced Russia's real GDP by 0.7 percent to 2.5 percent per year.[50] Overall, while the sanctions might have constrained Putin's eagerness to interfere further into Ukraine militarily, they have not succeeded in forcing Moscow to fully reverse its actions and end aggression in Ukraine. Despite falling oil prices in 2014, which in combination with Western sanctions caused a serious blow to Russia's economy, in subsequent years the Kremlin continued to take actions to project its power and influence in various world regions, including military deployments to Syria and Libya, a paramilitary deployment to the Central African Republic, and deepening economic ties with Nicolás Maduro's regime in Venezuela.[51]

Russia's entry into the Syrian civil war in 2015 to support Bashar al-Assad is particularly worth highlighting. The intervention allowed Russia to test some of its newly developed weapons as part of a broader endeavor to modernize its army.[52] This put an additional strain on relations with the United States, which was supporting Syrian groups in opposition to Assad.[53] When the United States partially withdrew from Syria, Russian troops promptly moved to occupy former US bases and supported Assad's brutal assault on Idlib Province, which resulted in a million refugees.[54]

By 2016, the dominant view in the Kremlin, as expressed in official statements and state media, considered the United States the top military power in the world and the leader of a hostile military alliance that relentlessly tried approaching Russian borders and used force and money to topple rival regimes. Kremlin's domestic attacks against independent media, civil society and NGOs, foreign aid, and control of strategic economic assets have thus, in its own thinking, all appeared justified as an effort to balance against an external Western threat.[55]

One additional major blow to United States–Russia relations was dealt by Russia's interference in the 2016 US presidential election campaign. According to the 2019 Mueller Report,[56] which documented the findings and conclusions of former Special Counsel Robert Mueller's investigation into Russian efforts to interfere in the 2016 presidential election, since as early as April 2014 Russia's St. Petersburg–based troll factory have actively used social media to exacerbate US political polarization, stoke divisions in the American electorate, and undermine legitimacy of democracy. The Kremlin particularly did not want Hillary Clinton, who ran for the US presidency in 2016, to win the presidential election due to her tougher stances on Russian policy issues, as well as her verbal support for Russia's civil society.[57] Therefore, it used these platforms to back candidates Donald Trump and Bernie Sanders over Hillary Clinton. The troll factory received guidance and funding from the wealthy Russian businessman Yevgeniy Prigozhin, who was closely tied to Putin and Russia's intelligence. The social media interference was a part of a three-pronged strategy, which also included an attempt to penetrate election machines in several US states, and a cyberattack on the Democratic National Committee email server, with subsequent release of confidential emails to the data dump WikiLeaks website. While Trump did become the US president, it is unclear to what extent the Kremlin's interference effort contributed to this result. One thing is certain: The Kremlin was elated about Clinton's defeat. Russia's deputies even celebrated Trump's victory by opening a bottle of champagne in Russia's parliament.[58] Election interference via social media continued into the 2020 electoral cycle.[59]

Whatever expectations Moscow might have had about Trump's presidency, they failed to materialize. Trump's periodic, amicable statements about Putin[60] in combination with the Kremlin's support for his candidacy in 2016 fueled suspicions of the so-called Russiagate—collusion by Trump's team with the Kremlin.[61] Concerned about Trump's alleged links to Russia, throughout Trump's presidency the US Congress kept imposing new rounds of sanctions on Russia. If anything, the cumulative sanctions dramatically expanded under Trump, more than they would have without the Kremlin's election interference. Trump's own foreign policy agenda did not seem to follow a particularly pro-Russian track either.[62]

The escalation in United States–Russia relations contributed to an expulsion and counter-expulsion of diplomats in both countries. Since 2016, US and Russian diplomatic missions were radically reduced in size through a series of tit-for-tat reductions. As a result of repeated expulsions of diplomats, Russia had to close its consulate general in San Francisco. The United States had to close the consulate general in Vladivostok, to suspend operations at the other remaining US consulate general in Russia in Yekaterinburg, while its Embassy personnel in Moscow was left badly understaffed, down from 1,200 personnel five years ago to just 120.[63] As part of another round of escalation in May 2021, the Kremlin added the United States to its "Unfriendly Country" list as a way to punish Washington for what it perceived as increased acts of aggression.[64]

New President Joe Biden's team, who took office in 2021, seems to have continued the policy track established through previous rounds of United States–Russia relations, attempting negotiations and sanctions when the Kremlin violates international agreements. At the same time, Biden's administration seems to be taking a cautious stance toward Russia, avoiding serious sanctions and offering in-person meetings with Putin. This partly stems from the Biden administration's explicit focus on China, where constraining Russia is not viewed as a priority. Some Biden administration team members who influence Russia policy, like John Kerry, were previously advocates of the reset policy with Russia under the Obama administration, when Biden was vice president. A more cautious approach is also based on the premise that Washington needs to work with Moscow on certain objectives, including mitigating climate change and nuclear arms control.[65]

Who Is at Fault?

Vladimir Putin, as Russia's president or prime minister, has continuously been in power since 1999 and has now seen a total of five US presidents rotating in office. Most of these US presidents, regardless of their personalities, backgrounds, and party affiliations, came to power with an agenda of deescalation of US relations with Russia.[66] All these presidents left office under another round of deteriorating United States–Russia relations.

This remarkable continuity in the United States–Russia antagonism over the last two decades has made observers wonder, why has it happened, and which side is to blame? Expert opinions on this question tend to fall into two camps.

Is It the West?

The first group of experts puts the blame on the United States for the unilateral exercise of unrestrained power after the Cold War that provoked Russia. This argument describes Russia as a defensive power, reacting to aggressive Western moves that violate its national interests and threaten its security. A particularly popular version of this argument is offered by scholars of the "realist" school of international relations. For example, according to Daniel Deudney and John Ikenberry, the deterioration in United States–Russia relations can primarily be explained by the ill-considered American policies that rejected the restraint exercised during the late Cold War in favor of a foreign policy that largely disregarded Russian interests, such as NATO expansion, the US withdrawal from the Anti-Ballistic Missile Treaty, decisions to deploy anti-missile systems, and disputes over pipeline routes from the Caspian region.[67]

The question of whether NATO enlargement threatened Russia's security is particularly widely discussed. This argument has been debated in the US policy community at least since George Kennan, who argued that the NATO expansion was "the most fateful error of American policy in the entire post-cold-war era."[68] More recently, John Mearsheimer, a leading realist scholar, famously blamed the Russo-Ukrainian war on the West. According to Mearsheimer, the West flagrantly violated the promises it previously made to Russia that NATO would not be expanding too far into the post-Soviet region.[69] Instead, the 2008 NATO summit in Bucharest introduced a guarantee that Georgia and Ukraine, two countries located on Russia's borders, would one day become NATO members. This utterly enraged Putin, leading to his August 2008 aggression against Georgia. But, according to Mearsheimer, the Georgian war did not teach the Western leaders the lesson they needed, and they continued promoting Western values and linkages in Ukraine. Eventually Putin "rightly" interpreted the 2014 Euromaidan as a Washington-backed coup and counteracted it by annexing Crimea and destabilizing Ukraine's east. According to this argument, any great power would have acted as Russia did when faced with the expansion of a hostile military bloc toward its borders.[70]

The NATO expansion argument faces a number of criticisms. First, it fails to address the timing of Russia's aggression against Ukraine. Russia did not seem to care much about NATO expansion until 2008. After NATO expanded into the Baltic region in 2004, Russia's land border with NATO countries became more than twice as large as its land border with Georgia, yet Putin did not seem worried.[71] In fact, in 2002, Putin himself stated that NATO enlargement to include the Baltics was "no tragedy," as long as no new military infrastructure was introduced.[72] And again in 2004, Putin reconfirmed that he had "no concerns about the expansion of NATO" because "today's threats are such that the expansion of NATO will not remove them."[73] At multiple meetings with President Obama over a five-year period, Putin and Medvedev never raised concerns over NATO expansion.[74]

Second, instead of fearing NATO, until 2008 Moscow had been developing an active partnership with it, participating in joint military exercises in Afghanistan and peacekeeping operations. In 2007, Moscow even ratified an agreement allowing NATO troops and arms to pass through Russia's territory in case of a military need. Until 2009, Russia's Kremlin-linked politicians occasionally raised the possibility of Russia's own future NATO accession.[75]

Third, if Russia is simply reacting to perceived threats from the United States and its allies, one would expect the Kremlin to react only to US provocations in its perceived sphere of influence and to develop military capabilities sufficient only to deter the United States and its allies.[76] However, that is not the case. Russia's interests expanded beyond simply countering the United States. In recent years, the Kremlin took multiple actions to project its power and influence in various world regions, including the Middle East and North Africa, Africa, and Latin America.

Is It Russia?

This pattern of Russia's expanding influence in various world regions and seeking to restore its great power status can also be explained by Russian leadership's own revisionist preferences. Various versions of this argument postulate that Russia, historically aggressive and imperialistic, has returned to its historical pattern of confrontation with the West under the rule of Vladimir Putin. An important part of this argument is based on the backgrounds of Putin and his closest elites in the Soviet security services (KGB),[77] which shaped their vision of the international system and the US role in it. These elites started to dominate Russia's policymaking circles by the mid-1990s, a process that accelerated when Yevgeny Primakov became Russia's prime minister, and eventually culminated under Putin's presidency in the 2000s. This dynamic helps explain the timing of deterioration in United States–Russia relations.

This argument has been popular among Russia hardliners in the US political spectrum, including John McCain (d. 2018), Hillary Clinton, and John Bolton,[78] as well as a number of scholars and policy experts. For example, according to Michael McFaul, a political science professor at Stanford who was a US ambassador to Russia under Obama, the United States and its NATO allies provided well-intentioned support for Russia's transition, only to have Putin reject a Western-dominated liberal order in favor of nationalist authoritarianism at home and revisionist adventurism abroad.[79] In the view of Philip Remler, the main task of Russian foreign policy in Putin's era has been to regain recognition of Russia as a world power like the Soviet Union was before it.[80] Russia's aggressive actions in the post-Soviet space, the ongoing information and/or hybrid warfare against the West, and its domestic ambitions in the Middle East, Latin America, and the Arctic all may indicate that Russia is a revisionist, not a status quo, power.[81]

Indeed, there are many examples of confrontational rhetoric and actions by Moscow that cannot be explained by, or that directly stem from, specific hostile US actions against Russia. These include Putin's 2007 Munich speech, repeated attacks and poisonings of individuals in Europe who were considered "traitors" or "enemies" by the Kremlin, such as former GRU agent Sergei Skripal,[82] information warfare, cyberattacks, and social media interference in the 2016 presidential elections.

Putin's view of the United States is closely linked to his worldview, which is connected to his KGB background and ideas, as well as his frustration with Washington's perceived neglect of Russia's great power aspirations. From this perspective, NATO expansion per se was not a decisive factor in "provoking Russia." According to Kimberly Marten, "Russia mourned its lost status more than it feared a new security danger, and no realistic alternative to NATO's geographic enlargement would have restored Russia's status in the system, especially given the expansion of NATO's mandates and the growth of US unilateralism."[83] In his speeches, Putin often expresses anger about what he sees as the US proclivity to ignore or downplay Russian interests. Examples of such public statements include his rejection of the criticism that he used excessive force to end the 2004 Beslan school siege (he countered that countries like the United States take advantage of such events to attack Russia because they "wish to tear from us a juicy chunk"), his declaration in response to criticism of Russia's heavy-handed activities in Ukraine that Washington had no business telling Moscow not to meddle in the affairs of its neighbors ("Comrade Wolf knows whom to eat; he eats without asking permission"), and his February 2007 accusation that the United States was the main destabilizing force in world affairs ("The US is overstepping its bounds in all areas").[84]

One particular concept that prominently figures in many of Putin's public talks is "sovereignty." This idea is central to Russia's foreign policy doctrine under Putin. But it is also conceptually distinct from what Western thinkers usually understand by "sovereignty." Putin views Russia's "sovereignty" quite broadly as the Kremlin's complete discretion over everything that happens in Russia domestically. The general picture looks as follows: External hostile forces in today's international system (the West, the United States, NATO, etc.) seek to destroy other states' sovereignty and subordinate them to their own domination. To do so, these hostile forces weaponize other countries' domestic problems by penetrating elements of civil society, financing them, and preparing color revolutions.[85] To prevent what Putin views as a catastrophic outcome, the preservation of sovereignty becomes the state's main responsibility and crucial for the nation's survival, which in Putin's view is the same as regime survival. And as a Russian president, Putin aims to maintain his country's sovereignty by ensuring that it has maximum freedom to maneuver, politically, economically, and militarily.[86] Western attempts to make Russia abide by the institutional rules of existing international systems will require Russia to give up too much of its sovereignty. This explains why

Putin and his officials often stress that Russia should not be part of any formal alliances that come with obligations and constraints.

The concept of "sovereignty" originates in Soviet Cold War thinking that the United States was out to destroy Soviet Russia. In Soviet times, the doctrine of sovereignty served as a fundamental ideological framework and emphasized the need to defend the socialist system from the aggression of world imperialism, led by the United States. The concept of "sovereignty" also legitimized and substantiated the state's right to control all spheres of life and suppression of dissent, which was equated to direct or veiled complicity with the enemy.[87]

One should not be surprised by Putin's ideological inclinations. He and his closest foreign policy advisors,[88] all have backgrounds in the Soviet secret service (KGB), where they served in Soviet security services during the peak of Soviet anti-Americanism, which followed the 1979 Soviet invasion of Afghanistan. The security services, which were exposed more to "dangerous" Western influences than the ordinary Soviet citizens, were particularly well indoctrinated by the Soviet system.[89] It is hardly surprising that decades later they continue to hold the same views of the international order and Washington's intentions, such as interpreting the US democracy-promotion efforts in the 1990s and 2000s as a continuation of the CIA's Cold War influence operations.[90]

The concept of sovereignty is closely connected to Russia's repeated emphasis on multipolarity, as opposed to the US hegemony. The Kremlin tends to define international politics by the relations, usually competitive, between sovereign actors. In this context "sovereign" refers to those few states on the international arena, which according to the Kremlin, can exercise genuinely independent choices—the United States, China, and Russia—and to a lesser extent, in specific areas, Germany, France, India, and Brazil. Under this logic, smaller states and multilateral organizations are objects or instruments of great power diplomacy, "a true sovereignty of world oligarchs distinguished from the limited sovereignty of their vassals,"[91] rather than independent actors. When Russian officials speak of "democratization of international relations," they usually imply the devolution of power from the alleged hegemon, the United States, to a group or "concert" of great powers, which includes Russia.[92]

This understanding of "sovereignty" also provides opportunity to address an apparent contradiction between Russia's emphasis on a "multipolar world" and a simultaneous proposition to return to Yalta world order. In Moscow's view, multipolarity is a prerogative of truly sovereign states, "great powers," while the rest of the world will have to be divided into one of the sovereigns' "spheres of influence." That is another holdover from the Cold War, when the USSR envisioned itself as one pole of a bipolar world, leading the "Socialist

Camp,"[93] but adjusted to the realities of today's world where, for example, China's growing role can no longer be ignored.

Three key takeaways for Russia's foreign policy stem from this worldview. First, Russia should consistently assert its primacy in its "sphere of interest," the post-Soviet space, and actively pursue closer integration among former Soviet republics. Of particular importance are Belarus and Ukraine, both of which would play a critical role in a possible conflict between NATO and Russia and constitute a springboard for Russian aggression against Poland or the Baltic states. Second, Russia should continue its efforts to weaken transatlantic institutions and the United States–led international order, including opposition to further NATO expansion. Third, to counter the United States–led world order, Russia should encourage a multipolar world, managed by a concert of major powers, by building its partnership with China.[94]

IS HYBRID WARFARE REAL?

Given the above analysis, challenging the United States and the United States–led world order is one of the key Kremlin goals. But it is a tough task given that Russia is inferior to the United States by an order of magnitude in terms of its military, economic, and technological strength—in almost all vital areas. The exceptions are nuclear weapons, which undergirds Russia's position in the world, its independence, and veto-power status in the UN Security Council. Despite Trump's shuddering presidency, the United States is still backed up by strong alliances on the international stage, while Russia has hardly any. Its de jure allies, Belarus and Kazakhstan, tend to practice a multi-vector foreign policy, although in recent years Belarus leader Lukashenko has become more dependent on Putin.[95] The Kremlin keeps its hopes high in the Sino-Russian axis, but China views Russia as a "junior" rather than an equal partner and selectively backs Russia only when it serves its own interest.[96] (See chapter 14.)

Accordingly, to compensate for its objective weaknesses relative to the United States, Moscow pursues an indirect approach, known as hybrid[97] or nonlinear warfare, over direct confrontation. Many analysts believe that the so-called Gerasimov doctrine is an operational concept developed for Russia's confrontation with the West.[98] The concept became known after Russia's Chief of the General Staff of the Armed Forces, Valery Gerasimov, published an article describing a new theory of modern warfare.[99] Its main presumption is that, in the twenty-first century, the "rules of war" have changed; "Wars are no longer declared and, having begun, proceed according to an unfamiliar template."[100] Because wars are never declared and transcend the boundaries between peace and war, the Gerasimov doctrine de facto describes a permanent conflict.[101] The role of nonmilitary (political, economic, informational, and humanitarian) tools in such conflicts has grown radically, and they often have exceeded the power of force and of weapons in their effectiveness.[102]

Under the Gerasimov doctrine, non-military tools are best combined with a military capable of using both deniable irregular and high-technology conventional forces. Hard power plays an indispensable role in Russia's international posture. Russia's military activities, which range from violations of its Baltic neighbors' airspace and harassment of US aircraft in international airspace over the Baltic and Black Seas to the Zapad exercises and the deployment of new weapons systems in Kaliningrad, complement its hybrid operations. Along with showcasing its military capabilities, these operations also seek to undermine the credibility of NATO's Article V security guarantee, especially among new NATO members (the Baltics). Without the engagement of hard power, hybrid warfare would not be as effective.[103]

This approach allows the Kremlin to act swiftly, remain active and visible, run higher risks, reach out to all relevant players, build regional and local advantages, use new tools, and act aggressively in the informational space.[104] As part of this approach, in recent years Russia has run a series of influence operations directed at the United States. Moscow holistically approaches information operations by combining the use of government intelligence and espionage capabilities through multiple intelligence agencies, cyber interference, traditional media, covert websites and social networks, online bots, trolls, and unwitting individuals unknowingly amplifying pro-Kremlin narratives. Russia's information operations aim to amplify existing American societal fissures over such divisive topics as race, nationalism, immigration, terrorism, and guns.[105] As the Mueller report discovered, through its influence operations, the Kremlin sought to suppress electoral participation, strengthen groups that share Russia's objectives or point of view, and create alternative media narratives that matched Russia's objectives.

In recent years, some US officials included the mysterious "Havana syndrome" as part of Russia's hybrid warfare. Havana syndrome refers to a set of medical symptoms experienced mostly abroad by US government officials and military personnel since 2016. The symptoms with unknown causes range from nausea, headaches, vertigo, dizziness, vomiting, ringing in the ears to cognitive difficulties (such as mental loss).[106] Some reports established that "directed, pulsed radio frequency energy" was the "most plausible" primary source of Havana syndrome. Russia's involvement, which since Josef Stalin had a history of using microwaves against the United States to disrupt intelligence operations, was suspected.[107] However, the exact origin of Havana syndrome is still unknown, and investigations are under way.

Moscow also challenges US interests in other regions, such as the Middle East and North Africa and Latin America, looks to increase its economic and military footprint in the Arctic, backs up radical and populist actors who seek to undermine the transatlantic alliance, and overall aims to "engender cynicism among foreign audiences, diminish trust in institutions, promote conspiracy theories, and drive wedges in societies."[108] Having practiced this approach in multiple contexts, Russia has refined a low-cost toolkit allowing it to bolster other illiberal regimes, amplify illiberal voices in developed democracies, abuse information ecosystems, and subvert elections and other democratic institutions. Therefore, despite a visible power asymmetry, Russia continues to be a challenge to the United States.

Unlike Moscow's well-developed approach, the United States lacks a coherent strategy to counter Russia's hybrid operations. US foreign policy shows a substantial continuity in that successive US administrations have tended to prioritize countering a rising China and ignore or dismiss the Russian challenge. It is popular among US policy analysts to discount Russia as a "declining power," which in the long term, will struggle to maintain its global influence due to a poor investment climate, stagnating workforce, a reliance on commodities with volatile prices, and a small economy.[109] This argument thus implicitly presumes that, if one ignores Russia, the problem will go away—the Kremlin will eventually run out of resources for its aggressive foreign policy. However, the case for Russian decline is usually overstated. Much of the evidence commonly raised to back this argument, such as Russia's shrinking population and its resource-dependent economy, is not as consequential for the Kremlin as many in Washington assume. There are reasons to see Russia as a persistent, rather than a declining, power.[110]

In the absence of a clear strategy toward Moscow, the United States prioritizes exerting pressure on Russia through sanctions. The idea is to impose enough burden on the Kremlin to curtail its ability to exert influence globally and inside the United States. In combination with Russia's presumed "decline," this approach should eventually force the Kremlin to change its course. The advantage of sanctions is that they do not require budget allocation. Furthermore, the United States bears a relatively low cost of sanctions, as compared to other countries closer and more economically connected to Russia, like the European Union. These considerations have made sanctions the default option in US policy on Russia, and they often substitute for alternative foreign policy tools, such as diplomacy, more coordination with allies, military deployment, etc.[111]

However, at least in the short term, Moscow is determined not to surrender to US pressure. It continues to build partnerships with autocratic regimes, like China and Belarus, to counter US influence, and hopes that countervailing international factors will work to its advantage. The Kremlin believes that weakening and polarizing democracy will accelerate the decline of US influence on the international stage, which is already happening vis-à-vis China, and hence will continue its efforts to challenge the United States on the international stage.

CONCLUSION

The paradox in United States–Russia relations over the last two decades is that while every single US administration has tried to reset or improve relations with Russia, they inevitably ended up in a worse situation than before. As US presidents rotated in power, Putin stayed at the top of Russia's regime, and his revisionist worldview remained unchanged. As long as Kremlin elites with a similar worldview stay in power (and following Russia's 2020 Constitutional amendments Putin can officially stay until 2036), the key pillars of Russian foreign policy will remain unchanged. They include the notion that Russia should assert its primacy in the post-Soviet space and work to undermine the transatlantic institutions and the United States–led international order. Russia's revisionist orientation will remain incompatible with the values and international commitments of the United States.

The current status quo is that both states view each other as security threats. For the Kremlin, perceived major threats are the American advantage in conventional weaponry, NATO expansion, and the threat of regime change in the form of democracy promotion. As for the United States, main concerns derive from Russia's emphasis on nuclear weapons modernization, electoral interference in the United States, willingness to interfere militarily in neighboring states, its support for rogue actors, and deepening Sino-Russian collaboration.[112] Russia also continues to orchestrate a series of hybrid operations against the United States and its allies across the globe.

While Russia remains one of the key disruptors of the international order and security threats, US policymakers tend to dismiss it as a declining power and prioritize a focus on China. The lack of a coherent strategy for dealing with a revisionist Kremlin in the long-term risks becoming a problem. The Kremlin has repeatedly demonstrated a tendency to wreak havoc, risking another crisis or even a military conflict. It also works to weaken NATO's standing by undermining the credibility of NATO security guarantees. These considerations are particularly important in light of the strengthening Sino-Russia alliance.

EDITOR'S POSTSCRIPT

The 2022 war in Ukraine brought US-Russian relations to a new low point. In justifying his invasion, Putin went beyond various complaints about Ukraine and its policies; he identified it with the struggle against the American "empire of lies." In a speech just prior to the invasion, Putin called Ukraine an American colony and a "puppet regime."[113] Nikolai Patrushev, head of Russia's National Security Council, in a lengthy interview in April, described the United States as having "long ago divided the world into vassals and enemies," whereas Russia opposed American dominance by defending "its sovereignty, firmly standing up for its national interests, its cultural and spiritual identity, traditional values and historic memory."[114]

From the beginning, the United States served as a major supporter of Ukraine, both diplomatically and militarily. The Biden administration helped solidify support in the West for far-reaching economic and financial sanctions against Russia. Not since the West imposed sanctions against Iran has a country been subjected to an economic offensive of this magnitude.

The United States provided Ukraine weapons and military assistance worth over $3 billion in just the first two months of the conflict. Initially, Biden was reluctant to supply the Ukrainian military, and he completely ruled out sending US military personnel, out of fear of setting off what Biden warned could become "World War III." Heavy offensive weapons (artillery, tanks, armored personnel carriers, as well as jet aircraft) were not offered at first; instead, the United States provided anti-tank weapons (Javelins) and shoulder-fired anti-helicopter weapons (Stingers) for carrying out defensive operations. By April 2022, this reluctance ended as Russian forces' mass killing of civilians was revealed, and the Ukrainian government demonstrated that it would fight to the end—a sharp contrast with the recent US experience with the government of Afghanistan. The Biden administration assembled a $40 billion package of military and economic aid for Ukraine, and for the first time since World War II, the United States adopted a lend-lease program to provide rapid assistance to Ukraine with minimal bureaucratic delay. It also provided Ukraine's military with real-time intelligence on Russian tactical goals, troop movements, and geocoordinates for mobile command posts and enemy weaponry.

Beyond preventing a Ukrainian defeat, what is the long-term goal of US policy toward Russia? In an unscripted remark during a speech in Poland, President Joe Biden declared that Putin should no longer be leader of Russia. Quickly his administration released a clarification to emphasize that there was no change in policy and that the United States was not seeking to overthrow Putin's regime. US policy now seems much more in line with a hardline version of Cold War containment policy, designed to isolate and weaken Russia. Any regime change would have to come from within. In the military sphere, Secretary of Defense Lloyd Austin publicly declared in April that the goal of US policy in Ukraine was to weaken Russia to eliminate the possibility of similar aggressive military actions by Russia against its neighbors. In the economic sphere, US and EU sanctions were designed to make it more difficult for Russia to finance this and any future wars.

The Kremlin's response was to adopt reciprocal diplomatic and economic measures and to warn the United States and NATO countries against further supplying Ukraine with advanced weaponry. Repeatedly, and perhaps for the first time since the Khrushchev era, Putin threatened the West with nuclear annihilation if it persisted in threatening Russian security.

—2022

DISCUSSION QUESTIONS

1. In your opinion, why has Russia's attitude toward the United States become more hostile over time? Was this development inevitable?
2. Are United States–Russia relations doomed to the cycle of attempted resets and subsequent downward spiral?
3. Is the "hybrid war" the Kremlin runs against the West real, or has it been exaggerated by the scholarship on the topic? Does the concept contribute to our understanding of today's relationship between Russia and the United States?
4. How much of a role has Russia played in causing or exacerbating the US domestic crises?
5. Should the United States make it a foreign policy priority to improve its relationship with Russia?
6. What can both countries do to repair their relationship? What other approaches could the United States take today to reengage with Russia peacefully?

SUGGESTED READINGS

Darden, Keith A. "Russian Revanche: External Threats & Regime Reactions." *Daedalus* 146, no. 2 (2017): 128–41.

Galeotti, Mark. "The 'Gerasimov Doctrine' and Russian Non-Linear War." https: //inmoscowsshadows.wordpress.com/2014/07/06/the-gerasimov-doctrine-and -russian-non-linear-war/.

Hill, Fiona. "The Russia Security Challenge." Brookings Institution, February 10, 2016, https://www.brookings.edu/testimonies/understanding-and-deterring-russia -u-s-policies-and-strategies/.

McFaul, Michael. "Putin, Putinism, and the Domestic Determinants of Russian Foreign Policy." *International Security* 45, no. 2 (2020): 95–139.

Mearsheimer, John J. "Why the Ukraine Crisis Is the West's Fault: The Liberal Delusions That Provoked Putin." *Foreign Affairs* 93 (2014), https://www .foreignaffairs.com/articles/russia-fsu/2014-08-18/why-ukraine-crisis-west-s-fault.

Pomerantsev, Peter, and Michael Weiss. *The Menace of Unreality*, https://imrussia .org/media/pdf/Research/Michael_Weiss_and_Peter_Pomerantsev__The_Menace _of_Unreality.pdf.

Rumer, E. "Thirty Years of US Policy Toward Russia: Can the Vicious Circle Be Broken?" (2019). Carnegie Endowment for International Peace.

Snegovaya, Maria. "What Factors Contribute to the Aggressive Foreign Policy of Russian Leaders?" *Problems of Post-Communism* 67, no. 1 (2020): 93–110.

Snegovaya, Maria, and K. Watanabe. "The Kremlin's Social Media Influence Inside the United States: A Moving Target." Free Russia Foundation, February 11, 2021, https://www.4freerussia.org/wp-content/uploads/sites/3/2021/02/The-Kremlins -Social-Media-Influence-Inside-the-United-States-A-Moving-Target-1.pdf.

NOTES

1. Tamer Fakahany, "End of History? 30 Years On, Does That Idea Still Hold Up?" Associated Press, November 7, 2019, https://apnews.com/article/syria-berlin-china -russia-islamic-state-group-5b8e1898db6246a9a8a82f66f35b8250.

2. Angela Stent, "Why Are US-Russia Relations so Challenging?," Brookings Institution, 2020, https://www. brookings.edu/policy2020/votervital/ why-are-us-russia-relations-sochallenging.

3. Gallup, Russia. https://news.gallup.com/poll/1642/russia.aspx.

4. Levada Center, "Attitudes towards the USA and Biden's Words about Putin," April 7, 2021, https://www.levada.ru/2021/04/07/otnoshenie-k-ssha-i-slova-bajdena -o-putine.

5. See Cold War History, https://www.history.com/topics/cold-war/cold-war -history.

6. George Kennan, "The Long Telegram." *Origins of the Cold War. The Novikov, Kennan, and Roberts "Long Telegrams"* (1946): 19–31, https://digitalarchive .wilsoncenter.org/document/116178.pdf.

7. See e.g., this quote by then Minister of Foreign Affairs Andrei Kozyrev: "Today we do not see any reasons that could prevent the promotion of fruitful cooperation between Russia and the United States. We do not share the fears voiced in certain quarters that the USA will now be dictating its will to us, emerging as the sole

superpower in the world etc. This approach could lead to a recurrence of old stereo-types. We do not threaten anyone, and we believe that no developed democratic civil society can pose a threat to us." T. Ambrosio, "The Russo-American Dispute over the Invasion of Iraq: International Status and the Role of Positional Goods," *Europe-Asia Studies* 57, no. 8 (2005): 1189–1210, 1189–90, 1193–94.

8. Communist-controlled parliament repeatedly blocked President Yeltsin's initia-tives and reform packages. As a result, in September 1993, Yeltsin suspended the Parliament and called for new elections to the lower house, accusing the deputies of obstructing reforms and usurping executive and judicial functions. Parliament's vice president Alexander Rutskoi called Yeltsin's decree unconstitutional and Russia's Constitutional Court called for his impeachment. The US president Clinton described Yeltsin's call for new elections "consistent with the democratic and reform course" and guaranteed Yeltsin support. On September 24, the Parliament voted to impeach Yeltsin and appoint Rutskoi as president. In response, Yeltsin ordered the cordoning off of the Parliament building, and shut off its utilities. After a day of rioting, Yeltsin moved to crush the rebellion with military force, which after a short standoff and tanks shelling the Parliament, led to surrender of Rutskoi and his followers.

9. David Frum, "The Bombs That Never Went Off," *Atlantic*, March 2021, https://www.theatlantic.com/ideas/archive/2021/03/the-quiet-end-of-kazakhstans-denuclearization-program/618424/.

10. Strobe Talbott, *The Russia Hand: A Memoir of Presidential Diplomacy* (Ran-dom House, 2007), 9.

11. Ralph R. Steinke, "A Look Back at NATO's 1999 Kosovo Campaign: A Ques-tionably 'Legal' but Justifiable Exception?," *Connections* 14, no. 4 (2015): 43–56: 47; "Clinton: Rwanda Guilt Led to Kosovo Intervention," *Balkan Insight,* November 2, 2009, https://balkaninsight.com/2009/11/02/clinton-rwanda-guilt-led-to-kosovo-intervention/.

12. Primakov's vision of the world order and Russia's role in it strongly influenced Putin's own thinking, see Rumer 2019.

13. W. Zimmerman, R. Inglehart, E. Ponarin, Y. Lazarev, B. Sokolov, I.Vartanova, and Yekaterina Taranova, "Russian Elite—2020," July 2013, Valdai Club, Moscow, http://vid-1.rian.ru/ig/valdai/Russian_elite_2020_eng.pdf, 31.

14. Keith A. Darden, "Russian Revanche: External Threats and Regime Reac-tions," *Daedalus* 146, no. 2 (2017): 128–41, 132–34.

15. Stent, "Why Are US-Russia Relations So Challenging?"

16. T. Ambrosio, "The Russo-American Dispute over the Invasion of Iraq: Inter-national Status and the Role of Positional Goods," *Europe-Asia Studies* 57, no. 8 (2005): 1189–90.

17. Ambrosio, "Russo-American Dispute over the Invasion of Iraq."

18. Fiona Hill, "The Russia Security Challenge," Brookings Institution, February 10, 2016, https://www.brookings.edu/testimonies/understanding-and-deterring-russia-u-s-policies-and-strategies/.

19. The concept of multipolarity stresses a need for a more equal distribution of international influence across many countries in opposition to the alleged US-driven unipolarity

20. Ambrosio, "Russo-American Dispute over the Invasion of Iraq."

21. Color revolutions are democratic mass uprisings in post-communist and post-Soviet regions against rulers from autocratic tendencies that often led to regime change in the region.

22. Maria Snegovaya, "Reviving the Propaganda State—How the Kremlin Hijacked History to Survive," *CEPA Brief, Center for European Policy Analysis,* (2018), https://cepa.org/cepa_files/2018-01-Reviving_the_Propaganda_State.pdf, 3.

23. Darden, "Russian Revanche," 134.

24. The Beslan school siege was a terrorist attack of an elementary school in the town of Beslan, North Ossetia, on September 1, 2004 (the beginning of a school year in Russia). Over 1,100 people were held hostages (including 777 children) by the terrorists. To liberate them, Russian security forces stormed the building with tanks, incendiary rockets, and other heavy weapons, and at least 333 people died as a result. The attack was followed by a series of political reforms in Russia, which further consolidated power in the Kremlin and reinforced the powers of the president.

25. Dov Lynch, "'The Enemy Is at the Gate': Russia after Beslan," *International Affairs* 81, no. 1 (2005): 154.

26. Lynch, "'The Enemy Is at the Gate,'" 141–61.

27. Darden, "Russian Revanche," 136.

28. Darden, "Russian Revanche," 134.

29. David Kramer, "What I Wish the U.S. Had Done About Putin Years Ago—And What Biden Should Do Now," *Politico,* September 4, 2021, https://www.politico.com/news/magazine/2021/09/04/us-president-putin-russia-democracy-504417.

30. Jeffrey Mankoff, "Russian Foreign Policy and the United States After Putin," *Problems of Post-Communism* 55, no. 4 (2008): 43.

31. Maria Snegovaya, "What Factors Contribute to the Aggressive Foreign Policy of Russian Leaders?" *Problems of Post-Communism* 67, no. 1 (2020): 98.

32. Vladimir Putin, "Speech and the Following Discussion at the Munich Conference on Security Policy," *President of Russia website,* February 10, 2007, http://en.kremlin.ru/events/president/transcripts/24034.

33. Vladimir Putin, "Speech and the Following Discussion at the Munich Conference on Security Policy," *President of Russia website,* February 10, 2007, http://en.kremlin.ru/events/president/transcripts/24034.

34. Luke Coffey and Alexis Mrachek, "End the Russian Veto on Georgian Accession," *The Atlantic Council,* October 14, 2020, https://www.atlanticcouncil.org/content-series/nato20-2020/end-the-russian-veto-on-georgian-accession/.

35. Michael Kofman, "The August War, Ten Years On: A Retrospective on the Russo-Georgian War," *War on the Rocks (2018),* https://warontherocks.com/2018/08/the-august-war-ten-years-on-a-retrospective-on-the-russo-georgian-war/.

36. Kofman, "The August War, Ten Years On."

37. Peter Baker, "US-Russian Ties Still Fall Short of' Reset'Goal," *New York Times* (2013), https://www.nytimes.com/2013/09/03/world/europe/us-russian-ties-still-fall-short-of-reset-goal.html.

38. On March 2011, a NATO-led coalition began a military intervention in Libya, to implement United Nations Security Council Resolution 1973, in response to events during the First Libyan Civil War.

39. Joby Warrick and Karen DeYoung, "From Reset to Pause: The Real Story Behind Hillary Clinton's Feud with Vladimir Putin," *Washington Post*, November 3, 2016; and Miriam Elder, "Vladimir Putin Accuses Hillary Clinton of Encouraging Russian Protests," *Guardian*, December 8, 2011, https://www.theguardian.com/world /2011/dec/08/vladimir-putin-hillary-clinton-russia.

40. Stent, "Why Are US-Russia Relations So Challenging?"

41. Hill, "The Russia Security Challenge."

42. Darden, "Russian Revanche," 135.

43. Steven Pifer, "Five Years After Crimea's Illegal Annexation, The Issue Is No Closer to Resolution," Brookings Institution. March 18, 2019, https://www.brookings .edu/blog/order-from-chaos/2019/03/18/five-years-after-crimeas-illegal-annexation -the-issue-is-no-closer-to-resolution/.

44. Hill, "The Russia Security Challenge."

45. Nicu Popescu, "Why A New Yalta Wouldn't End the Malaise Between the West and Russia," *European Council on Foreign Relations,* June 9, 2020, https://ecfr.eu/ article/commentarywhy_a_new_yalta_wouldnt_end_the_malaise_between_the_west _and_rus/.

46. Hill, "The Russia Security Challenge."

47. Julian E. Barnes and Eric Schmitt, "U.S. Warns Allies of Possible Russian Incursion as Troops Amass Near Ukraine," *New York Times,* November 19, 2021. https://www.nytimes.com/2021/11/19/us/politics/russia-ukraine-biden-administration .html?referringSource=articleShare&fbclid=IwAR0VSm6DUZRaxqqEXk3ob68 _AHKvJ_Eipd1QMP0bp8LmYqv5mPlifUNzxcc.

48. Brian Whitmore (2017), "The Daily Vertical: Why Minsk Failed" (Transcript), https://www.rferl.org/a/daily-vertical-why-minsk-failed-whitmore/28311078.html.

49. See e.g., Mark Galeotti, "The Minsk Accords: Should Britain Declare Them Dead?" Council on Geostrategy, May 24, 2021, https://www.geostrategy.org.uk/ britains-world/the-minsk-accords-should-britain-declare-them-dead.

50. Anders Åslund and Maria Snegovaya, "The Impact of Western Sanctions on Russia and How They Can Be Made Even More Effective," *Atlantic Council* (2021).

51. Eugene Rumer and Richard Sokolsky, "Grand Illusions: The Impact of Misper-ceptions About Russia on US Policy," Carnegie Endowment, June 13, 2021, https:// carnegieendowment.org/2021/06/30/grand-illusions-impact-of-misperceptions-about -russia-on-u.s.-policy-pub-84845.

52. Sebastien Roblin, "War-Torn Syria Became the Russia Military's Prov-ing Ground (Lots of Weapons Tests)," *National Interest*, August 26, 2020, https: //nationalinterest.org/blog/reboot/war-torn-syria-became-russia-militarys-proving -ground-lots-weapons-tests-167761.

53. To prevent unanticipated collisions, the United States and Russia have had to deconflict their air operations in Syria.

54. Stent, "Why Are US-Russia Relations so Challenging?"

55. Darden, "Russian Revanche," 146.

56. R. S. Mueller III, (2019), Report on The Investigation into Russian Interference in the 2016 Presidential Election, Special Counsel Robert S. Mueller, Volume 1, Washington, DC: U.S. Department of Justice, March, https://www.justice.gov/storage/report.pdf.

57. Michael Crowley and Julia Ioffe, "Why Putin Hates Hillary," *Politico*, July 25, 2016, https://www.politico.com/story/2016/07/clinton-putin-226153.

58. "Russian Leaders Literally Cheer Trump's Victory," *The World,* November 9, 2016, https://theworld.org/stories/2016-11-09/russian-leaders-literally-cheer-trumps -victory.

59. Maria Snegovaya and Kohei Watanabe, "The Kremlin's Social Media Influence inside the United States: A Moving Target," Free Russia Foundation, February 11, 2021, https://www.4freerussia.org/wp-content/uploads/sites/3/2021/02/The-Kremlins -Social-Media-Influence-Inside-the-United-States-A-Moving-Target-1.pdf.

60. David A. Graham, "Donald Trump's Pattern of Deference to the Kremlin Is Clear," *Atlantic,* January 15, 2019, https://www.theatlantic.com/politics/archive/2019 /01/trump-russia-putin-burden/580477/.

61. Which subsequently did not find confirmation in a special investigation concluded by Special Counsel Robert Mueller.

62. Maria Snegovaya, "Is Trump Putin's Agent?" Echo of Moscow, December 29, 2019, https://echo.msk.ru/blog/snegov_maria/2562475-echo/.

63. Congressional Research Service, "Russia: Foreign Policy and U.S. Relations— CRS Reports." April 15, 2021, https://crsreports.congress.gov R46761. 56; Isabelle Khurshudyan and John Hudson. "Amid Heightened Tensions, Russia and U.S. Make Quiet Breakthrough on Staffing at Moscow Embassy," December 3, 2021. Available at: https://www.washingtonpost.com/world/europe/russia-us-moscow-embassy/2021 /12/03/2a459f56-49fe-11ec-beca-3cc7103bd814_story.html.

64. Paul D. Shinkman, "Russia Adds U.S. to 'Unfriendly Country' List," *U.S.News.* May 14, 2021. Available at: https://www.usnews.com/news/world-report/articles /2021-05-14/russia-adds-us-to-unfriendly-country-list.

65. Nahal Toosi, "Biden Tried to Push Putin Aside. The Russian Isn't Having It," *Politico,* November 15, 2021, https://www.politico.com/news/2021/11/15/biden -putin-russia-522515.

66. Rebuilding relationship with Russia has been a US foreign policy objective starting from the Clinton administration in 1993. Biden is the first US president over the last two decades to verbally abandon attempts to "reset" US-Russia relations. Cassandra Sula, "Resetting the Reset: Looking Back at the Cycle of U.S.-Russia Relations," *Foreign Policy Research Institute*, August 9, 2017, https://www.fpri.org/ article/2017/08/resetting-reset-looking-back-cycle-u-s-russia-relations/.

67. Daniel Deudney and G. John Ikenberry, "The Unravelling of the Cold War Settlement," *Survival* 51, no. 6 (2009): 39–62, https://doi.org/10.1080/00396330903461666.

68. George F. Kennan. "A Fateful Error," *New York Times*, February 5, 1997, https: //www.nytimes.com/1997/02/05/opinion/a-fateful-error.html.

69. John J. Mearsheimer, "Why the Ukraine Crisis Is the West's Fault: The Liberal Delusions That Provoked Putin," *Foreign Affairs*, 93 (2014), https://www .foreignaffairs.com/articles/russia-fsu/2014-08-18/why-ukraine-crisis-west-s-fault. It

is worth pointing out that there is no confirmation that such guarantees of NATO non-expansion have ever been explicitly offered to Russia. Michael McFaul, Stephen Sestanovich, and John J. Mearsheimer, "Faulty Powers: Who Started the Ukraine Crisis?" *Foreign Affairs* 93, no. 6 (2014): 167–78, https://www.foreignaffairs.com/articles/eastern-europe-caucasus/2014-10-17/faulty-powers.

70. A similar argument has been put forward by Stephen Walt: "NATO expansion turned out to be a fundamental strategic misstep. It alienated Russia without making NATO stronger." Stephen M. Walt, "NATO Owes Putin a Big Thank-You," *Foreign Policy* 4 (2014): 156–79, https://foreignpolicy.com/2014/09/04/nato-owes-putin-a-big-thank-you/.

71. Maria Snegovaya, "Think of Russia as an Ordinary Petrostate, not an Extraordinary Superpower," The Monkey Cage (Political Science Blog), *Washington Post*, March 9, 2015, https://www.washingtonpost.com/news/monkey-cage/wp/2015/03/09/to-understand-russia-think-of-it-as-an-ordinary-petrostate-as-opposed-to-an-extraordinary-superpower/.

72. Kimberly Marten, "Reconsidering NATO Expansion: A Counterfactual Analysis of Russia and the West in the 1990s," *European Journal of International Security* 3, no. 2 (2018): 135–61.

73. Glenn Kessler, "NATO Seeks to Soothe Russia," *Washington Post* 3 (2004); Alexander Lanoszka, "Thank Goodness for NATO Enlargement," *International Politics* 57, no. 3 (2020): 451–70.

74. McFaul, Sestanovich, and Mearsheimer, "Faulty Powers."

75. Maria Snegovaya, "Ukraine's Crisis Is Not the West's Fault," *Moscow Times*, September 15, 2014, https://www.themoscowtimes.com/2014/09/15/ukraines-crisis-is-not-the-wests-fault-a39411.

76. Charles E. Ziegler, "A Crisis of Diverging Perspectives: U.S.-Russian Relations and the Security Dilemma," *Texas National Security Review* 4, no. 1 (2021): 11–33.

77. Fiona Hill and Clifford G. Gaddy, *Mr. Putin: Operative in the Kremlin*, Brookings Institution Press, 2015.

78. Ziegler, "A Crisis of Diverging Perspectives."

79. Michael McFaul, "Russia as It Is: A Grand Strategy for Confronting Putin," *Foreign Affairs* 97, no. 4 (July/August 2018): 82–91, https://www.foreignaffairs.com/articles/russia-fsu/2018-06-14/russia-it.

80. Philip Remler, *Russia at the United Nations: Law, Sovereignty, and Legitimacy*, Vol. 22, Carnegie Endowment for International Peace, 2020, https://carnegieendowment.org/2020/01/22/russia-at-united-nations-law-sovereignty-and-legitimacy-pub-80753.

81. Ingmar Oldberg, "Is Russia a Status Quo Power?" *UIPaper*, no. 1 (2016), published by the Swedish Institute of International Affairs, https://www.ui.se/globalassets/butiken/ui-paper/2016/is-russia-a-status-quo-power---io.pdf.

82. Maria Snegovaya, "Why Did Russia Poison One of Its Ex-Spies in Britain?" The Monkey Cage (Political Science Blog), *Washington Post*, March 30, 2018, https://www.washingtonpost.com/news/monkey-cage/wp/2018/03/20/why-did-russia-poison-one-of-its-ex-spies-in-britain/. Skripal went to Britain as part of an exchange

of captured former double agents in 2010 and was a British citizen at the time he was poisoned.

83. Marten, "Reconsidering NATO Expansion."

84. Jeffrey Mankoff, "Russian Foreign Policy and the United States after Putin," *Problems of Post-Communism* 55, no. 4 (2008): 42–51, 43.

85. Kirill Rogov, "The Doctrine of Sovereignty: What Tactical and Strategic Tasks Putin Is Solving," *Council on Foreign and Defense Policy*, July 25, 2014, http://svop .ru/news/12139/. See also Darden, "Russian Revanche."

86. Hill, "The Russia Security Challenge."

87. Rogov, "The Doctrine of Sovereignty." See also Darden, "Russian Revanche."

88. One of the most important among them is Secretary of the Security Council Nikolay Patrushev.

89. Maria Snegovaya, "What Explains the Sometimes Obsessive Anti-Americanism of Russian Elites?" Brookings Institution, February 23, 2016, https://www.brookings .edu/blog/order-from-chaos/2016/02/23/what-explains-the-sometimes-obsessive-anti -americanism-of-russian-elites/.

90. Hill, "The Russia Security Challenge."

91. Philip Remler, *Russia at the United Nations.*

92. Bobo Lo, *Russia and the New World Disorder* (London: Chatham House, 2015).

93. Remler, *Russia at the United Nations.*

94. Eugene Rumer, *The Primakov (Not Gerasimov) Doctrine in Action*, Vol. 5, no. 06, Carnegie Endowment for International Peace, 2019.

95. Mary Ilyushina, "For Belarus's Lukashenko, Russia Has Been a Lifeline for Decades. Here's Why," *Washington Post,* May 25, 2021, https://www.washingtonpost .com/world/2021/05/25/lukashenko-belarus-russia-putin/.

96. Dmitry Trenin, "Despite the Helsinki Summit, the Hybrid War Is Here to Stay," July 4, 2018, https://carnegiemoscow.org/commentary/76733; Angela Stent, "Russia and China: Axis of Revisionists," Brookings Institution (2020), 1–2.

97. Some analysts question the term "hybrid war," arguing that it has become all-embracive, and thus does not convene any new meaning. Mark Galeotti, "The mythical 'Gerasimov Doctrine' and the language of threat," *Critical Studies on Security* 7, no. 2 (2019): 157–61.

98. Andrew J. Duncan, "New 'Hybrid War' or Old 'Dirty Tricks'? The Gerasimov Debate and Russia's Response to the Contemporary Operating Environment," *Small Wars Journal* (17 September 2015); Victor R. Morris, William M. Darley, Michael Hoopes, Richard K. Snodgrass, Keith Nightingale, John J. Houser, Raashi Bhatia et al., "Grading Gerasimov: Evaluating Russian Nonlinear War Through Modern Chinese Doctrine," *Small Wars Journal,* September 17, no. 6 (2015).

99. Valeriy Gerasimov, "Tsennost nauki v predvidenii," *Voenno-promyshlennyi kur'er* 8, no. 476 (2013): 1–3.

100. Gerasimov, "Tsennost nauki v predvidenii," 2.

101. Rumer, *The Primakov (Not Gerasimov) Doctrine in Action.*

102. Trenin, "Despite the Helsinki Summit."

103. Rumer, *The Primakov (Not Gerasimov) Doctrine in Action.*

104. Trenin, "Despite the Helsinki Summit."

105. Mueller, Report on the Investigation; Eric Tucker, "FBI Official: Russia Wants to See US 'Tear Ourselves Apart,'" Associated Press, February 24, 2020, https://apnews.com/a55930e0a02d2e21d8ed2be7bc496a6f.

106. Matthew Lee and Nomaan Merchant. "State Dept. Names New Coordinator on 'Havana Syndrome' Cases," AP News, November 5, 2021, https://apnews.com/article/europe-health-antony-blinken-havana-injuries-8d1a7d35c9181bf565e6ac5aa3b54dc4.

107. Christina Pazzanese. "Rush to Stop 'Havana syndrome,'" *Harvard Gazette*, October 8, 2021, https://news.harvard.edu/gazette/story/2021/10/havana-syndrome-sees-uptick-in-cases-concerns-and-questions/.

108. Michael Kofman and Andrea Kendall-Taylor, "Why Moscow Will Be a Persistent Power," *Foreign Affairs*, November/December 2021, https://www.foreignaffairs.com/articles/russian-federation/2021-10-19/myth-russian-decline.

109. National Intelligence Council (US), ed. *Global Trends 2040: A More Contested World*, A Publication of the National Intelligence Council, US Government Printing Office, 2021.

110. Russia spends half of its annual defense budget—a far greater share than most Western militaries—on procuring new weapons, modernizing old ones, and researching military technology. It also has a viable technology sector and has developed its own successful analogs to popular online platforms. Kofman and Kendall-Taylor, "Why Moscow Will Be a Persistent Power."

111. Peter E. Harrell, "Trump's Use of Sanctions Is Nothing Like Obama's," *Foreign Policy* 5 (2019), https://foreignpolicy.com/2019/10/05/trump-sanctions-iran-venezuela-russia-north-korea-different-obamas. Åslund and Snegovaya, "The Impact of Western Sanctions on Russia."

112. Ziegler, "A Crisis of Diverging Perspectives."

113. Televised address to the nation, February 21, 2022.

114. Interview in *Rossiiskaya gazeta*, April 26, 2022.

Chapter 12

Relations with Former Soviet Republics

Darrell Slider

Russia's invasion of Ukraine, which began on February 24, 2022, marked a new and consequential stage in Russia's relations with neighboring states. Putin and other top Russian officials have often stated that former Soviet republics are within its sphere of influence, and that the region is critical to the national security of Russia. While some Russian nationalists have advocated expanding Russian borders to coincide more closely with what were Soviet borders, Vladimir Putin always rejected this as unwise. His strategy was generally directed at ensuring that former Soviet states remained loyal to and dependent on Russia. Ukraine could be seen as an example where failure to subjugate a neighbor led the Kremlin to adopt an aggressive, ultimately counterproductive, policy that resulted in many thousands of deaths and untold suffering.

After World War II, Europe was divided with most of East Europe consigned to the Soviet sphere of influence. The chief military alliance, under Soviet control, was the Warsaw Pact. Gorbachev oversaw the breakup of the Soviet bloc in 1989–1990, punctuated by the reunification of Germany and the dissolution of the Warsaw Pact. His policies ended a core principle of Soviet foreign policy that might be called the Stalin-Khrushchev-Brezhnev doctrine of "limited sovereignty." Under that doctrine, countries that had come under Soviet control at the end of World War II were not permitted to change their foreign policy orientation away from the Soviet bloc in favor of the West or even toward neutrality. Domestic political changes that threatened ruling communist parties were seen as equally threatening. The doctrine was enforced with invasions by Soviet and Warsaw Pact forces in Hungary in 1956 and Czechoslovakia in 1968. When reformers took power in Czechoslovakia in 1968 (the "Prague Spring") the Soviet Union invaded to put a halt to changes in the political and economic system that promised pluralism and extensive market reforms. Thus, the USSR used its overwhelming regional military position to dictate internal political decisions with its bloc.

With the breakup of the Soviet Union, and as Vladimir Putin consolidated power, Russia began to assert a "limited sovereignty" doctrine towards a new set of states that now formed Russia's new borderlands and "buffer" zones with the West—the former Soviet republics. Russia under Putin adopted the most fearful interpretation of NATO's role in the region: that it was not a defensive alliance designed to provide collective security to deter an attack but was instead an aggressive bloc seeking to (1) encircle Russia with new allies and military bases in order to (2) mount an attack, that would become (3) an invasion, and then (4) a military occupation, followed by (5) dismembering Russia and (6) stealing its natural resources. This was a trope familiar to Putin and those around him from their days in the KGB during the Cold War. There is nothing in the US public discourse, NATO files obtained by spies, or even the massive 2010 leak of secret State Department documents that would support this analysis. So Russian officials frequently resort to using fake quotes or documents purportedly from Allen Dulles (CIA director under Eisenhower) or Madeleine Albright (Secretary of State under Clinton). The image of NATO as an aggressive threat to Russian security implies that expansion of NATO is a conspiracy against Russia directed from Washington, and that countries join NATO because of pressure from Washington or other NATO capitals. The actual dynamic behind NATO expansion has always been fear of Soviet/Russian military aggression and a desire of would-be member states for the security that comes from membership and participation in joint military programs. For many new NATO members, the ultimate level of deterrence would be achieved by the stationing of US and NATO bases and facilities on their territory—to ensure that any attack on them would immediately trigger a response from their allies. Thus, the danger to Russia is not a potential attack from NATO, but the NATO response to any Russian military operations against a member state.

Putin's assumptions about NATO, the former Soviet republics, and Russia's "security interests" were encapsulated in a document that appeared in December 2021. Amid rising tensions from the buildup of Russian troops around Ukraine's borders, the Russian Ministry of Foreign Affairs published a draft of a "Treaty Between the United States of America and the Russian Federation on Security Guarantees."[1] Article 4 states that the United States "shall undertake to prevent further eastward expansion of the North Atlantic Treaty Organization and deny accession to the Alliance to the States of the former Union of Soviet Socialist Republics. The United States of America shall not establish military bases in the territory of the States of the former

Union of Soviet Socialist Republics that are not members of the North Atlantic Treaty Organization, use their infrastructure for any military activities or develop bilateral military cooperation with them." In essence, this was a call for the United States and Russia to sign a new Yalta Agreement, pressing the United States to accept a Russian sphere of influence in the former Soviet republics.[2] But whereas Yalta was largely a ratification of the existing state of play in 1945, corresponding to the areas where Soviet troops remained at the end of the war, this new treaty was presented with an implicit threat: agree to the terms or Russia will use its military force to impose its control in this region by preemptively acting against "security threats." In February 2022, Putin acted on his threat by announcing the start of a "special military operation" on Ukrainian territory.

HOW THE SOVIET UNION FELL APART

The collapse of the Soviet Union was not a single event or series of events at the end of 1991; in some respects, it is a process that continues to this day. The dominant Russian view on the meaning of the Soviet collapse has changed significantly over time. Yeltsin welcomed the break-up as a necessary precondition for Russia to gain true sovereignty. Putin has viewed the breakup as tragic, focusing on the loss of empire and status, as well as the supposedly precarious position of Russians left outside of Russia's new borders.

Putin's current position aligns more with the August 1991 coup-plotters, which included the then head of the Soviet KGB Vladimir Kryuchkov, rather than with Yeltsin and the "democrats." The leaders of the coup hoped to stop the disintegration of the USSR by establishing martial law. Tens of thousands of Muscovites responded, and put their lives on the line to deter a military takeover of the Russian parliament and the arrest of its leadership. At the time, Putin along with Leningrad mayor Anatoly Sobchak were allied with Yeltsin and resisted the coup. In retrospect, Putin has come to accept the hard-liners' view that the Moscow crowds who resisted the coup that presaged the collapse of the USSR were a manifestation in Russia of what would later be called "color revolutions."

The Soviet breakup was the result of Gorbachev's democratization agenda, growing national consciousness in many Soviet republics, and the outcomes of republic elections in 1990 and 1991.[3] In about half of the republics—in particular Latvia, Lithuania, Estonia, Georgia, Moldova, and Armenia—the communist political elite lost power to anti-communist leaders who emphasized republic sovereignty and national interests at the expense of centralized Soviet control. Advocates of preserving the USSR, including Gorbachev, point to the results of the March 1991 referendum which asked voters whether they supported the USSR as "a renewed federation of equal sovereign republics in which the rights and freedom of an individual of any ethnicity will be fully guaranteed." Fully 78 percent voted in favor, and this is presented as evidence that the collapse of the Soviet Union went against the popular will and could have been avoided. They often neglect to mention that "anti-Soviet" republic leaders in Lithuania, Estonia, Latvia, Moldova, Georgia, and Armenia were already strong enough to prevent the holding of the referendum on their territories. In the case of Russia, Yeltsin took advantage of the referendum to simultaneously conduct his own referendum on creating the post of president of Russia, a critical step that gave him the power and legitimacy to arrange Russia's exit from the union nine months later. Most republics, including those that boycotted the all-union referendum, in subsequent months held their own referenda on sovereignty/independence. Particularly important in this regard was the independence referendum in Ukraine on December 1, 1991, in which an independent Ukraine was supported by over 92 percent of those voting.[4]

Events of August-December 1991 accelerated the pace of the Soviet collapse. The attempted August coup by Soviet hardliners (including Gorbachev's vice president and prime minister) was a belated reaction against Gorbachev's reforms and the accelerating pace of self-determination efforts in many republics. At the time of the coup Gorbachev was planning to sign a new union treaty that would have granted significantly greater autonomy to the republics and could have perhaps delayed the Soviet collapse. The immediate result of the coup was the departure of the three Baltic republics from the USSR, a decision that was approved by Yeltsin and Gorbachev and then by Europe and the United States. By December 1991, the Ukrainian referendum, and the likely failure of any attempt to preserve the Union given Ukrainian leader Kravchuk's insistence on seceding prompted the leaders of the three Slavic republics—Russia, Ukraine, and Belarus—to announce the end of the Soviet Union. Gorbachev was not invited to the talks. They met in the Belovezha forest in Belarus and signed a hastily elaborated agreement creating a new entity, called the Commonwealth of Independent States (CIS). At the same time, they voided the 1922 agreement that had created the Soviet Union. Gorbachev resigned at the end of December 1991. By 1994 all former Soviet republics except for the Baltic states had become members of the CIS. This turned out to be a very weak association of equal members in which states were free to opt in or opt out of any agreement reached by the others.

At the time of the "divorce" there were minimal negotiations on the terms, but border issues did come up. The status of Crimea, for example, was apparently raised at one point by the Russian side in the Belovezha talks in December 1991. Leonid Kravchuk of Ukraine strongly objected to even discussing the topic, which led the Russian negotiators to drop the issue. The understanding reached was that the existing internal borders of the Soviet Union, however imperfect, would be used to determine the boundaries of the new post-Soviet states. Article Five of the Belovezha agreement stated that the parties "recognize and respect the territorial integrity of one another and the inviolability of existing borders . . . "[5] Attempting to redraw lines on the map so that disputed territories or nested minorities could secede would have opened the door to many new conflicts.

Which is not to say that the Soviet break-up was free of conflict. In the years that followed, Russia used its military strength and regional dominance to encourage and facilitate ethnic/separatist conflicts in several post-Soviet states—Moldova, Georgia, and most recently in Ukraine. Over time, these morphed into "frozen conflicts." Long-standing, unresolved conflicts are not rare internationally. Examples include Kashmir (India vs. Pakistan), Israel vs. Palestinians, and the Western Sahara/Morocco. They remain unresolved, not because they are "intractable," but because one of the parties to the conflict (or its outside sponsor) prefers the status quo to a peaceful settlement and is strong enough to both preserve the status quo and prevent effective international mediation. A bonus accruing to Russia's creation and maintenance of frozen conflicts is NATO's informal policy, advanced by France and Germany, that unresolved territorial conflicts disqualify a country from membership. This is to avoid NATO being pulled into a conflict with Russia due to Article Five of the NATO Treaty which considers an attack against one member state to be an attack against all.

Putin's attitudes toward the former Soviet states changed over time and drew into question the original 1991 agreement on borders. He has used a kaleidoscope of varying justifications for this position. Initially, Putin placed this issue in the context of Russians as a "divided people." Here he uses "Russians" to mean not just ethnic Russians, but those who share the Russian language and culture. This was the context for Putin's famous words in 2005 that the end of the Soviet Union was "the greatest geopolitical catastrophe of the twentieth century." In 2015, he called Russians "the largest separated people in the world." In a televised interview in June 2020, Putin asserted Russia's territorial claims in Moldova, Georgia, Ukraine, and potentially elsewhere, such as Kazakhstan and Belarus: Republics in the former USSR, when they joined the union, were given territory that was historically Russian. When they left, they should have left with what they came with. Instead, they were allowed to "drag with them" Russian lands, which he called "gifts from the Russian people."[6] In December 2021, Putin claimed that the collapse of the Soviet Union constituted the "collapse of historical Russia"—it lost "40 percent" of its territory, population, and productive capacity.[7] (The percent of territory "lost" by Russia was actually 24 percent, not 40 percent. The population "lost" [USSR minus Russia in 1989] was about 49 percent.)

Russia has also presented itself as the defender of repressed ethnic minorities in newly independent states. Stalin had employed a strategy to weaken non-Russian republics with a poison pill, incorporating into republics ethnic minorities that sometimes constituted a local majority. They were given special autonomous status, resulting in a "nested-doll" administrative structure. Usually "titular" minorities in these entities were given special privileges in staffing government agencies and other institutions on their territory. The end of the Soviet Union brought into question the status and privileges held by these minorities. Gorbachev was the first to use this as an instrument to undercut leaders of nationalist movements that sought to exit from the Soviet Union, when he offered minority autonomies new status as full-fledged subjects of a "renewed" federation. Russia pursued a similar policy to retain at least some influence in the new post-Soviet states.

There was a huge military imbalance between the newly independent states and Russia, which inherited most of what had been the Soviet military and took control of most Soviet military bases on the territory of former republics. This allowed Russia to play a role in emerging military conflicts and "peacekeeping" for years thereafter in the former Soviet space. An important contributing factor was the unwillingness of the United States and European countries to get involved in the region after the end of the Cold War. These powers were loath to interfere even in a bloody conflict located in the center of Europe, as Yugoslavia disintegrated into multiple military conflicts and attempted genocide. It was mostly thanks to the leadership of Gorbachev and Yeltsin during the breakup of the USSR that there was no bloodbath—in sharp contrast to that orchestrated by Serbian President Slobodan Milosevic and his compatriots in Bosnia in pursuit of a "Greater Serbia."[8]

One armed conflict in the post-Soviet space predated the Soviet break-up. Nagorno-Karabakh was the first ethnic/separatist conflict in the Soviet era, though the Soviet military played only a marginal role. In 1988 Armenian irregular fighters took advantage of Azeri weakness in the region to seize control of the majority ethnically Armenian territory of Nagorno-Karabakh and then defeated Azerbaijan's attempts to retake the region with military force. This territory had been awarded to Azerbaijan in the Stalin era, and there were a large Azeri minority in the region as well as a large Armenian minority in Azerbaijan. The term "ethnic cleansing" which found wide usage during the conflicts in Yugoslavia was first coined to describe Armenia's and Azerbaijan's policies of forcing ethnic minorities to give up their homes and flee for their lives through arson, rape, and murder. These crimes were committed by civilian mobs and irregular forces, instigated and organized by local nationalists and political leaders. Periodic clashes over the years broke out along the borders of the territory, but Nagorno-Karabakh maintained its status of an autonomous territory linked closely to Armenia. Azerbaijan, helped by

Turkey and enormous revenues from oil, rebuilt its military in the ensuing years. The situation changed dramatically in 2020 when Azerbaijan launched a successful military operation to return much of Nagorno-Karabakh to its control. Russia played a marginal role in the conflict over the years, though it sold weapons systems to both Azerbaijan and Armenia and was Armenia's chief military/strategic ally.

In Moldova, one of the first "frozen conflicts" developed around the Russian enclave of Transdniestria. Driven by fears that newly independent Moldova was about to merge with Romania, the Russian dominated territory east of the Dniester River declared independence in 1990. Armed conflict broke out in 1992, and the Russian military stationed in Transdniestria was decisive in defeating Moldovan forces. Since then, Russia has provided free energy supplies and other economic subsidies to the region, while helping to patrol the border with Moldova as part of a peace-keeping force. Talks on reintegration with Moldova have shown little movement, as Russia insists on special rights for the region that would give it a veto on Moldovan foreign policy, especially ties with the EU and NATO. Russia also wants to keep its military base in the region. Transdniestria's leaders, backed by periodic referenda, have proposed a different solution: that Russia simply annex the territory as it did with Crimea in 2014.

CONFLICT WITH GEORGIA, 2008

On the surface, instability in post-Soviet Georgia appeared to be based on rebellious ethnic minorities. All minorities in Georgia had legitimate complaints about their "second-class" status within the republic: Georgians were overrepresented in the central governmental institutions, instruction in the main universities was in Georgian, and Georgians held the top economic posts. The largest minorities in Georgia were Armenians (8.1% in 1989), Russians (6.3%), and Azeris (5.7%). Ossetians and the Abkhaz comprised only 3.0 percent and 1.8 percent, respectively, of Georgia's population in 1989; moreover, Ossetians were not concentrated geographically in South Ossetia but were spread throughout the republic. Nonetheless, the Abkhaz and Ossetians had advantages not possessed by other minorities in Georgia. Both had their own "autonomies"—nested administrative entities within Georgia which gave the titular ethnicity privileges in leadership bodies. Abkhazia and Ossetia had two other things in common: a border with Russia and a Russian military presence when the Soviet Union ceased to exist. These factors allowed successful separatist movements to arise in both regions.

The Abkhaz were vastly outnumbered by local Georgians, a product of past migrations. Yet when the Georgian military, national guard, and irregular

forces entered Abkhazia in 1992, the Abkhaz prevailed. A critical role was
played by Russian military units plus "volunteers," many recruited from
the neighboring North Caucasus republics in Russia. Among them were
Chechens, and the future rebel leader Shamil Basaev was one of their com-
manders. Weaponry from the Russian military began to appear in the region,
and there were occasional airstrikes by Russian jets against Georgian forces.
Both sides in the conflict committed atrocities against civilians. Systematic
ethnic cleansing of Georgians and other non-Abkhaz ethnic groups produced
hundreds of thousands of refugees and internally displaced persons; the population of Abkhazia was reduced by more than half when the conflict subsided.

South Ossetia, like Abkhazia, pushed for independence as the Soviet Union
broke apart. Unlike Abkhazia, Ossetians had direct economic and ethnic ties
across the border in Russia, in the republic of North Ossetia. As in Abkhazia,
there was a substantial local population of ethnic Georgians. Russia played
an important role in the region, supporting the separatist government militarily and economically. Some South Ossetian officials were ethnic Russians,
seconded there by the Russian government. Joint "peace-keeping" forces
included Russian, Georgian, and South Ossetian units.

How the 2008 Russian-Georgian war started is a matter of dispute,
but Georgia's right to establish control over its territory using its military
superseded Russia's right to cross into Georgian territory to stop it. Initial
reports, obviously false but spread widely on Russian state media, claimed
that Georgian troops had murdered 2,000 civilians in the initial attack on
Tskhinvali, an act of "genocide." This became the official justification
for a Russian "humanitarian intervention" on Georgian territory, which it
described as a "peace enforcement" operation. Later investigations—including by Russian prosecutors—found that the number of civilian dead was 162,
and that among those were an unknown number of Ossetian irregular forces
who fought Georgian forces in the streets. The armed confrontation lasted
only five days, as Russia was able to pour troops and equipment through a
tunnel linking South Ossetia to Russia. Russia had nearly complete control of
the airspace over the conflict zone, though several of its planes were downed
by Georgian forces or friendly fire. For Putin, the geopolitical context meant
much more was at stake than simply the fate of Russian-speakers in South
Ossetia. Georgian troops had participated previously in numerous NATO-led
operations in Afghanistan and Iraq, and NATO had, earlier in the year, promised Georgia and Ukraine eventual membership in the alliance.

Russia took advantage of the situation and immediately expanded to
conflict to Abkhazia, where Georgia had not sent its forces, and they ousted
the few remaining Georgian troops who controlled the Kodori Gorge.
Thousands of Georgians who had lived in South Ossetia were forced from
their homes, often by Ossetian irregular forces aided by Russian troops, and

fled to Georgia proper. At the end of the conflict, Russian troops entered Georgia proper where they burned, destroyed, and looted military installations, and sunk Georgian military vessels in port.[9] Russia recognized the independence of both South Ossetia and Abkhazia and formed economic and military alliances with both. Georgia lost control over more than 20 percent of its territory. A large part of the economy of both quasi-states is dependent on Russia, and most of the population had previously been issued Russian passports. South Ossetia has developed a close relationship with Russia and relies heavily on Russian subsidies. A 2020 agreement brought the economy of Abkhazia closer to Russia. Abkhaz elites have banned, however, Russian purchases of resorts or real estate in Abkhazia. Abkhazia has also resisted Russian efforts to control the domestic politics of the region; the candidate favored by Russia typically loses in Abkhaz elections.[10]

Putin's hostility toward Georgia was in part a reaction to the alternative model of governance presented there. Eduard Shevardnadze, Georgian leader since 1992, was willing to reach an accommodation with Russia on many issues, including the role of "peacekeepers" in Abkhazia and South Ossetia. His regime was heavily staffed by former communist officials from Shevardnadze's past stint as Georgian Communist Party First Secretary (1972–1985). Crime, corruption, and economic stagnation were the result. Shevardnadze repeatedly waged campaigns against corruption that had virtually no impact, and "young reformers" within the government eventually defected to form an opposition. Among them was Mikhail Saakashvili, a former Minister of Justice, who organized a new political party, the United National Movement. He and his party came to power at the end of 2003 through the "rose revolution" which was the first "color revolution" in a former Soviet republic. Mass demonstrations sparked by falsified results of the October 2003 parliamentary election forced Shevardnadze to resign. As president, Saakashvili introduced ambitious reforms directed at fighting corruption in government services and the police. These constituted the most far-reaching reform initiatives ever adopted in the post-Soviet space to root out illegality and improve governance. Georgia developed a reputation as one of the least corrupt post-Soviet states and became one of the safest countries in the world, with very high levels of public respect for the country's police force.[11] For Putin, both people-powered regime change and anticorruption reforms were anathema, for understandable reasons. (See chapter 1.) Interactions between Putin and Saakashvili were also hostile at a personal level, adding another layer to the 2008 conflict.[12]

In Georgia itself, hostility toward Putin and the Russian government (though not toward Russians, who are frequent visitors as tourists) is one of the few unifying principles in Georgian politics. Georgia's richest man, the billionaire Bidzina Ivanishvili initially supported Saakashvili but had a falling out and began supporting the opposition. Ivanishvili's wealth was produced in Russia, which has led the opposition to question his ultimate loyalties. The political coalition created by Ivanishvili, called Georgian Dream, defeated the Georgian National Movement in 2012 while Georgia transitioned from a presidential to a parliamentary democracy. Relations with Russia have been unremittingly poor for the entire period since 2008.

For Russia the lessons learned from the Georgia conflict would help in subsequent operations; it certainly did not serve as a warning to avoid similar conflicts. The problems exposed in military logistics and communication led to upgrades and reforms. (See chapter 16.) The Western response was more muted than expected, and many Western observers accepted the Kremlin's claims about who bore responsibility for starting the conflict. Nevertheless, the Kremlin was aware that Georgia won the public relations battle globally, and Russia began devoting more resources to this sphere—especially RT, the media operation directed primarily at foreign audiences.

CONFLICT WITH UKRAINE, 2014–2021

Over the period of its post-Soviet history, Ukraine has demonstrated political divisions between regions. Regions closer to Russia have traditionally supported more conservative leaders with a pro-Russian agenda. Western regions of Ukraine, particularly those added after the Second World War, were more aligned with Ukrainian nationalism and tended to see its future in stronger ties with Europe. Linguistic patterns closely followed along similar lines, though most of the population was bilingual—speaking or understanding both Ukrainian and Russian. Kremlin policy has been directed at intensifying internal divisions by "weaponizing" ethnicity in Ukraine.[13]

More than in any other post-Soviet state, Russia has actively and openly attempted to influence the domestic politics and foreign policy of Ukraine. In 2004, Putin endorsed Leonid Kuchma's chosen successor, Viktor Yanukovich. Yanukovich was from Donetsk and was supported by Ukrainians in the east and in Crimea. His opponent, Viktor Yushchenko, supported a more Western orientation. When initial election results showed Yanukovich as the winner, Putin immediately congratulated him on the victory. Evidence of overwhelming vote fraud, however, produced "orange" revolution protests and a new round of elections that was won by Yushchenko. Yanukovich ran again in 2009 and won the presidency, and he initially tried to steer a course between the EU and Russia.[14] An extensive association agreement with the EU was negotiated over several years, but when the document was set to be signed in November 2013 Yanukovich changed his position and rejected the agreement. Instead, he accepted a $15 billion credit from Russia, and appeared ready to align Ukraine more closely with Russia. Almost immediately, protests began in the center of Kiev, on Maidan Square, that turned into a permanent presence of several thousand demonstrators that swelled to many tens of thousands on days of mass protests. Attacks by police on demonstrators in December and January led to radicalization of the protests, manifested in the building of barricades, and taking up arms. In January 2014 Yanukovich introduced a series of new repressive laws to rein in protests, copied from recent Russian legislation and apparently following suggestions from Russian advisers. Violent attacks on protesters on February 20 resulted in over 100 deaths on the square. EU-mediated talks to find a compromise and set new elections were overtaken by events as the Yanukovich government lost control of security, even in the east of the country. With the help of the Russian military, Yanukovich fled Ukraine on February 22 and settled in Rostov, Russia.

In response to the chaos and the rapidly declining prospects for retaining influence over Ukraine, Russia within days began to secretly send irregular forces as well as soldiers and equipment without any identifiable insignia into Crimea and Eastern Ukraine.[15] The goal was to dismember Ukraine as it had Georgia, only this time in secret. Often in the guise of tourists, Russian operatives attempted along with local separatists to seize government buildings in eastern Ukraine as well as weapons stockpiles. "*Novorossiya*" (New Russia)—the regions of Ukraine that were targeted for Russian take-over—included large swaths of eastern and southern Ukraine, from Odessa to Kharkov. In the end, this effort was successful only in two areas, both predominately ethnic Russian: the area around Lugansk, which declared itself the "Lugansk People's Republic" (LNR, in the Russian acronym), and around Donetsk, called the "Donetsk People's Republic" (DNR).[16] In the Donbas, urban areas tend to be ethnic Russian, while the countryside is Ukrainian.

Crimea was a relatively new addition to Ukrainian territory; the peninsula was transferred to the republic in 1954. Most of the population was ethnic Russian, but from the perspective of Soviet economic planning subordination to Ukraine made more sense: electricity, railroad links, highways, and even water supplies all came from Ukrainian territory. The status of the port city of Sevastopol was more complicated, because of its role as a military base, headquarters of the Soviet Black Sea Fleet. After World War II and until 1991 the city was overseen, not by the Ukraine Republic government, but by Soviet authorities.

Putin, the Russian Foreign Ministry, and the Ministry of Defense repeatedly insisted that there were no Russian or Russian-supported military forces on Ukrainian territory. Some months later, Putin would admit that the Russian military played a direct role in Crimean events. The so-called "polite people" (*vezhlivye liudi*) had played a key role in securing the territory, isolating and disarming local Ukrainian military units, and organizing a quick referendum on joining the Russian Federation. The referendum, unsurprisingly, over-whelmingly (officially 97 percent) supported joining Russia, and Putin sub-sequently used the "self-determination" argument to justify annexation. This ignored both Ukrainian law and a basic convention in international practice that any such change in status requires negotiations with, and prior approval by, the government of the country from which a region is seceding.[17]

One event in particular crystallized attention to Russia's role in the fight-ing in the Donbas. A Malaysian airlines plane flying to Amsterdam to Kuala Lumpur, flight MH17, crashed in territory occupied by rebel forces. All 298 passengers, mostly Dutch, and crew were killed. Russia immediately sought to blame Ukraine, claiming that the plane was shot down by Ukrainian forces—either by a fighter jet pilot or a Soviet-era anti-aircraft missile based on Ukrainian soil. Russian media and government officials, including Putin himself, have continually denied any responsibility for what happened. Netherlands' investigators and the open-source research group Bellingcat found a wealth of contemporaneous evidence to the contrary, in the form of recorded phone conversations and countless social media messages, video, and photographs.[18] It turns out that Russian military equipment on highways and parked in fields attracted hundreds of amateur photographers—including Russian soldiers themselves posing for selfies in front of their vehicles—who posted evidence of the movement of the Buk launcher both to and from the site of the missile firing. Buildings and scenery in the background provided the means to identify exactly where the pictures were taken. Investigators determined that the 53rd Anti-aircraft Missile Brigade based in Kursk had transported the missile into Ukraine, shot down the plane, and then tried to cover the evidence by moving the launcher with the remaining missiles back to Russia. Russian official sources tried to dismiss the Bellingcat evidence as an elaborate fake concocted by Western intelligence agencies. In court in the Hague, where the Netherlands brought a case against three Russian officers and one Ukrainian fighter, the defense has engaged in delaying tactics and Russia refused to provide investigators access to suspects in Russia. Ultimately, the chain of command for this crime leads directly to Vladimir Putin.

Similarly, the larger Russian armed aggression against Ukraine has been thoroughly documented; again, the Russian government state has been to lie, repeatedly. Similar open-source investigations by Bellingcat and oth-ers have shown in detail the Russian role in the fighting that took place on Ukrainian territory in 2014 and after—identifying tanks and other equipment brought across the border and manned by rebels, by Russian irregular forces, by Russian military personnel "on leave," and at times by actively serving Russian units. An unusual additional source confirmed the presence of the Russian army: in December 2021 a court in Rostov convicted an official of corruption in supplying food to "units of the armed forces of the Russian Federation located in the DNR and LNR."[19]

The human cost of the conflict in eastern Ukraine was high—war-related deaths exceeded 14,000 by the end of 2021. Russian officials justified the fighting in the east as a legitimate response to Ukrainian nationalist forces who supposedly killed innocent civilians in the Donbas. Just as in South Ossetia, Russian state media broadcast false reports of atrocities—Channel One's story of a boy crucified and then displayed on the front of a tank was one of the most vivid accounts, reported by an "eyewitness." Ukrainian "fascists" were accused of mass killings of innocent civilians and hidden mass graves. In September 2014, all Duma fractions participated in a vigil in Moscow for "murdered innocents" in Donetsk that was a near exact copy of a vigil organized in 2008 by Kremlin youth organizations to mourn civilians supposedly murdered by Georgian troops in South Ossetia.[20] These reports helped shape Russian public opinion toward Ukraine and the conflict and also served as a recruiting device for irregular volunteers, often former military, who were trained, equipped, and transported to the front lines by Russia to fight on Ukrainian soil.

The Russian government in subsequent years denied the legitimacy of the post-Yanukovich governments as manifestations of a "military junta" that seized power illegally. They also claimed that Ukraine lacked real sovereignty in that "the West"—meaning the United States in particular—controlled the government and set its policies in all areas. As was the case with Georgia, part of Putin's antipathy toward Ukraine derived from the nature of its emerging political system. As in 1990s Russia, "oligarchs" played a strong role in Ukraine—dominant figures in various sectors of the economy who translated their economic power into political power through support of politicians, political parties, and media ownership. The lack of one dominant oligarch helped foster political pluralism in Ukraine. Unlike Russia after 2000, Ukraine has had an active political life characterized by hotly contested elections with outcomes that are unknown in advance and shifting parliamentary coalitions. During the time that Putin has been in power in Russia, Ukraine has had five presidents. It also has independent media and an active civil society. Corruption has remained high, but the country has instituted reforms after pressure from the EU and United States.[21] A National Anticorruption Bureau of Ukraine (NABU) has functioned since 2015 with significant powers and independence from the government. In the period after 2014, hundreds of Georgians who played a role in the Saakashvili administration moved to Ukraine and were involved in Ukrainian economic and police reforms. One of these Georgians, Gizo Uglava, became the first deputy director of NABU. Saakashvili himself, who has ties to Ukraine dating back to his university education, was for a time governor of Odessa province and was an advisor on reforms to both post-2014 Ukrainian presidents—Petr Poroshenko and Vladimir Zelensky.[22]

International efforts to end the conflict in eastern Ukraine stalled over the years, with Ukraine, the "people's republics," and Russia unwilling to make concessions. Russia refused to be treated as a participant in the conflict, though its support for the rebels was vital and undeniable. Negotiations in the immediate aftermath of the conflict stipulated steps that both direct parties to the conflict would consider political suicide: for example, Ukrainian official recognition of special status for the breakaway regions in Donbas. Similarly, the requirement that the DNR and LNR hold free elections based on Ukrainian law was also a nonstarter.

Russia increasingly integrated the breakaway regions into Russia, both economically and politically. The Russian ruble became the currency in use, and trade patterns shifted away from Ukraine proper to Russia. As in Georgia's breakaway regions and Transdniestria, Russia created a simplified path to citizenship for those living in the LNR and DNR. By mid-2021, over a half million Russian passports had been distributed to Ukrainian citizens living in these regions; large numbers of new citizens were bused to Russia to vote in the September 2021 Duma elections. In December 2021, leaders of both the DNR and LNR joined the Russian ruling party, United Russia.

For Ukraine, reintegration of these regions would present many problems. First, there is the question of what to do about those citizens who actively participated in crimes connected with military operations against the Ukrainian army and civilians. Even those internally displaced citizens who fled the conflict in Donbas for Ukraine proper were viewed with suspicion by many Ukrainians. Second, eastern Donbas as well as Crimea served as the political base for that part of the Ukrainian political spectrum that supported closer ties to Russia vs. the EU. Their return to Ukraine would cause at least a partial shift in the political balance away from reform and Westernization. Russia recommended a federal solution to Ukraine's problems, granting more autonomy to all regions—including in foreign policy. (This is the height of cynicism, given Putin's own systematic destruction of federalism in Russia. See chapter 3.) Many Ukrainians saw regional self-rule as a first step to dismantling the country, given Russia's past role in the east. As for Crimea, the Kremlin rejected even talking about returning Crimea to Ukrainian control, despite a lack of support for its annexation by any major country.

THE THREAT OF DEMOCRATIC
CHANGE IN BELARUS, 2020

Like Ukraine, Belarus's Slavic ethnicity and geographic location as a buffer between Russia and NATO members has led the Kremlin to view it as essential to Russia's security. Language has not been a critical factor in national identity. Both Russian and Belarusian are official languages, but Russian is clearly dominant. Most Belarusians speak Russian, and the Belarusian language is spoken in daily life by only 10–20 percent of the population. Still, Belarusians do not consider themselves part of "the Russian world" as Putin understands it. In 1991 Belarus, along with Russia and Ukraine, was one of the participants in (and the host of) the summit meeting that ended the USSR. But with the election of Alexander Lukashenko, a former state farm (*sovkhoz*) chairman, in 1994, Belarus preserved much of its Soviet past. Soviet-era institutions continued to function, sometimes without even renaming them; Belarus still has a KGB, for example. The Belarusian economic approach, like the Soviet model, continued to deliver income equality, job security, and social welfare payments, albeit at a low level. The regime refused to privatize the most important large-scale enterprises, and factories continued to provide housing, education, and other benefits to their employees, as they did in Soviet times.[23] As in Soviet times, Russia continued to play a major role in the Belarusian economy. Like Ukraine, Belarus lacked its own energy resources, but benefited by serving as a supply route for natural gas from Russia to Europe and goods from Europe flowing the opposite direction. Belarus was allowed to profit from the import of oil at subsidized prices, and then use its refinery to resell the output at world market prices, much as Cuba exploited its relationship with the Soviet Union in the 1970s.

Belarus was the only former Soviet republic to negotiate a "union" with Russia in the aftermath of the Soviet collapse. In December 1999, the two countries created a decision-making body, the Higher State Council, and a Council of Ministers of the Union Government. Negotiations on the terms of the union have been held over the years at both presidential and ministerial levels, but few agreements were finalized. Some of Lukashenko's proposals made it clear that he wanted Belarus to be an equal partner in the new union, and that he would was not going to join and become the lowly governor of the 86th subject of the Russian Federation. Under common currency provisions, for example, Lukashenko proposed that the Belarus national bank be given the right to issue rubles. At various points Lukashenko tried to improve his negotiating position with Russia by seeking opportunities for better relations with the United States and Europe. Disputes arose with Russia over several issues. The price of natural gas and oil was constantly a source of friction, as

Russia periodically sought to raise the price to world market levels. Russia without success sought military bases in Belarus to bring its forces closer to the borders of NATO members. At the same time, Belarus and Russian forces conducted joint military exercises on Belarusian territory. Belarus was also a major supplier of components to the Russian defense industry.[24] As was true of all other Russian allies, Lukashenko refused to recognize officially the annexation of Crimea. After the 2014 Ukrainian events, Lukashenko took advantage of Russian countersanctions against the West to minimally process and then reship to Russia items that would be contraband if imported directly from their countries of origin. Thus, there appeared such exports to Russia as "Belarusian shrimp" and salmon (Belarus has no fishing fleet and no access to the sea).

Over time Lukashenko shaped an increasingly harsh autocratic regime with a stifling bureaucracy and weakening economy. Violent suppression of the opposition, including murders of opponents, was widespread in Belarus long before Putin applied similar measures in Russia. Popular dissatisfaction, deepened by growing economic problems, rose over time and, by the time of the August 2020 presidential election, public opinion polls, if they had been allowed, would have shown that Lukashenko retained only a small core of supporters, primarily among the rural elderly. The strategy Lukashenko chose, in the face of his apparent unpopularity, was a combination of massive fraud carried out by a totally subservient election commission and by preventing his main opponents from appearing on the ballot.

Russia had no apparent role in Belarusian domestic politics in the runup to the 2020 elections, though Lukashenko clearly suspected Russia was acting on behalf of at least one of his opponents—Viktor Barbariko. Barbariko had ties to Russia since he was head of Belgazprombank, an affiliate of the bank operated by Russia's natural gas monopoly Gazprom. Further "proof" of supposed Russian interference was an incident involving a group of armed Russian irregular fighters who arrived in Belarus just before the election without Lukashenko's knowledge.[25] Belarusian police staged a raid of their quarters outside Minsk, and Lukashenko claimed they had planned to organize disturbances around the time of the elections. They were arrested and quickly returned to Russia.

Not content with merely preventing his main rivals from registering their candidacies, Lukashenko had two of them arrested and a third fled Belarus in the face of threats. Viktor Barbariko was accused of embezzlement. A popular video blogger, Sergei Tikhanovsky, who had a channel on politics and corruption in Belarus was arrested and falsely charged with assaulting a police officer. A third candidate, Valery Tsepkalo, had previously worked in the foreign ministry and was active in developing the country's growing IT sector. When his nominating documents were rejected, death threats prompted him to flee the country. Three women connected to the would-be candidates—Barbariko's campaign manager, Maria Kolesnikova, and the wives of the two other arrested candidates—organized a campaign nominating one of them, Svetlana Tikhanovskaya, to run for president.[26] Lukashenko allowed them to proceed with their campaign assuming that Belarusian voters would not support a female candidate with no political experience. This proved to be a major miscalculation. The three women drew large crowds at campaign rallies in all parts of Belarus and most likely Tikhanovskaya received more votes than any other candidate. The massive falsification of results produced an officially reported total of over 80 percent of the vote for Lukashenko.

The falsified election results triggered massive protests across the country that continued for weeks thereafter. These were immediately met with a harsh response: stun grenades, tear gas, armored personnel carriers, and roving bands of vigilantes. Thousands were arrested and many were systematically beaten and tortured, particularly in the main Minsk jail, Okrestina. At the height of the protests in August-September 2020, at least 1400 were injured by the police, with about 600 of those receiving their injuries after being arrested.[27] Several protesters were killed by the police or vigilantes. Arrests and trials of participants in the protests continued for over a year after the protests had ended. Many independent journalists who had reported on the protests, including from Russia, were also arrested, beaten, and forced to leave Belarus.

Russia's response to these events was initially restrained, though Putin was quick to congratulate Lukashenko on his "victory." For Putin, despite a frequently strained relationship in the past, Lukashenko's behavior contrasted favorably with that of former Ukrainian leader Yanukovich. Instead of temporizing and then fleeing his country, Lukashenko hit back hard against his opponents with all the resources he had. Once Lukashenko appealed to Putin for help, the Russian leader responded with massive loans to shore up the Belarusian economy. When strikes broke out at major enterprises, Putin sent in key personnel to assist. Employees of Belarusian state television walked off the job; within days a planeload of technicians and other strikebreakers from RT (formerly Russia Today) was dispatched to fill their positions and keep state television on the air. It quickly began to mirror Russian broadcasts in tone, and in a few cases, the accents of on-air news readers identified them as from Moscow.

Russia fully supported the repression Lukashenko directed at the opposition. There is no evidence of Russian participation in attacks on protestors and torture in jail cells, but at the end of August 2020, Putin agreed to Lukashenko's request to station a contingent of police reserves near the border with Belarus in case the situation got "out of control" and if, in Putin's words, "extremist elements, hiding behind political slogans, cross certain boundaries and begin looting, setting fire to cars, buildings, banks, take over administrative buildings, and so forth." This was the closest Russia had ever come to intervening in a neighboring state to put down protests. *Rosgvardiia*, the Russian National Guard tasked with curbing mass protests in Russia, signed an agreement in November 2020 on cooperation with the Belarusian Ministry of Internal Affairs "to protect public order, guarantee public safety, to protect important government sites, special shipments, and the fight against terrorism and extremism." They were to assist their Belarusian colleagues through training, joint exercises, as well as "other mutually acceptable forms of collaboration."[28]

Over time the opposition was systematically dismantled by Belarusia's *siloviki*. Their first target was Svetlana Tikhanovskaya, who was detained at the election commission when she attempted to file a formal protest of the results. She agreed to be escorted out of the country after the KGB threatened her children. She became the de facto president in exile and coordinated opposition activities from Lithuania. Maria Kolesnikova tore up her passport at the border to prevent a forcible deportation in September 2020 and was sentenced to eleven years in prison. In July 2021, former candidate Viktor Babariko was sentenced to fourteen years in prison for corruption; in December 2021, a court sentenced Sergei Tikhanovsky to eighteen years for allegedly organizing mass disturbances, interfering in the work of the Central Election Commission, and "inciting social enmity." Virtually all media that had reported on the protests were banned, with many editors and reporters arrested. Belarusian authorities were able to extradite, both through legal channels and through extralegal special operations, opposition supporters who had fled to Russia. In one case, viewed internationally as an act of air piracy or terrorism, a Ryan Airways flight in May 2021 from Cyprus to Lithuania was forced to make an emergency landing in Minsk for the purpose of arresting Roman Protosevich, cofounder of one of the most important online opposition resources. Rank and file protesters were also systematically rounded up, identified by photos and video from the scene. Anti-government "cyber-partisans" hacked Belarusian police files and discovered the names of some 4,500 government loyalists who had informed on their neighbors or fellow workers for participating in the September 2020 protests.[29]

Russia, for its part, fully supported these actions and provided diplomatic cover in the UN Security Council and elsewhere. Putin's support virtually guaranteed that Lukashenko would be under little pressure to take any conciliatory steps toward the opposition. Russian economic support was sufficient to replace much that was lost because of Western sanctions. Russian support for Belarus will likely come at a high price: a significant reduction of Belarusian sovereignty in many different spheres of their relationship. In November 2021, Lukashenko and Putin signed off on a series of arrangements that would further integrate Belarus into Russia in many areas—though, as in past negotiations, the initial documents made clear that the details were still under discussion. At the end of November 2021, Lukashenko in an interview on Russian state television made a symbolic concession to the Kremlin and for the first time recognized Crimea as part of Russia, "both de facto and de jure."

RUSSIA'S INVASION OF UKRAINE, 2022

Putin and other Russian officials assumed that the "anti-Russia" component in Ukrainian politics was imposed on Ukraine by the West. It should be obvious that Russia's aggression toward Ukraine, which began openly in 2014, would produce a backlash among Ukrainians. By law, Ukraine had a policy of neutrality in its security policy. Nevertheless, Ukraine took Russian security interests into account, and in 2010 Prime Minister Yanukovich signed a long-term lease for Russia to continue to station its Black Sea Fleet in Sevastopol until 2042. (Of course, once Russia annexed Crimea, it stopped paying the basing fees to Ukraine.) In 2014, membership in NATO for Ukraine was supported by a small minority of the population. Over the years, the security threat posed by Russia caused a major shift in public opinion and, by 2021, a solid majority of Ukrainians were in favor of joining NATO. Prior to 2014, Ukraine put few resources into the military, and a significant part of that was drained by corruption. In the period from 2014 to 2021, Ukraine increased military spending and undertook major reforms of its armed forces.

Putin repeatedly called admitting Ukraine to NATO as a step that would cross a "red line"; at the same time he must have understood that Germany and France were opposed to giving Ukraine any prospect of joining the alliance in the foreseeable future. In October 2021, Putin downplayed the significance of formal membership of Ukraine in NATO with the argument that the alliance was already "taking over" (he used the word *osvoenie*) Ukraine through military assistance programs and potentially putting in "NATO infrastructure" and that this "really poses a threat" to Russia.[30] In late 2021 and early 2022, Russian forces massed along the Ukrainian border both in Russia and Belarus, threatening a new and more serious conflict. A state propaganda campaign began that echoed the charges made against Georgia in 2008: that Ukraine was massing troops along its internal border with the breakaway regions to return them by force—though no such redeployment was in fact happening. Once again, Putin claimed that Ukrainian "Russophobe" policies necessitated the military buildup, and that Ukraine's actions toward the breakaway regions were "reminiscent of genocide."[31]

On February 24, 2022, Russia launched a multipronged invasion of Ukraine, intended to "shock and awe" Ukraine into submission. A few days earlier, Russia had recognized the two breakaway republics as independent states and accepted their claims to the parts of Donetsk and Lugansk provinces that were under Ukrainian control. Putin declared that the purpose of the intervention was to stop genocide directed at the DNR and LNR specifically and Russia-speakers in general. A favorite retort by Russian propagandists to opponents of the war was "where have you been for the past 8 years?"— implying that Ukrainian forces had been killing civilians in DNR and LNR since the regions broke away in 2014. (In fact, civilians on both sides of the dividing line died mostly in the early years of the conflict, especially in 2014–2015. In the period from January 2020 to September 2021, a total of 44 civilians were killed on both sides, most often by landmines.[32])

Putin's other justifications for the invasion appear to mimic George W. Bush's excuses for the Iraq war: Ukraine supposedly presented a future threat to Russia, and so the war was to prevent a potential attack. Russia charged that the United States had sponsored biolabs in Ukraine that were preparing attacks on Russia and that Ukraine was supposedly striving to obtain nuclear weapons. Ukraine could, in Putin's eyes, also serve as a platform for advanced NATO weaponry that would threaten Russia.

Initially, there were two announced goals for the invasion: "de-Nazification" and "de-militarization" of Ukraine. De-militarization meant destroying Ukraine's armed forces and their weaponry, thus removing any security threat to Russia emanating from Ukrainian territory. The Russian understanding of what was meant by de-Nazification was quite elastic. "Neo-Nazis" sometimes referred to members of extreme right-wing groups that exist in Ukraine (and many other countries including Russia) that espoused white supremacist, anti-Semitic views and held torchlight parades. These groups have no significant role in Ukrainian politics. Frequently mentioned was the Azov Brigade, initially an irregular force created by a far-right group to respond to separatist attacks in eastern Ukraine in 2014. Later, however, it was integrated into the Ukrainian National Guard and is part of Ukraine's military command structure. At other times, de-Nazification was a call for regime change, depicting the Ukrainian government as illegitimate and guilty of massive violations of the rights of Russian speakers. Vladimir Zelensky, Jewish by ethnicity, was called a neo-Nazi and antisemite. In the most expansive usage, de-Nazification targeted Ukrainian nationalism and Ukrainian identity itself. "De-Ukrainization" was a variant of de-Nazification that, in its most extreme form, was a call for genocide to eliminate anyone considering themselves Ukrainian. During the conflict, the Kremlin completely stopped using the word "Ukraine" (much as they refused to say the name "Navalny"); instead, when criticizing Ukrainian actions Putin ascribed them to "Kiev."

Whatever the real basis for Putin's decision to invade, the assumptions about how the war would proceed were egregiously out of touch with reality.

Paradoxically, Russians knew little about contemporary Ukraine, but many Russians—including Vladimir Putin who published two lengthy articles on the topic—considered themselves experts. Their image of Ukraine was based on past visits, contacts with Ukrainians living in Russia, and the voluminous but biased discussions about Ukraine on Russian state television. The Russian foreign policy community had also not developed expertise on Ukraine, and Putin and other top decision makers appear to have relied heavily on accounts from a small number of pro-Russian Ukrainians who were in opposition to the Kiev government. Putin apparently believed that a significant portion of the Ukrainian population was pro-Russian and would greet arriving Russian armed forces as liberators. While a few Ukrainians became collaborators as Russians took over cities in the south and east, most—including Russian-speakers and political leaders from pro-Russian political parties (such as the mayors of Odessa and Kharkov)—rallied around their identity as Ukrainians in the face of brutal Russian aggression. *The New York Times* reported that Yanukovich-era officials who had fled with him to Russia in 2014 called former colleagues and members of the pro-Russian opposition as the invasion began in an attempt to recruit them for a new Russian-sponsored government. The typical response was a categorical rejection, punctuated with expletives.[33]

Deeply enmeshed in a "groupthink" mode,[34] Russian policymakers assumed that the Ukrainian military would quickly collapse, much like the Iraqi Army did at the beginning of the Iraq War in 2003 and like Ukrainian military units did in Crimea in 2014. In fact, Ukrainian forces had developed significantly since 2014, aided in part by NATO advisers, and had combat experience on the front lines in the Donbas region. This misreading of Ukraine was reflected in the composition of the invading force, geared toward a quick victory (many predicted it would take at most three days) and lacking long-term logistical support, including sufficient fuel and food supplies. The Russian force included a large component of *Rosgvardia* forces, whose main function was not to win battles but put down opposition protests—just as they do in major Russian cities.

Russian forces committed countless war crimes—all of course denied in the Russian media—including torture, rape, looting, and mass executions of civilians in cities that they occupied. Bombing of Ukrainian cities was often indiscriminate, but there was deliberate targeting of civilian infrastructure that provided water and electricity, as well as hospitals and schools. Ukrainian cultural sites were also targeted, and museums looted. In one of the worst crimes, a large bomb was dropped on the main theater in the center of Mariupol, killing an estimated 600 civilians who had sought shelter in the building's basement. The war produced a massive population exodus, both within Ukraine and outside its borders. In the first two months of the war, an estimated five million Ukrainians, mostly women and children, fled the country.

At the time of writing (May 2022), the final outcome of the conflict is uncertain. Initial plans to take over all of Ukraine were abandoned, and Russia concentrated its forces on the south and east of the country. Ukraine showed no sign of being willing to accept even a partial occupation of its territory. The results of the war will most likely be the opposite of what Putin intended: Instead of returning to Russian control, postwar Ukraine will be hostile to Russia and Russians for generations to come. Instead of de-Ukrainization, the war deepened a sense of Ukrainian identity. Instead of de-militarization, Ukraine has become a country where the military is the most prominent and trusted institution, and Western-supplied arms will make the country more capable of defending itself than it was on the eve of the invasion. Instead of blocking Ukraine's reorientation toward the West, Ukraine is now on track to join the European Union and has forged a close relationship with the United States (which was a big contrast with Trump-Ukraine relations). Instead of stopping NATO's spread and rolling back the alliance, the war solidified ties among allies, and set in motion a new round of expansion as Finland and Sweden applied to join. NATO member states, including Germany, decided to increase their military spending to counter the obvious threat posed by a hostile and aggressive Russia.

CONCLUSION

One can imagine an enlightened Russian foreign policy strategy toward the post-Soviet states that would pursue mutual benefits. A policy along these lines would seek to take advantage of past ties and soft power attractions to convince former republics that their future development would benefit from pursuing common interests with Russia. A self-confident Russian policy would respect their independence and sovereignty and would understand that it was in Russia's interest for its neighbors to be stable and prosperous. In practice, the de facto, unstated Russian policy is quite different. Putin appears most comfortable with regimes that mirror his own: regimes that are autocratic, corrupt, run sham elections, fully control the press, and ruthlessly put down any attempted popular revolutions. Regime change in the region is viewed with trepidation by the Kremlin, whether it occurs through elections or popular revolution. Russia views governments in the post-Soviet space that seek to distance themselves from Russia and exercise their sovereignty as a threat to Russian security. Russian policy has been to weaken them; unstable states, in the Kremlin's view, would remain economically and militarily dependent on Russia. In 2022, a more extreme goal was set for Ukraine: a military takeover followed by anti-democratic regime change to the benefit of Russian interests—perhaps even incorporation of Ukraine into Russia.

What have been the concrete results of Russia's policies toward the former Soviet republics?

1. *Russia has no close allies nor a functioning alliance system.* Under Putin, Russia created organizations open to former Soviet republics to enhance economic cooperation and to coordinate security efforts. Much like Comecon and the Warsaw Pact—alliances that mimicked the European Economic Community (the precursor to the EU) and NATO—Russia formed the Eurasian Economic Union (from 2015, earlier it was called the Eurasian Economic Community) and the Collective Security Treaty Organization (CSTO, formed in 2002, the Russian acronym is *ODKB*). Of the eleven potential member states (comprising former Soviet republics minus the Baltic states), only a handful have consistently participated in these organizations. Belarus and Kazakhstan have been the most constant, along with Kyrgyzstan and Tajikistan among Central Asian states. Turkmenistan has opted out, while Uzbekistan has joined both organizations temporarily and tentatively for various periods. Armenia has maintained close economic and military ties with Russia for reasons peculiar to that country: it is the only post-Soviet state in a state of undeclared war with two neighbors—Turkey and Azerbaijan. Georgia, Ukraine, and Moldova refuse to participate for understandable reasons.

Countries that are part of Russia's weak economic community and military alliance system are wary of Russia. Paradoxically, the strong Russian presence in these organizations weakens them and makes them less attractive to member states. In part this is a result of Russia's overwhelming dominance in terms of economic and military power compared to its potential allies. By contrast, the European Union was a more attractive alliance to potential members because no one country was powerful enough to dominate the organization, and it therefore adopted consensus rules. Russia insists on being at least "first among equals" with veto power, if not dictating every facet of the organization. Russia has an outsize voice in the structures it has sponsored—leadership, staffing, and missions are determined by Russia.

"Joint" military operations are in fact mostly Russian, just as the "Warsaw Pact" invasions of Hungary and Czechoslovakia were mostly Soviet military actions in terms of troops, weaponry, and logistics. Russia takes its interests as paramount to the interests of member states, as Armenia discovered in 2020 when its forces in Nagorno-Karabakh were attacked by Azerbaijan and Russia intervened only when the conflict subsided and only as a mediator and "peacekeeper." (The CSTO's Article Four parallels NATO's Article Five—an attack on one member is supposed to be treated as an attack on all.) In 2018, Armenia could itself have been subject to a CSTO intervention. Serzh Sargsyan, president for ten years and a close Russian ally, tried to extend his rule by shifting to a parliamentary form of government and taking the post of prime minister. Mass street protests led by an anti-corruption reformer, Nikol Pashinyan, forced Sargsyan to resign. Pashinyan became prime minister, and his supporters won a majority in parliamentary elections held some months later. Pashinyan made it clear that he wanted stronger ties with the EU and United States, while maintaining close relations with Russia. The CSTO treaty, changed in reaction to the 2011 "Arab Spring," specifically allows for interventions to prevent "color revolutions" in member states, but Sargsyan never requested an intervention, and Russia sat on the sidelines despite obvious dissatisfaction with the outcome. Russian media mostly ignored the street protests, while the Kremlin seemed politically paralyzed by the events.[35]

The first time CSTO forces were used to stabilize a regime faced with popular protests was in January 2022 in Kazakhstan. Mass protests and unrest sparked by rising fuel prices threatened the political position of the president, Kassym-Jomart Tokayev. The loyalty to the regime of factions within the military and police was wavering. Tokayev requested a CSTO force be sent, and the request was approved the next day. Putin claimed he saw in these events "international terrorist aggression" from fighters who trained abroad and who were using what he called "Maidan technologies."[36] The force that was sent was overwhelmingly Russian with token representation from other member states. CSTO intervention signaled to regime opponents that Russia backed Tokayev and was willing to use force to support him. The result of the intervention, even though it consisted of only a few thousand men, was a shift in the internal balance of power in Kazakhstan. Former president Nursultan Nazarbayev and his clan were removed from positions of influence in Kazakhstan's political institutions, secret police, and economy. Some of Nazarbayev's allies were accused of stoking the protests. Since CSTO intervention was conditioned on evidence of foreign intervention, Kazakhstan's police arrested and tortured several visitors from Kyrgyzstan to force them to confess to being part of a foreign terrorist operation. The official narrative was undermined when it turned out that one of those tortured was a well-known Kyrgyz jazz musician who was performing in Almaty.

Putin's view of the former empire is clear to its neighbors: Russia has a sense of loss and is still in denial about its decline as a superpower. The result is a long list of grievances that, following the example of Crimea, could at any moment turn into an existential threat to neighboring states. For Putin's Russia, current borders are changeable due to circumstances, and true sovereignty is possessed solely by Russia, the ultimate arbiter within its imagined sphere of influence. (See chapter 11.) The leaders of neighboring states saw that there was no warning to Ukraine about Crimea, no long-expressed desire by Russian elites to return it to Russia. Yet Ukraine lost control of Crimea in a matter of weeks. Any state in the region could conceivably find itself in Ukraine's position, given Putin's comments about "gifts" made by Soviet leaders to non-Russian republics. This is of special concern to Belarus and Kazakhstan but is generally applicable to any state with a common border with Russia or hosting a substantial Russian military presence.

In its economic relationships in the former Soviet space, Russia benefits from its energy resources and the Soviet-era pipeline infrastructure. It uses these assets to reward or punish its neighbors (see chapter 15). Russia faces competition in all former Soviet republics with China (see chapter 14 and trade data in table 14.1), and Russia's declining economic potential sharply contrasts with that of China, making it a less attractive ally. Closer economic integration with Russia on tariffs and technical standards reduces opportunities for trade with the much larger market of the European Union.

2. *Russia's policies have produced bad outcomes for the people in territories they have "liberated."* "Successful" breakaway regions quickly learned the consequences brought by indeterminate status. The chief beneficiaries of Russia's policies have been local elites who remained in power with Russia's economic and political support. The consumer economy is dependent on Russia for crucial supplies and economic assistance. Health care and education have deteriorated. The population, despite receiving Russian passports, are often unable to travel anywhere but Russia. Many do go there out of economic necessity; there are few jobs in their home territories. Pseudo-states are unable to attract foreign investors, other than Russians, and even Russian businesses with global interests are fearful of violating sanctions. Economic activity is dominated by criminal groups, and smuggling became perhaps the most profitable form of economic activity in almost all these regions. Transdniestria, for example, has specialized in the trade and production of illegal arms. In Abkhazia, most of the homes and buildings destroyed during the conflict thirty years ago remain in ruins. Other infrastructure has been allowed to deteriorate, including sites that could have served as tourist attractions. South Ossetia has lost most of its population and its economy is on life support (from Russia). Once thriving enterprises in the breakaway areas of the Donbas were either shuttered or were taken over by groups with ties to local rulers appointed by Moscow.

3. *The West and the international community have punished Russia for its behavior toward its neighbors, and no end to sanctions is in sight.* Russia and Putin's government have been targets of increasingly damaging sanctions in response to its behavior toward post-Soviet states. While the war in Georgia brought little international reaction, war in Ukraine led many countries to reassess their policies toward Russia. Economic and financial sanctions have been the main response by the United States and European Union, to impose a cost for Russian actions in Ukraine. (See chapters 11 and 13.) Annexation of Crimea has been roundly condemned by most countries as an aggressive

violation of international conventions; China, which has its own problems with breakaway regions, has refused to endorse Russia's actions. The 2022 war in Ukraine produced an array of new Western policies that promised to set back the Russian economy for decades and would isolate it even more completely than did the Cold War's "iron curtain."

War crimes investigations have also followed Russian actions in the former Soviet space. Though Russia, like the United States, did not join the International Criminal Court (ICC), it has carried out military operations in countries that are under the Court's jurisdiction. Georgia is a member state, and the 2008 war has resulted in investigations of war crimes and crimes against humanity. Ukraine did not ratify the Rome Treaty that established the ICC, but in November 2013 it accepted jurisdiction of the Court over actions on its territory after that date. Potential criminal activity by Russia in Crimea and Eastern Ukraine since 2014 are under active investigation. Russia is open to charges stemming from ethnic cleansing (Georgians in South Ossetia), aggression against a sovereign state (Ukraine and Georgia), deliberate targeting of civilians and civilian institutions (Eastern Ukraine), killing and kidnapping of civilians, and discrimination against ethnic minorities (Ukrainians and Tatars in Crimea).[37] And, as mentioned above, atrocities committed by Russian forces in the 2022 war in Ukraine will produce thousands of new indictments.

At the same time, there are limits to Western punitive measures. Economic sanctions and the international criminal justice system work slowly, sometimes taking many years. The contrast with the fate of Serbian leader Slobodan Milosevic is instructive. Initially, it took years for Western countries to step in to put an end to his genocidal policies toward former Yugoslav republics. But when they did, NATO forces used air power to change the balance of forces, and Milosevic and his allies were forced to the negotiating table. Serbian reversals in Bosnia and Kosovo were met with popular protests and an election loss, followed by his successor's quick decision to send Milosevic to the Hague for trial. Putin's aggression toward Georgia and Ukraine was comparable to Milosevic's in its brutality and its challenge to international norms, but it took place, not immediately, but over a long period after the breakup of the USSR. Orchestrating a replay of the fall of Milosevic was considerably more difficult in Putin's case: Milosevic had no nuclear weapons, nor did he have a veto in the United Nations Security Council. And, like Lukashenko in Belarus, Putin created an electoral system in Russia that makes defeat impossible.

4. *Russia's behavior has largely negated its potential for "soft power" influence in the post-Soviet space.* Russian policies in the former Soviet Union illustrate how the use of "hard power" instruments such as the military and economic pressure can undermine "soft power" advantages that Russia

possessed at the end of the Soviet era. The previous soft power attraction of Russia from Soviet times was strong: educated citizens in post-Soviet republics spoke Russian as their second language, and for many it was their primary language. In Georgia, a country that always took pride in its own ancient language and culture, most educated Georgians had an extensive library of Russian classics. After the 2008 conflict, young people stopped learning Russian. As the Georgian composer, Gia Kancheli, put it in an interview, his grandchildren do not speak Russian "thanks to Putin."[38] Georgian schools shifted to focus on English as the standard second language requirement, and established programs that brought in hundreds of American teachers who were sent not just to the cities, but even to rural schools.

In Ukraine, after the Russian military incursion and annexation of Crimea, the Ukrainian language was promoted as an important marker of national identity. Many who had grown up speaking Russian and used it daily began working on improving their spoken Ukrainian. Putin's 2022 war invasion will do more than any other event in Ukrainian history to push Russian-speaking Ukrainians to shift to Ukrainian as their main language at home and at work. Before the Russian-supported repression, most Belarusians had a positive view of Russia and were ambivalent about closer European integration. After Lukashenko used violence to solidify his grasp on power with Putin's assistance, Russia's reputation was likely permanently damaged for the Belarusians who opposed Lukashenko. Russia, not even trying to expand its influence by presenting an attractive model of culture and society, has engaged in "influence operations" designed to affect the internal politics of neighboring states. Many former Soviet republics have taken countermeasures to block broadcasts of Russian television channels on their territory— Georgia, Ukraine, the Baltic states, Moldova, and even Armenia.[39]

Russia continues to be a magnet for migrant workers from many former Soviet republics, especially Tajikistan and Uzbekistan. By far the largest number are unskilled workers motivated by poverty and poor economic prospects in their home countries. They frequently live in crowded, squalid conditions in Russia so that they can remit most of their earnings to their families back home. The experiences of labor migrants in Russia do not help improve Russia's image for migrants and their compatriots. Employers frequently take advantage of them and refuse to pay or delay paying wages. Migrants are not eligible for free health care or other government services. "Guest workers" whose legal status is narrowly circumscribed by strict limits on work and residence permits, face bureaucratic and legal obstacles that can often only be overcome through bribes. Ethnic discrimination and hostility from the local population, directed at migrants from the Caucasus and Central Asia in particular, is widespread and at times erupts in ethnic riots or other indiscriminate violence.

Overall, Kremlin policies have failed to preserve what Putin has come to see as Russia's natural sphere of influence. Instead, his policies drove both leaders and publics in several key republics to reject Russian influence and its self-proclaimed "older brother" role. This then sets up potential conflicts with neighboring states as Russia attempts to achieve its goals through coercion, which only further isolates Russia internationally and alienates the citizens of targeted countries. So far, Putin has not paid a domestic political price for his international behavior—a consequence of state control over the messaging and the views of many Russians who are still experiencing the psychological trauma of Russia's lost status as the center of an empire. The catastrophic consequences of Putin's 2022 war on Ukraine may well change this pattern.

DISCUSSION QUESTIONS

1. What are the chief motives underlying Putin's policies toward the former Soviet republics?
2. If you were trying to convince Russians of the correctness of the government's policies toward Russia's neighbors, what propaganda points would best resonate?
3. What advantages, if any, does Russia possess in the struggle for influence in the post-Soviet states? How do these advantages compare with those of the United States, the EU, or China?

SUGGESTED READINGS

Asmus, Ronald D. *A Little War That Shook the World: Georgia, Russia and the Future of the West.* New York: Palgrave/Macmillan, 2010.
Kotkin, Stephen. *Armageddon Averted: The Soviet Collapse, 1970–2000.* Oxford: Oxford University Press, 2001.
Plokhy, Serhii. *The Last Empire: The Final Days of the Soviet Union.* New York: Basic Books, 2014.
Wilson, Andrew. *Ukraine Crisis: What It Means for the West.* New Haven: Yale University Press, 2014.

NOTES

The transliteration and spelling of names in this chapter largely correspond to Russian rather than local usage in the former Soviet republics.

1. The text of the draft treaty, dated December 17, 2021, is at https://mid.ru/en/foreign_policy/news/1790809/.

2. The 1945 Yalta (which is in Crimea) agreements, signed by Stalin, Churchill, and Roosevelt, accepted Stalin's demand for a Soviet sphere of influence in Central and Eastern Europe, roughly corresponding to areas Soviet troops liberated from Nazi control. For detailed accounts, see Diane Shaver Clemens, *Yalta* (Oxford University Press, 1972), and Serhii Plokhy, *Yalta: The Price of Peace* (Viking, 2010).

3. The author described these events at greater length in Stephen White, Graeme Gill, and Darrell Slider, *The Politics of Transition: Shaping a Post-Soviet Future* (Cambridge University Press, 1993), 79–97.

4. Independence was supported by a majority of those voting in all regions of Ukraine, including Crimea and the Donbas region in the east.

5. Gennady Burbulis, "Epokha El'tsina: sozidaya dostoijuyu Rossiyu i novyi miroporiadok. Politosofiya nadezhdy," Report from the Conference sponsored by the Fifth Yeltsin Forum (Moscow, December 14, 2016), 30.

6. "Putin—o moral'noi rane ot Zelenskogo i 'podarkakh' russkogo naroda," https://www.vesti.ru/article/2423246 (June 21, 2020).

7. "Putin nazval raspad SSSR tragediei i 'raspadom istoricheskoi Rossii'" https://www.rbc.ru/politics/12/12/2021/61b5e7b79a7947689a33f5fe (December 12, 2021).

8. Stephen Kotkin, *Armageddon Averted: The Soviet Collapse 1970–2000* (Oxford: Oxford University Press, 2001).

9. For a recent assessment see Samuel Charap et al., *Russia's Military Interventions: Patterns, Drivers, and Signposts* (Santa Monica: RAND, 2021), 75–98. Also, Ronald D. Asmus, *A Little War That Shook the World: Georgia, Russia, and the Future of the West* (New York: Palgrave Macmillan, 2010).

10. Pål Kolstø, "Biting the Hand That Feeds Them? Abkhazia-Russia Client-Patron Relations," *Post-Soviet Affairs* 36, no. 2 (2020): 140–58.

11. *Fighting Corruption in Public Services: Chronicling Georgia's Reforms* (The World Bank, 2012).

12. Putin, without naming his domestic archrival, has referred to Aleksei Navalny as "a Russian Saakashvili." Saakashvili allegedly mocked Putin as "Lilliputin" in private.

13. Erika Harris, "What Is the Role of Nationalism and Ethnicity in the Russia–Ukraine Crisis?" *Europe-Asia Studies* 72, no. 4 (May 2020): 593–613.

14. Paul Manafort, who was later to be Donald Trump's 2016 campaign manager, was paid over $60 million for his services as a political consultant to Yanukovich. "Paul Manafort Made More than $60 Million in Ukraine, Prosecutors Say," *Washington Post,* July 30, 2018.

15. For details on how the conflict unfolded, see Roy Allison, "Russian 'Deniable' Intervention in Ukraine: How and Why Russia Broke the Rules," *International Affairs* 90, no. 6 (2014): 1255–97; and Tetyana Malyarenko, "A Gradually Escalating Conflict: Ukraine from the Euromaidan to the War With Russia," in Karl Cordell and Stefan Wolff, eds., *The Routledge Handbook of Ethnic Conflict,* 2nd ed. (London: Routledge, 2016), 349–68.

16. For an analysis of why only Donetsk and Lugansk fell to separatists, see Silviya Nitsova, "Why the Difference? Donbas, Kharkiv and Dnipropetrovsk After Ukraine's Euromaidan Revolution," *Europe-Asia Studies* 73, no. 10 (December 2021): 1832–56.

17. Recent examples of negotiations prior to a region's secessionist referendum vote include Quebec (the referendum failed), Scotland (failed), and South Sudan (seceded). The absence of a prior agreement through negotiations led Spain to declare Catalonian referenda on secession illegal, and it issued arrest warrants for the organizers.

18. On Bellingcat's role in the MH17 investigation, see Eliot Higgins, *We Are Bellingcat: Global Crime, Online Sleuths, and the Bold Future of News* (London: Bloomsbury, 2021). Details are in the Bellingcat report *MH17 - Potential Suspects and Witnesses from the 53rd Anti-Aircraft Missile Brigade* (February 23, 2016).

19. "Rostovskii sud ob'iasnil prigovor s 'rossiiskimi chastiami v DNR i LNR,'" *rbc.ru* (December 16, 2021). The Kremlin later contended that the court's statement was the result of "a mistake."

20. "Miting 'Donetsk: nevinno ubiennye' na Poklonnoj gore. fotoreportazh," *rbc.ru*, September 27, 2014.

21. Daria Kaleniuk and Olena Halushka, "Why Ukraine's Fight Against Corruption Scares Russia," *Foreign Policy,* December 17, 2021. https://foreignpolicy.com/2021/12/17/ukraine-russia-corruption-putin-democracy-oligarchs/.

22. Saakashvili secretly returned to Georgia in October 2021 in advance of elections there and was arrested a few days later. He was imprisoned on charges for which he had been sentenced in absentia.

23. In other post-communist countries, these functions were transferred to local government. Viachaslau Yarashevich, "Political Economy of Modern Belarus: Going Against Mainstream?" *Europe-Asia Studies* 66, no. 10 (December 2014): 1703–34.

24. Aleksandr Golts, "Belarus and Russia: Military Cooperation but with Different Goals," in Andis Kudors, ed., *Belarusian Foreign Policy: 360°* (Riga: University of Latvia Press, 2017), 87–100.

25. Veterans of Russia's irregular forces who fought in eastern Ukraine, they had been lured to Belarus by Ukraine's intelligence service, for the purpose of arresting them when their connecting flight was to have flown through Ukrainian airspace. See the Bellingcat report, "Inside Wagnergate: Ukraine's Brazen Sting Operation to Snare Russian Mercenaries" (dated November 17, 2021).

26. For a profile of Tikhanovskaya, see Dexter Filkins, "The Accidental Revolutionary Leading Belarus's Uprising: How Sviatlana Tsikhanouskaya Came to Challenge Her Country's Dictatorship," *New Yorker*, December 13, 2021.

27. A detailed accounting was done by Russian independent journalists in "Minsk izbityi. Kak siloviki kalechili protestuiushchikh," *Mediazona*, October 13, 2020.

28. The agreement was not announced until a full month after it was signed. "MVD Belorussii i Rosgvardiia zakliuchili soglashenie o sotrudnichestve," *Interfax* (December 18, 2020).

29. https://charter97.org/ru/news/2021/12/18/448054/.

30. At Valdai Discussion Club meeting, http://en.kremlin.ru/events/president/news/66975 (October 21, 2021).

31. "Developments in Donbass Look Like Genocide—Putin," TASS, December 9, 2021.

32. United Nations Human Rights Monitoring Mission in Ukraine, "Conflict-related Civilian Casualties in Ukraine," report dated October 8, 2021.

33. Andrew E. Kramer, "Russia's Grave Miscalculation: Ukrainians Would Collaborate," *The New York Times*, May 7, 2022.

34. Groupthink is a phenomenon described by Irving L. Janis, in which decision makers exclude dissenting points of view and reach a consensus that is often based on wishful thinking. See his *Groupthink: Psychological Studies of Policy Decisions and Fiascoes,* 2nd Edition (Boston: Houghton Mifflin, 1983).

35. Pavel K. Baev, "What Made Russia Indifferent to the Revolution in Armenia," *Caucasus Analytical Digest*, no. 104 (July 23, 2018): 20–23.

36. "Session of CSTO Collective Security Council," http://en.kremlin.ru/events/president/news/67568.

37. Michael Newcity, "Why Russia Withdraws from the International Criminal Court," *Russia Direct* (November 24, 2016). Other participants in these conflicts are also under investigation, but the chief focus has been on Russian actions.

38. From an interview with Kancheli in a documentary about his life that aired on Russia's independent channel *Dozhd'* (TVRain) after the composer's death in 2019.

39. In a law adopted July 16, 2020, by the Armenian parliament.

Chapter 13

Relations with the European Union

Jeffrey Mankoff

Russia's relationship with the European Union (EU) is deeply paradoxical. The European Union is simultaneously Russia's most important economic partner and a multilateral, sovereignty-questioning, value-based organization that fits uncomfortably with Moscow's state-centric view of international relations. Though Russia is deeply tied by history and culture to Europe, and all three of its post-Soviet presidents (Boris Yeltsin, Vladimir Putin, and Dmitry Medvedev) have at times described Russia as part of Europe, the organizing principles of Russian politics and foreign policy are far removed from those at the heart of the EU. As the crisis and war in Ukraine—sparked initially by Russian demands that Kyiv back away from an EU association agreement—suggest, Moscow has come to see the EU's normative and regulatory power as a threat, even as the two sides remain locked in an interdependent economic relationship despite escalating sanctions.

Despite the structural incompatibilities between Russia's geopolitical, power-centric approach and the EU's emphasis on rules and norms, Moscow and Brussels maintained a generally functional relationship for most of the two decades following the Soviet collapse and the signing of the Maastricht Treaty. During this period, EU-Russian relations were based on an integrationist, transformationalist paradigm, premised on the lack of clearly defined alternatives to the model of democratic capitalism that predominated at the end of the Cold War. Europe, though, never developed a viable framework for Russian integration into the existing economic and security architecture, while Russia's expected democratic transition failed to take root. More recently, Europe's attractiveness as a model suffered in the aftermath of the 2008–2009 financial crisis and ensuing upheavals around migration, Brexit, and the rise of xenophobic populism. Following Vladimir Putin's return to the presidency in 2012 in the face of large-scale protests dominated by urban, middle-class Russians (many of whom had spent time in Europe or the United States), Russia took a more confrontational approach, seeking to leverage Europe's populist furies for its own ends. As part of its legitimating mythology, Putin's Russia also began asserting the fundamental incompatibility between an allegedly decadent Euro-Atlantic West and a Russia that remained a bulwark of supposedly "traditional" values.[1]

Using a wide range of tools, Moscow promoted this "traditional values" narrative to European voters who felt that Brussels had been ignoring their concerns, seeking to mobilize their resentment as a wedge against the process of European and Euro-Atlantic integration. Russian efforts to promote these values through its support of antiestablishment political parties in Europe, such as the UK Independence Party, France's Front National, Hungary's Fidesz, and Germany's Alternative für Deutschland (AfD), helped export this clash of values into the domestic politics of several EU countries. What these parties share is less an ideology (while most are right-wing populists, Russian support has also found its way to leftwing parties and candidates such as Greece's Syriza) than hostility to the EU and its promotion of pooled sovereignty and values-based politics. Similarly, Moscow promotes this antiestablishment, anti-EU narrative through its growing presence in European media, including broadcast stations such as RT and Sputnik, as well as through manipulation of social media to amplify anti-EU, nativist, and anti-American voices. Underpinning this support is Russia's significant financial role in much of Europe, particularly its investment in real estate, energy, infrastructure, and other assets, often with local partners who provide political cover for Russian money. This financial penetration has dissuaded some governments from taking serious steps to push back against Russian influence at the state level or from reaching consensus at the EU level about an appropriate response.

Similar tactics have, of course, been a staple in Russian relations with its post-Soviet neighbors, which Moscow regards as part of its own sphere of influence and where it has sought to check the expansion of European values and institutions. Indeed, the borderlands between Russia and the EU—Belarus, Moldova, Ukraine, and, to a lesser degree, the South Caucasus and the Western Balkans—have been on the front lines of the unfolding confrontation between Moscow and Brussels. From the mid-1990s to the mid-2010s, Brussels (along with Washington) promoted the eastward expansion of the EU's regulatory framework—with or without the promise of formal membership—as the path to stability and prosperity not just in these borderlands, but in Russia itself. In the wake of the global financial crisis and Putin's contested return to the Kremlin, Moscow came to reject the idea of European regulatory expansion as either necessary or desirable. It eventually articulated its own vision of Russo-centric "Eurasian" integration as an alternative to the further extension of Brussels' influence. Throughout the ensuing contretemps, EU officials struggled to understand, much less respond to Russia's alignment with the forces of Euroskepticism, wedded as they were to the belief that the EU existed on a separate plane from the geopolitics of Europe's past.[2]

Ukraine has been affected the most, with Russia's annexation of Crimea and military intervention in Donbas a direct consequence of Kyiv's attempt to sign an association agreement with Brussels that would effectively preclude membership in the Russian-sponsored Eurasian Economic Union (EEU) for good. Belarus now faces a similar dilemma, as a younger, more nationalist and more pro-European cohort seeks to pull the country away from its longstanding dependence on Russia, which has in turn moved to consolidate its control of Belarusian state institutions. Similar, if less dramatic, dynamics are at play in Armenia, Moldova, and Georgia, which are also being asked to choose, perhaps irrevocably, between moving toward Europe or a Russian-dominated Eurasia. Underlying what has become a geopolitical competition over the post-Soviet periphery is Russia's own failure to find a secure path to Europe and the resulting effort to build up the EEU as an alternative geopolitical pole based on values incompatible with those of the Euro-Atlantic West.

The relationship has also been profoundly shaped by the deep economic and institutional crisis affecting all of Europe, including Russia itself. Russia's comparatively strong recovery in the wake of the 2008 financial crisis, coupled with the continued shift of economic dynamism to Asia, helped strengthen a perception in Moscow that the era of Western leadership was ending. European and American sanctions, applied initially in response to Russia's aggression against Ukraine, impacted Russian growth, but have also accelerated Moscow's pursuit of import substitution and attempts to seek alternatives to integration with the West. Since the onset of the Ukraine conflict, then, both Russia and the EU have pursued policies to reduce their interdependence. Russia's belief in Europe's diminishing global importance underpins Russian efforts to promote a Eurasian alternative, to seek closer economic and political cooperation with China and other Asian powers, as well as its calls to reconfigure the framework of global governance to give non-Western powers a larger say through the promotion of alternative institutions such as BRICS and the Shanghai Cooperation Organization (SCO).

Within the EU, a decade and a half of crisis has precipitated a fundamental debate about the nature of European identity, while forcing many governments and the EU itself to focus relentlessly on shoring up the institutional and political case for European integration in the face of migration, populism, Brexit, and an increasingly difficult relationship with Beijing as well as Moscow. At the same time, difficult economic circumstances have left

European leaders to choose between aggressively sanctioning Russia in ways that might harm their own economies and failing to aggressively defend the values and principles at the core of the European political model. This dilemma has been made more difficult by questions about the durability of the transatlantic tie with Washington and the role of Russophile populists like Viktor Orbán's Hungary within the EU itself.

Despite the criticisms of Orbán and other central and eastern European populists for being soft on Russia, it is the large Western European states that have the most developed economic relationships with Russia and whose security is least affected by Russian revisionism. The post-communist states of Eastern Europe, especially Poland and the Baltic states, have been most alarmed at the emergence of a more aggressive Russia, one that is not only deploying troops in Ukraine but also carrying out provocations in many other European states. Meanwhile, EU member states like Hungary and the Czech Republic, and some of the Balkan countries that aspire to EU membership have elected governments that are more tolerant of, if not openly supportive of, Russia's civilizational narrative and financial inducements. They have focused on softening EU pressure on Moscow in response to the invasion of Ukraine and other provocative steps.

This chapter focuses on the dilemma facing Europe, between a carefully cultivated interdependence with Russia and the challenge of an aggressively revisionist Russia that increasingly sees the EU—in addition to NATO—as a rival.

RUSSIA'S PLACE IN EUROPE

The EU's very existence challenges some of the fundamental assumptions underpinning official Russia's view of the world—namely, that states reign supreme and that cold calculation of national interests trump the abstract values driving European integration. The EU's emphasis on liberal values has often put it at odds with Russia, whose foreign policy has always been driven much more explicitly by the pursuit of narrowly defined interests and the personal profit of its elites.[3] The EU has pursued varying degrees of integration toward both Russia and its neighbors to promote democratic transition in Russia itself, even as many EU member states maintain a more realpolitik approach to Moscow. As Putin's Russia has come to reject important elements of the liberal democratic model in vogue at the end of the Cold War and instrumental to the EU project, it has turned to emphasizing bilateral ties with European states over efforts to engage constructively with Brussels.

Even if Russia would never join the EU itself, Brussels in the 1990s pursued a course whose outlines conformed with Willy Brandt's concept of

Wandel durch Annäherung, or "change through engagement." The basic aim was to use the prospect of improved access to European markets as an inducement for the post-Soviet countries to assimilate European values relating to human rights, democracy, and respect for international law.[4] Similar agreements were signed with a range of post-Soviet countries on the assumption that with the proper mix of incentives, the EU could bring about their gradual adoption of European values.

In practice, Russia's post-communist transition did not follow the smooth path many Europeans foresaw during the institution-building boom of the early 1990s. The spat over Russia's war in Chechnya provided one of the first indications that, even in its post-Soviet guise, Russia did not share many of the fundamental values driving the process of European integration. This gap would be a recurring theme, one more problematic in the context of EU-Russia relations than in Moscow's relationship with the United States, which like Russia remains jealous of its sovereignty and more comfortable with the use of large-scale military force. Since the EU is as much a moral community as a geopolitical entity, Russia's rejection of the liberal principles underlying European integration remains a barrier.

Even if Russia would never find its way into the EU, Brussels did gradually expand eastward, taking in most of the post-communist states of Central and Eastern Europe. While Moscow consistently opposed NATO expansion, it was, until the leadup to the crisis in Ukraine, comparatively sanguine about the prospect of a larger EU. The EU's new members though helped push Brussels into taking a more assertive stance toward Russia based on their own difficult history and continued fear of Russian revanchism. And if Russia did not initially raise much objection to the "widening" of the EU, it was generally more concerned by the parallel process of "deepening," to the extent that it entailed the EU's development into an autonomous security player through initiatives like the European Defense and Security Policy (EDSP) and Common Foreign Policy (CFP).[5]

With the waning of hopes for a democratic breakthrough in Russia following Vladimir Putin's ascension to the presidency in 2000, the gap between Russian and EU political practice widened. European officials and multilateral institutions frequently condemned Russia's seeming retreat from democratic liberalism and its still spotty record on human rights—as demonstrated in the state's takeover of private television channels, the seizure of Mikhail Khodorkovsky's Yukos oil company, assassinations of journalists and opposition figures, and efforts to consolidate what Putin termed the "power vertical" (*vertikal vlasti*) in place of democratic elections.

Russia strongly defends its own sovereignty and argues that European values are not universal—and that consequently its own history and traditions steer it in a different direction. Moscow thus rejects the premise that Europe has a right to pass judgment on Russian behavior. This gap between the EU's promotion of what it views as universal rights and Russia's invocation of sovereignty as an absolute principle—at least for major powers—remains among the most significant barriers to integration as a model for structuring relations between Russia and the EU.

A deep chasm in values and institutions overlays increasingly extensive economic ties between Russia and Europe. In recent years, this chasm has widened dramatically as Putin has emphasized Russia's Eurasian (as opposed to European) identity and midwifed a set of "Eurasian" institutions like the EEU designed as an alternative to Euro-Atlantic integration for states in Russia's wider neighborhood. Moscow has also challenged such pillars of European security as the now-suspended Conventional Armed Forces in Europe (CFE) Treaty, the 1975 Helsinki Final Act, the 1987 Intermediate-Range Nuclear Forces (INF) Treaty (from which the United States withdrew in 2019), and the 1990 Charter of Paris. Emphasis on the "traditional values" narrative coupled with Russian support for Brexit and anti-EU populists in other member states also suggest an effort to divide Europe from within. Yet Russia and the EU are nevertheless bound together in many ways, notably through an interdependent economic relationship, and may find themselves enmeshed ever deeper in the event of a waning US commitment to uphold the pillars of transatlantic unity.

THE RUSSO-EUROPE ECONOMIC PARTNERSHIP

Taken as a whole, the EU is by far Russia's most important economic partner, both as a source of investment capital and as a trade partner. The EU is Russia's largest trading partner, accounting for 37.3 percent of Russian foreign trade in goods in 2020, while Russia is the EU's fifth largest trading partner. The total value of EU-Russia trade has fallen since 2013 though, largely as a result of sanctions and Russia's adoption of import substitution policies in response.[6] Individual EU countries, including Germany and the Netherlands, are among Russia's leading trade partners and sources of foreign investment as well (much of the money flowing into Russia from the Netherlands and other popular offshore jurisdictions like Cyprus and Malta originated in Russia before finding its way through offshore financial institutions to avoid taxation).[7]

A broader objective of policy in both Brussels and Moscow for much of the post–Cold War era has been to deepen mutual economic dependence, creating a community of interests within both the political elite and the business community, an effort symbolized by the successful campaign to bring

Russia into the World Trade Organization (WTO).[8] These economic ties have traditionally provided ballast in relations with countries such as Germany and Italy that have the most extensive economic relationships with Russia. This interdependence can, though, complicate political decision making around sanctions or controversial investment projects. A notable example is the Nord Stream-2 offshore gas pipeline from Russia to Germany. Despite the opposition of the European Commission and many states in central and Eastern Europe (not to mention the United States), Berlin pressed ahead with the project, which promised investment, cheap energy, and jobs for German workers until the 2020 invasion of Ukraine.[9]

Energy remains the biggest source of interdependence, notwithstanding Brussels' efforts to develop alternatives to Russian oil and gas. This dependence has been the source of repeated problems, as deliveries from Russia have been curtailed on multiple occasions because of tensions between Russia and transit states Ukraine and Belarus. As Ukraine was long the site of major energy disputes (related to unpaid bills for Russian gas, but underpinned by Kyiv's efforts to break out of the Russian geopolitical orbit), for over a decade now, Russia has sought to minimize Ukraine's role in its lucrative energy relations with Europe. To cut Ukraine (and Belarus) out of the picture, Moscow has built several offshore pipelines (Nord Stream, Blue Stream, Turkish Stream), that bypass these problematic transit states and link key Russian partners like Germany and Turkey.

Energy and other economic linkages also provide a vehicle for corruption, which in turn is a prominent source of Russian influence in Europe. Through investment in real estate or critical infrastructure like power plants, the Russian state and state-connected businesses, many with underworld ties, have been able to establish a toehold in many European economies. Illicit finance from Russia (or other sources) requires the cooperation of European banks, law firms, investment houses, and other businesses, in turn enmeshing European companies and businesspeople in complex webs of corruption that "ensnare foreign elites and form ready-made Kremlin lobbies."[10] This corruption also extends to political parties that take financial and other assistance from Russian sources.

SPECIAL RELATIONSHIPS

Given its own state-centric worldview and the fact that the EU itself has been in continuous flux since its creation in 1993, Russia prefers dealing directly with individual European states rather than EU structures. Russia's special relationships with many of the larger EU states, as well as the deep economic ties that resulted, have long been a source of tension within Europe. The rise of populist, pro-Kremlin parties and political figures in several Central and Eastern European countries have turned this pattern on its head, as figures like Hungary's Orbán and the Czech Republic's Miloš Zeman bring the Kremlin's anti-EU narrative to the center of European politics and fuel concern about illicit Russian influence.

Germany has always been the key player among the European states. Not only is Germany the largest economy in the EU and one of Russia's top trade and investment partners, but its economic success relative to the rest of Europe during the crisis, along with its long tradition of *Ostpolitik*, have allowed Berlin to eclipse Brussels as the main driver of European policy toward Russia. Of course, Germany possessed another asset during the most recent period of confrontation with Moscow: Chancellor Angela Merkel, who served in that post from 2005 until the end of 2021. Her upbringing in communist East Germany, coupled with her political dominance inside Germany and unmatched standing among European leaders, left her singularly equipped to understand and address the challenge posed by a more revisionist Russia on Europe's doorstep.[11] Notwithstanding the influence of voices in Berlin sympathetic to Russian concerns, however, Moscow has deployed its disruptive toolkit in Germany since the onset of the conflict in Ukraine in 2014, cultivating the far-right AfD and promoting disinformation through both its state-controlled media and social networks.

As Russia emerged as an increasingly revisionist power in Europe, it was Merkel who played the largest role in building a consensus for a more assertive response, both within Germany and in Europe as a whole, particularly on the question of Ukraine and wider European sanctions. Merkel's departure from the chancellorship represented a potential watershed in Russo-German relations, with Germany ruled for at least the near future by a coalition headed by the Social Democrat Olaf Scholz. Before the Ukraine invasion Berlin seemed likely to tack back towards its *Ostpolitik* tradition, prioritizing mutually beneficial economic agreements with Moscow in the belief that Russia must be part of the solution to Europe's insecurity.

While Germany has been Russia's most important partner within the EU, other Western European states have also forged strong bilateral relationships with Moscow that have at times been the source of tension with their post-communist neighbors in Eastern Europe, and with the European Commission in Brussels. Particularly during its decade of leadership by Silvio Berlusconi (2001–2006 and 2008–2011) and Romano Prodi (2006–2008)—both of whom are deeply entangled with Russian business—Italy sought to position itself as a mediator between Russia and Europe, while in the process developing mutually beneficial economic ties.[12] France, too, has often pursued an independent policy toward Russia that frustrated many of its European allies. While French President Emmanuel Macron has been forthright in his criticism of Russia's authoritarian rule and aggression toward its neighbors, his promotion of Europe's "strategic autonomy" from the United States also entails calls to fundamentally refashion relations with Russia since, in Macron's view, "the European continent will never be stable, will never be secure, if we do not ease and clarify our relations with Russia."[13] Macron's interest in making Russia into a pillar of European security lines up with longstanding Russian calls for a more inclusive European security architecture (notably former President Dmitry Medvedev's call to negotiate a new treaty on European security), but was strongly resented in central and eastern Europe, as well as in the United States, which remains wary of any step that would diminish NATO's relevance.

The UK was long something of an outlier among large Western European states in generally favoring a harder line against Russia, especially in the aftermath of the poisoning of the Russian defector Alexander Litvinenko in London in 2006 and again following the botched poisoning of the double agent Sergei Skripal in 2018. Yet the UK too was constrained by economic ties, in its case by the outsized role Russian money played in the City of London and in the British real estate market. The departure of the UK from the EU, following a referendum in which Russian money and disinformation played an important role, helped further shift the balance of power within the European Council toward France and Germany, states favoring a more accommodating approach to Moscow.

If Germany (and France and Italy to a lesser degree) traditionally served as Russia's bridge to the EU, Poland, Sweden, and the Baltic states have been the wariest of European attempts to engage and integrate Russia. A long history of Soviet (and in many cases, tsarist) occupation inclined the newly sovereign states of Eastern Europe to seek rapid integration with Euro-Atlantic structures following the 1989 revolutions to guard against any renewed danger from the East. Many of them continued to regard Russia as an ongoing threat to their independence and urged the EU (and NATO) to play a more active role in defending them from this perceived threat. They were instrumental in developing new policy instruments to engage post-communist states that remained outside the EU and NATO, including the Yugoslav successor states in the Western Balkans and Russia's European post-Soviet neighbors (Belarus, Ukraine, and Moldova). They were also instrumental in pushing Brussels into taking a harder line with Moscow, for instance, over the 2008 war between Russia and Georgia or sanctions in response to the Ukraine conflict.

The rise of populism and the victory of populist figures in a number of Central and Eastern European countries have scrambled this traditional geographic divide. Poland's relationship with Russia has remained frosty despite the election of a populist government under the Law and Justice (PiS) party, but escalating tensions between Warsaw and Brussels over PiS's attempts to subvert the rule of law badly damaged Polish influence within Europe. Meanwhile, populist leaders in the Czech Republic, Hungary, Slovakia, and elsewhere have openly courted Moscow. In part, the affinity appears ideological, as the Kremlin narrative of European decadence at odds with "traditional" values resonates with many supporters of the Czech, Slovak, and Hungarian leaders. At the same time, analysts point to financial and other forms of assistance from Moscow that potentially aided the populists' cause. In Hungary, Orbán's shift to a more pro-Russia orientation coincided with the award of a contract to Russia's state-owned nuclear monopoly Rosatom to build two new reactors in Hungary and the concomitant weakening of anticorruption laws shortly before Hungary's 2014 elections, fueling concern about illicit Russian funding of Orbán's campaign. This concern has intensified with Brussels ramping up pressure over Orbán's assaults on Hungarian institutions and the rule of law.[14]

Russian attempts to cultivate individual partners in Europe aims at weakening EU solidarity and undercutting the legitimacy of the EU's model of pooled sovereignty and normative politics. Russia's energy policy has long sought to provoke divisions within Europe, using differential pricing and destination clauses to pit consumer states against one another. Moscow also appears to be behind various environmental NGOs that have spoken out against hydraulic fracking (which would reduce Europe's need to import Russian gas).[15] Support for pro-Russia and anti-EU populist parties plays a similar role.[16] To the extent that these parties entrench themselves in national or European politics, the more "Europe" itself becomes the topic of debate, rather than Russia.

Many of these parties have aligned themselves with Russia's "traditional values" narrative, emphasizing that, as Putin remarked in 2013, many Western states were "denying moral principles and all traditional identities: national, cultural, religious and even sexual."[17] Such claims of Western decadence are part of a deliberate strategy to portray Russia as the embodiment of a more authentic "European" identity than the supranational, multicultural model embodied by the European Union. Moscow aims in the process to mobilize opposition to the project of European integration both within current EU member states and, perhaps more importantly, in the borderlands between the EU and Russia itself.

RUSSIA, THE EU, AND THE SHARED NEIGHBORHOOD

The ability of the EU to confer prosperity and security on its members has made integration an appealing prospect for nonmembers, including many of

Russia's post-Soviet neighbors. Russia's turn to a more revisionist foreign policy and elaboration of a Eurasian alternative are intimately connected to preventing these states' drift into the EU's orbit. For many years, Russia argued strenuously against NATO's eastward expansion. Yet it remained sanguine about the prospect of a wider European Union that would both enhance the economic prospects of Russian trading partners and, thanks to the EU's free trade rules, improve Russian companies' access to the wider European market. Hostility to the EU, encompassing both a geopolitical struggle over states like Ukraine and Moldova, as well as efforts to undermine EU institutions from within, have emerged more starkly since Putin returned to power in 2012. The crisis in Ukraine grows directly out of this confrontation, which also shaped the contours of upheaval in Armenia (2018) and Belarus (2020).

At the heart of this confrontation are competing narratives about the post-Soviet states and about Russia's own position vis-à-vis Europe. While Brussels argues that it is in Russia's interests to have secure and prosperous neighbors and that the smaller states of the former Soviet Union have the sovereign right to choose for themselves whether and how to integrate with Europe in line with the principles contained in the Paris Charter and other agreements, Moscow fears that Brussels' gravitational pull represents a threat to Russian influence in countries like Ukraine and Belarus (of course, this fear runs counter to Russia's portrayal of a decadent, declining Europe).[18] The ten eastern EU members (the original eight were joined by Bulgaria and Romania in 2007) have pushed Brussels to pay more attention to the still unstable area between the EU's new eastern borders and Russia.

Europe's "neighborhood" policies have focused on reforms that would erode the institutional links between Russia and its former dependencies, while Moscow's idea of Eurasia is portrayed as an alternative to direct integration with Europe. For Brussels, part of the problem has been a lack of strategic vision driving outreach to the post-Soviet East. Bureaucratic inertia is one challenge; so too, though, are divisions between European states about the importance of this region relative to other security and economic challenges facing the EU. To Poland and other Eastern European EU members, this lack of attention to the "neighborhood" has both weakened Brussels' hand in dealing with Moscow and undermined European security by allowing corruption and poor governance to flourish just beyond EU borders. At the same time, many Western European powers see the main threats emanating from elsewhere, particularly since the outbreak of the Arab Spring and the subsequent migration crisis.

Brussels has often struggled, however, to engage the region in a coherent way, given the competing interests of member states and a lack of clarity regarding ultimate goals—not to mention the welter of other challenges facing the EU in the decade since the start of the financial crisis—from migration to Brexit. For much of the post–Maastricht Treaty era, Brussels crafted agreements with neighboring states on a bilateral basis. These accords were designed as an à la carte menu of steps to promote cooperation between the EU and former Eastern Bloc states. For some, these agreements were portrayed as a stepping-stone to full EU membership, whereas for others they were more limited agreements designed to address specific problems but lacking the force of law. The European Neighborhood Policy (ENP), which Brussels unveiled in 2003, was the first attempt at developing a unified strategy for the countries east (and south) of the EU including, initially, Russia itself. While the association agreements signed under the auspices of the ENP would be tailored to the interests of each partner state, they were all designed to encourage convergence on the basis of the EU's *acquis communautaire* (that is, the basic statutes defining the obligations of EU membership).[19] Since Russia was not an aspiring EU member, it rejected the argument that it should adjust its legislation to be in line with the *acquis*, particularly since Moscow had no role in writing them.

Largely to balance a perceived tilt toward the south during France's 2008 European Council presidency, Poland and others proposed the Eastern Partnership (EaP) in May 2008 to focus on the six post-Soviet states around Russia's borders: Belarus, Ukraine, Moldova, Azerbaijan, Armenia, and Georgia. The EaP sought to channel EU funds to these six countries for economic and institutional development, to improve border management, and to enhance EU energy security.

The EaP also held out to partner countries the opportunity to sign association agreements with the EU that would promote deeper convergence with EU norms and standards. The association agreements would contain language on the creation of a so-called Deep and Comprehensive Free Trade Area (DCFTA) between the partner states and the EU. The six EaP countries all had extensive economic ties to Russia; one consequence of a DCFTA would be to reorient their trade toward Europe, while reforms demanded as part of the association agreement process would help sever their institutional ties to Russia.

Moscow thus viewed the EaP as an attempt by the EU to carve out a new sphere of influence and weaken Russian access to European energy markets.[20] This skepticism was not entirely off the mark. Though Brussels rejected the suggestion that it was engaged in geopolitical competition with Moscow, the Russo-Georgian war encouraged the EU and its members to downplay reservations about the poor state of political freedom and human rights in several of the EaP states out of concern that Moscow had rejected the post-1991 territorial status quo.[21]

Russia's response emphasized both deterring its neighbors from pursuing deeper integration with the EU and developing a separate multilateral framework mirroring the institutional basis of the EU. Moscow exerted enormous pressure on its neighbors to reject the promised association agreements in favor of affiliation with the Russian-sponsored Customs Union and Eurasian Union, which Putin had described as "an essential part of Greater Europe united by shared values of freedom, democracy, and market laws."[22]

Russia used a variety of inducements to make its case, including offers of discounted energy and financial assistance, as well as various types of threats. In the run-up to the EU's November 2013 Vilnius Summit, Russian pressure succeeded in convincing Armenia to backtrack from its association agreement and instead opt for the EEU. Similar pressure was applied to Ukraine, leading President Viktor Yanukovych to also announce a last-minute change of plans just weeks before Vilnius. It was Yanukovych's change of heart that sparked the first protests on Kyiv's Maidan Nezalezhnosti (Independence Square) in late 2013, ultimately leading to Yanukovych's fall from power, followed by Russia's annexation of Crimea and military intervention in eastern Ukraine in early 2014. Significantly, the new Ukrainian government, headed by President Petro Poroshenko, made signing the EU association agreement one of its first tasks. Georgia and Moldova also signed their association agreements in the face of Russian opposition, while Armenia signed a watered-down version after then-President Serzh Sargsyan agreed to join the EEU.

UKRAINE AND THE FUTURE OF EUROPE

The competition between a Brussels-centric Europe and a Moscow-centric Eurasia culminated with the war in Ukraine. Sharply divided between a Ukrainian-speaking west, much of which was under Austro-Hungarian or Polish rule until World War II, and a Russian-speaking east and south that was long part of the Russian Empire, Ukraine continues to live up to its name (the word *Ukraina* means "borderland"). Within the Ukrainian elite, relations with Russia and the EU served as a proxy in power struggles between competing regional factions, at least until the Maidan protests, the fall of Yanukovych, and Russia's military intervention consolidated support for deeper integration with Europe across the population. Until his sudden about-face in September 2013, even Yanukovych and his Party of Regions supported deeper economic integration with the EU as the key to the country's future development and prosperity (not to mention the preservation of their own assets), as well as a hedge against overweening Russian influence. Much of the Russian elite, conversely, continues to regard Ukrainian identity as artificial, a product of foreign powers' efforts to divide and undermine an organic all-Russian nation encompassing Great, Little (Ukrainian), and White (Belarusian) Russians.[23]

Moscow exerted enormous pressure on Kyiv to back away from the association agreement that Yanukovych had committed to sign at the Vilnius Summit. The Maidan protests began the same night that Yanukovych announced, following a meeting with Putin in Moscow, that he would not sign the association agreement. For perhaps the first time ever, tens of thousands of protesters took to the streets waving the blue and yellow EU flag, calling on Yanukovych to embrace the European future he had long promised. Over the course of subsequent months, Ukraine plunged into a state of near collapse due to a combination of its leaders' own mismanagement and deliberate Russian provocations. At the same time, relations between the EU and Russia deteriorated to levels not seen since the Cold War. After Russia's February 2014 seizure of Crimea, Brussels followed Washington in imposing sanctions, even though the interdependence of the Russian and EU economies made sanctions more difficult for the Europeans.[24]

Ambivalence expressed in opinion polls diminished as the confrontation deepened, but Europeans remained concerned about the economic consequences of the crisis, especially as many EU states faced the possibility of renewed recessions.[25] Through the Normandy format, European leaders took the lead in negotiating and seeking to uphold the cease-fire that brought an uneasy halt to the most serious fighting in the fall of 2015.

The conflict in Ukraine set the stage for the rapid deterioration of EU-Russia ties across the board, which dovetailed with escalating Russian pressure on the EU. Russia accelerated efforts to de-integrate its economy from Europe, including through the cultivation of China and other non-Western partners, as well as to destabilize European politics. In addition to support for populist, anti-EU candidates, Russia has employed a range of asymmetric tools to exacerbate social tensions and undermine the efficacy of liberal institutions throughout Europe (not to mention in the United States). These include dissemination of propaganda through both traditional and social media designed to highlight cleavages around issues like immigration, as well as promotion of a "traditional values" narrative to amplify the backlash against the allegedly decadent stewards of what Russian propaganda started calling "Gayropa."[26] Russia also appears to have used its disinformation capabilities to influence the outcome of the Brexit referendum and (unsuccessfully) Catalonia's referendum on independence from Spain.[27]

CONCLUSION

Moscow's ambivalent position with respect to Europe reflects in some ways a centuries-old dilemma of Russian identity. Russia is in Europe, but not of it. The EU's challenge lies in learning to reconcile values and interests in its dealings with Russia—a task for which the strategy of integration it has pursued for much of the past two decades appears inadequate. Since the outbreak of the crisis in Ukraine, relations between Russia and the EU have deteriorated dramatically. The leaders of even traditionally sympathetic states such as France and Germany have at times portrayed Putin's Russia as a threat to European stability, even as they push for diplomacy and strive to normalize relations with Moscow.

Russia continues to see in the European project a threat not only to its influence in the post-Soviet region but to the very legitimacy of Russia's authoritarian government. Even with Russia-friendly governments in power in places like Budapest, and with the UK having departed entirely, intra-EU dynamics appear to have shifted substantially against Moscow in less than a decade. The old paradigm of *Wandel durch Annäherung* has largely given way to one based on bolstering Europe's defenses against Russian interference and cutting off connections that appear to either reward Russia or serve as a source of Russian leverage.

At the same time, Europe's own challenges continue unabated. Brexit highlighted the dangerous lack of legitimacy from which the EU suffers in many quarters. The rise of anti-EU populists in Central and Eastern Europe—including in countries like Poland that have benefited enormously from EU membership—adds to the challenge, even if these states are unlikely to follow Britain out the door (if only because of the financial benefits they receive as members). Relations with the United States grew increasingly complicated with the election of Donald Trump, America's first Euroskeptic president. While Trump maintained a puzzling affinity for Putin's Russia that prompted his impeachment, the Biden administration began its term in office calling for restoring "stable and predictable" relations with Moscow. It nonetheless struggled to remain on the same page with its European allies, as when France recalled its ambassador following the announcement of a new US defense partnership with the UK and Australia (AUKUS) and Canberra's decision to cancel a contract for French submarines.[28] Even if the worst predictions about the fragility of Europe's peripheral economies have not yet come true, much of the continent remains economically fragile more than a decade after the onset of the financial crisis.

The still-simmering conflict in Ukraine will ultimately determine much not only about the nature of EU-Russia relations, but about the EU itself. As the EU has suffered from a democratic deficit and rising populism at home, the Maidan protesters' willingness to face down both Yanukovych's goons and the Russian military speak to the continued attractiveness of European ideals at least in part of the continent. Ensuring that Ukraine's transition succeeds, and that Kyiv retains a "European perspective" even if the idea of formal membership in the EU or NATO remains out of reach, is in the EU's vital interests. Not only will instability (never mind active conflict) on Europe's borders eviscerate Europe's security, but failure to make good on its promises to Kyiv will damage the soft power advantage that Europe continues to enjoy in its wider neighborhood. Failure would also reinforce Russia's narrative about European decadence and raise the likelihood of additional challenges from Moscow in the years to come.

Despite the challenge posed by Ukraine, the EU and Russia will continue to have a complex, interdependent relationship, one driven in no small part by the continued willingness of the United States to underwrite Europe's security amid its widely touted "pivot" to Asia. A Europe less confident of American backing is one in which voices calling for an accommodation with Moscow are liable to get louder. Regardless of US policy, Europe will remain Moscow's indispensable economic partner for the foreseeable future, including in energy. Similarly, Europe's quest for diversification is beginning to bear fruit, but given existing infrastructure and future uncertainty, Europe for now has little choice but to continue buying large quantities of Russian natural gas.

Nor can Europe's major security challenges be solved without Russia playing a constructive role. In addition to Ukraine, these include the protracted conflicts in Moldova and the South Caucasus, the war in Syria and the resulting refugee crisis, instability in North Africa and the Eastern Mediterranean, and arms control (nuclear as well as conventional) in Europe itself. Russia's perception of European, and American, decline mean that, at least for the foreseeable future, these tensions are likely to remain. Only if the European Union can get its own house in order and present a united front to Moscow will it have any hope of being able to restore a modicum of stability.

AUTHOR'S POSTSCRIPT

The outbreak of large-scale war on the European continent in February 2022 led the EU to accelerate dramatically its effort to decouple from Russia, even as the danger of a wider conflict loomed. A few months in, the war appears likely to have massive and long-lasting consequences for the EU. The economic interdependence that emerged at the end of the Cold War is being unwound with breathtaking speed. Defense spending is set to rise by amounts unthinkable before February 24—notably in Germany, where Chancellor Scholz spoke of the war as marking a *Zeitenwende* (loosely, a change of eras) signifying an end to the period of seeking "change through engagement" with Moscow.[29]

What replaces it remains to be seen. On the one hand, the extent of popular and official support for Ukraine has been impressive, allowing officials to press ahead with policies that would have been difficult in more stable times. On the other, the economic effects of decoupling from Russia, especially in energy, and of hosting millions of Ukrainian refugees, could be serious. If, as now appears likely, the war drags on for months or years, piling up victims with little prospect of resolution, European interest and enthusiasm for confronting Russia could wane. Inflation and a new generation of refugees could revive support for Euroskeptic populists, whose backing for Russia has left them wrongfooted by the invasion. One way or another, the combination of moral outrage and rapid decoupling suggests that there is no going back to the pre–February 24 world, certainly for as long as Vladimir Putin remains in power. The EU's challenge lies in girding its populations for a long struggle, while laying the foundations now for a more stable postwar order.

The speed and scale of the European (and American) reaction to the invasion of Ukraine seems to have caught observers in Moscow by surprise. After all, Europe's response to the 2008 invasion of Georgia was insignificant, and while the 2014 annexation of Crimea and intervention in Donbas sparked sanctions and promises to reduce dependence on Russia, as the initial shock wore off, voices in Europe calling for engagement reemerged. Even Merkel remained committed to the Nord Stream-2 project, which had widespread support within Germany. Perhaps in part, the different response to the full-scale invasion of Ukraine was a culmination of mounting frustration with a decade and a half of Russian revisionism. It also seems informed by Europe's own haunted past. Putin's rejection of Ukrainian identity as such, war crimes committed by Russian forces in occupied areas, and the brazen attempt to oust a democratically elected government by force too clearly echo the crimes of the twentieth century in a continent that has long vowed "never again."

The EU itself was constructed as an alternative and an antidote to the wars of conquest that repeatedly tore Europe apart. If Russia's previous assaults on its neighbors could be explained away as part of the unfinished business of the Soviet collapse, the invasion of Ukraine and all the horrors that have ensued was simply too much for even the most pragmatically cynical European leaders to downplay. Nor could it be written off as what Russian bard Aleksandr Pushkin termed "a quarrel among Slavs/ an old familiar struggle/ . . . a problem that will not be resolved by you."[30] As much as Putin justified the war through tendentious claims about Russians and Ukrainians as "one people," the conflict has larger stakes that the EU and its member states cannot ignore.

The fact that the armed struggle for Ukraine was triggered by Yanukovych's foiled bid to sign a trade agreement with the EU indicates the extent to which Moscow has come to view the spread of European influence as a threat. And with the efforts to destabilize Europe from within through support of Euroskeptic parties, disinformation, and other dark arts, Moscow has made the struggle not only about where Ukraine (or Moldova, Georgia, or other European post-Soviet states) fit in the wider balance between Moscow and Brussels, but also about the future of the European project as such. However instrumental, Putin's embrace of the "traditional values" narrative, which predates the Euromaidan and "Revolution of Dignity," represented an effort to challenge the EU's normative foundation, with its emphasis on humanistic values and individual rights. In that sense, the war in Ukraine is also about what being "European" means. At a moment when the EU faces its own internal threats, a Russian success would represent a triumph for the atavistic forces of imperialism, wars of aggression, and ethnic cleansing that Europe sought to banish in the wake of the Second World War.

Aware of the stakes, the EU and its members have thus far committed to supporting Ukraine both militarily and economically. They are welcoming millions of Ukrainian refugees—not long after an influx of refugees from the Middle East helped destabilize European politics and accelerate the rise of anti-EU populists. Poland, recently on the verge of being sanctioned over the PiS government's assault on the rule of law, has taken on a pivotal role in welcoming refugees and facilitating the transit of weapons and other supplies to Ukrainian forces.[31]

The pivot away from Russia as an energy supplier and source of investment has been particularly notable. In April 2022, the EU announced plans for a total ban on Russian coal imports.[32] Many EU members also called for gradually moving away from Russian oil and gas—even though the economic impacts would be much larger. In early May 2022, Commission President Ursula von der Leyen proposed a total embargo on Russian oil, despite resistance from Hungary, Slovakia, and other Central European states that receive the bulk of their oil from Russia.[33] Meanwhile, Gazprom's decision to cut gas supplies to Poland and Bulgaria accelerated plans to substitute Russian gas with pipeline gas from other suppliers, LNG, and renewables.[34] Driving the effort to decouple from Russian energy are both moral revulsion at Russian actions in Ukraine as well as recognition of the vulnerability that such dependence creates—an argument long championed by Poland and other member states along the EU's eastern flank, but resisted in Germany and many other western and southern EU member states.

Notwithstanding the moral and strategic case for decoupling, the economic effects are liable to be serious. In 2019, Russia provided more than a quarter of the EU's crude oil imports.[35] Though oil is a fungible global commodity, fully replacing Russian crude will be a challenge, requiring European states to pay a premium for boosting supplies from the Middle East, North America, Africa, or elsewhere. Compared to oil, the impact of removing Russian gas from the energy mix will be even greater, since spot markets are less central to the gas trade, where long-term contracts continue to play a significant role.

Though Europe has gradually reduced its dependence on Russian gas through market integration, anti-trust measures, and construction of interconnector pipelines and LNG terminals, Russia still supplied around 155 billion cubic centimeters of pipeline gas to Europe in 2021. Those volumes comprised 30 percent of Europe's total gas imports—and a far greater share in the Baltic states, Finland, and much of Central Europe and the Balkans.[36]

Thus far, the backlash against Russia's invasion has provided European officials an opening to make far-reaching decisions. As the conflict drags on, the accumulation of economic consequences (not to mention the possibility of the conflict spreading beyond Ukraine) could impose new constraints. The immediate spike in crude prices following von der Leyen's announcement of plans for an oil embargo suggest the potential for further economic turbulence as Europe unwinds its energy dependence on Russia. Meanwhile, the influx of Ukrainian refugees continues. By early May 2022, the United Nations High Commissioner for Refugees estimated that around five million Ukrainians had already arrived in neighboring EU members Poland, Romania, Slovakia, and Hungary since the start of the war.[37]

The dilemma facing European leaders will lie in balancing what they perceive to be the strategic and moral stakes of decoupling with the economic consequences that could drive further inflation and, potentially, renew the populist backlash to European integration that spiked after the migration crisis of the mid-2010s. Given Russia's interest in seeing the European project fail, Moscow would welcome such a development. Indeed, it can be expected to try fueling it, as it earlier did through information campaigns stoking hostility against migrants and supporting anti-EU parties like Germany's AfD.[38] Elections in both Germany (2021) and France (2022) saw pro-Russian populists lose ground, though they remain influential actors—in Berlin and Paris, as well as in the capitals of many smaller states. Along with von der Leyen and her colleagues in Brussels, Scholz, French President Emmanuel Macron, and other key national leaders have a window of opportunity to show that the EU can cope with the unprecedented challenge that Russia's war has unleashed. They must navigate the tricky shoals between confronting Russia and maintaining political and economic stability at home. Achieving something like victory in Ukraine over the longer term will require European politicians to recognize that not only the future of the European project itself is at stake, but that their own societies and politics will remain part of the battle space.

—2022

DISCUSSION QUESTIONS

1. Why has Russia's attitude toward the EU, and especially the expansion of the EU's influence in the post-Soviet region, become more hostile over time? Was this development inevitable?
2. What were the goals of the EU's Eastern Partnership (EaP)? Are these goals incompatible with Russian interests?
3. Given the failure of Europe's strategy of change through engagement, what other approaches could the EU take today?
4. How much of a role has Russia played in causing or exacerbating Europe's internal crises?

SUGGESTED READINGS

Forsberg, Tuomas and Hiski Haukkala. *The European Union and Russia.* London: PalgraveMacmillan, 2016.
Gower, Jackie, and Graham Timmins, eds. *The European Union, Russia, and the Shared Neighbourhood.* London: Routledge, 2013.
Janning, Josef. "Russia, Europe, and the New International Order." European Council on Foreign Relations, April 9, 2014. http://www.ecfr.eu/article/commentary_russia _europe_ and_the_new_international_order245.
Maçães, Bruno. *The Dawn of Eurasia: On the Trail of the New World Order.* New Haven, CT: Yale University Press, 2018.
Milosevich, Mira. "Russia's Westpolitik and the European Union," Center for Strategic and International Studies. July 2021. https://www.csis.org/analysis/ russias-westpolitik-and-european-union.

NOTES

The views expressed in this article are those of the author and are not an official policy or position of the National Defense University, the Department of Defense, or the US Government.

1. Irina du Quenoy and Dmitry Dubrovskiy, "Violence and Defense of 'Traditional Values' in the Russian Federation," in Olga Oliker, ed., *Religion and Violence in Russia: Context, Manifestations, and Policy* (Washington, DC: Center for Strategic and International Studies, 2018), 93–116, https://www.jstor.org/stable/resrep22453.
2. Christian Nitoiu and Monika Sus, "Introduction: The Rise of Geopolitics in the EU's Approach in its Eastern Neighbourhood," *Geopolitics* 24, no. 1 (2019): 1–19.
3. Jeffrey Mankoff, *Russian Foreign Policy: The Return of Great Power Politics*, 2nd ed. (Lanham, MD: Rowman & Littlefield, 2011), 1–21, 77–79. Also see Philip

Hanson and Elizabeth Teague, "Big Business and the State in Russia," *Europe-Asia Studies* 57, no. 5 (2005): 657–80.

4. "Partnership and Cooperation Agreements (PCAs): Russia, Eastern Europe, the Southern Caucasus, and Central Asia," http://europa.eu/legislation_summaries/ external_relations/ relations_with_third_countries/eastern_europe_and_central_asia/ r17002_en.htm.

5. Dov Lynch, "Russia's Strategic Partnership with Europe," *Washington Quarterly* 27, no. 2 (2004): 100.

6. European Commission, "Countries and Regions: Russia," 2021, https://ec .europa.eu/trade/policy/countries-and-regions/countries/russia/.

7. Anastasia Stognei, "Russia Targets Offshore Tax Dodges," *The Bell*, August 8, 2020, https://thebell.io/en/russia-targets-offshore-tax-dodges/.

8. Russian Ministry of Foreign Affairs, "Programma effektivnogo ispol'zovaniia na sistemnoi osnove vneshnepoliticheskikh faktorov v tseliakh dolgosrochnogo razvitiia Rossiiskoi Federatsii," May 11, 2010, http://www.runewsweek.ru/country/34184.doc. Also see Angela Stent and Eugene Rumer, "Russia and the West," *Survival* 51, no. 2 (2009): 95.

9. Jeffrey Mankoff, "With Friends Like These: Assessing Russian Influence in Germany," Center for Strategic and International Studies, July 2020, https://csis-website -prod.s3.amazonaws.com/s3fs-public/publication/200724_Mankoff_FullReport_v3 .pdf.

10. Brian Whitmore, "Putin's Dark Ecosystem: Graft, Gangsters, and Active Measures," Center for European Policy Analysis, September 2018, https://cepa.org/cepa _files/2018-09-Putins_Dark_Ecosystem.pdf.

11. For a good profile of Merkel, see George Packer, "The Quiet German," *New Yorker*, December 1, 2014. Also see Klaus Larres and Peter Eltsov, "Merkel in the Middle," Politico, July 17, 2014, http://www.politico.com/magazine/story/2014/07/ merkel-in-the-middle-109071. html.

12. Nadezhda Arbatova, "Italy, Russia's Voice in Europe?" *Russie.Nei.Visions*, no. 62, Institut Français des Relations Internationals, September 2011, https://www.ifri .org/sites/default/files/atoms/files/ifrirussieitaliearbatovaengsept2011.pdf.

13. Emmanuel Macron, "Discours du Président de la République à la conférence des ambassadeurs," Élysée (French Ministry of Foreign Affairs), August 27, 2019, https://www.elysee.fr/emmanuel-macron/2019/08/27/discours-du-president-de-la -republique-a-la-conference-des-ambassadeurs-1.

14. See Heather Conley et al., "The Kremlin Playbook: Understanding Russian Influence in Central and Eastern Europe," Center for Strategic and International Studies, October 2016, https://csis-prod.s3.amazonaws.com/s3fs-public/publication /1601017_Conley_KremlinPlay book_Web.pdf.

15. Andrew Higgins, "Russian Money Suspected behind Fracking Protests," *New York Times*, November 30, 2014, http://www.nytimes.com/2014/12/01/world/russian -money-suspected-behind-fracking-protests.html.

16. These parties and affiliated groups have all supported Russian actions in Ukraine (including sending observers to the Russian-organized referendum on Crimean independence) and may also receive direct backing from the Kremlin. Uniting these

groups is an illiberal ideology at odds with the values of the Euro-Atlantic West, as well as hostility to the European Union and a desire to reassert national sovereignty against Brussels. See Mitchell Orenstein, "Putin's Western Allies," *Foreign Affairs*, March 25, 2014, http://www.foreignaffairs.com/articles/ 141067/mitchell-a-orenstein/ putins-western-allies. For a more detailed analysis, see "The Russian Connection: The Spread of Pro-Russian Policies on the European Far Right," Political Capital Institute (Budapest), March 14, 2014, http://www.riskforecast.com/useruploads/files/ pc_flash_report_russian_connection.pdf; "Russia's Far Right Friends," Political Capital Institute (Budapest), December 3, 2009, http://www.riskforecast.com/post/in -depth-analysis/russia-s-far-right-friends_349.html; and Timothy Snyder, "Fascism, Russia, and Ukraine," *New York Review of Books*, March 20, 2014.

17. Vladimir Putin, "Meeting of the Valdai Discussion Club," The Kremlin, September 19, 2013, http://en.kremlin.ru/events/president/news/19243.

18. F. Stephen Larrabee, "Russia, Ukraine, and Central Europe: The Return of Geopolitics," *Journal of International Affairs* 63, no. 2 (2010): 33–52; Filippos Proedrou, "Ukraine's Foreign Policy: Accounting for Ukraine's Indeterminate Stance between Russia and the West," *Southeast European and Black Sea Studies* 10, no. 4 (2010): 443–56.

19. European Commission, "The Policy: What Is the European Neighborhood Policy?," October 30, 2010, http://ec.europa.eu/world/enp/policy_en.htm.

20. Valentina Pop, "EU Expanding Its 'Sphere of Influence' Russia Says," *EU Observer*, March 21, 2009, http://euobserver.com/9/27827.

21. Ahto Lobjakas, "EU's Eastern Partnership Strains to Juggle Interests, Values," Radio Free Europe/Radio Liberty, April 29, 2009, http://www.rferl.org/content/EU _Eastern_ Partnership_Summit_Strains_To_Juggle_Interests_And_Values/1618551. html.

22. Vladimir Putin, "Novyy integratsionnyy proyekt dlya Yevrazii—budushcheye, kotoroye rozhdayetsya segodnya," *Izvestiya,* October 3, 2011, https://iz.ru/news /502761.

23. Vladimir Putin, "Article by Vladimir Putin 'On the Historical Unity of Russians and Ukrainians,'" The Kremlin, July 12, 2021, http://en.kremlin.ru/events/president /news/66181.

24. "Western Powers Move to Punish Russia," Al Jazeera, March 6, 2014, http://www. aljazeera.com/news/europe/2014/03/western-powers-move-punish-russia-2014361546437093 28.html.

25. Adrian Croft, "Most Europeans in Poll Think EU Should Offer Ukraine Membership," Reuters, September 10, 2014, http://www.reuters.com/article/2014/09/10/us -ukraine-crisis-poll-idUSKBN0H524620140910.

26. Andrew Foxhall, "From Evropa to Gayropa: A Critical Geopolitics of the European Union as Seen from Russia," *Geopolitics*, 24, no. 1 (2019): 174–93.

27. Robin Emmott, "Spain Sees Russian Interference in Catalonia Separatist Vote," November 13, 2017, https://www.reuters.com/article/us-spain-politics -catalonia-russia/spain-sees-russian-interference-in-catalonia-separatist-vote -idUSKBN1DD20Y.

28. "Secretary Blinken's Meeting with Foreign Minister Lavrov," U.S. Department of State, May 19, 2021, https://www.state.gov/secretary-blinkens-meeting-with -russian-foreign-minister-lavrov/.

29. Olaf Scholz, "Regierungserklärung von Bundeskanzler Olaf Scholz am 27. Februar 2022," German Federal Government, February 27, 2022, https://www .bundesregierung.de/breg-de/aktuelles/regierungserklaerung-von-bundeskanzler-olaf -scholz-am-27-februar-2022-2008356.

30. Aleksandr Pushkin, "Klevetnikam Rossii [To Russia's Slanderers]," 1831, https://www.culture.ru/poems/4966/klevetnikam-rossii.

31. Andrew Higgins, "Long on Europe's Fringe, Poland Takes Center Stage as War Rages in Ukraine," *New York Times*, March 22, 2022, https://www.nytimes.com/2022 /03/25/world/europe/poland-ukraine-russia.html.

32. Frédéric Simon, "EU's von der Leyen to Present Russia Oil Ban in Parliament Today," EurActiv, May 4, 2022, https://www.euractiv.com/section/energy -environment/news/eus-von-der-leyen-to-present-russia-oil-ban-in-parliament-today /.

33. Ursula von der Leyen, "Speech by President von der Leyen at the EP Plenary on the Social and Economic Consequences for the EU of the Russian War in Ukraine— Reinforcing the EU's Capacity to Act," European Commission, May 4, 2022, https:// ec.europa.eu/commission/presscorner/detail/en/speech_22_2785.

34. "Ukraine War: Russia Halts Gas Exports to Poland and Bulgaria," BBC, April 27, 2022, https://www.bbc.com/news/business-61237519.

35. "The EU Just Proposed a Ban on Oil from Russia, Its Main Energy Supplier," NPR, May 4, 2022, https://www.npr.org/2022/05/04/1096596286/eu-europea-russia -oil-ban.

36. "Gas Supply Stop by Russia: EU Would Have to Reduce Consumption Already by Summer," University of Cologne, Institute of Energy Economics, May 2, 2022, https://www.ewi.uni-koeln.de/en/news/gas-analysis/.

37. UN High Commissioner for Refugees, Operational Data Portal: Ukraine Refugee Situation, https://data2.unhcr.org/en/situations/ukraine.

38. Jeffrey Mankoff, "With Friends Like These."

Chapter 14

Russia-China Relations

Jeanne L. Wilson

In the last few years, the Russian-Chinese relationship has become steadily closer, indicating, as noted in their 2021 Joint Statement, that the relations between the two states "have reached the highest level in their history."[1] This development is all the more notable given the often fractious and discordant nature of the interactions between the two states. Ties attained a newfound stability with the coming to power of Vladimir Putin as the Russian president in 2000 and the signing of the "Treaty of Good-Neighborliness and Friendly Cooperation between the People's Republic of China and the Russian Federation" in July 2001. Even so, skepticism about the primary basis of the relationship and the extent of trust between the two states has been widespread. Bobo Lo famously characterized the relationship between the two states as an "axis of convenience" in his 2008 book, a judgment that he has partially revised.[2] There seems little doubt that the Russian-Chinese relationship has become more substantive, resting on an increasing convergence of views on the nature of the international political system, and identified mutual interests. At the same time, latent (and not so latent) tensions underlie a key number of issues central to the relationship. The most problematic feature of the interactions between these two states lies in their increasingly asymmetrical power relations. China is virtually universally considered to be a rising power, whereas Russia is, at least in a relative sense, a power in decline.[3] This dynamic, moreover, has been further accentuated by China's newly assertive foreign policy under the Xi Jinping leadership, in which China has largely cast off its former policy of maintaining a low profile and sought to expand its global presence, including within the post-Soviet space.

This chapter provides an overview of the Russian-Chinese relationship with a focus on its evolution since the start of Putin's third term as president in 2012. First, I address the most convergent aspects of Russian-Chinese relations. The two states share a largely consensual view of the dynamics of political interactions in the international system as well as a shared sense of political values that form one component of each state's evolving national identity. I then turn to other aspects of the relationship that are more complex, indicating underlying tensions that are often rooted in economic disparities. This includes a brief discussion of the key economic factors that serve to frame the relationship, the Russian response to China's Belt and Road Initiative (BRI), defense cooperation, Russian demographic concerns and the status of the Russian Far East, and an emergent competition between Russia and China in Central Asia. The final section examines the implications of these developments for the future evolution of the Russian-Chinese relationship.

RUSSIA AND CHINA: THE INTERNATIONAL DIMENSION

A considerable body of scholarly, journalistic, and policy-oriented work assumes that a realist perspective explains the Russian-Chinese relationship. In this view, Russia and China act as self-interested states seeking to counterbalance the hegemonic dominance of the West, notably the United States. Russia, to a greater extent than China, has actively promoted the thesis that US hegemony is giving way to the rise of a multipolar world. Russia and China correspondingly occupy separate poles in a multivectored system that also includes regional organizations such as the Shanghai Cooperation Organization (SCO), the Eurasian Economic Union (EEU), and BRICS (Brazil, Russia, India, China, and South Africa) that present an alternative to Western-dominated security and financial institutions. Although realism accurately depicts the role of the West—and the United States in particular—as a factor contributing to the strengthening of ties between the two states, it fails sufficiently to recognize the extent to which Russia and China have come to share a convergent ideational perspective as to the nature of the international political system. Here, constructivist assessments of Russian and Chinese motivations play a complementary role in emphasizing the importance of norms and values as a motivating factor in state behavior. Gilbert Rozman, in particular, has stressed the importance of identity as a factor that brings these two political outliers in the international system closer together. He argues that this development is a reflection of their shared Marxist-Leninist heritage (which is, however, not immutable to change).[4] Although consensual norms and values partly indicate the commonalities of a similar political tradition—for example, a preference for strong leadership, centralized control, and political stability—Russia and China are also drawn together by their shared view of the world that rejects the validity of Western interpretations of human rights and liberal democracy as universal. Rather, Russia and China continuously reaffirm their commitment to themes of a Westphalian order. The 2016 Russia-China Joint Declaration on the Promotion of Principles of International Law stresses, moreover, the authority of the United Nations as a source of international law and the sanctity of state sovereignty, sovereign equality, a respect for the right of all states to choose their own political system, and noninterference in the internal affairs of other states.[5] This position was reaffirmed in a 2021 Joint Statement by the Russian and Chinese foreign ministers that reiterated the sanctity of international law and the importance of the UN Charter as a bedrock precept of global governance.[6]

It is not the case, however, that Russian and Chinese views coincide fully. China has managed to maintain a position of polite neutrality on Crimea and the Ukrainian crisis, while Russia has typically sought to distance itself from unqualified support for Chinese actions in the South China Sea. Geography also plays a role. Russia is more invested, for example, in the topic of NATO enlargement than China, but considerably less concerned than China about the status of Taiwan. Nonetheless, it is largely the case, as the Russian and Chinese leaderships constantly reaffirm, that these two players do share a set of views that can be distinguished from that of the Western states on major international issues.

In recent years, Russia and China have paid increasing attention to matters of arms control. The topic is addressed in 2016 and 2019 joint statements on global strategic stability, and extensively discussed in their 2021 joint statement.[7] The United States, moreover, is explicitly singled out for criticism for abandoning previous agreements concluded between the United States and the Soviet Union (and subsequently with Russia) including the withdrawal in 2001 from the Anti-Ballistic Missile Treaty (ABM) and the cessation in 2019 of compliance with the Intermediate Nuclear Forces Treaty (INF). Russia and China also continuously reaffirm their allegiance to multilateral forms of arms control such as the Nuclear Non-Proliferation Treaty (NNPT), and the Comprehensive Nuclear Test Ban Treaty (CTBT), as well as opposing any efforts for the militarization of outer space. The most contentious issue, however, for both Russia and China has been that of the construction of missile defense systems.

The topic of missile defense has a long and complicated history. The US withdrawal from the ABM Treaty in 2001 set the stage for the proliferation of various proposals for the deployment of ABM systems. The original rationale adopted by the United States and its allies for the deployment of missile defense was twofold: deterrence was considered obsolete, and rogue regimes—notably Iraq, Iran, and North Korea—constituted an "axis of evil" that posed a threat, if not directly to the United States, at least to its NATO allies in Europe and its defense treaty partners, specifically South Korea and Japan, in East Asia. Not only were Russia and China unpersuaded by this argument; they viewed themselves as the designated targets of a system that could at least theoretically render second-strike capability inoperable. At present, Russia and China are primarily concerned about the deployment of the Aegis Ashore ballistic missile defense system in Europe and the possible deployment of the Terminal High Altitude Area Defense (THAAD) missile defense system in Northeast Asia. The July 2017 Russian-Chinese joint statement on the "Current Situation in the World and Important International Issues" was highly succinct in specifying that the deployment of ABM systems in Europe and the Asia-Pacific Region would "negatively affect the international and regional strategic balance, stability and security" and that Russia and China were "strongly opposed to such a policy."[8]

Russia and China also largely share coincident views on such prominent international issues as the civil war in Syria, the Iranian nuclear crisis, and the atmosphere of chronic turbulence on the Korean peninsula. Russian intervention in the Syrian civil war in September 2015 through the carrying out of air strikes was largely unanticipated and was likely the result of a number of external calculations not directly related to Syria—for example, Russia's desire to project itself as a great power, as well as an outright defiance of the West in the wake of the annexation of Crimea. In contrast, China's role in the Syrian conflict has been largely passive, providing support to Russia, especially within the United Nation's Security Council. Nonetheless, Russia and China are united in their fundamental assessment of the Syrian conflict and its international repercussions: they support the inviolable sovereignty of the Syrian state under the leadership of Bashar al-Assad and call for the resolution of the Syrian crisis through political and diplomatic means, under the auspices of the United Nations.[9] Similarly, Russia and China are supportive of the efforts of the United Nations to monitor the Iranian nuclear program (and thus prevent the emergence of Iran as a nuclear weapon state) but are opposed to the implementation of sanctions against Iran. Both states, however, have a common vested interest in maintaining the non-proliferation regime of nuclear weapons.

This opposition to nuclear non-proliferation also prevails in the case of North Korea (although in this case North Korea has already attained the status of a nuclear power). North Korea lacks any real allies, but China and secondly Russia can lay claim to having the closest ties globally with this isolated and reclusive state. In certain respects, Chinese and Russian policy conforms to the position laid out by the Western powers. They support the application of sanctions and call for the denuclearization of North Korea. Nonetheless, both states, although China more so than Russia, bear the brunt of criticism from the West as well as from the United Nations for tolerating North Korean efforts to evade sanctions as well as for providing the economic support necessary (as in the sale of Chinese coal) that helps to ensure the survival of the regime. Neither China nor Russia (nor South Korea for that matter) has an interest in the collapse of the Kim Jong-un leadership and its likely destabilizing and chaotic consequences. Russian-Chinese joint statements, including a July 2017 statement signed by the Russian and Chinese Foreign Ministries on the problems of the Korean Peninsula, express concerns over North Korean missile launches but are unequivocal in rejecting attempts to resolve the situation through military means. Rather, they propose a step-by-step process by which North Korea ends nuclear testing and the United States and South Korea refrain from large-scale joint exercises as well as the deployment of THAAD antimissile systems. Ultimately, in their view, any resolution of the situation mandates a diplomatic path of negotiations and consultation.[10]

In the last several years, Russia and China have not only become bolder in their critique of the international political situation but more assertive in setting themselves up as examples for global emulation. The global order is characterized as one of increasing turbulence and instability, a situation that confers upon Russia and China a responsibility to work toward ensuring international order. On the one hand, Russia and China are depicted as agents of change, but the development of polycentricity and a multipolar world is also depicted as an "irreversible historical process."[11] This theme is reiterated in their 2021 Joint Statement that posits that "Russia and China have formed a model of a new type of international relations" that plays an important role in "ensuring international and regional security and stability."[12] At least in terms of rhetoric, Russia and China are issuing a challenge to the hierarchy of power relationships in the international system and US primacy.

In fact, Russia and China are firmly united in viewing the hegemonic position of the West, along with its professed values and interventionist activities, as nothing less than an existential threat. The threat is no less dangerous because it is perceived as primarily employed by Western actors—above all, the United States—using soft power measures that seek to infiltrate and subvert the regime from within. Tactics include democracy promotion, efforts to create a civil society, the establishment of NGOs (often with foreign funding), use of the Western media, and the mobilization of youth. For the Kremlin and Beijing, these were the tactics employed in the color revolutions in Georgia (2003) and Ukraine (2004), during the political protests that occurred in 2013–2014 in Ukraine that led to the replacement of President Viktor Yanukovych, and in demonstrations in Hong Kong in 2014 during the so-called Umbrella Revolution. In the eyes of both the Russian and Chinese leaderships, regime survival necessitates a strategy of resistance to Western norms and values as well as the development of an alternative legitimating ideology. Neither state has yet managed to construct a fully cohesive national identity, but they both stress their divergence from neoliberal precepts embraced by the West.

RUSSIAN-CHINESE RELATIONS: THE ECONOMIC DIMENSION

Economic ties have historically been considered a weak link—in fact the weakest link—in the Russian-Chinese relationship. This is in part a reflection of the economic disparity between the two states. China's GDP, according to the purchasing power (PPP) measures used by the CIA *World Factbook*, has surpassed that of the United States and, at an estimated $22.5 trillion (2019 estimate), is over five and a half times that of Russia ($4 trillion).[13] In the post-Soviet era, moreover, Russia has struggled to regain its status as an industrial powerhouse, but without a great deal of success. Russia's economic profile, rather, is closer to that of an underdeveloped country dependent on raw materials as a source of exports. The loosening of previous prohibitions on Chinese involvement in foreign investment and the purchase of high-technology items, notably in the military sector, has intensified the Kremlin's fear that it could turn into a raw materials appendage of China. In the wake of the imposition of foreign sanctions by the West, the Kremlin felt compelled, as a matter of necessity, to turn to China as an alternative economic partner.

Estimates of the extent of Chinese foreign direct investment (FDI) in Russia are highly imprecise and vary widely. According to statistics from the Chinese Ministry of Commerce, China's accumulated FDI stock in Russia reached US$12.8 billion by the end of 2019, accounting for .6 percent of China's total accumulated FDI. In 2019, moreover, Chinese FDI was actually negative (minus US$379 million), as Chinese investors mainly in the mining industry (a category that includes oil and gas) repatriated their investments back to China. This amounted to a reverse flow of US$1.13 billion, or more than 42 percent of total Chinese investment.[14] Although Chinese FDI to Russia accounts for only .6 percent of its total accumulated investment (US$137 billion in 2019), these figures dwarf corresponding Russian investment in China, which according to statistics from the Russian Central Bank comprised US$43 million in 2019.[15]

China is Russia's number-one trade partner, although Russia ranked fourteenth as China's trade partner in 2019.[16] Since 2016, the total volume of Russian-Chinese trade has increased by 57 percent, growing from US$69.7 billion in 2016 to reach US$109.7 billion in 2019. This figure only accounts for about 2.5 percent of China's total trade volume and is almost five times less than Chinese trade with the United States, China's largest trading partner.[17] The lack of diversification in Russia's commodity trade profile is evident. In 2019, fuels constituted 71 percent of Russian exports to China, compared to 63 percent in 2016. The profile of Russian exports to China centers on a variety of raw materials, including wood (7.6 percent), minerals (3 percent), and metals (3 percent). In contrast, by 2019, machinery and electrical items constituted 38 percent of Chinese exports to Russia, up from 35 percent in 2016, and the single largest category in Chinese-Russian exports (although consumer goods as a collective whole constituted 45 percent of Chinese exports to Russia). It is testimony to Russia's lack of global competitiveness that by 2019 the number-one import from China was capital intensive equipment, drawing upon China's rapidly developing high technology.

As the data for Russian-Chinese trade indicate, the Chinese leadership is primarily interested in developing economic ties with Russia in the energy sector. Negotiations between Russia and China have been protracted and often contentious as to pricing. Nonetheless, the Eastern Siberia Pacific Oil (EPSO) oil pipeline began operations with a spur to China in 2011, followed by a second link that began commercial operations in January 2018. The two states signed a deal in 2014 to construct a gas pipeline, the Power of Siberia, that became operational in 2019. A memo of understanding signed in 2017 provided for a Power of Siberia 2 but doubts have been expressed as to its economic feasibility. After several years of indecision, the project was revived in 2020, with the rerouting of the pipeline to bring gas from existent fields in Western Siberia through Mongolia, rather than developing entirely new gas fields in Eastern Siberia.

To date, the hope that China could become an economic substitute for the loss of Western investments because of sanctions has not been realized. Nonetheless, it is notable that Chinese investment has been critical in maintaining the operations of certain key Kremlin-supported projects targeted for sanctions. This includes the purchase of 9.9 percent of shares in the Yamal liquefied natural gas (LNG) project and the extension of a $12 billion loan and the purchase of 10 percent of the shares of Sibur, a petrochemical complex. Chinese targeting of large-scale energy projects for investment also indicates the co-mingling of political and economic motivations. The Chinese seem especially interested in special deals with a select group of individuals having close ties to President Putin. Perhaps the most controversial deal that involved Chinese financing was the advance payment that Igor Sechin, the head of the Russian oil firm Rosneft, received in 2013 from the Chinese oil companies CNPC and Sinopec, which Sechin then used to repay debt that the company generated in absorbing rival TNK-BP. Sechin, who shares a *siloviki* background with Putin, is considered his most trusted associate. Similarly, both the Yamal LNG project and the Sibur petrochemical complex are co-owned by Gennady Timchenko, a close friend of Putin, who was one of the first people to be placed on the US sanctions list. Chinese financing of Russian projects has typically been by state-owned banks rather than commercial banks, which are reluctant to bear the economic consequences of violating the West's sanctions regime. Vladimir Milov, a Russian opposition politician and a former Deputy Minister of Energy has pointed out that Russia is supplying energy to China at hugely discounted prices relative to the global energy market with special deals that in many cases ensure their tax free and highly subsidized status. This is a practice that provides extensive benefits to friends of Putin but supplies little to the federal budget.[18]

There is little doubt that the trajectory of Russian-Chinese economic relations indicates an increasing disparity between the two states in terms of the structure of trade and their respective economic and technological capabilities. Putin has classified the predominance of energy exports to China as a "natural" phenomenon, but others, such as Milov, have concluded that Russia is evolving into a "raw materials appendage of Beijing."[19] China has replaced Germany as a source of industrial equipment and high technological imports, and Chinese high-tech companies are making increasing inroads into China. The Chinese telecommunication firm Huawei has been active in the installation of 5G technology, with capabilities that exceed that of Russian companies. In the past few years, moreover, the Russian Central Bank has been moving to hold a greater percentage of its currency reserves in yuan rather than the dollar. In short, there is an increasing penetration of Chinese economic interests within the Russian economy.

China's Silk Road Initiative: A Challenge to Russia

In the fall of 2013, Xi Jinping proposed in a speech at Nazarbayev University in Kazakhstan that China and the states of Central Asia cooperate to establish trade and economic linkages through a modern version of the Silk Road to promote regional cooperation. Eventually, this initiative morphed into a megaproject that includes a maritime component and a global scope. Variously known as the Silk Road, One Belt One Road (OBOR), and now the Belt and Road Initiative (BRI), this endeavor focuses on the construction of large-scale infrastructure projects financed through China's Silk Road Fund and the Chinese-sponsored Asian Infrastructure Investment Bank (AIIB). The BRI poses a direct challenge to Russia as it directly targets the post-Soviet space, and most particularly Central Asia, which is viewed by Russia as a sphere of influence critical to Russia's status as a great power.

The Russian leadership's reaction to the BRI has evolved to date through several stages. In the first instance, the Kremlin simply chose to ignore the BRI and turned down the invitation to join the AIIB. However, when Xi Jinping met Putin in February 2014 in Sochi, he indicated that China welcomed Russian participation in the BRI and alleviated some of Russia's concerns by proposing the creation of an economic corridor, which would connect with the Trans-Siberian railway through Mongolia. At the March 2015 Boao Forum in Beijing, the Russian delegation, led by First Deputy Minister Igor Shuvalov announced that Russia was willing to cooperate with the BRI. Subsequently, at the 2015 meeting of Putin and Xi, the two states agreed to link the BRI with the EEU, the regional economic integration project promoted by Russia, an initiative devised by Russia.[20] The Sino-Russian Joint Declaration on Cooperation between the EEU and the Silk Road Economic Belt, signed during Xi's visit to Moscow, pledged to seek to coordinate the two initiatives, as well as envisioning BRI participation in ventures located in Russia.[21] In essence, the Russian leadership's acquiescence to the BRI was an acknowledgment of the reality that it had little choice but to endorse the project and get the best deal possible under the circumstances.

To date, there is not much evidence of Russian-Chinese coordination of the EEU and Silk Road policies, nor of any Silk Road–sponsored projects within Russia. The 2015 agreement mandated that the EEU and China begin negotiations on a trade and investment agreement. In May 2018, China and the EEU signed an economic and trade cooperation agreement, which came into effect in October 2019.[22] The agreement, contrary to Chinese desires makes no mention of the operation of a free trade area or preferential arrangements between states. None of the forty projects proposed by the EEU for Chinese consideration have to date been funded.[23] Although the package of agreements signed at the 2015 meeting endorsed the construction of a high-speed railway between Kazan and Moscow as a signature Silk Road undertaking, the initiative has been mired in dissention over construction and cost issues and seems unlikely to be realized. There are two BRI projects in Russia that exist independently of the negotiations between the EEU and China: the previously noted Yamal LNG project and the Sibur gas-processing and petrochemical complex, both of which are financed through the Silk Road fund. The Kremlin's efforts to have the Chinese tie the Trans-Siberian and Baikal-Amur railroads to BRI initiatives have been unsuccessful and the BRI transport corridors avoid Russia and go through Central Asia.

The Kremlin has portrayed the agreement between the BRI and the EEU as a mutually beneficial endeavor between two equal partners. However, the reality is that Russia cannot compete with China economically in the post-Soviet space. Table 14.1 provides comparative data on the extent of Russian and Chinese trade with the former Soviet republics (except for the Baltic states), as well as the percentage increase (or decrease) in total trade for the two states since 2016. Both Russia and China reported higher levels of trade in 2019 compared to 2016 apart from Tajikistan for China and Turkmenistan for Russia. China's total trade volume in 2019 was higher than that of Russia for

Table 14.1. Chinese and Russian Imports, Exports, and Total Trade with the Post-Soviet States 2019 ($US millions)

	Imports		Exports		Total Trade		Percentage Change	
	China	Russia	China	Russia	China	Russia	China	Russia
Armenia	.54	.85	.22	1.7	.76	2.6	+95%	+100%
Azerbaijan	.86	.86	.62	2.3	1.5	3.3	+95%	+55%
Belarus	.91	13.7	1.8	21.7	2.7	35.4	+81%	+51%
*China	—	54.1	—	57.3	—	114.4	—	+58%
Georgia	.81	.45	1.4	.88	2.2	1.33	+176%	+21%
Kazakhstan	3.5	5.7	12.8	14.3	16.3	21.3	+24%	+64%
Kyrgyzstan	.07	.32	6.3	1.6	6.4	1.9	+12%	+58%
Moldova	.05	.38	.12	1.3	.17	1.7	+70%	+42%
*Russia	60.3	—	49.5	—	109.8	—	+58%	—
Tajikistan	.08	.04	1.5	.95	1.6	.99	-10%	+43%
Turkmenistan	8.7	.54	.43	.15	9.1	.69	+142%	-23%
Ukraine	4.5	4.8	7.4	6.6	11.9	11.4	+77%	+21%
Uzbekistan	2.2	1.2	5.0	3.9	7.2	5.1	+100%	+89%

Percentage Change in Total Trade Relative to 2016

Sources: World Bank: World Integrated Trade Solution Data (WITS); https://wits.worldbank.org/ CountryProfile/en/Country/RUS/Year/2019/TradeFlow/EXPIMP/Partner/by-country; https://wits.worldbank .org/CountryProfile/en/Country/CHN/Year/2016/TradeFlow/Export/Partner/by-country; https://wits .worldbank.org/CountryProfile/en/Country/RUS/Year/2016/TradeFlow/Export; https://wits.worldbank.org/ CountryProfile/en/Country/CHN/Year/2019/TradeFlow/Export/Partner/by-country

Note: Percentages compiled from World Bank 2016 data.

*World Bank Data for Russian and Chinese Imports and Export are not internally consistent.

every Central Asian state except Kazakhstan.[24] Moreover, in 2019, China's total trade volume was higher than Russia's in Georgia and Ukraine, which was not the case in 2016. In fact, in 2019 China became Ukraine's largest trading partner (although total trade with the states of the European Union remains greater as a cumulative bloc). In cases such as Armenia and Moldova the percentage increase in Chinese trade is less meaningful given the low level of trade but the percentage increases in a three year period in Georgia (176 percent), Turkmenistan (142 percent), Uzbekistan (100 percent), Ukraine (77 percent), and even Belarus (81 percent) indicate the increasing penetration of China in the post-Soviet space spurred on by projects connected to the BRI. The BRI, moreover, has morphed into more than an economic infrastructure project, with the development of the "digital silk road" in 2014, and a "health silk road" in 2017. More recently, the Chinese have begun to link the Silk Road to their Arctic ambitions. During Russian prime minister Dmitry Medvedev's November 2017 visit to Beijing, Xi called on Russia and China jointly to develop and cooperate on the utilization of the North Pole sea route and build a Silk Road on ice.[25] It is notable, furthermore, that the "white paper on China's Arctic policy" released in January 2018 explicitly refers to a "Polar Silk Road" as a component of the BRI.[26] Although there are no overt tensions between Russia and China regarding China's emerging Arctic policy, Russia is committed to its quest to maintain predominance in the Arctic as a matter of national sovereignty and territorial integrity.

In the last several years, there has been increasing unease among Russian political elites about the perceived expansionist tendencies of the BRI in the former Soviet region, as well as a growing sense that the BRI is not beneficial to Russian interests.[27] Putin was a keynote speaker at the 2017 BRI conference in Beijing (placed second on the agenda after the inaugural address of Xi Jinping) and also spoke at the second BRI forum in 2019. However, Sergei Lavrov, the Russian foreign minister, declined to appear at the 2020 virtual BRI conference, sending a subordinate to attend, a possible indication of official disenchantment.[28]

RUSSIAN-CHINESE DEFENSE COOPERATION

In the last several years, forms of defense cooperation have deepened between Russia and China. This is seen in all three areas of the bilateral defense relationship: military exercises, high-level military-to-military contacts, and forms of military technical cooperation.[29] China and Russia first participated in combined military exercises in 2003, and, especially since 2014, the exercises have become increasingly complex. This includes peacekeeping mission exercises conducted under the auspices of the SCO and joint naval exercises conducted in the Mediterranean in 2015, the South China Sea in 2016, and the Baltic Sea in 2017. Although Russia has sought to remain neutral with respect to Chinese territorial claims in the South China Sea, its participation in the 2016 bilateral exercises could be interpreted as an implicit approval of the Chinese position. The same logic applies to suggest Chinese acquiescence to Russia's interpretation of the Mediterranean and Baltic Seas as legitimate spheres of Russian influence. In 2018 and 2019 China participated in the Vostok-2018 and Tsentr-2019 exercises in Russia, while in 2021 Russian forces participated for the first time in military exercises in Ningxia Hui Autonomous Region adjacent to Xinjiang province in China.

Russia and China engage in defense contacts through a multitude of ongoing bilateral and multilateral meetings, which have also increased over time. These include the China-Russia Intergovernmental Joint Commission of Military-Technical Cooperation, exchanges between services, and Staff Headquarters Strategic Consultations. Since 1990, Russia and China have held over one hundred high-level meetings, the most prominent of which involved meetings between the Russian and Chinese ministers of defense and the vice chairman of the Central Military Commission of the Chinese Communist Party (CCP), deputy defense ministers, and deputy chiefs of the Russian and Chinese armed forces.[30] Although the leaders of both states support closer defense ties, the intensification of military contacts appears to be a special priority of the Chinese, who seek to benefit from Russia's deeper experience in military planning, communication, and coordination.

Military-technical cooperation constitutes a key component of the Russian-Chinese relationship that extends beyond arms sales to encompass a broader range of activities that includes joint research and development, weapon licensing agreements, and technology transfers. After the collapse of the Soviet Union, arms sales to China kept key sectors of the Russian military-industrial complex afloat in a period when domestic purchases were almost nonexistent. Chinese arms sales reached their peak in 2005–2006 and subsequently declined. Still, according to the Stockholm International Peace Research Institute (SIPRI) arms transfer database, China was Russia's second largest customer in 2019 and 2020 (after India), with arms deliveries from Russia totaling US$1.7 billion.[31]

A chronic irritant in the Russian-Chinese military-technical relationship has been Russian objections to the Chinese practice of reverse engineering weapons systems they have purchased from Russia. For example, the Russians complained that the Chinese repackaged the Su-27 fighter aircraft as the J-11 fighter aircraft, which in the Russian view violated the original licensing agreement for production.[32] Since 2014, however, the Russians have loosened the informal prohibitions that existed on the transfer of high-technology armaments to China. In 2015, the two states signed two high-profile deals on the sale of advanced weapons systems. The agreements arrange for the supply of six battalions of Russian S400 antiaircraft missile systems and twenty-four Sukhoi Su-35 fighter aircraft. In 2019, speaking at a meeting of the Valdai Discussion Club, Putin surprised his audience by disclosing that Russia was helping China to build a missile defense system, although further details about this endeavor were not made public.[33] Russia and China have also increased the range of joint production agreements and technology transfers.[34]

Russian motivations for expanding its military-technical relationship with China are governed by a mix of political and economic factors. Chinese objectives are simpler, and largely rooted in a desire to use Russia's capabilities in arms production—itself a product of the Soviet legacy—to enable domestic production of weapon systems. Although the Russian military-industrial complex is not as financially strapped as it was in the 1990s, it is still chronically short of cash. The most prominent joint production deal between Russia and China has been a 2015 agreement to produce heavy-lift helicopters, an undertaking that is entirely dependent on Chinese funding.

China, moreover, has been explicit in outlining its terms for production, which include the use of aviation engines produced at the Motor Sich enterprise in Ukraine, rather than Russian manufactured models.[35] Russian superiority in the military technical field has been threatened by an increasing reliance on Chinese components, such as electronics and navy diesel engines, which it can no longer receive from European sources.[36] In 2019, the Russian military analyst Pavel Felgenhauer published an article in Novaya Gazeta that accused the Russian producers of the anti-aircraft missile in the S-400 series destined for China of deliberately sabotaging its shipment to China because they had not yet mastered the technologies for its successful implementation. The article, provocatively entitled "The Dependence of Russia on China Is Growing with Each Day," lasted on the *Novaya Gazeta* website two days before it disappeared, an indication of the sensitivity of the topic.[37]

Although economic considerations are important in Russian arms sales to China, there is also the sense that Russia needs China's political support, despite the risks that China could become a competitor in selling arms through reverse engineering, or worse, a military threat in the event of worsening relations.[38] But the dynamics of this relationship are rooted in short term calculations: it seems that it is only a matter of time before China surpasses Russia in its technological mastery of armaments production.[39]

RUSSIAN-CHINESE RELATIONS AND THE RUSSIAN FAR EAST

The Russian Far East was severely affected by the collapse of the Soviet Union and the subsequent loss of government subsidies. Over a million inhabitants left the region, leaving a population of approximately 6.3 million in an area that constitutes 36 percent of Russia's territory.[40] During the Soviet era, moreover, the border was highly militarized, leaving its residents isolated from contact with their Asian neighbors. The signing of the 2004 border agreement between Russia and China put the long-standing territorial dispute to rest and eased security concerns along the 2,400-kilometer border.

In the last few years, the Kremlin has shown a greater commitment to the economic development of the Russian Far East. The Ministry for Development of the Russian Far East was established in 2012. This has been accompanied by the acknowledgment that China is a necessary partner in the revitalization of the area.[41] This is not to say, however, that the population has outgrown its suspicions and outright hostility toward foreigners—especially the Chinese. Although not condoned by the Kremlin, the media as well as some members of the political class continue to propagate highly exaggerated and xenophobic accounts asserting that millions of Chinese migrants are overrunning the Russian Far East. Precise figures on the Chinese presence in Russia are not available, but regional official and academic data estimate the number of Chinese migrants as between four and five hundred thousand, more than half of whom reside in European Russia, with the largest population in Moscow.[42] It is by no means clear, moreover, that the average wage of migrants is higher in Russia than in China, and in recent years worsening economic conditions in Russia have led to a reverse flow of migrant workers back to China. The closure of the border with the onset of the coronavirus pandemic also reduced the migration of Chinese to Russia, notably agricultural workers who came for seasonal employment.

Previously, Russia sought to restrict Chinese economic activity in the Russian Far East, notably in the extractive industries, an exclusion that did not apply to the Japanese and Koreans. As late as 2012, Prime Minister Dmitry Medvedev warned that the Russian Far East could become a raw materials appendage to China because of China's "excessive expansion."[43] Since 2014, these constraints have been reduced, and additional programs to encourage Chinese investors have been initiated. The lack of border crossings has been a serious impediment to cross-border trade, although the first vehicle road bridge between Blagoveshchensk and Heihe was finished in December 2019, and a rail bridge in the Jewish Autonomous Region between Nizhneleninskoye and Tongjiang was completed, in August 2021. Since 2014, Russia and China have established various formats to encourage the Chinese presence in the local economy, with an eye not only toward large-scale extractive industries that are favored by Beijing—such as the Chinese purchase of shares in the Yamal LNG plant—but also smaller-scale ventures. In 2018, Russia and China signed a six-year cooperation plan for the Russian Far East which recommended investment projects in such areas as agriculture, tourism, and transport infrastructure.[44] In smaller scale ventures, the Chinese presence is especially notable in agriculture, forestry, and construction. Chinese activity in the agricultural sector ranges from large-scale ventures leased by local officials to Chinese agribusiness to individual farmers renting land. A 2019 report by the BBC estimated that Chinese citizens owned or leased at least 350,000 hectares of land in the Russian Far East (out of 2.2 million hectares used for agricultural purposes).[45] In the Jewish Autonomous Region, Chinese farmers are estimated to have leased up to 80 percent of the land.[46] These statistics, however, predate the pandemic, which prevented Chinese seasonal workers from entering Russia.

Statistics on the Chinese economic presence in the Russian Far East are highly unreliable especially since most planned projects are never realized. China does not rank among the major foreign investors in the Russian Far East. The positive spin put on economic cooperation in the Russian and Chinese media typically focuses on deals signed rather than realized results. According to Denis Suslov, an economist at the Far Eastern Branch of the Russian Academy of Sciences: "less than 10 percent of announced deals reach the pre-investment stage, and only 1 to 2 percent of them get actually implemented."[47] Here, too, the situation in the Russian Far East exemplifies the tensions in the Russian-Chinese relationship born out of economic asymmetry. Russians in the region fear the potential consequences of opening up to the Chinese economic juggernaut. Chinese agricultural workers are grudgingly admired for their work ethic but resented for their very presence on Russian soil. For their part, Chinese investors are not necessarily eager to invest in the Russian Far East, where they encounter a maze of bureaucratic obstacles, a lack of infrastructure, uncertain profits, and an often-hostile reception. Other locales, in contrast, are more attractive and present fewer challenges. Despite evidence of enhanced goodwill on the part of the Kremlin and greater attention to structural reforms within the region, it is not clear that current efforts to stimulate economic activity between Russia and China will lead to a better outcome than previous attempts.

INCREASING COMPETITION IN CENTRAL ASIA

In the last several decades, the Chinese presence in Central Asia has increased markedly, a process accelerated by China's launching of the BRI in 2013. As table 14.1 indicates, China is now the major economic actor in the region. Chinese economic interaction with the states of Central Asia, however, does not rely solely on trade. Chinese FDI far exceeds that of Russia, and all of the states in Central Asia are in debt to China. The situation is particularly acute in Kyrgyzstan and Tajikistan, the two smallest states in the region bordering China. A total of 45 percent of Kyrgyz external borrowing is from China, while China holds 52 percent of Tajik foreign debt.[48] All of the states of Central Asia except Turkmenistan receive funding from the AIIB through the BRI, while China is increasingly seeking to link Central Asia to a Chinese hub by providing digital technology.

The official Russian reaction to these developments is to deny that Russia and China have any conflicting interests in Central Asia. According to Sergei Lavrov: "we do not see China as a rival [in Central Asia]. . . . The plans that Russia and China have for the region and Eurasia overall do not contradict each other."[49] The dominant narrative on the region is that Russia and China coexist more or less harmoniously due to an informal division of tasks between them: China focuses on economic issues, while Russia is the security provider for the region. There are, however, at least two interrelated problems with this assessment. First, China has increased its activities in Central Asia along a host of other dimensions, most notably in the military realm, developing its linkages with the regional political elites, and implementing a soft power program that projects a positive image of China. Second, the Russian political class has generally ignored or downplayed the newly assertive foreign policy of the Xi Jinping leadership that considers Central Asia to be a key focus of its periphery diplomacy.

In the last several years, China has dramatically raised the profile of its military linkages with the Central Asian states, by increasing the number of bilateral joint military exercises with Central Asian states, expanding arms transfers (including technologically advanced equipment), and developing programs to train officers. In addition, China has established what is sometimes referred to as a military base in the Gorno-Badakhshan Autonomous Region of Tajikistan, although it is officially designated a border guard station. China supplied 1.5 percent of Central Asian arms imports between 2010–2014, but by 2015–2018 the amount had increased to 18 percent of the total. Uzbekistan and Turkmenistan purchased more arms from China than Russia in the period from 2014–2018.[50] China is in the process of leveraging its economic presence in the region to strengthen ties with regional leaders, who benefit economically.[51] China has also provided funds for Chinese language teaching and scholarships for Central Asia students to study at Chinese Universities. The number of Confucius Institutes and classes per capita, is reportedly greater in Central Asia than anywhere else in the world.[52]

These actions show a deliberate effort by the Xi Jinping leadership to increase its influence in Central Asia. In October 2013 and November 2014, the CCP held two conferences that set the direction of Chinese foreign policy under Xi Jinping. The first meeting focused on Chinese diplomacy toward states bordering China, a category that includes Central Asia as well as Russia. This was reportedly the first major meeting dealing with foreign policy since 2006 and the first forum devoted specifically to periphery diplomacy in PRC history.[53] At the 2013 meeting, Xi reportedly outlined four key priorities: (1) enhance political good will; (2) deepen regional economic integration; (3) increase China's cultural influence; and (4) improve regional security cooperation. As Xi further noted in his 2014 speech, regional cooperation must expand to encompass "shared beliefs and norms of conduct for the whole region."[54] In other words, Chinese diplomacy cannot be limited to the pursuit of purely economic goals. It also includes a civilizing mission, reflected in Xi's exhortations on the need to create a "community of common destiny," which can be construed as an extension of distinctly Chinese values and norms.

To be sure, Russia and China share several important goals in Central Asia, which include, above all, maintaining regional stability and joint efforts to combat Islamic militarism. It is too soon, at the time of writing, to predict the impact of the Taliban victory in Afghanistan, but for both Russia and China this is a troubling development—although both are likely to take a pragmatic approach in dealing with the new Afghan leadership. In particular, China has sought to ensure that the Taliban do not provide support to Uighur dissidents in Xinjiang province. The Shanghai Cooperation Organization (SCO)—which includes Russia, China, the Central Asian states (except Turkmenistan), and most recently India and Pakistan—has been largely ineffective in conducting counter-terrorist activities, and it seems unlikely that it will pursue this matter now, given Pakistan's history of support for the Taliban. Chinese dissatisfaction with the SCO was probably a factor in its decision in 2016 to establish the Quadrilateral Cooperation and Coordination Mechanism, a multilateral organization composed of China, Tajikistan, Pakistan, and Afghanistan (but notably not Russia), which focuses on security issues in the region.[55]

Nonetheless, the burgeoning presence of China in Central Asia makes it harder for Russia to continue to present itself as the dominant regional power, which serves as an important underpinning for Russia's claim to great power status. Maintaining Russian influence in Central Asia has been increasingly important in the wake of the decisive movement of Ukraine into the Western camp after 2014. Russian anxieties about the need to preserve its image factor into the Kremlin's plan for the Greater Eurasian Partnership. First announced in a 2016 speech by Putin at the St. Petersburg International Economic Forum, the Partnership is in some ways a reworking of the Kremlin's long-standing efforts to lure the Europeans into establishing an economic space "between Lisbon and Vladivostok."

By situating Russia at the center of the Eurasian land mass, serving as a bridge between Europe and Asia, the concept is also an effort to address Russia's position in Central Asia and its relationship with China. Russian commentary in this context has often been contradictory on the issue of how to deal with China. Some accounts see Russia and China as part of a mutual effort to establish the partnership, while for others, the partnership is explicitly designed to contain China.[56] In any case, the construct is, as David Lewis has stressed "a geopolitical imaginary," existing only in the virtual realm.[57]

CONCLUSION

Russian and Chinese officials routinely describe their relationship as at historically high levels. At the 2020 meeting of the Valdai Discussion Club, Putin acknowledged, albeit in oblique terms, the possibility of a military alliance between Russia and China, a statement that immediately set off a furor of speculation in media circles.[58] There is no doubt that the two states share a largely consensual perspective in the international realm, rooted in their joint animosity toward the West. Their ties are not merely a result of structural counterbalancing against the West but indicate an ideational convergence in their joint rejection of many of the norms and values of the liberal international order, notably the West's commitment to a vision of human rights and democratic practice that sanctions intervention in the internal affairs of sovereign states. In the last several years, the level of military cooperation between the two states has also intensified. Ostensibly the two states interact as equal partners, a maxim that serves as a fundamental underpinning of their relationship. The constant repeating of this mantra, however, cannot conceal the increasing asymmetry in the distribution of power between Russia and China. This is a dynamic driven by economics but that spills over into other issue areas of their relationship.

The reality is that Russia is increasingly on the defensive in its relationship with China and in a subordinate position. This is seen in trade patterns between Russia and China in which Russia has essentially assumed the role of a raw material—chiefly fossil fuels—supplier to China. In the military sphere, Russia has begun to turn to China as a provider of technologically advanced component parts that Russia cannot produce domestically. The efforts to coordinate the EEU with the BRI have failed, and China is now posing a challenge to Russian claims to dominance in Central Asia. This list could be expanded but it demonstrates the increasing asymmetry that divides these two neighbors and fellow outliers in the international political system.

In the last few years, the rumblings of discontent with the disparities in the Russian Chinese relationship have increased on the Russian side although they remain muted, presumably out of a reluctance to criticize the Kremlin leadership.[59] Since the collapse of the Soviet Union, China has distinguished itself from the other major powers in its policy of treating Russia with scrupulous respect as an equal partner. With Xi Jinping's increasingly assertive foreign policy, however, that deference is diminishing. As Gilbert Rozman has noted: "China has been content to flatter Russia with words of equality even as it shows reduced respect."[60] This sentiment is echoed by the Russian Sinologist, Alexander Lukin, who argues that the peak of Sino-Soviet rapprochement has passed.[61]

In the United States, a growing perception of China as a threat to American hegemony led a number of analysts to advocate that US foreign policy seek to exploit tensions in the Russian-Chinese relationship to entice Russia to return to the Western fold.[62] This reasoning, rooted in realpolitik and reminiscent of the maneuverings of the Nixon White House in the 1970s in seeking to isolate the Soviet Union by opening up to China, did not find a receptive audience in Moscow. Russian analysts, and presumably the Kremlin leadership too, are well aware of Russia's vulnerabilities in its interactions with China, but there is also a sense that, at least for the present, maintaining strong ties with China is in the national interest.[63] This speaks to the depth of Russia's estrangement from the West as well as its concern to avoid a replay of the Sino-Soviet split, with its potential for destabilization along the 4,200-kilometer border. The assessment that strong ties with China are beneficial in the short run rests on the questionable assumption that an increasingly subordinate Russia will be able to extricate itself from the network of ties that bind it to China in the future should its sovereignty be imperiled. But it is China, not Russia, that has the upper hand, in this increasingly asymmetrical relationship.

DISCUSSION QUESTIONS

1. To what extent do you believe that the Russian-Chinese relationship rests on geopolitical factors? Justify your answer.
2. What is the weakest link in the Russian-Chinese relationship? How might the Russian state overcome this problem?
3. To what extent do you feel that Russian policy toward China threatens to turn Russia into a resource appendage of China?
4. To what extent do you see the cordial relationship between Russia and China continuing in the future?

SUGGESTED READINGS

Kaczmarski, Marcin. *Russia-China Relations in the Post-Crisis International Order*. London: Routledge, 2015.
Lo, Bobo. *A Wary Embrace? What the China-Russia Relationship Means for the World*. Lowy Institute. Docklands, Australia: Penguin Random House, 2017.
Lukin, Alexander. *China and Russia: The New Rapprochement*. New York: Polity, 2018.
Rozman, Gilbert. *The Sino-Russian Challenge to the World Order*. Stanford, CA: Stanford University Press, 2014.

Trenin, Dmitri. *From Greater Europe to Greater Asia? The Sino-Russian Entente.* Moscow: Carnegie Moscow Center, 2015.

Wishnick, Elizabeth. "In Search of the 'Other' in Asia: Russia-China Relations Revisited." *Pacific Review* 30, no. 1 (2017): 114–32.

NOTES

1. "Joint Statement of the Russian Federation of the People's Republic of China on the Twentieth Anniversary of the Treaty of Good Neighbourliness and Friendly Cooperation between the Russian Federation and the People's Republic of China," The Kremlin, June 28, 2021, http://static.kremlin.ru/media/events/files/en/Bo3RF3JzGDvMAPjHBQAuSemVPWTEvb3c.pdf (accessed September 6, 2021).

2. See Bobo Lo, *Axis of Convenience* (London: Chatham House, 2008); and *Russia and the New World Disorder* (London: Chatham House, 2015).

3. See Simon Saradzhyan, "Is Russia Declining?," *Demokratizatsiya* 24, no. 3 (2016): 339–418.

4. Gilbert Rozman, *The Sino-Russian Challenge to the World Order: National Identities, Bilateral Relations, and East versus West in the 2010s* (Stanford, CA: Stanford University Press, 2014). Also see Elizabeth Wishnick, "In Search of the 'Other' in Asia: Russia-China Relations Revisited," *Pacific Review* 30 (2016): 114–32.

5. Kenneth Anderson, "Text of Russia-China Joint Declaration on Promotion and Principles of International Law," Lawfare, July 7, 2016, https://www.lawfareblog .com/text-russia-china-joint-declaration-promotion-and-principles-international-law (accessed January 28, 2018).

6. Interestingly, this statement also includes an affirmation by both parties to human rights as universal, and democracy as "one of the achievements of humanity." At the same time, the statement makes it clear that it does not adhere to Western interpretations of these concepts, with Western practices condemned as interfering in the internal affairs of other states which possess the right to determine their own practices. See "Joint Statement by the Foreign Ministers of China and Russia on Certain Aspects of Global Governance in Modern Conditions," Ministry of Foreign Affairs of the Russian Federation, March 23, 2021, https://www.mid.ru/en/foreign_policy/news/-/asset_publisher/cKNonkJE02Bw/content/id/4647776 (accessed September 9, 2021).

7. "Sovmestnoe zaiavlenie prezidenta Rossiiskoi Federatsii i predsedatelia Kitaiskoi Narodnoi Respubliki ob ukreplenii rlobal'noi stratericheskoi stabilnosti," The Kremlin, June 25, 2016, http:www.kremlin.ru/supplement/5098 (accessed September 3, 2017); "Sovmestnoe zaiavlenie Rossiiskoi Federatsii i Kitaiskoi Narodnoi Respubliki ob ukreplenii rlobal'noi stratericheskoi stabil'nosti v sovremennuyu epoku," The Kremlin, June 5, 2016, http://kremlin.ru/supplement/5412 (accessed December 2, 2019); "Joint Statement on the Twentieth Anniversary."

8. "Sovmestnoe zaiavlenie Rossiiskoi Federatsii i Kitaiskoi Narodnoi Respubliki o tekyshchei situatsii v mire i vazhnykh mezhnunarodnykh problemakh," The Kremlin, July 4, 2017, http://kremlin.ru/supplement/5219 (accessed April 17, 2018).

9. See ibid. and "Sovmestnoe zaiavlenie Rossiiskoi Federatsii i Kitaiskoi Narodnoi Respubliki," The Kremlin, June 25, 2016, http://www.kremlin.ru/supplement/5100 (accessed March 23, 2018).

10. "Joint Statement by the Russian and Chinese Foreign Ministries on the Korean Peninsula's Problems," Ministry of Foreign Affairs of the Russian Federation, July 4, 2017, http://www.mid.ru/en/foreign_policy/news/asset_publisher/cKNonkJE02Bw /content/id/2807662 (accessed April 17, 2018).

11. "Sovmestnoe zaiavlenie Rossiiskoi Federatsii i Kitaiskoi Narodnoi Respubliki o tekyshchei situatsii v mire."

12. The idea of a "new type of international relations" is a Chinese construction, initially advanced by Xi Jinping to describe a new type of great power relationship between the United States and China. See "Joint Statement of the Russian Federation and the People's Republic of China on the Twentieth Anniversary." http://static .kremlin.ru/media/events/files/en/Bo3RF3JzGDvMAPjHBQAuSemVPWTEvb3c .pdf (accessed September 6, 2021).

13. Central Intelligence Agency, *The World Factbook*, www.cia.gov/the-world -factbook/countries/china/#economy; https://www.cia.gov/the-world-factbook/ countries/russia/#economy (accessed September 11, 2021).

14. 2019 Statistical Bulletin of China's Outward Foreign Direct Investment, Ministry of Commerce of the People's Republic of China, http://images.mofcom.gov.cn/ hzs/202010/20201029172027652.pdf (accessed September 16, 2021).

15. The Central Bank of the Russia Federation, http://www.cbr.ru/eng/statistics /macro_itm/svs/#highlight=investment%7Cdirect (accessed September 11, 2019); also see Vasily Kashin, "Is China Investing Much in Russia?," Valdai Club, September 6, 2017, http://valdaiclub.com/a/ highlights/chinese-investments-in-russia (accessed March 24, 2018).

16. World Bank, Indicators by Trading Partner, China 2019, https://wits.worldbank .org/CountryProfile/en/Country/CHN/Year/2019/TradeFlow/EXPIMP/Partner/by -country (accessed September 11, 2021).

17. Percentages extrapolated from World Bank, Indicators by Trading Partner, China 2019, World Bank, Indicators by Trading Partner, China 2016; https://wits.worldbank .org/CountryProfile/en/Country/CHN/Year/2016/TradeFlow/EXPIMP (accessed September 11, 2021); Indicators by Trading Partner Russia 2016, https://wits .worldbank.org/CountryProfile/en/Country/RUS/Year/2016/TradeFlow/EXPIMP/ Partner/RUS/Product/all-groups; Indicators by Trading Partners Russia 2019, https:// wits.worldbank.org/CountryProfile/en/Country/RUS/Year/2019/TradeFlow/EXPIMP /Partner/RUS/Product/all-groups (accessed September 16, 2021).

18. Vladimir Milov, "The 'Manchurian President': Vladimir Milov on How Russia Became a Raw-Materials Appendance of Beijing," *The Insider*, June 30, 2021, https: //theins.ru/en/opinion/vladimir-milov/242596 (accessed August 30, 2021).

19. Vladimir Putin, "Valdai Discussion Club Session," The Kremlin, October 3, 2019, http://en.kremlin.ru/events/president/news/61719 (accessed November 12, 2019); Milov, "How Russia Became."

20. The members of the EEU are Russia, Kazakhstan, Belarus, Armenia, and Kyrgyzstan.

21. "Zhonghua renmin gongheguo yu eluosi lianbang guanyu sichou zhi lu jingji dai jianshe he jianshe duijie hezuo de lianhe shengmin (quanwen)," May 9, 2015, http://www.qstheory.cn/ zhunqu/zywz/2015-05/09/c_1115229503.htm (accessed September 16, 2015).

22. "Guanyu 2018 nian 5 yue 17 ri quanshude 'Zhonghua Renmin Gongheguo yu Ouya Jingji Lianmeng Jingmao Hezuo Xieding' shengxiaode lianghe shengming," *Renmin Ribao*, October 26, 2018.

23. "Sopriazhenue EAES i EPshP priobretaet real'nye ochertaniia: soglasovan spisok infrastrukturnykh proektov," January 3, 2017, http://www.eurasiancommission .org/ru/nae/news/Pages/2-03-2017-1.aspx (accessed November 4, 2020).

24. In 2016, the World Bank data reported China having a greater total trade volume for Kazakhstan than Russia.

25. Zhang Yunbi and Zhang Yue, "Xi Backs Building of Polar Silk Road," *China Daily*, November 2, 2017, http://www.chinadaily.com.cn/world/cn_eu/2017-11/02/ content_ 34007511.htm (accessed April 10, 2018).

26. "China's Arctic Policy," State Council Information Office, January 2018, http://english.gov.cn/archive/white_paper/2018/01/26/content_281476026660336.htm (accessed April 11, 2018).

27. Alexander Gabuev, and Ivan Zuenko. "The 'Belt and Road' in Russia: Evolution of Expert Discourse." *Russia in Global Affairs* 16, no. 4 (2019): 142–163.

28. Ankur Shah, "Russia Loosens Its Belt," Foreign Policy, July 16, 2020, https://foreignpolicy.com/2020/07/16/russia-china-belt-and-road-initiative/ (accessed August 1, 2020).

29. See Ethan Meick, "China-Russia Military-to-Military Relations: Moving Toward a Higher Level of Cooperation," US-China Economic and Security Review Commission, Staff Research Report, March 20, 2017; and Dmitry Gorenburg, "An Emerging Strategic Partnership: Trends in Russia-China Military Cooperation," World Press, April 29, 2020, https://russiamil.wordpress.com/2020/04 /29/an-emerging-strategic-partnership-trends-in-russia-china-military-cooperation/ (accessed August 8, 2020).

30. Meick, "China-Russia Military-to-Military Relations," 18.

31. SIPRI, TIV of arms exports from Russia 2019–2020, https://armstrade.sipri.org /armstrade/html/export_values.php (accessed September 17, 2021).

32. See Sebastien Roblin, "China Stole This Fighter from Russia—and It's Coming to the South China Sea," *National Interest*, July 24, 2016.

33. Vladimir Putin, "Zasedanie Diskussionnogo Kluba Valdai," October 3, 2019, http://kremlin.ru/events/president/news/61719 (accessed June 23, 2020).

34. Schwartz, "Russia-China Defense Cooperation," 6–7.

35. Nina Sidorkova, "Serdukov rasskazal o sud'be kontrakta c Kitaem po tiazhelomu vertoletu AHL," *Politika,* November 8, 2018, https://www.rbc.ru/politics/08/11 /2018/5be309289a794718634661b8 (accessed February 1, 2020). Of course, technically the importation of Ukrainian aircraft engines into Russia is a violation of the Ukrainian trade embargo, but such transfers continue, if at a reduced volume.

36. Gorenburg, "An Emerging Strategic Partnership."

37. Pavel Felgenhauer, "Gruz-400: Zavisimost' Rossii ot Kitaia narastaet s kazhdym dnem," Info Resist, February 22, 2019, https://inforesist.org/zavisimost-rossiya -ot-kitaya-narastaet-s-kazhdym-dnem/ (accessed August 28, 2021); "Russian Newspaper Deletes Article by Defense Analyst Who Accused Moscow of Sabotaging Long-Range Missile Shipment to China," Meduza, February 25, 2019, https://meduza .io/en/feature/2019/02/25/russian-newspaper-deletes-article-by-defense-analyst-who -accused-moscow-of-sabotaging-long-range-missile-shipment-to-china (accessed August 28, 2021).

38. Denis Abramov, "In Arms Trade, China Is Taking Advantage of Russia's Desperation," *Moscow Times*, November 1, 2016.

39. See Dimitri Simes, Jr., "China Rises from Russian Customer to Competitor in Arms Industry," *Nikkei Asia*, January 22, 2021, https://asia.nikkei.com/Politics /International-relations/China-rises-from-Russian-customer-to-competitor-in-arms -industry (accessed September 19, 2021); Michael Kofman, "The Emperors' League: Understanding Sino-Russian Defense Cooperation, War on the Rocks," August 6, 2020, https://warontherocks.com/2020/08/the-emperors-league-understanding-sino -russian-defense-cooperation (accessed September 18, 2021).

40. Paul Stronski and Nicole Ng, "Cooperation and Competition: Russia and China in Central Asia, the Russian Far East, and the Arctic," Carnegie Endowment for International Peace, February 2018, https://carnegieendowment.org/2018/02 /28/cooperation-and-competitionrussia-and-china-in-central-asia-russian-far-east-and -arctic-pub-75673 (accessed February 7, 2018).

41. See Stephen K. Wegren, Alexander M. Nikulin, and Irina Trotsuk, "Russia's Tilt to Asia and Implications for Agriculture," *Eurasian Geography and Economics* 56, no. 2 (2015): 127–49.

42. Alexander Gabuev and Maria Repnikova, "Why Forecasts of a Chinese Takeover of the Russian Far East Are Just Dramatic Myth," Carnegie Moscow Center, July 14, 2017, https:// carnegie.ru/2017/07/14/why-forecasts-of-chinese-takeover-of-russian-far-east-are-justdramatic-myth-pub-71550 (accessed August 2, 2017).

43. Stronski and Ng, "Cooperation and Competition," 18.

44. Dmitri Simes, Jr. and Tatiana Simes, "Moscow's Pivot to China Falls Short in the Russian Far East," *South China Morning Post*, August 29, 2021, https:// www.scmp.com/week-asia/politics/article/3146505/moscows-pivot-china-falls-short -russian-far-east (accessed September 18, 2021).

45. Andrei Zakharov and Anastasia Napalkova, "Why Chinese Farmers Have Crossed the Border into Russia's Far East," BBC Russian Service, November 1, 2019, https://www.bbc.com/news/world-europe-50185006 (accessed November 2, 2019).

46. Alexander Gabuev and Gary Shtraks, "China's One Belt, One Road Initiative and the Sino-Russian Entente" (policy Q & A, National Bureau of Asian Research, August 9, 2016), https://carnegie.ru/2016/08/09/china-s-one-belt-one-road-initiative -and-sino-russian-ententepub-64297 (accessed August 15, 2016).

47. Simes and Simes, "Moscow Pivot to China Falls Short."

48. Jeanne Wilson, "Russia and China in Central Asia: Deepening Tensions in the Relationship," *Acta Via Serica* 1 (June, 2021): 1–24, doi: 10.22679/ sbd.3032.6.2.003; Temur Umarov, "China Looms Large in Central Asia," Carnegie

Moscow Center, March 30, 2020, https://carnegiemoscow.org/commentary/81402 (accessed April 5, 2020).

49. Sergei Lavrov, "Vystuplenie i otvety na voprosy ministra inostrannykh del Rossii S.V. Lavrova v Rossiisko-Tadzhikskom (Slaviznskom) Universitete, Dushanbe, 5 fevralia 2019 goda," Russian Ministry of Foreign Affairs, May 2, 2019, https://www.mid.ru/ru/maps/tj/-/asset_publisher/VfByAd5UOwu3/content/id/3501226 (accessed August 5, 2020).

50. Bradley Jardine and Edward Lemon, "In Russia's Shadow: China's Rising Security Presence in Central Asia." *Kennan Cable*, no. 52, 2020, May. Wilson Center, https://www.wilsoncenter.org/publication/kennan-cable-no-52-russias-shadow-chinas-rising-security-presence-central-asia (accessed June 4, 2020).

51. Niva Tsz Yan Yau, Governance Effects of China in Central Asia. Program Event. Foreign Policy Research Institute, December 10, 2020; Temur Umarov. "Dangerous Liaisons: How China is Taming Central Asian Elites." *Carnegie Moscow Center*, January 29, 2021, https://carnegiemoscow.org/commentary/83756 (accessed February 3, 2021).

52. Erzhan Kerimbaev, Nabizhan Mukhametkhanuly, Aynur Turgenbay, and Zaura Nabizhankyzy. "Main Factors of China's Soft Power in Central Asia." *Central Asia and the Caucasus*, February 1, 2020; https://www.ca-c.org/online/2020/journal_eng/cac-01/02.shtml (accessed January 2, 2021).

53. Michael Swaine, "Chinese Views and Commentary on Periphery Diplomacy," *Chinese Leadership Monitor*, 44 (Summer), 2014, https://www.hoover.org/research/chinese-views-and-commentary-periphery-diplomacy (accessed January 5, 2015).

54. Xi, Jinping "The Central Conference on Worker Relations to Foreign Affairs Was Held in Beijing," Ministry of Foreign Affairs, November 29, 2014, https://www.fmprc.gov.cn/mfa_eng/zxxx_662805/t1215680.shtml (accessed April 16, 2021).

55. It is not clear, however, how effective this body can be given the likelihood of disparate aims among its membership.

56. See, for example, Alexander Lukin, "Sino-Russian Cooperation as the Basis for Greater Eurasia," *Human Affairs* 30 (2020): 174–188. Sergei Karaganov, "From East to West or Greater Eurasia?," *Russia in Global Affairs*, October 25, 2016, https://eng.globalaffairs.ru/articles/from-east-to-west-or-greater-eurasia/ (accessed January 2, 2017); Valdai Report, *Toward the Great Ocean—6: People, History, Identity, Education*, Valdai Discussion Club, 2018, https://valdaiclub.com/files/19357/ (accessed February 2, 2019).

57. David Lewis, "Geopolitical Imaginaries in Russian Foreign Policy: The Evolution of 'Greater Eurasia,'" *Europe-Asia Studies* 70, no. 10 (2018): 1612–37.

58. Vladimir Putin, "Zasedanie Diskussionnogo Kluba Valdai," October 3, 2019; http://kremlin.ru/events/president/news/61719. (accessed November 2, 2019).

59. See Country Reports: Russia (January 2021), The Asan Forum, http://www.theasanforum.org/country-report-russia-january-2021 (accessed March 3, 2021).

60. Gilbert Rozman, "Multipolarity Versus Sinocentrism: Chinese and Russian Worldviews and Relations," The Asan Forum, August 27, 2020, https://theasanforum

.org/multipolarity-versus-sinocentrism-chinese-and-russian-worldviews-and
-relations/ (accessed January 12, 2021).

61. Alexander Lukin, "Have We Passed the Peak of Sino-Russian Rapprochement?," *Washington Quarterly* 44, no. 3 (2021): 155–73; see also Igor Denisov and
Aleksander Lukin, "Korrektsiia i Khedzhirovanie," *Rossiia v Global'noi Politike* 4
(2021): 154–72.

62. See, for example, Charles Kupchan, "The Right Way to Split China and Russia:
Washington Should Help Moscow Leave a Bad Marriage," *Foreign Affairs*, August
4, 2021, https://www.foreignaffairs.com/articles/united-states/2021-08-04/right-way
-split-china-and-russia (accessed August 4, 2021); Andrea Kendall-Taylor and David
Shullman, "A Russian-Chinese Partnership Is a Threat to U.S. Interests," *Foreign
Affairs*, May 14, 2019; https://www.foreignaffairs.com/print/1124283 (accessed May
20, 2019).

63. See Xie Wenting and Bai Wenyi, "US Cannot Break China-Russia Strategic
Partnership as It's Based on National Interests: Alexander Lukin," *Global Times*, July
12, 2021, https://www.globaltimes.cn/page/202107/1228458.shtml (accessed July 15,
2021); Alexander Gabuev, "As Russia and China Draw Closer, Europe Watches with
Foreboding," Carnegie Moscow Center, March 19, 2021 (accessed March 30, 2021).

Chapter 15

Energy

Stefan Hedlund

In Russia, everything is about oil. This is the very essence of being a "petro-state." The importance of revenue from oil exports is such that pretty much any important change in socioeconomic indicators may be traced back to fluctuations in the price of oil. This holds true across the board, for GDP growth, manufacturing, budget performance, consumer expenditure, and more. Perhaps most importantly, the dollar/ruble exchange rate has tended to follow the dollar price of oil very closely.[1]

This said, the Russian energy complex also includes a large gas industry. In terms of energy content, the two are just about equal, producing around five hundred million tons of oil equivalent each year. But their respective roles are miles apart. While Russia exports three-quarters of its oil output, it consumes nearly two-thirds of its gas at home, at low regulated prices. In the words of Thane Gustafson, "without much exaggeration, one could say there is a division of roles: oil pays the bills abroad, while gas subsidizes the economy at home."[2]

One of many implications of the dependence on oil revenue is that any ambition to forecast the performance of the Russian economy has boiled down to forecasting movements in the price of oil. Since analysts do not have a particularly impressive track record in forecasting the price of oil, it is not surprising that forecasts of Russian economic performance have also tended at times to be rather far removed from reality.

These observations not only underscore how hard it has been to get matters right in assessing developments in Russia. They also illustrate how hard it is to govern a petro-state, as well as how economic policy is made hostage to the vagaries of international markets for oil and to infighting between powerful vested interests vying for access to ground rents.

This chapter provides an account of the emergence and development of the Russian energy complex. Following a brief look at historical legacies, it focuses on events after the collapse of the USSR. It describes how the oil and gas sectors went through very different processes of privatization, with different implications for corporate governance and for foreign involvement. It also provides an account of Russian pipeline politics and of the ambition to transform Russia into an "energy superpower." The chapter concludes with an outlook of what the future may hold.

SOVIET ENERGY

The history of Russian oil antedates that of the Soviet Union. The first discovery was made in the region around Baku, in present-day Azerbaijan, in the mid-nineteenth century.[3] The takeoff was marked in 1873, when a real gusher was struck.[4] That year also saw the arrival of the Swedish Nobel family, founders of the Nobel Brothers Petroleum Company. Over the coming decades Baku would constitute the hub of an oil boom that entailed the introduction of the world's first oil tanker and the world's first oil pipeline.

In the post–World War II era, Soviet oil production was marked by a geographical shift. Damage done to oil installations in Azerbaijan during the war caused efforts to be aimed instead at fields in the Volga basin and the Ural Mountains, where output continued to increase until about 1970.

The real game changer would prove to be Western Siberia. With the discovery, in 1969, of the supergiant Samotlor field, the region was poised for a spectacular takeoff. Over the years from 1970 until 1977, annual output increased sevenfold. Stephen Kotkin may well be right in stating that "without the discovery of Siberian oil, the Soviet Union might have collapsed decades earlier."[5] It was a tremendous bonanza, producing a strong sense of complacency.

As fields in the Volga-Urals region went into decline, the Soviet oil industry became increasingly dependent on fields in the Tyumen region, especially Samotlor. Little was done to explore for new fields that might have broadened the basis. As oil is a "wasting resource," meaning that pumping will inevitably lead to exhaustion, this was a recipe for deep trouble down the road. In 1977, the CIA produced a set of three reports predicting that Soviet oil and gas output would peak in 1980 and decline sharply thereafter.[6]

In that same year, General Secretary Leonid Brezhnev ordered a massive increase in resource inputs. By 1982, investment in the oil sector had nearly doubled, leading to a boost in output that, temporarily, more than offset the decline in older fields.[7] But it was no more than a quick fix, failing to address the endemic problems of lack of exploration, escalating costs of drilling, and a complete neglect of energy conservation.

Another short-term reprieve was found in an all-out wager on natural gas. In 1980, it was announced that the output of gas would be increased by nearly half over the coming five years. As the bulk of the reserves again were in Western Siberia, exploitation was coupled with the construction of six huge trunk lines to the European parts of the USSR. One of these, named Druzhba, or "Friendship," would extend all the way to Western Europe, allowing gas to be sold for badly needed hard currency. It remains to date the longest pipeline in the world.

The combined stories of Soviet oil and gas provide important insights into one of the main shortcomings of the Soviet economic growth strategy, namely, the belief that falling efficiency in resource use may be offset by boosting the input of resources. In the short term, this generates an illusion of success.

During 1970–1988, the volume of Soviet net energy exports increased by 270 percent, and in the early 1980s, energy exports brought in 80 percent of desperately needed hard currency earnings.[8] The downside of these achievements was that the energy sector crowded out investment in other sectors. In 1981–1985, it absorbed 90 percent of total industrial investment growth.[9]

The forced production techniques that were used to meet exaggerated production targets also caused damage to reservoirs, which led to lower ultimate recovery rates. Most important, the depletion rate for oil, that is, the share of new oil that simply offsets decline in older fields, was rising. By 1985, it had reached 85 percent.[10]

It was at this inauspicious point in time that Mikhail Gorbachev succeeded to power, as the last leader of the Soviet Union. When he set out to implement reforms he hoped would revitalize the Soviet order, he was hostage to an energy complex that had been transformed from an engine of growth into a millstone around his neck; it has even been suggested that the sharp fall in energy prices that marked the 1980s played an important part in the collapse of the USSR.[11]

The core of the economic legacy that was left for Gorbachev's successors may be defined as an overwhelming dependence on revenues from an energy complex that was running dry. Entailed here was a geographic dilemma that still haunts Russian economic policymakers. As the once supergiant West Siberian oil fields are being depleted, new reservoirs must be found and developed. This means moving into Eastern Siberia and the Far East, under highly complex geological and offshore conditions.

Gustafson sums up the contrast between old and new oil rather elegantly, noting that while the conditions of geology in Western Siberia had represented "an oilman's dream," those in the eastern regions represent "an oilman's nightmare."[12] The bottom line is that success will require new infrastructure and modern technology, neither of which is readily available without foreign assistance.

The story of Russian energy during the first couple of decades after the collapse of the USSR would on this count be marked by an ambition to have the cake and eat it too, to invite foreign energy companies to join while making every effort to deny them true ownership in the process. It was simply bound to lead to conflict and to a failure to realize potential long-term gains from true cooperation.

RUSSIAN ENERGY

The collapse of the Soviet Union has often been portrayed as being both sudden and unexpected. This is not entirely true. Although the abrupt nature of the endgame may have come as a bit of a surprise, well-placed insiders had sensed well in advance what was about to happen. And they had made their moves accordingly, in some cases with striking success in amassing vast personal fortunes.

The core feature in post-Soviet reform was privatization. As various members of the Russian elites rushed to agree that former Soviet state property must be privatized, they also began maneuvering for positions to secure the best cuts for themselves.

Some of those who moved to pick up major stakes in newly created private enterprises were insiders, senior bureaucrats with ample experience, and networks in the relevant ministerial structures. Others were outsiders, former operators in the Soviet underground economy who had developed skills that would be helpful in working the emerging market economy. Across the board, the process would be marked by at times egregious rigging and bending of the rules.

Given the sorry state of Soviet manufacturing (outside the military industries), the biggest prize in the process of mass privatization was commodities, mainly in the mining and energy industries. The latter in particular would prove to be a battlefield for at times heated struggles between different sets of actors, to the detriment of the formulation of a much-needed long-term development strategy.

Privatizing Russian Gas

An outstanding example of skills in "insider privatization" was provided by the last Soviet minister of gas, Viktor Chernomyrdin. His first step, taken already in August 1989, was to transform his ministry into a joint stock company, the RAO Gazprom, which he placed under his own leadership. Rumors have it that a sizable part of the stocks ended up in his own pockets, via holding companies controlled by him and his family and friends.

When Chernomyrdin was appointed prime minister by President Boris Yeltsin in December 1992, he handed the reins of power over Gazprom to his close associate Rem Vyakhirev. Throughout the Yeltsin era, the two would run in such a tight tandem that many began to question if it was the Kremlin that controlled Gazprom or if it was perhaps the other way around. In the important December 1995 elections to the State Duma, Chernomyrdin even launched a political party. Formally named "Our Home Is Russia," it was quickly nicknamed "Our Home Is Gazprom."

His hold on power would last until September 1998, when he was replaced by Sergei Kiriyenko. By then, Gazprom would have provided ample illustration of the impact of predatory corporate governance on corporate performance. The company abused its monopoly control over gas export pipelines to variously punish and reward foreign countries, and it developed elaborate schemes to "tunnel" profits into the accounts of privately owned companies serving as middlemen.

A case in point was ITERA, an opaque trading company headquartered in Florida. Founded in 1992 to trade consumer goods with Turkmenistan, it soon began exploiting its powerful connections to tap into the trade in natural gas. This move brought the company into a relation with Gazprom that would prove to be strikingly successful.

ITERA would over the coming years evolve into a small business empire of its own, expanding from an intermediary in trade to a major independent gas producer. It would pocket substantial margins on reselling Gazprom gas and would even assume effective control over some of its gas fields. By 2001, it had become the largest supplier of gas to other CIS states (former Soviet republics).

The spectacular growth of ITERA was remarkable, given that it operated in a sector that was so economically important and so heavily politicized. Over the decade from 1991 until 2001, Gazprom sales of gas to other CIS states were more than halved. What remained, moreover, was chiefly deliveries as payment for the transit of gas via Ukraine, Belarus, and Moldova. By the end of the Yeltsin era, Gazprom had withdrawn almost fully from trade with other CIS states.

In the meantime, the company had achieved little to no increase in gas production. Its failure to exploit the substantial resources under its control was especially striking when compared to the performance of independent Russian gas producers like Novatek, Nortgaz, and indeed ITERA. Its lackluster performance would last well into the Putin era.

Privatizing Russian Oil

The fate of Russian oil would be very different. The last Soviet minister of oil did not have the clout to rival the achievement of Chernomyrdin in preserving his ministry as a monolith. In September 1991, the Ministry of Oil was transformed into a joint stock company, named Rosneftegaz. But its assets would not long remain under unified control.

The Russian oil industry was subjected to subdivision and privatization, resulting in a near dozen formally independent oil companies. The leading actors would come from a variety of directions, representing insiders as well as (initial) outsiders. Some would be skilled managers, meaning that despite shady operations and massive personal enrichment, some companies would perform quite well in their core business of oil production. Across the board, the oil industry would also be opened up to participation by foreign oil majors in a process that would be rife with serious controversy.

The first spinoff from Rosneftegaz was created in November 1991, when the acting minister of oil, Vagit Alekperov, set aside three oil fields—Langepaz, Urengoi, and Kogalym—that he packaged into a new entity named Lukoil. Placed under his own control as CEO, Lukoil remains to date one of the major Russian oil companies.

In 1993, two further companies of subsequent renown—Yukos and Surgutneftegaz—were spun off. While the former would end up controlled by Mikhail Khodorkovsky, destined to become the wealthiest of all the Russian oligarchs, the latter was taken over by another prominent insider, Vladimir Bogdanov, whose role at the Ministry of Oil had been to supervise precisely that entity.

Although greatly diminished, the parent company, now renamed Rosneft, still accounted for more than 60 percent of the country's oil output. This was soon to change. The real watershed in the transformation of the Russian oil industry arrived in 1995.

Being in dire need of funds to cover gaping holes in the budget, the government embarked on a process of "loans for shares," whereby a group of private bankers advanced credits against collateral in the form of government-held blocks of shares in strategic industries. As the government did not and perhaps never even intended to repay the loans, the banks were allowed to recover their money by auctioning off the collateral. This they did to themselves, in rigged proceedings where there was rarely more than one bidder.

The end result was that a small set of well-connected operators were allowed to acquire major stakes in the country's most valuable industries at rock-bottom prices. This was the origin of the creation of the Russian "oligarchy" that would dominate Russian politics for decades to come. Private financial fortunes amassed via short-term speculation on currency markets and in government securities could now be transformed into substantial holdings of real assets with serious worth.

Given the prominent role that would be played by Rosneft in Vladimir Putin's subsequent "authoritarian restoration," it is intriguing to note how close it too came to being thrown to the wolves, along with the rest of the assets of the former Ministry of Oil. In 1998, still desperate to cover gaping holes in the budget, the Kiriyenko government tried but failed to auction it off.

ACCEPTING FOREIGN PARTNERS

Proceeding to the parallel involvement of foreign energy companies, the first steps were taken on Sakhalin Island, located off the east coast of the Russian mainland. The presence in this region of substantial hydrocarbon reserves had been known since the late nineteenth century, but due to the severity of the climate and the need to engage in technologically challenging offshore drilling, no serious operation was undertaken in the Soviet era.

Following the Soviet breakup, the Russian government decided to allow the entry of foreign companies. This implied accepting production sharing agreements (PSAs), whereby the foreign partner would be allowed to recoup all costs before the sharing of proceeds could begin. Although the Kremlin would later express great regret over this decision, at the time it did not have much choice. With the price of oil at just over $20 per barrel, Russia was in a financially and politically weak position.

The first PSA was concluded in 1994, for Royal Dutch Shell to explore the giant Sakhalin II gas field. Having acquired 55 percent of the shares, it assumed control over operations with no Russian participation. Phase 1 involved a giant offshore production platform that began delivering Russia's first offshore oil in 1999. Phase 2 also involved a liquefied natural gas plant that reached full capacity by the end of 2010.

A second PSA was concluded with ExxonMobil in 1996 to develop the Sakhalin I oil and gas field. Compared to the Shell venture, ExxonMobil took longer to get online, beginning production only in 2005. It was different also in having major Russian participation; although ExxonMobil assumed operating responsibility, it had no more than a 30 percent share. Again, in contrast to Sakhalin II, Sakhalin I passed cost recovery after only three years of operation.

The high-water mark of foreign involvement was reached in June 2003 with a joint venture between BP and the Russian Alfa Group. The merger called for the two sides to contribute their respective assets in Russian oil and gas, creating the country's third-largest oil company. It was not only the size of the deal—$14 billion—that caused banner headlines to appear. Even more important was the fact that BP would enter into the new venture—named TNK-BP—as an equal partner.

Markets hailed what was then generally viewed as the start of a new era of strategic energy cooperation between Russia and the West. The anticipated next step was a deal between ExxonMobil and Yukos, at the time Russia's flagship oil company. The stated vision of Mikhail Khodorkovsky, the CEO of Yukos, was to create a privately owned—and thus controlled—route for the export of Russian oil via Murmansk to the United States.

If successful, he would have provided himself with important outside protection in his increasingly confrontational relation to President Putin. But within the coming year, the Kremlin reversed course and proceeded to roll back the influence of foreign oil on all fronts.

Privatizing Exploration

During the Soviet era, responsibility for geological mapping and exploration rested with the Ministry of Geology. It enjoyed high political priority, being staffed by highly professional specialists educated at fine academic institutions. During the turbulent 1990s, that all changed. As government financing plummeted, massive reductions in staff led to cutbacks in exploration, which in turn increased the dependence of Russian oil and gas industries on a small number of supergiant fields that were entering terminal decline.

The government appears to have believed that the newly privatized energy companies would find it in their own interests to shoulder the burden of continued exploration. This might also have happened had they been provided with adequate incentives to make longer-term commitments. But that was not to be.

As the Putin era unfolded, it was becoming clear that the outlook for both oil and gas had become heavily contingent on new fields being brought online and on cutting-edge technology to make that possible. At a July 2008 meeting in Severodvinsk, Putin frankly noted, "The potential for growth based on the former resource base and outdated technologies has in fact been exhausted."[13] Knowing what was broken, however, was not the same as knowing how to fix it.

In the case of gas, large new discoveries had been made, ranging from the giant Kovytka field in Eastern Siberia to several smaller but jointly important fields on the Yamal Peninsula and the giant Shtokman field in the Barents Sea. The core question here concerns when and if these fields will be brought online. The track record of poor governance at Gazprom must in this respect be viewed as very serious.

The case of oil is again different. During the chaos of the Yeltsin era, the output of oil plummeted, from levels over ten million barrels per day (bpd) at the end of the 1980s to an average of six million bpd during the 1990s. In stark contrast to the continued stagnation of gas, the Putin era would witness substantial recovery, to over nine million bpd by 2008.

The latter was partly due to the skills of the new private owners, but the real key to the production upsurge in the early 2000s was that "the most profitable private companies are the ones that have squeezed the cream of their reserves the hardest." The inevitable consequence of this "predatory approach" was an enhanced need for more intensive exploration.[14]

PIPELINE POLITICS

When the Soviet Union built its first export pipelines to Europe, there was an obvious ambition to trade gas for much-needed hard currency. But there was also the added benefit of making the Europeans dependent on that gas. As this took place at the peak of the Cold War, it was not surprising that US president Ronald Reagan issued stark warnings to his NATO partners about willingly accepting such dependence. But the Europeans would not listen. Today, in consequence, the EU depends on Russia for about one-third of its gas, and the politics surrounding this dependence has become increasingly conflict ridden.

The key feature of a pipeline is that once it has been built, the parties are locked into mutual dependence. If the relation is purely commercial, this need not be much of a problem, but if it becomes politicized, then there will be no end to trouble. In the wake of the Soviet breakup, the Kremlin soon enough discovered that the dependence of states in its neighborhood on piped Russian gas could be exploited for political gain.

While governments that were deemed to be "friendly" would be offered discounted prices and secure deliveries, those that were not would be required to pay "market" prices and face threats of delivery disruptions. Those that found themselves in the "unfriendly" category would voice loud complaints about how Russia was wielding its "gas weapon" to make neighbors more pliant.

Although Ukraine was far from alone in getting the rough end of the stick, its size and strategic location between Russia and the EU would ensure that it was at the forefront of such confrontations. On two occasions, in January 2006 and again in January 2009, a standoff between Moscow and Kiev over the pricing of gas led Gazprom to shut down its deliveries. Since gas consumed by Ukraine is taken from pipelines that also transport gas to Europe, shutting down the flow to Ukraine also implied shutting down the flow to countries that had now become EU member states.

In its ambition to counter this type of behavior, the EU has been marred by the absence of consensus on how to manage the overall relation to Russia.

While Germany has remained positive toward increasing its dependence on Russian gas via the Nord Stream pipelines that transport gas via the Baltic from Vyborg in Russia directly to Greifswald in Germany, Poland and the Baltic states have voiced strong opposition, to the point of even conjuring up the threat of a new Russo-German pact against Poland.

Although the tensions over Ukraine have created banner headlines, Russian pipeline politics have been about much more than merely Gazprom and Ukraine. Relations with the newly independent republics in Central Asia and in the South Caucasus have also figured prominently.

While Moscow was the center of Soviet power, emphasis was placed on developing energy resources within the Russian Federation. When the Soviet Union collapsed, the governments in newly independent republics to the south turned to foreign energy majors for help in developing their long-neglected energy resources. As a result, Kazakhstan, Turkmenistan, and Azerbaijan were found to possess substantial reserves, mainly but not exclusively offshore in the Caspian Sea. These finds would have important implications, commercial as well as geopolitical.

Frequent reference would be made to the Great Game over Central Asia that was played out in the nineteenth century between the Russian and British Empires. This time around, the players had multiplied to include not only Russia and Britain but also China, America, and the European Union. China in particular would enter the fray with a voracious appetite for energy to feed its booming economy.

The problem for the new actors was that absent means of transportation, energy in the ground has no value. Gas extraction in particular would simply not be possible without pipelines, and the existing pipeline grid was controlled by Russia. Further developments would in consequence be heavily focused on pipelines. In the early stages it looked like Moscow would be able to retain its control, but that would change.

The first challenge to Russian hegemony emerged from Kazakhstan, where exploitation of the giant Tengiz field would serve to redraw the map of global oil. Already discovered in 1979, it is the sixth-largest oil field in the world. Development began in 1993. In 2000, the role of Kazakhstan was enhanced even further with the discovery of the giant offshore Kashagan field, held at the time to be one of the most important discoveries in the world in the past thirty years. Following numerous delays, commercial production was finally begun in 2016.

When exploitation of the Tengiz field began, Moscow was successful in ensuring that the export pipeline was routed over Russian territory to the Russian Black Sea port of Novorossiisk. While Kazakhstan and its foreign partners thus remained firmly within the Russian orbit, the case of Azerbaijan would present a very different story.

In 1994, Azeri president Heydar Aliyev concluded a PSA with a BP-led consortium to begin exploiting the country's giant offshore oil and gas fields. Hailed as the "deal of the century," between 1997 and 2007 output from the Azeri-Chirag-Gunashli oil field would rise more than fourfold, triggering a boom that transformed both Azerbaijan and the way in which the regional game over oil is played. In 1999, BP added to its success with discovery of Shah Deniz, one of the largest gas condensate fields in the world.

The main reason that Azerbaijan would prove to be so important was that it dealt Russia the first real blows to its inherited transport hegemony. First was the Baku–Tbilisi–Ceyhan (BTC) pipeline, built to allow Azerbaijan to export oil via Georgia to the southern Turkish port of Ceyhan. Promoted by Washington for political reasons, it is the second-longest oil pipeline in the world after the previously mentioned Soviet-era Druzhba that links Western Siberia with Europe. First oil was pumped in 2005.

Then followed the Baku–Tbilisi–Erzurum (BTE) gas pipeline that became operational at the end of 2006. Also known as the South Caucasus Pipeline, it transports gas from the Shah Deniz field via Georgia to Turkey. The launch of the BTE was even more important than that of the BTC, in the sense that it could serve as a crucial link in a chain designed to transport substantial volumes of gas to Europe without crossing Russian territory. The reason this has remained hypothetical is that Azeri gas reserves are much too limited for this link to assume any strategic importance on its own.

A real game changer would be to construct a Trans-Caspian Pipeline (TCP) to link Azerbaijan with Turkmenistan. While total reserves in Azerbaijan are estimated at no more than 30 billion cubic meters (bcm), the combined long-term potential of gas from Kazakhstan, Uzbekistan, and above all Turkmenistan is in the range of 150–200 bcm, corresponding to about two-thirds of Russia's long-term potential.[15]

The possibility of actually building the TCP had been under periodic discussion since the mid-1990s but had been repeatedly delayed by disputes over the exploitation of oil and gas resources in the middle of the Caspian Sea. The speedy and successful construction of the BTE provided new impetus. By proposing to build its own pipeline, Nabucco, to transport gas into southeastern Europe, the EU threatened to deprive Moscow of its hegemony over energy flows from the Caspian basin to customers in Europe.

This challenge in turn placed in focus the need to secure long-term control over the sources of gas in Central Asia. Recalling the new Great Game, this is where Turkmenistan enters center stage. During the Soviet era, it had been an important provider of gas to other Soviet republics. Following independence, it embarked on a dual policy of exploiting this position, demanding higher prices and breaking its dependence on pipelines leading north to Russia.

The outcome on the former count was a long series of incidents involving pricing disputes and delivery disruptions. Given that the bulk of the gas it took from Turkmenistan was destined for Ukraine and onward to Europe, Gazprom agreed to substantial price hikes, firmly convinced it would be able to pass the burden on to its customers in the EU.

The threat of finding alternative routes for gas out of Central Asia was more serious. It was brought to a head in 2006 when China concluded a deal on a seven-thousand-kilometer pipeline that would allow it to purchase gas for thirty years starting in 2009. Although Russia would remain the major route for Turkmen export, the China deal indicated that the playing field was being widened. The Kremlin could no longer count on retaining its hegemony. The main cause for concern was that the pipeline to China would be followed by a pipeline route to Europe in the form of a TCP and Nabucco.

Estimates of total Turkmen gas reserves ran so high, to potentially twenty-two trillion cubic meters, that there was plenty of room to play a "multi-vectored" game of courting several partners. In 2006, the newly discovered Yolotan-Osman field was claimed to hold no less than seven trillion cubic meters of gas, representing more than double the reserves in Russia's giant Shtokman field. Yet, although Ashgabat embarked on gradually increasing foreign policy activism, Russia still appeared to have the upper hand.

The peak of the Kremlin's ambition to secure the Caspian basin was reached in the spring of 2007. Following lengthy negotiations, President Putin finally managed to secure a deal with Kazakhstan, Turkmenistan, and Uzbekistan to build a "Pre-Caspian," or Prikaspiiskoe, gas pipeline. Designed to hug the northern shore of the Caspian, it was to ensure that the bulk of Central Asian gas would continue flowing north into the Russian grid. The deal was generally viewed as a final Russian victory in the Great Game.

It was at this time, when it began to look as though a resurgent Russia was about to walk off with the spoils, that the notion of an emerging Russian "energy superpower" made its appearance. In the words of Fiona Hill, "Russia is back on the global strategic and economic map. It has transformed itself from a defunct military superpower into a new energy superpower."[16]

AN ENERGY SUPERPOWER

The first two terms of Vladimir Putin's presidency were marked by a truly seismic shift in Russian oil revenues. In market economies, price and quantity normally move in opposite directions. In the case of Russian oil, they began rising in tandem, and quite dramatically too. The price per barrel for benchmark Brent oil went from a low of $9.82 in December 1998 to $25.51

in January 2000 and to a peak of $144.5 in July 2008. Meanwhile, production volumes increased by more than 50 percent.

The sudden spike in petrodollar inflow had two rather unfortunate political consequences. One was that it generated a sense of complacency that put an effective end to the ambitions for radical economic reform that marked Putin's first years in power. By 2003, that game was for all intents and purposes over. Why engage in politically painful reforms when you can live high off the hog on oil revenues?

Even more sinister was that the overarching ambition to make Russia great again had found a tempting outlet. The deep economic depression during the 1990s had brought devastation to the country's erstwhile military superpower. Hopes in the early 2000s that rapid economic growth would build an economic superpower were also quickly frustrated. As the petrodollars began gushing in, the Kremlin was deluded into believing that by wielding its "energy weapon" it would succeed in reclaiming its coveted role as a major player in global affairs.

The envisioned creation of a Russian "energy superpower" would proceed along three tracks. First was the need to break the hold of the oligarchs and restore state control over the energy complex. Second was the associated need to roll back the influence of foreign oil companies, and third was the need to harness control over pipelines as a means of getting a stranglehold over the energy supply to other countries, including those inside the EU.

Breaking the Oligarchs

The task of restoring state control over the country's energy assets yet again brings home the difference between oil and gas. Viktor Chernomyrdin's success in preserving the assets of the former Ministry of Gas under unified control meant that restoring state control over Gazprom would mainly be a question of a changing of the guard. Once he had been elected president, Vladimir Putin proceeded to do precisely that.

In June 2000, Chernomyrdin was replaced by Dmitry Medvedev as chairman of the board, and in May the following year, Vyakhirev was in turn replaced by Aleksei Miller as CEO. Both of the new appointments were "friends of Putin," harking back to his days in St. Petersburg. While the new management team would prove quite successful in clawing back assets transferred to ITERA under Yeltsin, their skills as managers of a gas company would not be as impressive.

While independent gas producers like Novatek and Nortgaz scored a real takeoff and oil companies greatly increased their output of "associated gas," Gazprom registered a slight decline in output. Merely changing the guard had not led to improvement in the company's performance as a gas producer.

Restoring state control over the oil industry would be an altogether different matter. The process of insider privatization had created companies that in some cases provided their owners with ample resources to challenge the Kremlin. A case in point was Yukos, whose CEO, Mikhail Khodorkovsky, escalated his conflict with Putin to an open challenge for the presidency. The Kremlin retaliated by arresting and imprisoning him and by destroying Yukos.

The company was first presented with a claim for back taxes that would eventually reach $28 billion. It then had its assets frozen, meaning it could not settle the tax claim, and in conclusion its assets were sold at a series of rigged auctions. The prized asset was Yuganskneftegaz, representing about 60 percent of the Yukos total. On December 19, 2004, it was sold at an auction to recoup outstanding taxes.

Although Gazprom had been the originally intended buyer, the risk of international legal action to seize its assets abroad was deemed to be so large that a last-minute swap was made. The designated main beneficiary instead turned out to be Rosneft, at the time the only piece of the old Soviet oil industry that remained in state hands.

The single bidder at the auction was an obscure company named Baikal Finance Group, which had been created only two weeks before the event. The price it paid was $9.3 billion, representing just over half of the estimated market value. Only days later, it was in turn taken over by Rosneft, which also had been the source of financing for the deal.

The destruction of Yukos Oil stands out as one of the most controversial events of the Putin era. The degree of sheer vengefulness was such that Yukos, in Gustafson's words, "was not so much plundered as lynched."[17] Andrei Illarionov, at the time still Putin's senior economic adviser, also blasted the auction of Yuganskneftegaz as the "scam of the year."[18]

Following the absorption of Yuganskneftegaz, Rosneft emerged as Russia's second-largest oil company, producing 74.4 million tons. By 2010, with the giant Vankor field online, the company reached 115.8 million tons. It was then also one of the leading independent gas producers in Russia, with an annual output of natural and associated gas of about 12 bcm. The CEO of Rosneft, Igor Sechin, emerged as one of the most powerful men in Russia, with very close links to President Putin.

Gazprom, however, would not be left without gain. The conclusion of the Yukos affair had sent a powerful message to other members of the oligarchy, who would prove more than willing to bow to the Kremlin's demands. In September 2005, oligarch Roman Abramovich accepted to surrender the Sibneft oil company to Gazprom for $13.1 billion. It was the biggest-ever takeover in Russia, and it brought the company a fair bit of the way toward becoming an energy supergiant.

Rolling Back Foreign Oil

The ambition to roll back the influence of the foreign oil majors began where the first steps toward foreign involvement had been taken, namely, at Sakhalin. The Kremlin was particularly angered by the PSAs, which most observers would subsequently agree had been inherently unfair to Russia. Speaking in 2007, Putin would describe the Sakhalin II PSA as a "colonial project" that had nothing to do with the interests of the Russian Federation.

There were grounds for resentment. The PSA with Shell was signed when Russia was on its knees, giving the company the right to recoup all costs plus a 17.5 percent rate of return before Russia would get a 10 percent share of the proceeds. The Kremlin felt vindicated in its anger by the fact that the cost of the project had ballooned from an original estimate of $10 billion in 1997 to $20 billion in 2005, postponing the time when Russia would begin to receive income. This said, the means that were used to redress the imbalance came close to sheer extortion.

Shell suddenly found itself the target of a campaign claiming that serious ecological damage was being done. Faced with threats of a $50 million lawsuit and the risk of having its concession revoked, by December 2006 the company agreed to reduce its stake from 55 to 27.5 percent, allowing Gazprom to pick up 50 percent plus one share. Following this transfer of control, nothing more would be said about ecological damage.

The next victim was the TNK-BP joint venture. At the time of the original deal, BP had nurtured grand ambitions to develop the giant Kovytka gas field in East Siberia. Those plans had entailed building a pipeline to China, which Gazprom refused to accept. Faced with an added blank refusal to have its gas pumped westward, the company was restricted to the local market. As this fell far short of volumes stipulated in the licensing agreement, TNK-BP was faced with the same threat that had confronted Shell, namely, losing its license. In June 2007, it agreed to sell its stake.

Then followed ExxonMobil. Its operation of the Sakhalin I oil and gas field had also been linked from the very outset with plans for exports to China. In October 2006, it signed a preliminary agreement with the China National Petroleum Corporation. But Gazprom instead insisted that the full output from Sakhalin I be sent via its own Sakhalin–Khabarovsk–Vladivostok pipeline. In May 2009, the consortium agreed to sell 20 percent of Sakhalin I gas to Gazprom.

Leaving Sakhalin Island and Eastern Siberia, Gazprom would also become embroiled in controversy at the other end of the country. Offshore in the Russian sector of the Barents Sea lies the Shtokman field, one of the world's largest natural gas fields. Discovered in 1988, its estimated final output is comparable to the annual gas output of Norway.

Due to the extreme Arctic conditions prevailing in the area and a sea depth that varies from 320 to 340 meters, it was realized early on that Gazprom would not be able to go it alone. But the Kremlin was no longer ready to accept genuine partnership with foreigner companies. In 2008, Gazprom agreed with Total and StatoilHydro that they would be involved in organizing the design, financing, construction, and operation of the Shtokman infrastructure. Upon completion, their shares would be transferred to Gazprom.

It was symptomatic of the changing times that where the early Sakhalin pioneers—Shell and ExxonMobil—had succeeded in getting the Kremlin to accept PSAs that were clearly biased against Russia, in the Shtokman case the foreigners ended up offering their technology for a mere fee rather than an ownership stake or even a share in output. Putin's Russia had morphed into a very different kind of partner than that presided over by Yeltsin. The times of bargain basement dealing had come and gone.

Rounding off the story of trouble faced by Big Oil in Russia, in the summer of 2008, TNK-BP was shaken by a bitter internal power struggle that caused its CEO, Robert Dudley, to flee the country and be replaced by the president of the Russian Alfa Group, Mikhail Fridman. Given that TNK-BP accounted for a quarter of BP's output and a fifth of its total reserves, this was no small matter. But the saga of BP involvement in Russia was set to continue, with surprising new twists and turns.

In January 2011, markets were stunned by the announcement of a major deal between BP and Rosneft, aimed at exploring the Kara Sea on Russia's Arctic continental shelf. The deal entailed a share swap whereby BP would become the biggest nonstate shareholder in Rosneft, which is 75 percent controlled by the Russian government, and Rosneft would become the second-largest shareholder in BP.

The deal seemed to ensure ironclad political protection from the very top. Yet when the Russian Alfa Group co-owners of TNK-BP brought legal action, Prime Minister Putin did not have any objection. Following a four-month legal battle, BP had to face the fact that its proposed alliance with Rosneft had collapsed. The prize of Arctic hydrocarbon exploitation was again back on the market.

The next round was a strategic exploration partnership between Rosneft and ExxonMobil. Having long and positive experience of working together on Sakhalin, in August 2011 the two announced the first in a series of agreements that would entail investing up to $500 billion in developing Russia's Arctic and Black Sea oil reserves. In October 2012, Rosneft added that it would itself take over TNK-BP. The Alfa Group was paid $28 billion in cash to get out, and BP was offered a package of cash and a close to 20 percent stake in Rosneft.

The stage appeared to be set for long-term cooperation between Rosneft and ExxonMobil, taking the exploration for oil to entirely new levels. But then followed the crisis in Ukraine and the imposition of Western sanctions that target both Rosneft and its CEO, Igor Sechin. Following a drawn-out conflict with the US Treasury Department, in March 2018 ExxonMobil announced it was walking away from its Russian ventures, excepting that on Sakhalin.

A Pipeline Stranglehold

The very mention of the notion of an "energy superpower" presumes that the possession of large reserves of energy may be somehow "weaponized," which is a highly dubious proposition. It can, to begin with, not include oil. Oil does mean revenue, which in turn may help boost military production and thus indirectly support ambitions to achieve power. But oil cannot be construed as a "weapon" in its own right.

To the extent that Russia does possess an "energy weapon," it is in the form of pipelines for gas. Threats by suppliers of oil to cut off deliveries may be countered by turning to other suppliers, who may reroute their tankers. In the case of gas, that is not possible. Countries connected to the Russian grid of gas export pipelines would find that they were vulnerable to Russian pressure.

As discussed above, Gazprom has not been shy about using political pricing, coupled with threats of supply shutoffs, to reward countries that were loyal and to punish those that were not. Ukraine would find itself over time on both sides of the fence. Following the gas wars in 2006 and 2009, the Kremlin turned around and began offering substantial discounts on gas in return for political concessions. If Kiev abstained from seeking deeper relations with the EU, it would get both credits and cheap gas. Following the collapse of the Yanukovych government in 2014, all such concessions were withdrawn.

On a parallel track, the Kremlin also launched a project to reduce its dependence on Ukraine as a transit country by constructing bypass pipelines. To the north was the Nord Stream project that would pump gas to Germany via the Baltic Sea. To the south was South Stream, designed to pump gas via the Black Sea into the Balkans and Central Europe.

The outcome of this ambition at first was mixed. While Nord Stream I came online in 2011, South Stream was blocked by EU regulators. But by 2021 Gazprom had inaugurated its replacement Turk Stream in the south and added Nord Stream II in the north. As a consequence, Gazprom no longer needed Ukraine. Given the importance to its budget of transit fees, this greatly exacerbates Kiev's vulnerability to Russian pressure.

An additional ambition from the Gazprom side was to increase its commercial presence inside the EU by purchasing downstream assets. In Germany and the Netherlands in particular, it was very successful in picking up stakes in gas distribution companies. The crunch came in 2006, when British regulators moved to block an anticipated bid by Gazprom for Centrica, Britain's largest gas distributor. Gazprom CEO Aleksei Miller responded with a thinly veiled threat that the EU should not block Gazprom's "international ambitions" or the company could redirect its gas instead to markets in China and Japan.

By the time Putin handed over power to Dmitry Medvedev, who was duly elected president in March 2008, the rhetoric from the Kremlin was assertive. With only months to go before the global financial crisis would strike, the Russian elites seemed confident that their country had been returned to its rightful place as a great power.

The Europeans did have cause to be concerned. A complete cessation of the Russian gas flow at the time would have been calamitous for municipal heating systems and for energy-intensive industries. But as subsequent events would show, the Kremlin's assertive foreign policy rested on a serious underestimation of the opposition. The outcome would be a classic case of "policy blowback."

Western democracies may be slow to respond to challenges, but once they do, they are capable of harnessing considerable soft power. Propelled into action by the 2009 gas war, which left several EU member states freezing in the dead of a very cold winter, the EU took a series of highly effective measures to diversify sources of supply, to construct connector pipelines that allow gas to be transported between EU member states, and to implement conservation measures.

The core of its Third Energy Package, adopted in the fall of 2009, was a call for "ownership unbundling," meaning that gas producers would not also be allowed to operate transmission systems. This clause was so clearly pointed at Russia that it came to be known as the "Gazprom clause." Yet, in a further illustration of the lack of internal EU cohesion, the call for unbundling was not implemented. Germany continued to support Nord Stream and ruled that it was exempt from unbundling requirements.

This said, by the time Putin was elected to the presidency for a third term, in March 2012, the situation had been fundamentally transformed. A complete shutdown of the Russian gas flow to Europe would be problematic but no longer catastrophic. The edge of the "gas weapon" had been blunted.

OUTLOOK

The outlook for Russian energy is heavily marked by the fact that all the major fields in operation, oil as well as gas, have long since reached their peak and are now being depleted. In the case of Samotlor, so much water has been injected to maintain pressure that what comes to the surface is 90 percent water, causing it to be branded "the largest water company in the world."[19] Given how dependent the Russian economy has become on revenues from energy exports, this has serious long-term implications.

During the good years of abundant petrodollar inflow, the Russian government acted prudently to set aside a considerable part of that income into a precautionary Reserve Fund, to serve as a cushion against drops in the price of oil. In the aftermath of the global financial crisis, as oil prices increased, it served that purpose very well. The fund had been used up by the end of 2017, but the Ministry of Finance ensured that the federal budget would break even at oil prices just over $50 per barrel, less than half of what had been the case when the price of oil peaked. By 2020, the budget break-even price of oil had been reduced to $40 per barrel, allowing the government to add even more to its Reserve Fund.

While this shows that the consequences of being heavily dependent on oil revenue can be managed, skillful fiscal policy cannot remove the fact that Russia remains dependent on resource extraction, chiefly, albeit not exclusively, of energy.

The outlook for energy production in the short term is that Russia will remain on a plateau of reasonably stable output levels. Although there is little to suggest that Gazprom will improve its performance anytime soon, it is likely going to be able to maintain current output levels for some years to come.

The oil companies have for their part succeeded in "creaming" their existing fields to allow a continued uptick in output. Even if these increases have only been marginal, they have allowed new records of production to be set. Such forced extraction is clearly not sustainable. New fields must be both discovered and brought online, and this is not achievable without foreign cooperation, which in turn will not materialize while Western sanctions remain in place.

The precise impact of the sanctions on the regime is difficult to assess. There is general agreement that the economic sanctions have had a negative impact on economic growth; this is the case in particular for restricting access to financial markets. But the fact that the introduction of sanctions coincided with a sharp fall in oil prices has made the actual impact hard to assess; it has been drowned out by the sharp fall in petrodollar inflow.

Even greater controversy pertains to the impact on Russian actions. While it is clear that sanctions have not caused Russia to reverse its action in Ukraine, some have argued that they had the effect of deterring further Russian aggression, an argument that can never be proven since it hinges on presuming to know what the Kremlin may have had in mind.

With specific regard to energy, the sanctions were designed to exclude the gas sector and the impact on the oil sector has been iffy. Denying access to sophisticated technologies from service companies like Halliburton and Schlumberger has not prevented Russian oil companies from creaming their reservoirs. It is probably true that there will be an impact on greenfield exploration, but this is also in question.

Russia does have abundant reserves in the ground. The Arctic offshore in particular has been estimated by the US Geological Survey to hold one-fifth of all still undiscovered global reserves of oil and gas. It was the lure of these riches that prompted ExxonMobil to conclude its massive deal with Rosneft.

Yet, even if sanctions were to be lifted, this would not automatically translate into a renewed Russian energy boom. Arctic offshore drilling presents challenges that make it a very long-term undertaking, requiring high energy prices to be commercially viable. The sensitive ecosystem also makes it vulnerable to environmental protests, driven by concern over climate change. Similar caution pertains to new fields in Eastern Siberia and the Far East that are marked by severe cold and difficult geology. Successful exploration and exploitation will require cutting-edge technology that again makes the costs of extraction very high.

While the longer-term outlook for sustained Russian energy production must in consequence be viewed as gloomy, the more political shorter-term outlook for the construction of pipelines presents a more nuanced picture.

In its relations to the EU, Gazprom looks set to have continued success. With the Biden administration's decision to side with Germany and abandon sanctions on Nord Stream II, the path was cleared for it to come online. Last minute German licensing problems caused it to be postponed, again, in November 2021. Although South Stream had been blocked, that project did help to fatally undermine the EU's proposed Nabucco, which may well have been the real purpose. And the replacement Turk Stream came online in early 2020. All in all, Gazprom retains a form grip over the European market for natural gas. Looking toward the east, the Kremlin has been less successful in building pipelines to China. While Russia was in a financially weak position, Beijing was keen to strike megadeals on Russian oil that created banner headlines. It was not equally keen to do the same in gas. Its main priority there was to build an extensive network of pipelines into Central Asia that ensures it has an adequate supply of gas for its western provinces.

The combined outcome for Gazprom has been that its previously mentioned ambition to ensure continued hegemony over the flow of gas out of Central Asia via a "Pre-Caspian" pipeline has been blocked, and that long-discussed plans to build an Altai pipeline to pump gas from Western Siberia to China have been placed in doubt. This enhances the company's geographical dilemma of having its main reserves in the east and its main markets in the west.

Some relief is provided via the "Power of Siberia" pipeline, which finally came on line in 2019. It carries gas from Russian fields in the Far East to the northeastern part of China, where gas is in short supply. As in the case of oil, however, Beijing is presumed to have secured a bargain on price. And it still leaves open the question of broader infrastructure development that will be needed to fully exploit the energy complex in Eastern Siberia and the Far East.

Looking further into the future, plans are being drawn up for a Power of Siberia II pipeline that would take gas from western Siberia into eastern China via Mongolia, but when and if this will happen is shrouded in uncertainty.

The bottom line of the story of Russian energy is that the country has locked itself into a long-term strategy of dependence on resource extraction, coupled with authoritarian, predatory governance that impairs the introduction of efficient markets and production techniques. This is a legacy that will be very hard to overcome, even if Western sanctions are lifted and cooperation is resumed.

AUTHOR'S POSTSCRIPT

Russia's decision to launch an all-out war against Ukraine provided instant closure on three long-standing debates about Russian energy policy.

The *first* was to finally vindicate those who had issued persistent warnings about Russian use of energy as a weapon. The main purpose of Russian pipeline construction had allegedly been to create a situation where the gas flow to "unfriendly" countries could be shut down, without disturbing the flow to "friendly" countries like Germany. When Gazprom announced it was shutting down gas supply to Poland and Bulgaria, because they had refused to pay for gas in rubles, the European Union was forced to call an emergency meeting on its energy policy. Further reliance on Russian energy was suddenly viewed as deeply disturbing.

The *second* was to finally vindicate all those who had warned, ever since the 1970s, about the wisdom of Germany making itself so dependent on Russian energy. The German government had persisted in claiming that energy relations were purely commercial and must not form part of the security discussion. When Russia went to war, Berlin was forced into a deeply painful reassessment of decades of *Ostpolitik*, of claims that it knew better than the United States how to manage relations with Moscow. Its last-minute decision to scrap certification of the Nord Stream II pipeline was symbolic of how the roof had caved in, and of how Germany may now look forward to a deeply painful restructuring of its energy policy.

The *third* was to finally vindicate those who had argued that Russia must wean itself of dependence on hydrocarbon exports. Although the German government fought a valiant rearguard action to exempt energy from the sanctions regime, it was clear from the outset that Moscow would be faced with a future where Europe will wean itself of all energy imports from Russia. The impact on Russian gas exports will be massive, rendering all pipelines to Europe obsolete, and highlighting the absence of adequate infrastructure to pump gas towards the east. The impact on oil will be different, in the sense that oil is not entirely dependent on pipelines. Loss of the European market may be partly made up for by exporting oil to other markets, but this will be at higher transport cost, at lower prices, and under conditions where insurance companies will not want to touch Russian cargoes. In a landmark decision, Shell Oil announced it would not accept any blending of Russian crude into its oil supply.

—2022

DISCUSSION QUESTIONS

1. Why is it important to distinguish between oil and gas in the Russian energy complex?
2. What is the "geographic dilemma" of Russian energy?
3. Has the history of foreign involvement in Russian oil been a success?
4. How has Russia wielded its "gas weapon"?
5. Who are the players in the new "Great Game" over energy in Central Asia?

SUGGESTED READINGS

Fortescue, Stephen. *Russia's Oil Barons and Metals Magnates: Oligarchs and the State in Transition.* New York: Palgrave Macmillan, 2006.

Goldman, Marshall I. *Petrostate: Putin, Power, and the New Russia.* Oxford: Oxford University Press, 2008.

Gustafson, Thane. *Wheel of Fortune: The Battle for Oil and Power in Russia.* Cambridge, MA: Belknap, 2012.

Hedlund, Stefan. *Putin's Energy Agenda: The Contradictions of Russia's Resource Wealth.* Boulder, CO: Lynne Rienner, 2014.

Stulberg, Adam N. *Well-Oiled Diplomacy: Strategic Manipulation and Russia's Energy Statecraft in Eurasia.* Albany: State University of New York Press, 2007.
Yergin, Daniel. *The Prize: The Epic Quest for Oil, Money, and Power.* London: Simon & Schuster, 1991.

NOTES

1. A new set of fiscal rules introduced in 2015 finally caused the direct link between oil price and exchange rate to be broken. But the role of oil revenues remains overpowering.

2. Thane Gustafson, *Wheel of Fortune: The Battle for Oil and Power in Russia* (Cambridge, MA: Belknap, 2012), 3.

3. Steve Levine, *The Oil and the Glory: The Pursuit of Empire and Fortune on the Caspian Sea* (New York: Random House, 2007), chaps. 1–2 passim.

4. The story of early oil, and of early conflicts around oil, is told in Daniel Yergin, *The Prize: The Epic Quest for Oil, Money, and Power* (London: Simon & Schuster, 1991), part 1.

5. Stephen Kotkin, *Armageddon Averted: The Soviet Collapse, 1970–2000* (Washington, DC: Brookings Institution, 2001), 15.

6. Gustafson, *Wheel of Fortune,* 28–29.

7. Thane Gustafson, *The Politics of Soviet Energy under Brezhnev and Gorbachev* (Princeton, NJ: Princeton University Press, 1989), 64.

8. Gustafson, *The Politics of Soviet Energy,* 55–56.

9. Gustafson, *The Politics of Soviet Energy,* 39–40.

10. Gustafson, *The Politics of Soviet Energy,* 67.

11. Yegor Gaidar, *Collapse of an Empire: Lessons for Modern Russia* (Washington, DC: Brookings Institution, 2007).

12. Gustafson, *Wheel of Fortune,* 466.

13. Arild Moe and Valery Kryukov, "Oil Exploration in Russia: Prospects for Reforming a Crucial Sector," *Eurasian Geography and Economics* 51, no. 3 (2010): 313.

14. Leslie Dienes, "Observations on the Problematic Potential of Russian Oil and the Complexities of Siberia," *Eurasian Geography and Economics* 45, no. 5 (2004): 325 passim.

15. Roland Götz, "The Southern Gas Corridor and Europe's Gas Supply," *Caucasus Analytical Digest,* no. 3 (2009): 2.

16. Fiona Hill, *Energy Empire: Oil, Gas and Russia's Revival* (London: Foreign Policy Centre, 2004), i, http://fpc.org.uk/fsblob/307.pdf.

17. Gustafson, *Wheel of Fortune,* 314.

18. "Putin Aide Slams Yukos Selloff," BBC News, December 28, 2004, http://news.bbc.co. uk/2/hi/europe/4129875.stm.

19. Gustafson, *Wheel of Fortune,* 191.

Chapter 16

The Military

Bettina Renz

The rapid annexation of Crimea and the surprise Russian involvement in the Syrian civil war led many commentators to conclude that the West had seriously underestimated Russian military capabilities. There may be some truth in that, but now overestimation is the greater danger.

—Tor Bukkvoll (2016)

For more than two decades following the end of the Cold War, Western interest in the Russian military steadily decreased. Given the ongoing decay of the country's armed forces and the significant operational shortcomings their troops routinely displayed in the various conflicts they fought across the former Soviet region, it seemed that Russia's days as a global military power were over and that it was of relevance, at best, as an example of a "failed exercise in defense decision making."[1] Following the annexation of Crimea in spring 2014, developments in the Russian military and questions over the Kremlin's plans for using it reemerged as a major concern not only for its neighbors, but also for the West. It was clear that Russian military capabilities were significantly higher than they were during the 1990s and Moscow demonstrated increased willingness to use armed force as a tool of foreign policy. However, as noted by Tor Bukkvoll above, some Western assessments tended to overstate the scale of the changes that occurred, as Russia's poor operational performance in its escalation of the war against Ukraine in spring 2022 demonstrated. This chapter aims to provide some important historical, political, and international context required for a nuanced analysis of recent events. Outlining military reforms, developments in Russian military thinking, and continuity and change in the Kremlin's views on the utility of military force as an instrument of foreign policy, it suggests that the transformation of

Russian military capabilities and defense policy was neither as sudden nor as comprehensive as it appears.

THE RUSSIAN ARMED FORCES AND
POST-SOVIET TRANSITION

The sudden collapse of the Soviet Union did not take only the outside world by surprise. It presented the leaders of the fifteen newly independent states, including Boris Yeltsin as the president of the Russian Federation, with the unprecedented task of creating the political, societal, and economic structures and conditions required for their countries to function on an even basic level. Given the scale of the mission of state building, and the fact that Cold War tensions were much diminished, systematic military reforms were not considered the highest priority. Various programs initiated during Yeltsin's time in office demonstrated an awareness of the need for such reforms; but none of them resulted in fundamental modernization.[2] The country's conventional military capabilities deteriorated, as did the image of its armed forces, both internationally and within Russia itself. Yeltsin's failure to push through reforms was often attributed to his unwillingness to go against the wishes of the armed forces' conservative leadership.[3] It is important to consider, however, that other significant obstacles stood in the way of structured reforms during the 1990s.

The fate of the defunct Soviet armed forces, the personnel and assets of which were located across a vast region, including in Eastern Europe, was the most immediate concern. The process of relocating military personnel back to the Russian Federation alone was costly and preoccupied the leadership for several years.[4] Negotiations with the other newly independent states over the ownership of Soviet military hardware and bases were another difficult and time-intensive endeavor. In the case of particularly sensitive and valuable installations, such as the Sevastopol naval base, disputes were not resolved until well into the 1990s.[5] Given the weakness of the Russian economy at the time, even a comparatively high proportion of the gross domestic product (GDP) spent on defense—around 4 percent throughout Yeltsin's time in office—amounted to very little, especially compared to the volume of funding the Soviet armed forces had grown accustomed to during the Cold War.[6] The necessity to relocate personnel and assets back to Russia, in addition to the costs attached to retiring tens of thousands of former soldiers in order to reduce the size of the military to a more realistic level, meant that little time and money were left for significant modernization in the early post-Soviet years.

The newly created Russian armed forces were also immediately drawn into various violent conflicts that had erupted across the former Soviet territory, for example, in Transdniestria, Abkhazia, Tajikistan, and within Russia's own borders in Chechnya from 1994. These deployments were of significant scale, with estimates of around forty thousand Russian troops engaged in regional wars by the mid-1990s.[7] All of these conflicts continued for many years. Russian soldiers fought in some of these areas even before the country's Ministry of Defense was set up in May 1992, let alone before there had been a chance to reform or to prepare them for conflict scenarios other than conventional warfare in a European theater, for which they had been trained during the Cold War. The management of these ongoing conflicts preoccupied the political and military leaderships and made the pursuit of structured and well-thought-out reforms less likely, if not impossible.

Finally, while it is one thing to note that Russian military reforms during the 1990s were botched, it is quite another thing to assume that there was a clear pathway toward successful reforms that the leadership simply failed to follow. Yeltsin's government faced a task that went far beyond merely *reforming* or *modernizing* an already existing military. Instead, the Russian leadership had to *create* armed forces for a newly established state, operating in a domestic and global context that was fundamentally different from what went before. Military reforms in Russia were not a simple matter of downsizing, professionalization, or procuring up-to-date technology. Instead, all-encompassing structural, organizational, and doctrinal changes were required to make the armed forces suitable for the country's new system of governance and the post–Cold War security environment. When the Soviet Union had collapsed, it was far from clear what kind of military Russia needed or wanted, because its future, especially regarding its role as a global actor in a changing international security environment, was so uncertain.[8]

Russian military reforms were never going to be an easy undertaking and, for the reasons outlined above, very little systematic change was achieved during the 1990s. It is important to note, however, that Moscow's desire to reestablish and maintain a powerful military per se was never in question. Russia's self-perception as a great power has been a central feature in the country's identity dating back centuries.[9] This did not change when the Soviet Union collapsed in 1991. In the words of Margot Light, in the early post-Soviet years, "Russia was clearly not a superpower; indeed, it was questionable whether it was a Great power. Yet to ordinary people, as well as to politicians, it was unthinkable that Russia could be anything less than this."[10] Although military power is not the only characteristic on which a country's status in the international system is based, it has always been an indispensable symbol of strength for any great power, including for Russia.[11] As the Russian armed forces decayed during the 1990s, so did the country's standing as a global actor. It soon became apparent to the political leadership that a strong nuclear deterrent alone was not enough to uphold the country's great power status. The Russian Federation's first military doctrine, issued in 1993, already reflected the intention to maintain parity in conventional military strength with other great powers.[12] For the first decade of the post-Soviet era, however, this remained nothing but an unattainable ambition.

VLADIMIR PUTIN AND MILITARY MODERNIZATION

When Vladimir Putin rose to political prominence, first as prime minister in 1999 and then as president in March 2000, he made the restoration of Russia's international status as a great power, including a strong military, a priority from the outset.[13] The Second Chechen War, which commenced in autumn 1999 and was overseen by Putin as the new prime minister, revealed significant operational difficulties and reinforced the need for reforms. In a speech delivered in November 2000, Putin presented the conclusions reached from various meetings on military policy held by the Russian Security Council. Recognizing the work of service personnel operating in Chechnya, he explained that the conflict had demonstrated the armed forces' lack of preparedness to "neutralize and rebuff any armed conflict and aggression" against Russia, which, in his words, could "come from all directions." He also noted that the operations there had come at too high a cost and that the loss of soldiers' lives was "unpardonable," making reforms a necessity. In particular, Putin emphasized the need to restore the prestige of the Russian military within the country itself, including the image of the military career as a profession, which had suffered significantly during the troubled 1990s: "The problem is directly linked with national security interests. The trust of the army in the state and having the army 'feel good' about itself is the bedrock foundation of the state of the Armed Forces."[14]

Aided by a recovering economy, supported not least by rising oil and gas prices from 2000 onward, ambitions to rebuild Russia's conventional military power became yet again a realistic prospect, even without significantly raising the percentage of GDP spent on defense. Various areas of military reform that had already been identified during the Yeltsin years, such as increasing the number of professional soldiers, strengthening permanent readiness, procuring modern equipment, and rooting out corruption, returned to the agenda. The five-day war with Georgia in 2008, which resulted in a swift strategic victory for Russia but also demonstrated a number of ongoing operational difficulties, provided the impetus for accelerated reforms.[15] A wide-ranging military modernization program was announced the same year, supported in 2010 by an ambitious procurement plan, the State Armament Program to 2020.

Under the leadership of a civilian defense minister with a background in finance and accounting—Anatoly Serdiukov—the 2008 modernization program, which focused on making the Russian armed forces more usable by increasing their efficiency and cost-effectiveness, was implemented with unprecedented determination and financial backing. The program encompassed a wide spectrum of changes. A move from divisions to smaller brigades was intended to improve the mobility and combat readiness of the ground forces. Understaffed mobilization units—a remnant of the Soviet past—were disbanded to create room for more units with permanent readiness. Central command bodies were streamlined, and the size of the officer corps, which had made the Russian military too top-heavy, was slashed. Efforts were made to enhance the recruitment of professional soldiers and to lessen the reliance on conscription, including measures aimed at improving the image of military careers, such as higher salaries and better welfare provisions. The education of soldiers was adjusted to make it relevant for the twenty-first-century security environment.[16] Large-scale interservice exercises, which had not been held during the 1990s for financial reasons, were reintroduced.[17] Finally, Serdiukov's reforms were accompanied by an ambitious procurement plan, seeking to modernize 70 percent of the military hardware by 2020.

It is beyond doubt that these reforms have been an unambiguous success in making the Russian military incomparably better than it was during the 1990s. Although very little physical force was used for the annexation of Crimea, the operation there suggested vast improvements in command and control and showed that Russian military planners were able to fine-tune tactics to the requirements of a specific situation, rather than relying on overwhelming force as they had done in the past. The air campaign over Syria commencing in 2015 showed that Moscow's conventional military reach was no longer restricted to its immediate neighborhood. It also exhibited a range of new technologies that Russia had not used in armed conflicts before. The operations in Crimea and Syria heightened Russia's international image as a serious military actor and also vastly improved the prestige of the military as an organization and employer domestically.[18] Improvements in capabilities, performance, and image compared to the 1990s did not mean, however, that all obstacles in the way of reforming the military have been decisively overcome, or indeed that Russia had achieved the parity in conventional military power with the West that it desired.

Russia's outdated defense industry precluded the modernization of military hardware during the 1990s, and problems in this area are still a restraint on Moscow's ambitions. Although the need to overcome the technology gap between Russian and Western producers was addressed in the reform plans of 2008, systemic deficiencies, like outdated management practices, an obsolete manufacturing base, a lack of innovation culture, and corruption, could not be rooted out in a few years. On the one hand, the State Armament Program to 2020 resulted in impressive technological modernization of the armed forces. The interim target of updating 30 percent of equipment by 2015 was even exceeded in certain areas, with particularly notable upgrades of the strategic nuclear arsenal, air defense systems, and a large number of new aircraft made available to the air force.[19] On the other hand, the State Armament Program has been less successful in delivering equipment that would make Russian technology truly modern, especially compared to the most advanced armed forces of the West. Plans for the serial production and delivery of next-generation platforms, such as the Armata main battle tank and the fifth-generation PAK FA fighter, which have been in development for many years, have not been realized.[20]

In the last few years, under President Putin's advocacy, ambitious plans for Russia's progress in Artificial Intelligence (AI) have been laid out and AI research and development is rapidly growing. A National Strategy for the Development of Artificial Intelligence Development up to 2030 was unveiled in October 2019.[21] However, Russia entered the AI race relatively late, and it has been noted that its capabilities in this area should not be overstated.[22]

Most significantly for global power projection, the restoration of the Russian navy turned out to be a difficult undertaking.[23] Although a large proportion of funding from the State Armament Program to 2020 was allocated to naval modernization, the defense industry has been unable to deliver the quantity and quality of large surface vessels required for a blue-water navy. Western sanctions on the export of military and dual-use equipment into Russia were particularly painful in this respect because many electronic components on Russian ships were foreign made.[24]

In spring 2018 a new State Armament Program to 2027 was introduced.[25] It was noted that its outlook was "more cautious and conservative in terms of ambition" than its predecessor, prioritizing further modernization of the nuclear triad and upgrading existing systems at the expense of new and innovative products. Most notably, in view of the production problems experienced since 2011, naval ambitions were apparently lowered significantly, with a shift in focus from the creation of a blue-water navy to strengthening existing capabilities in coastal protection.[26]

Owing to official secrecy and the difficulties of comparing defense expenditures across nations, accurate estimates of Russia's defense budget are difficult. Comparisons based on market exchange rates, like the numbers offered by SIPRI, indicate that the country is spending up to ten times less on its military than, for example, the United States and that its budget is much closer in scale to medium-sized states like the UK or France. Economic experts have noted, however, that such comparisons can be misleading, because costs (for example, of technology and salaries) vary significantly between countries. As such, estimates of Russian military expenditure based on purchasing power exchange rates indicate that its budget, although lower than that of the United States and China, is more substantial than often claimed.[27] This does not mean, however, that financial factors are no longer a restraint on the Kremlin's military ambitions. Given the economy's reliance on energy exports, the Russian defense budget is subject to volatile gas and oil prices. When global energy prices declined in the years up to 2015, military expenditure required to sustain the modernization plans pushed up defense spending to more than 5 percent of the GDP.

The size of the Russian armed forces is set at a maximum of just over one million soldiers by presidential decree. This figure has been difficult to achieve, even with the continuing practice of filling the ranks with conscripts. Although exact numbers are not known, and even official Russian estimates are often contradictory, according to Defense Minister Sergei Shoigu, the numerical strength of the armed forces by 2020 stood at approximately 900,000 soldiers, of which around 225,000 were conscripts, 405,100 contract soldiers, and the rest officers.[28] A reduction in the terms of conscription from two years to one year in 2008 reportedly helped diminish problems with draft evasion and *dedovshchina*—a brutal practice of hazing that had made military service particularly unpopular.[29] On the flip side, shorter service also had a negative impact on the levels of training and experience gained by conscripts before they enter into the reserves, and thus on their preparedness to engage in any potential combat operation. 2014 plans to increase the number of contract soldiers to 499,200 were subsequently revised down to 425,000 and then increased again to the current aspiration of 475,600 by 2027.[30] There are questions whether, even with adequate funding, this number will be achievable. As a Russian journalist noted in 2016, although the popular image of the military in the country had massively improved in recent years, "the popularity of the army is growing quicker than the actual willingness to serve."[31] There is also evidence to suggest that many professional soldiers do not renew their contract after an initial three-year term, indicating, as Aleksandr Golts claimed, "that the conditions of service must not be as attractive as described by the military propagandists."[32]

Russian military modernization since 2008 has successfully overcome many of the problems the country's armed forces experienced due to the long period of neglect following the collapse of the Soviet Union. Wide-ranging reforms, supported by significant financial backing, drove up their capabilities and combat readiness and restored their image as a formidable military both at home and abroad. At the same time, as their poor operational performance during the war against Ukraine in spring 2022 showed, modernization was far from complete, and the prowess of Russia as a global military power, especially when it comes to its conventional capabilities, still has serious limitations. Although the operations in both Crimea and Syria were a far cry from the often-shambolic efforts in the past, both were limited in scope and scale. As the performance of Russian forces in spring 2022 demonstrated, neither gave an insight into their capacity to conduct a large, combined combat operation against a near-peer state opponent. As was the case in the past, Russia's position as a military great power today is based, above all, on its massive nuclear arsenal.

HYBRID WARFARE IN RUSSIAN STRATEGIC THOUGHT

As noted above, military modernization cannot be achieved with structural changes and the procurement of advanced technology alone. It also requires adjustments to doctrine and strategic thinking in order to prepare the armed forces for dealing with a variety of possible conflict scenarios and threats, which will vary from country to country and change over time.[33] Before the annexation of Crimea, analysts believed that the Russian military leadership's inability to move on from Cold War thinking on conventional war fighting had been a major obstacle in the way of reforms, while the West had made the transition to small wars and insurgencies.[34] This perception fundamentally changed in 2014, when the seemingly effortless annexation of Crimea, achieved with a minimum level of violent force, led some observers to conclude that Russia had developed "new and less conventional military techniques."[35] These techniques quickly became known as "hybrid warfare," a concept that became a focal point in Western discussions of Russian military capabilities. As Russia's all-out war against Ukraine in spring 2022 showed, it was problematic to evaluate the salience of the hybrid warfare concept from the operations in Crimea alone. In other words, the view of hybrid warfare as a new war-winning approach was too simplistic. The concept had to be understood within the context of wider developments in Russian military thinking.

It is by now a widely acknowledged fact that the term "hybrid warfare" (*gibridnaia voina*) did not originate in Russian military thinking. Although Russian strategists and commentators today often refer to it, they have done so only since 2014, once it had become popularized by Western authors.[36] The term itself is often traced back to a US author, Frank Hoffman, who had written a piece on the rise of hybrid wars in 2007.[37] Broadly speaking, Hoffman characterized hybrid warfare as a mix of traditional military tactics with unconventional and nonphysical approaches, including information and psychological tools. The use of hybrid warfare, in his eyes, could explain how, in some cases, weaker opponents could gain an advantage over technologically and numerically superior adversaries. Hybrid warfare seemed an apt description of Russia's approach in Crimea, because it was mostly unconventional and nonphysical tools, such as subversion and the use of "little green men,"[38] disinformation and propaganda, rather than reliance on traditional military approaches that led to the success in this case. The concept was useful insofar as it drew attention to the success of Russian military modernization in certain areas and highlighted potential new challenges for its neighbors and the West. As various scholars quickly noted, however, the success of the hybrid warfare approach in Crimea was due to a particularly favorable operational environment for Moscow, including the availability of troops already stationed on the peninsula, the lack of a coordinated response from the Ukrainian authorities and the international community, and a large pro-Russia civilian contingent that welcomed, rather than resisted, the annexation. A significantly strengthenen Ukrainian military since 2014 and an uncompromising national will to resist Russian aggression made a successful repetition of such an approach impossible in spring 2022.[39]

Since 2014 a body of literature has started to emerge on Russia's use of private military companies (PMCs), such as the notorious Wagner group, as a part of its "hybrid warfare toolbox."[40] Although Russian PMCs emerged in the mid-2000s, their involvement in the annexation of Crimea and in the war in Ukraine attracted broad international attention. Experts estimate that there are between ten and twenty Russian PMCs with personnel numbering into the tens of thousands.[41] Although some of these companies are purely commercial entities, the status of others remains murky and the boundaries between state and private interests are often blurred. Wagner, for example, acts mostly for Russian state agencies and evidence suggests that it is closely linked to Russian military intelligence and the Ministry of Defense. As such, groups like Wagner are better described as semi-state security forces, rather than PMCs in the Western understanding of the word.[42]

In recent years, Russian PMCs have also operated in countries as diverse as Syria, Libya, the Central African Republic, and Sudan, fulfilling a large array of tasks ranging from the guarding of infrastructure, personal protection, and training of local security forces to fully blown warfighting. Contemporary Russian military theory and doctrine does not yet suggest a clear vision of the role of PMCs in strategy, portraying such companies mostly as a Western phenomenon.[43] However, given their increasing visibility in various regions of the globe it seems clear that the Kremlin is experimenting with PMCs as a tool for achieving various foreign policy objectives. As Åse Østensen and Tor Bukkvoll concluded in their 2021 study of the role of PMCs in Russian foreign policy, their utility is not clear cut, and the deployment of PMCs can carry serious political risk in some cases. At the same time, the use of PMCs as war-fighting proxies has afforded the Kremlin plausible deniability for its actions, for example in eastern Ukraine between 2014 and 2022 and Syria. Moreover, the increasingly visible activities of PMCs in various African states have served to further Russia's great power ambitions and image by demonstrating its participation in the geopolitical contest for influence over the continent.[44]

Although the use of nonmilitary and unconventional tools in warfare, such as disinformation and psychological operations, or the use of semi-state security forces like the Wagner group, merits detailed study, such approaches never were the focus of Russian military thinking. As Charles Bartles pointed out in 2016, "Russia is experimenting with some rather unconventional means to counter hostile indirect and asymmetric methods, but Russia also sees conventional military forces as being of the utmost importance."[45]

Russian approaches to war fighting are grounded in a long history of strategic thought that is much more complex than a simple "Cold War tradition" and new "hybrid warfare" divide suggested. Even during the Cold War, conventional theater warfare with intensive firepower and mass militaries was only one strand in the debate.[46] Thinking about the utility of indirect and unconventional approaches, including information and psychological operations, also has always been part of the Russian military tradition.[47] During Soviet times in particular, a number of thinkers became known internationally for innovative, forward thinking regarding the role of advanced technology in future wars. During the 1970s they devised the concept of the "Military-Technical Revolution," the intellectual origin of the "Revolution in Military Affairs," which came to dominate US strategic thought during the 1990s.[48] The modern version of this forward-thinking and technology-focused view on warfare is the work by Russian authors writing about "sixth-generation war," where information, communication, and command and control are increasingly seen as the keys to success. As Timothy Thomas has noted, it is this tradition in strategic thought, rather than something completely new, that best characterizes the writings of those contemporary Russian authors that are often identified in the West as the originators of hybrid warfare.[49]

As the outline of Russia's military modernization in the previous section shows, the development of hybrid warfare approaches has not been a major focus. The aspiration of achieving an army of one million soldiers and developing its potential for global conventional power projection, in addition to maintaining and upgrading a strong nuclear deterrent, clearly demonstrates that Russia sought to modernize across the full spectrum of military capabilities. "Hybrid" methods that led to success in Crimea are likely to figure in low-intensity conflict scenarios in Russia's neighborhood and beyond in the future. However, it is also clear that the mastery of such methods does nothing for Moscow's feelings of insecurity vis-à-vis more powerful opponents or for its belief that a strong military is a prerequisite for great power status recognition. As demonstrated by Russia's escalation of the war against Ukraine in spring 2022, conventional war fighting remains a central concern of Russian strategic thought and military planning.

After the annexation of Crimea, the understanding of the hybrid warfare concept in the West has broadened. It came to be used not only to describe Russian military tactics, but the Kremlin's approach to foreign policy in general. For example, the use of disinformation aimed at Western audiences via state-sponsored media outlets like RT or Sputnik, or through social media and so-called troll factories, was often described as an expression of a hybrid war launched against the West.[50] From an analytical point of view, this conceptual stretching was always problematic. As Michael Kofman noted, the notion became almost meaningless as a result: "The term now covers every type of discernible Russian activity, from propaganda to conventional warfare, and most that exists in between. What exactly does Russian hybrid warfare do, and how does it work? The short answer in the Russia-watcher community is everything."[51]

THE MILITARY AS AN INSTRUMENT OF RUSSIAN FOREIGN POLICY

The reason the world's attention was sharply drawn to developments in the Russian military in 2014 was probably not so much the fact that the Crimea operation demonstrated stunning new military prowess or a new, war-winning hybrid warfare approach. More likely, it was because for the first time in the history of the Russian Federation, the country's leadership used armed force for territorial expansion. Such infringements of another state's sovereignty had not occurred in Europe since the end of World War II, and Moscow's actions were a blatant violation of international law. The fact that Russia had used its military in this way aroused suspicions that military reforms had been pursued by Putin, above all, to enable the goal of further territorial expansion. It created fears that Moscow's actions in Ukraine denoted a dramatic turnaround in foreign policy, a "paradigm shift," that when supported by modernized armed forces would lead to a "seismic change in Russia's role in the world."[52] There were expectations that the annexation of Crimea was part of a bigger plan and that further territorial conquest was highly likely. As the former US secretary of defense Leon Panetta noted, "Putin's main interest is to try and restore the old Soviet Union. I mean, that's what drives him."[53] Considering Moscow's ongoing military aggression against Ukraine since 2014 and the launch of a full-out war in spring 2022, these concerns were certainly justified especially regarding the threat this posed to the sovereignty of Russia's closest neighbors.

As mentioned above, Russian soldiers have been involved in sizable operations across the territory of the former Soviet Union since the end of the Cold War.[54] As such, Moscow's preparedness to use military force as an instrument of foreign policy is not a new development. Already during the early post-Soviet years, these interventions led to concerns that Russia's foreign policy in this region was driven by an imperialist agenda. As Zbigniew Brzezinski wrote in 1994, "regrettably, the imperial impulse remains strong and even appears to be strengthening. . . . Particularly troubling is the growing assertiveness of the Russian military in the effort to regain control over the old Soviet empire."[55]

Russia's imperial legacy has informed its decision to use military force in its neighborhood since the end of the Cold War. When the Russian Federation was established, its future role in the region and the world was uncertain. However, the idea that, owing to its history, the country had a special role to play in its neighborhood quickly established itself as a consensus view.[56] The 1993 Russian foreign policy concept unambiguously laid out what Moscow saw as its interests, rights, and responsibilities as the dominant security provider in what it often refers to as its "near abroad." At the same time, the Kremlin made clear its expectation that what it saw as Russia's privileged position should be acknowledged by the international community. As Yeltsin asserted in 1993, "Russia continues to have a vital interest in the cessation of all armed conflict on the territory of the former USSR. Moreover, the world community is increasingly coming to realize our country's special responsibility in this difficult matter. I believe the time has come . . . to grant Russia special powers as a guarantor of peace and stability in this region."[57] The Kremlin's desire to protect what it sees as its "privileged sphere of influence," by military force if necessary, has been a constant feature in Russian foreign policy ever since.

Military interventions in its "near abroad" since the early 1990s have been variously justified with reference to what the Kremlin described as its responsibility to provide security in the region. However, Russia's feeling of responsibility as a guarantor of security was not the only reason for the use of force. Military power was also applied to strengthen the grip over what the Kremlin views as its "sphere of influence," an important element in the country's great power identity and status. During the 1990s Moscow not only used force to bring to an end the "hot" phase of civil wars; in all cases, it also established a lasting military presence in the countries affected, gaining both strategically important outposts as well as a powerful lever of political influence. This has contributed to Russia's lasting control over the region. Perhaps unexpectedly for Russia, Yeltsin's appeal to the international community to accept the country's "privileged position" in the former Soviet sphere was never heeded. As neighboring states established their own foreign and security policies, they cooperated with Moscow when it suited them but also explored other options. The West justifiably believed that, as sovereign states, all newly independent states should be allowed to pursue their own interests. Moscow's view that its dominant position in the region was under threat has resulted in increasingly aggressive military action there.

The perception of outside, and specifically Western, encroachment into its "near abroad" has become a dominant theme in the Kremlin's foreign policy discourse. Criticism of NATO's eastward enlargement since the mid-1990s, and since the early 2000s the phenomenon of "color revolutions" in former Soviet states, which Moscow routinely claimed were Western instruments used to weaken its position, has been a central theme in this discourse. The war in Georgia in 2008 was justified by the Kremlin in part by the need to provide regional security and to defend Russian troops and citizens against what it described as "Georgian bellicosity toward South Ossetia."[58] However, it is clear that status concerns and the growing feeling that its control over the "near abroad" was weakening were important motivations for the use of force. Unlike the military interventions of the 1990s, this war occurred against the backdrop of an increasingly confrontational tone in Russian foreign policy rhetoric toward the West.[59] Since the so-called Rose Revolution in 2003, Moscow had perceived a sovereign Georgia as a potential locale for Western intrusion into its "sphere of influence." Georgian president Mikhail Saakashvili, who was elected in 2004, pursued an openly pro-Western foreign policy with the long-term goal of joining NATO, an aspiration that was officially welcomed by the alliance in 2008.[60]

From 2004 onward, Russia's relationship with Georgia had steadily deteriorated, and evidence suggests that Moscow both expected and had planned for the escalation of these tensions.[61] A shelling by Georgian artillery of the South Ossetian capital in 2008 gave the Kremlin an excuse to intervene and force the country firmly back into its orbit. The war left Georgia weakened and made the solution of the territorial disputes over South Ossetia and Abkhazia ever more unlikely. As such, the outcome of the war diminished the prospect of Georgia's NATO membership. As Roy Allison concluded, weakening Georgia in this way "was not just a goal but an *instrument* for Russia"[62] in the pursuit of higher-order foreign policy objectives: the preservation of its perceived "sphere of influence" and, ultimately, the assertion of its great power aspirations.

When it comes to the use of force in Ukraine in 2014, a similar confluence of factors determined Moscow's decision making. As was the case in Georgia in 2008, Moscow acted on its claim that political developments in Ukraine since the Orange Revolution in 2004 had been engineered by the West in its efforts to encroach into its "sphere of influence." When in February 2014 the United States and other Western governments officially welcomed the new

Ukrainian government shortly after the change in power had occurred as a result of the Maidan revolution, the Kremlin portrayed this as evidence of the West's efforts to bring to power a government in Kiev that "would move Ukraine toward the EU and even NATO."[63] That this was a motivation for the use of force in this case was confirmed later by Putin's heavy emphasis on what he claimed was the West's responsibility for Russian actions in his "Crimea speech."[64] Counting on the fact that the new Ukrainian leadership was not in a position to stage an effective military response, Moscow exploited the situation and intervened.

Unlike in Georgia, where the Kremlin chose to recognize the "independence" of South Ossetia and Abkhazia, in Ukraine in 2014 it opted for the outright annexation of Crimea in blatant disregard of international law. One explanation for this was that Crimea has been of extreme strategic importance to Russia, because the Sevastopol naval base is central for power projection in the Black Sea region and beyond. Disputes over Russian basing rights in Crimea had led to tensions in the past, and fears that this could lead to a war with Ukraine were already being expressed during the 1990s.[65] As Russia's subsequent actions against Ukraine demonstrated, however, regional and international status concerns were the major driver for its military aggression, starting with the annexation of Crimea in 2014 and the war in the country's east, and escalating into a full-out war in spring 2022. Seeking to deny Ukraine's sovereignty in this way, Moscow sent a signal to its neighbors and to the world that what it claimed as its dominant position in the region was nonnegotiable and would be defended, if required, by any means.

The intervention in the Syrian civil war in 2015 differed from previous uses of force inasmuch as, for the first time since the end of the Cold War, the Kremlin unilaterally intervened beyond the borders of its immediate neighborhood. The reasons for resorting to military power in this case, however, were in line with Moscow's broader views on the utility of force. As was the case in previous interventions, strategic interests and security considerations played a role in Syria. Russia's relations with the latter date back to the Cold War, and the continuation of President Bashar al-Assad's government was seen as conducive to the preservation of its material interests in the country. However, these interests alone were unlikely to have been significant enough to merit an expensive military operation.[66] Russia also had long been concerned with the international reach of religiously motivated extremist and terrorist groups, not least because of the security situation in the North Caucasus. Assisting Assad in defeating groups like the Islamic State, in the Kremlin's eyes, would not only help to return stability and security to Syria but also restrict the potential spread of their activities beyond the Middle East, for example, to Central Asia and, ultimately, to Russia itself.[67]

It is likely that a major motivation for the use of force in Syria was connected to the Kremlin's determination to assert the country's international status. As Angela Stent put it, "Putin's decision to intervene in Syria is rooted in . . . Russian concerns over power and influence."[68] Throughout the post-Soviet years, Moscow had increasingly voiced its indignation not only about what it saw as the West's encroachment into its "sphere of influence," but about what it saw as a unipolar world order and a monopoly on the use of force dominated by the United States. It came to believe that the loss of great power recognition, not least owing to its military weakness, had excluded Russia from having a say in global developments beyond its immediate neighborhood. Its inability to prevent NATO's Operation Allied Force against the Serbian regime in 1999 was of particular importance in this respect.[69] Subsequently, military modernization was prioritized, because this was seen as necessary to reassert Russia's great power status. As Putin noted in 2012, developing military potential was indispensable "for our partners to heed our country's arguments in various international formats."[70] Having been unable to prevent Western-led regime change in Serbia in 1999, as Russia saw it, a stronger military enabled it to prevent a similar scenario in Syria. As Fyodor Lukyanov concluded, by acting not only in Ukraine but also in Syria, "Russia made clear its intention to restore its status as a major international player."[71]

Moscow used military force as a tool of foreign policy since the early 1990s, especially in its so-called near abroad. Military modernization since 2008 made the Russian armed forces more capable, and it has given the Kremlin more opportunity and confidence to use them. Russia's preparedness to use force for maintaining a dominant position in its perceived "sphere of influence" and to reassert its status as a great power by any means is an existential threat to those sovereign states it considers to be within this sphere, as the escalation of the war against Ukraine in spring 2022 demonstrated. For the West, also, the potential escalation of tensions with Russia is a serious concern.

CONCLUSION

Successful reforms pursued over the past decade have made the Russian armed forces considerably more capable than they were for much of the post–Cold War years. This has made the country's political leadership more confident in using them. Coupled with an increasingly assertive foreign policy, this has resulted in more aggressive military action and posturing, culminating in the violation of Ukraine's territorial integrity and sovereignty in blatant disregard of international law. All of this has serious implications for international security and for Russia's relationship with its neighbors and with the West.

This volume was about to go to press when the Kremlin launched its full-out assault on Ukraine in spring 2022. The poor operational performance of Russia's armed forces during the initial stages of the war confirmed the chapter's argument that Russia was far from achieving its ambition of maintaining armed forces rivalling those of the world's strongest states. The ease with which Russia was able to achieve its objectives in Crimea in 2014 and partially also in Syria led to overconfidence in the level of effectiveness its armed forces had achieved. These limited operations, in addition to scripted exercises even if they were impressive in scale, were a bad predictor of capabilities required for large combined force operations against a state adversary. Moreover, at the time of the Crimea annexation Moscow was able to exploit a temporary political vacuum in Kyiv and Ukrainian armed forces that had suffered from years of malign neglect under President Viktor Yanukovich. By spring 2022, the Ukrainian leadership, society and the armed forces were fully prepared for what was to come.

The heavy losses Russian forces experienced in spring 2022 suggest that many of the achievements of military modernization since 2008 have been undone, and this will be difficult to reverse. Financial limitations were already an obstacle to overcoming shortcomings in manpower and technology even before spring 2022. The unprecedented sanctions since spring 2022 that are unlikely to be lifted any time soon will make Moscow's achievement of its military ambitions even more unlikely.

The annexation of Crimea and full invasion of Ukraine violated core principles of international law and were acts of aggression with serious consequences that are by now as good as irreversible. The Kremlin's actions will taint Russia's international image and its relations with Ukraine, its other neighbors, and the West for decades to come. Its actions have also heightened fears about the security of Europe and beyond with grave consequences for international peace and stability. Moscow's decision to push its quest for great power status and a preeminent position in what it has long claimed as its "sphere of influence" to the limit already has caused unspeakable loss and damage to Ukraine. It will also come at a high price ultimately to Vladimir Putin's regime and to Russia.

DISCUSSION QUESTIONS

1. Why did Russia embark on a program of military modernization in 2008?
2. Is contemporary Russia a military great power?
3. Is "hybrid warfare" a threat to Russia's neighbors and to the West?
4. How should the West respond to a more militarily assertive Russia?

SUGGESTED READINGS

Allison, Roy. *Russia, the West, and Military Intervention.* Oxford: Oxford University Press, 2013.

Connolly, Richard, and Cecilie Sendstad. "Russian Rearmament: An Assessment of Defense-Industrial Performance." *Problems of Post-Communism* 64, no. 3 (2017): 112–31.

Fridman, Ofer, *Russian Hybrid Warfare: Resurgence and Politicization,* Oxford: Oxford University Press, 2018.

Østensen, Åse Gilje, and Tor Bukkvoll. "Private Military Companies—Russian Great Power Politics on the Cheap?," Small Wars & Insurgencies, DOI: https://doi.org/10.1080/09592318.2021.1984709 (published online September 29, 2021).

Renz, Bettina. "Russia and Hybrid Warfare." *Contemporary Politics* 22, no. 3 (2016): 283–300.

———. *Russia's Military Revival.* Cambridge: Polity, 2018.

Westerlund, Fredrick, and Susanne Oxenstierna, eds. *Russian Military Capability in a 10-Year Perspective—2019.* Swedish Defense Research Agency FOI Report, Stockholm, 2019. https://www.foi.se/report-summary?reportNo=FOI-R--4758--SE.

NOTES

1. Carolina Vendil Pallin, *Russian Military Reform: A Failed Exercise in Defense Decision Making* (London: Routledge, 2009).

2. Anne Aldis and Roger McDermott, eds., *Russian Military Reform, 1992–2002* (London: Frank Cass, 2003).

3. Zoltan Barany, "Defense Reform, Russian Style: Obstacles, Options, Opposition," *Contemporary Politics* 11, no. 1 (2005): 35.

4. Dmitri Trenin, *Post-Imperium: A Eurasian Story* (Washington, DC: Carnegie Endowment for International Peace, 2011), 76.

5. Brian Taylor, *Politics and the Russian Army: Civil-Military Relations, 1689–2000* (Cambridge: Cambridge University Press, 2003), 274.

6. SIPRI Military Expenditure Database, "Data for All Countries 1949–2020," https://www.sipri.org/databases/milex (accessed October 4, 2021).

7. Pavel Baev, "Peacekeeping and Conflict Management in Eurasia," in *Security Dilemmas in Russia and Eurasia,* ed. Roy Allison and Christoph Bluth (London: Royal Institute of International Affairs, 1998), 218.

8. Bettina Renz, "Russian Military Capabilities after 20 Years of Reform," *Survival* 56, no. 3 (2014): 69.

9. Iver Neumann, "Russia as a Great Power 1815–2007," *Journal of International Relations and Development* 11, no. 2 (2008): 128–51.

10. Margot Light, "Russian Foreign Policy," in *Developments in Russian Politics,* eds. Stephen White, Richard Sakwa, and Henry Hale (Basingstoke: Palgrave, 2010), 229.

11. Bettina Renz, "Why Russia Is Reviving Its Conventional Military Power," *Parameters* 46, no. 2 (2016): 24–26.

12. Richard Pipes, "Is Russia Still an Enemy?," *Foreign Affairs* 76, no. 5 (1997): 75–76.

13. Bettina Renz, *Russia's Military Revival* (Cambridge: Polity, 2018), 61–83.

14. Vladimir Putin, "TV Address to the Citizens of Russia," March 24, 2000, http://en. special.kremlin.ru/events/president/transcripts/24201 (accessed May 12, 2018).

15. Carolina Vendil Pallin and Frederick Westerlund, "Russia's War with Georgia: Lessons and Consequences," *Small Wars and Insurgencies* 20, no. 2 (2009): 400–24.

16. Margarete Klein, "Towards a 'New Look' of the Russian Armed Forces? Organizational and Personnel Changes," in *The Russian Armed Forces in Transition: Economic, Geopolitical and Institutional Uncertainties*, ed. Roger McDermott, Bertil Nygren, and Carolina Vendil Pallin (London: Routledge, 2012).

17. Johan Norberg, "Training to Fight: Russia's Major Military Exercises, 2011–2014," Swedish Defense Research Agency FOI Report, 2015, https://www.foi.se/reportsummary? reportNo=FOI-R—4128—SE (accessed February 21, 2018).

18. Pavel Aptekar' and Ivan Prosvetov, "Otnoshenie k armii v Rossii perevernulos," *Vedomosti*, February 22, 2018.

19. Julian Cooper, "Russia's State Armament Program to 2020: A Quantitative Assessment of Implementation, 2011–2015," Swedish Defense Research Agency FOI Report, 2016, 51–52, https://www.foi.se/rapportsammanfattning?reportNo=FOI-R--4239--SE (accessed November 1, 2017).

20. PAK FA stands for "Perspectivney aviatsionnyi kompleks frontovoi aviatsii."

21. Sergey Sukhankin, "Russia Adopts National Strategy for Development of Artificial Intelligence," *Jamestown Eurasia Daily Monitor* 16, no. 163 (2019), https://jamestown.org/program/russia-adopts-national-strategy-for-development-of-artificial-intelligence/.

22. Kevin Dear, "Will Russia Rule the World through AI? Assessing Putin's Rhetoric against Russia's Reality," *RUSI Journal* 164(5–6) (2019): 36–60.

23. Paul Goble, "Russian Navy Ever Less Able to Support Putin's War Plans," *Jamestown Eurasia Monitor* 16, no. 59 (2019), https://jamestown.org/program/russian-navy-ever-less-capable-of-supporting-putins-war-plans/.

24. Richard Connolly and Cecilie Sendstad, "Russian Rearmament: An Assessment of Defense-Industrial Performance," *Problems of Post-Communism* 64, no. 3 (2017): 112–31; Richard Connolly and Philip Hanson, "Import Substitution and Economic Sovereignty in Russia," Chatham House Research Paper, 2016, https://www.chathamhouse.org/publication/import-substitution-and-economic-sovereignty-russia (accessed November 1, 2017).

25. Richard Connolly and Mathieu Boulège, "Russia's New State Armament Program: Implications for the Russian Armed Forces and Military Capabilities," Chatham House Research Paper, 2018, https://www.chathamhouse.org/publication/russia-s-new-state-armament-programme-implications-russian-armed-forces-and-military (accessed May 10, 2018).

26. Douglas Barrie, "Russia's State Armament Program 2027: A More Measured Course on Procurement," International Institute for Strategic Studies, February 13,

2018, https://www.iiss. org/en/militarybalanceblog/blogsections/2018-f256/february-1c17/russia-state-armamentprogramme-d453 (accessed May 1, 2018).

27. Michael Kofman and Richard Connolly, "Why Russian Military Expenditure Is Much Higher than Commonly Understood (As Is China's)," War on the Rocks blog, December 16, 2019. https://warontherocks.com/2019/12/why-russian-military -expenditure-is-much-higher-than-commonly-understood-as-is-chinas/ (accessed October 3, 2021).

28. "Chapter Five: Russia and Eurasia," *The Military Balance* 121, no. 1 (2021): 170.

29. Aptekar' and Prosvetov, "Otnoshenie k armii v Rossii." For a detailed account of the problem of *dedovshchina* before the recent reforms, see Dale Herspring, "Dedovshchina in the Russian Army: The Problem That Won't Go Away," *Journal of Slavic Military Studies* 18, no. 4 (2005): 607–29.

30. "Chapter Five: Russia and Eurasia," 170.

31. Sviatoslav Ivanov, "Khotiat li russkie sluzhit?," Gazeta.ru, February 22, 2016, https:// www.gazeta.ru/army/2016/02/22/8081159.shtml (accessed May 1, 2018).

32. Aleksandr Golts, "How Many Soldiers Does Russia Have?," *Jamestown Eurasia Daily Monitor* 14, no. 144 (2017).

33. Renz, *Russia's Military Revival*, 160–88.

34. Barany, "Defense Reform, Russian Style," 35.

35. House of Commons Defense Committee, "Towards the Next Defense and Security Review: Part Two—NATO," Third Report of Session 2014–15, HC358, July 31, 2014, http:// www.publications.parliament.uk/pa/cm201415/cmselect/cmdfence/358 /358.pdf (accessed August 12, 2017).

36. Ofer Fridman, *Russian Hybrid Warfare: Resurgence and Politicization* (Oxford: Oxford University Press, 2018).

37. Frank Hoffman, *Conflict in the 21st Century: The Rise of Hybrid Wars* (Arlington, VA: Potomac Institute, 2007).

38. Russian special forces, whose presence in Crimea was initially denied by Putin, who claimed that these unmarked soldiers were "armed civilians," were referred to in the media at the time as "little green men."

39. Johan Norberg, "The Use of Russia's Military in the Crimean Crisis," Carnegie Endowment for International Peace, March 13, 2014, https://carnegieendowment.org /2014/03/13/useof-russia-s-military-in-crimean-crisis-pub-54949 (accessed August 4, 2017); Maxim Bugriy, "The Crimean Operation: Russian Force and Tactics," *Jamestown Eurasia Daily Monitor* 11, no. 61 (2014), https://jamestown.org/program/the -crimean-operation-russian-force-and-tactics (accessed August 4, 2017).

40. Åse Gilje Østensen and Tor Bukkvoll, "Private Military Companies—Russian Great Power Politics on the Cheap?," *Small Wars & Insurgencies,* DOI: https://doi.org /10.1080/09592318.2021.1984709 (published online September 29, 2021), 5.

41. "Russia's Use of Its Private Military Companies," *Strategic Comments* 26, no. 10 (2020): vii.

42. Kimberly Marten, "Russia's Use of Semi-State Security Forces: The Case of the Wagner Group," *Post-Soviet Affairs* 35, no. 3 (2019): 181–204.

43. Tor Bukkvoll and Åse G. Østensen, "The Emergence of Russian Private Military Companies: A New Tool of Clandestine Warfare," *Special Operations Journal* 6, no. 1: 4.

44. Østensen and Bukkvoll, "Private Military Companies."

45. Charles Bartles, "Getting Gerasimov Right," *Military Review* 96, no. 1 (2016): 36.

46. Dima Adamsky, *The Culture of Military Innovation: The Impact of Cultural Factors on the Revolution in Military Affairs in Russia, the US, and Israel* (Stanford, CA: Stanford University Press, 2010), 42–43.

47. Dima Adamsky, "Cross-Domain Coercion—the Current Russian Art of Strategy," *Proliferation Papers* 54 (2015): 25; Raymond Garthoff, "Unconventional Warfare in Communist Strategy," *Foreign Affairs* 40, no. 4 (1961): 566–75.

48. Dima Adamsky, "Through the Looking Glass: The Soviet Military-Technical Revolution and the American Revolution in Military Affairs," *Journal of Strategic Studies* 31, no. 2 (2008): 257–94.

49. Timothy Thomas, "The Evolution in Russian Military Thought: Integrating Hybrid, New-Generation and New-Type Thinking," *Journal of Slavic Military Studies* 26, no. 2 (2016): 555.

50. See, for example, Peter Apps, "Putin's Nuclear-Tipped Hybrid War on the West," May 1, 2018, https://www.reuters.com/article/us-apps-russia-commentary/commentary-putins-nuclear-tipped-hybrid-war-on-the-west-idUSKCN1GD6H2 (accessed May 10, 2018).

51. Michael Kofman, "Russian Hybrid Warfare and Other Dark Arts," March 11, 2016, https://warontherocks.com/2016/03/russian-hybrid-warfare-and-other-dark-arts (accessed November 10, 2017).

52. Peter Rutland, "A Paradigm Shift in Russia's Foreign Policy," *Moscow Times*, May 18, 2014.

53. Cited in Centre for Strategic and International Studies (CSIS), "Global Security Forum 2016: Welcoming Remarks and Plenary I—Navigating 21st Century Security Challenges," December 1, 2016, https://www.csis.org/events/global-security-forum-2016-welcoming-remarks-and-plenary-i-navigating-21st-century-security (accessed May 10, 2018).

54. Renz, *Russia's Military Revival*, 121–59.

55. Zbigniew Brzezinski, "The Premature Partnership," *Foreign Affairs* 73, no. 2 (1994): 72.

56. Roy Allison, *Russia, the West, and Military Intervention* (Oxford: Oxford University Press, 2013), 122–23.

57. Cited in Stephen Page, "The Creation of a Sphere of Influence: Russia and Central Asia," *International Journal* 49, no. 4 (1994): 804.

58. Andrei Tsygankov and Matthew Tarver-Wahlquist, "Duelling Honors: Power, Identity and the Russia-Georgia Divide," *Foreign Policy Analysis* 5, no. 4 (2009): 307.

59. Angela Stent, "Restoration and Revolution in Putin's Foreign Policy," *Europe-Asia Studies* 60, no. 9 (2009): 1090.

60. NATO, "Bucharest Summit Declaration" (press release 49, 2008), https://www.nato.int/cps/ua/natohq/official_texts_8443.htm (accessed August 10, 2017).

61. Mark Kramer, "Russian Policy toward the Commonwealth of Independent States: Recent Trends and Future Prospects," *Problems of Post-Communism* 55, no. 6 (2008): 7.

62. Roy Allison, "Russia Resurgent? Moscow's Campaign to 'Coerce Georgia to Peace,'" *International Affairs* 84, no. 6 (2008): 1065.

63. Samuel Charap and Timothy Colton, *Everyone Loses: The Ukraine Crisis and the Ruinous Contest for Post-Soviet Eurasia* (London: International Institute for Strategic Studies, 2017), 126.

64. Vladimir Putin, "Address by the President of the Russian Federation," March 18, 2014, http://en.kremlin.ru/events/president/news/20603 (accessed May 10, 2018).

65. Dmitri Trenin, *Post-Imperium: A Eurasian Story* (Washington, DC: Carnegie Endowment for International Peace, 2011), 44–46.

66. Roy Allison, "Russia and Syria: Explaining Alignment with a Regime in Crisis," *International Affairs* 89, no. 6 (2013): 800–807.

67. Vladimir Putin, "A Plea of Caution from Russia," *New York Times*, September 11, 2013; Derek Averre and Lance Davies, "Russian Humanitarian Intervention and the Responsibility to Protect: The Case of Syria," *International Affairs* 91, no. 4 (2015): 820–21.

68. Angela Stent, "Putin's Power Play in Syria: How to Respond to Russia's Intervention," *Foreign Affairs* 95, no. 1 (2016): 108.

69. Derek Averre, "From Pristina to Tskhinvali: The Legacy of Operation Allied Force in Russia's Relations with the West," *International Affairs* 85, no. 3 (2009): 571–91.

70. Vladimir Putin, "Being Strong: Why Russia Needs to Rebuild Its Military," *Foreign Policy*, February 21, 2012, http://foreignpolicy.com/2012/02/21/being-strong (accessed August 10, 2017).

71. Fyodor Lukyanov, "Putin's Foreign Policy—the Quest to Restore Russia's Rightful Place," *Russia in Global Affairs*, May 4, 2016, http://eng.globalaffairs.ru/redcol/Putins- Foreign-Policy-18133 (accessed August 12, 2017).

Index

Page numbers followed by *f* refer to figures and *t* to tables.

427

About the Contributors

Alfred B. Evans Jr., professor emeritus of political science at California State University, Fresno. He is the author of *Soviet Marxism-Leninism: The Decline of an Ideology* (1993). He is also editor or co-editor of three books, including *Russian Civil Society: A Critical Assessment* (2006). He has published many book chapters and articles in scholarly journals. His current research focuses on civil society in Russia, with particular emphasis on organizations that engage in public protests.

Stefan Hedlund, professor of Russian studies at Uppsala University, Sweden. His research has mainly focused on institutional dimensions of Russian economic development and attempted reforms through a lens of historical and cultural legacies. He has published many articles and some two dozen books, most recently *Invisible Hands, Russian Experience, and Social Science: Approaches to Understanding Systemic Failure* (2011) and *Putin's Energy Agenda: The Contradictions of Russia's Resource Wealth* (2014).

Kathryn Hendley, Roman Z. Livshits and Theodore W. Brazean Professor of Law and Political Science at the University of Wisconsin, Madison. Her research focuses on legal and economic reform in the former Soviet Union and on how law is actually experienced and used in Russia. Her research has been supported by grants from the National Science Foundation, the Social Science Research Council, the National Council for Eurasian and East European Research, and the International Research and Exchanges Board. She has been a visiting fellow at the Woodrow Wilson Center, the Kellogg Institute for International Affairs at Notre Dame University, the Russian Economic School (Moscow), and the Program in Law and Public Affairs at Princeton University. She has published widely in journals such as *Post-Soviet Affairs*, *Law and Social Inquiry*, and the *American Journal of Comparative Law*.

Janet Elise Johnson, professor of political science at Brooklyn College, City University of New York. She is the author of *Gender Violence in Russia: The Politics of Feminist Intervention* (2009) and *The Gender of Informal Politics: Russia, Iceland and Twenty-First Century Male Dominance* (2018) and co-editor (with Katalin Fábián and Mara Lazda) of *The Routledge International Handbook to Gender in Central-Eastern Europe and Eurasia* (2022). She has published articles in *Post-Soviet Affairs*, *Slavic Review*, *Perspectives on Politics*, the *Journal of Social Policy*, *Politics & Gender*, *Communist and Post-Communist Studies*, *Signs: Journals of Women in Culture and Society*, and *Aspasia* as well as online in the *Washington Post*'s Monkey Cage, the *Boston Review*, and the *New Yorker*. Over her career, she has been affiliated with various Russian studies institutes, including at Indiana, Miami, and Columbia Universities as well as the University of Helsinki. She writes extensively on gender and politics in Russia.

Maria Lipman is a senior associate visiting fellow at the Institute of European, Russian and Eurasian Studies (IERES), George Washington University, and coeditor of *Russia Post*, russiapost.net, published by IERES. She reviews books on Russia and East Europe for the journal *Foreign Affairs*. Lipman taught courses on Russia at Indiana University (Bloomington) in 2017–2018, and at Grinnell College in 2019–2021. From 1995 until 2019 Ms. Lipman was the editor or deputy editor of various Russian-language publications, and, most recently, she edited *Point & Counterpoint*, published online by the IERES, George Washington University. From 2003 to 2014 she was an associate at the Moscow Carnegie Center and the editor of its policy journal, *Pro et Contra*. Ms. Lipman was cofounder and deputy editor of two Russian weekly magazines: *Itogi* (Results), the first weekly newsmagazine in Russia, published in association with *Newsweek*, and *Ezhenedel'ny Zhurnal* (Weekly Journal). From 2001 until 2011, Ms. Lipman wrote an op-ed column on Russian politics, media, and society for the *Washington Post*. From 2012 to 2017 she wrote a blog for the *New Yorker* online. She has published widely in the United States and Russia, and contributed to, edited, or coedited several volumes on Russian media, politics, and society. Ms. Lipman holds an MA from Moscow State University.

Jeffrey Mankoff, distinguished research fellow at National Defense University's Institute for National Strategic Studies. He was previously senior fellow and deputy director of the Russia and Eurasia Program at the Center for Strategic and International Studies, an adviser on Russian affairs at the Department of State, adjunct fellow at the Council on Foreign Relations, and associate director of International Security Studies at Yale University. He has also held fellowships at Harvard, Yale, and Moscow State universities.

The author of *Russian Foreign Policy: The Return of Great Power Politics* (2011), his new book is *Empires of Eurasia: How Imperial Legacies Shape International Security*. He holds a PhD in diplomatic history from Yale.

Alexandra Novitskaya, PhD candidate in women's, gender, and sexuality studies at Stony Brook University, SUNY. Her research interests are in the intersections of sexuality, national identity, migration studies, and queer theory. Her work has been published in *NORMA: International Journal of Masculinity Studies*, *The Russian Review*, and in *Post-Soviet Affairs*. Her doctoral dissertation explores the experiences of post-Soviet LGBTQ migrants in the United States.

Nikolai Petrov is a senior research fellow in the Russia and Eurasia Program at Chatham House in London and was professor of political science at the Higher School of Economics in Moscow. He is a member of the Program on New Approaches to Research and Security in Eurasia (PONARS Eurasia) and the author or editor of numerous publications dealing with analysis of Russia's political regime, post-Soviet transformation, the socioeconomic and political development of Russia's regions, democratization, federalism, and elections. His works include the three-volume *1997 Political Almanac of Russia* and annual supplements. He is the coauthor of *Between Dictatorship and Democracy: Russian Post-communist Political Reform* (2004); *The Dynamics of Russian Politics: Putin's Reform of Federal-Regional Relations*, in two volumes (2004, 2005); *Russia 2025: Scenarios for the Russian Future* (2013); *The State of Russia: What Comes Next?* (2015); and *The New Autocracy: Information, Politics, and Policy in Putin's Russia* (2018).

Elizabeth Plantan is an assistant professor of political science at Stetson University. From 2018–2020, she held a China Public Policy Postdoctoral Fellowship at the Ash Center for Democratic Governance and Innovation at Harvard Kennedy School. Her research focuses on environmental activism, civil society, and authoritarian politics, particularly in China and Russia.

Bettina Renz is professor of international security in the School of Politics and International Relations at the University of Nottingham, United Kingdom. She has written and published widely on Russian defense and security policy. Her most recent book is *Russia's Military Revival* (2018).

Richard Sakwa is professor of Russian and European politics at the University of Kent, a senior research fellow at the Higher School of Economics University in Moscow, and an honorary professor in the Faculty of Political Science at Moscow State University. He has published widely on

Soviet, Russian, and post-communist affairs. His recent books include *Putin Redux: Power and Contradiction in Contemporary Russia* (London and New York, Routledge, 2014), *Frontline Ukraine: Crisis in the Borderlands* (London, I. B. Tauris, 2016), *Russia against the Rest: The Post-Cold War Crisis of World Order* (Cambridge University Press, 2017), and *Russia's Futures* (Cambridge, Polity, 2019). His latest books are *The Putin Paradox*, published by I. B. Tauris (Bloomsbury) in 2020 and *Deception: Russiagate and the New Cold War* (Lexington Books, 2022).

Louise Shelley, Omer L. and Nancy Hirst Endowed Chair and University Professor at the School of Policy and Government, George Mason University. She founded and directs the Terrorism, Transnational Crime and Corruption Center (TraCCC). Her most recent books are *Dirty Entanglements: Corruption, Crime, and Terrorism* (2014); *Human Trafficking: A Global Perspective* (2010); and *Dark Commerce: How a New Illicit Economy Is Threatening Our Future* (2018), which was written while she was an inaugural Andrew Carnegie fellow. She is the author of many articles and book chapters on transnational crime, Soviet and Russian crime and justice, and money laundering. Professor Shelley served for six years on the Global Agenda Councils of the World Economic Forum, first on the illicit trade council and then as the inaugural cochair of organized crime. Dr. Shelley appears frequently in the media, lectures widely at universities and multinational bodies, and has testified on numerous occasions before Congress. She is a life member of the Council on Foreign Relations.

Darrell Slider is professor emeritus in the School of Interdisciplinary Global Studies at the University of South Florida. He received a PhD in political science from Yale University. His past work has covered many areas of Soviet and Russian politics, with a particular emphasis on federalism and regional politics in Russia and Georgian politics. Dr. Slider's publications include *The Politics of Transition: Shaping a Post-Soviet Future* (1993, coauthored with Stephen White and Graham Gill), as well as numerous book chapters and articles in journals such as *Post-Soviet Affairs*, *Demokratizatsiya*, *Europe-Asia Studies*, *Slavic Review*, and *Journal of Communist Studies and Transition Politics*. He has been awarded grants in support of his research by the Kennan Institute for Advanced Russian Studies, the International Research and Exchanges Board (IREX), and the National Council for Eurasian and East European Research. Twice Dr. Slider has been a Fulbright Research Scholar in Moscow at the Higher School of Economics, in 2004–2005 and in 2017–2018.

Maria Snegovaya received her PhD from Columbia University. She is a post-doctoral fellow at the Center for Eurasian, Russian and East European Studies (CERES) at Georgetown University's Walsh School of Foreign Service, a visiting scholar at the Institute for European, Russian, and Eurasian Studies and the Illiberalism Studies Program at George Washington University, and adjunct senior fellow at the Center for New American Security. She is also a member of PONARS Eurasia, a George Washington University–based network of academics advancing new approaches to research on politics and society in Russia and Eurasia. She specializes in comparative politics, international relations, and statistical methods. The key focus of her research is Russia's domestic and foreign policy, as well as democratic backsliding in Eastern Europe. Her research has appeared in policy and peer-reviewed journals, including *West European Politics, Party Politics, Journal of Democracy, Post-Soviet Affairs, Problems of Post-Communism,* and the *Washington Post*'s political science blog, the Monkey Cage. Her research has been referenced in publications such as the *New York Times, Bloomberg, BBC,* the *Economist,* and *Foreign Policy.* Throughout her career she has collaborated with multiple US think tanks and is frequently invited to give talks at US universities and research centers.

Laura Solanko is senior adviser at the Bank of Finland Institute for Emerging Economies (BOFIT).

Pekka Sutela was head of the Bank of Finland Institute for Emerging Economies (BOFIT). His publications include *The Political Economy of Putin's Russia* (2012) and *Trading with the Soviet Union* (2014).

Stephen K. Wegren is distinguished university professor and professor of political science at Southern Methodist University. He is the author or editor of nineteen books on the political economy of post-communist nations and has published numerous articles and book chapters in a wide range of journals and books. His research has been supported by the Social Science Research Council, the National Council for Eurasian and East European Research, the Ford Foundation, the International Research and Exchanges Board, OXFAM, and the Norwegian Research Council. Recent books include *Food Policy and Food Security: Putting Food on the Russian Table* (2018); *Russia's Food Revolution: The Transformation of the Food System* (2021); and *Russia's Role in the Contemporary International Agri-Food Trade System* (2022).

Jeanne L. Wilson is an emeritus professor of political science at Wheaton College in Norton, Massachusetts, and a research associate at the Davis Center for Russian and Eurasian Studies at Harvard University. Her research interests are focused on comparing Russian and Chinese foreign policy behavior, especially with respect to questions of identity and status, as well as their position as outliers in the international political system. She is also interested in the question of China's increasingly active foreign policy behavior in the former Soviet republics and its implications for the Russian-Chinese relationship. She is the author of *Strategic Partners: Russian-Chinese Relations in the Post-Soviet Era* (2004) and a number of articles and book chapters, including recent articles in *International Politics, Problems of Post-Communism, Acta Via Serica,* and the *Journal of Soviet and Post-Soviet Politics and Society.*

Lightning Source UK Ltd.
Milton Keynes UK
UKHW011820080922
408544UK00001B/2

"This newly revised and updated eighth edition of *Putin's Russia* offers a thorough and comprehensive understanding of the way the Russian regime has evolved from the end of the Soviet era through the 2022 invasion of Ukraine. The authors are leading specialists in their fields, and the volume is written in a clear and accessible style. Discussion questions and suggestions for further reading accompany each chapter. The book will be useful for instructors and anyone looking for an authoritative and up-to-date treatment of the current state of the Putin regime."

—Thomas F. Remington, Emory University

"This volume brings together renowned American, European, and Russian experts to cover important aspects of Russia's political system, economic and social dynamics, and foreign policy. Slider's introduction provides a lucid treatment of the Soviet era and how it has shaped Vladimir Putin's leadership since 2000. Each subsequent chapter traces the evolution of its subject from the 1990s to today, revealing the dynamics that have led to the current situation. The volume will be valuable for students beginning their study of Russia as well as those seeking more in-depth coverage of specific topics."

—William M. Reisinger, University of Iowa

Thoroughly revised, expanded, and updated, this classic text provides the most authoritative and current analysis of contemporary Russia. Leading scholars explore the domestic and international problems Russia confronts by considering a comprehensive array of economic, political, foreign policy, and social issues.

Contributors

Alfred B. Evans Jr., Stefan Hedlund, Kathryn Hendley, Janet Elise Johnson, Maria Lipman, Jeffrey Mankoff, Alexandra Novitskaya, Nikolai Petrov, Elizabeth Plantan, Bettina Renz, Richard Sakwa, Louise Shelley, Darrell Slider, Maria Snegovaya, Laura Solanko, Regina Smyth, Jeanne L. Wilson

DARRELL SLIDER is pr

ROWMAN &
LITTLEFIELD
800-462-6420 | www.rowman.c

Cover images: (top) © Reuters / Alan
(bottom) courtesy of Darrell Slider